TRADING THE
MARKETS
THE POINT &
FIGURE WAY

TRADING THE MARKETS THE POINT & FIGURE WAY

Become A Noiseless Trader And Achieve Consistent *Success In Markets*

PRASHANT SHAH

Notion Press

Old No. 38, New No. 6
McNichols Road, Chetpet
Chennai - 600 031

First Published by Notion Press 2018
Copyright © Prashant Shah 2018
All Rights Reserved.

ISBN 978-1-64249-224-8

CONTENTS

ACKNOWLEDGEMENTS

The assistance and support of many people have contributed in turning the dream of this book into a reality.

Thanks to my Father, Pravin Shah, and Mother, Rekha Shah, for all the support and guidance and for moulding me into the person I have become today.

To my grandmother (*Baa*), late Savita Shah, who single-handedly raised my father since he was a few months old. I know the sacrifices she has made to give us a life. She taught me to be a fighter –determined and persistent in life – and how to have a never-give-up attitude. Her late night stories on bravery and victory of good over evil have left an indelible mark on my persona. I try to continue her legacy and teach the same things to the apple of my eye, Ahaan, who makes me smile every day.

Many thanks to my precious wife and best friend Isha for all the encouragement and support she has given me in writing this book – be it international exams while working or me leaving a job only to write a research paper and eventually a book. All this after a marriage is only possible when there is a companion like her, an unending inspiration.

I am fortunate to have very understanding in-laws, Kiran and Subhash Gupta. They have always supported me in every decision and have stood by me during good and bad times. I am blessed to receive their unwavering emotional support and encouragement.

To the hero of my life, Ravi mama (maternal uncle) – the one I have always looked up to. The childhood memories I have of him and his love and support at every stage of my life are strong pillars on which my life has been built. I thank him for existing.

I am truly thankful to my colleagues at Definedge, Vinay Shah, Nitin Gajbhiye, Abhijit Phatak and Raju Ranjan. They have greatly contributed to this book and my thought process while writing it. Special thanks to B. Krishnakumar for proof-reading and editing the book and for keeping me in line. His writing skills are beyond my abilities, and his efforts are truly appreciated. Thanks to Biren Patel, who first taught me OHLC and sent me to a seminar on technical analysis during 2005, my first ever training on the topic. I have benefited from many helpful suggestions and comments from Nitin Mude, Rajesh Badiye, Prashant Gupta, Sumeet Jain, Brijesh Bhatia, and K. Anant Rao. I feel a debt of gratitude to so many professionals, traders and market practitioners. Parts of this book are inspired by many subject practitioners, technical analysts, traders, authors and teachers from whom I have learned. I thank you all and many others for your support, friendship, and willingness to impart your knowledge of investing and trading in the markets.

At the outset, I would like to express my sincere gratitude to Jeremy du Plessis, Thomas Dorsey including all other authors having mastery on Point & Figure, who generously shared such valuable knowledge on Point & Figure. It would be no exaggeration to admit that, without Jeremy du Plessis, I wouldn't be in position to write this book. I have learnt almost everything about Point and Figure charting, including but not limited to its history, construction, naming the chart and advanced methods like applying indicators on them from his works. He is an authority on the subject, and any study on Point & Figure is totally incomplete without studying his works on this subject. Thomas Dorsey has also brilliantly worked on Breadth and Relative Strength matrix using Point & Figure charts and same can be referred from his works. This has had a big positive impact on my approach towards analyzing markets. I can't thank these two enough for their contribution and the influence they have had on my approach to Point & Figure charts.

Thanks to the CMT Association and International Federation of Technical Analysts (IFTA), through which I was introduced to the best of the works in the field of technical analysis. They have greatly contributed to my knowledge of trading and analysis.

Thanks to all my students, event participants and product subscribers for keeping me on my toes with their wonderful observations and queries.

My special thanks to Notion Press (the publisher of the book) as well as the editor of this book and the project manager, Charmine Joseph, along with the rest of the staff members behind the scenes whom I have not known directly.

All the charts in this book are from TradePoint software by Definedge Solutions. Though I am a founder member of the company, the software and company is a result of the unwavering hardwork of many. It is because of them that this book has become a reality today.

I presented the concepts the way I understood them with consistent practice of so many years. Everything that I wrote about is borrowed in one way or the other from ancestors and brilliant minds in the field of trading, P&F and technical analysis. Credit for anything that you learn from this book goes to them. What you don't like is my weakness.

– **Prashant Shah**

Chapter 1

INTRODUCTION & CONSTRUCTION

Hi, I am Prashant...your friend in this wonderful journey of learning Point & Figure technique of market trading and analysis. It is good if you know nothing about P&F when reading this book, because I will explain everything right from the beginning. I hope you enjoy the process of becoming a proficient P&F analyst and a trader.

1.1: INTRODUCTION & CONSTRUCTION

Broadly, there are two types of market analyses: financial and technical. Financial or fundamental analysis is about understanding the business of the company, its balance sheet and other financial reports and studying the micro- and macro-economic factors. Technical analysis, on the other hand, studies the behavior of the price action and the demand-supply equation based on it.

Below are the basic tenets of technical analysis, from the classic work by Robert D. Edwards and John Magee, *Technical Analysis of Stock Trends*:

1. The price moves in trends, and a trend will continue until reversed.
2. Stock prices are determined by the interaction of demand and supply, and the shifts in them cause the reversal in trends.
3. Price discounts everything. Shifts in demand and supply can be detected in charts.
4. History and chart patterns tend to repeat themselves.

Line, bar and candlestick charts are very popular among technical analysts. Image 1.1.1 explains their construction.

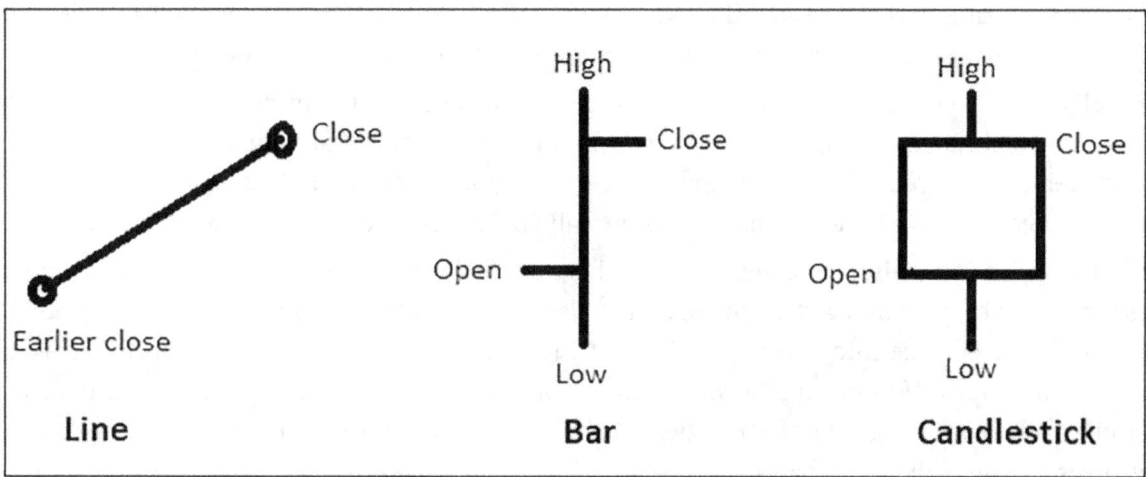

Image 1.1.1: Line, bar and candlestick

Line charts are drawn by connecting closing prices. In bar charts, a bar is bullish when its closing price is higher than the earlier period; it is bearish when closing price is lower. For candlestick charts, a candle is bullish when close of a period is higher than open, else it is bearish.

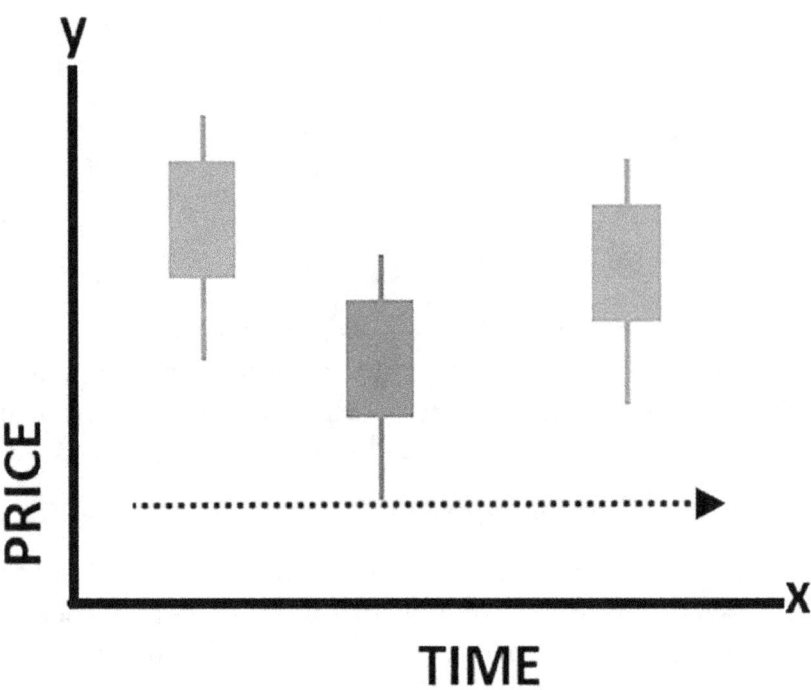

Image 1.1.2: Price and time chart

Image 1.1.2 shows a price and time chart. There are two dimensions to these charts: price and time. In these charts, time is plotted on the *X* axis and price on the *Y* axis. They can be a viewed on different time frames such as daily, weekly, monthly or even intraday time intervals such as 60 min, 30 min, 15 min, etc. Two-dimensional charts move with the passage of time.

Point & Figure

Point & Figure (P&F) charting has a long history and is known to be the oldest charting method. It was very popular before computers came into existence. Bar and Candlestick charts gained more popularity due to simple plotting and the availability of software platforms. We are quite used to these modern charting methods today; in fact, most techniques of technical analysis are designed using them.

But P&F has its own place and is also being actively and successfully implemented today. The recent advancement in technology has made it possible to explore the clarity and simplicity of P&F. It is a complete charting system, objective in nature and applicable on all types of financial instruments. In fact, because there is more objectivity and science that makes me call P&F charts a tool relevant for the next-generation.

P&F is one of the noiseless categories of charting techniques. Noiseless, because it filters out unnecessary data and presents a clear picture. It is also known as the timeless or one-dimensional chart because it only takes price into account while plotting. P&F formations help us in clearly defining the market structure over different time horizons. Clear formations remove the confusion while placing the trades and enable easy designing of strategies. Once understood and practiced, it would be difficult to trade or invest without the P&F charts.

Let us begin with understanding their construction, which is the most important part of P&F analysis. I want you to spend enough time understanding the basics before moving on to patterns and trading. In my talks on P&F, people usually are more interested in knowing trade setups immediately; they don't focus much on the basics and struggle later while discussing the trading strategies.

Construction

As mentioned earlier, P&F charts have a long history and an interesting journey that began from the figure charts. Unlike the usual candlestick or bar charts, P&F charts are plotted vertically. They are explained stepwise below. It is said that plotting of prices began from these charts, and I am sure you will find it very interesting to learn the method.

Figure Charts

Figure charts are plotted in the tabular format. We draw a line chart by connecting the closing prices of a particular time period. Instead of that, figure charts are plotted by writing the prices in the boxes that move vertically (see Image 1.1.3).

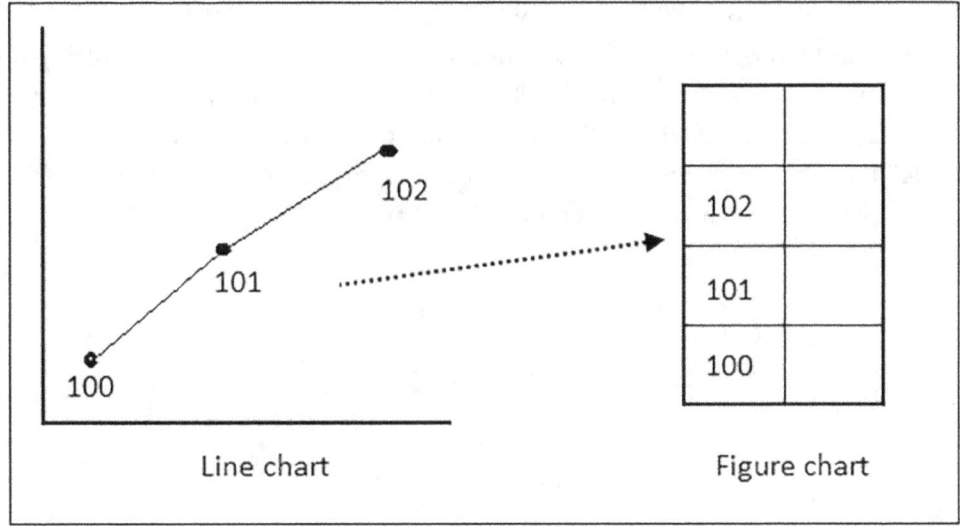

Image 1.1.3: Figure chart construction

A line chart connects all the prices, even if the price has been flat or has not moved much. A figure chart moves only when the price moves by a particular predefined range; nothing gets marked if the price remains flat. That range or move must be decided by the user to plot the figure chart. For example, if a stock is trading at 100, we may decide to plot the price only when it moves by 1 rupee or 1 point. So the next figure will be written only if the price moves by 1 box or more. Any price move below 1 will be treated as insignificant and will not be plotted. Image 1.1.4 shows how the plotting will look if the price moves from 100 to 101.

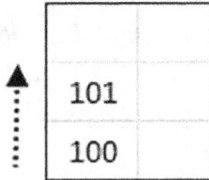

Image 1.1.4: Figure chart construction

If the price goes up further by 1 point to 102, it will be written in the next higher box. Note that it should be at or above 102 to qualify for plotting. New price will be written in the boxes as and when the price moves up by 1 point. If the price goes straight to 105, all the boxes in between will be marked. Image 1.1.5 shows the plotting if the price moves to 105.

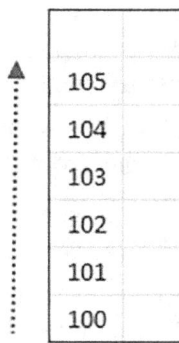

Image 1.1.5: Figure chart construction

In the above example, price gets plotted only if it moves by 1 point, hence size of the box is 1.

Further, if price goes to 106, it will be marked in a similar manner. Repeated plotting doesn't happen in these charts. So if price trades at the same level, the charts will not move. So here, if price remains at 105, we will not write 105 again; the chart will simply remain the same. But, what if the price turns down and goes below 104? It can't be marked in the same column, right? Hence, the column needs to be changed and 104 should be written in the subsequent column (see Image 1.1.6).

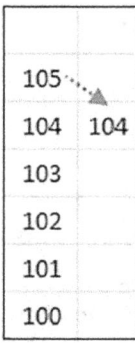

Image 1.1.6: Figure chart construction

Notice one thing here: '105' is not written in the next column because we begin marking from 104, that is, when it started moving down. The definition of moving down is: when the price went below the previous box-price of 104. So that means the column needs to be changed when the price changes its direction. This is quite interesting, since there are columns in the figure chart that show the number of times the price has changed direction. And figures in each column will display the extent the price has traveled before changing direction again.

In the above example, the price is falling now. And if it goes down to 103, it will be written in the same column, as shown in Image 1.1.7.

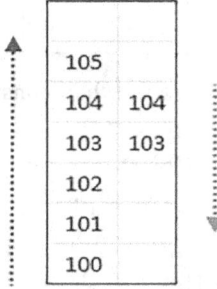

Image 1.1.7: Figure chart construction

4

The current figure is 103, and if it goes to 102, plotting will be continued in the same column and it will not be changed as long as the price continues to move in the same direction. The column will be changed if the price goes higher. The definition of going higher is: when the price moves above the previous box-price of 104. So, if price goes to 104, then the column needs to be changed again. Image 1.1.8 shows the plotting if the price goes to 105 again from 103.

105		105
104	104	104
103	103	
102		
101		
100		

Image 1.1.8: Figure chart construction

This is how figure charts are plotted. Notice that every column that moves down begins with one box lower than the last high price and the column that moves up begins with one box higher than the lowest price in the previous column.

The size of the box in the above example was 1. It can be plotted with 2 points, 5 points or any other number for that matter. So a figure chart can be plotted with various box-sizes; but, the method of plotting remains the same. It can be easily imagined that if box-size is kept high then plotting will be less and if box-size is kept low, plotting will be more. We discussed that a column is changed when price changes direction. The requirement of change of direction can also be defined. In the above example, the column was changed when price moved back to 104 from 105 or it went back to 104 from 103. So the column was changed when the price changed direction by one box, this is known as reversal value. So the figure chart shown above is a one-box reversal chart. Had this reversal value been 2 instead of 1, price had to go below 103 from 105 to change the column.

So there are two parameters when plotting the figure chart: box-value and reversal value. In the above chart, both are 1. The same chart can be plotted with a three-box reversal method also; meaning that a column will be changed only when price has changed direction by three boxes. So price will have to go at or below 102 from 105 to change the column. This is also applicable to price changing direction from down to up. The price at 102 will have to go at or above 105 to change the column from down to up. The counting is quite simple: count three boxes below 105 to arrive at reversal price of 102 and three boxes above 102 to arrive at reversal price of 105 (see Image 1.1.9).

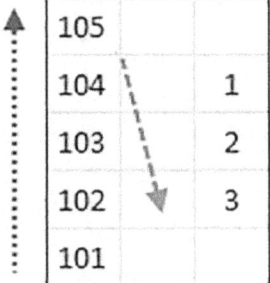 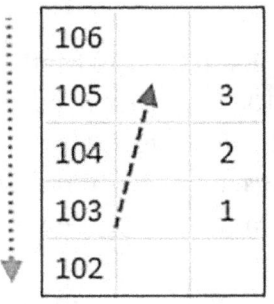 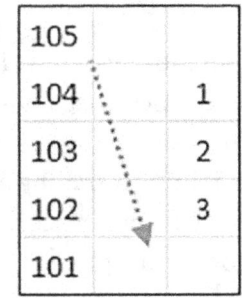 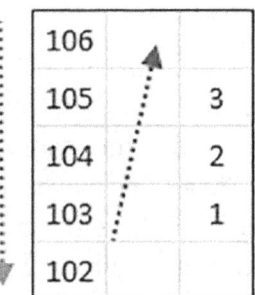

Image 1.1.9: Figure chart construction

There is another way to calculate this. Three boxes are 3 points in the above example because box-value is 1. Had there been 5, reversal points would have been 15. Hence, multiply the box-value by 3 to calculate the points that need to be deducted from the high price or added to the low price to arrive at a reversal price.

Note that this three-box requirement is not for continuation plotting; price has to reverse by three boxes to qualify for the change of column. Once the column is changed, every box will be plotted; it will need to go in the opposite direction by three boxes to change the column again. As a result, reversal will not be plotted frequently as small price fluctuations will be ignored while plotting the chart.

In the same example, if the price goes below 102 from 105, then the column needs to be changed and all the numbers to arrive at 102 are written in that column. In the same way, if price goes above 105 from 102, all the three figures to arrive at 105 are written (see Image 1.1.10).

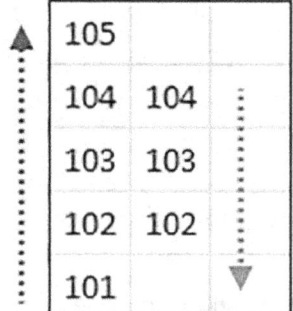 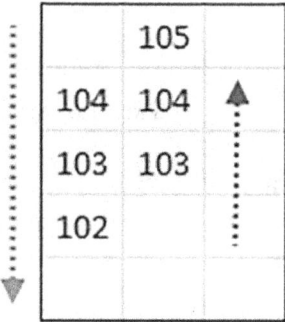

Image 1.1.10: Figure chart construction

So a three-box reversal chart will have a minimum three filled boxes in any column. Image 1.1.11 shows the three-box reversal figure chart with price moving to 102 and then 105.

105		105
104	104	104
103	103	103
102	102	
101		
100		

Image 1.1.11: Figure chart construction

Though these charts are not plotted when price doesn't move, continuation price and reversal price is known at every point in time. If price goes above 106 in the above chart, it will be written in the same column. If it moves down to or below 102, the column will be changed again. If it remains between 106 and 102, nothing will get plotted. So, if price is trading at 104, figure will remain same, hence actual price can be different from the current figure chart box-price. Note that continuation or reversal prices were calculated from last figure price and not from actual price.

Image 1.1.12 is a figure chart of Hindalco plotted using daily closing prices between 13th of June, 2013 to 26th of July, 2013.

Hindalco - Figure chart

				105		105	
104				104	104	104	104
103	103			103	103	103	103
102	102	102		102	102		102
101	101	101	101	101			101
100	100	100	100	100			100
99	99	99	99				99
98	98	98					98
97	97	97					97
96	96	96					96
95	95	95					95
94	94						

13 June 2013 to 26 July 2013

Image 1.1.12: Figure chart

The box-value in the above chart is 1 and the reversal value is 3, which can be changed as per requirement. Simple observation of the above chart will help you to know the levels where price has traded most and where it has seen more demand or supply.

Point Charts

It is not always practically feasible to write figures in the boxes. Imagine the pain especially when it is a four or five digit price and during the time when there were no computers. The clever thing is to make an index of figures at the left-hand side and just point (mark) the chart instead of writing the figures whenever the requirement of filling the box is met. Charts plotted with this method were called point charts. Image 1.1.13 is the same Hindalco chart plotted as a point chart.

Hindalco - Point chart

105					X		X	
104	X				X	X	X	X
103	X	X			X	X	X	X
102	X	X	X		X	X		X
101	X	X	X	X	X			X
100	X	X	X	X	X			X
99	X	X	X	X				X
98	X	X	X					X
97	X	X	X					X
96	X	X	X					X
95	X	X	X					X
94	X	X						

13 June 2013 to 26 July 2013

Image 1.1.13: Point chart

It looks better than the figure chart and is easy to maintain as well. But a major issue remains with both figure charts as well as point charts: We don't know whether a column is representing rising or falling prices; visually it is difficult to differentiate between them.

Point & Figure Chart

The solution was found by using different markings for both types of columns: Rising prices were marked with a cross-mark and falling prices were marked with a circle. Eventually, cross-marks became 'X' and circle became 'O'. Image 1.1.14 shows the same chart of Hindalco plotted with 'X' and 'O' columns, representing up and down moving prices respectively.

Hindalco - Point & Figure chart

105					X		X	
104	X				X	O	X	O
103	X	O			X	O	X	O
102	X	O	X		X	O		O
101	X	O	X	O	X			O
100	X	O	X	O	X			O
99	X	O	X	O				O
98	X	O	X					O
97	X	O	X					O
96	X	O	X					O
95	X	O	X					O
94	X	O						

13 June 2013 to 26 July 2013

Image 1.1.14: Point & Figure chart

The chart seems clean and complete. Charts plotted in this manner are known as Point & Figure charts. We plotted the above chart with 1 box-value and 3 reversal value, hence it is known as '1 × 3 Point and Figure chart.' Had the same chart been plotted using 10 as box-value, it would be named '10 × 3 Point and Figure chart.'

Three-box reversal charts are popular and widely used because reversal is weighed more, and that effectively reduces the noise. The box-price is the price of the 'X' or 'O' box. Remember, we calculate box-value and reversal value from the last box-price and not the actual price. So, for a P&F analyst, it is box-price that matters and continuation or reversal levels should always be calculated from box-price. The major feature of P&F charts is that 'X' represents rising price and 'O' represents falling price. Time or volume is not considered while plotting them. Only price is plotted – nothing else; which is exactly why they are also known as one-dimensional charts.

Exercise

As said earlier, the basics and construction of P&F charts should be very clear before one begins analyzing them. If you don't spend enough time on construction, confusion might arise while discussing patterns. Here is an exercise you have to complete, however boring it may seem.

Table 1.1.1 is a table for construction exercise of a 10 × 3 P&F chart.

Table 1.1.1: Point & Figure chart construction

Sr No	Price	Reversal	Sr No	Price	Reversal
1	2300.00		14	2494.90	
2	2339.65		15	2529.70	
3	2359.30		16	2499.25	
4	2336.55		17	2577.50	
5	2302.65		18	2611.05	
6	2320.25		19	2539.70	
7	2412.55		20	2674.95	
8	2393.60		21	2644.00	
9	2376.10		22	2517.90	
10	2353.65		23	2463.05	
11	2412.00		24	2519.25	
12	2363.55		25	2432.45	
13	2412.60		26	2324.10	

The table depicts the actual prices of a stock. You may wish to plot the chart on your own and then compare it with the final plotting. Put reversal price against every price in the above table after plotting the chart in Excel sheet, as shown below. Reversal price is a level that will fulfill the criteria to change the column.

2680												
2670												
2660												
2650												
2640												
2630												
2620												
2610												
2600												
2590												
2580												
2570												
2560												
2550												
2540												
2530												
2520												
2510												
2500												
2490												
2480												
2470												
2460												
2450												
2440												
2430												
2420												
2410												
2400												
2390												
2380												
2370												
2360												
2350												
2340												
2330												
2320												
2310												
2300												

A better option is to plot simultaneously and follow stepwise explanation. You can complete the exercise on your own after the 6th price and compare with the final chart. We are plotting a 10 × 3 chart, so continuation price will get plotted at every 10-point move in price. A reversal price is 30points away from the last box-price. If the price is in a column of X, then reversal price will be 30-points below the high price in column of X and vice versa.

1. The first price is 2300. Nothing can be done at this price, because we don't know whether price will move higher or lower and it will require starting the plotting with 'X' or 'O'. Plotting will begin with column of 'X' if price goes 10 points higher to 2310, and it shall begin with column of 'O' if it goes 10 points lower to 2290.

2. Price is moving higher and reaches 2339.65. So, plotting will begin with column of 'X' which will get marked up to box-price 2330. Box-price of 2340 is not marked because it has not been reached. The current box-price is 2330; hence, reversal price is 2300, which is 30 points less or three boxes away from box-price of 2330.

3. The next price is 2359.30. Price is moving higher, so we continue to fill boxes in the same column of 'X' up to the box-price of 2350. Reversal price would be 2320, so the column will turn to 'O' if price falls below 2320. Continuation box-price is 2360; meaning that even if price goes up by 70 paise from the current price, a new box will be plotted.

4. The price is 2336.55. It has not gone above 2360 to mark 'X', nor is it below the reversal value of 2320 to flip over to column of 'O'; hence, nothing can be plotted. Chart will not move, so reversal level would remain unchanged.

5. The price is 2302.65. It has gone below reversal value 2320, so column needs to be changed from 'X' to 'O'. Box-price of 2300 would not get filled because price has not gone below it. So, marking of 'O' would stop at box-price 2310 and reversal price would be 2340, which is 30 points added to the current box-price of 2310.

6. There will be no marking at 2320.25. It has not gone below 2300 to plot continuation box, nor gone above 2340 to plot reversal.

Image 1.1.15 shows the status of plotting so far.

Sr No	Price	Reversal
1	2300.00	-
2	2339.65	2300
3	2359.30	2320
4	2336.55	2320
5	2302.65	2340
6	2320.25	2340

2360		
2350	X	
2340	X	O
2330	X	O
2320	X	O
2310	X	O
2300	X	

Image 1.1.15: Point & Figure chart construction

7. Price goes up to 2412.55. As the price has moved well above the reversal price of 2340, flip over to a column of X and plot X upto the box-price of 2410. The reversal price now is 2380, 30-points below the last price of 2410.

8. It is status quo. Price is at 2393.60, which doesn't qualify for plotting either way.

9. Price goes down to 2376.10. It has fulfilled reversal criteria of going below 2380; hence, column needs to be changed to 'O' up to box-price 2380. Reversal price is 2410.

10. Price continues to go down up to 2353.65. Box-price of 2360 gets filled, but 2350 will not be marked because price has not gone below it. Reversal price is 2390 where column will be changed to 'X'.

11. Price is 2412 again, which has qualified for the reversal. So, column will turn to 'X', which will be plotted up to box-price 2410. Reversal price would be 2380.

12. Price goes down to 2363.55 to mark the reversal. So column will be changed to 'O', which will get filled up to box-price 2370. Reversal price is 2400.

13. Price has come to 2412.60 again. Column will turn to 'X' again up to box-price 2410. This is the third occurrence of this box-price getting tested. Reversal price would be 2380.

Image 1.1.16 shows the plotting so far.

Sr No	Price	Reversal
1	2300.00	-
2	2339.65	2300
3	2359.30	2320
4	2336.55	2320
5	2302.65	2340
6	2320.25	2340
7	2412.55	2380
8	2393.60	2380
9	2376.10	2410
10	2353.65	2390
11	2412.00	2380
12	2363.55	2400
13	2412.60	2380

Price							
2430							
2420							
2410			X		X		X
2400			X	O	X	O	X
2390			X	O	X	O	X
2380			X	O	X	O	X
2370			X	O	X	O	
2360			X	O			
2350	X		X				
2340	X	O	X				
2330	X	O	X				
2320	X	O	X				
2310	X	O					
2300	X						

Image 1.1.16: Point & Figure chart construction

14. The resistance at 2410 gets broken finally. Price went up to 2494.90, which qualifies for plotting continuation boxes up to 2490. Reversal price is 2460.

15. Price is 2529.70. Plotting will continue in the same column of 'X' up to 2520. Box-price of 2530 does not qualify for plotting. Reversal price is 2490.

16. Price is 2499.25. Nothing gets plotted.

17. Price is 2577.50. So, it has continued to move up further, which qualifies for continuation plotting of 'X' in the same column up to box-price 2570. Reversal price is 2540.

18. Price continues to move up to 2611.05. Column of 'X' will get plotted up to box-price 2610. Reversal price is 2580.

19. Price is 2539.70. It has gone much below reversal price requirement of 2580. Column will be changed to 'O', which will get filled up to box-price 2540. Had the price been at 2541, box-price of 2540 would not have been marked. Reversal price is 2570.

Image 1.1.17 shows the plotting so far.

Sr No	Price	Reversal
14	2494.90	2460
15	2529.70	2490
16	2499.25	2490
17	2577.50	2540
18	2611.05	2580
19	2539.70	2570
20	2674.95	
21	2644.00	
22	2517.90	
23	2463.05	
24	2519.25	
25	2432.45	
26	2324.10	

Price	1	2	3	4	5	6	7	8
2610							X	
2600							X	O
2590							X	O
2580							X	O
2570							X	O
2560							X	O
2550							X	O
2540							X	O
2530							X	
2520							X	
2510							X	
2500							X	
2490							X	
2480							X	
2470							X	
2460							X	
2450							X	
2440							X	
2430							X	
2420							X	
2410			X		X		X	
2400			X	O	X	O	X	
2390			X	O	X	O	X	
2380			X	O	X	O	X	
2370			X	O	X	O		
2360			X	O				
2350	X		X					
2340	X	O	X					
2330	X	O	X					
2320	X	O	X					
2310	X	O						
2300	X							

Image 1.1.17: Point & Figure chart construction

20. The next price is 2674.95, which qualifies for the reversal. Bulls have got the control back to change the column to 'X' and fill the boxes up to box-price 2670. Reversal price is 2640.

21. Price is 2644. Nothing gets plotted.

22. Price tumbles to 2517.90, which qualifies for reversal to column of 'O' up to box-price 2520. Reversal price is 2550.

23. Price goes down further to 2463.05. Box-price of 2470 gets filled in the same column of 'O'. Reversal price is 2500.

24. Price goes up to 2519.25, which qualifies for column reversal to 'X' up to box-price 2510. Reversal price is 2480.

25. Price falls to 2432.45, which qualifies for reversal to column of 'O' that will get plotted up to box-price 2440. Reversal price is 2470.

26. Price is 2324.10. So, box-price of 2330 gets marked in the same column of 'O'. Reversal price is 2360.

Image 1.1.18 shows the final plotting of the chart.

Sr No	Price	Reversal	Sr No	Price	Reversal
1	2300.00	-	14	2494.90	2460
2	2339.65	2300	15	2529.70	2490
3	2359.30	2320	16	2499.25	2490
4	2336.55	2320	17	2577.50	2540
5	2302.65	2340	18	2611.05	2580
6	2320.25	2340	19	2539.70	2570
7	2412.55	2380	20	2674.95	2640
8	2393.60	2380	21	2644.00	2640
9	2376.10	2410	22	2517.90	2550
10	2353.65	2390	23	2463.05	2500
11	2412.00	2380	24	2519.25	2480
12	2363.55	2400	25	2432.45	2470
13	2412.60	2380	26	2324.10	2360

Image 1.1.18: Point & Figure chart construction

Price												
2680												
2670									X			
2660									X	O		
2650									X	O		
2640									X	O		
2630									X	O		
2620									X	O		
2610							X		X	O		
2600							X	O	X	O		
2590							X	O	X	O		
2580							X	O	X	O		
2570							X	O	X	O		
2560							X	O	X	O		
2550							X	O		O		
2540							X	O		O		
2530							X			O		
2520							X			O		
2510							X			O	X	
2500							X			O	X	O
2490							X			O	X	O
2480							X			O	X	O
2470							X			O		O
2460							X					O
2450							X					O
2440							X					O
2430							X					O
2420							X					O
2410			X		X		X					O
2400			X	O	X	O	X					O
2390			X	O	X	O	X					O
2380			X	O	X	O	X					O
2370			X	O	X	O						O
2360			X	O								O
2350	X		X									O
2340	X	O	X									O
2330	X	O	X									O
2320	X	O	X									
2310	X	O										
2300	X											

Image 1.1.19: Point & Figure chart construction

13

The prices in the exercise table (Image 1.1.20) are actual daily prices of Bajaj Auto between September 2014 and January 2015. Only relevant prices were taken into account to explain the plotting, and even among these, notice that plotting didn't happen at every price.

It must be now clear that the P&F chart moves only when price moves. There were instances where we did not plot anything. At any point in time, the continuation and reversal price level will be known. Nothing gets plotted until price either trades at or above the continuation or reversal level.

Box-Value

Figure 1.1.1 shows the 10 × 3 chart of Bajaj Auto that we constructed in the exercise using Excel sheet.

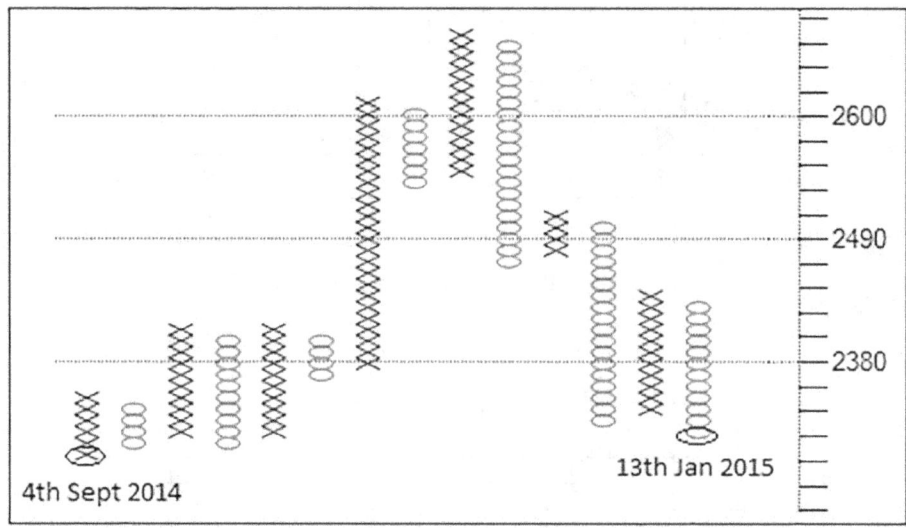

Figure 1.1.1: Bajaj Auto daily 10 × 3 Point & Figure chart

We plotted the above chart using 10 boxes. It can be plotted using any other box-value in a similar manner. The look of the chart will be different when box-value is changed. Figure 1.1.2 and Figure 1.1.3 show the same period P&F charts plotted using 5 and 20 box-values, respectively.

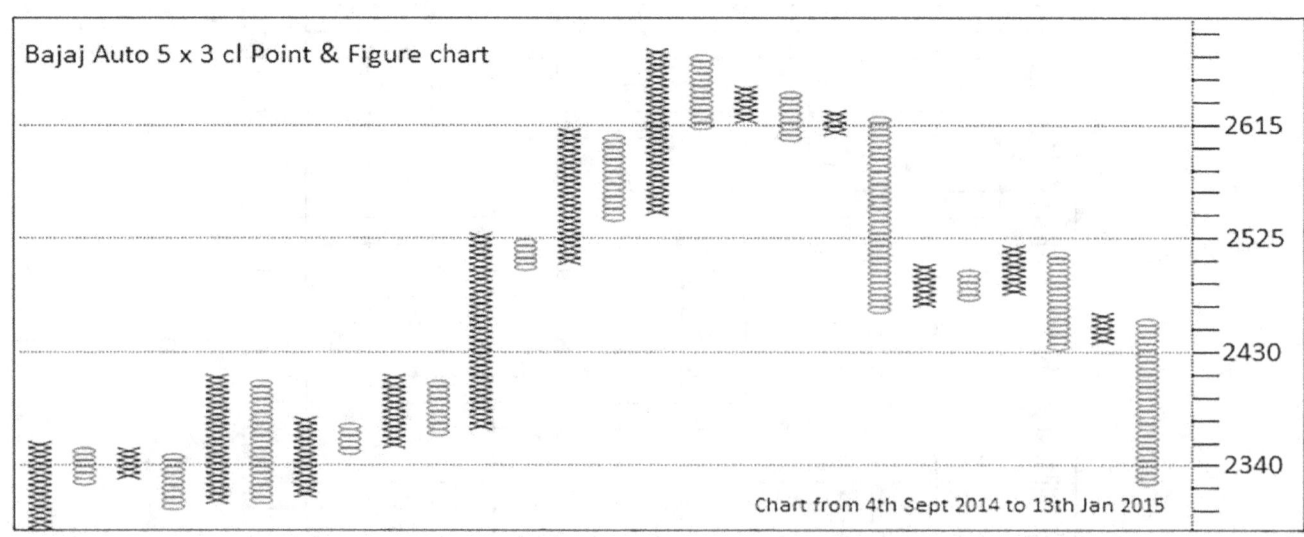

Figure 1.1.2: Bajaj Auto daily 5 × 3 Point & Figure chart

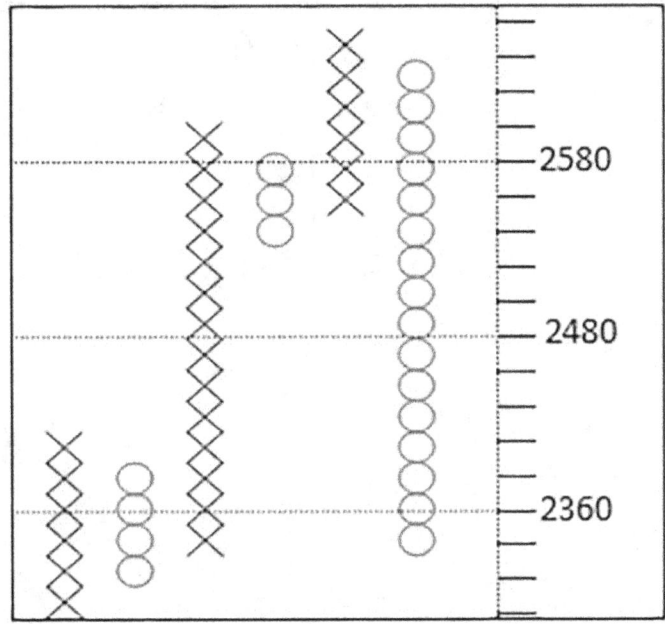

Figure 1.1.3: Bajaj Auto daily 20 × 3 Point & Figure chart

Notice that the chart plotted with box-value 5 has more columns than the chart with box-value 20. The number of columns can be increased or decreased further by changing the box-value. I am sure most of you will be thinking about which box-value is appropriate and how does one determine it. We will discuss this at length in Chapter 5. By now, it must be clear that changing the box-value alters the amount of information captured in the chart.

Log Charts

Charts plotted with 5, 10, 20, etc., are known as absolute box-value charts, since 5, 10, etc. are absolute numbers. The major problem in plotting a chart with them is that they become less relevant when price range changes. For example, Suzlon was trading at 200 at a particular time and it traded at 20 as well. Box-value of 2 when it was trading at 200 was 1% of the price, but the same box-value cannot be used when it is trading at 20 – as it would constitute 10% of the price, and it would require a 30% move to plot the reversal. There are many such examples of stocks moving in wide ranges where the same box-value cannot be used at all price levels.

P&F charts can also be plotted on a log scale where box-value will be defined as a percentage. A chart plotted with 1% box-value will need a 1% move from the last box-price to plot the continuation box and a column reversal needs a 3% price move. The manner of construction remains the same but log box-value is used instead of absolute. This makes the chart consistent in terms of box-value, and price patterns become more relevant.

Log charts should be used when analyzing a medium-term or long-term picture. Figure 1.1.4 depicts the 1% × 3 P&F chart of Nifty.

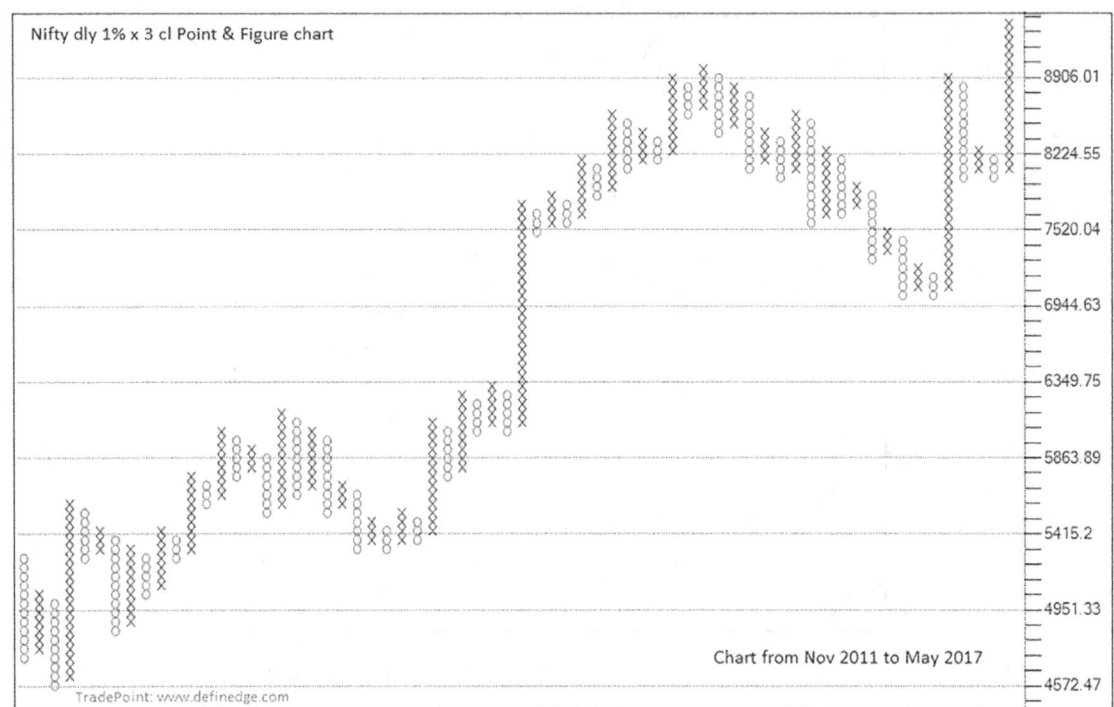

Figure 1.1.4: Nifty daily 1% × 3 Point & Figure chart

Continuation box requires 1% move in the chart shown above, and price needs to be reversed by 3% to qualify for change of column.

Unlike the regular candle or bar chart, the P&F chart does not move with time. Hence, the X axis in the chart does not capture time.

Numbers or alphabets are written instead of 'X' and 'O' in the column when month is changed: 1 instead of 'X' or 'O' is plotted in the column when month turns to January, 2 when it is February and so on. A, B and C are written for October, November and December, respectively. But I prefer plotting clear P&F charts with 'X' and 'O', and all charts in the book are shown in the same manner – the period of chart is written on it.

Reversal Value

We plotted a chart with reversal values 1 and 3. Reversal value can be any other number, but the logic of construction remains the same. Reversal values between 1 and 5 are normally used. A five-box reversal chart plotted with 10-point box-value needs 50 points for a column reversal and a two-box chart will need 20 points for a column reversal. Three-box reversal chart is the most popular P&F technique and widely followed. We would focus on three-box reversal charts for a while. We will discuss other reversal values in Chapter 6.

Chart Type

You may have noticed 'cl' used in the name of the charts shown earlier. It shows that chart is plotted with closing prices. P&F charts can be plotted using only one price. All charts shown above are plotted using closing prices. They can also be plotted using high or low price of the period but only one price needs to be selected for plotting.

In High–Low method of plotting, if previous column is of 'X', high price is considered for plotting and low is ignored. If high price does not qualify for the plotting of continuation box, then low price is taken into account to check if it qualifies for the reversal and column is changed to 'O' if it does. Similarly, low price is taken into account and high price is ignored if previous column is 'O'. If low price doesn't qualify for plotting, then high price is considered to check whether it qualifies for reversal.

The method and usefulness of High–Low charts are discussed at length in Chapter 5. 'HL' is used in the chart name when chart is plotted using High–Low price. People also use the term HiLo. Importantly, a chart name should clearly mention box-value, reversal value and data-type (High–Low or close) used for the plotting. There are other methods of plotting the prices as well, which are discussed in Chapter 5.

Time Frame

P&F charts can be plotted on all time frames. They can be plotted using daily, weekly, monthly, etc., prices or intraday prices such as hourly, half-hourly, ten minutes and even one minute. It can be plotted using tick-by-tick prices also, which is actually the origin of P&F charts. These were plotted on a piece of paper when rates used to appear on ticker tape during earlier times. But prices plotted on one-minute time interval display clearer patterns than tick-by-tick data.

Time frame is basically a data frequency to plot the charts. I recommend increasing the box-value on daily charts to look at the larger picture instead of plotting weekly or monthly charts. A weekly chart is locked at the end of the week, but plotting higher box-value daily chart gets locked every day. Box-value is the most significant variable for a P&F analyst and a most useful tool to analyse patterns.

Which box-value should be used is discussed at length in Chapter 5. But to begin with, the following are some suggestions for stocks on daily time frame:

- ⋏ 0.25% × 3 for short-term analysis
- ⋏ 1% × 3 for medium-term analysis
- ⋏ 3% × 3 for long-term analysis

It is similar to daily, weekly and monthly time frames. Volatility is different for index. As the stock market index are not as volatile as individual stocks, it would be inappropriate to use the same box-size settings for index. Hence, the following box-values may be considered for indices:

- ⋏ 0.10% × 3 for short-term analysis
- ⋏ 0.25% × 3 for medium-term analysis
- ⋏ 1% × 3 for long-term analysis

You can play around with different box-sizes to find the most suitable based on the volatility of the instrument and your trading time frame. Though, chapter on box-value post discussion over patterns will give you more understanding about using them.

Understanding P&F

P&F charts are plotted vertically and move up and down in columns of X and O respectively. So what we can see in large horizontal price–time charts will be captured in several columns in P&F charts. An up move seen over several candles in the candlestick chart can be captured in a single column in the P&F chart. A single column of X or O in the P&F chart can represent price action of anywhere between 1-day to several days, as long as the reversal criteria is not met. Image 1.1.21 shows two columns of 'X' and 'O' that are picked from the Nifty 10 × 3 chart plotted with daily closing prices.

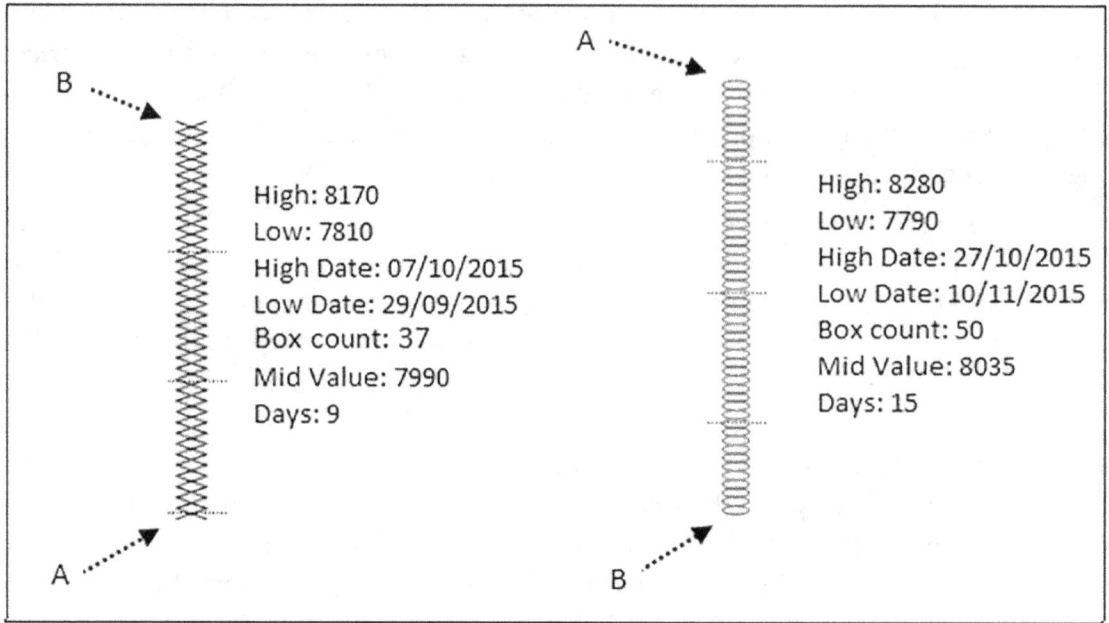

Image 1.1.20: Point & Figure chart columns

Point A is a beginning date in both the columns and Point B is the end date. Column of 'X' represents rising price, so low date is where the column begins and column of 'O' represents falling prices and hence high date is where column started, both marked by point A.

Column of 'X' that started on low date 29th September 2015, ended at high date 7th October 2015 at point B, capturing 9 days of up move. It went from 7810 at point A to 8170 at point B, which is the low and high price of the column, respectively. The total number of boxes in the column is 37, which shows a 370-point move in the same direction without a reversal of 30 points. Please re-read the construction part if there is difficulty in understanding this.

Column of 'O' started on high date 27th October 2015 marked by point A and ended on low date 10th November 2015 marked by point B. Therefore, column represents price move of 15 days. High price of the columns is 8280 at point A and low price is 7790 at point B. Number of boxes are 50 in the column, which shows a 500-point fall without a reversal of 30 points. The mid-value of each column is also mentioned, the purpose behind the same will be explained in a later chapter. Every P&F column provides all these information about the price trend in the column.

The method of construction is the unique feature of P&F charts that removes noise from the data. The chart captures price action that is significant, which is defined via the box-size and reversal value. At every plotting of 'X' that marks new high price, reversal level is being trailed up and with every new 'O' that takes the price down, reversal level is trailed down. Objectivity is the most wonderful part of P&F charts and I believe it is an integral part of trading. Everything in P&F is objective and all techniques that are going to be discussed in this book are objective in nature. With its unmatchable features, P&F complements all other methods of trading and subjective analysis.

Market Phases

There are mainly four types of market phases: Uptrend, Downtrend, Sideways and Broadening Phase, as shown in Image 1.1.22. All market trends can be divided into these phases. Each of these has different characteristics, and a strategy that works in one phase may not work in another.

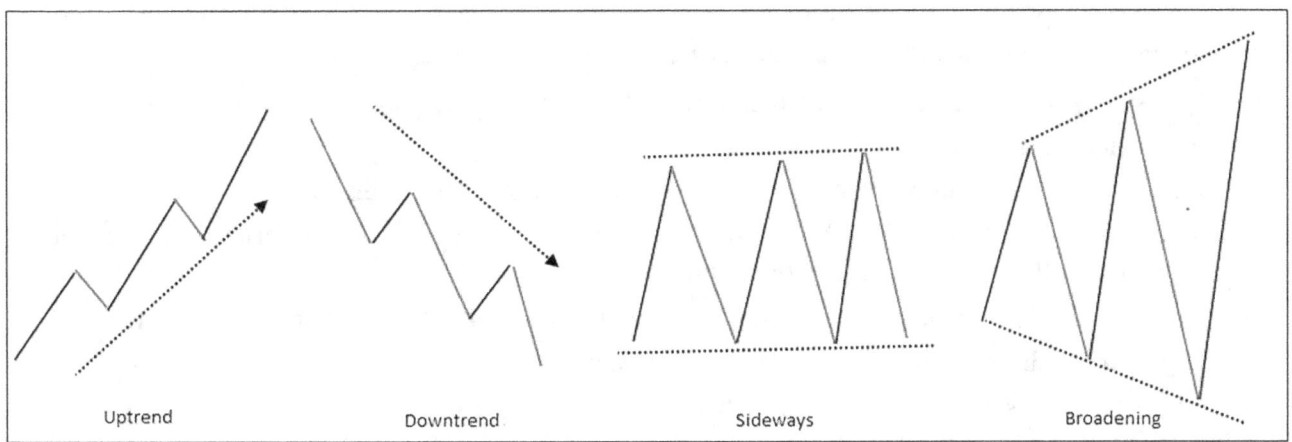

Image 1.1.21: Market phases

Every instrument will see these phases on all time frames – they are inevitable. By accepting this, we understand that any single strategy will not work in all the phases. Buying at low is a nice idea in an Uptrend, but may not be a sensible idea in a downtrend. Selling on rise or negative breakout would be effective in Downtrend. Trading supports-resistances will work during Sideways and avoiding breakout, rather going contra, should be the strategy during the Broadening Phase. Knowing this is fine but implementation is not that simple because phase identification is a difficult task. To make it more complex, volatility can be different and each time frame can have different phases. P&F is not immune to all these, but it has the major advantage of noiselessness. To a larger extent, the Sideways phase is handled during plotting itself; charts hardly move during such phases.

Sideways markets are difficult to handle. Apart from boredom and frustration, a major issue a trader faces during this period is overtrading. Markets keep generating clues but do not produce strong moves; breakouts fail and frequent trading eats out the gains made during the trending period. Trading success will be far improved only if these periods are ignored. The P&F chart is truly an effective technique here. As the P&F chart filters noise, irrelevant price moves are eliminated. Hence, overtrading too is curtailed to a big extent while using them.

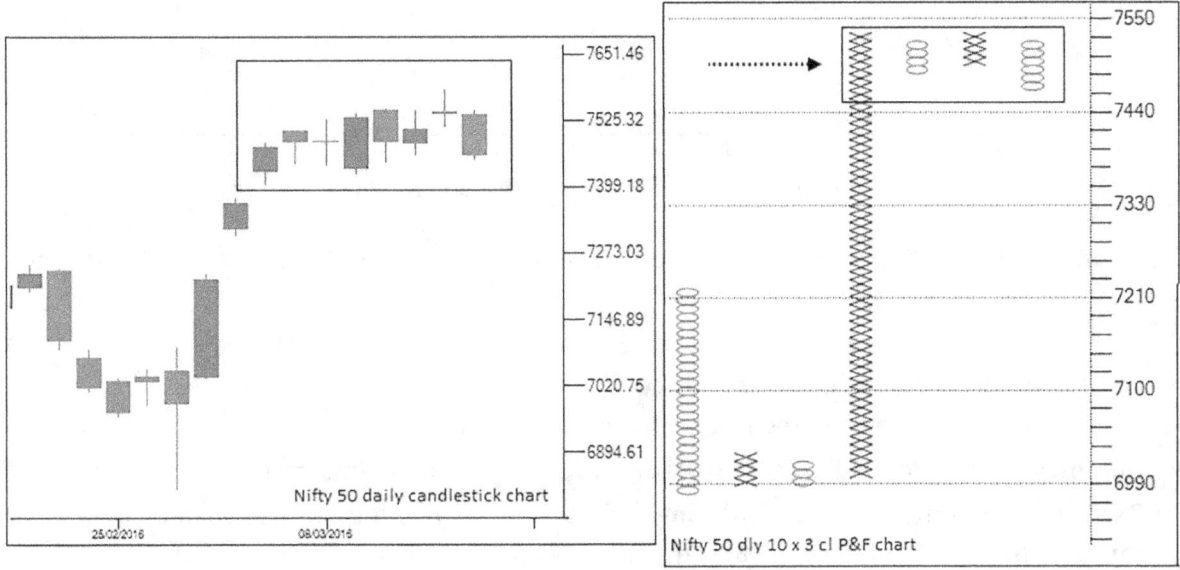

Figure 1.1.5: Nifty daily candlestick chart and daily 10 × 3 Point & Figure chart

The basic concepts of box-value, reversal value and type of charts are essential to be understood to plot a P&F chart. For revision, the terminologies are explained in brief again as follows:

- ⅄ **Box-size/Box-value:** Size of each box defined by the user.
- ⅄ **Box-price:** Price of a box of 'X' or 'O'.
- ⅄ **Reversal value:** Column reversal criteria. Normally it ranges between 1 and 5.
- ⅄ **Reversal price:** Price arrived by calculating reversal value from last box-price. A price level, if recorded, will result in change of the column.
- ⅄ **Close-only:** Charts plotted with closing price method are called closing only P&F charts.
- ⅄ **High–Low:** Charts plotted with High–Low price method are called High–Low P&F charts.
- ⅄ **Absolute charts:** Charts plotted with absolute box-value numbers.
- ⅄ **Log charts:** Charts plotted on log scale with percentage or log box-values.
- ⅄ **Continuation plotting:** Box plotted in the same column because price has continued the trend is known as continuation plotting.
- ⅄ **Column reversal:** Column switch from 'X' to 'O' or 'O' to 'X' because price reversal criteria are met.

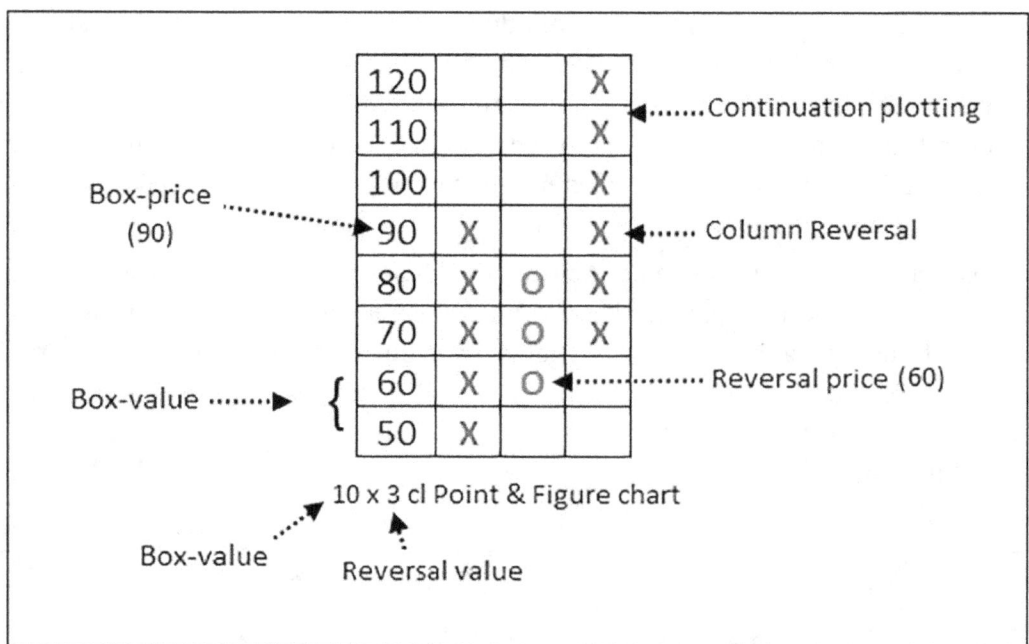

Image 1.1.22: Point & Figure chart terminologies

We begin the next section with discussion on techniques of reading P&F charts using basic patterns.

Summary

- ⅄ P&F chart moves only when price moves.
- ⅄ Column of 'X' represents rising prices and column of 'O' falling prices.
- ⅄ Continuation and reversal prices are known to a trader at all points in time.
- ⅄ P&F charts compress the data. The long and horizontal price formations in time-based charts are captured in several columns in P&F charts.
- ⅄ It is not that P&F charts don't plot trendless phases. They display price congestions and not the time.

- P&F charts can be plotted using any price – daily, weekly, monthly, yearly or any other intraday time interval. The patterns and their interpretation is the same, irrespective of time frame chosen. I prefer daily over other charts and one minute over other time interval charts.
- Plot 3% box-value charts for investing, 1% for medium-term trading and 0.25% for short-term trading in stocks. Plot 1%, 0.25% and 0.10%, respectively, for indices.

1.2: PATTERNS

Construction of Point & Figure charts is unique, and effective P&F analysis will be very difficult unless it is properly understood. Point & Figure charts move vertically in alternating columns of 'X' and 'O'. The combination of the columns produces patterns that are objective and simple to identify. I have segregated patterns into different types to ensure stepwise explanation and smooth sailing through them.

Basic and most simple Point & Figure formations are explained in this chapter. No other pattern, trading or analysis is conceivable without these formations, hence though basic, this is one of the most important chapters of the book and integral to understand of the Point & Figure methodology.

Basic Patterns

Basic patterns are formed with the combination of two or three columns and no signal in P&F charts can be formed without them. They are objective in nature, very simple to understand and can be identified easily with little practice. There are two types of basic patterns explained below.

1. Column Reversal

We discussed in the construction part that column switchover happens in P&F chart only when reversal criteria is met. In a three-box reversal chart, price needs to be reverse by three-times the box-value to change the column from 'X' to 'O' and vice versa. It is not only an important feature of P&F charts but also provides us significant information. This switchover from column of 'X' to 'O' or vice versa is known as column reversal. There are two types of column reversal – Positive & Negative.

As explained in Image 1.2.1, in positive column reversal, column of 'O' turns to column of 'X' and in negative column reversal, column of 'X' turns to column of 'O'.

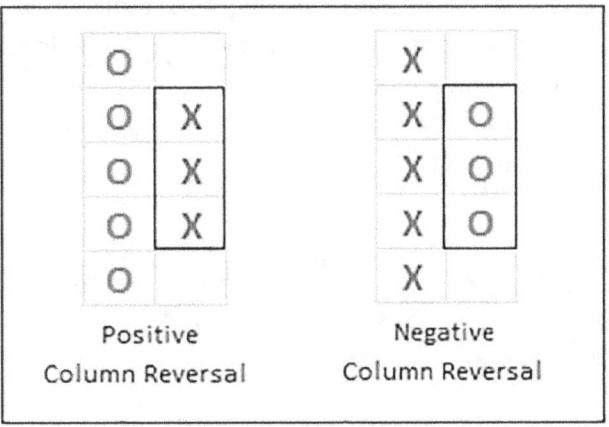

Image 1.2.1: P&F column reversal

Column reversal is a key feature of P&F charts. Interestingly, it is a pattern that is formed at every column. We discussed earlier that any column in a three-box reversal chart will have at least three boxes in it; hence, this formation takes place at the occurrence of the third box in every column. So, the third box-price of every column is a price that qualifies the formation (see Image 1.2.2).

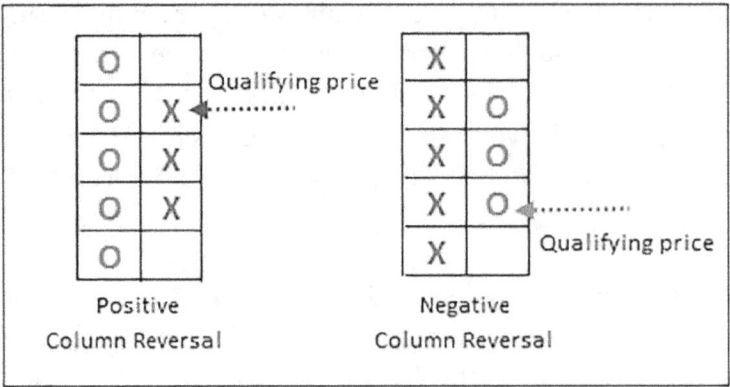

Image 1.2.2: P&F column reversal

P&F charts can be plotted using other than three-box reversal values also. In such cases, the first, second or fifth box of every new column in case of 1-box, 2-box and 5-box reversal chart, will be the qualifying price. As discussed in the construction part, at any point in time, we know the reversal price where the column will be changed. Hence, the box-price that will qualify the column reversal pattern is always known in advance.

P&F charts are basically swing charts. Every time a column is turned to 'O' or a negative column reversal takes place, it forms a swing high, which is the high box-price of column of 'X' from which it is turning. Similarly, a swing low is marked at low box-price of column of 'O' when positive column reversal takes place. This basic information and simple formation is underused by many practitioners in the field. It is very useful while designing various price setups and also a very important formation when higher box-values are used.

2. Basic Buy-Sell signals

Basic Buy and Sell signals of P&F charts are known as Double Top Buy and Double Bottom Sell patterns. Name is unfortunate because Double Top is a bearish formation and Double Bottom is a bullish formation in traditional technical analysis, which is exactly the opposite in case of P&F. In the usual price–time charts, Double Top is when two peaks are at similar position and price trades below neckline of the pattern, and the pattern is Double Bottom when two bottoms are formed at identical levels and price trades above the neckline of the pattern, as shown in Image 1.2.3.

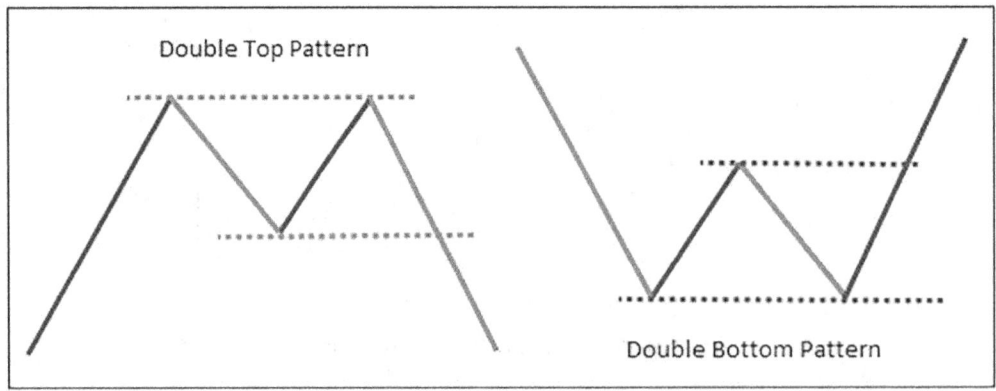

Image 1.2.3: Double Top and Double Bottom patterns

P&F Double Top is a bullish pattern and Double Bottom is a bearish pattern, which are also known as basic Buy and basic Sell signals, respectively. P&F Double Top is a Buy signal that indicates that price has tested previous top and broken out. In the same way, P&F Double Bottom is a Sell signal that is formed when previous bottom gets broken (see Image 1.2.4).

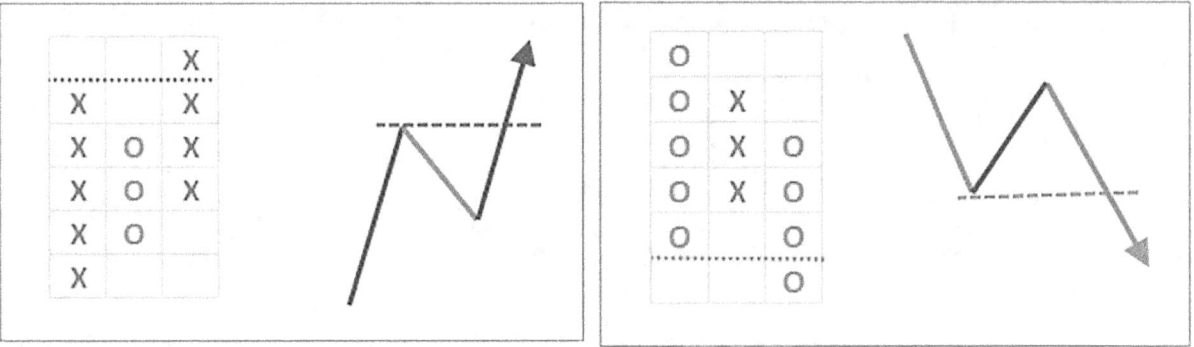

Image 1.2.4: P&F Double Top Buy and Double Bottom Sell patterns

Double Top Buy is a three-column pattern which is formed when a column of 'X' exceeds immediate previous column of 'X'. It is basically a breakout above a previous swing high and the signal is generated when the price moves one box above the high of the previous column of 'X'. In the same way, Double Bottom Sell is a three-column formation that shows downside breakout of previous swing low. It is formed when column of 'O' falls below immediate previous column of 'O'.

It is important to understand that the breakout happens when a new box is plotted above top of previous column of 'X' in case of Buy pattern and below low of previous column of 'O' for Sell pattern.

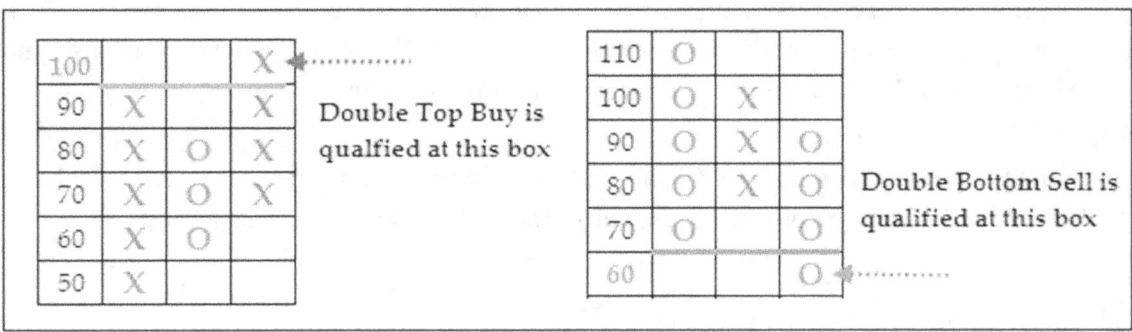

Image 1.2.5: P&F Double Top Buy and Double Bottom Sell patterns

See patterns in Image 1.2.5. A Double Top Buy signal gets generated when price goes above 100. It is not a Double Top pattern unless price marks a box above previous column of 'X'. In the second figure in the image, Double Bottom Sell signal gets generated when box-price of 60 is marked. So the formation is objective in nature and there cannot be an argument over its occurrence; whether and how to trade them is a separate discussion.

Note that a Double Top is qualified when price exceeds immediate previous column of 'X' or Double Bottom is qualified when price falls below immediate previous column of 'O' and not necessarily columns before that. Hence, it is a three-column formation and you have to refer to only the previous column to identify these patterns. There are only two possibilities with every column of 'X': either it will be above previous column of 'X' or not, hence either it will be a Double Top buy column or not. Similarly, every column of 'O' is either a Double Bottom Sell column or not.

To begin with, when you are looking at a column of 'X', just compare it with the immediate previous column of 'X' to mark the Double Top Buy signals. Figure 1.2.1 shows the Double Top formations in the 10 × 3 P&F chart of Bajaj Auto.

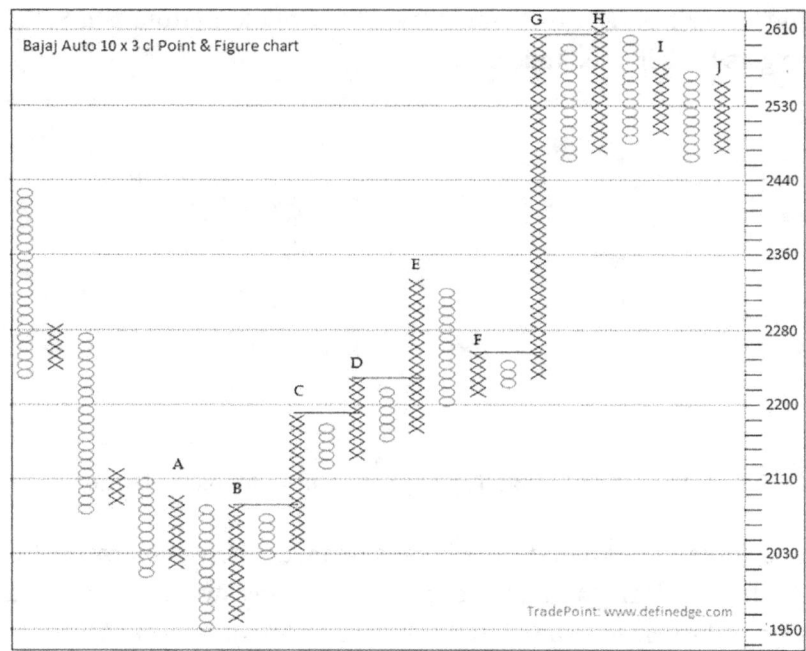

Figure 1.2.1: Bajaj Auto daily 10 × 3 cl Point & Figure chart

There is no Double Top Buy signal in column A because high price of that column is not above high price of its previous column of 'X'. There is no Buy signal in column B as well for the same reason. But high price of column C has gone above high price of column B, hence it qualifies for the Double Top Buy formation at box-price when it crossed higher price of column B. Column D and column E also qualify for Double Top Buy signals. There is no Buy pattern in column F. Column G and H qualify for Buy pattern. Column I and J do not qualify.

To mark the Sell signals, a column of 'O' should be compared with immediate previous column of 'O'. Figure 1.2.2 shows only Double Bottom Sell signals in the 10 × 3 P&F chart of Bajaj Auto.

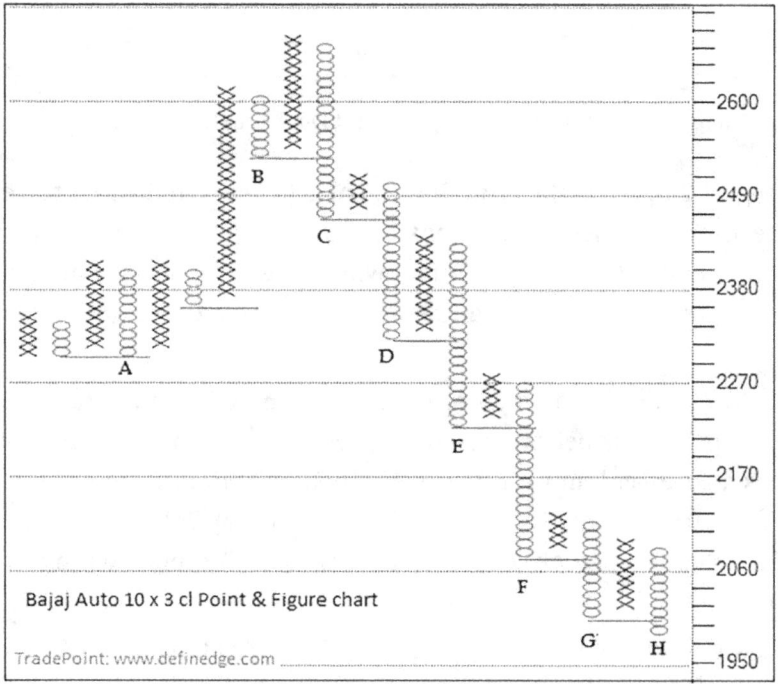

Figure 1.2.2: Bajaj Auto daily 10 × 3 cl Point & Figure chart

There is no Double Bottom Sell signal at column A because it is at the same level of the previous bottom of 'O'. There is no sell signal in column B as well, because it is not below the low of its previous column of 'O'. The Double Bottom Sell signal is marked at column C at box-price when it fell below low price of column B. There are Double Bottom Sell signals in columns D, E, F, G and H, because low price of each column is below the low price of its immediate previous column of 'O'. A sell signal is marked as soon as a new box of 'O' gets formed below the low of its previous column of 'O'.

The criteria of breakout are certain; hence, it is possible to know in advance about the box-price that would generate the signal. See the first chart of Image 1.2.6. Current box-price is 90; a Double Top Buy signal will be generated if box-price of 100 is marked. In the second chart of the same image, recent box-price is 70; a Double Bottom Sell signal will be formed if price falls below 60. So the price level at which the Buy or Sell signal will be formed is always known in advance.

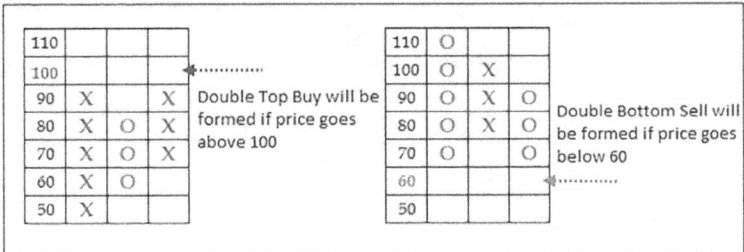

Image 1.2.6: P&F Double Top Buy and Double Bottom Sell patterns

Double Top Buy and Double Bottom Sell signals are the most basic P&F formations that display swing breakouts. When a column of 'X' rises above previous column 'X', it is basically a bullish swing breakout and a column of 'O' going below previous column of 'O' is a bearish swing breakout. The first column of these three-column formations represents a trend. The second column represents correction and the third represents breakout or resumption of previous trend.

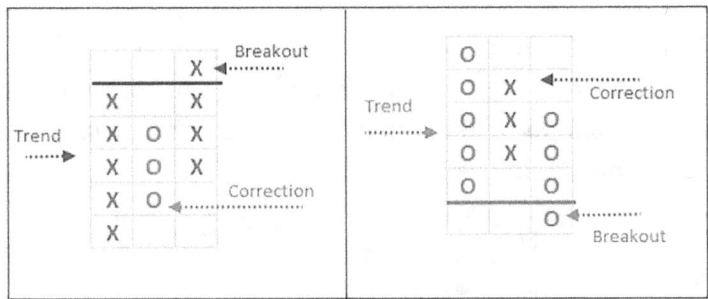

Image 1.2.7: Trend, correction and breakout

Hence, a bullish swing breakout is a Buy signal and Bearish swing breakout is a Sell signal. So it is possible to mark a P&F chart with clear Buy-Sell signals. Can one trade these simple patterns? Can a swing trading method using these objective signals be designed? Wait ... there is more to discuss before we come to that.

Columns and Signals

Figure 1.2.3 shows a three-box reversal P&F chart of Nifty daily price plotted with 20-point box-value. There are 17 columns of 'X' and 16 columns of 'O' in this chart, of which a Double Top buy pattern has been formed in 10 columns of 'X' and Double Bottom Sell pattern has formed in only 7 columns of 'O'. Signals are marked on the chart.

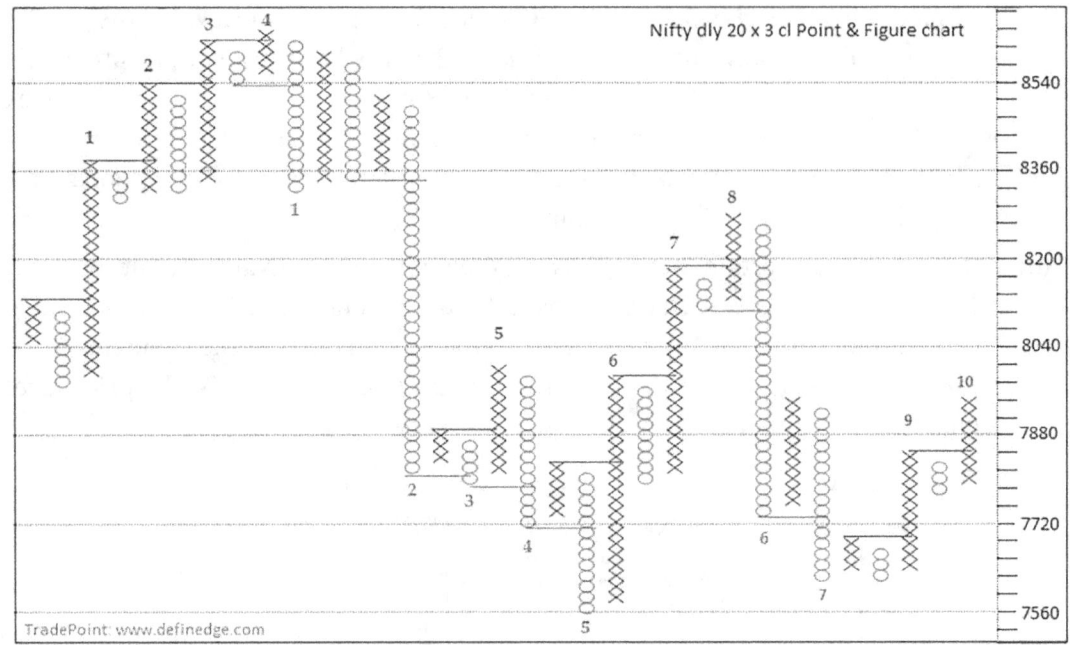

Figure 1.2.3: Nifty daily 20 × 3 cl Point & Figure chart

In a P&F chart, column of 'X' appears after column of 'O' and vice versa. Hence, on a given time period, a P&F chart will have equal number of 'X' and 'O' column. The P&F method compresses the price data and presents a larger picture of price behavior plotted across several columns. Insignificant data are ignored while plotting, so we say they are noise-free and can result in increased productivity of trades. Now you know that not every column generates even basic Buy or Sell signal!

Swing Chart

P&F charts are best swing charts. As explained earlier, 'X' when turned to column of 'O' marks swing high and 'O' when turned to column of' X' locks swing low. There are three figures shown in Image 1.2.8. The first figure is a P&F chart and the second is a chart drawn with line connecting the top of every column of 'X' and the bottom of every column of 'O', which are the important swing points. The same lines are shown in the third figure by removing the P&F chart.

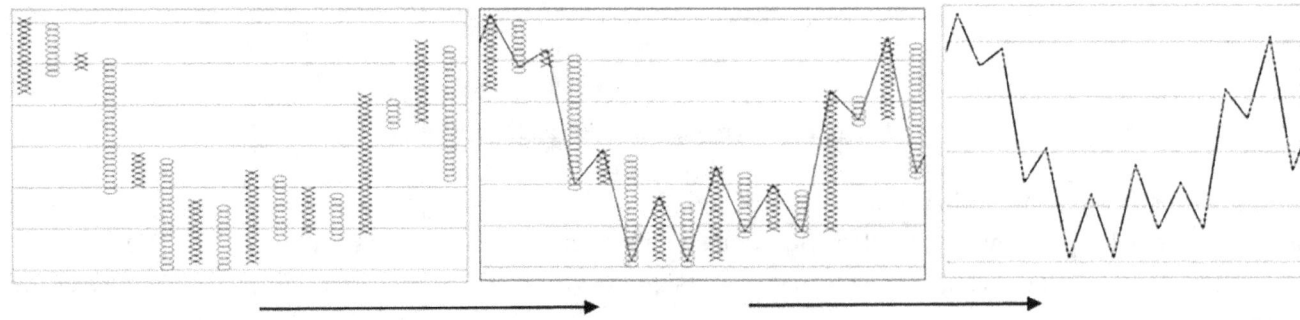

Image 1.2.8: P&F swings

So, basically a P&F chart is a curve-less line chart showing the swing points. If lines are drawn instead of columns, then a P&F chart of figure 1 will look like figure 3. Given below are charts that explain the importance of this. Figure 1.2.4 is a line chart of Tata Motors drawn by connecting the daily closing prices during late 2015.

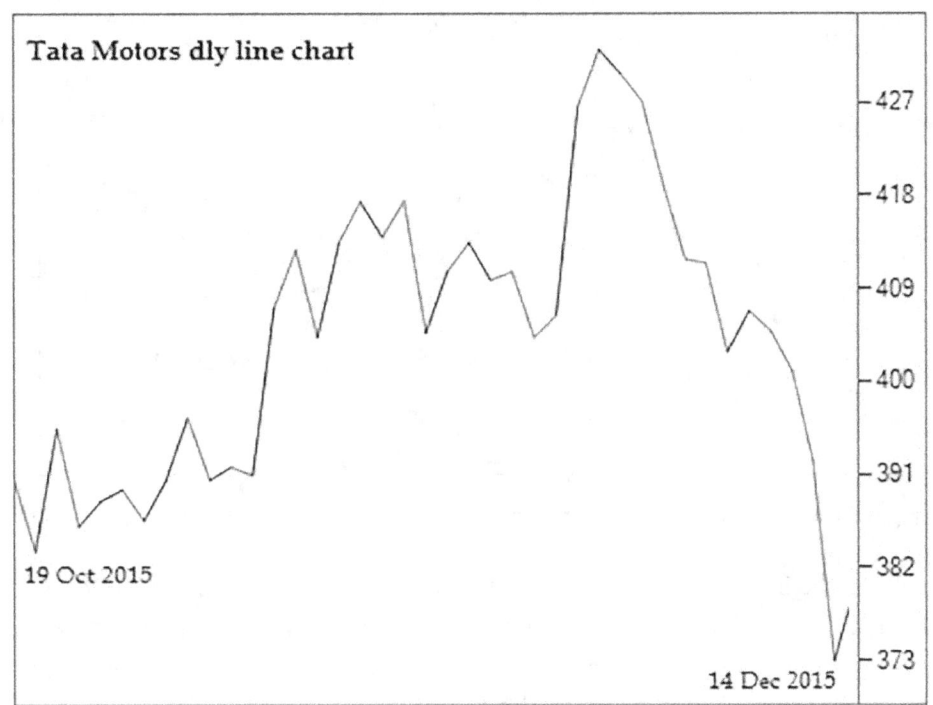

Figure 1.2.4: Tata Motors daily line chart

Figure 1.2.5 is a 0.25% × 3 P&F chart of the same line chart of Tata Motors. Basic Buy-Sell signals are marked in the chart. Patterns that are quite difficult to define on the line chart can be easily defined on P&F.

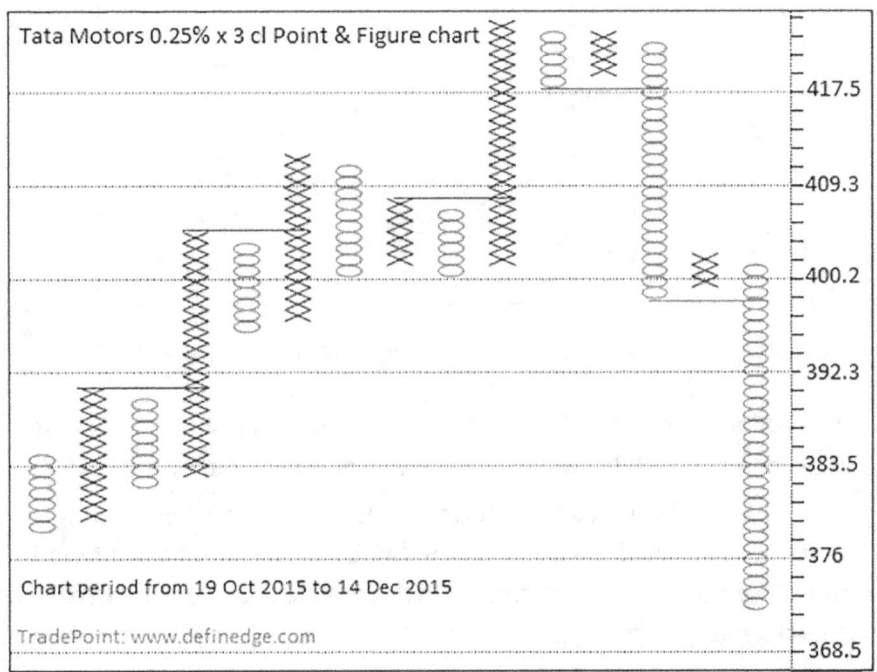

Figure 1.2.5: Tata Motors daily 0.25% × 3 cl Point & Figure chart

If swing points of the P&F chart shown in Figure 1.2.5 are connected, then it will look like Figure 1.2.6. Compare it with the line chart shown in Figure 1.2.4 and you will observe that a lot of noise is removed, besides availability of simple and objective patterns.

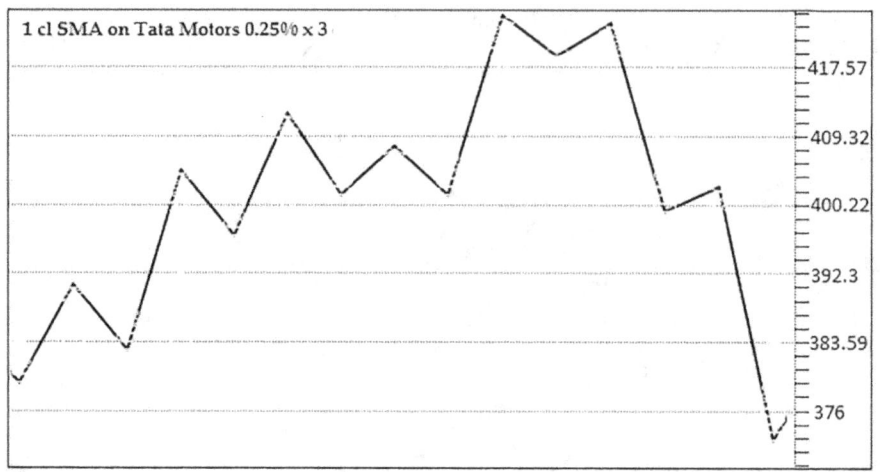

Figure 1.2.6: One column SMA line on Tata Motors 0.25% × 3 cl Point & Figure chart

The chart explains the importance of noise-free plotting and simple unmatchable formations that P&F throws. Noise can be removed further if box-value is increased. Figure 1.2.7 is the same chart plotted with 0.75% × 3 parameters. The entire formation is confined to four columns!! So sensitivity of P&F charts can be defined and altered by the user by changing the box-size.

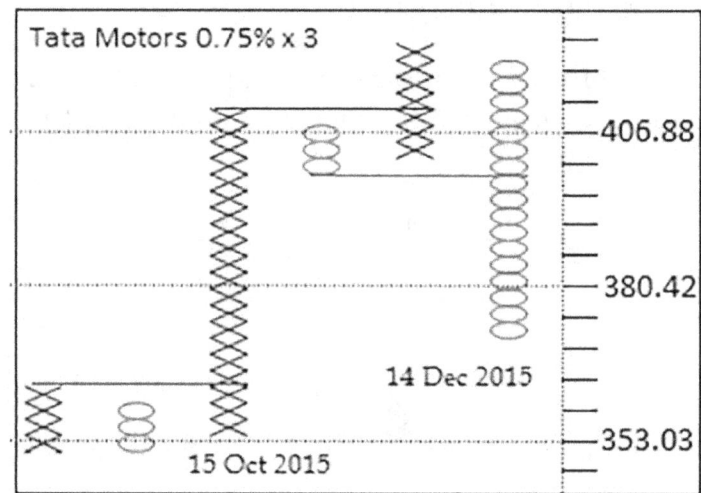

Figure 1.2.7: Tata Motors daily 0.75% × 3 cl Point & Figure chart

Using different box-values produces different setups. Box-value with 1% will show lesser columns than box-value 0.25% – the latter will have more noise and more information.

Any type of price move (column) can be defined and setups can be created by combining them. Knowing P&F in this manner will enable you to understand, analyse and trade them in a better way. It is not always easy to find those moves in price–time charts because there is time involved. As time elapses, it stretches the chart horizontally in price–time charts.

The major advantage of making things objective is that we can scan the patterns periodically and back-test them to study the environment that is most suited. These basic signals and all patterns that we are going to discuss remain valid for all P&F charts whether they are plotted with closing prices or other methods. Interpretation of patterns is quite different on High–Low charts; they are wider than charts plotted with closing prices. Several patterns are found more on wider charts and should be looked for. We will discuss them in detail in Chapter 5 on parameters.

Fresh and Continuation Signals

Not all P&F columns are Buy-Sell columns, and not all Buy-Sell columns are Fresh signals. A bullish breakout that happened at Double Top Buy signal remains open until formation of Double Bottom Sell signal. There can be Double Top Buy signals in between, which are known as Continuation Buy signals. Fresh Buy signal is a first Double Top Buy pattern coming after a Sell signal. Similarly, first Double Bottom Sell pattern coming after buy signal is a Fresh Sell signal; all the Double Bottom Sell signals in between are Continuation Sell signals. Figure 1.2.8 is the ABB chart that shows the Fresh and Continuation signals.

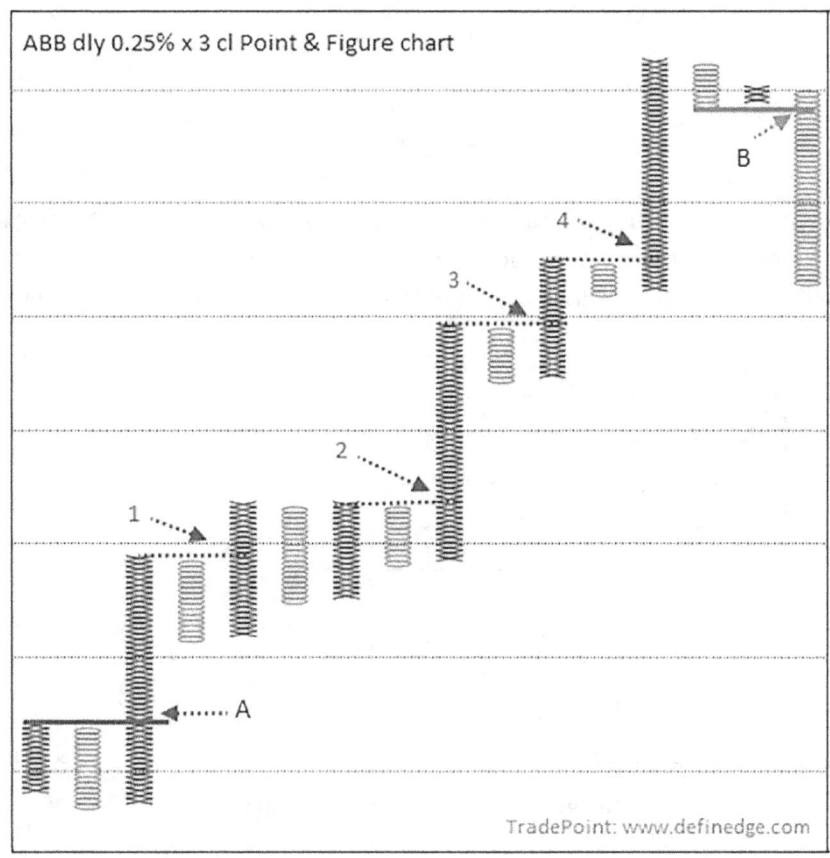

Figure 1.2.8: ABB daily 0.25% × 3 cl Point & Figure chart

If these basic signals are traded on the above chart, buy trade taken at Fresh Double Top signal at point A remains open until point B. Four Double Top Buy signals shown in between are Continuation bullish signals.

In simple words, one can trade long based on Double Top Buy and exit when Double Bottom Sell signal occurs. One can sell at Double Bottom Sell signal and cover when Double Top Buy pattern triggers. We will discuss this further.

Exit Method

We discussed that it is possible to know beforehand the price at which these Buy and Sell signals will be generated. In the method discussed above, when an instrument is bought upon Double Top Buy formation, the exit pattern is Double Bottom Sell pattern. While placing the buy trade, it will be possible to determine the price at which exit or Sell signal will get triggered. See Image 1.2.9. Double Top Buy is generated when box-price of 100 is marked. The stop can be placed at 50, simply because Double Bottom Sell pattern will be triggered if price falls to or below 50.

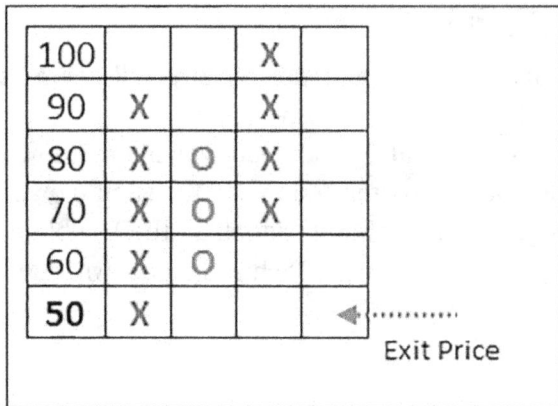

Image 1.2.9: Point & Figure pattern

See Image 1.2.10, in continuation of the above chart. Price recovered again after forming the column of 'O'. For long trade initiated at 100, exit price becomes 90 because that is the level at which Double Bottom Sell signal will be formed now. So stop-loss is trailed from 50 to 90 as price has moved up in the favor.

130			X		X	
120			X	O	X	
110			X	O	X	
100			X	O		
90	X		X	◄		◄ Exit Price
80	X	O	X			
70	X	O	X			
60	X	O				
50	X					

Image 1.2.10: Point & Figure pattern

So exit price can be known in advance at every point in time. Vice versa is applicable to short signals.

So with this method, initial stop-loss is always known while placing the trade and also there is a trailing mechanism that keeps one in the trade when trend is in favor and until it is reversed. There is no need to ask any one when you should exit your position!

Basic Method – SAR

So, can a Double Top Buy signal and Double Bottom Sell signal be traded alone? Yes. This is known as an asymmetric approach and defines the basic method of trading P&F charts. It is an objective trading system that becomes a SAR (Stop and Reverse) method of trading, meaning that an instrument is bought when a Double Top Buy signal is formed and sold when a Double Bottom Sell signal is triggered. While exiting bullish trade, Fresh short should also be initiated, which will be covered when Double Top Buy signal has been generated and Fresh long is also initiated. A trading position always remains open when SAR method of trading is implemented. Figure 1.2.9 is a P&F chart of Reliance.

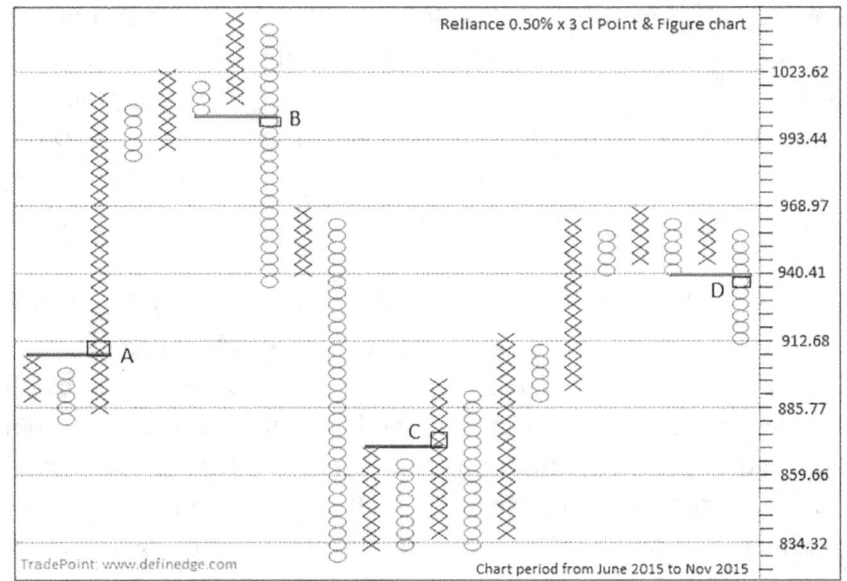

Figure 1.2.9: Reliance daily 0.50% × 3 cl Point & Figure chart

SAR trading method discussed above is marked on the chart. Point A is Double Top Buy formation, which is a Buy signal. The Buy trade remains active until a Double Bottom Sell signal is formed, which happened at Point B, and which is a first Sell signal after Double Top Buy pattern triggered at point A. Long positions should be liquidated and Fresh shorts may be initiated if SAR method is followed. Point C is the first Double Top Buy since point B, hence short trades should be covered and Fresh long trades should be created. Long trades should be kept open until point D, where a first Sell signal since point C forms. So longs should be exited and Fresh shorts should be created at point D. Hence, there are a total four trades in this chart: two long trades and two short trades.

Figure 1.2.10 is a P&F chart of ABB. Signals based on the same trading method are marked on the chart.

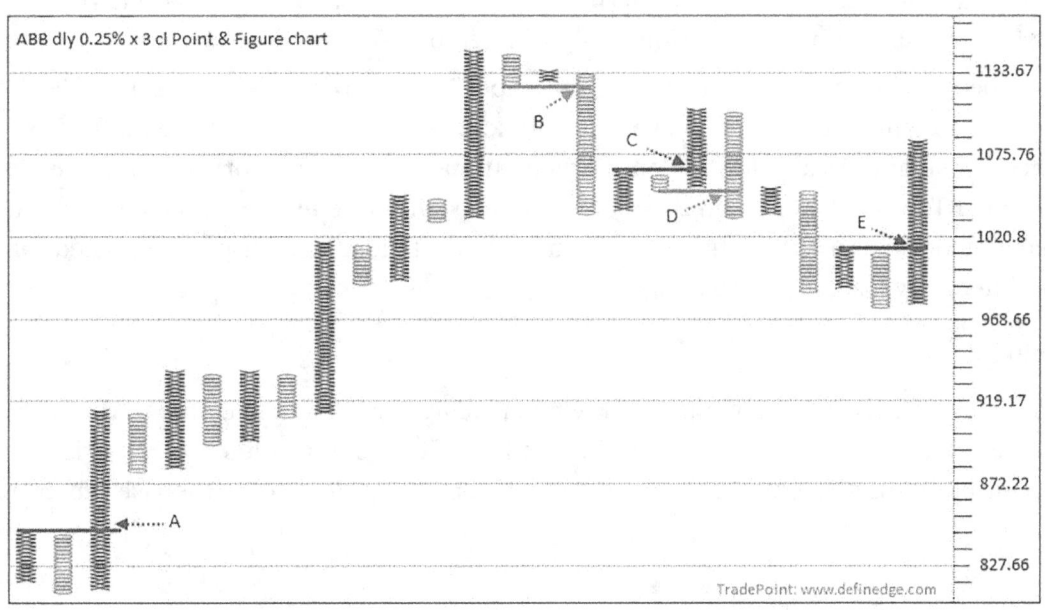

Figure 1.2.10: ABB daily 0.25% × 3 cl Point & Figure chart

Point A is a Double Top Buy formation where a long trade or Fresh Buy should be initiated. Buy trade remains active until point B, where a first sell signal is formed after buy signal. So what is bought at Point A should be sold and Fresh short positions should be created here. Point C is Double Top Buy formation, hence short positions should be covered and Fresh Buy signal is generated. Point D is where longs should be exited and Fresh short can be initiated. Point E is where short trades should be liquidated and Fresh longs should be initiated, being the first buy signal since point D. So there are a total 5 trades in this chart: 3 long and 2 short.

The above charts explain the SAR method of trading using basic P&F Buy-Sell signals clearly. It is an objective method of trading and a trend-following method which will generate returns when there is a trend. The whipsaws or losses will happen when there is a volatility but it can be understood that they can be comparatively much less than other methods mainly because major portions of Sideways trend gets eliminated due to the manner of plotting of P&F charts. Hence, plotting is curtailed; not every column generates Buy-Sell signals and not every Buy-Sell signal is traded. There will be fewer signals during congestion period; hence, number of trades is significantly reduced with better productivity.

It is not that only this asymmetric approach is traded. More analysis can be performed and Continuation signals can also be traded using different methods, but one should be able to identify the Fresh signals and Continuation signals.

A 'long-only' approach can also be followed using the same method. Meaning that a Buy signal is taken when there is a Double Top Buy pattern and it is liquidated when a first Double Bottom Sell pattern occurs after a Buy signal. Short trades are not initiated and there is no position during such times. The 'long-only' approach will keep one out from the bearish markets.

Though position sizing is beyond the scope of this book, it is important to mention that P&F signals can be effectively utilized for designing position sizing rules. For example, enter 50% upon breakout and add 50% upon next continuation breakout, and exit all when reversal signal gets formed. This is known as pyramiding – P&F basic method flourishes with it. The major advantage is that if trade is immediately reversed, stakes are not very high, and when there is a strong trend, you are in with maximum positions. Pyramiding is a popular method of position sizing adopted by many successful traders.

What has been the past performance of this method? What box-value is more suitable to trade this? All these questions will be answered later in this book. The best thing about the method is objectivity. You don't need great analytical skills to identify them. It may or may not work, but occurrence cannot be argued. A Double Top Buy will remain a Double Top Buy signal whenever you open the chart, no matter what has happened subsequently. It is of utmost importance that subjectivity gets reduced for successful implementation of any trading methodology.

Affordability

We discussed, that we always know initial risk while placing the trade itself. Due to this, affordable and non-affordable trades can be determined easily. Number of boxes in a column of 'O' prior to Buy signal and number of boxes in a column of 'X' prior to Sell signal help determine the risk when trading (see Image 1.2.11).

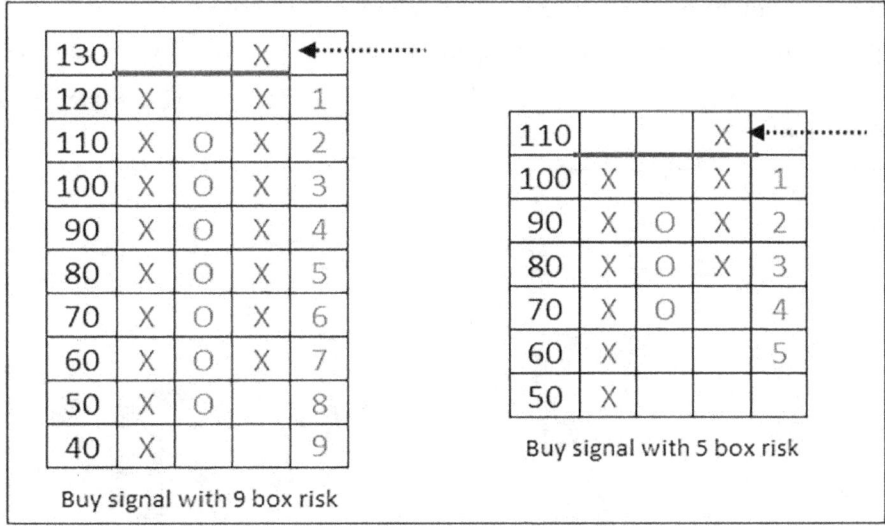

130			X	← · · · · · · · · · · · ·
120	X		X	1
110	X	O	X	2
100	X	O	X	3
90	X	O	X	4
80	X	O	X	5
70	X	O	X	6
60	X	O	X	7
50	X	O		8
40	X			9

Buy signal with 9 box risk

110			X	← · · · · · · · · · ·
100	X		X	1
90	X	O	X	2
80	X	O	X	3
70	X	O		4
60	X			5
50	X			

Buy signal with 5 box risk

Image 1.2.11: Affordability

The first figure in Image 1.2.11 has a long column of 'O' before the Buy signal. There are seven 'O's in the column, but it will take nine boxes for a Double Bottom Sell signal to be generated. A trade with three boxes as reversal, shown in the second figure column will take five boxes to generate the Sell signal. Two boxes get added to the number of boxes prior to the signal while calculating the risk.

Logic dictates that a trade with minimum boxes in the previous column offers a trade with lesser risk. A three-box reversal chart will have minimum three boxes in the column before the signal, a two-box will have minimum two boxes and a five-box will have minimum five boxes.

If the risk is measurable and known, it is easy to differentiate the trade as affordable or unaffordable. While affordability can be subjective, to put it in simple words, risk that you are not comfortable taking is unaffordable trade. When a trade is offering unaffordable risk, ignore it and wait for the next opportunity. Overall risk–reward is attractive when only affordable trades are initiated. The quantum of risk depends on the box-value used, which we will discuss in length subsequently.

The above calculation is applicable when exit method is a basic sell signal. There are other ways of exiting the trades as well; risk can be calculated in each case in similar manner. Exciting trading opportunities come by when affordable trades are triggered from the major patterns, which we will discuss in the next chapter.

Exercise

I have ensured that more time is spent on the basic formations and every aspect of these is discussed. P&F becomes real fun and takes you into another zone if this part is very well understood and pondered upon. And it can become complicated or can confuse you if they are hurriedly overlooked and deserved time is not spent. People take it for granted and the overall subject becomes difficult for them. Take a break before going ahead and spend some time to think more on the formations and methods that we have discussed. Let the questions occur; you may note them somewhere, to seek the solutions in the sections to come.

There is an exercise to ensure that you are completely comfortable with these basic formations. Mark every Double Top Buy and Double Bottom Sell signal on charts shown below, and count the number of long and short Fresh signals in each of them. Read this section again if you are still not clear on the formation of the basic patterns.

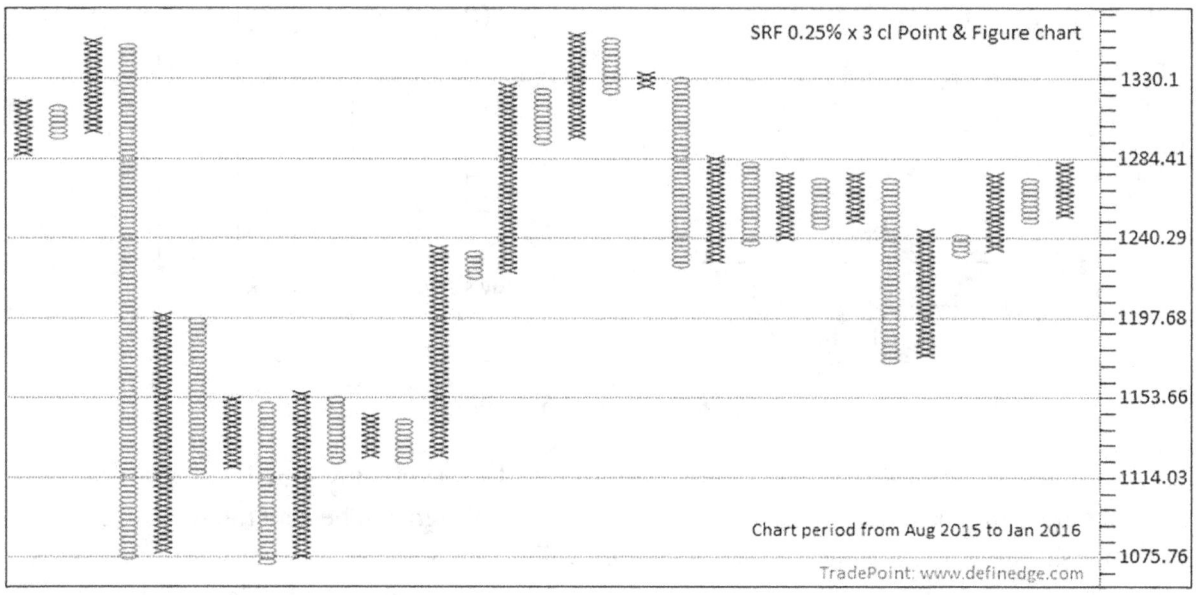

Figure 1.2.11: SRF daily 0.25% × 3 cl Point & Figure chart

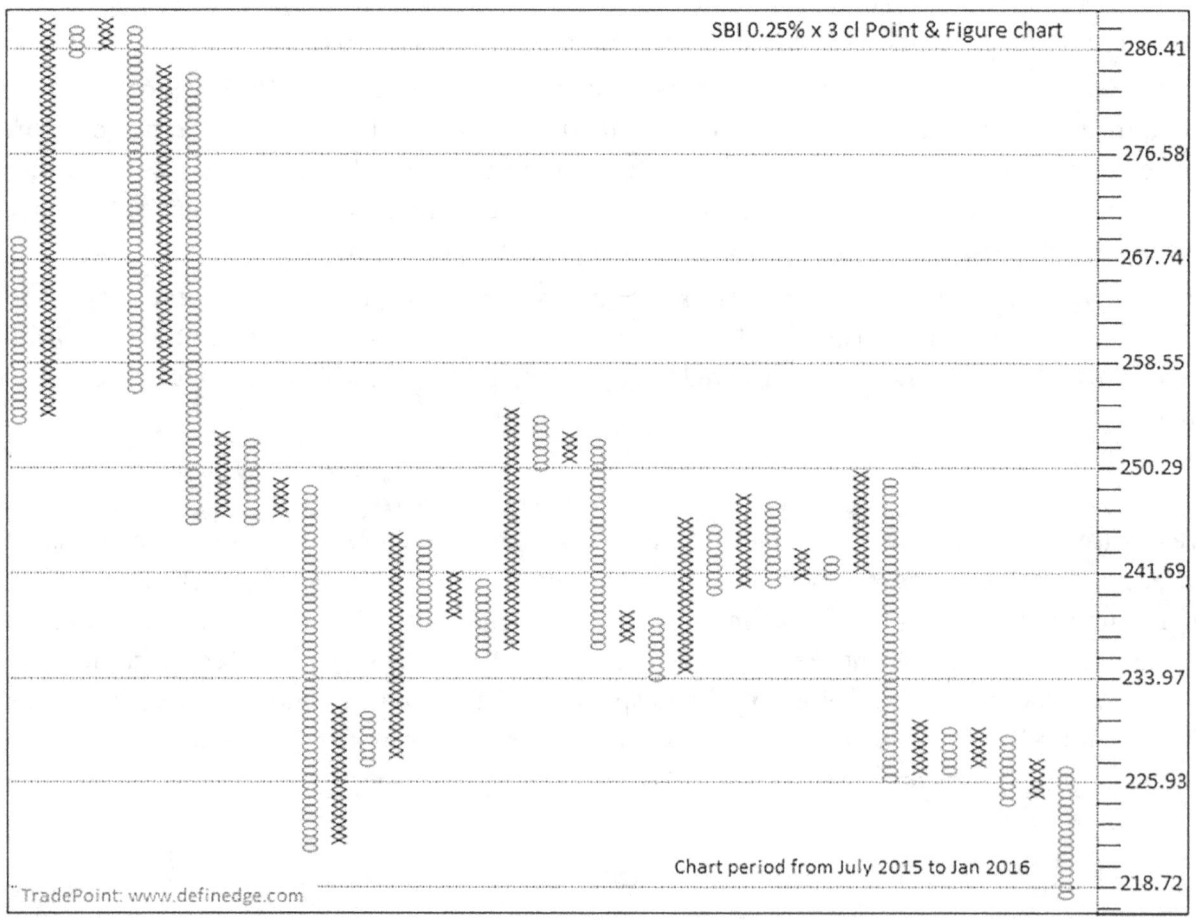

Figure 1.2.12: SBI daily 0.25% × 3 cl Point & Figure chart

Figure 1.2.13: Tata Steel daily 1% × 3 cl Point & Figure chart

Markings of Fresh signals on these charts are shown at the beginning of the next discussion. If you could locate them easily and are clear with what we have discussed so far, then we are on for the fascinating journey of understanding price structures. Open some P&F charts and observe these basic Buy-Sell signals. Having observed these patterns on practical charts before moving on to the next section will improve your understanding further. Please note that practice should be limited to observations only. Chapter 2 on patterns will slowly lead you on the path to unveil exciting formations that are the outcome of different market actions.

If you wish to open a P&F chart, then the first question arises with regard to box-value. A 1% box-value P&F chart will generate a box at every continuation move of 1% and a column reversal will get formed at a 3% move in the opposite direction. Double Top Buy or Double Bottom Sell will form later, depending on the length of the column. Similarly, 0.25% chart will generate reversal at a 0.75% move, but the basic Buy signal depends on the length. (See Image 1.2.12)

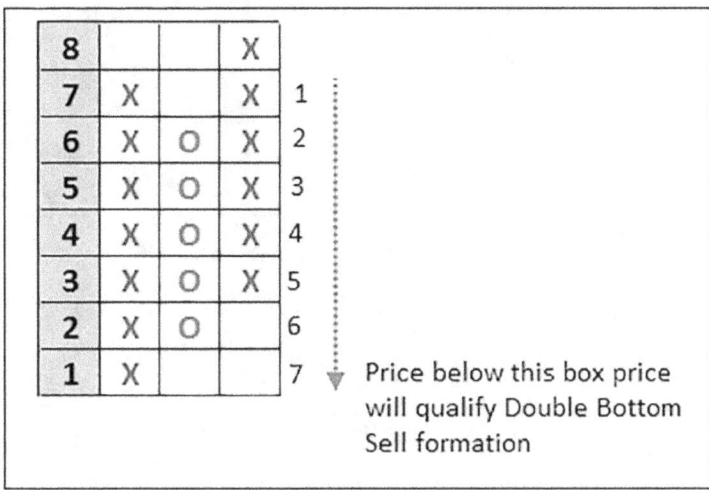

Image 1.2.12: Affordability

Price generated Buy signal at box number 8. If it reverses immediately from this box and begins marking 'O's in the next column, then it will have to fall till box number 1 to generate Sell signal. If this chart is 1% × 3, then the initial risk of the trade is 7%; if this is a 2% × 3 chart, then risk is 14% and if it is a 0.25% × 3 chart, then risk the is 1.75%. Start with 0.25% or 1% box-value of daily prices for observation of the basic signals. I know I have initiated a thought; we will discuss the concept of box-value in detail in Chapter 5.

Summary

- ▲ There are only two possibilities in every column of 'X' or 'O': either they will produce a basic pattern or they will not.
- ▲ There are Fresh and Continuation basic signals.
- ▲ Trading all basic signals is a SAR strategy.
- ▲ Objectivity is the biggest advantage of Point & Figure charts. They produce less frequent and more productive trades, risks can be clearly measured and setups can be tested.
- ▲ P&F charts help a trader stay away from consolidation zones, which are basically non-trending phases, which eat away most of the gains made during trending moves. The plotting is reduced during such periods and patterns filter the things further.
- ▲ Avoid unaffordable trades and ride the trends.
- ▲ P&F columns produce cyclic pattern behavior. Congestion patterns are followed by smooth signals and vice versa.

It is very important for a trader to understand and know when not to trade or control the position sizing. P&F chart addresses these issues to a significant extent.

Chapter 2

PATTERNS

2.1: MAJOR PATTERNS

We discussed construction and basic P&F formations in the earlier chapter. It must be clear now that a column reversal is a two-column formation and basic Buy-Sell signals are three-column formations. If you have observed several P&F charts before reading this section, then it will benefit in understanding further. Nonetheless, correct marking of charts given as exercise at the end of Chapter 1 will ensure you are on the right track. Marking of Fresh signals on them are shown in Figures 2.1.1 through 2.1.3.

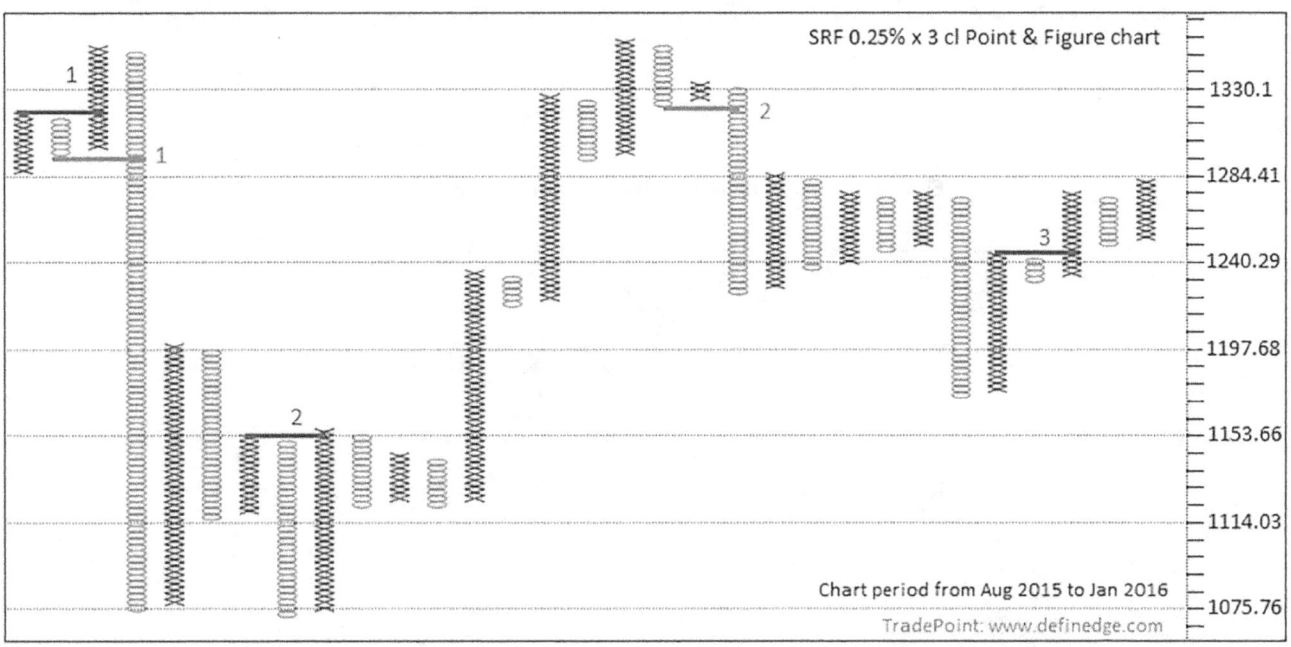

Figure 2.1.1: SRF daily 0.25% × 3 cl Point & Figure chart

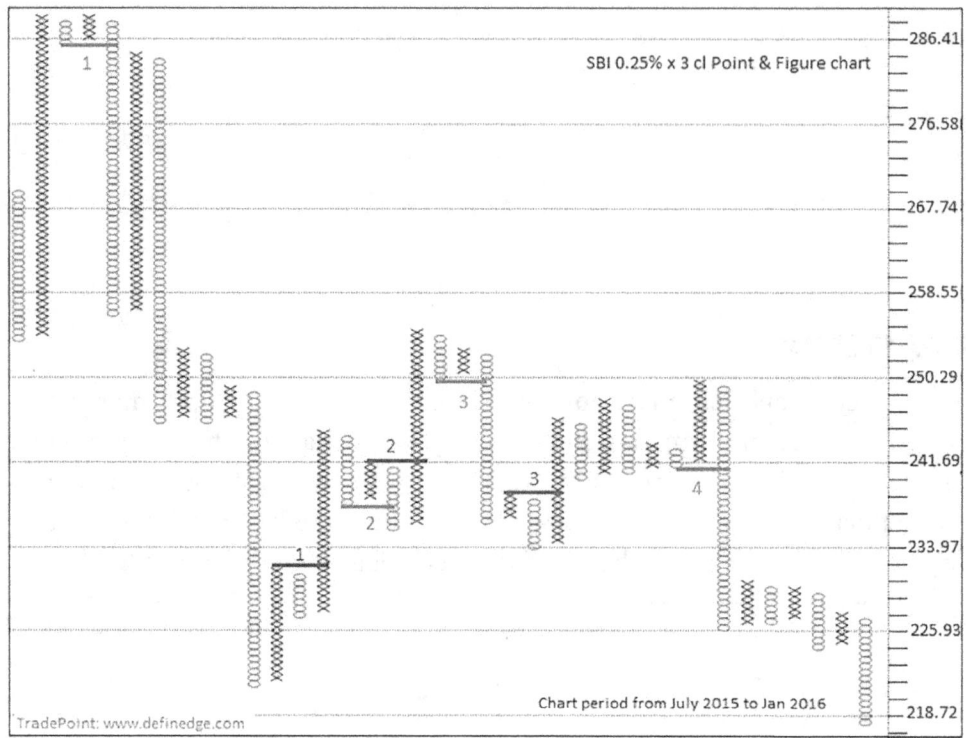

Figure 2.1.2: SBI daily 0.25% × 3 cl Point & Figure chart

Figure 2.1.3: Tata Steel daily 1% × 3 cl Point & Figure chart

You are ready for further discussion if your markings are correct. Please re-read the previous chapter if there is any confusion.

Differentiation between Fresh and Continuation signals is important irrespective of trading methodology. We discussed a basic P&F pattern trading method in the previous chapter. Like any other price-following method, period of Sideways or horizontal trend generate whipsaws with this method as well, but it is comparatively less, for reasons we discussed in the earlier chapter. Chapter 9 on back-testing begins with the testing of this basic method and its past performance on different box-values. This method can be explored further when universe size is small, if one wants to trade in fewer instruments like Nifty, Bank Nifty or some other selected instruments on a consistent basis.

Most traders are not system traders and they like to trade specific patterns or setups that have high probability and better risk–reward, etc. We will discuss P&F patterns from both aspects: system trading and setup trading.

From the trading perspective, let me begin with the method of exit. There are infinite ways to enter the trade, but to define exit is the most difficult and important task in trading. The objectivity of P&F patterns is really useful from this perspective. With the learning so far, one can define that a long position should be exited when Double Bottom Sell signal is triggered and short position should be closed if Double Top Buy signal is triggered. Though various exit methods are possible, to be defined as we discuss the subject further, let's begin with this basic rule. A good driver is not known by how well he or she can accelerate but on their control over the brakes. In the same way, a good trader should have exits in control. A well-defined exit method also provides opportunity to back-test the performance of various patterns.

Major Patterns

We discussed three-column basic patterns. There are many other P&F patterns, but most of them are extensions or variations of major patterns discussed in this chapter. You will master P&F if these major price patterns are understood well. They are more than just three-column formations that tell us more about the price structure. A little practice of these patterns will make you understand and analyse any type of technical chart setup.

As stated earlier, basic Double Top Buy or Double Bottom Sell cannot be traded when you are looking for a pattern on a large universe or group of stocks. Advanced setups would help you to identify Buy patterns that are more bullish or Sell patterns more bearish. Apart from filtered basic signals, multi-column, advanced formations provide more information about market sentiments, and help us to determine the best trading opportunities.

Triple Top - Triple Bottom

If high box-price of two consecutive columns of 'X' happens to be at the same level from which column has turned to 'O', then it becomes a strong resistance area. It displays strong supply area because three-box reversal has been produced from the same level twice. Similarly, if low box-price of two consecutive columns of 'O' is at the same level and price turns to the column of 'X', then it shows strong support area where price has witnessed demand. See Image 2.1.1.

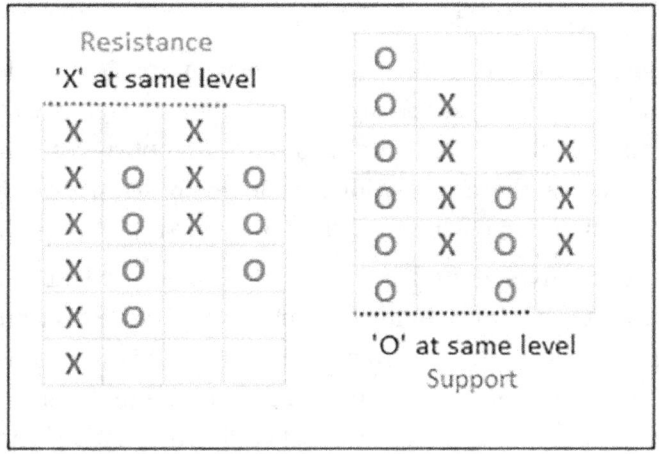

Image 2.1.1: Resistance and support

The two adjacent columns of 'X' are at the same level, indicating strong resistance. A breakout above this level will indicate strong buying interest. Two adjacent columns of 'O' that are the same level represent significant support. A break of this level will indicate breach of a significant support level.

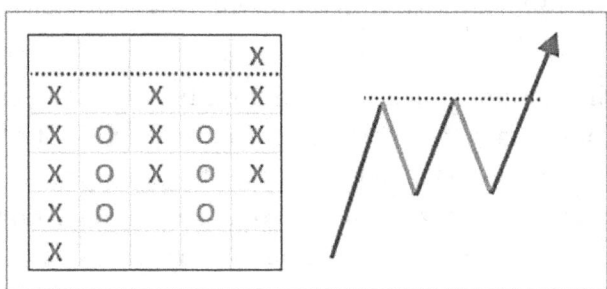 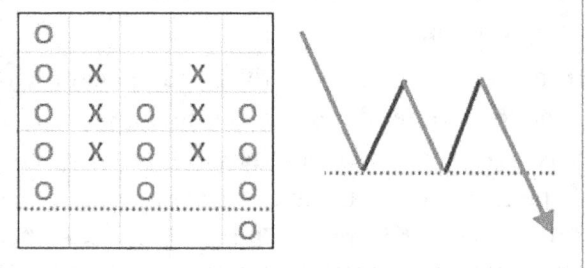

Immediate breakout is required to qualify as Triple Top Buy or Triple Bottom Sell formation. Hence, it is strictly a five-column formation, where the first two columns of 'X' have high box-price at the same level and there is a breakout above these highs in the fifth column of 'X'. Similarly, Triple Bottom Sell signal is strictly a five-column pattern, where low box-price of the first two columns of 'O' are at the same level and 'O' in the fifth column has gone below the same. Refer Image 2.1.2.

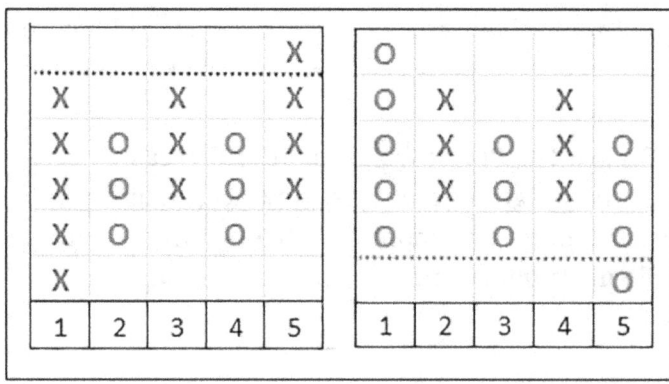

Image 2.1.2: Triple Top Buy and Triple Bottom Sell pattern

All the above rules should be met to qualify as a valid Triple Top Buy or Triple Bottom Sell formation; any inconsistency will disqualify the setup. So if someone asks, is it ok if it is a six-column setup instead of five, or 'X' is not exactly at the same level? The answer is 'No'. To begin with, let's be rigid and make it more of science than art. We may need to forgo a few opportunities but let's accept it – after all, money is made in markets by deciding what not to do!

Triple Top Buy and Triple Bottom Sell are popular patterns in the P&F world. Think of it, a Triple Top Buy formation is also a Double Top buy pattern and a Triple Bottom Sell pattern is a Double Bottom Sell pattern as well. One more column at same level defines strong support–resistance area and increases the significance of the breakout; hence, these formations are logically stronger than basic formations. Triple Top Buy is a resistance breakout pattern, whereas Triple Bottom Sell is a support breakout formation.

On a daily P&F chart, it is a five-column pattern, but as discussed in the earlier chapter, it is not necessarily a five-day pattern. It is a minimum five-day pattern, and the maximum could be any duration. The higher the box-value, the more are the number of days. This aspect is discussed in detail in a subsequent chapter of the book. But understand one thing, if it is a one-month bullish Triple Top pattern, then it means that there was a supply at a particular level during the last one month, and price has broken out from that level.

Figure 2.1.4 shows Triple Top Buy and Triple Bottom Sell formations that occurred in chart of Bajaj Auto.

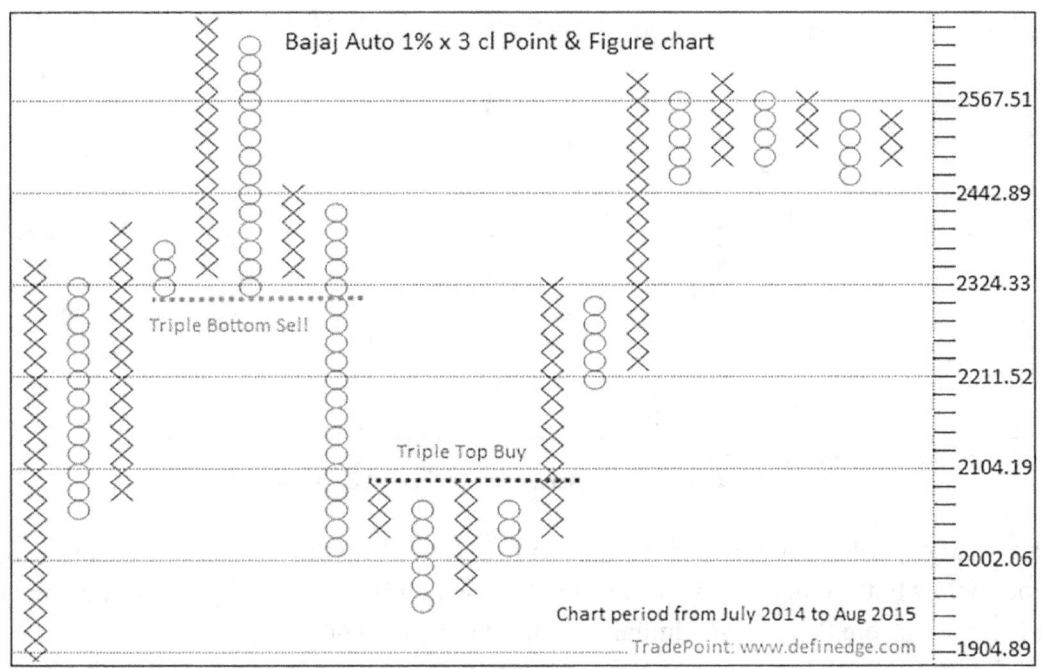

Figure 2.1.4: Bajaj Auto daily 1% × 3 cl Point & Figure chart

The formation is easy to find on P&F charts once the rules are understood. With practice, one can easily find the structure of price overcoming significant supports and resistances. The BEML chart shown in Figure 2.1.5 shows Triple Bottom Sell signal that occurred during October 2015, which was effective because price corrected significantly thereafter.

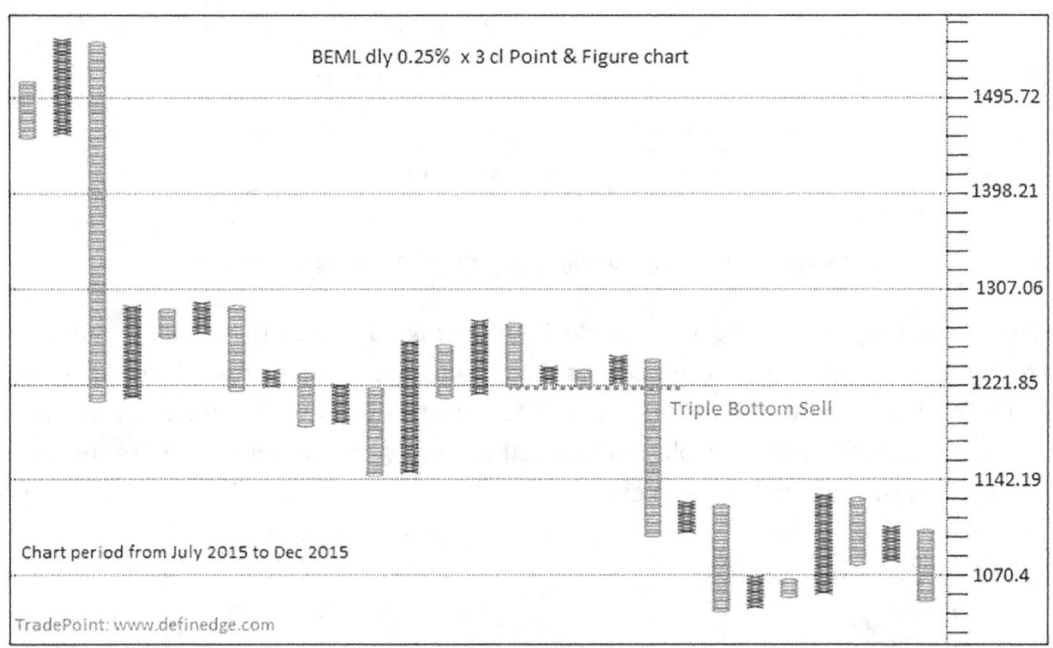

Figure 2.1.5: BEML daily 0.25% × 3 cl Point & Figure chart

There are three occurrences of Triple Top Buy formation in the 2.5-year duration chart of Dr. Reddy, shown in Figure 2.1.6, where the first two were followed by favorable move and the third failed.

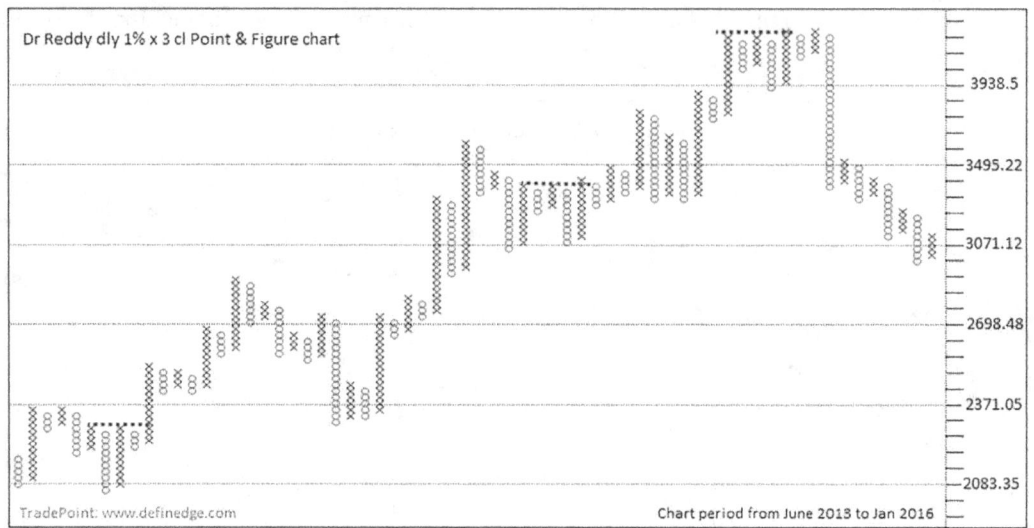

Figure 2.1.6: Dr. Reddy daily 1% × 3 cl Point & Figure chart

Price can witness pullback or fail to rise after forming Triple Top Buy Signal. If price in the five-column buy setup goes below bottom of the fourth column of 'O', which is the column prior to the breakout, then it will trigger Double Bottom Sell signal. Similarly, if price fails to go down immediately after Triple Bottom Sell signal and goes above the top of the fourth column of 'X' of the pattern, then it will generate Double Top Buy signal. Refer Image 2.1.3.

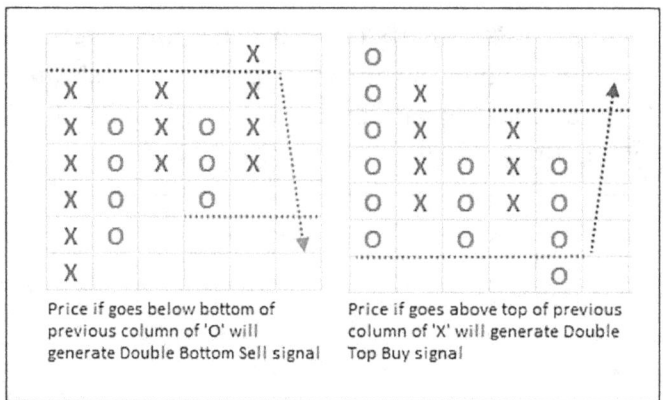

Image 2.1.3: Triple Top Buy and Triple Bottom Sell pattern

Double Bottom Sell signal coming after Triple Top Buy Signal can be the signal to exit the trade. But the pattern remains valid unless its bottom gets broken. Bottom level of a Triple Top Buy formation is the lowest 'O' of the entire formation. In other words, the pattern does not fail unless price falls below the lowest 'O' In the pattern. Similarly, Triple Bottom Sell pattern remains active, unless top of the pattern (highest level of 'X' in the pattern) is taken out.

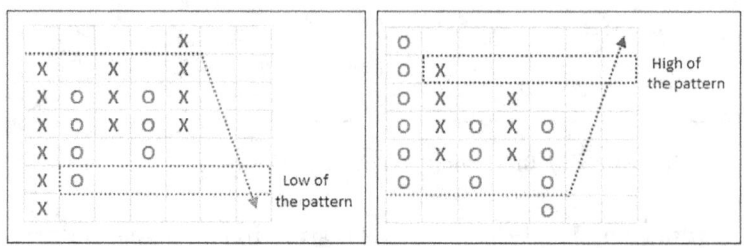

Image 2.1.4: Triple Top Buy and Triple Bottom Sell pattern failure levels

The pattern that has not failed becomes a reference area for future trends. A Triple Top Buy pattern can also be traded using bottom of the formation as a stop, and similarly, Triple Bottom Sell can be traded with stop placed at top of the pattern.

You might want to check the exercise charts of the last chapter again. There were three Triple Bottom Sell signals in Figure 2.1.3 of Tata Steel P&F chart. Two of them are Fresh Double Bottom Sell signals and one is Continuation Double Bottom Sell signal.

Using different box-values of P&F helps to reveal many structures and traditional breakout formations, which at times are difficult to scan or view in usual charts. Triple Top Buy formation that occurred in higher box-value charts capture significant breakouts. They represent significant breakout from last congestion zone from accumulation patterns such as cup and handle, rounding pattern, Inverted Head and Shoulder, etc. Figure 2.1.7 is the daily candlestick chart of Kotak bank. It is almost a year-long accumulation pattern which broke out during April 2014. P&F chart of the same time plotted with a 3% box-value is shown in Figure 2.1.8.

Figure 2.1.7: Kotak bank daily candlestick chart

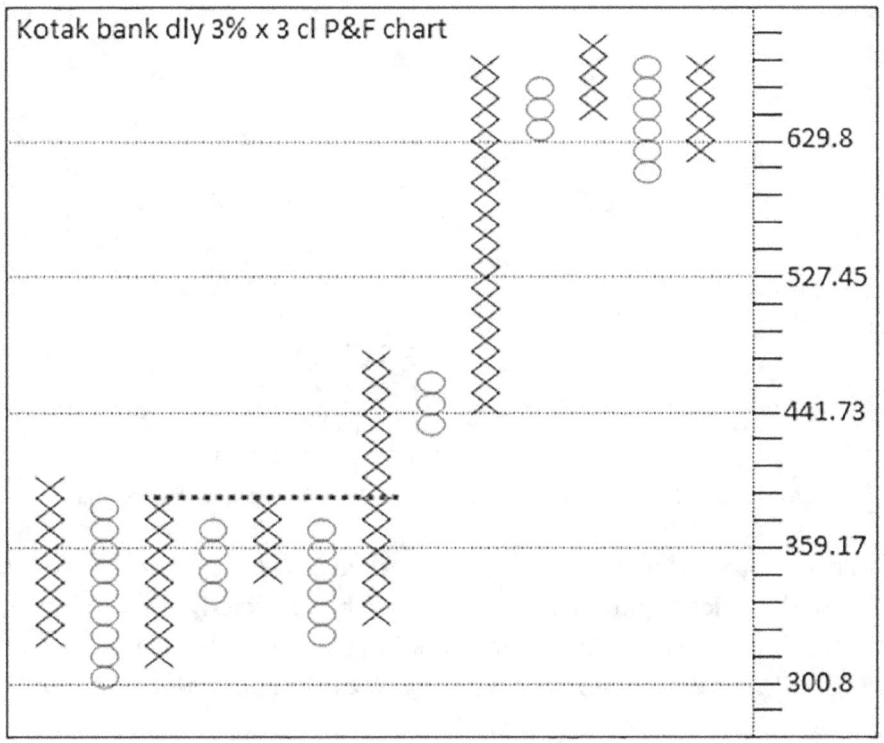

Figure 2.1.8: Kotak bank daily 3% × 3 cl Point & Figure chart

It occurred as a Triple Top Buy formation in a P&F chart. This multi-column breakout formation easily shows us breakout formation from long period of consolidation or accumulation. Such breakout patterns, especially in higher box values, are very significant events. It is far easier to identify and scan for such breakout patterns in P&F charts, which may be difficult to do with other charting methods. High box-value and their utilization will be discussed in Chapter 5, but the principle is applicable in all types of P&F charts and time frames.

There could be a long accumulation formation in intraday time-frame charts when we come across Triple Top Buy in daily charts. Similarly, Triple Bottom Sell formation displays significant distribution pattern on lower box-value or time-frame charts. Figure 2.1.9 shows a 10 × 3 P&F chart of Nifty futures on 1 min time interval.

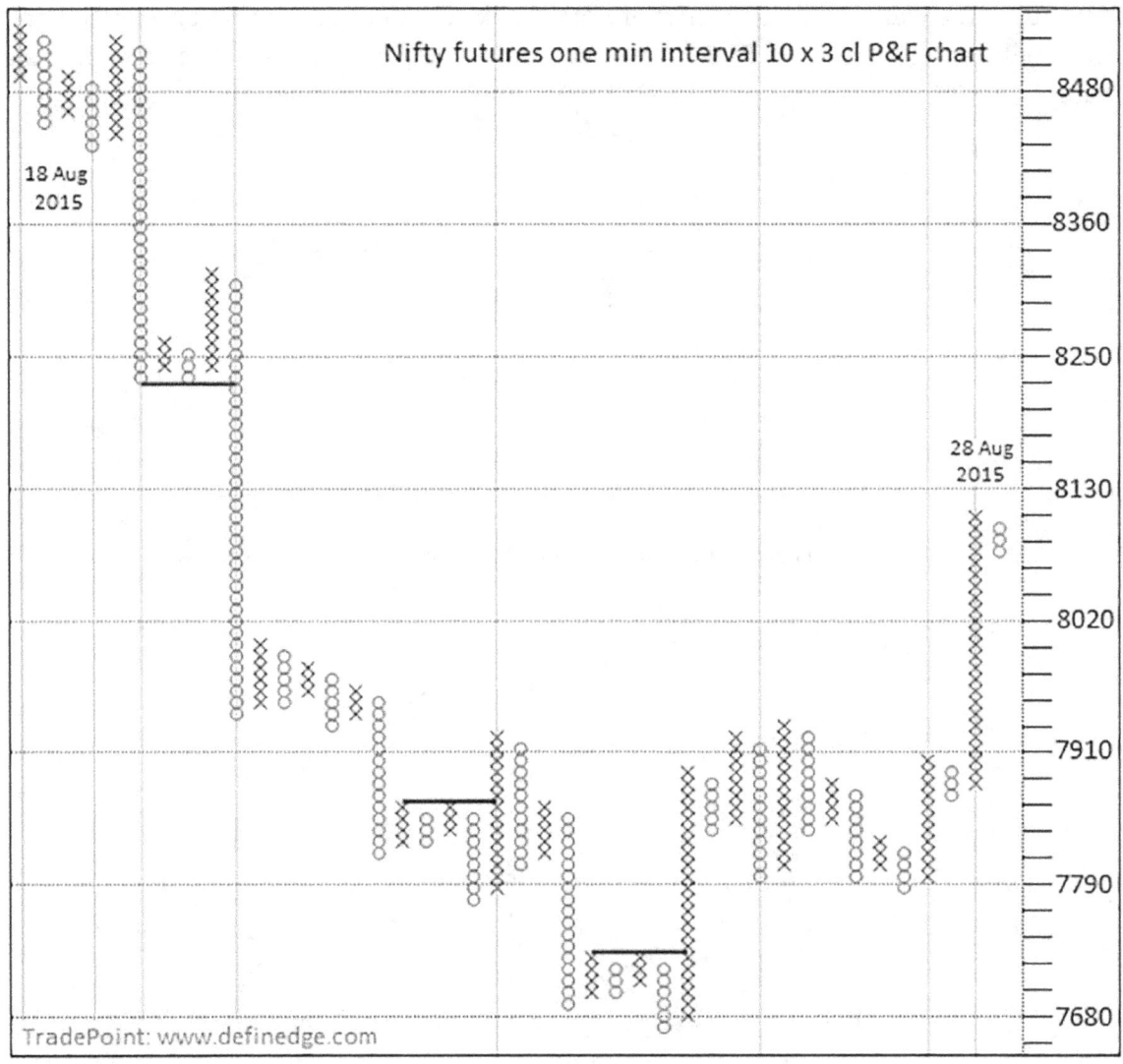

Figure 2.1.9: Nifty-I futures 1 min interval 10 × 3 cl Point & Figure chart

There are two Triple Tops and one Triple Bottom marked in the chart for observation. The pattern is quite rare to find due to the strict requirement of having two boxes exactly at similar level before breakout. The most advantageous thing is a strong breakout formation coming with the clear rules of entry and exits. The formation which occurred during horizontal trends is part of congestion and it often results in a trap or failure.

Have a look at the daily candlestick chart of Reliance Capital shown in Figure 2.1.10.

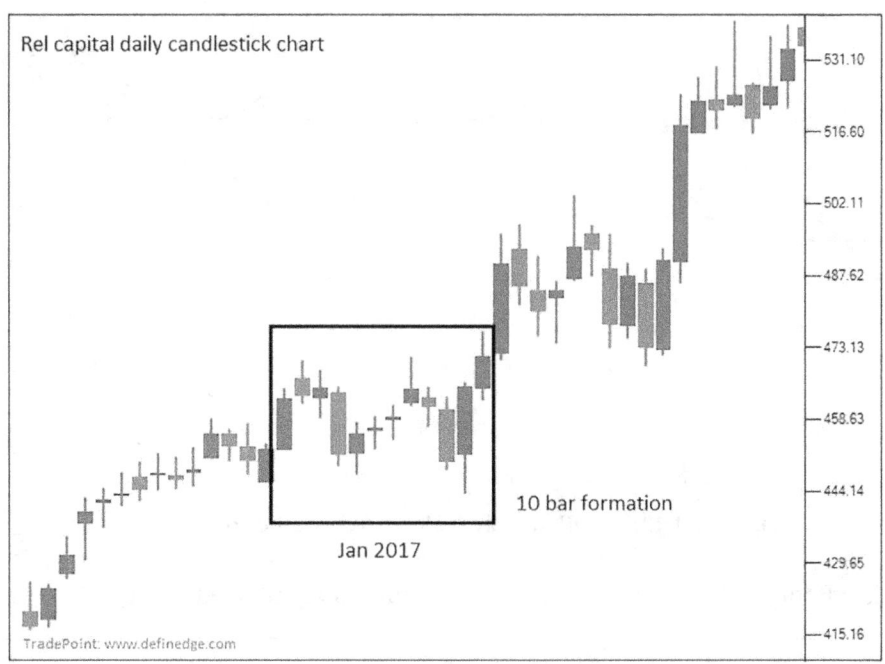

Figure 2.1.10: Reliance Capital daily candlestick chart

Figure 2.1.11 is a 0.25% × 3 P&F chart of Reliance capital, which shows 10 bar consolidation pattern as Triple Top Buy breakout.

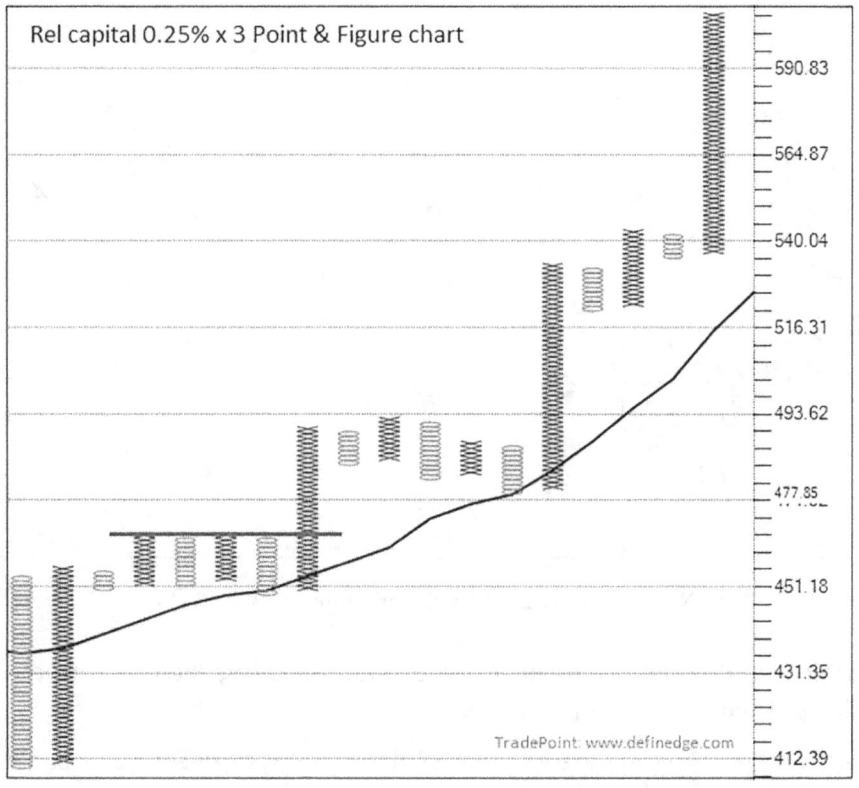

Figure 2.1.11: Reliance Capital daily 0.25% × 3 cl Point & Figure chart

Whatever the instrument and time frame, objective setups can turn out to be a profitable trading strategy if execution is focused upon. Figure 2.1.12 is a 0.25% × 3 P&F chart of USDINR showing examples of Triple Top Buy patterns.

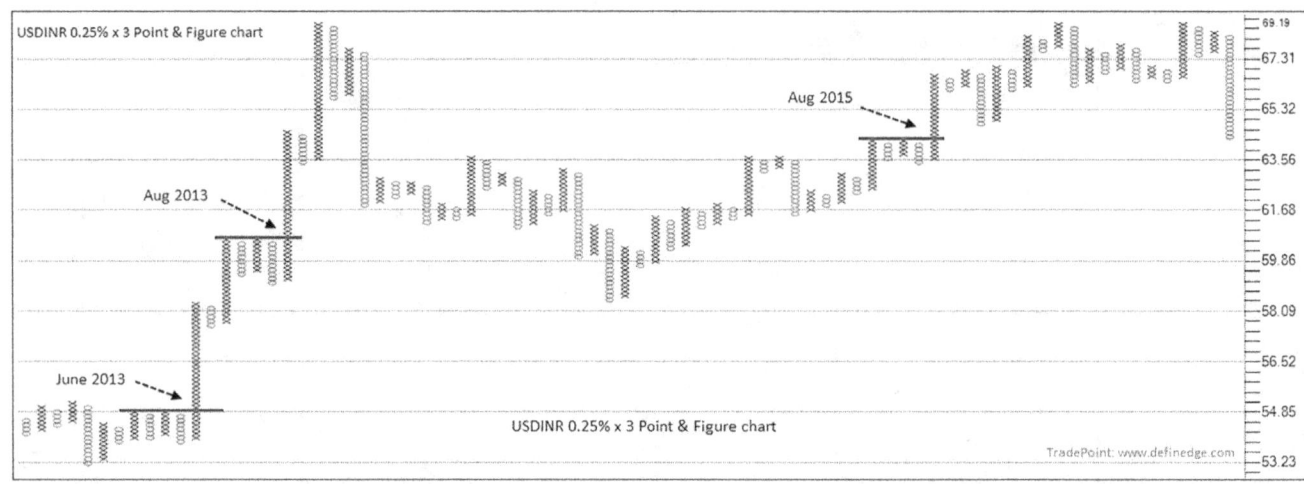

Figure 2.1.12: USDINR daily 0.25% × 3 cl Point & Figure chart

Figure 2.1.13 is a Bank Nifty 21500 call option premium chart plotted using 3% × 3 during April 2017.

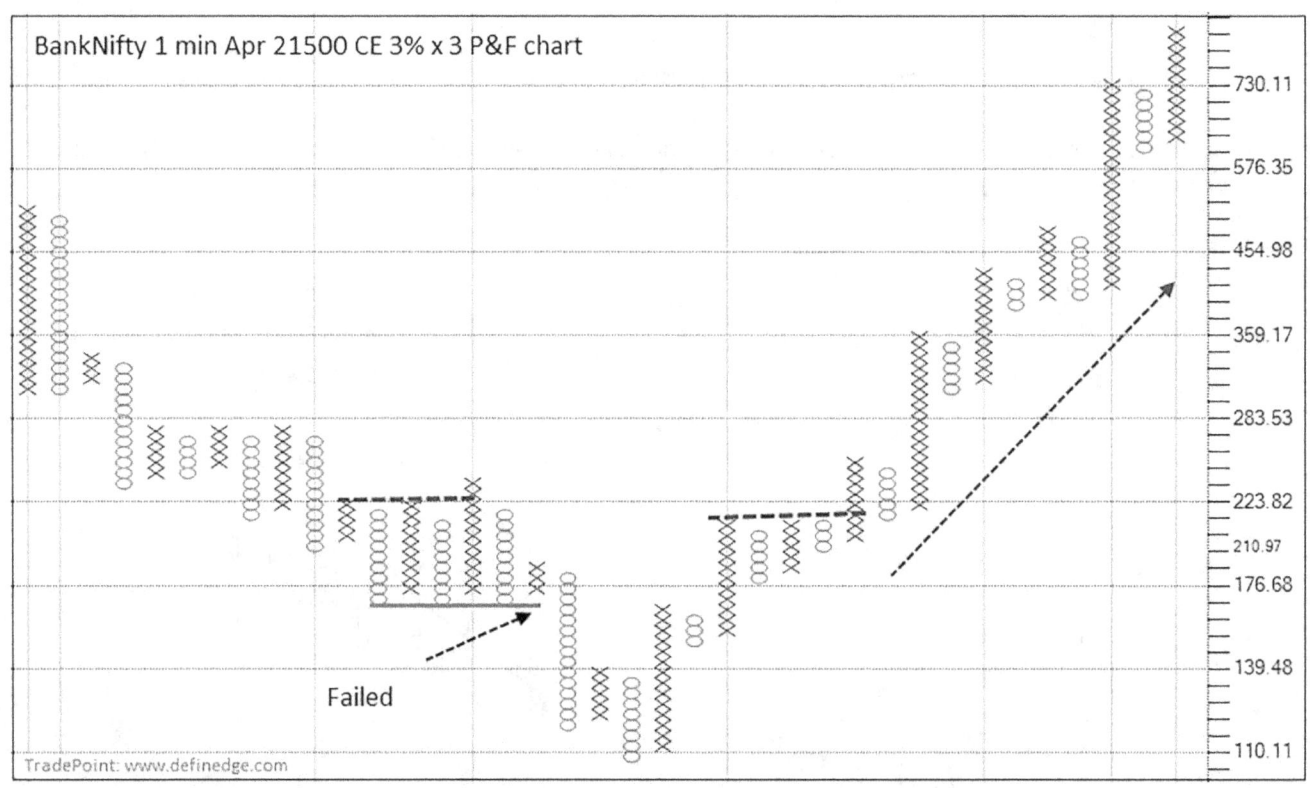

Figure 2.1.13: Bank Nifty Apr 2017 21500 CE 1 min interval 3% × 3 cl Point & Figure chart

There was a Triple Top Buy pattern formed earlier that failed but the one formed later worked well. Option chart analysis is discussed in the latter part of the book.

Figure 2.1.14 is the 1% × 3 Point & Figure chart of daily prices of JP Associates. Mark Triple Top Buy and Triple Bottom Sell formations on the chart. Markings will be shown at the beginning of the next chapter.

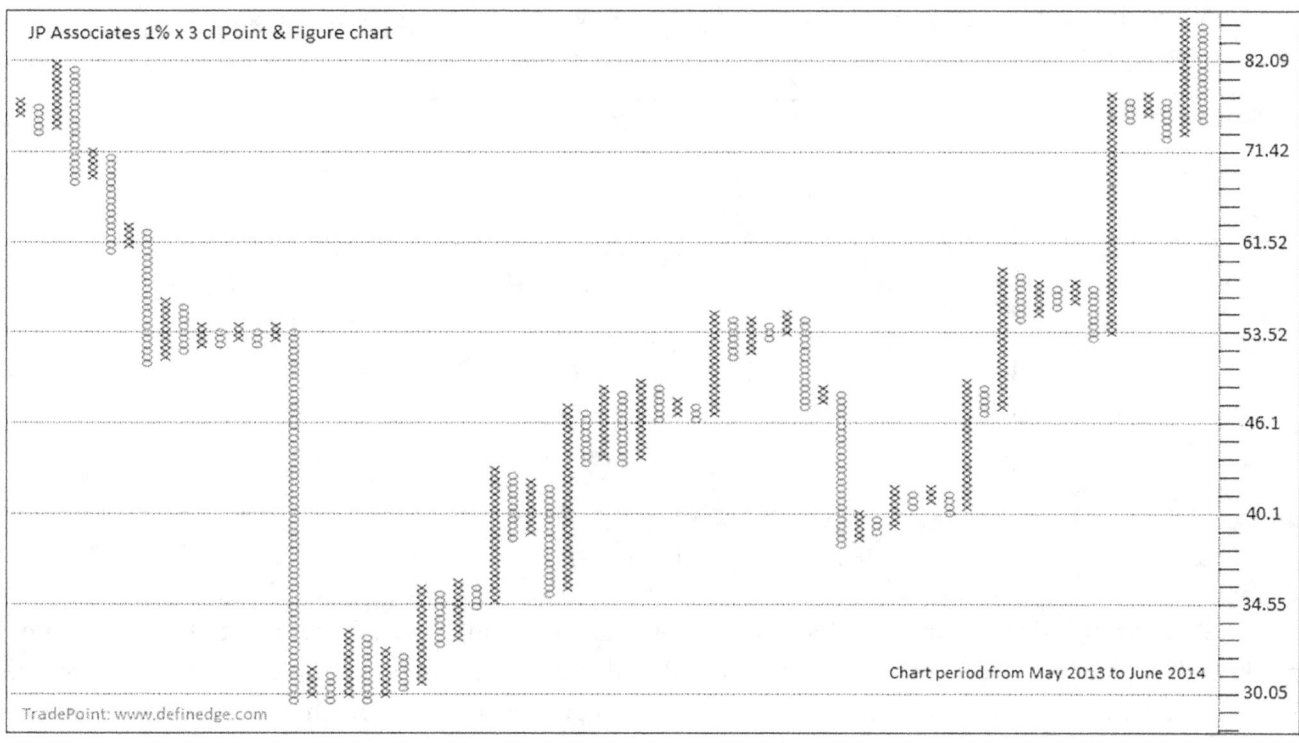

Figure 2.1.14: JP Associates daily 1% × 3 cl Point & Figure chart

Trap

Trap should be a familiar word to market participants. We fall prey to it often. Getting trapped can be simply defined as getting stuck in a trade that has moved against the entry.

Double Top Buy is a bullish swing breakout formation. A column of 'O' may occur after such breakout which represents correction, but if the same column keeps extending lower and falls below the low box-price of previous column of 'O', then Double Bottom Sell signal gets generated and a buy pattern that was triggered in the prior column gets reversed immediately. It's a kind of shock to bulls. This setup represents trapped bulls, hence the name. In other words, when a sell pattern occurs immediately after a buy pattern, it is a Bull Trap formation. See Image 2.1.5.

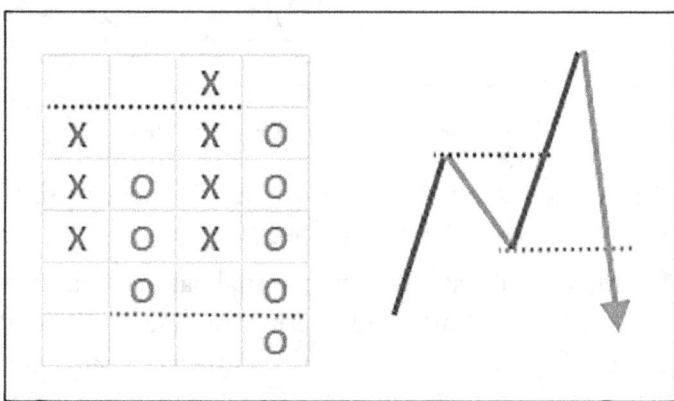

Image 2.1.5: Bull Trap

Similarly, it is a Bear Trap pattern if Double Top Buy signal is triggered immediately after Double Bottom Sell signal. Refer Image 2.1.6.

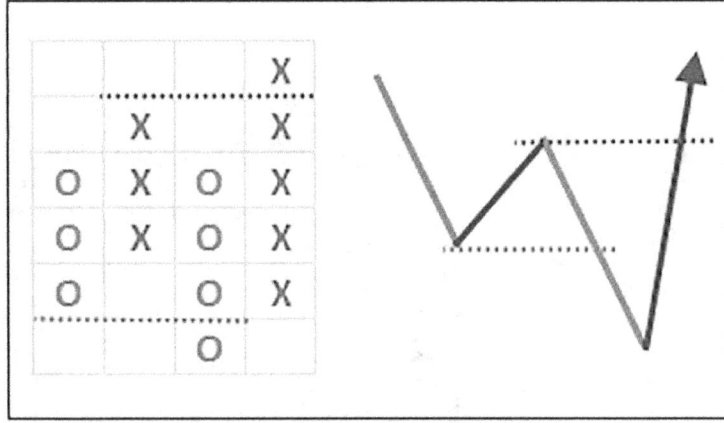

Image 2.1.6: Bear Trap

The reverse signal comes immediately after the breakout column; hence, these are strictly four-column patterns. Bull Trap is a bearish pattern that gets qualified at fourth column at box-price that forms Double Bottom Sell pattern and Bear Trap is a bullish pattern that gets qualified at fourth column box-price when Double Top Buy pattern gets formed. See Image 2.1.7, explaining the same.

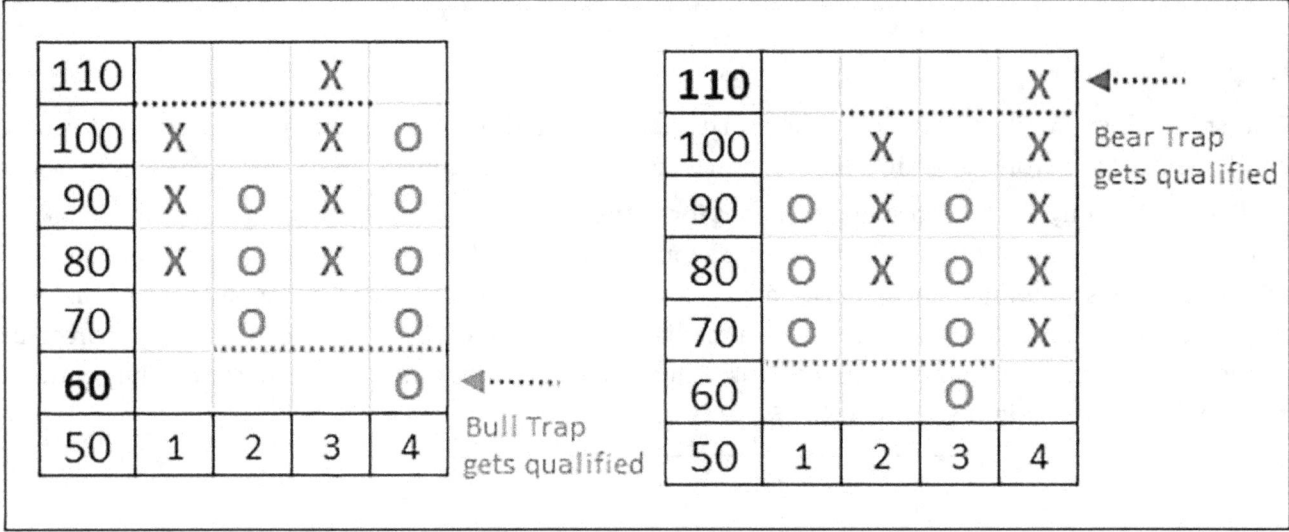

Image 2.1.7: Bull Trap and Bear Trap

Bull Trap in Image 2.1.7 is formed at fourth column when 'O' appears at box-price 60 and Bear Trap is formed at fourth column when 'X' is formed at box-price 110.

We often use words like trap or whipsaws in conventional pattern analysis. By that we usually mean pattern failures or false breakouts, but it is difficult to define the rules to figure it out. Objectivity of Point & Figure patterns helps us in defining this kind of structure. Observe the formations in 1% x3 chart of Bata India, shown in Figure 2.1.15.

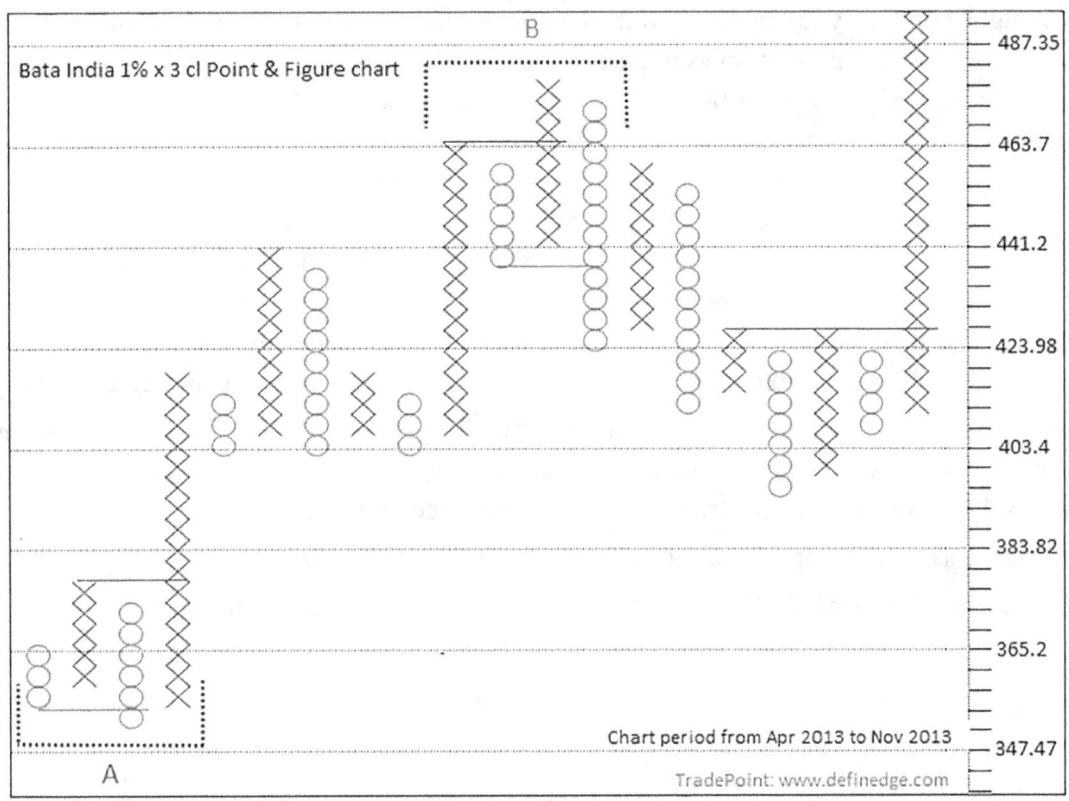

Figure 2.1.15: Bata India daily 1% × 3 cl Point & Figure chart

Pattern A is a Bear Trap because Double Top Buy pattern has formed immediately after Double Bottom Sell. Pattern B is a Bull Trap because Double Bottom Sell has occurred immediately after Double Top Buy. The last pattern in the chart is Triple Top Buy.

Figure 2.1.16 shows occurrences of traps shown in the Reliance capital chart.

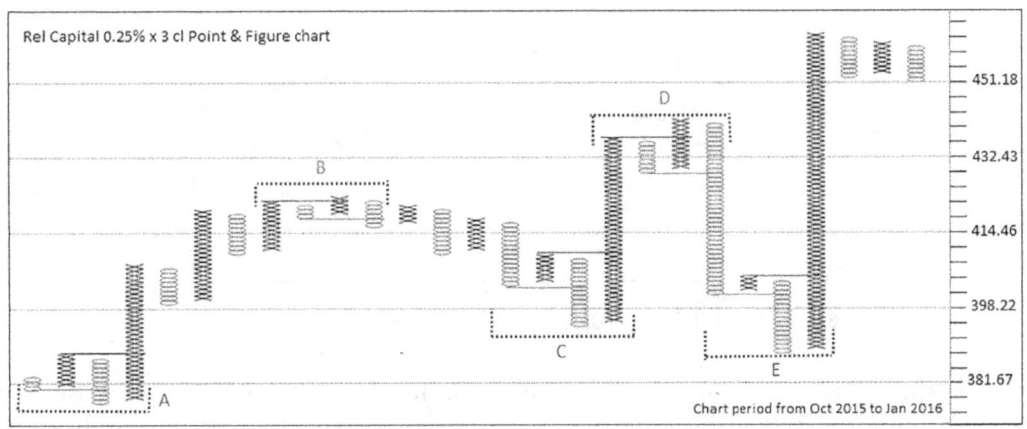

Figure 2.1.16: Reliance capital daily 0.25% × 3 cl Point & Figure chart

Points A, C and E are Bear traps, while B and D are Bull traps. A little practice is required to train the eyes to find such formations but objectivity makes the job easy for us. A trap is a trap, irrespective of what happens subsequently and a discussion over occurrence is pointless.

Did a thought come to your mind as to how to know in advance and avoid getting trapped? It is a frequently asked question when I discuss traps. Let me tell you a secret: There is no way of doing that! And another secret: It is possible to never be trapped in markets! Understand that one gets trapped only when there is uncertainty about the method of exit. If exit to a bullish pattern is defined as Double Bottom Sell, then one has to liquidate the position when that happens. It is unfortunate that it happened immediately but that was a calculated risk and a part of the game. The loss being booked is a temporary phenomenon and an important aspect of a strategy. That means you don't get trapped when you follow the patterns and your method of exit is certain. Being trapped is a bigger issue and it usually indicates the lack of any meaningful exit plan. Usually, it is left to the judgment of expert opinions and other sources; such subjective decisions play major role in getting stuck in a trade and seeing unmanageable losses.

Moreover, if one is not looking at simple basic formations, one may not have a position when coming across a trap formation. Knowing that one party is stuck in the trade can become interesting information to such traders, because they can contribute in taking the prices further.

An interesting aspect of trap formation is shown in the following charts.

Figure 2.1.17 is a 0.25% × 3 P&F chart of Maruti marked with only Bear traps.

Figure 2.1.17: Maruti daily 0.25% × 3 cl Point & Figure chart

Observe it carefully and make sure that you were able to identify the formations. Bear traps in this chart look interesting, don't they? Price seems to be coming in favor more often than not after the Bear Trap pattern being formed. Have a look at the 0.25% × 3 P&F chart of Tata Steel shown in Figure 2.1.18, marked with only Bull traps.

July 2014

Tata steel 0.25% x 3 cl Point & Figure chart

TradePoint: www.definedge.com

March 2015

Figure 2.1.18: Tata Steel daily 0.25% × 3 cl Point & Figure chart

They look yummy in the above chart and price seems to be waiting for them to record sharp falls. Bear traps in chart of Maruti and Bull traps in the chart of Tata Steel look like profitable formations for a simple reason which you may have noticed. There is an important difference in both the charts: price was in an Uptrend in the first chart and in a Downtrend in the second. You got the idea then. Bear traps in Uptrend and Bull traps in Downtrend are effective setups and nice opportunity for traders.

Understand the logic of the setup. People look for resistances and predict tops when price is rising. They become confident when swing low is broken, which is where Double Bottom Sell pattern is typically generated. Bears feel comfortable because instrument has gone up 'a lot' and there can be a serious correction which has just begun. Weak longs also get shaken out. But price reverses immediately and resumes the Uptrend. Traders who are short will run for cover and exited longs will feel the pain of missing the bus looking at the soaring prices. Fresh breakout traders will find a candidate. Stock is being shifted into strong hands. Hence, bear traps are logical and more profitable formation when the instrument is in Uptrend.

Similarly, people keep finding Bottoms and supports when the price is in Downtrend. It is more comfortable to buy stock when it has corrected because risk– reward looks favorable. Bullish swing breakout or Double Top Buy formations provide confidence to the bulls because it seems that it has bottomed-out. But price reverses immediately and generates Double Bottom Sell signal. This comes as a shock to bulls and leveraged traders panic. Their selling results in more downside. Hence, Bull Trap is a more favorable and profitable pattern in Downtrend.

So the trap in the direction of trend is a logical trading setup. You may want to look for Bull traps in chart of Uptrend in Figure 2.1.17 and Bear traps in chart of Downtrend in Figure 2.1.18. We will discuss trend identification techniques in Chapter 3. It is pertinent to note in this context that Bear traps are also Fresh Double Top Buy signals because Buy signal has come after sell signal and Bull traps are also Fresh Double Bottom Sell signals.

If price reverses immediately after Bear Trap and generates Double Bottom Sell signal, then pattern fails. Similarly, if price reverses immediately after Bull Trap and generates Double Top Buy pattern, then Bull Trap fails. Hence, the basic Buy-Sell signal and pattern failure level is the same in case of traps. We will discuss various methods of analysis and different setups in the chapters to come; in all of them, when trap is a part of the setup it increases the chances of success.

Figure 2.1.19 is a 1% × 3 Point & Figure chart of DLF. Mark Bear Trap and Bull Trap formations in the same. Marking will be shown at the beginning of the next chapter.

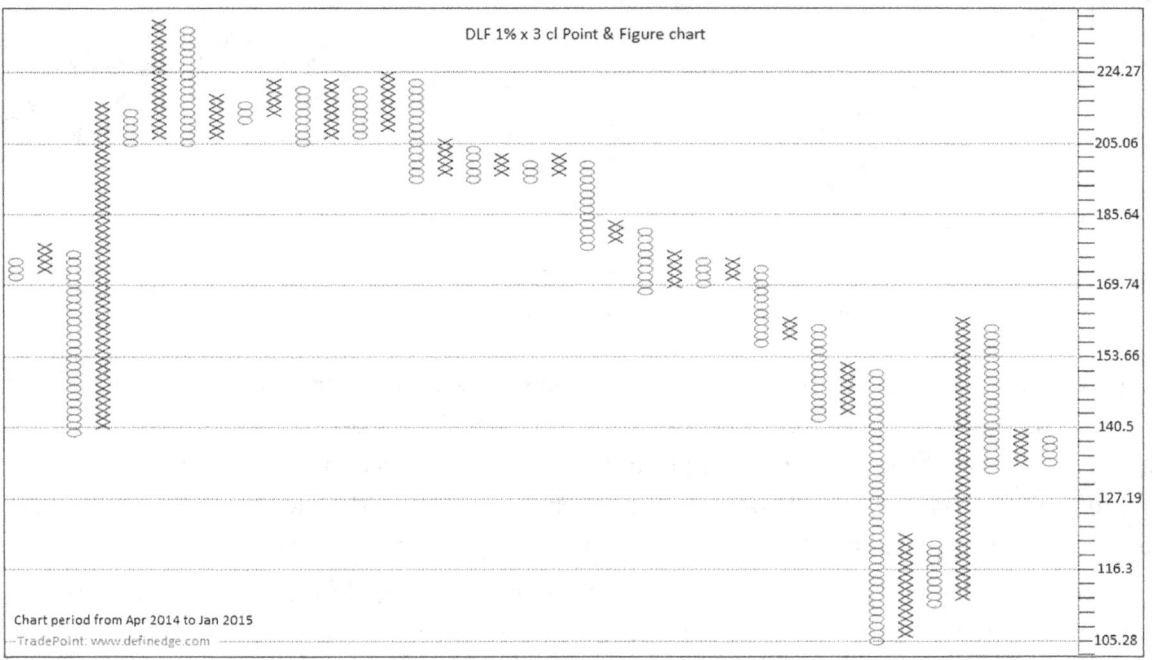

Figure 2.1.19: DLF daily 1% × 3 cl Point & Figure chart

Pole

Pole formation is truly a gift from Point & Figure to the world of technical analysis. It is a matchless and useful pattern even from the perspective of designing systems. Pole doesn't get generated upon Double Top Buy or Double Bottom Sell signal; hence, it is a reversal formation and not a breakout or continuation. There are two types of poles: High Pole, which is a bearish formation, and Low Pole, which is a bullish formation.

People often find pole a difficult pattern to identify or remember. Below is a stepwise explanation of them for better understanding.

High Pole

The following are three stages that qualify as a High Pole formation:

1. **Double Top Buy pattern**: There must be a basic bullish breakout pattern.
2. **Minimum five boxes in favor after Buy signal**: Price must have traveled by at least 5-boxes or more after the buy signal. Refer Image 2.1.8. Double Top Buy pattern has been formed at box-price 100; price traveled five boxes after the same till box-price 140.

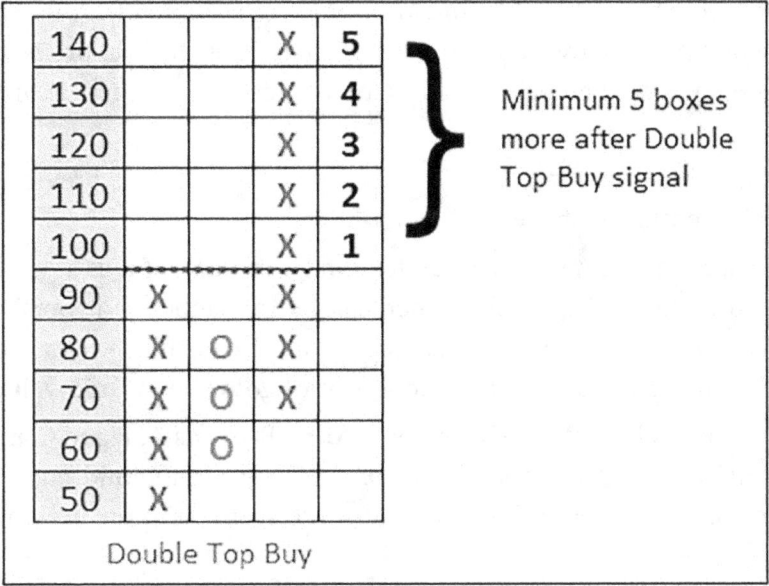

140			X	5
130			X	4
120			X	3
110			X	2
100			X	1
90	X		X	
80	X	O	X	
70	X	O	X	
60	X	O		
50	X			

Minimum 5 boxes more after Double Top Buy signal

Double Top Buy

Image 2.1.8: Five-box move after Double Top Buy

Note that requirement is minimum five boxes, so any number of boxes above that qualifies for the next stage of pole. The five-box requirement is after breakout and not for the total number of boxes in the column.

3. **Column of 'O' falling below previous mid-price:** Once price has traveled five boxes after breakout, if the immediately following column of 'O' falls below the midpoint of the previous column of 'X', it then fulfills the High Pole pattern criteria. Note that it is a mid-price of total number of boxes in 'X' and not boxes after breakout.

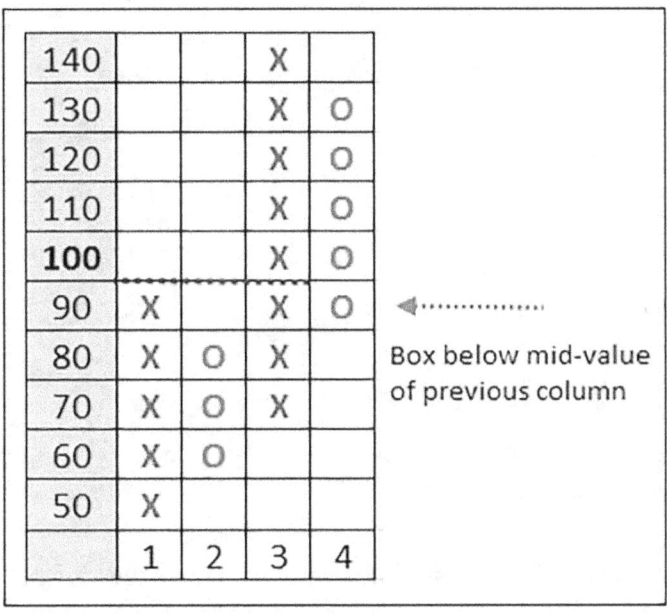

140			X	
130			X	O
120			X	O
110			X	O
100			X	O
90	X		X	O
80	X	O	X	
70	X	O	X	
60	X	O		
50	X			
	1	2	3	4

Box below mid-value of previous column

Image 2.1.9: High Pole

The total number of boxes in the column of 'X' is 8 in the above example (Image 2.1.9). Mid-box is the fourth box. Mid-price can also be calculated in the following manner.

Mid-box-price of column: (High Box-price + Low Box-price)/2

High box-price in the column of 'X' is 140 and low box-price is 70, so mid-value is 105 as per the above calculation. Immediate box-price below 105 is 100, so that becomes the box-price at which High Pole will get formed. We considered box-price below mid-value because the column is of 'O', which represents falling prices.

High Pole gets formed the moment 'O' falls below mid-box-price of previous column of 'X' after meeting all three criteria mentioned above.

It is explained stepwise to make it simple to understand, but think of it as a whole. There are basically three requirements to forming the High Pole, which can be remembered as breakout, long column and 50% retracement, all happening over four columns. Breakout is basic bullish signal, long column is defined as minimum five boxes in favor and 50% retracement is price going below mid-value of previous column.

Figure 2.1.20 is 10 × 3 P&F chart of hourly prices of Nifty. Patterns A, B and C are High Pole which got formed when box shown by arrow got marked. High price, low price and mid-box-value are shown in the chart for better understanding. It is basically at least 50% retracement to the previous swing move.

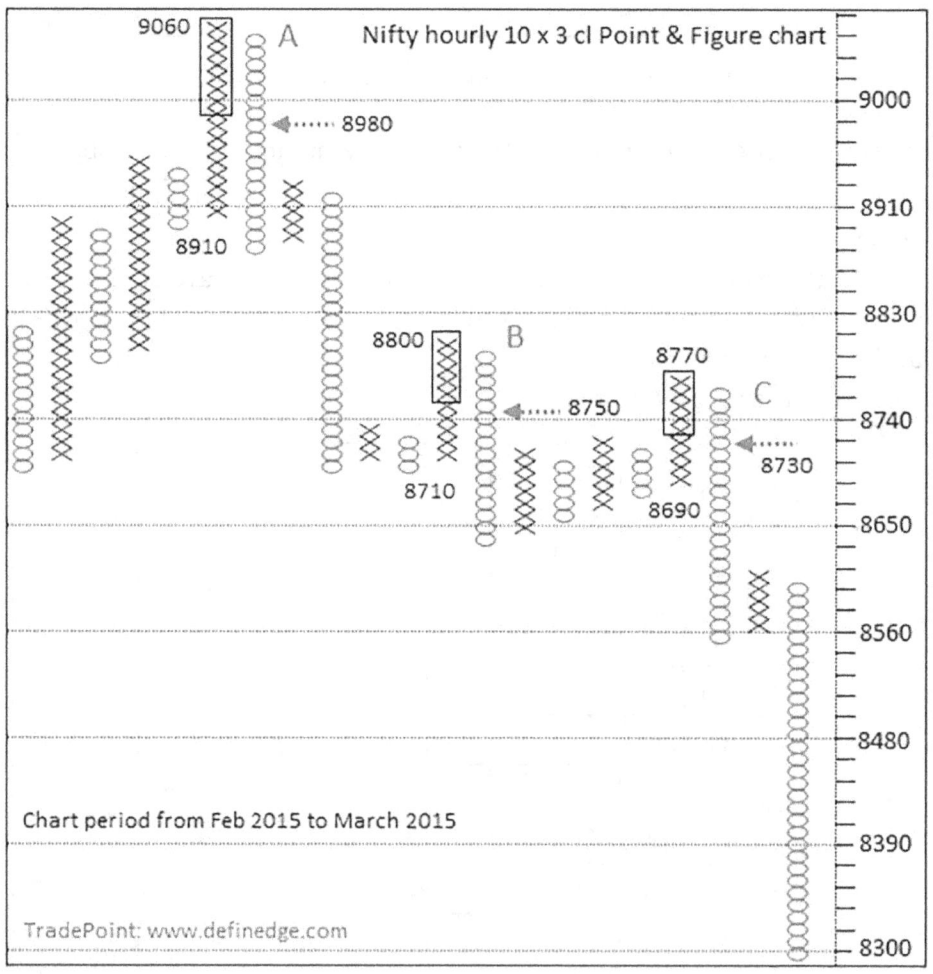

Figure 2.1.20: Nifty-I futures 60 min interval 10 × 3 cl Point & Figure chart

Low Pole is exactly the opposite of High Pole. The following are the three stages of Low Pole formation:

1. **Double Bottom Sell signal:** Basic bearish breakout pattern.

2. **Minimum five boxes in favor after Sell signal:** Price has traveled at least five boxes more after Sell signal. See Image 2.1.10. Double Bottom Sell signal has been formed at box-price 90. Price has traveled five boxes after the same till box-price 50.

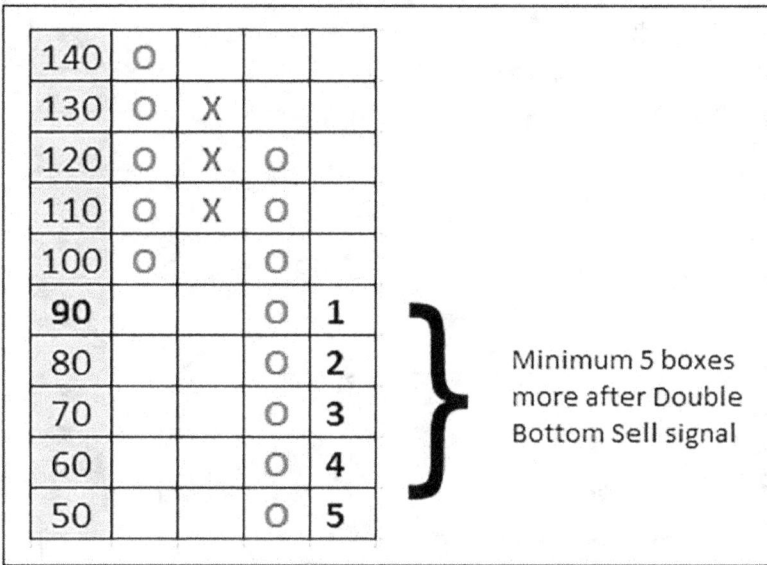

Image 2.1.10: 5 box move after Double Bottom Sell

3. **Column of 'X' that rises above previous mid-price:** Column of 'X' appearing immediately after the breakout rises further to go above mid-box-price of previous column of 'O'. In Image 2.1.11, total number of boxes in the column of 'O' is 8. High box-price in the column of 'O' is 120 and low box-price is 50, hence mid-value is 85. Immediate box-price above 85 is 90, which becomes the box-price above which the Low Pole will get formed. We looked at box-price above mid-value because it is a column of 'X' that represent rising prices and needs box-price higher than mid-price to call it a breach.

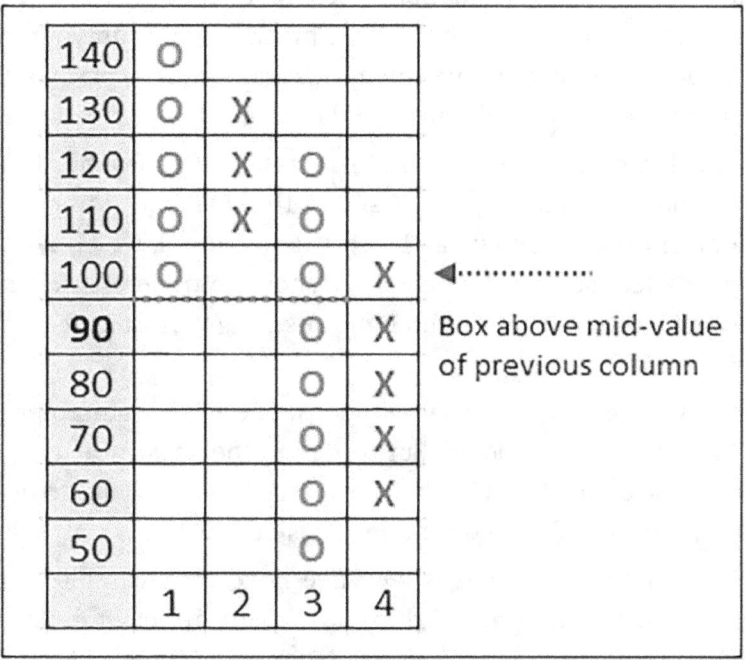

Image 2.1.11: Low Pole

Figure 2.1.21 is the same Nifty spot hourly chart plotted using 10 × 3 parameters. Patterns A, B and C are Low Pole formations. Levels are shown in the chart for better understanding.

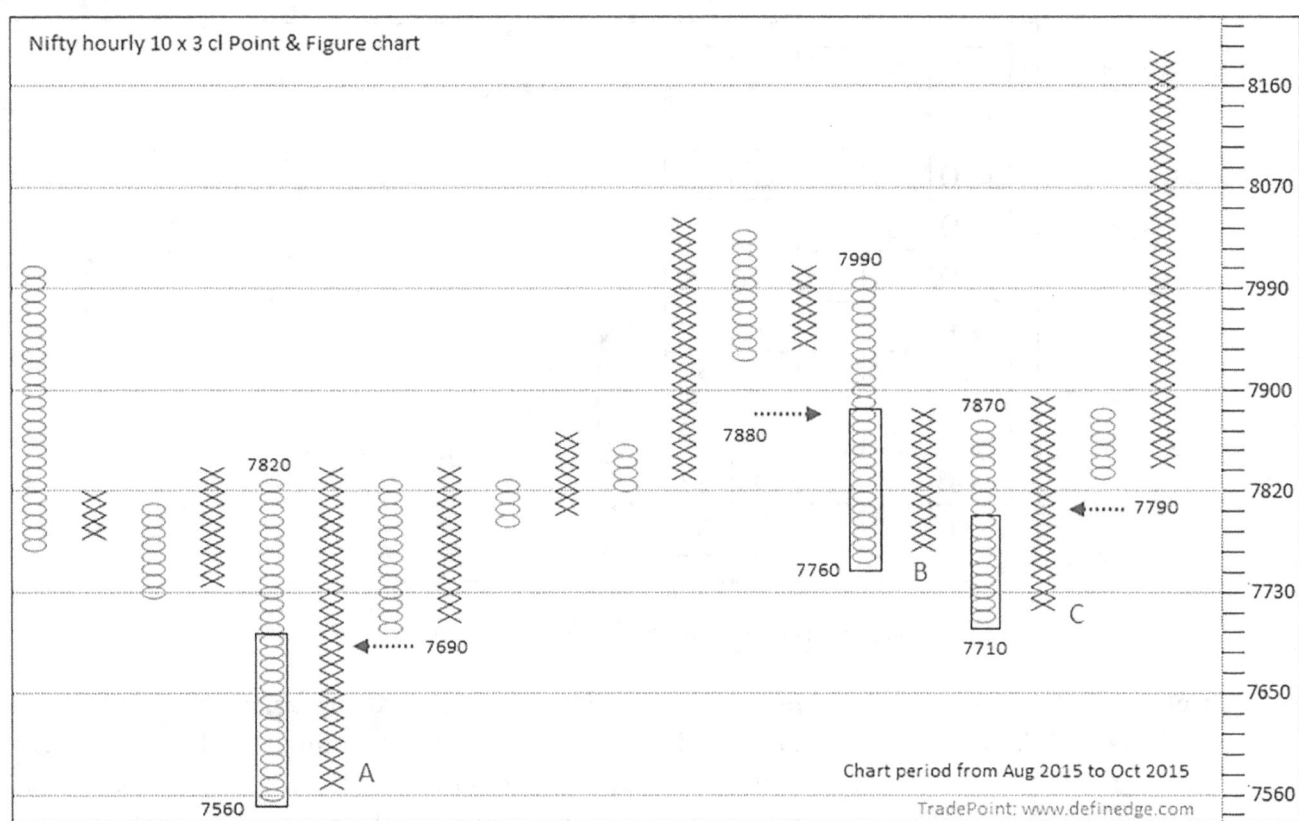

Figure 2.1.21: Nifty-I futures 60 min interval 10 × 3 cl Point & Figure chart

Note that Low Pole gets formed in the column of 'X', being bullish formation, and High Pole gets formed in the column of 'O', being bearish formation. Poles are thought-provoking four-column formations. Software may show you ready-made plotting but a little practice will train your eye to spot it on charts. Don't let the mid-value requirement complicate things. It's simply a mid-price of long column which can be observed. The trick is to look for long columns and then check the 50% retracement.

Requirement of long column defines strength of the trend. After Double Top Buy formation, when price advances further to produce more boxes, it shows that bulls got immediate move in favor. The column can have any number of boxes and it can be very large as well, which typically happens in strong trends. Immediate reversal after such strong trends is a shock to traders. Price getting retraced by 50% leads to significant erosion in potential profit and hints at strong vertical price reversals known as 'A' or 'V' shaped reversals.

You may find different versions of poles in other books. There is a requirement of some consolidation or congestion before the occurrence of poles. But to define the pattern of congestion is not easy and people remain subjective while doing that. The three criteria discussed above to define poles are clear and help in keeping it objective. One can define what one needs before poles or after it for further analysis.

Another thought that can come to mind is why five boxes and why 50%? Few authors have also mentioned a three-box requirement for poles. I think five boxes suffice; it defines the large column and favorable move. But this can be customized. Similarly, 50% requirement can be replaced by some Fib number like 61.8 or 38.2 or any other number. Such customizations can be made as per the preference and can be back-tested before actual implementation in trading.

You may want to do such experiments once you practice the charts more and the concept is grasped. For the moment, these basic rules to define poles are sufficient. Clear definition of pattern is the most important aspect of trading because execution becomes simple thereafter. Moreover, 50% is mid-value of previous columns, hence easy to remember and identify.

High price of breakout column of 'X' is the highest point of the High Pole formation; pattern fails if price goes above the same. Low price of breakout column of 'O' is the lowest point of Low Pole formation. Price going below the same negates the pattern. See Image 2.1.12 for more explanation.

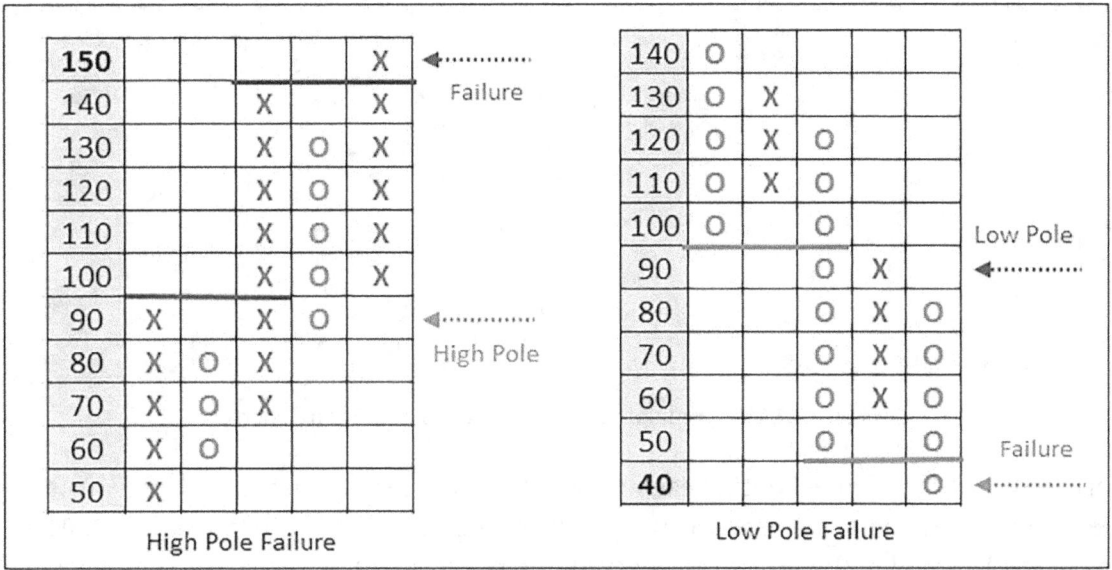

Image 2.1.12: Pole failures

Figure 2.1.22 is 0.50% × 3 daily P&F chart of CESC.

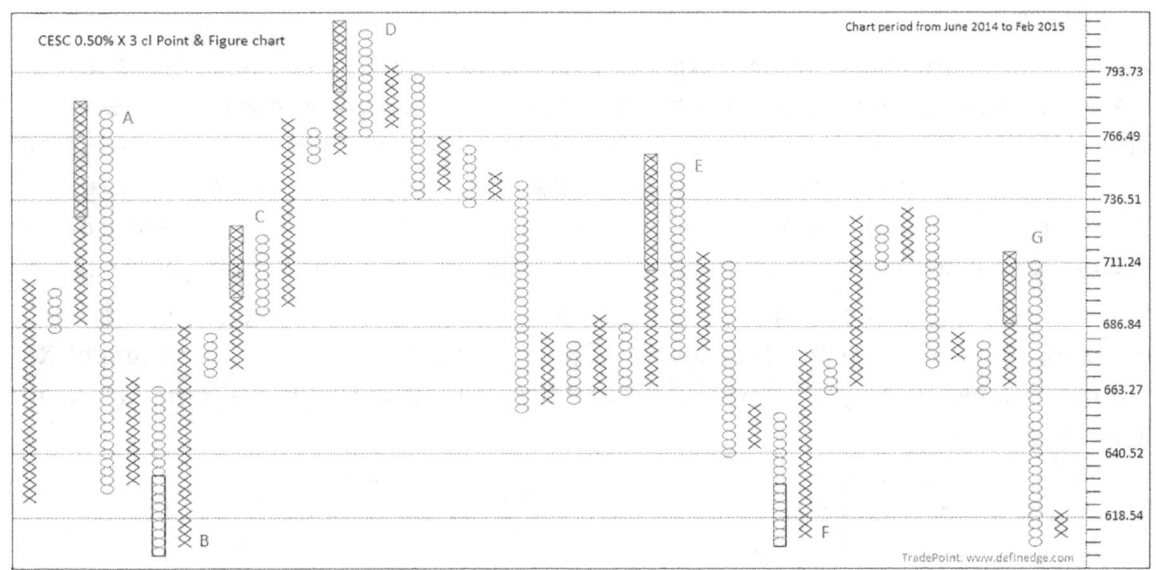

Figure 2.1.22: CESC daily 0.50% × 3 cl Point & Figure chart

Pattern A is High Pole that occurred during July 2014. Price went lower and Low Pole was formed at pattern B later in the same month. Pattern C was High Pole that failed and price soared further to mark high box-price at 813 during September 2014 where pattern D occurred which is a High Pole. Price went down till 656 box-price. It formed High Pole again at pattern E, which was followed by lower prices. Low Pole got formed at pattern F at box-price 632. Price went higher post that and marked box-price of 732 during February 2015. Pattern G is the High Pole that witnessed sharp fall in the same column itself.

Observe P&F chart of Arvind shown in Figure 2.1.23.

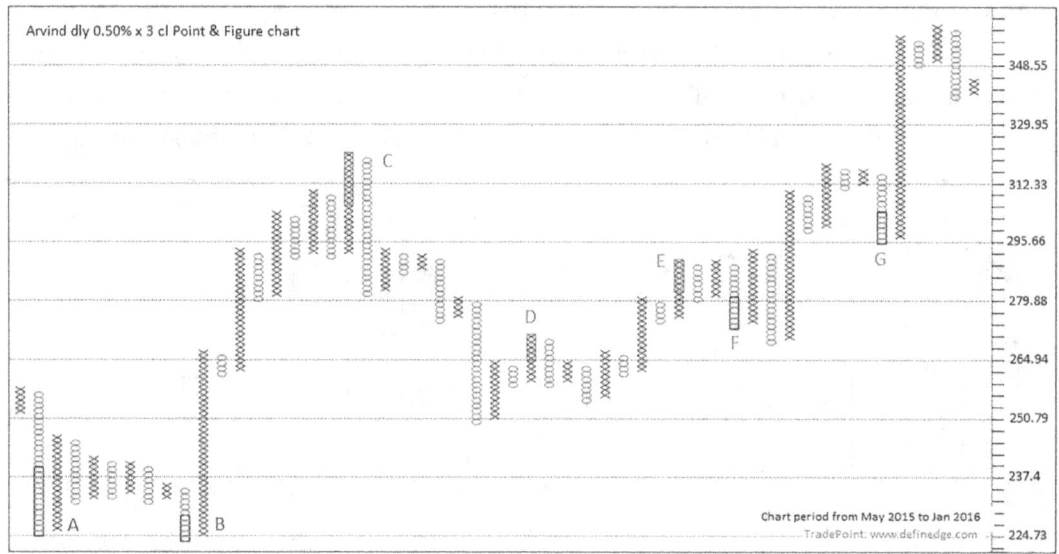

Figure 2.1.23: Arvind daily 0.50% × 3 cl Point & Figure chart

Pattern A is Low Pole formed during early May of 2015 but price consolidated after the same. Again Low Pole occurred around same levels at pattern B during June 2015 at box-price 229. That was the beginning of the Uptrend in the prices that marked box-price of 320 on the chart. High Pole occurred at pattern C, which resulted in correction till box-price of 250. Patterns D and E formed High Pole, resulting in column consolidation phase. Low Pole at Pattern F failed but price immediately bounced and regained the previous territory. Pattern G was another Low Pole in an Uptrend, which took prices to 361 in the month of January 2016.

A P&F column represents a swing move and large columns display strong trends. Poles represent vertical reversal and swift 50% retracement to such large swings. Moreover, it is only a previous column, hence recent price swing gets retraced by more than 50% – this recent swing is very difficult to define otherwise. Hence, Pole is a unique setup and one of the important features of P&F charts that provides us truly meaningful information about the price structure. Pole is the only reversal pattern of P&F; most others are breakout patterns and get generated when Double Top or Double Bottom pattern is completed.

What is important to understand here is that whenever price exceeds five boxes after breakout, it qualifies for the High Pole, which will be formed if price goes below mid-price of column of X. Hence, in case of reversal, bearish High Pole will get formed before Double Bottom Sell formation in the same column. Refer Image 2.1.13.

140		X				130	O			X	◄··········
130		X	O			120	O	X		X	Double Top Buy
120		X	O			110	O	X	O	X	
110		X	O	High Pole		100	O	X	O	X	
100		X	O	◄··········		90	O		O	X	
90	X		X	O		**80**			O	X	◄·········
80	X	O	X	O		70			O	X	Low Pole
70	X	O	X	O		60			O	X	
60	X	O		O	Double Bottom Sell	50			O	X	
50	X			O	◄·········	40			O		

Image 2.1.13: Poles

So, poles provide early signals of reversal many of the times and can be utilized as an exit pattern along with basic sell signal. If pole is considered as an exit pattern, the stop should be brought to mid-column price if a Buy signal exceeds five boxes in the same column, simply because it will be qualified for High Pole formation in that case. Similarly, a stop should be trailed to mid-column price if a sell signal is followed by five or more boxes in favor in the same column.

You can remember these patterns as 50% pole. P&F charts are swing charts and patterns it produces are 'M's and 'W's that are visible when we connect them with high and low prices of the columns, as shown in Image 1.2.8 in previous chapter. It now has 'A's and 'V's also due to the poles! Interesting? Take a break before going ahead to ponder over it.

Poles can act as reference points: Low Pole occurring frequently in the same area shows demand zone and High Pole appearing in the same area indicates supply zone. Observe the Ajanta Pharma chart shown in Figure 2.1.24.

Figure 2.1.24: Ajanta Pharma daily 0.25% × 3 cl Point & Figure chart

Boxes on the chart show the area where poles have occurred frequently. Low Pole occurring around the same level shows demand area, indicating bullishness. And High Pole occurring frequently in the same price zone indicates supply zone or bearishness. The area when broken indicates that price is changing orbit. Support becoming resistance and resistance becoming support is known as polarity principle, which is applicable here and highlighted in the chart above.

Figure 2.1.25 is a chart of Apollo Tyre showing demand and supply areas.

Figure 2.1.25: Apollo Tyre daily 0.25% × 3 cl Point & Figure chart

Using poles as exit strategy results in excessive trades but seems effective.

Figure 2.1.26 is a P&F chart of Glenmark. Mark High Pole and Low Pole formations on it. Correct markings are shown at the beginning of Section 2.2.

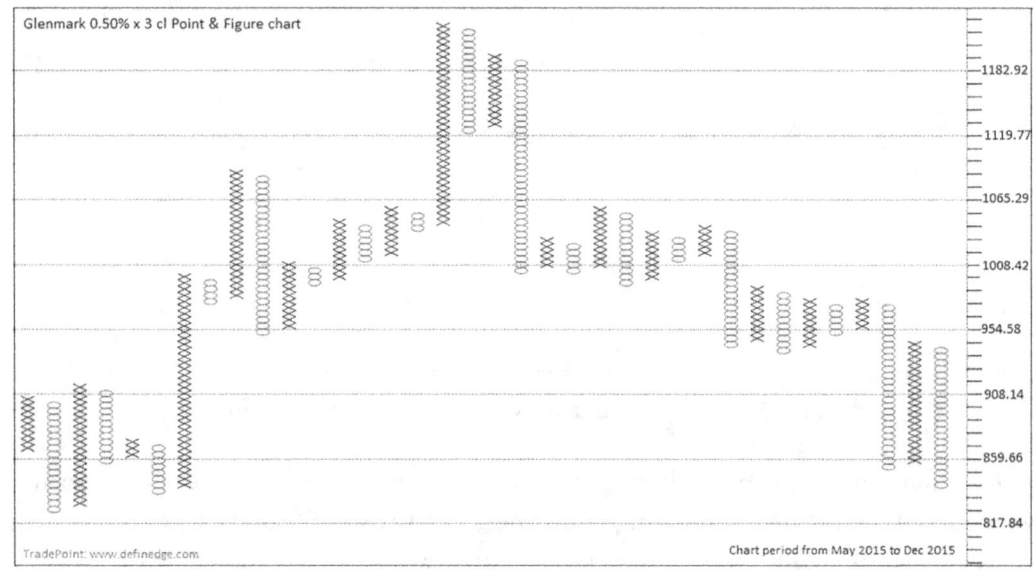

Figure 2.1.26: Glenmark daily 0.50% × 3 cl Point & Figure chart

Triangles

The Triangle is another unique feature of P&F charts. No other method can display converging formation in such an impressive manner. I need to explain Inside Column before discussing triangles.

Inside Column

As the name suggests, Inside Column is a column that is confined within the previous column; meaning that the high of the inside column is below the high of its previous column and low is above the low of its previous column. (See Image 2.1.14) I borrowed this concept from Inside Bar or Harami candlestick formation, but remember a P&F column is not a bar or candle representing a particular time period – it represents a price swing. So when range of a swing move is within the range of its previous swing move, an Inside P&F Column is formed.

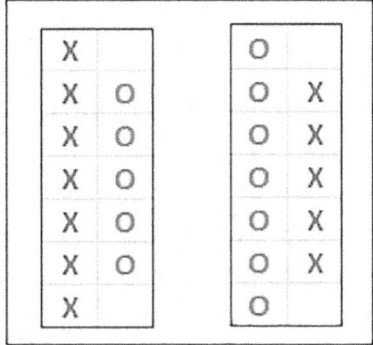

Image 2.1.14: Inside columns

It is also important to understand that an Inside Column actually forms upon occurrence of third column because second column is moving until then and there is a possibility that it doesn't remain an Inside Column. Occurrence of third column locks the Inside Column pattern.

Inside Columns are simple yet powerful formations that are easy to identify. It shows that current swing points are within the prior swing points that indicate price congestion. Consecutive Inside Columns display prolonged price congestion. (See Image 2.1.15).

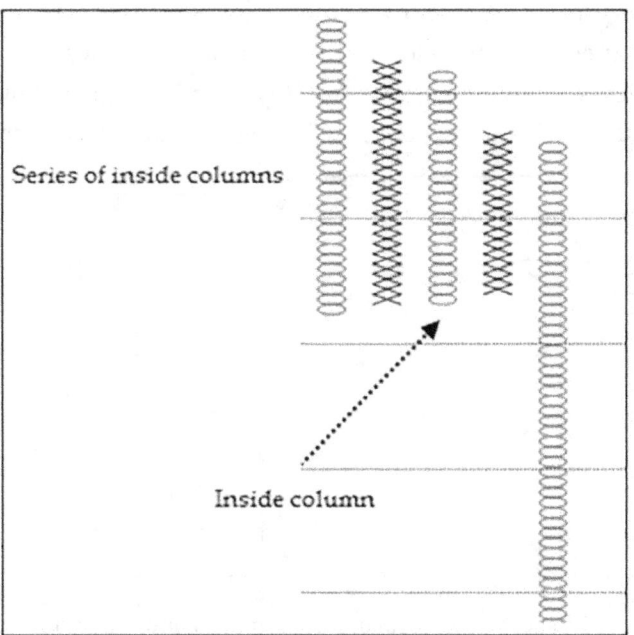

Image 2.1.15: Series of Inside Columns

Triangles

Triangles must be a familiar pattern for someone having even a basic knowledge of Technical Analysis. It is a pattern of convergence where the length of each price leg is smaller than its previous price leg. With Point & Figure, an Inside Column shows inside swing move. Series of Inside Columns display converging price pattern. Image 2.1.16 shows three consecutive Inside Columns that create a symmetrical triangular price formation. It becomes a four-column Triangle pattern where price range of every column is within the range of its previous column.

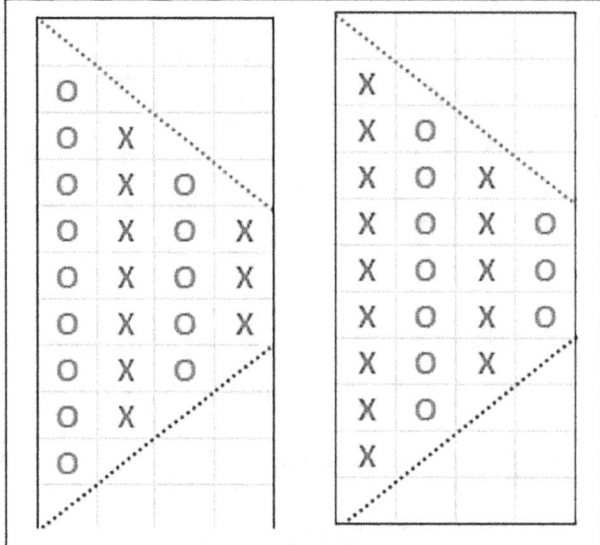

Image 2.1.16: Four-column triangle

Such is the beauty of Point & Figure charts that converging formation is also made objective and well defined. A convergence indicates price consolidation and it remains a consolidation until broken out. A four-column Triangle indicates strong congestion where previous three swing trends have been within their earlier trends; it is very difficult to define convergence in this manner otherwise. Breakout after such kind of congestion is expected to be followed by expansionary move. Breakout is well defined in P&F charts via basic Buy-Sell signals. Hence, a Double Top Buy after Triangle is a bullish Triangle breakout and Double Bottom Sell signal after Triangle is a bearish Triangle breakout pattern.

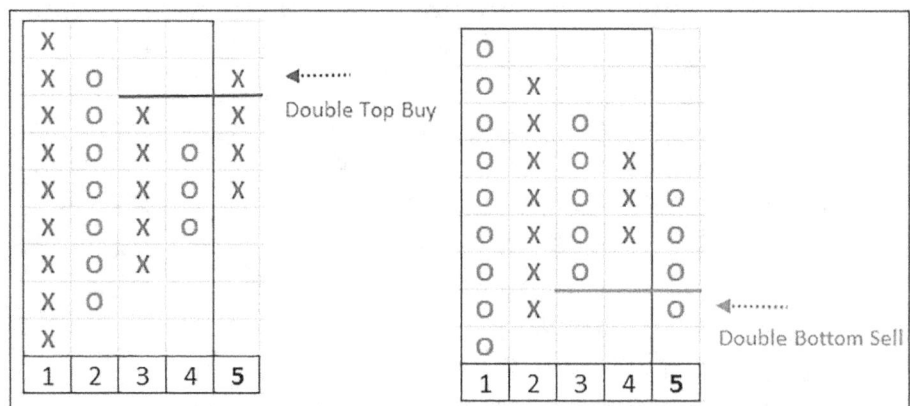

Image 2.1.17: Breakout from four-column Triangle

So, note that it is not a bullish triangle if last column is of 'X' and bearish Triangle if last column is of 'O'. Breakout can happen in the fifth column or any column after that; it is possible that price keeps consolidating for few more columns and generates breakout subsequently. Triangle is a neutral formation and it becomes bullish or bearish based on the direction of the breakout that may happen in any column after triangle. P&F Triangles are also important from the point of view that they don't plot time and display price congestions only. Figure 2.1.27 is a chart of Wipro showing four-column Triangles that occurred between December 2014 and June 2015.

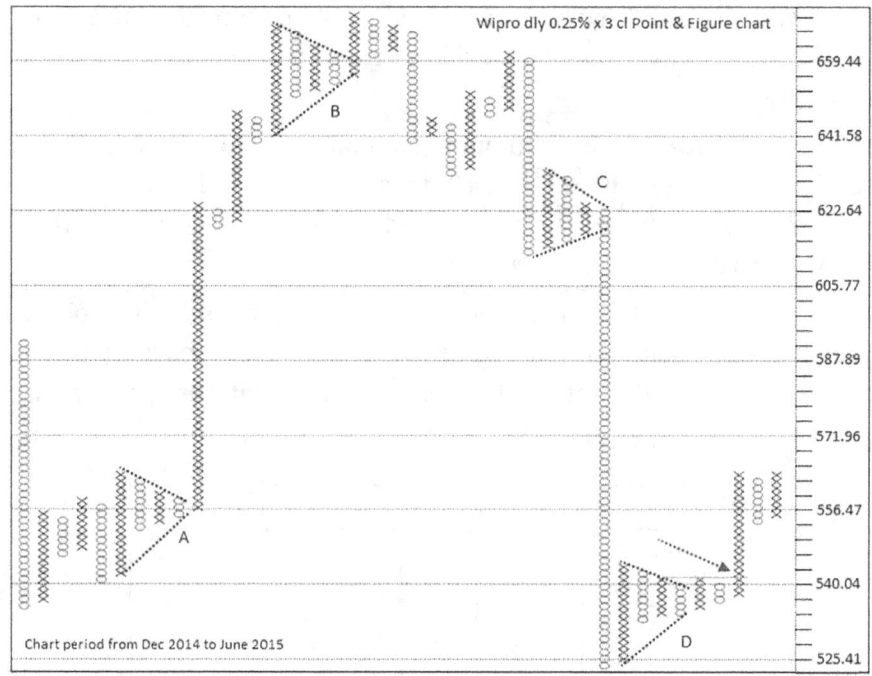

Figure 2.1.27: Wipro daily 0.25% × 3 cl Point & Figure chart

Breakout from pattern A was very effective but the same from pattern B didn't last long. Breakout from pattern C was equally effective. All three breakouts occurred in the fifth column of Triangle but breakout from pattern D didn't occur immediately. The fifth column didn't register the breakout and it eventually happened in the seventh column, which also happens to be a Triple Top Buy.

Exit based on Double Top Buy and Double Bottom Sell signal is recommended from bearish and bullish triangle breakouts, respectively. As mentioned earlier, the Triangle pattern displays congestion, and many of the times, first breakout from tight congestion proves to be a false breakout that traps the trader who expected the expansion after tight range-bound activity. It is similar to head fake formation described by John Bollinger (see Bibliography Point 2) that usually happens after a significant band squeeze. To make it relevant here, often the first Triangle breakout fails and the breakout in reverse direction produces a strong move. This failure of Triangle breakout is also a tacit pattern in the reverse direction. For this reason, there is a different rule for failure level of this pattern.

Triangle formation when followed after bullish breakout remains valid until price falls below recent 'O' of the pattern. Similarly, bearish breakout after Triangle formation remains valid until price goes above recent 'X' of the pattern. Refer Image 2.1.18.

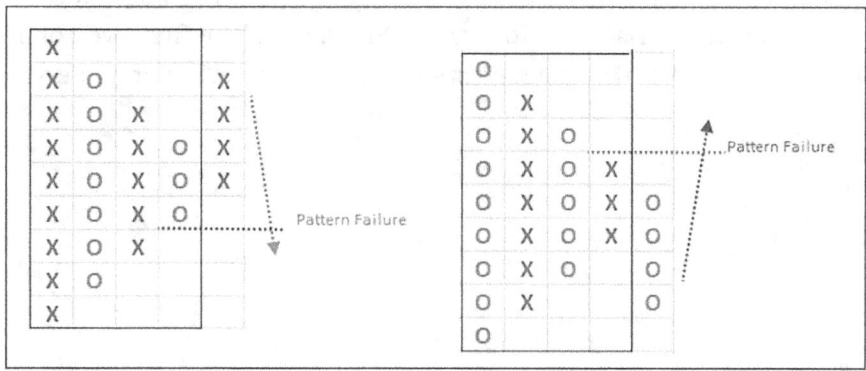

Image 2.1.18: Triangle failure

It is possible that Inside Column keeps appearing and a four-column Triangle turns out to be a bigger one. Hence, there could be five, six or more column in a Triangle. Triangle with larger number of columns indicates some serious price congestion.

A four-column Triangle breakout is minimum five-column pattern because the earliest possible breakout happens in the fifth column. It becomes a Triangle only upon the occurrence of the fifth column when the fourth column as inside formation gets locked. Four-column Triangles that display prolonged price congestion are quite rare.

But breakout appears many of the times in the fourth column itself. It is observed over so many charts that even series of two Inside Columns can be as effective and important as four-column patterns. So the three-column Triangles are also interesting congestion formations that generate effective trading opportunities.

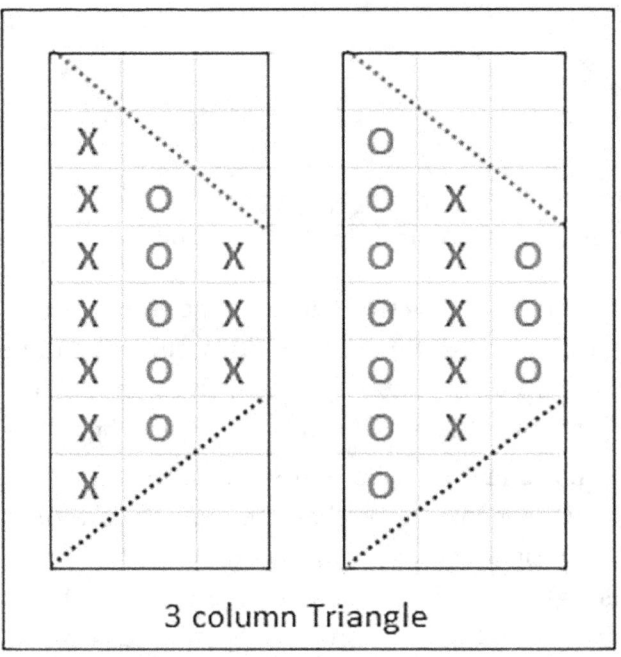

3 column Triangle

Image 2.1.19: Three-column Triangle

Image 2.1.19 shows three-column Triangles, which is a series of two Inside Columns.

Three-column Triangles are equally effective though their occurrence could be more frequent. Breakout and all other things remain same with three-column triangles as well.

If you notice, when the first column is very large in a three-column Triangle, it suggests consolidation after trend but does not become a triangular formation. Similarly, if the first two columns are very large, then it doesn't satisfy the essence of triangle formation. Refer Image 2.1.20 to understand this.

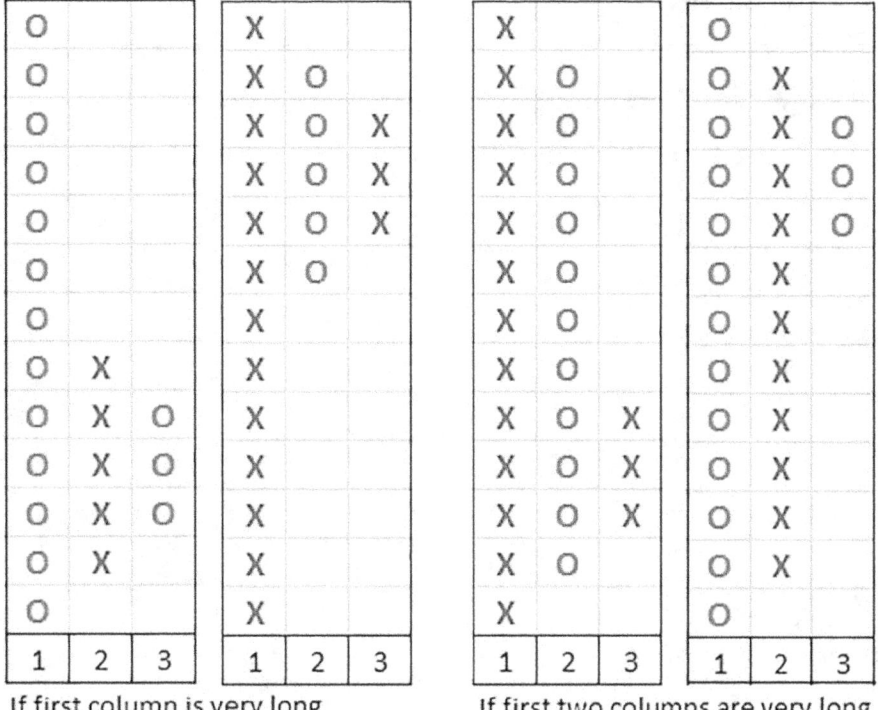

If first column is very long   If first two columns are very long

Image 2.1.20: A 50% three-column Triangle

To deal with this, I have defined a rule. Each column in the series of three-column triangle should be at least half the length of its previous column. So, column 1 shouldn't be more than double that of column 2 and column 2 shouldn't be more than double that of column 3 in length. These are the prerequisites of three-column Triangles.

I do not wish to complicate things, but this rule was essential to be made. To keep it simple, there are two types of three-column Triangles: without 50% rule and with 50% rule. To begin with, you can forget all these and observe all three-column Triangles (without 50% rule). You can read this later when you have mastered the formation. Note that 50% rule is not required in case of four-column Triangle.

Remember, a three-column Triangle gets locked over appearance of fourth column, and breakout happens at fourth column or thereafter (see Image 2.1.21).

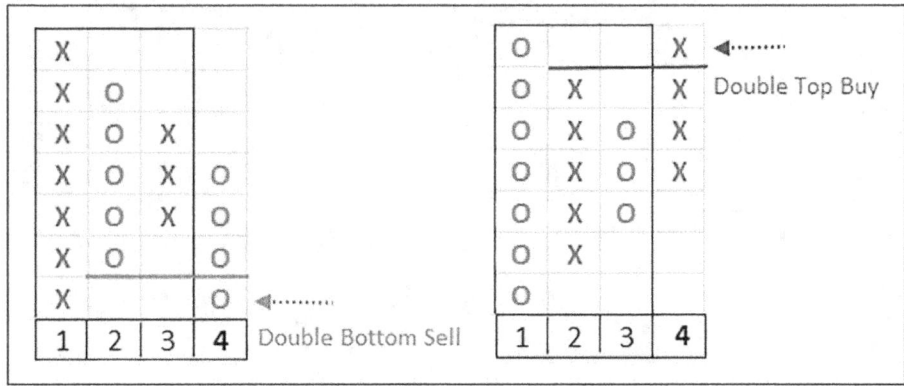

Image 2.1.21: Breakout from three-column Triangle

Figure 2.1.28 is a 1% × 3 P&F chart of BPCL.

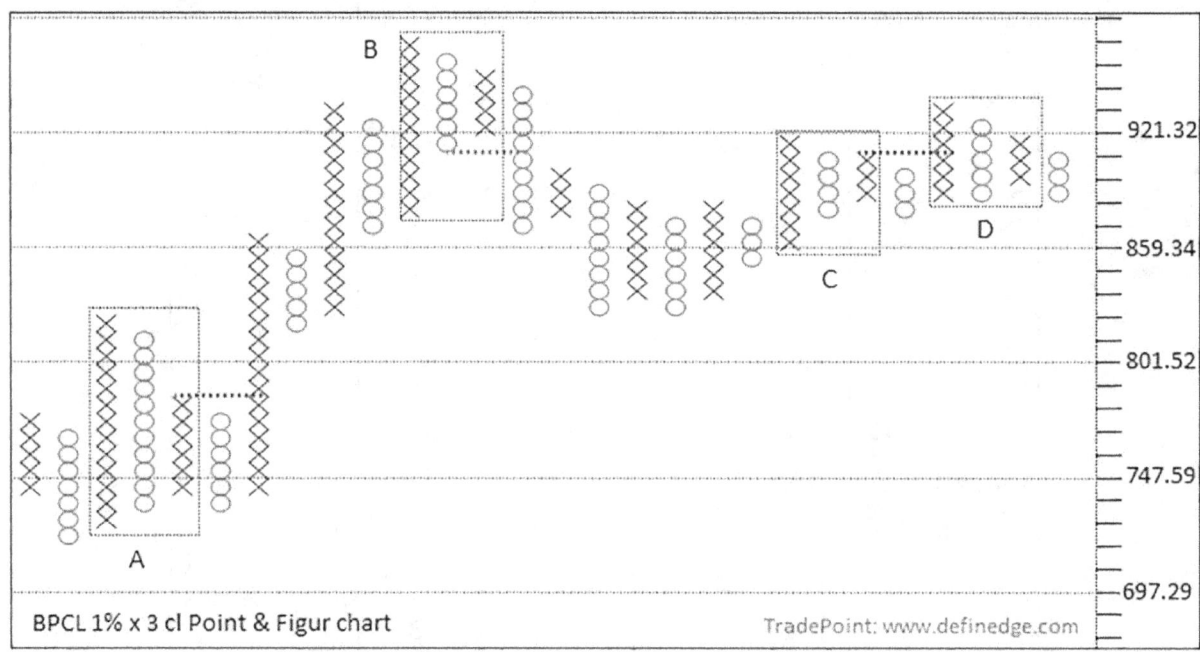

Figure 2.1.28: BPCL daily 1% × 3 cl Point & Figure chart

Pattern A is a three-column triangular formation. 'O' at fourth column happened to be at same level of previous 'O' so there was no breakout. It broke out to the upside in the fifth column. Pattern B is another three-column Triangle broken out at the fourth column. Breakout from pattern C also triggered in fifth column but followed by another Triangle shown at pattern D. It is important to understand that Triangles display congestion and breakouts are expected but they should not be pre-empted; consolidation can be prolonged and breakout direction is uncertain. If you have a feeling that breakout is certain in a particular direction, then don't trade it! Markets often surprise us and the best of trades happen when we are least comfortable in making them.

Figure 2.1.29 is a daily P&F chart of Axis bank.

Figure 2.1.29: Axis bank daily 0.25% × 3 cl Point & Figure chart

There are five occurrences of triangles in the Axis bank chart over the 1-year period it displays. Patterns A and B are three-column triangles around the same zone that witnessed breakout in immediate column. Patterns C, D, E and F are four-column Triangles that also witnessed immediate breakouts. The formations on this chart have been effective. Breakout after pattern C was retraced back immediately but it was a pullback to the pattern and price resumed the Uptrend soon afterwards.

Note in the chart that breakouts from patterns B and E were compelling. There is another observation applicable to them, described in Section 2.3 on Follow-through. Nonetheless, Triangles come with predefined exit to play breakout from consolidating price formation. Risk is usually low and a thrust is expected.

Figure 2.1.30: Tech Mahindra daily 1% × 3 H-L Point & Figure chart

Figure 2.1.30 is a 1% × 3 High–Low P&F chart of Tech Mahindra. High–Low charts are aggressive in nature and have more columns than charts plotted with closing prices. Breakout levels on these charts can help traders to refer levels in real time also and they need not wait till closing prices. Breakout didn't happen immediately from three-column Triangle shown at pattern A. It happened to be Triple Top Buy after Triangle formation. Negative breakout after pattern B didn't sustain much and price reversed eventually to resume the Uptrend. Pattern C witnessed effective negative breakout. Downside breakout from pattern D proved to be false and price reversed immediately. But it faced stiff resistance at the area of strong supply zone, displayed by multiple 'X's seen around the same levels. Breakout from three-column triangle at pattern E didn't happen immediately and was followed by Triple Bottom Sell.

P&F doesn't plot time consolidation. Triangles that we can see in three–four P&F columns may have larger congestion area in usual price–time charts with many consolidating bars or candles. Triangles are clean congestion breakout setups which are objective in nature, along with clearly defined entry and exit signals. Triangles are also important reference zones when price revisits the consolidation area. Converging pattern of the last three–four trends displayed by P&F is another matchless feature of these charts.

If you observe carefully, you will understand that if first column of a triangle is of 'X', immediate three-column Triangle breakout will be bearish only and four-column Triangle breakout will be bullish only. Hence, in a way, direction from three-column Triangle breakout is certain and it depends on type of last column. But all that is required to remember is the level when the breakout from Triangle will occur.

Have a look at the exercise charts of the last chapter to find Triangles. They are seen on all charts except Tata Steel. Figure 2.1.31 is a 1% × 3 Point & Figure chart of daily prices of PNB. You need to mark Triangles on it. Correct markings will be shown at the beginning of the next section.

Figure 2.1.31: PNB daily 1% × 3 cl Point & Figure chart

The major patterns discussed in this chapter along with basic signals are the most important P&F formations. It is interesting to understand that all Tops and Bottoms will have one of these formations. Broadly, there can be two types of Tops and Bottoms: 'W' or 'M' shaped that show gradual reversal or 'V' or 'A' shaped that are vertical reversals. There will be a P&F pattern in both of these cases. Refer Image 2.1.22 to understand the same.

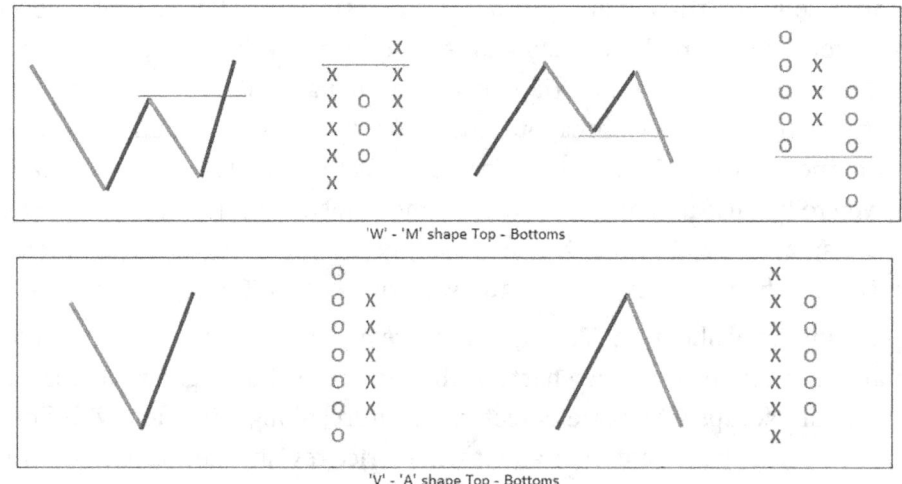

Image 2.1.22: W, M, V and A shaped Tops and Bottoms

Every other pattern apart from pole is also a basic Buy-Sell pattern. We don't know about top or bottom when they are being formed and not every occurrence of these formations indicates that. But knowing this may help in evaluating and to analyse the significance of these patterns occurring at particular price level/zone.

There are exercise charts at the end of the discussion on every pattern. You may want to go back to all those charts again and mark all major patterns. Take a break before going ahead and make sure you have understood these patterns. Don't be in hurry to analyse charts now.

A P&F column can have any number of days, but the minimum will be one. Hence, a four-column setup on daily chart will consist of a minimum four days. The same setup when seen on larger box-value represents a bigger picture. Triple Top formation in 1% box-value will have larger width and more number of days compared to the same setup on a 0.25% box-value.

Every pattern comes with the predefined entry and exit levels. Practice and experience will sharpen the skills of spotting them correctly.

Section 2.2 will begin with all exercise charts marked with major patterns. The focus has been more on understanding of the patterns so far. The practical aspects of trading using all these information are discussed in the latter part of the book.

Summary

- ⋏ Triple Top Buy is a resistance breakout pattern, whereas Triple Bottom Sell is a support breakout formation.
- ⋏ Traps = failure + breakout.
- ⋏ Traps should be traded in the direction of trend.
- ⋏ Poles are A and V shaped reversal patterns.
- ⋏ Poles are not the breakout patterns and can be utilized as an exit pattern. Them occurring at the same area shows demand and supply zones.
- ⋏ Traps and Poles can work as important support and resistance points when markets are in a bracketed phase.
- ⋏ Triangle is a converging formation; there are three-column Triangles, and multi-column Triangles. It is an objective P&F formation that offers a trade with attractive risk–reward ratio.
- ⋏ The pattern that has not failed becomes a reference area for future trends.

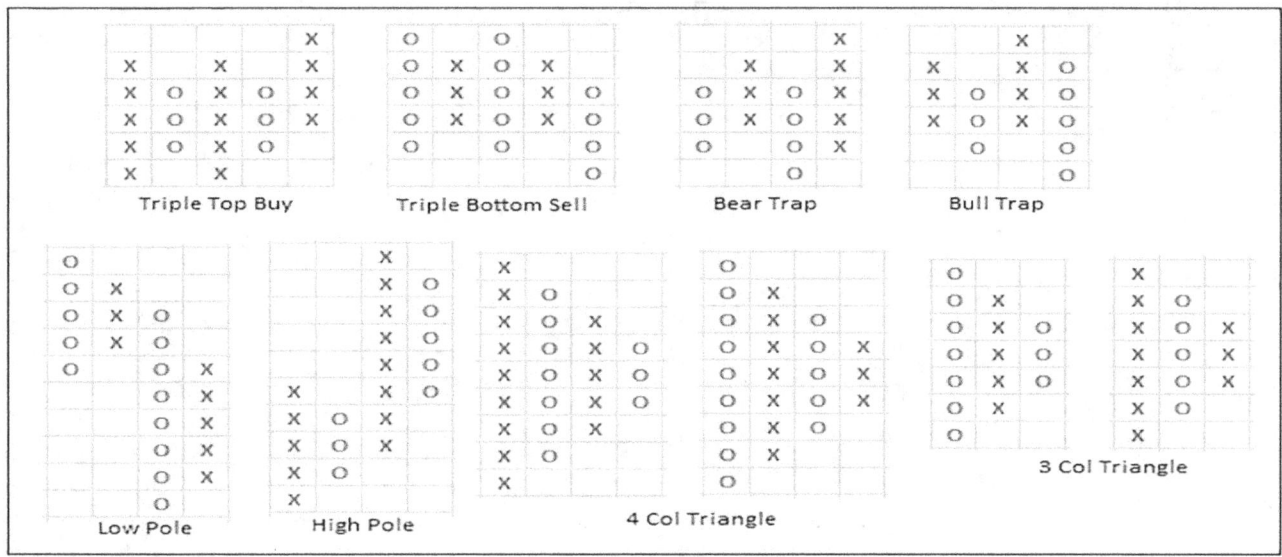

Image 2.1.23: P&F Major Patterns

2.2: OTHER IMPORTANT PATTERNS

Charts were given for exercise after every discussion in the previous section. All those charts are shown below with all four major patterns marked on them.

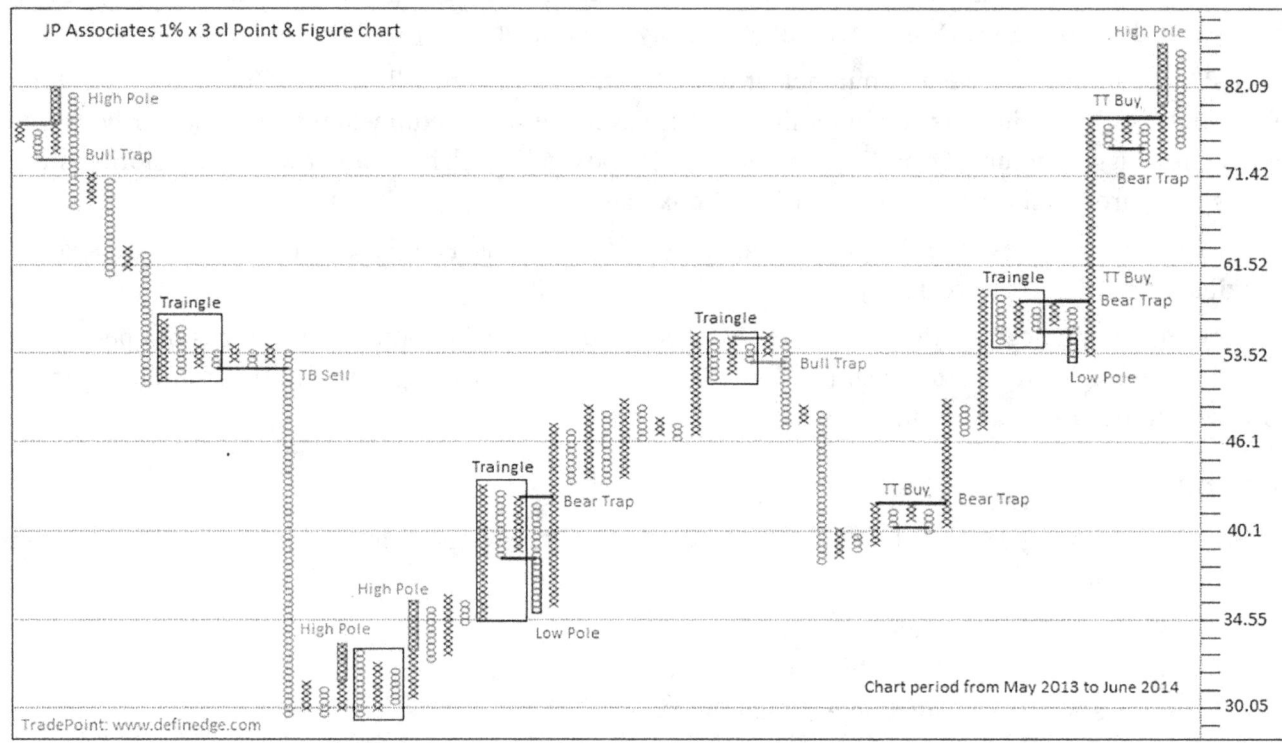

Figure 2.2.1: JP Associates daily 1% × 3 cl Point & Figure chart

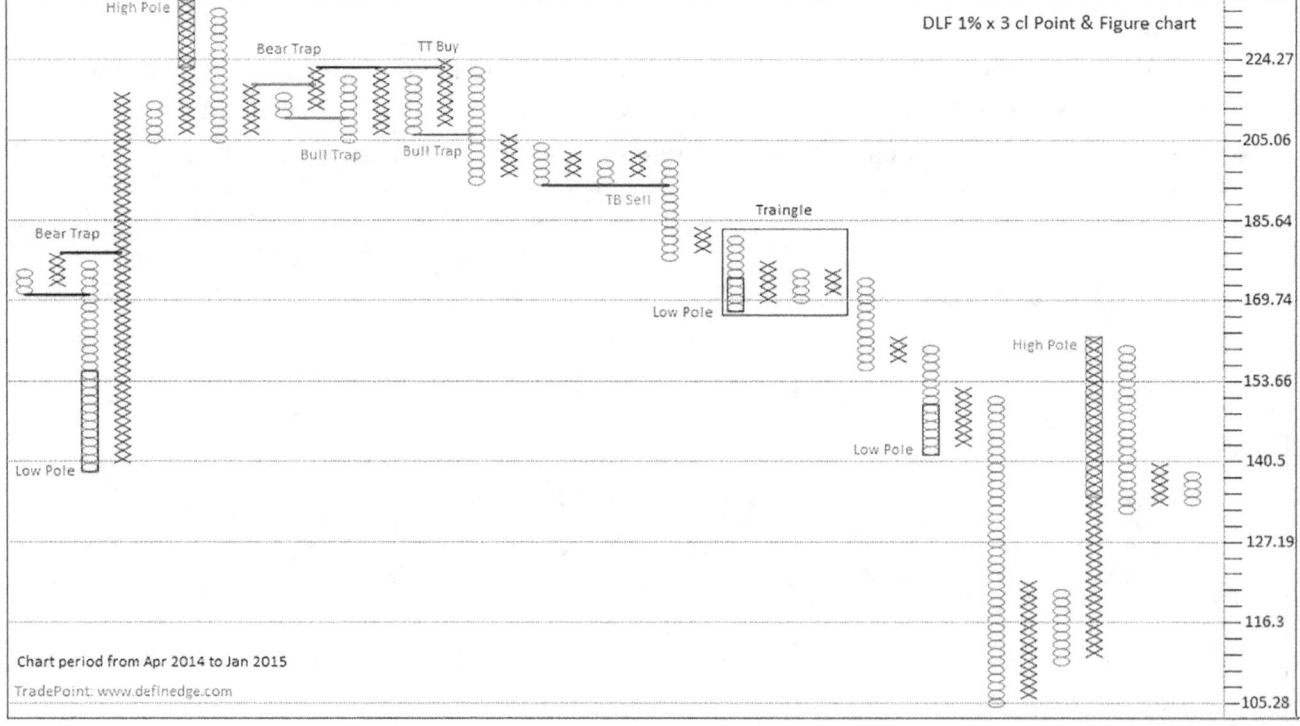

Figure 2.2.2: DLF daily 1% × 3 cl Point & Figure chart

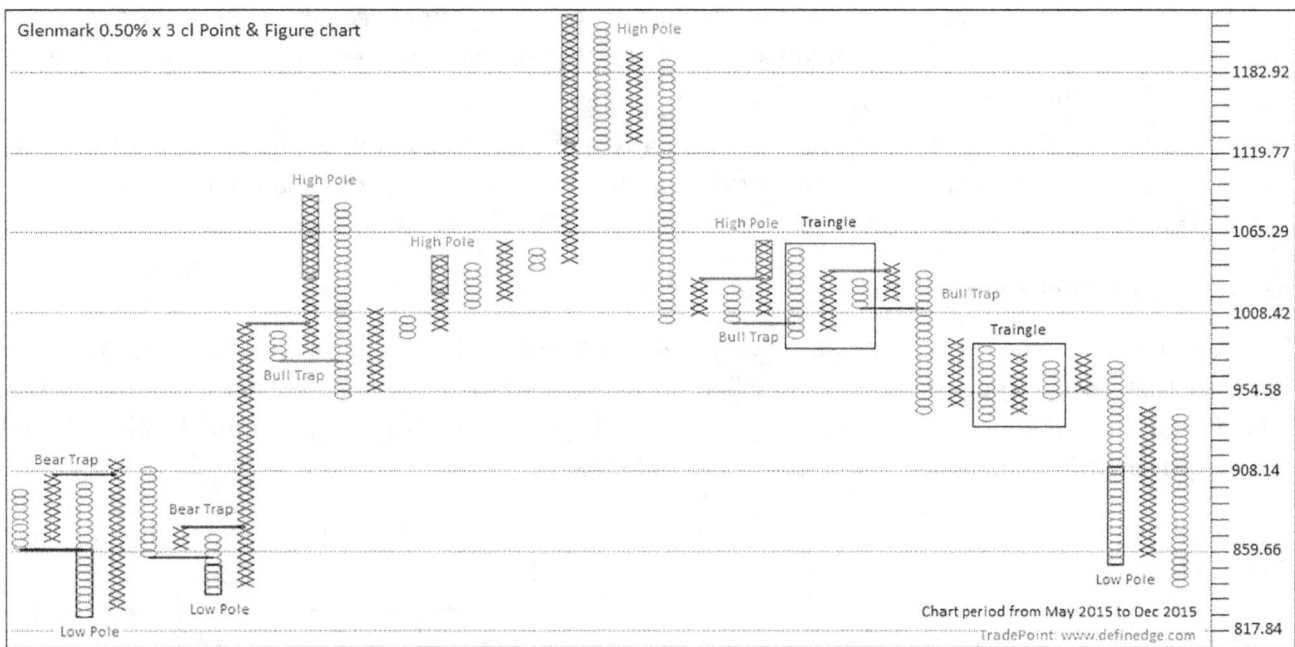

Figure 2.2.3: Glenmark daily 0.50% × 3 cl Point & Figure chart

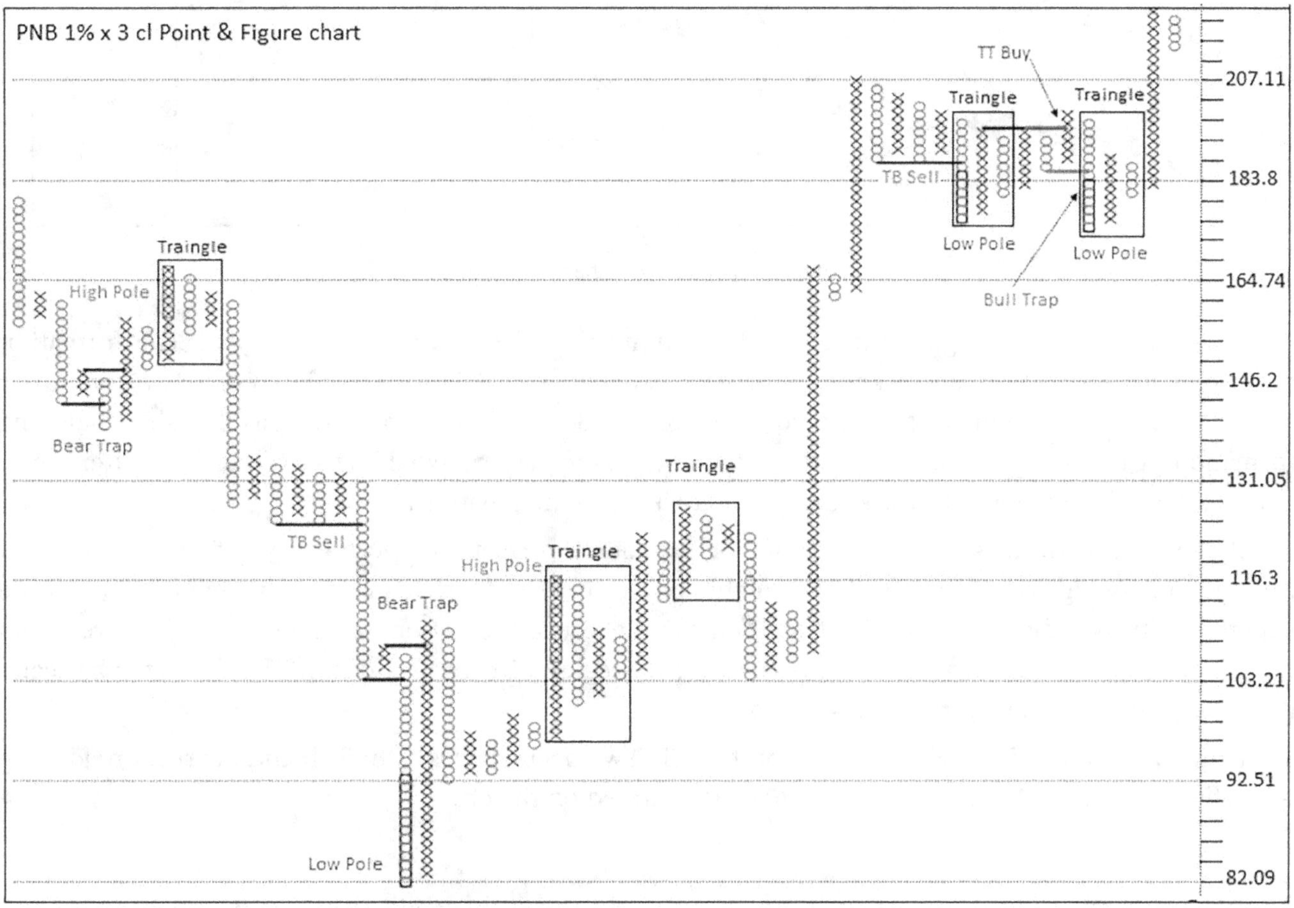

Figure 2.2.4: PNB daily 1% × 3 cl Point & Figure chart

The rest will be a cakewalk if you have been able to spot these patterns correctly. Read the section on patterns again if you face problems in identifying any of the formations. Eventually you will realize the importance of all these exercises.

This section deals with patterns which are derivatives or extensions of major patterns. But they have greater significance due to additional information that they provide. Having understood the major patterns will help you grasp them easily. Let us discuss them.

Broadening Formation

Trap formation was discussed in the previous section. Recollect and revise them before going ahead. We discussed that Double Top Buy pattern immediately followed by Double Bottom Sell pattern is a Bull Trap. What if Bull Trap fails immediately and forms another buy pattern? Or Bear Trap is immediately followed by a Sell pattern? It will look like Image 2.2.1, shown below.

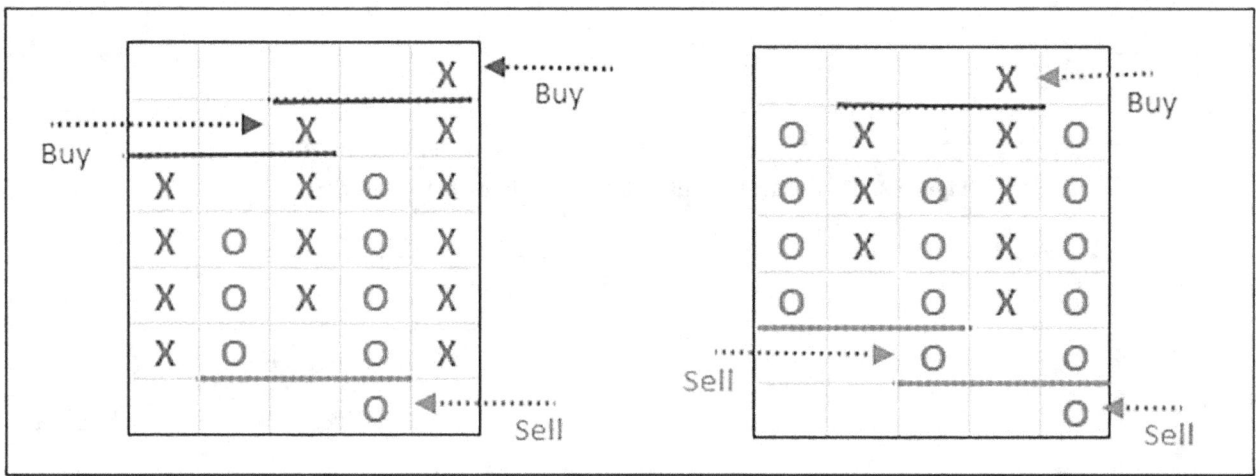

Image 2.2.1: Broadening formation

So, it traps the smart guy who entered assuming that the other side is trapped! The formation represents widening swing and is known as a Broadening pattern. A buy pattern immediately formed after Bull Trap is a five-column pattern with consecutive Buy-Sell–Buy patterns known as Bullish Broadening formation. And a Sell pattern, immediately after a Bear Trap pattern, would be a five-column pattern with consecutive Sell-Buy-Sell patterns known as Bearish Broadening pattern.

Broadening pattern is like a megaphone or expanding formation where every swing is wider than the previous swing. This is one of the inevitable phases in the life cycle of any instrument, on any time frame. It is truly a difficult phase for trend followers because they often get stopped out and breakouts fail miserably. It is a phase where trend-following strategies witness drawdown. The market is basically behaving 'wild' and there is no clear direction.

Figure 2.2.5 is a daily 0.25% × 3 P&F chart of LT. Two occurrences of Bullish and Bearish Broadening formations between May and November 2015 are marked on the chart.

Figure 2.2.5: LT daily 0.25% × 3 cl Point & Figure chart

Bullish Broadening formation is a failed Bull Trap and it is also a Bull Trap formation immediately followed by a Bear Trap. Similarly, Bearish Broadening pattern is a failed Bear Trap and also a Bear Trap immediately followed by a Bull Trap. The last three columns of both the patterns are basic signals. Do not get confused with the multitude of patterns being described. The idea is to explain the concept of patterns within a pattern. A multi-column formation is a combination of patterns and knowing it in this manner will help you understand price structure and design your own observations going further.

Bullish Broadening pattern is formed when Buy signal is generated in the fifth column and Bearish Broadening pattern is formed when Sell signal is generated in the fifth column.

Broadening pattern failure happens when the price either falls below the lowest 'O' of Bullish Broadening pattern or rises above the highest 'X' of Bearish Broadening pattern. (See Image 2.2.2).

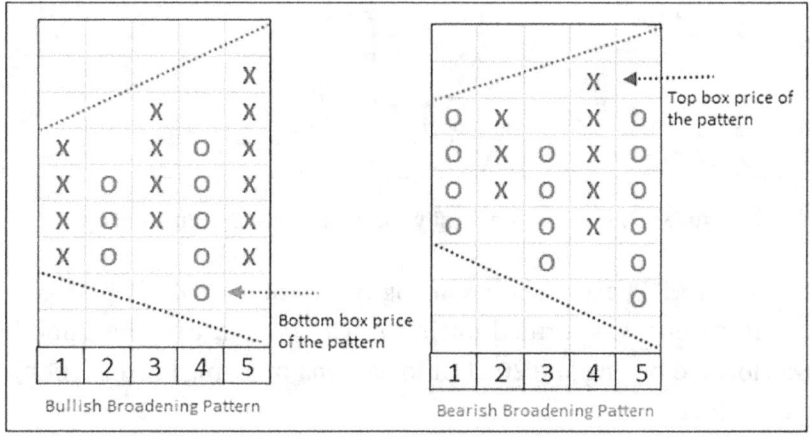

Image 2.2.2: P&F Broadening formations

If Broadening formations are failed traps, then it would be interesting to know the ratio of traps that fail immediately; in other words, how many times a Trap formation becomes a Broadening formation. The table featured below details the number of occurrences of all Traps and Broadening patterns in stocks from the Nifty 500 index (defined by the National Stock Exchange). The calculation is based on the 20-year price data from 1ˢᵗ January 1996 to 31st March 2015. They are derived from a total of 8 box-values starting from 0.25% up to 2%. Table 2.2.1 shows the number of occurrences and the ratio.

Table 2.2.1: Number of occurrences of Trap and Broadening patterns in Nifty 500 stocks from 1-1-1996 to 31-12-2015

Pattern	Occurrences	Pattern	Occurrences
Bear Trap	133648	Bull Trap	124099
Bearish Broadening	24432	Bullish Broadening	25201
Ratio	18.28%	Ratio	20.31%

Roughly about 20% of Traps have become Broadening formation in the past. In other words, 80% of Traps don't fail immediately.

Figure 2.2.6 is a P&F chart of Jindal Steel. Two occurrences of Bullish and Bearish Broadening formations between August and December 2015 are marked on the chart.

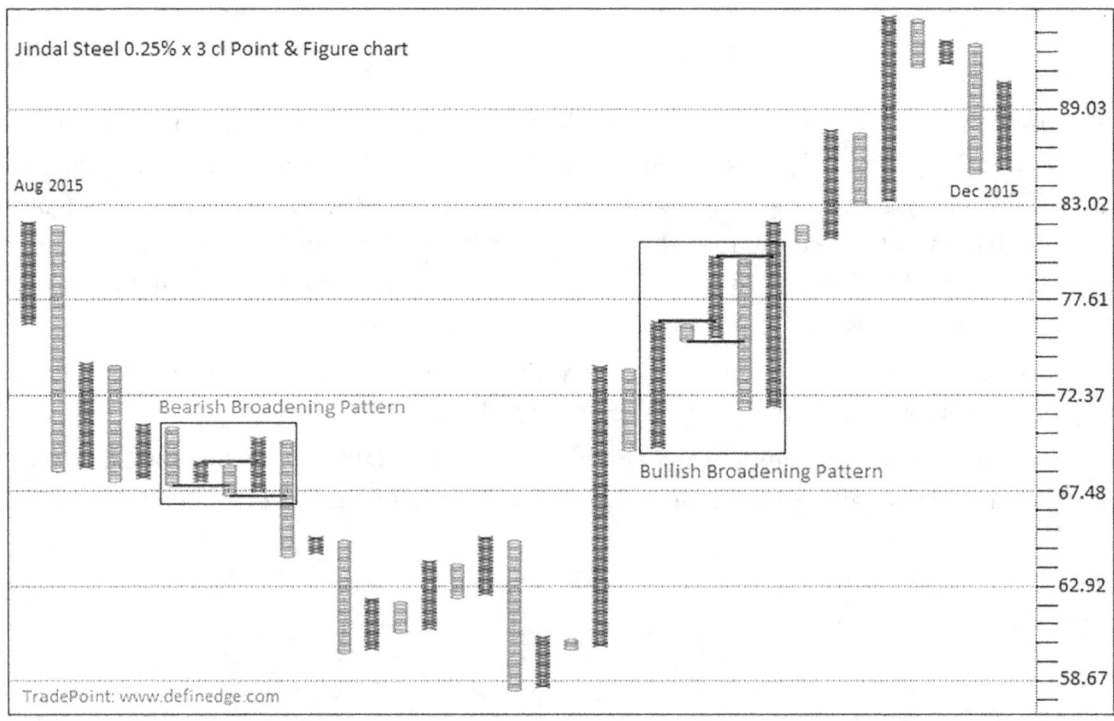

Figure 2.2.6: Jindal Steel daily 1% × 3 cl Point & Figure chart

Figure 2.2.7 is a 1% × 3 P&F chart of daily closing prices of Bata India between May 2011 and July 2014. Bullish Broadening pattern was formed during April 2013 around the same levels where Bearish Broadening pattern was formed during late 2011. It locked major swing bottom then, and price surged till box-price 740 during early 2015.

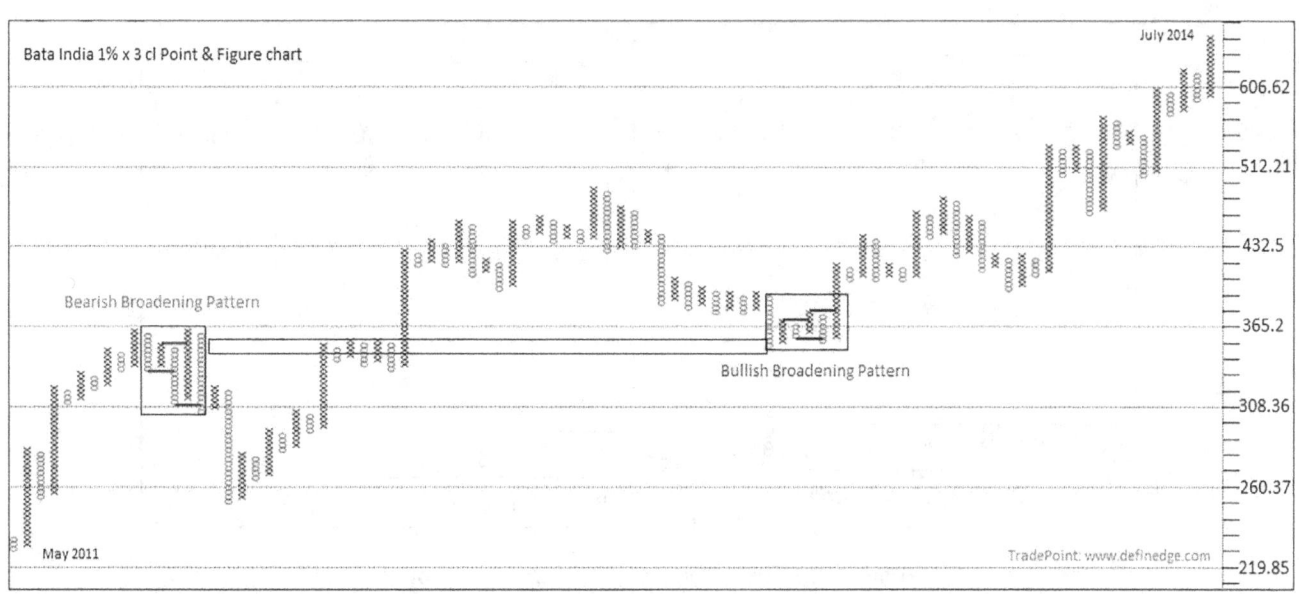

Figure 2.2.7: Bata India daily 1% × 3 cl Point & Figure chart

The Broadening pattern is just an inverse of the Triangle pattern. Converging formations like triangles display dull and consolidation phase but swing traders are fine with it because not much trade signals are generated during that phase. The advantage of a noiseless chart is that the plotting is reduced during such phases and the patterns restrict a lot of trading signals; hence, those phases can be nicely dealt with using these charts. Broadening phases, however, produce wild and volatile moves, which is a difficult period to deal with. The one who is trading the instrument regularly may witness whipsaws during this phase, but it is an important information to others sitting on the sidelines. Normal expectation is that such difficult phases would be followed by a trending phase.

Initial basic reversal signal of Broadening formations usually goes quite far; hence, at times they become unaffordable from the trading perspective. Follow-through pattern is discussed in the next section to understand how to deal with this. You can, however, run a scan and shortlist candidates where Broadening pattern has occurred. This will be handy as Broadening phase is typically followed by a trending move.

Even Broadening formations can fail in the immediate column. This may happen when Broadening phase gets extended, volatility is all-pervasive in such cases and there is no strength in the trend. This is called a Double Broadening formation, because the Broadening pattern is followed by another Broadening pattern!

Double Broadening Formation

Bullish Broadening pattern when fails in immediate column generates Bearish Double Broadening formation. Similarly, Bearish Broadening pattern that immediately fails triggers Bullish Double Broadening pattern. It is a typical case of back-to-back Broadening formations, which are known as Double Broadening patterns (see Image 2.2.3).

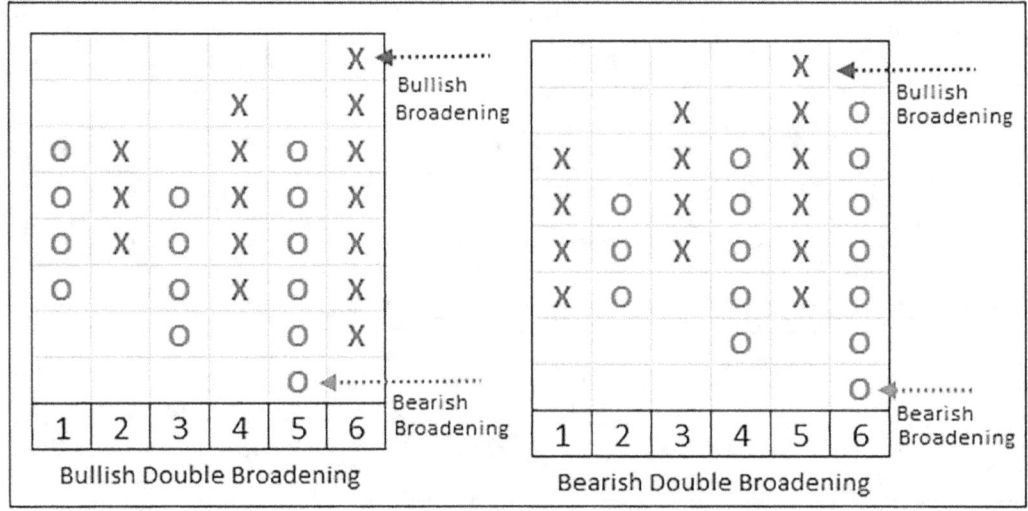

Image 2.2.3: P&F Double Broadening formations

In nutshell, Bullish Double Broadening formation is a consecutive Sell-Buy-Sell-Buy pattern where Bearish Broadening pattern is immediately followed by Bullish Broadening pattern. Same way, Bearish Double Broadening formation is a consecutive Buy-Sell-Buy-Sell pattern where Bullish Broadening pattern is immediately followed by Bearish Broadening pattern. So they are six-column patterns with Buy or Sell signal in each column. This type of formation is quite rare.

Look at below chart of Reliance Infra.

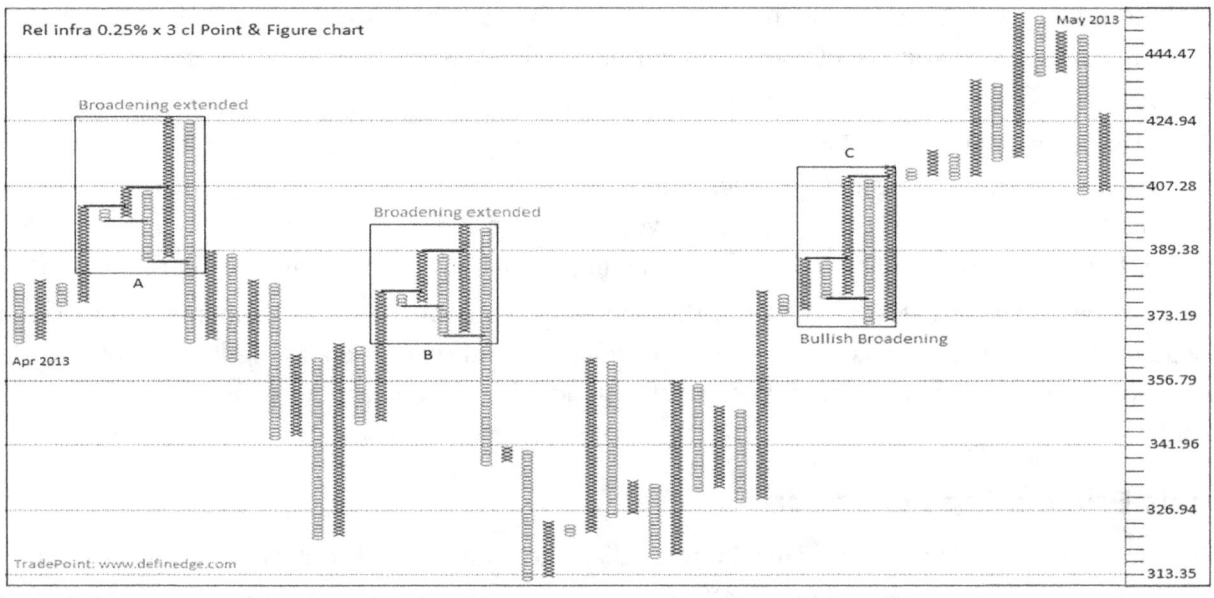

Figure 2.2.8: Reliance Infra daily 0.25% × 3 cl Point & Figure chart

Pattern A and Pattern B are Bearish Double Broadening formations where sixth column produced Double Bottom Sell pattern to fail the Bullish Broadening pattern immediately. Pattern C is a five-column Bullish Broadening pattern.

It is quite rare to see the Broadening formation failing at the sixth column itself. We saw the number of occurrences of Broadening formations in Nifty 500 stocks over a period of 20 years. Table 2.2.2 shows the ratio of Broadening formations failing immediately, based on the number of occurrences during the same period.

Table 2.2.2: Number of occurrences of Broadening and Double Broadening patterns in Nifty 500 stocks from 1-1-1996 to 31-12-2015

Pattern	Occurrences	Pattern	Occurrences
Bearish Broadening	24432	Bullish Broadening	25201
Bullish Double Broadening	3587	Bearish Double Broadening	3326
Ratio	14.68%	Ratio	13.20%

Hence, Broadening patterns don't often fail immediately and the ratio goes down further as box-value increases. Double Broadening is extended Broadening which has lower failure ratio.

The other side of objectivity that noiseless charts display is that you can see whipsaws clearly. You can see periods of trouble also. This is not displayed so clearly in the usual charts. You can easily see the periods of Broadening and Double Broadenings where trend followers might have been in trouble.

Broadening is an inevitable phase of every instrument and every time frame. It is unavoidable but can be dealt better with the help of position sizing. Reduce the bet when stop is far; remember the affordability part we discussed in the Chapter 1.

Broadening formations provide very important reference points. It is the area of battlefield of the Bulls and Bears where one side eventually took over.

100% Pole

We discussed pole formation in the previous chapter. A pole is formed when a column is retraced by 50% immediately after the long breakout column – you can call it 50% Pole. It is possible that after forming 50% Pole, the trend continues in the same column and retraces the prior swing by 100% or more. Such a pattern qualifies as a 100% Pole!

High Pole is formed when column of 'O' retraces previous long column of 'X' by 50%. If same column of 'O' continues the down move and retraces the prior move entirely to generate Double Bottom Sell pattern in the same column, then it is a bearish 100% Pole. Similarly, after forming Low Pole, if 'X' continues to rise and generate Double Top Buy formation in the same column, then it is a bullish 100% Pole (See Image 2.2.4):

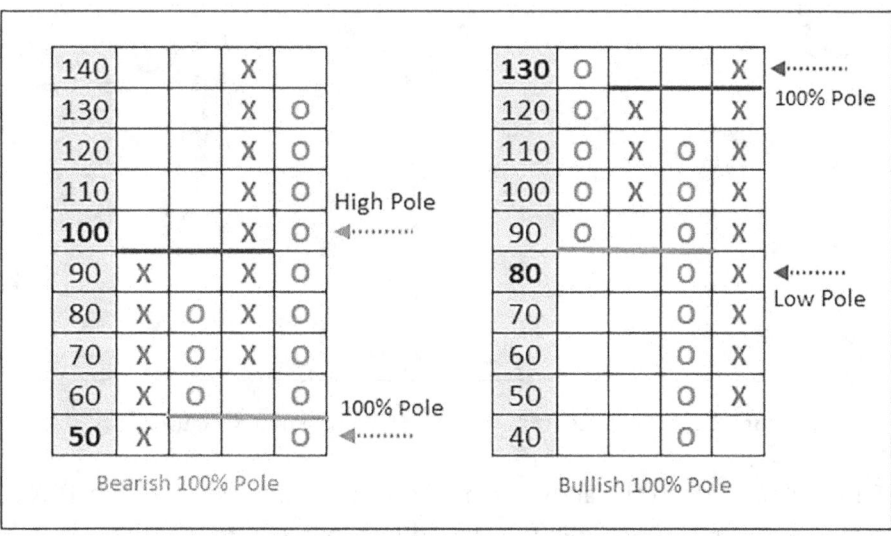

Image 2.2.4: P&F 100% poles

Understand that a 100% Pole pattern is a usual Pole formation as well and prior conditions about the pole pattern remain the same. There should be at least a five-box move after the breakout, and retracement column should happen immediately. The difference is that the retracement is deep enough to go up to 100%. You might have noticed this pattern while reading poles. I segregated 100% Pole from usual pole because it provides indication of more bullishness or bearishness than 50% Pole. It shows a steep reversal that has retraced prior move completely. In this instance, the prior move by itself was a strong move, representing a breakout of at least five boxes or more. A strong move after breakout that gets completely retraced would come as a shock to the traders.

They are called 100% Poles because they retrace prior swing move by more than 100%. Simple names help in remembering the formations. I also used to call it 'back to pavilion' initially, and asked people to remember it by name bullish or bearish engulfing, mainly because of their resemblance with engulfing candlestick formation and due to the popularity of candlestick charts. Many people call the column a candle, it is fine as long as the concept is understood. Daily candlestick chart engulfing pattern shows that the previous day candle is engulfed, whereas daily P&F engulfing column pattern shows that the previous swing move is engulfed and retraced entirely. You will often find instances of 100% Poles at major Tops and Bottoms.

Have you observed that a 100% Pole is a trap formation as well? In fact it is a combination of three patterns. A bearish 100% Pole is a High Pole, a Bull Trap and a Double Bottom Sell as well. Similarly, a bullish 100% Pole is a Low Pole, a Bear Trap as well as a Double Top Buy pattern. So it is a powerful formation and occurs on all time frames but seen more on lower box-value charts.

Figure 2.2.9 is a 0.25% × 3 daily P&F chart of Reliance Infra.

Figure 2.2.9: Reliance Infra daily 0.25% × 3 cl Point & Figure chart

There are several 100% Poles in the above chart. Pattern A and B are bearish 100% Pole followed by lower prices. Pattern C is bullish 100% Pole that failed but followed by bearish 100% Pole at pattern D, which was a timely occurrence. Pattern D is also a Bearish Broadening formation if looked at carefully.

Pattern E is Low Pole and not 100% Pole. Pattern F is a bullish 100% pole followed by bearish 100% pole at pattern G that failed. Patterns H and I are bullish 100% Poles that was followed by a sharp spike in price.

Figure 2.2.10 is the intraday time interval chart of Nifty, plotted using 5 × 3 parameters with closing prices of every minute. Vertical lines are day-separating lines.

Figure 2.2.10: Niftyfutures 1 min interval 5 × 3 cl Point & Figure chart

Patterns A and B are bullish 100% Poles that occurred around same levels, which resulted in a steady upswing. Pattern C is bearish 100% Pole that occurred as shock to the bulls who were riding the trend smoothly. The price follow-through was significant. Low Pole formation that failed subsequently can be seen at the end of the chart.

So, a Pole can turn out to be the 100% Pole. Table 2.2.3 shows occurrences of Poles and 100% Poles in the all stocks of Nifty 500 over 20 years.

Table 2.2.3: Number of occurrences of Poles and 100% Pole patterns in Nifty 500 stocks from 1-1-1996 to 31-12-2015

Pattern	Occurrences	Pattern	Occurrences
Low Pole	147465	High Pole	165157
Bullish 100% Pole	60768	Bearish 100% Pole	56556
Ratio	41.21%	Ratio	34.24%

Ratio of Low Poles becoming bullish 100% pole is quite high; hence, exit based in Low Pole seems a sensible approach. For entry, waiting for 100% Pole helps in filtering poles. The ratio of pole becoming 100% Pole gets reduced as box-value is increased.

Bullish 100% Pole fails when bottom of the pattern is broken and bearish 100% Pole fails when top of the pattern gets broken, as shown in Image 2.2.5.

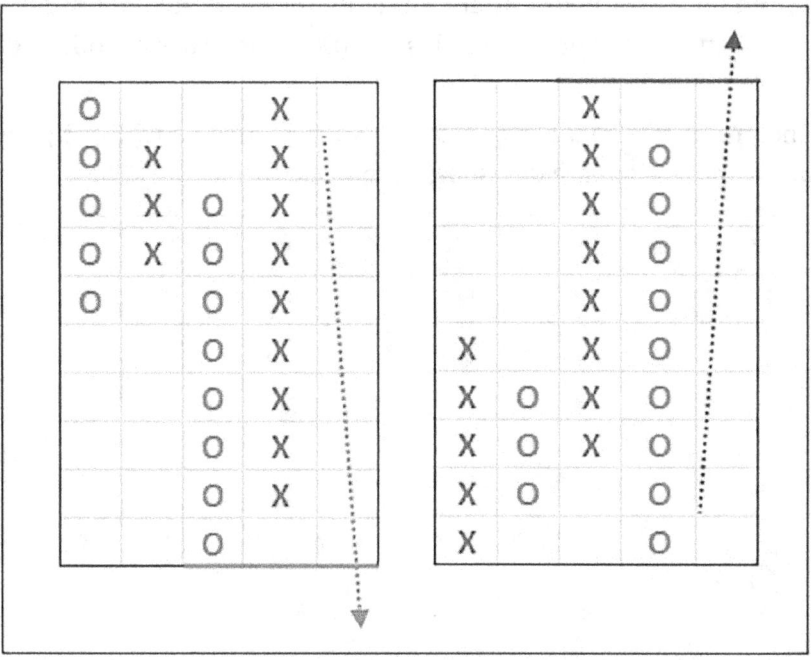

Failure of 100% Pole

Image 2.2.5: Failure levels of 100% Pole

While I said that High Poles and Low Poles can be good exit patterns, 100% Poles are entry patterns. The problem, however, is that the initial risk is very high with an entry using 100% Poles. Section 2.3 on Follow-through will help in dealing with it.

If 100% Pole fails in immediate column, it will become a Broadening formation. We saw the occurrences of 100% Pole in Table 2.2.3. Table 2.2.4 shows number of 100% Poles becoming Broadening formations.

Table 2.2.4: Number of occurrences of 100% Pole and Broadening after Pole patterns in Nifty 500 stocks from 1-1-1996 to 31-12-2015

Pattern	Occurrences	Pattern	Occurrences
Bearish 100% Pole	56556	Bullish 100% Pole	60768
Bearish Broadening after pole	7913	Bullish Broadening after pole	8095
Ratio	13.99%	Ratio	13.32%

The ratio of 100% Poles that fail immediately has been very low. The 100% Poles do not typically offer an affordable trade. A subsequent entry based on a Follow-through can be a rewarding trading opportunity.

The 100% Pole formations are important reference patterns when we analyse the chart of an instrument. There is an extra flavor of bullishness or bearishness associated with the pattern. There is an ingredient of failure of one side along with strength of the overpowering side.

Spend some time on observing charts as we discuss the patterns. There are not many rules and a little practice is required to gain proficiency in identifying these patterns. More importantly, these patterns are objective in nature, hence once understood, will be etched in memory quite easily. Broadenings are an extension of Traps and 100% Poles are an extension of 50% Poles. I am covering P&F formations that are different from each other, but are complementary in nature.

Let us shift focus to the bullish and bearish patterns that reversed. These patterns provide key insights about the state of the market.

Pattern That Reversed

Bearish and bullish patterns that reversed are reversal formations and not really an extension to any pattern that we have discussed so far. I wish their names were different to make them less confusing and easy to remember. Nonetheless, they are useful and important formations that can easily be understood. Bearish pattern that reversed is a bullish pattern and bullish pattern that reversed is a bearish pattern.

These patterns indicate a trend reversal. A Buy signal formed after a bearish trend can be classified as a bearish pattern that reversed. Bearish trend for this formation is defined as a series of two Double Bottom Sell patterns. Hence, a Buy signal happening after two consecutive sell signals, becomes a bearish pattern reversed.

Similarly, a Double Bottom Sell pattern immediately coming after two consecutive Double Top Buy patterns, is called a bullish pattern that reversed.

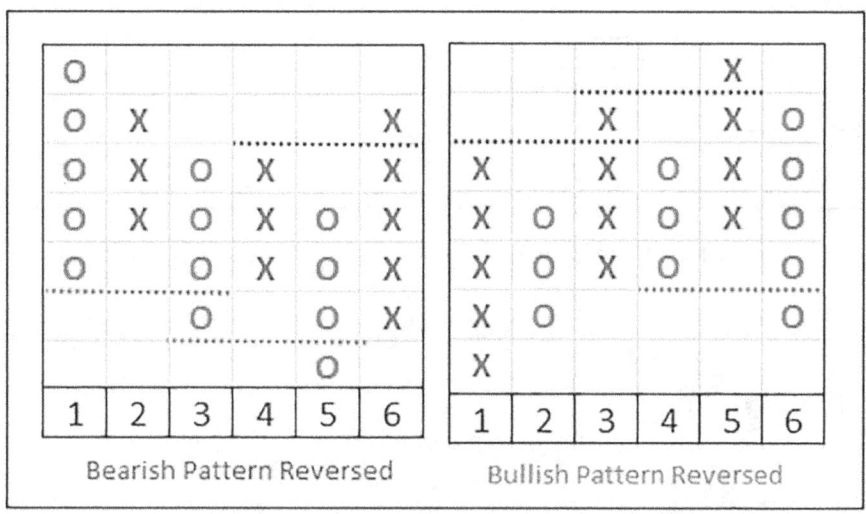

Image 2.2.6: Bearish and bullish pattern reversed

It is a six-column reversal formation where a trend gets reversed in the sixth column. Note that there shouldn't be a Buy signal before the sixth column, meaning that column of 'X' in second and fourth column shouldn't have produced Double Top Buy pattern to qualify for bearish pattern reversed. Similarly, there shouldn't be a Double Bottom Sell pattern before sixth column to qualify for the bullish pattern reversed formation.

In other words, column 3 or 5 shouldn't be a Bull Trap in case of bearish pattern reversed and shouldn't be a Bear Trap in case of bullish pattern reversed.

As you can see in images, it is a reversal pattern in an established trend. The formation has a distinct importance when found in Uptrend or Downtrend. Bearish pattern reversed is a bullish flag-like formation when appearing in the Uptrend. It shows that the correction to the prior trend is over and becomes an effective pullback setup. Similarly, bullish pattern that reversed in Downtrend resembles bearish flag. Figures 2.2.11 and 2.2.12 are P&F charts of LIC Housing.

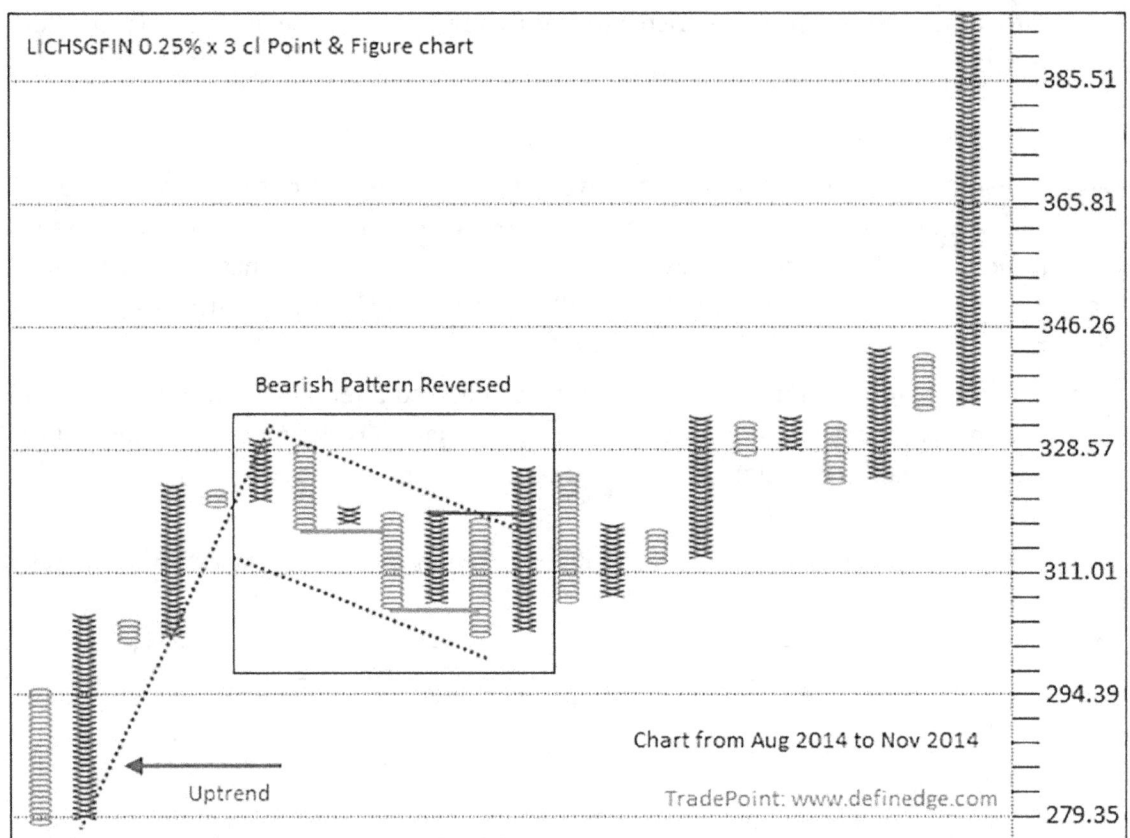

Figure 2.2.11: LIC housing finance daily 0.25% × 3 cl Point & Figure chart

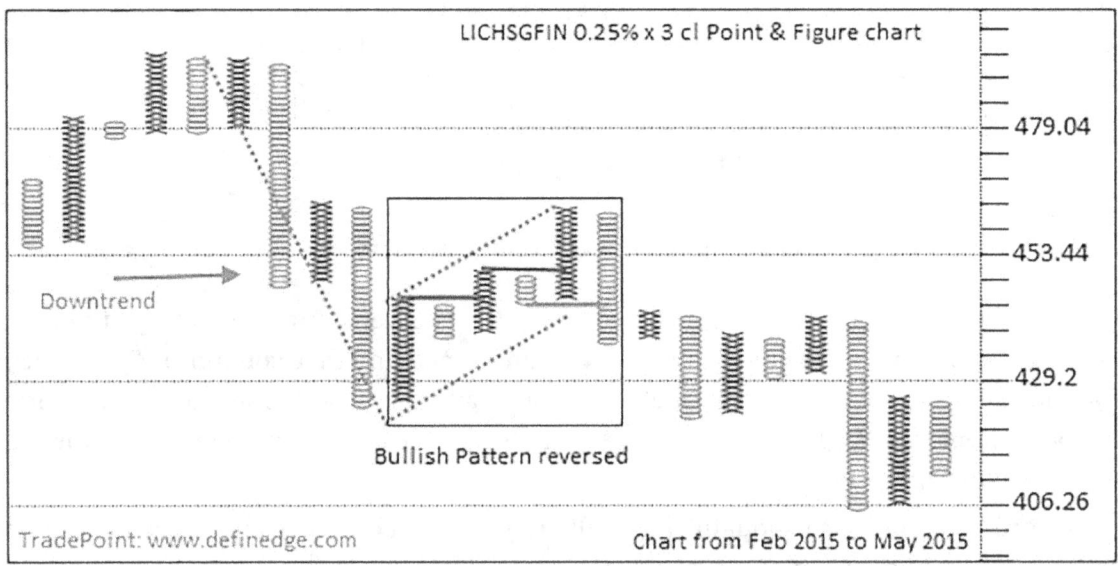

Figure 2.2.12: LIC housing finance daily 0.25% × 3 cl Point & Figure chart

Bearish pattern reversed in Figure 2.2.11 looks like bullish flag formation because prior trend was up, and bullish pattern reversed in Figure 2.2.12 looks like bearish flag formation because prior trend was down. The pattern is more effective and should be traded when occurring in the direction of the trend.

Bearish pattern reversed in Downtrend and bullish pattern reversed in Uptrend are patterns against the trend and look like wedge formations many of the times. Figure 2.2.13 is a P&F chart of Dish TV; both formations shown in the chart are against the trend.

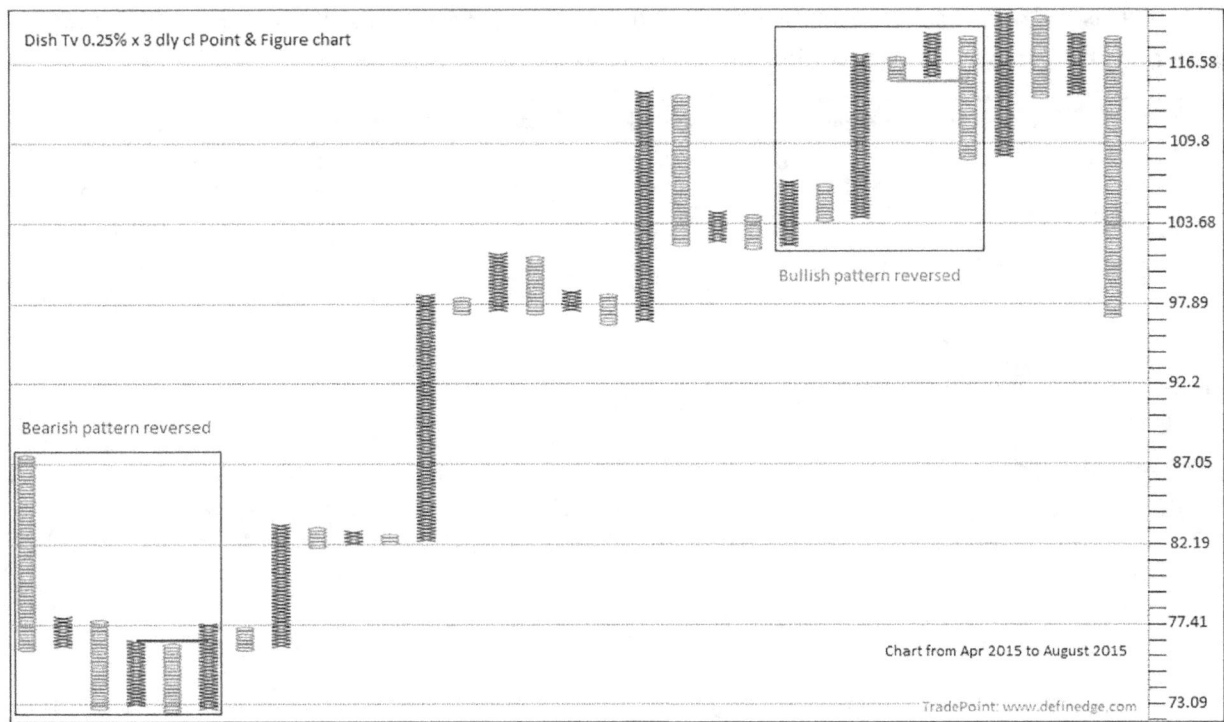

Figure 2.2.13: Dish tv daily 0.25% × 3 cl Point & Figure chart

Pattern against the trend can be referred to and provides opportunity when there is confirmation from other tools or indicators. It should be avoided when the instrument is trading in the new zone; meaning that a bullish pattern reversed should be ignored when an instrument is trading at new high.

Bearish pattern reversed will be negated when bottom of the pattern gets broken and bullish pattern that reversed is negated when top of the pattern gets broken, as shown in Image 2.2.7.

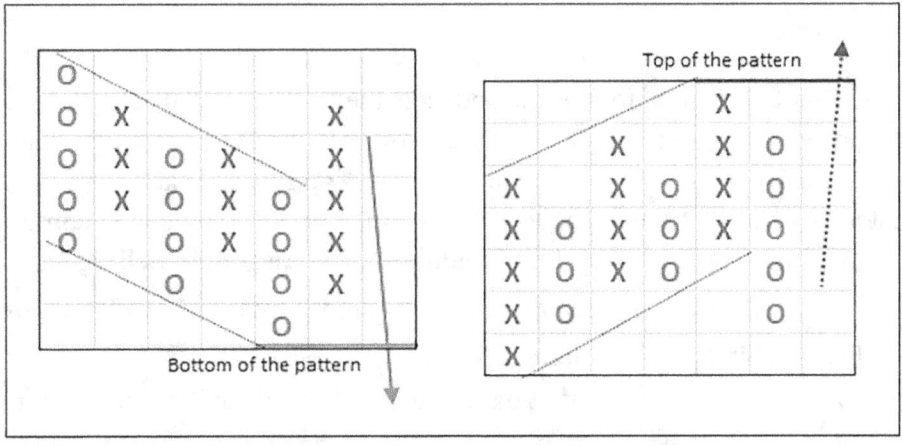

Image 2.2.7: Bearish and bullish pattern reversed

It would be interesting to note that the last four columns of this pattern form a trap pattern. The last four columns of bearish pattern reversed is a Bear Trap and that of bullish pattern reversed is a Bull Trap. Conditions prior to the occurrence of trap distinguish it from this formation. If it fails in the immediately following column, then it would become a Broadening formation.

Figure 2.2.14 is a 10% × 3 P&F chart of TVS Motors plotted with daily closing prices. Bearish pattern reversed was marked in the bottom during May 2009. Same pattern is seen in the chart during October

2013, which is a Continuation formation and a bookish setup that looks like a flag. It is interesting to observe that the number of boxes in the column of 'X' in both the cases is 24.

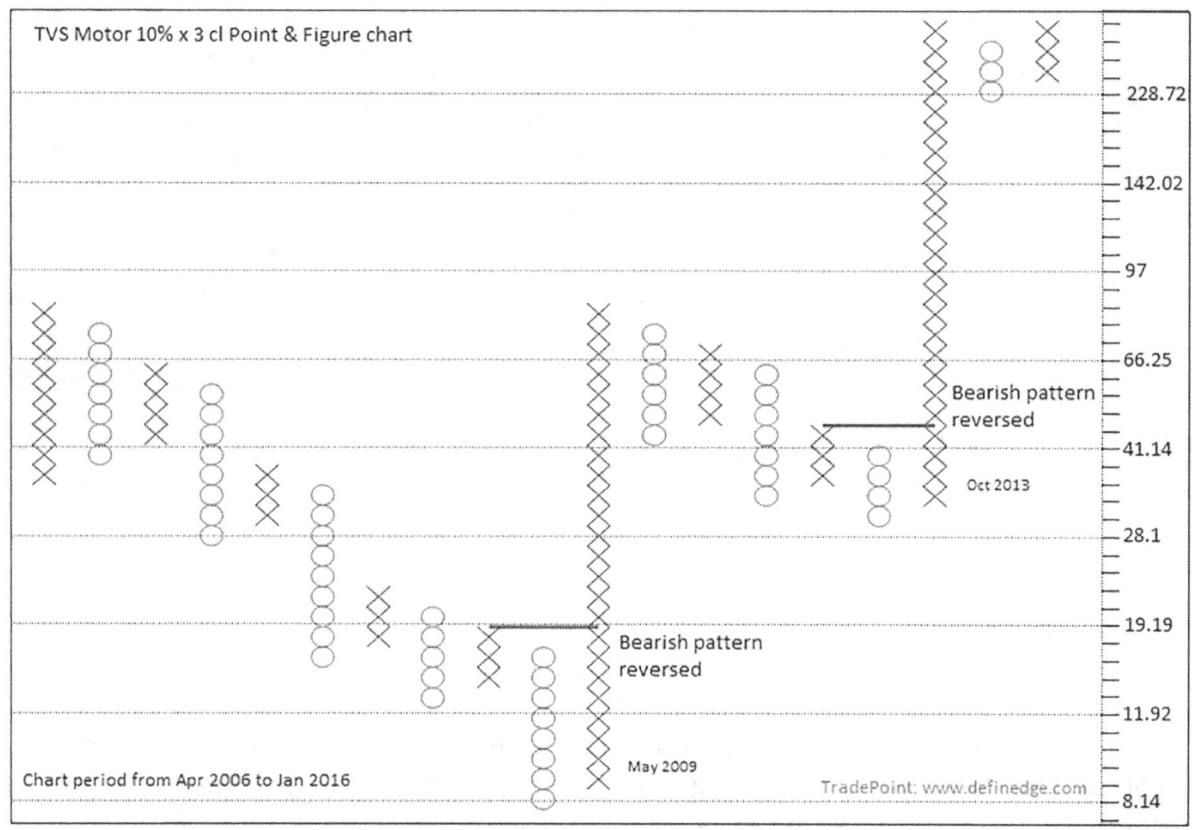

Figure 2.2.14: TVS motor daily 10% × 3 cl Point & Figure chart

A 10% box-value! We will discuss more about it in the chapter on box-values.

Catapult

Catapult is popular Point & Figure formation and considered as a reliable pattern from the trading perspective. Two consecutive patterns in the same direction form a Catapult, where a strong Buy signal is followed by Continuation Buy signal. Traditionally, a Triple Top Buy formation is considered as a strong Buy signal; when it is followed by Double Top Buy formation, it becomes bullish Catapult. The retracement of column of 'O' occurring after Triple Top Buy should not have triggered a Sell signal.

Hence, a bullish Catapult can be defined as a seven-column formation with the following criteria:

⬥ Triple Top Breakout in the fifth column.

⬥ Column of 'O' in the sixth column that has not generated a Double Bottom Sell pattern.

⬥ Column of 'O' in the sixth column should be below high price of the third column of 'X'.

⬥ Double Top Buy in the seventh column.

Similarly, the criteria for bearish Catapult formation are:

⬥ Triple Bottom Breakout in the fifth column.

⬥ Column of 'X' in the sixth column has not generated a Double Top Buy pattern.

⬥ Column of 'X' in the sixth column should be above low price of third column of 'O'.

⬥ Double Bottom Sell in the seventh column.

Both the setups are shown in Image 2.2.8.

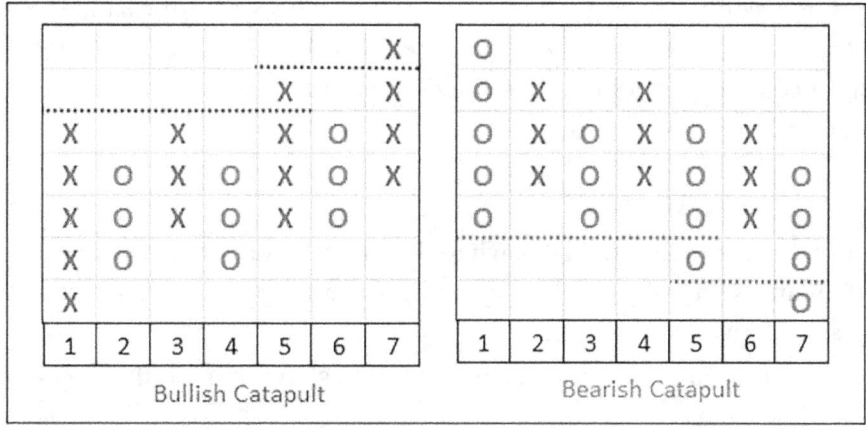

Image 2.2.8: P&F Catapult pattern

Figure 2.2.15 is a 1% × 3 P&F chart of IOB.

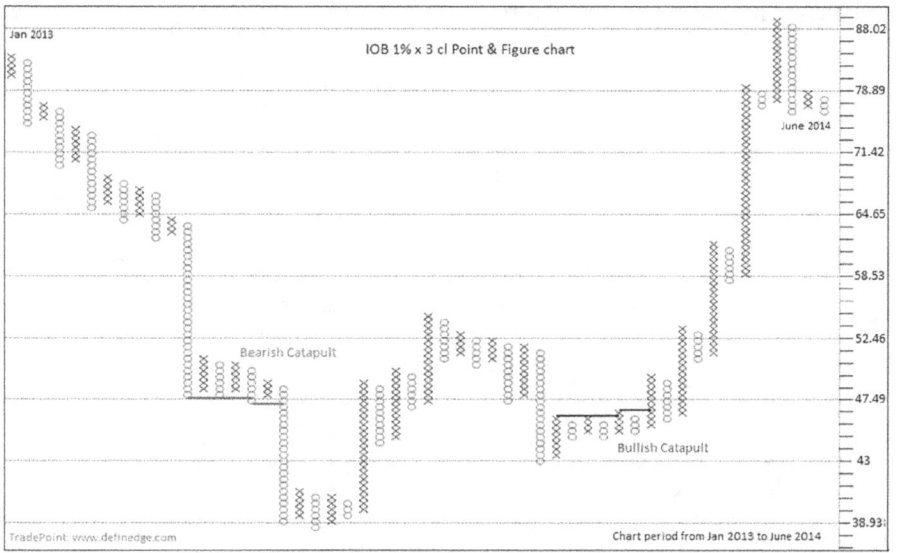

Figure 2.2.15: IOB daily 1% × 3 cl Point & Figure chart

Bearish Catapult that occurred during July 2013 witnessed immediate fall in prices. Bullish Catapult that occurred during February 2014 resulted in smooth upswing.

Bullish Catapult fails when price falls below bottom of the pattern; lowest 'O' of all seven columns is the low of the pattern. Similarly, bearish Catapult fails when price goes above the highest 'X' of the entire pattern (see Image 2.2.9).

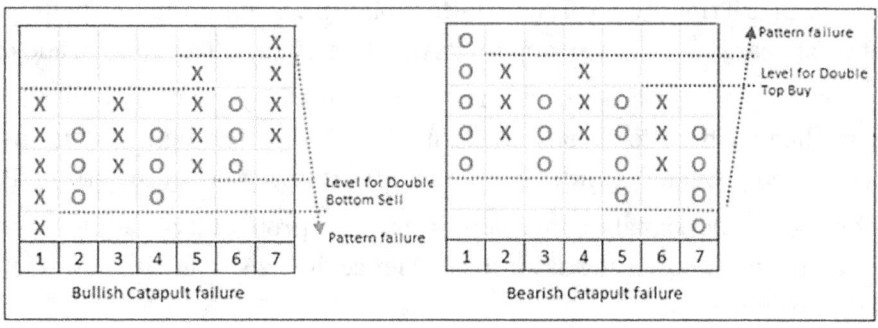

Image 2.2.9: Catapult failure levels

Catapult is rare but a significant formation. It usually produces an affordable trade opportunity and its strength lies in the follow-through to the strong breakout. Refer Image 2.2.9 again. In case of bullish Catapult, can the sixth column, not going below previous column low, provide some early opportunity to trade? We will discuss this further, subsequently.

Summary

- ↗ It is interesting to know the candidates where breakout trades are in trouble. Such difficult period for trend-following is typically followed by a strong trending phase. Hence, Broadening and Double Broadening are interesting formations.

- ↗ The 100% Pole is a combination of three patterns and shows more bullishness or bearishness than High Pole and Low Pole.

- ↗ Bullish and bearish patterns reversed with the trend resemble a flag pattern and indicate that short-term price correction is over. They resemble wedge formations when found against the trend.

- ↗ Deep correction and follow-through to Triple Top Buy pattern are important ingredients of the Catapult pattern. They don't occur often.

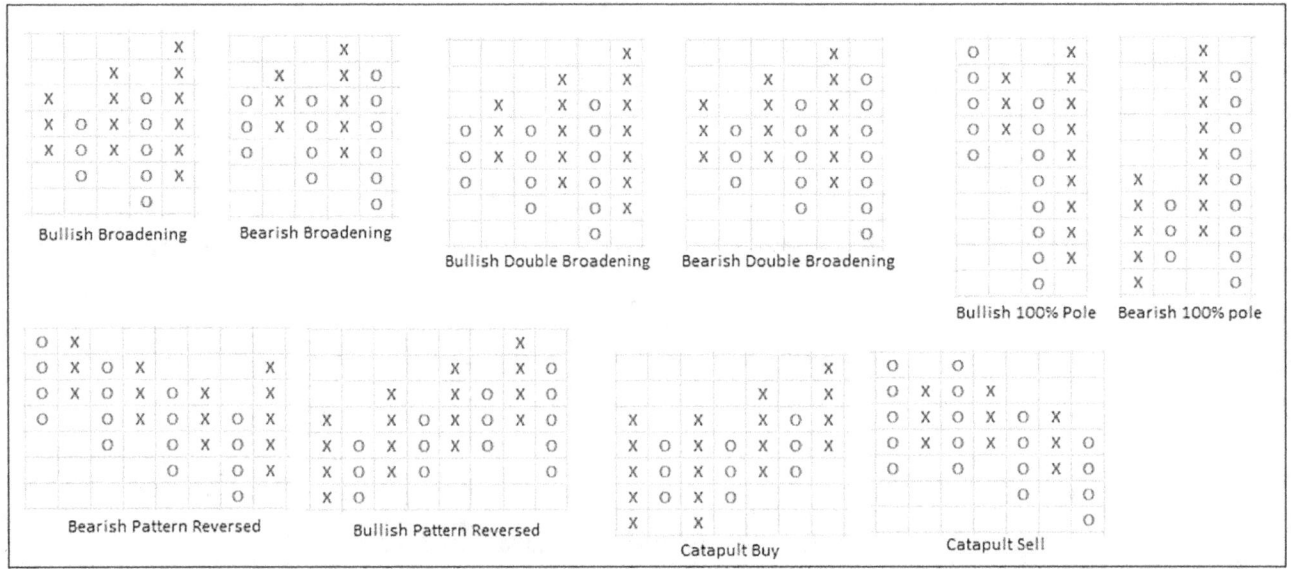

Image 2.2.10: P&F other important patterns

2.3: FOLLOW-THROUGH

Follow-through is an important concept and I cannot stress enough about its significance. If there is strength in the move, it shall witness a follow-through. We discussed the Catapult formation which is basically a follow-through to Triple Top or Triple Bottom pattern, Double Top Buy pattern is otherwise also a bullish signal but its appearance after a strong formation like a Triple Top pattern adds to its bullishness.

If the major patterns that we discussed till now are followed by a basic Double Top Buy or Double Bottom Sell pattern, then such basic signals are termed as Follow-through formations. Follow-through makes powerful setups and provides affordable trading opportunities. They are strong P&F signals.

Such Follow-through trade signals come across as high probability trading opportunity. Follow-through indicates that the initial pattern has strength. Hence, it is a simple yet powerful formation. Clear P&F signals enable us to define it easily.

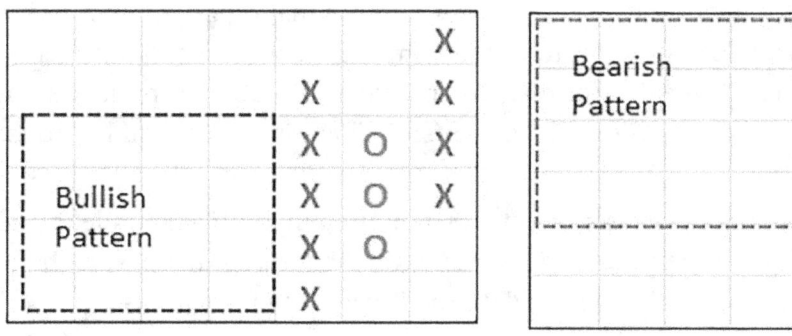

Bullish follow-thorugh   Bearish follow-through

Image 2.3.1: Follow-through

Usually, initial reversal levels in case of Traps or Poles are quite far. Hence, Bear Trap or Low Pole if followed by Double Top Buy signal indicates not only the strength behind the pattern, but provides a low-risk trading opportunity as well. Similarly, Double Bottom Sell signal after High Pole or Bull Trap is a bearish Follow-through signal. See Images 2.3.2 and 2.2.3 that show Follow-through to Trap and Pole formations.

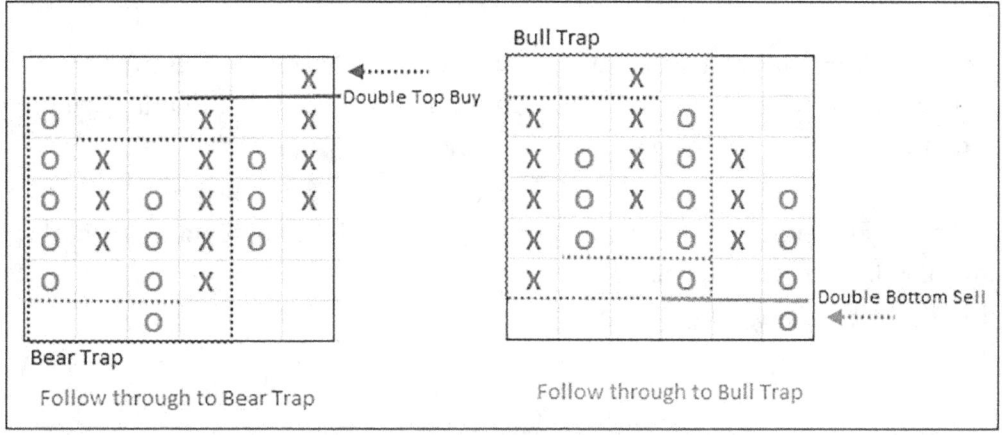

Image 2.3.2: Trap Follow-through

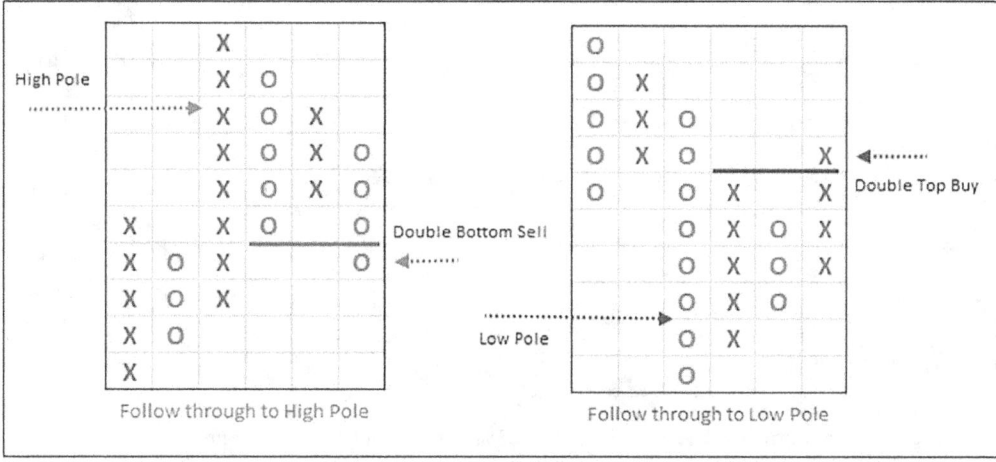

Image 2.3.3: Pole Follow-through

Follow-through is a Continuation signal and indicates that the major pattern is in control. Note that it is not necessary that Follow-though must occur in the immediate column; it can happen in subsequent columns as well. Remember, a bullish Follow-through formation is valid only if price has not gone below the bottom of the initial bullish pattern. Similarly, a bearish Follow-through is valid if price is below the top of the initial bearish pattern.

Broadening formation is an interesting setup but may not offer an affordable trade due to large initial reversal level. A Follow-through to the signal makes it an affordable setup that has the benefit of strong formation as well. Image 2.3.4 shows Follow-through to the Broadening formations.

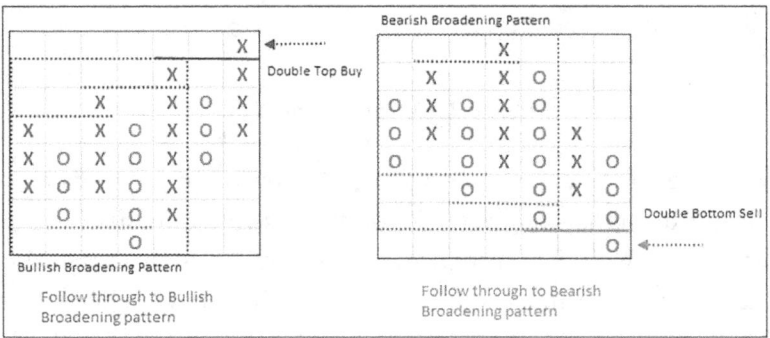

Image 2.3.4: Broadening Follow-through

Thus, there are two important aspects of Follow-through. First is that it proves the strength of the initial move. The other aspect is that several formations are difficult to trade initially due to wide stop; they can be traded when Follow-through appears.

The Follow-through formation entry signals could be quite lagging but they are more efficient. It filters the signal that gets reversed immediately; hence it is a logically acceptable scenario. Given below are charts showing Follow-through formations.

Figure 2.3.1 is a 0.25% × 3 P&F chart of CEAT Ltd.

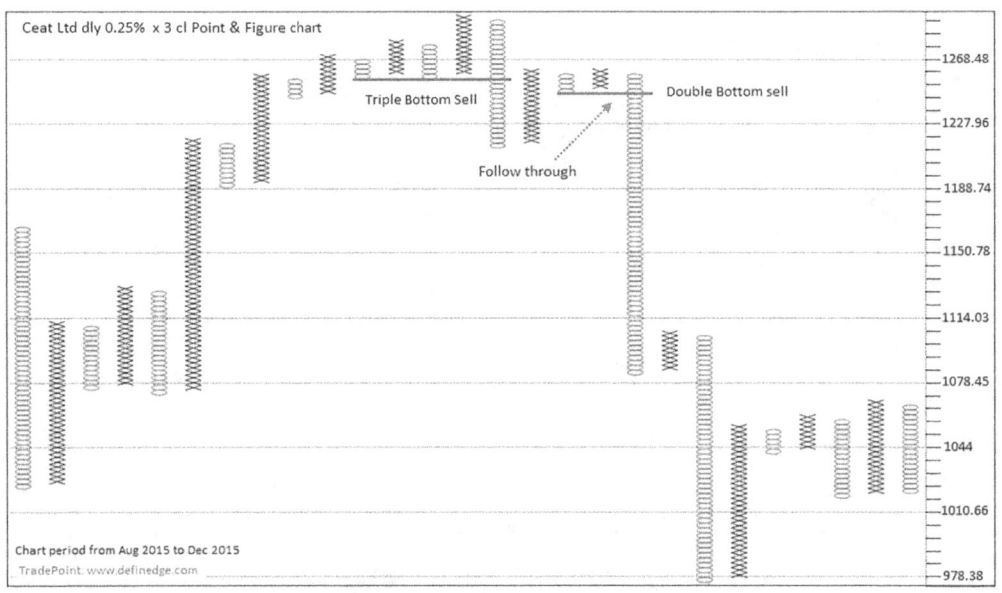

Figure 2.3.1: CEAT daily 0.25% × 3 cl Point & Figure chart

Triple Bottom Sell signal in the above chart occurred right at major swing top during October 2015 followed by price consolidation. Follow-through in the form of Double Bottom Sell signal without negating the initial pattern provided the opportunity to short with better risk–reward proposition.

A pattern remains valid unless negated; it can be traded for a profit target based on vertical or horizontal counts that will be discussed later. The other option is to trail the position with stop-loss placed either at the bottom of the bullish formation or top of the bearish formation. Other patterns instead of basic Buy-Sell signals coming after valid strong patterns are also Follow-through formations, rather stronger in nature.

Figure 2.3.2 is a 0.25% × 3 P&F chart of Rcom.

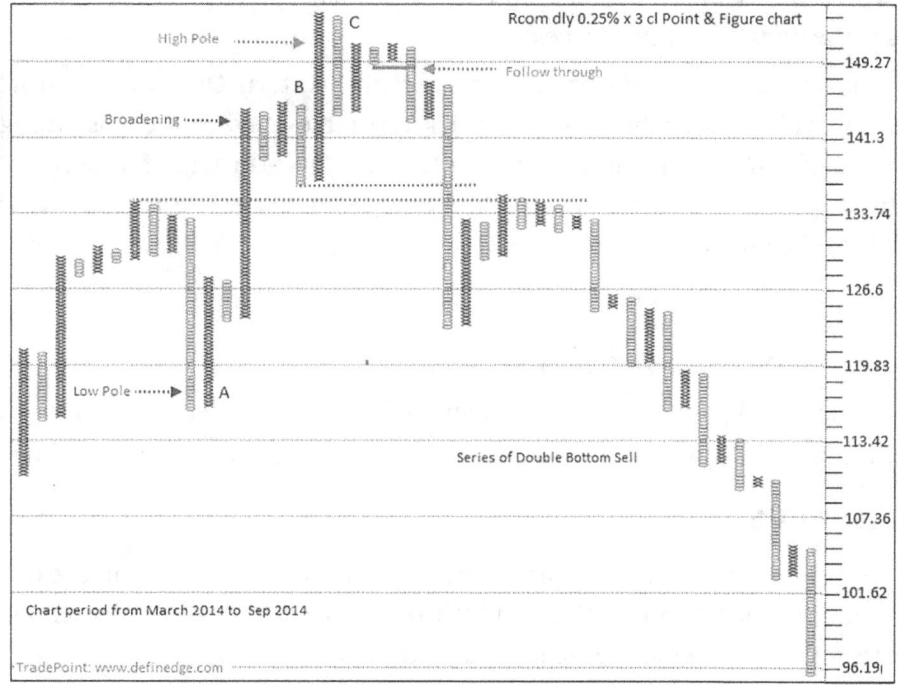

Figure 2.3.2: Rcom daily 0.25% × 3 cl Point & Figure chart

Pattern A is Low Pole followed by Double Top Buy signal, which is a Follow-through to Low Pole. Pattern B is Bullish Broadening formation. Pattern C is High Pole formation that occurred during June 2014, which was followed by price consolidation. But Follow-through provided another affordable setup, which resulted in severe crash that generated a series of basic Double Bottom Sell signals.

Figure 2.3.3 is a 0.25% × 3 P&F chart of JSW Steel.

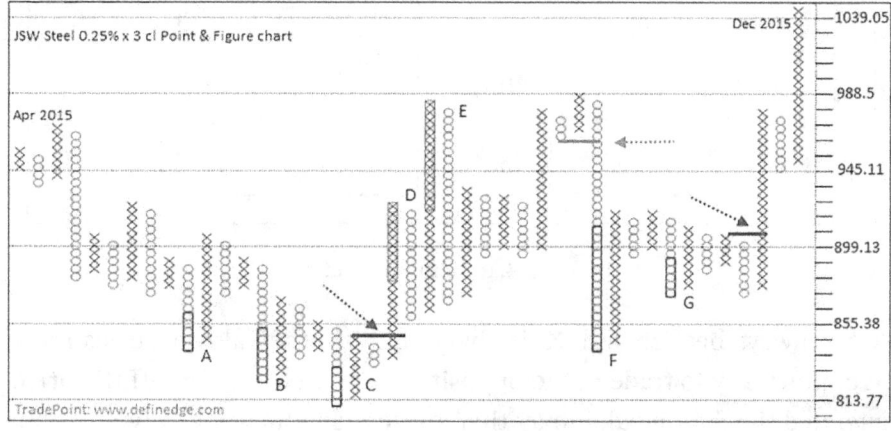

Figure 2.3.3: JSW Steel daily 0.25% × 3 cl Point & Figure chart

Pattern A is a 100% Pole that did not witness Follow-through. Pattern B is a Low Pole which did not see Follow-through as well. So price is witnessing initial thrust in the Downtrend but not being able to see sustained demand. Pattern C is Low pole that witnessed the Follow-through. Pattern D is High Pole which got negated immediately. Pattern E is High Pole followed by price consolidation. Pattern F is a Low Pole followed by consolidation and another Low Pole at Pattern G. Both of them eventually witnessed the Follow-through resulting in sharp rise in prices.

Note that patterns A, B, D and G in Figure 2.3.3 could be avoided because there was no Follow-through formation. It can significantly improve the performance of pattern trading. Follow-through makes Poles an affordable entry signal. A P&F analyst should understand which signals are to be traded. Follow-through formation increases the odds of trading success.

Follow-through is a key concept and is an extremely reliable pattern. Once practiced, it helps in filtering the affordable setups, which generally results in quick favorable move if there is strength in the trend. Patterns occurring against the trend will not usually see the Follow-through if underlying trend is strong. Concepts to be discussed later, relating to trend and analysis, will help in identifying the environment conducive to look for follow-through formations.

Summary

- ➤ Follow-through is the best P&F formation.
- ➤ It indicates that initial pattern has strength and offers better risk–reward proposition.
- ➤ Pay attention to larger duration breakouts and major patterns; trade their Follow-throughs.

2.4: COLUMN REVERSAL

Although column reversal is the most basic formation of a P&F chart, using it from the trading perspective needs understanding of major P&F formations and a little practice. It can provide very affordable trading opportunity but one must know which setup should be traded.

We discussed the affordability aspect while discussing the basic patterns. There can be another way of looking at the affordable trades or trades with lower risk. Refer Image 2.4.1.

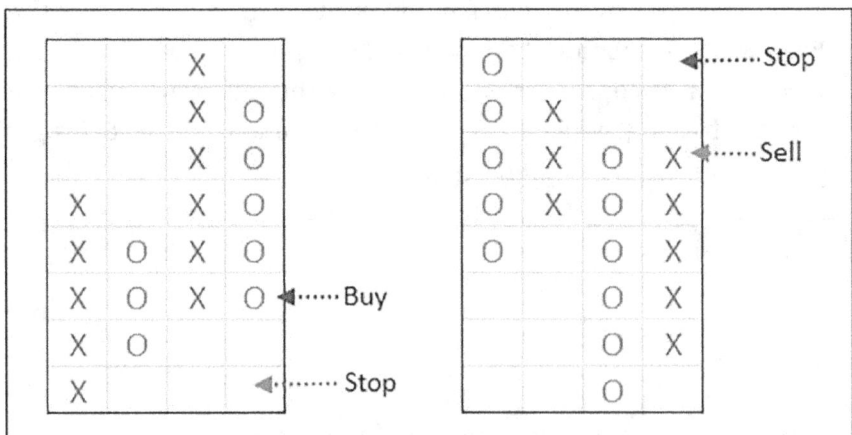

Image 2.4.1: Column reversal

It is not that 'O' is always bearish and 'X' is always bullish; they also occur as retracement to strong trends, which is an opportunity to trade in the opposite direction of column. If the price is in a column of 'O' that has not generated the Sell signal, it may then present an affordable buying opportunity. Similarly, column of 'X' occurring after Sell signal, which has not generated a Buy signal, could turn out to be an affordable setup to trade short. Exit the trade when basic opposite signal is generated. Long signal with this kind of setup can be traded when trend is bullish and short signal when trend is bearish. The major problem with this setup is that short-term trend is bearish when there is a Buy setup and bullish when there is a Sell setup. It is akin to the adage of catching a falling knife. To overcome this, column reversal comes to the rescue.

Bullish setup followed by positive column reversal can become an efficient entry setup if occurs in the Uptrend. Similarly, a negative column reversal after bearish pattern is an efficient entry point if it occurs in a downtrend. (See Image 2.4.2)

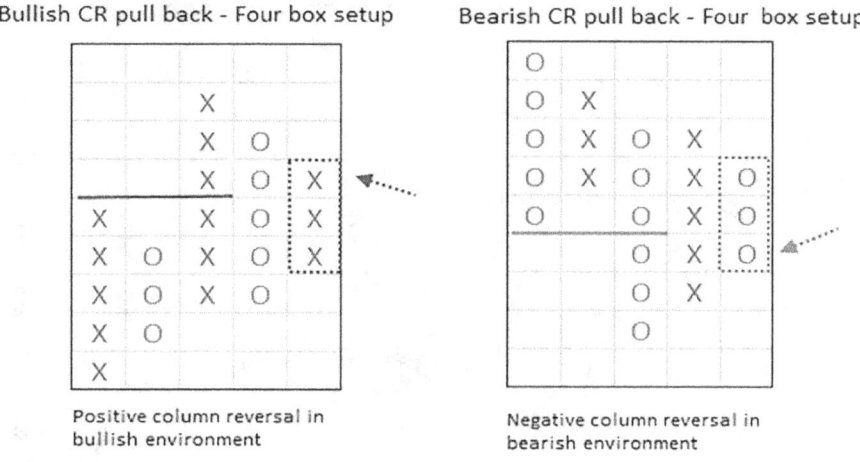

Image 2.4.2: Column reversal pullback

Though the column reversal pattern offers a low-risk entry, it is crucial to figure out when to take it. A bullish pullback is an effective setup in bullish environment. Bullish environment can be defined as bullish formation in an Uptrend. Similarly, a bearish pullback is effective when there is bearish formation and the trend is down. It is a more compelling setup for charts with higher box-values. The section on box-value deals with it at length.

Figure 2.4.1 is a 3% x3 P&F chart of Tata Comm plotted with daily closing prices.

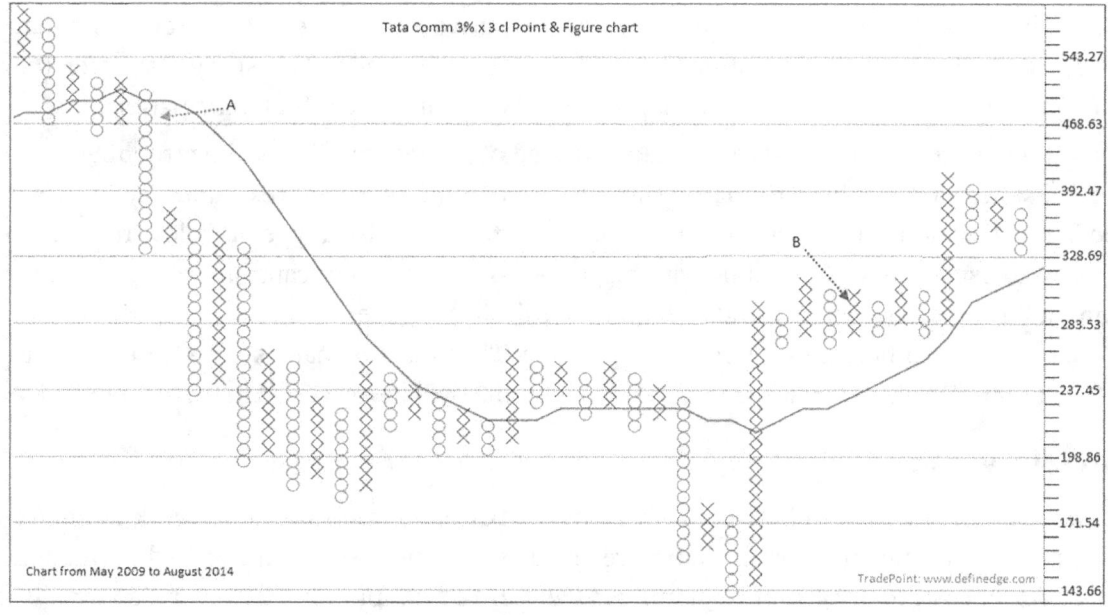

Figure 2.4.1: Tata Comm daily 3% × 3 cl Point & Figure chart

The black line in the above chart demarcates the trend filter. The trend is bearish if the price is below the line and vice versa. We will discuss it in the section on indicators. Point A in the chart above is a bearish pattern followed by negative column reversal. Pattern failing to cross average line indicates weakness. Point B is a positive column reversal after a Bear Trap formation with large column of 'X' and bullish pattern in the Uptrend that forms a bullish pullback setup.

Major patterns instead of simple Double Top or Double Bottom patterns are more meaningful setups. The major advantage of column reversal is the opportunity it provides with attractive risk–reward ratio. Figure 2.4.2 is a 0.25% box-value chart of Yes bank.

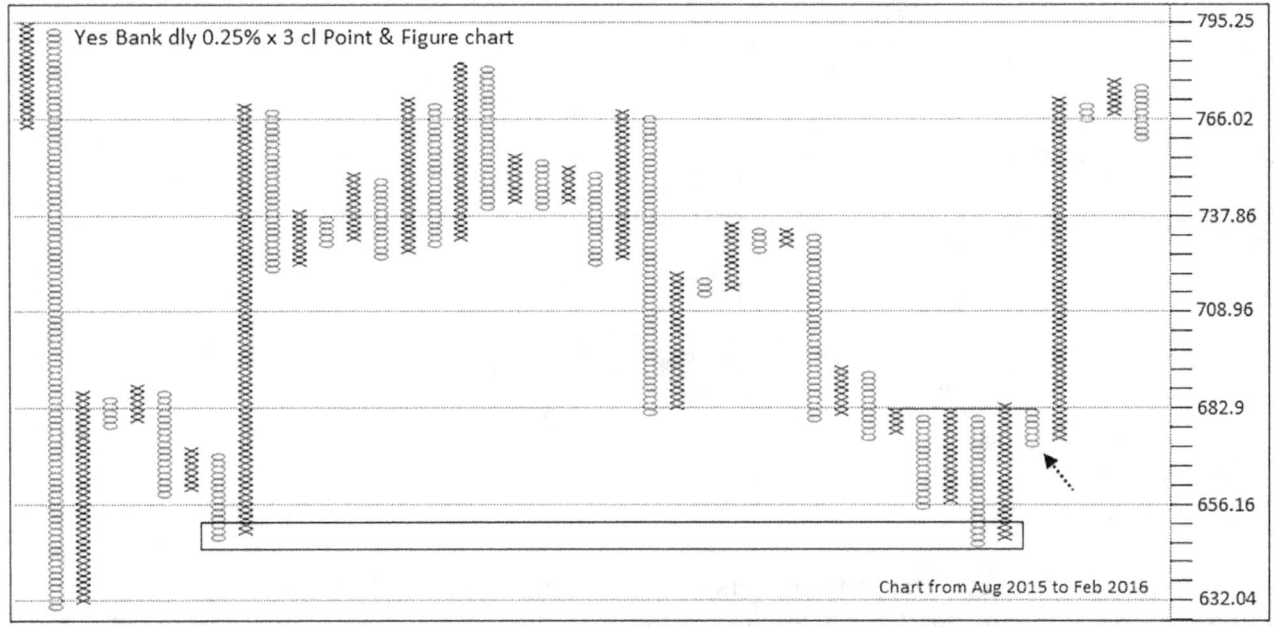

Figure 2.4.2: Yes bank daily 0.25% × 3 cl Point & Figure chart

Arrow on the chart points at column of 'O' appearing after Triple Top Buy formation occurring at previous support level. The long column of 'X' that completed the Triple Top Buy formation provides entry but with relatively wide stop. The next column of 'O', provides better risk–reward trade but remember the trend is down as the price is in a column of 'O'. Positive column reversal after this column of 'O' indicates strength in the setup and offers a better risk–reward trade. The sharp rise after the column reversal formation took the price at earlier supply zone where it formed Bull Trap pattern.

Trades based on column reversal can be taken instead of basic signals in a strong trending environment. Column reversal can provide an affordable entry with limited risk at key resistance/support zone but it should be in the direction of the setup and after a major pattern. It is also a type of Follow-through formation and may be used especially when dealing with bigger box-size. A word of caution: we are essentially trying to pre-empt a Buy or Sell signal by using column reversal. This is generally a risky proposition and must be resorted to, only after sufficient experience and practice. There can be many setups designed with column reversal formation; a weak breakout is one such formation that will be explained in this chapter subsequently.

Column Mid-Value

We discussed about trading a follow-through to major patterns when the initial risk is unaffordable. I explored the idea of trading them with column reversal as the stop-loss, but it resulted in frequent trading and higher impact cost. Mid-value of a column is an effective tool for exit whenever a column is long and initial risk is high – it is a solution derived from Poles. A stop can be placed at mid-value for long columns. This would be interesting particularly from the system trading perspective where every signal needs to be followed. Even setup traders can follow this rule to trade Traps, Broadenings or 100% Poles where initial basic signal stop is quite far.

Summary

- ⅄ Column reversal is the most basic formation but needs experience to trade.
- ⅄ It is more applicable on higher box-values and when trader wants to play strength of the initial pattern.
- ⅄ Overall analysis of trend can improve success ratio of trading this basic formation.
- ⅄ Beware of pre-empting and overtrading.
- ⅄ Mid-value as a stop when initial basic signal is far can be a sensible alternative.

2.5: PATTERN RETEST

Price retesting of previous pivotal levels are traditionally considered as important supports and resistances and proves very effective most of the time; but trading them is quite tricky and needs confirmatory tools. Below is a quick look at the formations seen on usual charts when price retests the previous peaks or troughs.

1. Double Bottom and Double Top

Double Bottom and Double Top patterns I am referring to here are the traditional formations that are popular reversal patterns. Double Bottom formation is a bullish pattern that forms when price takes support at previous trough and bounces back to breach the neckline of the pattern. Similarly, Double Top is a bearish pattern that is formed when two peaks occur at the same level and price falls below neckline of the pattern. The height of the pattern is extended from neckline to derive the target that price can travel.

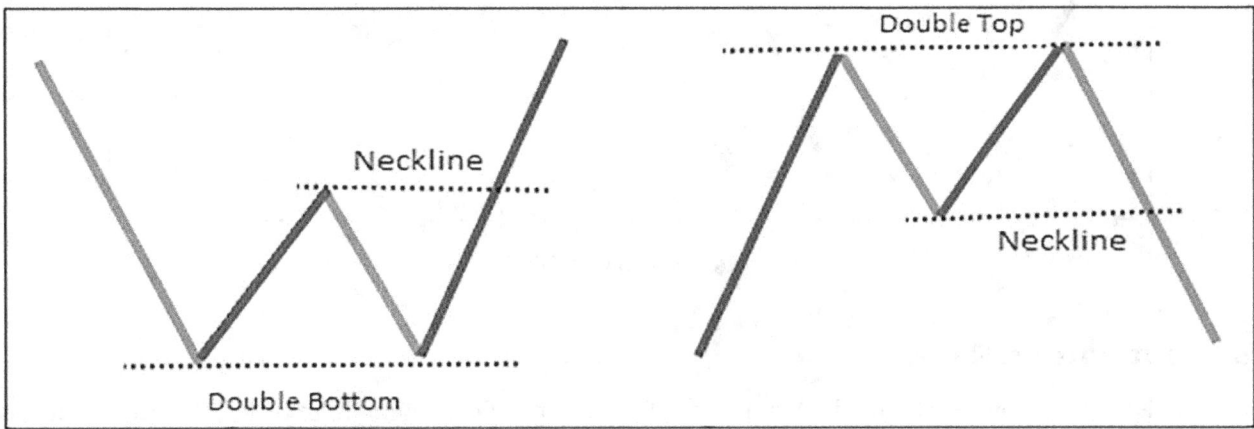

Image 2.5.1: Traditional Double Tops and Double Bottoms

2. Rising Bottom and Falling Top

Another bullish pattern is Rising Bottom, which is formed when price marks a bottom higher than the previous bottom. It indicates the rising demand; hence, it is a bullish pattern that marks higher low. If price falls short of previous top, it is called Falling Top formation, which forms lower high and indicates falling demand and hence is a bearish formation.

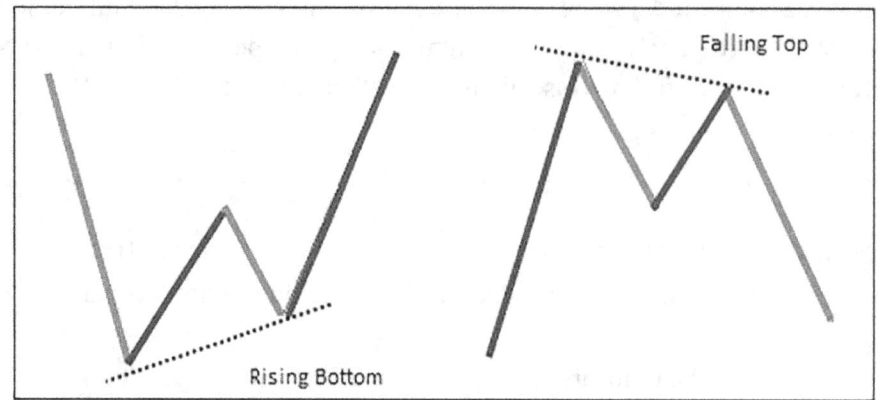

Image 2.5.2: Rising bottom and Falling top

3. Swing Failure

Swing failure is one of my favorite patterns and it is a very significant one too. It is a bullish swing failure pattern when previous bottom is broken but price quickly recovers from the lower levels and moves above the broken bottom. Hence, it is a kind of a trap formation also known as false breakout or spring bottom. Bearish swing failure is formed when price breaches the previous peak but is unable to sustain and falls back below the top. It is also known as up-thrust formation that traps traders who bought on the breakout above the swing high.

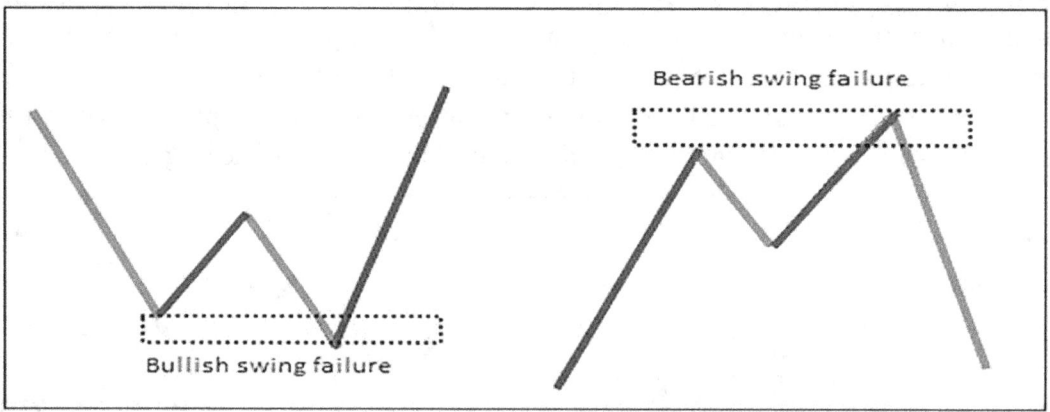

Image 2.5.3: Swing failure

It's about Pattern Retest

Patterns discussed above are formed when price retests the previous swing high or low. These formations have different names but they are variations of price testing the previous swing high or low. Price may bounce from the same level, or a little higher or generate false breakout to trap traders. These are good formations but difficult to trade because the type of pattern is unknown prior to occurrence. It is also possible that the prior swing high or low is ignored completely and there is no reaction in their vicinity. Hence, trades based on anticipation might prove dangerous.

With P&F, we trade patterns. When I analyse all the above scenarios on different charts, I can simply call them a 'pattern testing a previous pattern.' See Image 2.5.4 shown below.

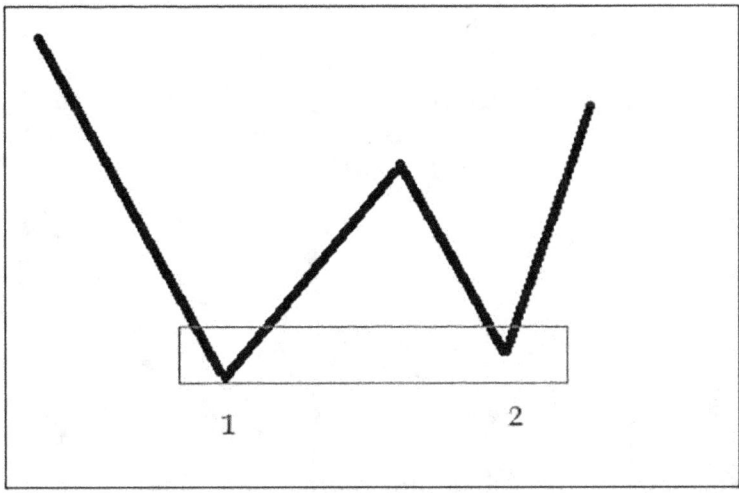

Image 2.5.4: Retest

If there is a bullish P&F pattern at point 1 and price comes to retest the same price zone and forms another bullish pattern at point 2, it is a bullish pattern retest setup. Point 2 can be at same level or little higher or little lower than the previous bottom but it should be near point 1 pattern area. This way, it considers all the scenarios discussed above and confirms the trading opportunity upon occurrence of bullish P&F pattern at point 2. It is not necessary that both patterns are the same; they could be different in nature. While trying to find bottom is like catching the falling knife, the odds are definitely better while using the pattern retest concept. Similarly, a bearish pattern being formed at previous bearish pattern area is bearish pattern retest. (See Image 2.5.5).

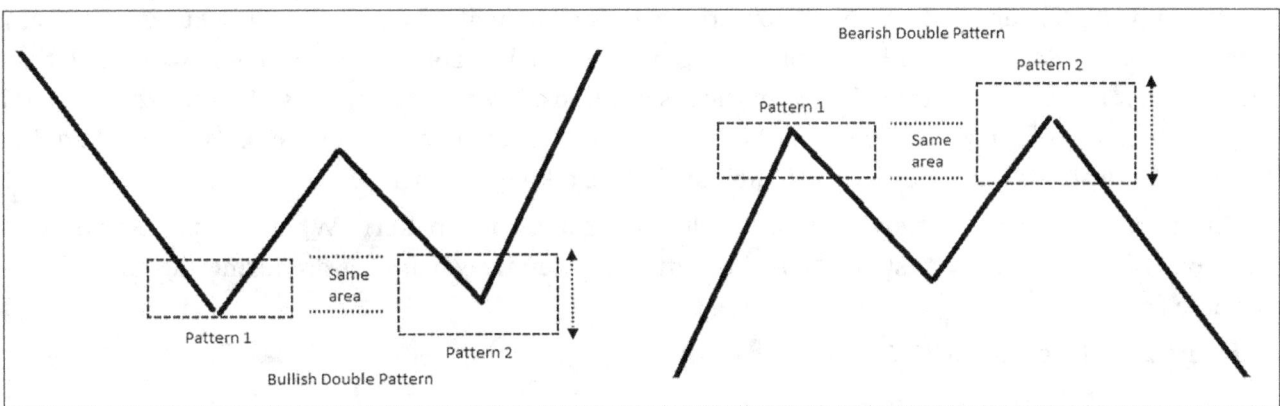

Image 2.5.5: Bullish and bearish double patterns

The major patterns that we have discussed are important reference point when revisited. Figure 2.5.1 is a 1% × 3 P&F chart of Tata Steel. There is a bullish 100% Pole pattern at point 1 and bullish 100% Pole pattern at point 2. The recurrence of bullish pattern at Point 2 confirms that buyers are still active and confirms the underlying bullishness.

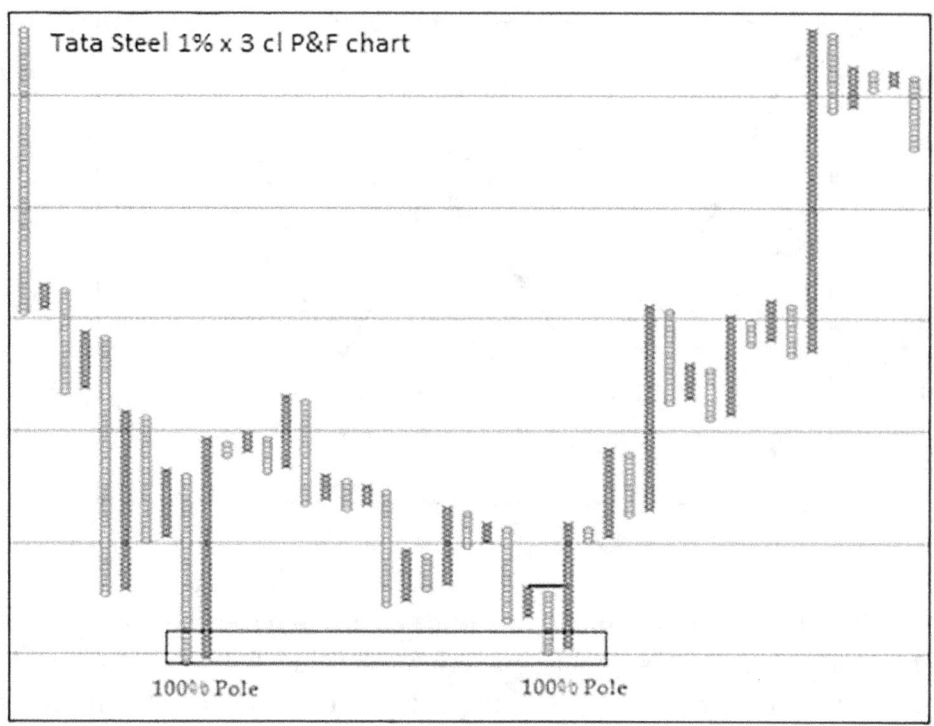

Figure 2.5.1: Tata Steel daily 1% × 3 cl Point & Figure chart

It is about looking for a pattern in the same area of the previous pattern. It is only logical to expect buying interest to resurface at price levels where the buyers were active earlier. We look for another bullish pattern as a confirmatory tool to ensure that buyers are indeed present at the same price zone. Looking for a pattern at the prior demand or supply zone removes the element of subjectivity and guesswork that is normally is associated while trading at prior support or resistance zones. Patterns come with predefined entry and exit levels that are traded and not the assumptions. If we trade patterns, then we know when it will get negated. The entry may have some lag but will have better chances of success. Patience is required and one must wait for the pattern to be completed before taking trades.

There are two types of pattern retests: double pattern and triple pattern. When two patterns occur at same level to form pattern retest, it is a double pattern. When three patterns are formed at same level, it is a triple pattern.

Figure 2.5.2 below a is 0.25% × 3 P&F chart of LT.

Figure 2.5.2: LT daily 0.25% × 3 cl Point & Figure chart

Both are instances if a bearish double pattern, wherein two bearish P&F patterns occurred at the same price zone, confirming the presence of sellers.

It is important to ride the trend once entered at the correct level. P&F provides a nice trend-riding technique. There is no point in entering a trade right at the top or bottom, only to book out for a nominal profit. It is always better to enter late but ride the trend to extract maximum mileage from the move.

Remember, second pattern of double pattern formation should fall within the area of the earlier pattern. To avoid confusion and keep things objective, there should be at least three columns between the two patterns to call it a valid double pattern retest formation. Previous peak or trough is also defined via pattern. The message here is simple and important: it shows the strength of demand and supply at a particular price zone.

Figure 2.5.3 is a 0.25% × 3 P&F chart of Maruti.

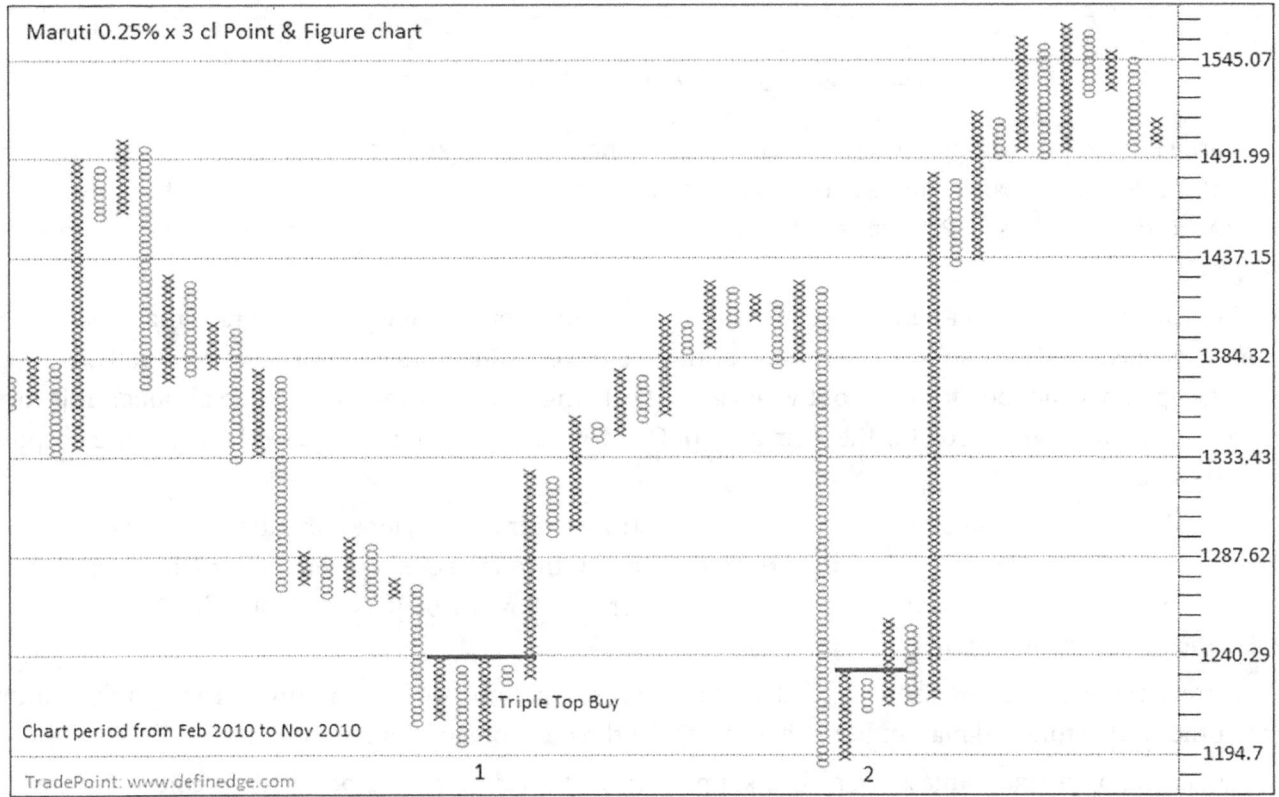

Figure 2.5.3: Maruti daily 0.25% × 3 cl Point & Figure chart

Pattern at point 1 is Triple Top Buy formation and that at point 2 is Double Top Buy formation. It is a swing failure formation where price edged below previous bottom and bounced back again to trap the bears.

The strength of swing failure formation lies in the Rejection. Price fails to go down any further, and the subsequent bullish pattern is a pointer that the bullish camp is active at the price zone. Hence, the pattern at spot 2 has got strength of rejection, which makes the setup interesting.

There are chances of price retesting the same zone for a third time, which will then be similar to the Triple Top or Triple Bottom pattern that we discussed earlier. Pattern at point 3 should be referred to; formation is named as Triple pattern. Terminology is kept simple and relevant, which helps in remembering and recollecting the setups easily.

Figure 2.5.4 is 0.25% × 3 P&F chart of daily prices of Infy.

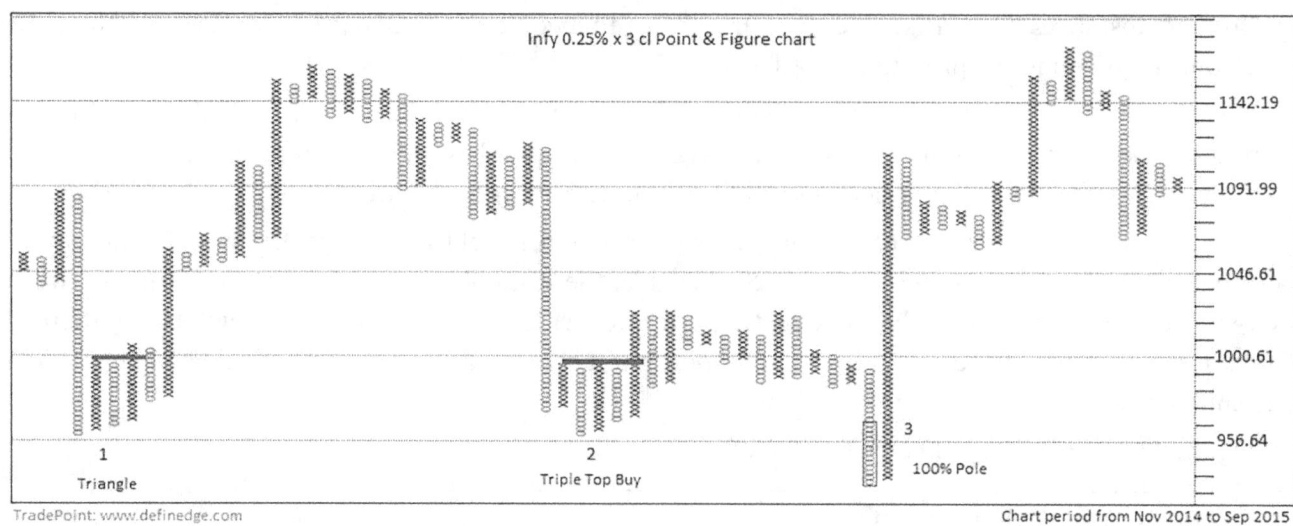

Figure 2.5.4: Infy daily 0.25% × 3 cl Point & Figure chart

Three bullish formations occurred at same price zone, which makes it a bullish Triple pattern. Pattern 3 is a 100% Pole at the same zone where two bullish patterns occurred earlier, which shows the strength of demand at that price zone. Pattern retest, especially in large cap stocks, could prove to be very rewarding trade setups.

I would like to mention here about retest of an area for a fourth time. It is very rare that price takes support or faces resistance for a fourth time at the same zone. They often get broken eventually. Hence, avoid the pattern and look for breakout when a level is being tested for the fourth time although it is rare to find. This is also why I look for the formation of Quadruple Tops and Bottoms, explained in the chapter on variations.

The idea is that instead of looking at the top or bottom at same level, look for patterns occurring at the same zone, which is why it is called pattern retest. Follow-through setups formed after Double or Triple patterns are one of the best setups of P&F charts. Observe Follow-through coming at point 2 in the charts of LT and Maruti shown above.

Pattern retest in the direction of trend is a powerful setup. Look for Follow-through and confirmation from other indicators and market breadth, to increase the odds of success even further.

Avoid taking a trade unless there is a supporting P&F pattern at the price zone. One option is to look for confirmatory P&F patterns in the lower time-frame chart to get into a trade early. Objectivity and noiselessness associated with P&F charts are of great advantage and these types of filtrations to the patterns make them high-probability trade setups.

Summary

- ⋏ Pattern retest is a smart way of trading prior important pivot points.
- ⋏ Pattern retest in large cap stocks is a very rewarding formation.
- ⋏ It provides confirmation and offers tradable opportunities with better chances of success.
- ⋏ Two patterns at same level is a double pattern retest and three patterns occurring at same level is a triple pattern retest.
- ⋏ Follow-through to pattern retest is something that should not be missed.

2.6: TURTLE TRADING ON P&F

There are a lot of books and write-ups on Turtle trading system. Legendary traders Richard Dennis and William Eckhardt conducted the turtle experiment in 1983. I recommend to search for the Turtle method online, if you are not aware of it. It is a must-read story. Turtle is a complete trading system along with money management and position-sizing rules. It is a simple trend-following system that considers 20-day, 10-day or 55-day price breakouts. I am not discussing the Turtle system or its history but exploring the same idea on P&F.

Similar kind of systems can also be designed on P&F charts. To underline the difference between both, P&F columns are swing moves and not fixed time interval candles. It is also the reason that parameters for breakout needs to be adjusted in comparison to price–time charts.

A simple yet effective breakout strategy can be designed on Point & Figure charts by defining multi-column breakouts. A column of 'X' rising above multiple columns displays stronger breakout than the one going above just the previous column. For example, a bullish breakout may be defined as a column of 'X' rising above the prior 10-columns of 'X'. And a bearish breakout can be defined as column of 'O' going below previous 10 columns of 'O'.

Figure 2.6.1 is a 0.50% × 3 P&F chart of Balaji Tele showing the pattern discussed above.

Figure 2.6.1: Balaji Tele daily 0.50% × 3 cl Point & Figure chart

You may find it similar to breakout strategies on usual charts such as price breakout above the high of several number of days. Only difference is that it is columns in case of P&F that represent trend. A 10-column breakout on vertically moving P&F charts would have a number of days and not necessarily 10-days. It would significantly reduce the number of trades and also result in improved odds of trading success.

This strategy is applicable to all time frames and box-values. It is also effective on lower box-values, because number of occurrences is reduced to a large extent. Figure 2.6.2 is a 0.50% × 3 chart of Bharat Forge that illustrates how a significant trend can be captured with this strategy.

Figure 2.6.2: Bharat Forge daily 0.50% × 3 cl Point & Figure chart

Figure 2.6.3 is a 10 × 3 Bank Nifty derivative chart on one-minute time frame showing the 10-column bullish and bearish breakouts.

Figure 2.6.3: Bank Nifty-I 1 min interval 10 × 3 cl Point & Figure chart

Any other breakout parameter can be utilized instead of 10. It is a SAR (Stop and Reverse) method of trading if single parameter is defined for bullish and bearish breakouts. Parameter for long and short can be different. For example, a strategy can be designed for entry based on 20-X breakout and exit based on 10-O breakout. It can be any other number for that matter.

Figure 2.6.4 is a Tech Mahindra chart of more than 7 years plotted with 1% × 3 parameters. It shows long setup for investment based on 10-X breakout and exit based on 5-O breakout. Whipsaws must be considered as the premium paid for timely exits before significant fall in prices that may occur any time, and particularly when everything looks good!

Figure 2.6.4: Tech Mahindra daily 1% × 3 cl Point & Figure chart

Other filters such as indicators, to be discussed in Chapter 3, can be applied to fine-tune the entry. The simpler the strategy, the more effective it is.

Summary

- ⌁ P&F is not limited to a few column patterns; it can be tweaked to suit personal style and preference.
- ⌁ 'X' or 'O' coming out of previous 10 or 20 columns show significant price consolidation breakout. It offers very few but more productive trades. Various strategies can be built around such occurrences.

2.7: MORE PATTERNS AND VARIATIONS

This section is relatively advanced and will take you to the next level of understanding the patterns. We have discussed the major P&F formations, which are completely objective in nature. Meaning that there cannot be an argument over their occurrence, irrespective of what happens subsequently. Words like 'strict' were used while explaining the column requirements for every pattern. That kind of rigidity is required in the initial learning process to keep the objectivity aspect intact. Effective tweaking of rules is possible only when rules are understood thoroughly. Read this section for knowledge and ideas; implement them once you are comfortable with basic formations.

We discussed earlier that a column of 'X' can either be a Double Top Buy or not. There are two other possibilities if it is not a Double Top Buy. Either it will be a falling 'X' or 'X' occurring at the same level. Similarly, any column of 'O' has three possibilities: Double Bottom Sell, Rising 'O' or 'O' at same level.

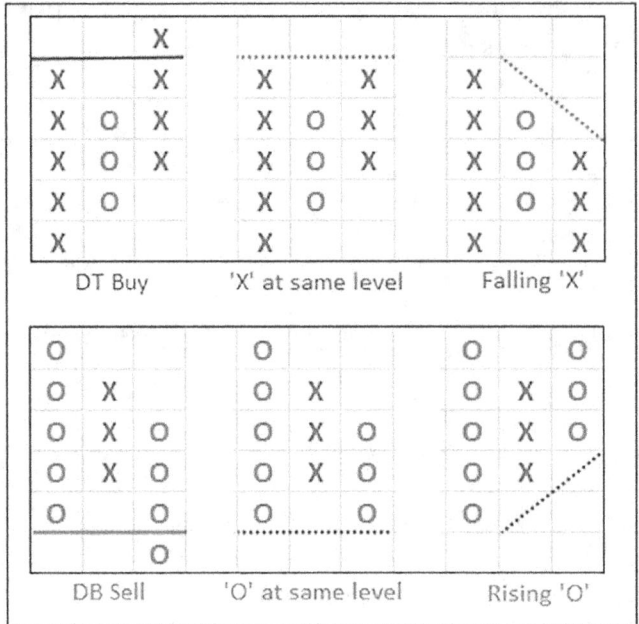

Image 2.7.1: Three-column formations

Observe Image 2.7.1 very carefully. It will help you understand P&F in a much better manner. Every column falls in one of the three categories shown in the image. We have discussed Double Top Buy and Double Bottom Sell patterns at length. Let us discuss the other two formations.

At Same Level

When column of 'O' stops falling exactly at the low of previous column of 'O', it indicates demand at that price level. If it changes the column and turns up again from the same level instead of triggering a Double Bottom Sell signal, it is then a sign of strong demand at the level where twin 'O' occurred. Similarly, 'X' at same level indicates supply or strong resistance. Hence, a pattern that turns around from same levels indicates strong support or resistance area (see Image 2.7.2).

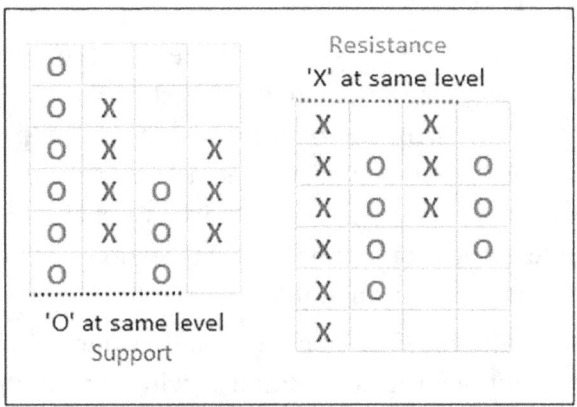

Image 2.7.2: 'O' and 'X' at same level

After forming 'O' at the same level, if price turns around and generates a Double Top buy signal in the immediate next column of 'X', the pattern is called "Double Top Buy after support.."The exactly opposite set of conditions is required to complete a "Double Bottom Sell after resistance pattern.."(See Image 2.7.3)

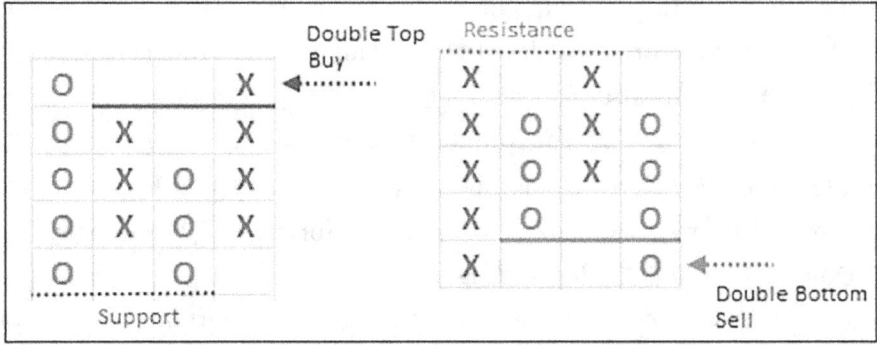

Image 2.7.3: Double Top Buy after support and Double Bottom Sell after resistance

Although this pattern may come across as a basic pattern with a slight twist, such distinction between basic patterns is necessary as they convey extra-bit of information about the supply-demand equation. Besides, defining various patterns "with subtle variations" will be helpful while scanning and back-testing the past occurrence of the pattern and their performance.

'X' and 'O' at same level are particularly important information when higher box-values are used. We will discuss it in the section on box-values.

Rising 'O'–Falling 'X'

If the top of the current column of 'X' is lower than the high of the previous column of 'X', it is a sign of diminishing demand. Similarly, if the low of current column of 'O' is higher than the low of the previous column of 'O', then it is a pattern of Rising 'O', suggesting strong buying interest or demand. (See Image 2.7.4)

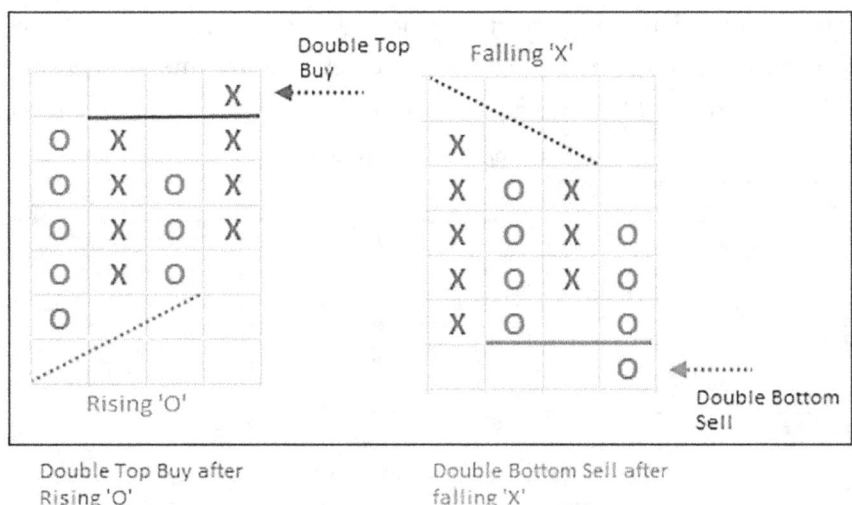

Image 2.7.4: Rising 'O' and Falling 'X'

Basic Buy pattern after such formation displays breakout when demand is rising and a sell pattern shows downside breakout when demand is falling. These patterns typically occur as continuation buy-sell signals in the midst of a trending move.

This means that any Double Top Buy and Double Bottom Sell pattern can be classified in the following categories:

- ▲ Rising Double Top Buy (Rising column of 'O' before Buy signal)
- ▲ Double Top Buy after Support (Buy signal after forming 'O' at same level)
- ▲ Bear Trap (Double Top Buy after Sell signal)

Similarly, any Double Bottom Sell has the following three possibilities:

- ▲ Falling Double Bottom Sell (Falling column of 'X' before Sell signal)
- ▲ Double Bottom Sell after Resistance (Sell signal after forming 'X' at same level)
- ▲ Bull Trap (Double Bottom Sell after Buy signal)

This distinction is not very necessary in early stages. But, it is important to understand the variations as they can provide meaningful information and insights.

I reiterate that objectivity is the major feature of P&F methodology. Variations to the basic patterns are useful only when someone gets proficient with the basic patterns to begin with.

Multiple Top–Bottoms

You may recall that a Triple Top Buy pattern is a five-column pattern where two consecutive columns of 'X' are at the same level. What if they are not at same level and there is one box higher or lower in the middle column? Or, there can be one or more columns of 'X' in between, before the buy signal is triggered. This will make the pattern a seven-column formation. This would not be a valid Triple Top pattern but the interpretation of the pattern is the same. The underlying message is that there is a breakout above a significant resistance level. Markets are dynamic in nature and variations are inevitable. While it is okay to ignore pattern variations, it makes a lot of sense to understand and incorporate them in trading and analysis. A seven-column Triple Top formation is known as spread Triple Top Buy formation. It is still a breakout from resistance; they can also simply be defined as multi-column breakout patterns. All the factors discussed above are equally relevant on the Sell side as well. Defined variations can be back-tested for the number of occurrences and their profitability, and to know more about the behavior of a particular instrument.

Triple Top pattern is not a common pattern as prices do not always line-up at the same level. They tend to exceed or fall short of prior levels. Once the basic patterns are internalized, the variations will be far easier to comprehend. Look at Image 2.7.5.

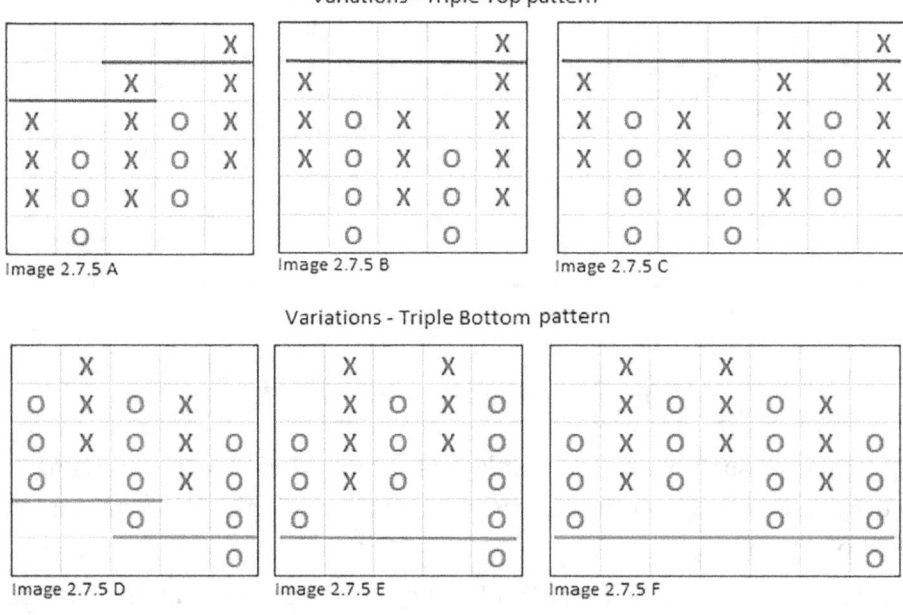

Image 2.7.5: Variations of Triple Top and Triple Bottom patterns

Look at Image 2.7.5 A and B: It could have been a Triple Top Buy pattern had middle column not exceeded the previous column by one box. They are known as diagonal patterns. Image 2.7.5 C and E are known as spread Triple Top and spread Triple Bottom formation, respectively. When Triple Top has Rising bottom, it becomes ascending Triangle. When Triple Bottom has Falling Tops, it becomes descending Triangle. Though there may be many such pattern variations, what needs to be understood is that these variations are nothing but multi-column breakouts.

Quadruple Top–Bottoms

If a there is a Double Top Buy signal after three 'X's at similar level instead of two, then it is known as Quadruple Top Buy signal. It displays the successful breakout above a stiff resistance on the fourth attempt. Quadruple Buy and Sell signals are shown in Image 2.7.6.

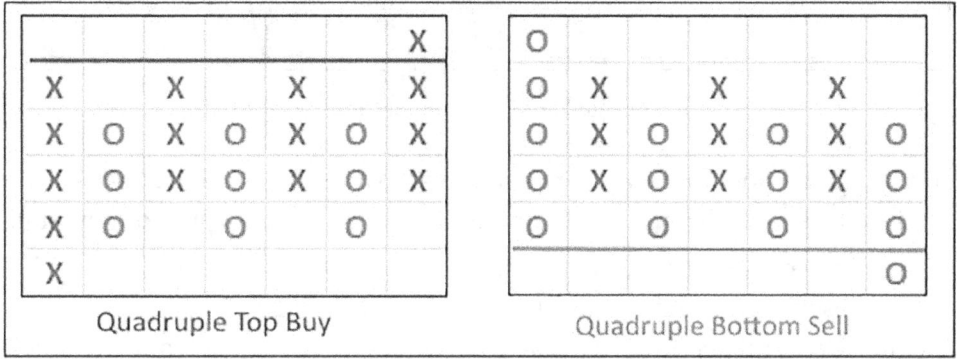

Image 2.7.6: Quadruple breakout pattern

These are very rare formations but relatively stronger when found. Strength of the bulls or bears defending the level gets exhausted and results in catastrophic move when they start giving up.

Six-Column Traps

Bull Trap and Bear Trap are basically four-column formations. A Buy signal is required immediately after Sell signal to call it a Bear Trap. But it is possible that a Buy signal may not happen immediately and there is a column of 'X' in between. Core of the pattern, however, remains the same. It can still be a Trap formation with variation, as shown in Image 2.7.7.

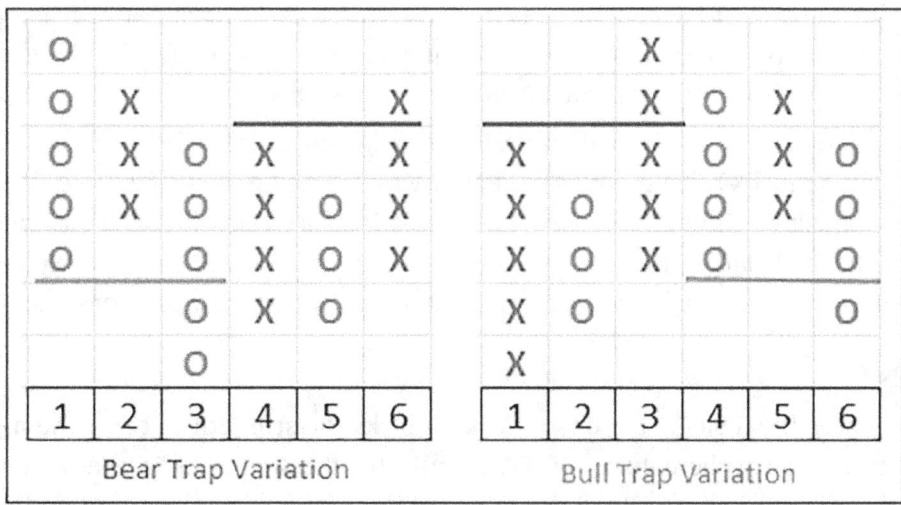

Image 2.7.7: Variation of trap patterns

It can be called a six-column Trap instead of four. It is probably more tradable than actual traps due to lower risk, making them an affordable setup. If I draw a line through the six columns connecting the high of column of 'X' with low of the subsequent column of 'O', then it looks like Image 2.7.8 shown below.

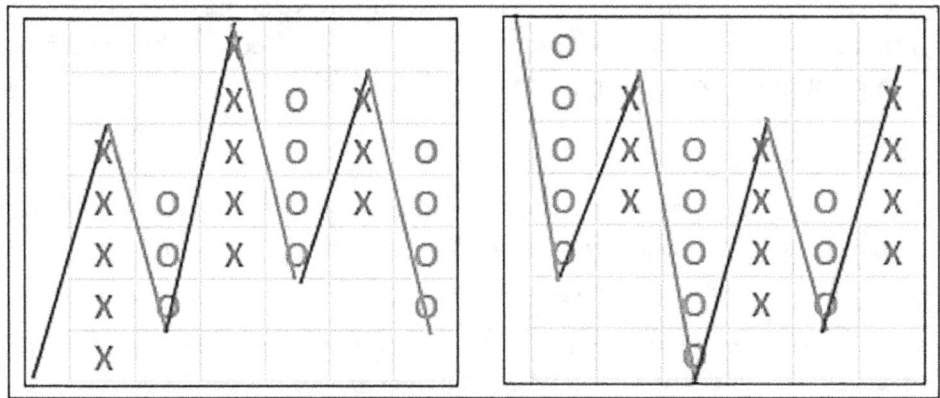

Image 2.7.8: Six-column traps

Don't they resemble the popular Head & Shoulder pattern in time-based candlestick or bar chart? It turns out to be an interesting finding then that formation can be defined with combination of columns!

It is fascinating to understand that many such setups can be defined and identified with combinations of P&F columns. We observe and come across various price structures that can be designed in a similar manner and brought close to objectivity, so that they can be scanned across many stocks and a list of probable candidates can be generated.

A lot can be written on variations. Possibilities of combination are infinite; it is a function of one's creativity. Understand the essence of the pattern and deal with it once you get proficient with the basic patterns. With sufficient practice, these P&F patterns can be identified in real time as they will capture your attention automatically.

My objective here is to make you understand the possibilities and learn to tweak the basic rules going forward. Once you understand how to define such combinations, then you can formulate and design various trading systems using them. Defining the patterns in an objective fashion has several advantages: They can be back-tested and scanned, making the job of trading in real time relatively stress free and objective.

You may find setups with different names on websites and elsewhere. All are valid but names don't matter much. Understanding of P&F columns is important. You must have noticed that all other setups are variations or extensions of major formations. Small columns show congestion, large columns display trend. We will explore this further in Chapter 7 on building systems.

While it is fine to initially ignore the pattern variations, knowing them is definitely important, especially once you gain expertise in P&F methodology. That is why no charts were featured in this section and the concepts were explained through images. These variations are also objective patterns in themselves that can be traded. But as I said earlier, knowledge of P&F in this manner helps in exploring further and designing different formations – below are examples of few patterns that I have designed on P&F.

Weak Breakout

Basic formations display breakout. If a bullish breakout lacks the strength to carry the move further and reverses immediately to form the column of 'O', it indicates the weakness in the pattern and demands further investigation. There is a possibility of false breakout and it can turn out to be the trap going forward. We can define it using a combination of columns.

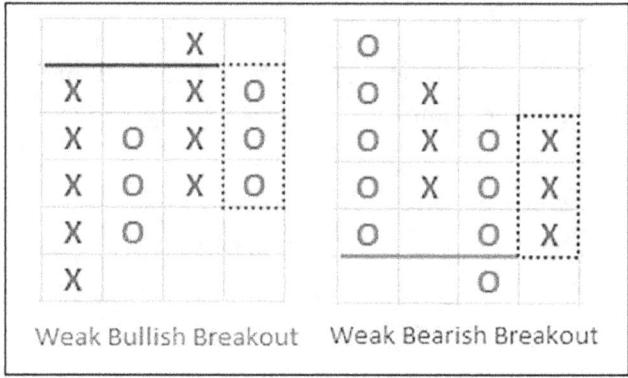

Image 2.7.9: Weak breakouts

If there are only one or two boxes of 'X' after a Double Top Buy signal and if the price flips to a column of 'O' thereafter, such a pattern is defined as a Weak Bullish Breakout. Similarly, if price forms just one or two 'O's after Double Bottom Sell signal and changes the column to 'X', then it is defined as a Weak Bearish Breakout (see Image 2.7.9). The weak breakout points can be the reference points for further analysis. It is a potential trap formation if price continues in the same column. A consolidation phase can have a series of weak breakouts.

Figure 2.7.1 is a 3% P&F chart of Reliance Infra.

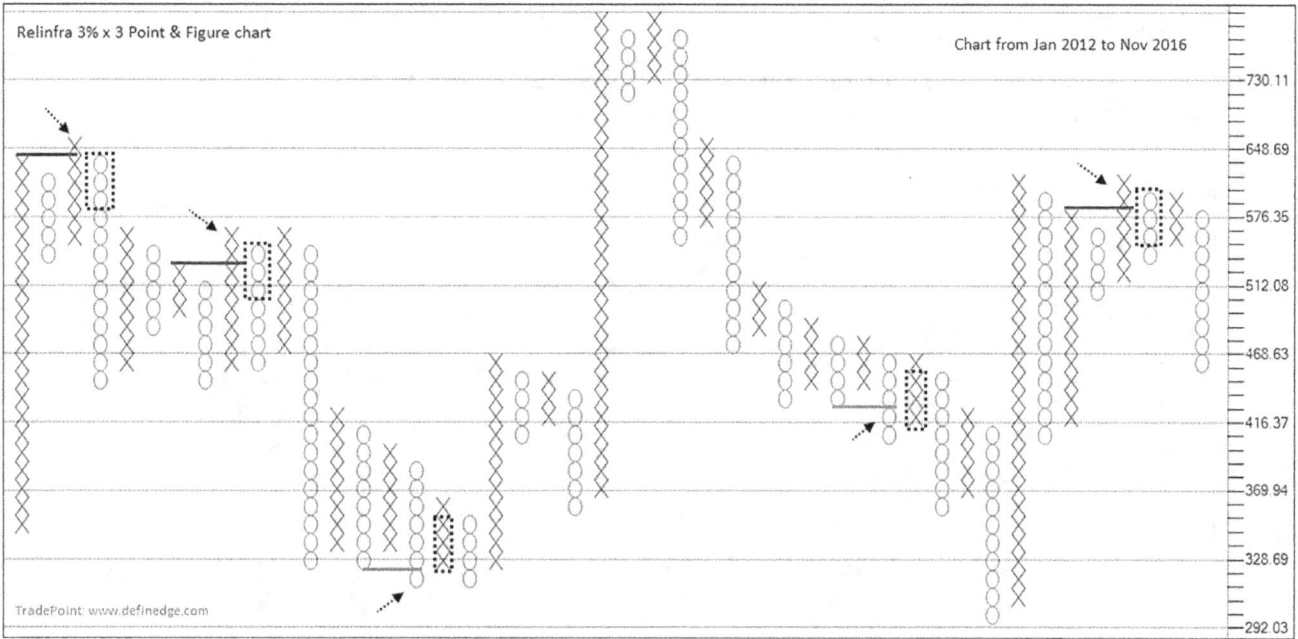

Figure 2.7.1: Reliance infra daily 3% × 3 cl Point & Figure chart

Weak breakouts are shown by a box around the column. Arrow shows that price could not travel more than 2 boxes after the breakout, indicating the weakness of the breakout.

Weak breakout signals become important when found at important lows or near pullback setups. Though it is applicable on all box-values and time frames, it should be typically applied on higher box-values, as explained in Chapter 5. Weak breakouts can be traded upon column reversal signals; hence, they offer attractive risk–reward trades. They can become effective when traded in direction of the trend. Techniques of analyzing trend are discussed in Chapter 3.

Five-Box Traps

We discussed Trap formation in the section on major patterns. If weak breakout turns out to be a trap, it becomes a five-box trap. Image 2.7.10 explains it.

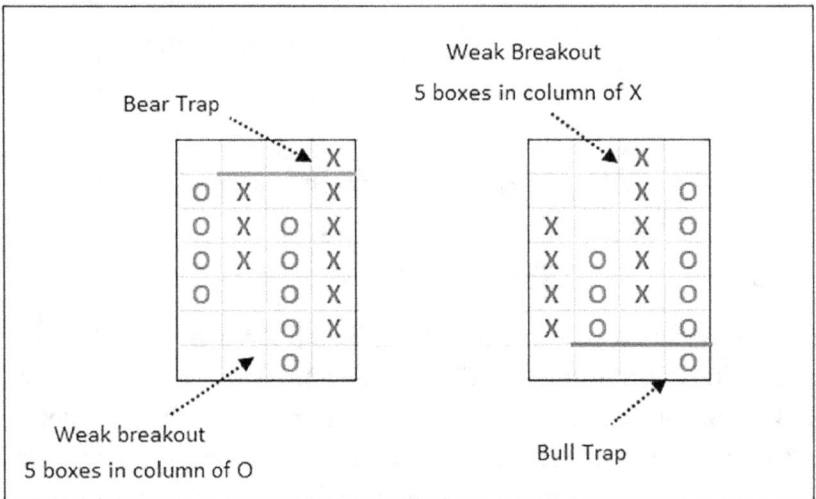

Image 2.7.10: five-box traps

It is a five-box Trap because the number of boxes in the column preceding the breakout is less than 5. If weak breakout is of just one box that turns out to be a Trap, it will be a four-box Trap formation.

Figure 2.7.2 is a 3% × 3 chart of Tata Steel showing five-box Trap patterns.

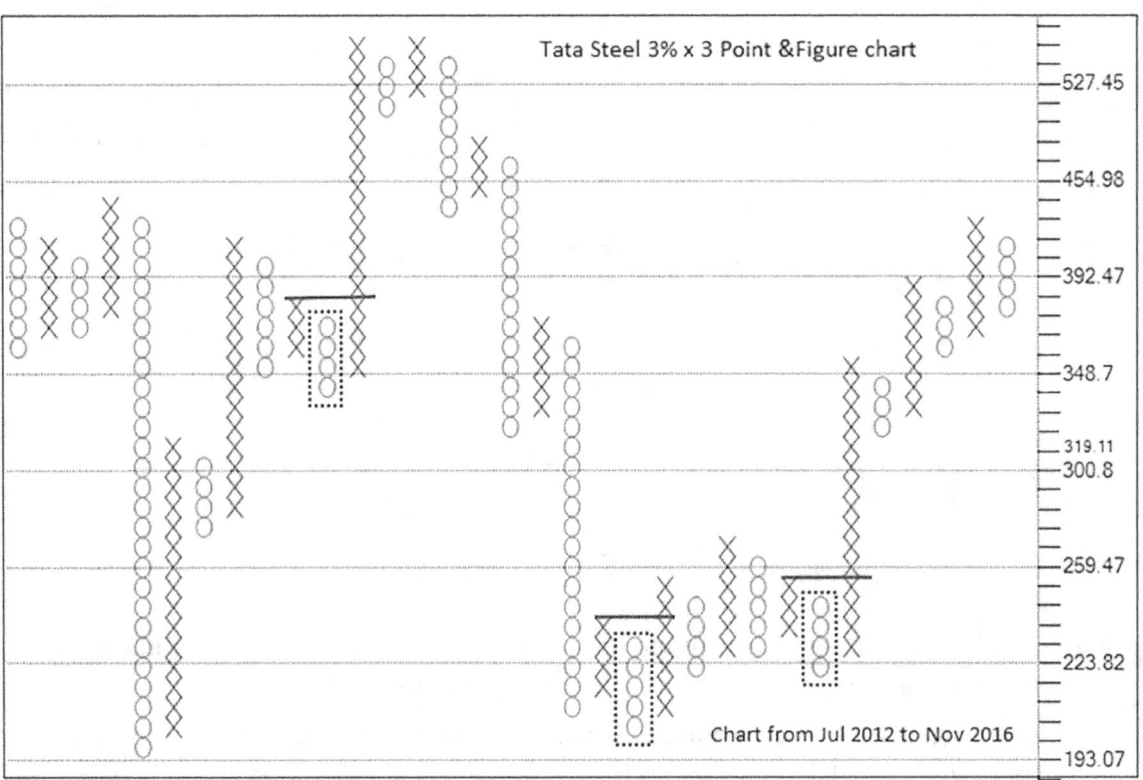

Figure 2.7.2: Tata Steel daily 3% × 3 cl Point & Figure chart

From affordability and risk management perspective, initial risk with five-box Traps is less compared to other traps.

Ziddi Bulls and Ziddi Bears

Ziddi in Hindi means stubborn. Image 2.7.11 explains why this formation is given this name.

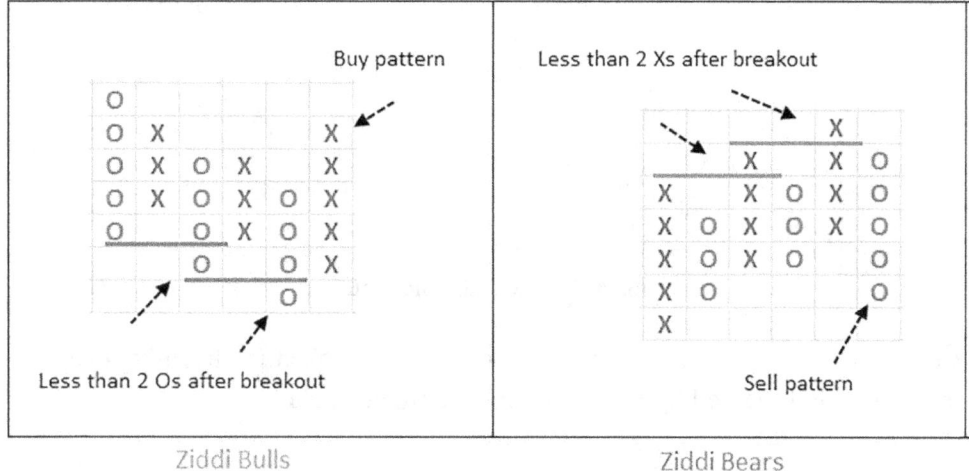

Image 2.7.11: Ziddi bulls and Ziddi bears

Consecutive weak breakouts followed by trap are called Ziddi formations. Ziddi bulls is a formation showing bulls that did not let price travel even by three boxes twice after breaking down and then formed the Bear Trap. It shows the stubbornness or strength of the bulls that are not letting price fall twice after bearish breakout, and weakness of bears that were unable to push the prices lower. Ziddi bear pattern indicates the inability of bulls to push the price higher on two occasions and strength of the bears that succeeded in pushing the prices lower to form the Bull Trap.

Figure 2.7.3 is a 1% P&F chart of Pidilite Industries showing Ziddi Bulls formation.

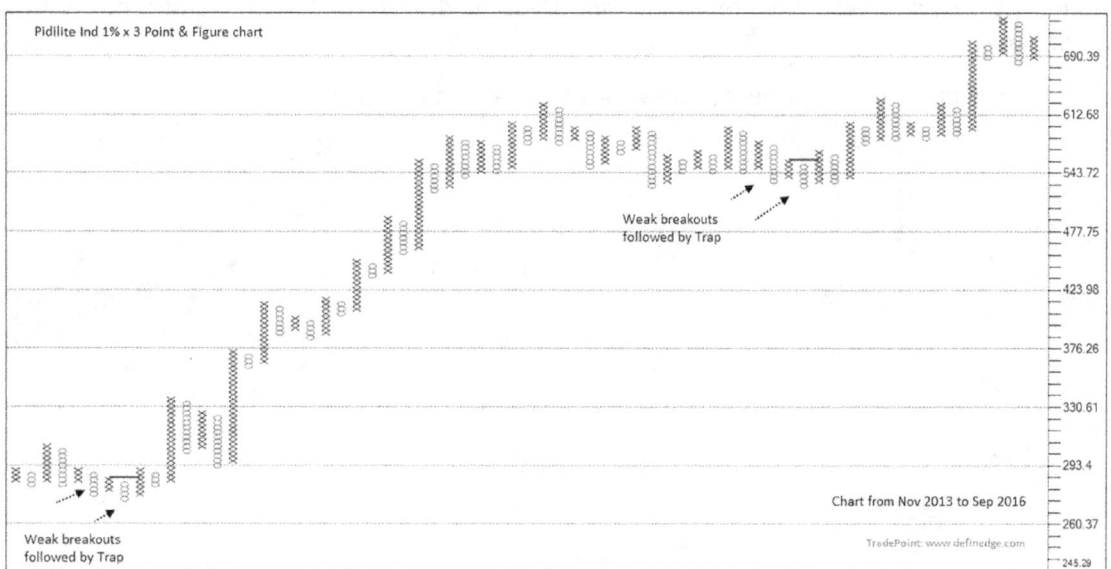

Figure 2.7.3: Pidilite Industries daily 1% × 3 cl Point & Figure chart

For Ziddi bulls, there shouldn't be a Buy pattern in the earlier columns of the pattern. Similarly, there shouldn't be a Sell pattern in the earlier columns to qualify for Ziddi bears.

Note that Ziddi bulls is also a Bear Trap and Ziddi bears is also a Bull Trap, but prior formations make them very interesting and provide us opportunity to trade *zid* or stubbornness of one side.

P&F Diamond

Diamond is a popular chart pattern which is considered as a strong formation that usually occurs when price is forming a significant top or bottom. Image 2.7.12 shows a diamond pattern.

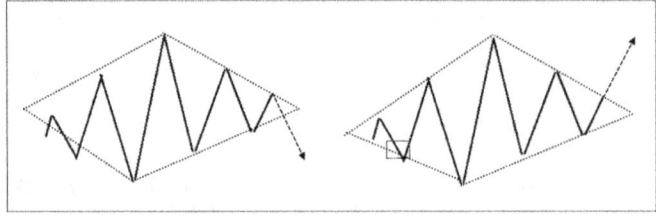

Image 2.7.12: Diamond pattern

The same can be designed on Point & Figure as well. If you look at it carefully, it can be described as a P&F Broadening formation followed by P&F triangle. See Image 2.7.13.

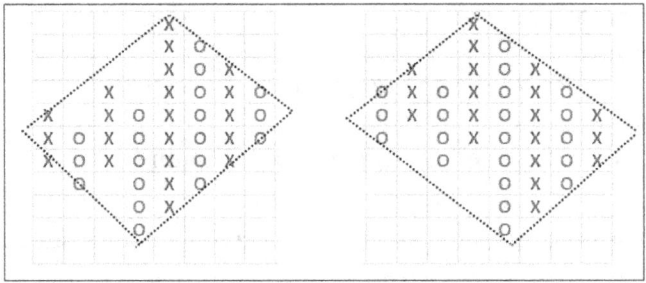

Image 2.7.13: P&F diamond pattern

There could be variations of that also, but this is how we can make it objective and which makes it simple to identify, test or scan. Shape of the diamond will be determined by the length of the Broadening and Triangle patterns.

Figure 2.7.4 is a chart of JSW Energy showing P&F diamond pattern.

Figure 2.7.4: JSW Energy daily 0.25% × 3 cl Point & Figure chart

Diamond breakout is also a Triangle breakout; hence, rules of trading the Triangle pattern are applicable here as well. But here, the triangle pattern occurs after the Broadening pattern, making it a Diamond.

Super Pattern

I couldn't find a better name for this pattern. While the rules of the pattern are very simple, it turns out to be one of the profitable and reliable patterns in my several years of trading P&F charts. The most advantageous thing about P&F is that we can segment price into boxes. Buy after small pullback is a general statement, but buy at four-box retracement after a ten-box move is more objective and is practically feasible with P&F charts. Trend, pullback or retracement can be easily and objectively defined using P&F boxes.

Image 2.7.14 explains the Super pattern.

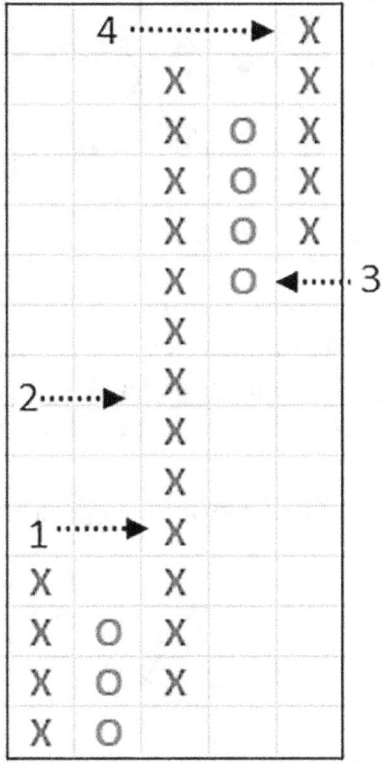

Image 2.7.14: Bullish Super pattern

Point 1 - Basic Double Top Buy pattern

Point 2 - Price travels minimum ten boxes after Buy signal, representing a strong trend after breakout

Point 3 - Immediate column of 'O' forming less than or equal to four boxes, shows small retracement

Point 4 - Follow-through Buy that reinforces strength of the trend

Bullish Super pattern is completed at the Double Top Buy pattern at point **4.**

Long column after breakout pattern suggests strong momentum, which is all that a trader wants. Small retracement and immediate breakout shows strength of the trend that offers a trade with low initial risk. It could indeed be a super formation.

Bearish Super pattern is just the opposite of bullish Super pattern. The conditions are basically the same. Image 2.7.15 explains the same.

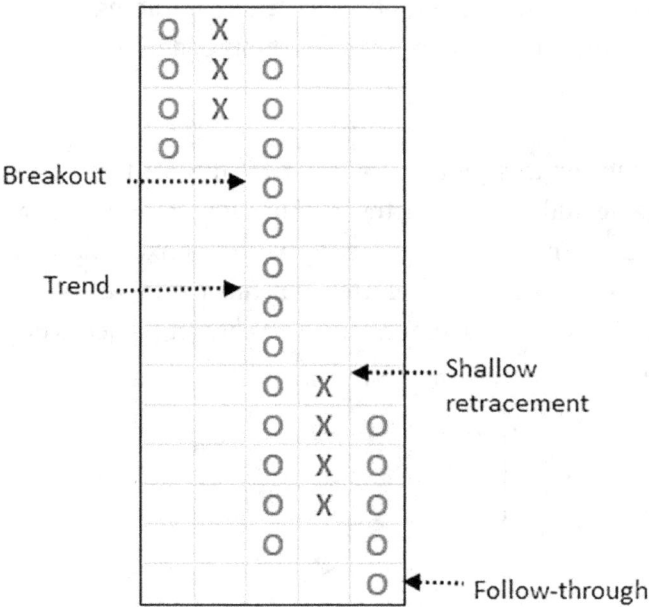

Image 2.7.15: Bullish Super pattern

Bearish Super pattern qualifies at Double Bottom Sell box-price of Follow-through; 10 or 4 are the parameters of this pattern, which can be modified as per the preference. It can be Super 8 when retracement is defined as less than eight boxes instead of four. Or it can be Super 3 where trades with only three-box reversal after strong trend are entertained. For bearish trades, reducing the retracement can prove more advantageous.

Figure 2.7.5 is a 1% box-value chart of Jindal Steel showing Super pattern.

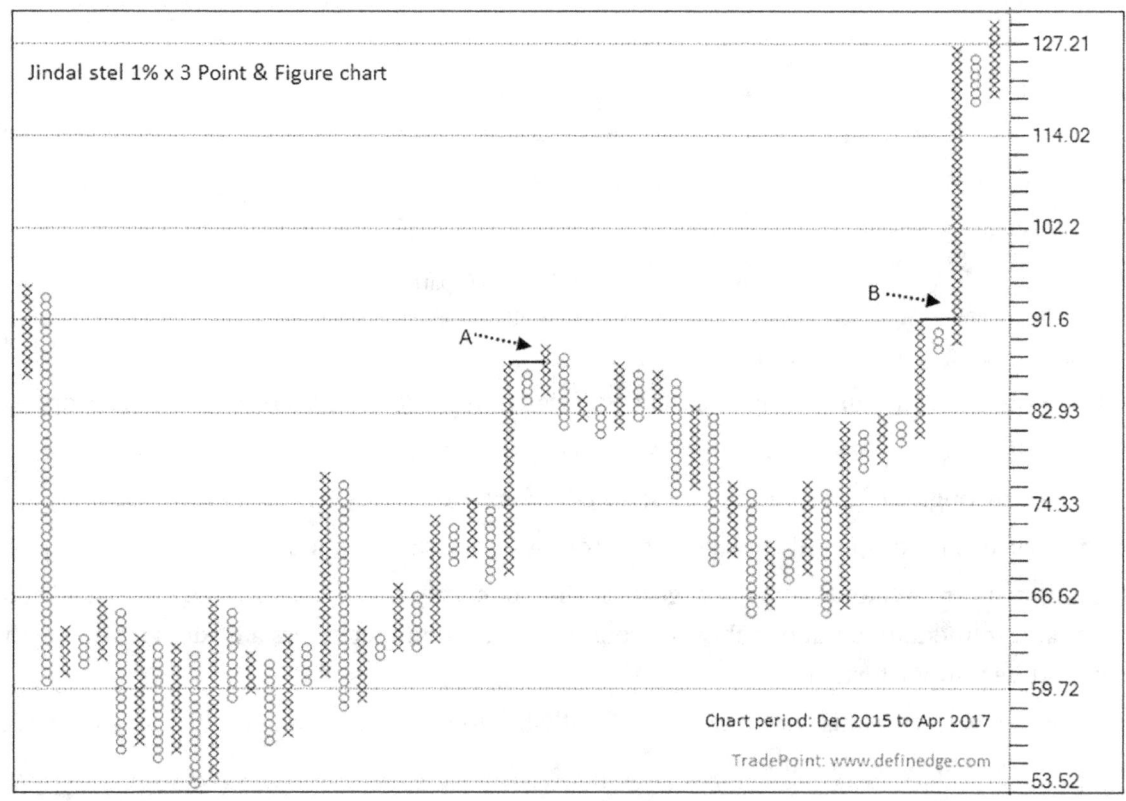

Figure 2.7.5: Jindal Steel daily 1% × 3 cl Point & Figure chart

Pattern A and B are Super patterns; pattern A immediately reversed and failed whereas pattern B resulted in a nice move post breakout. Apart from objectivity, momentum as an ingredient and low initial risk makes this pattern an attractive proposition from a trading perspective.

Super pattern is a remarkable structure that offers Follow-through with defined and limited risk. All that a trader needs is momentum and an affordable trade setup. The setup explained above perfectly fits in and, most importantly, makes it objective.

Summary

- ⅄ Diagonal and spreads are variations of Triple Top and Triple Bottoms.
- ⅄ Six-column traps are variation to traps.
- ⅄ Quadruple Tops and Bottoms are significant breakout patterns.
- ⅄ Variations shouldn't become a license to do anything. Define them to derive objective patterns having variation.
- ⅄ Understand the essence of the pattern and deal with it once you practice the basic patterns.
- ⅄ Weak breakout, four- to five-box traps, Ziddi Bulls and Bears, Diamonds and Super pattern are patterns that we identified and developed because of the extensive knowledge of pattern variations. These patterns are thoroughly back-tested and are a outcome of several years of practice and research.

2.8: FAILURE

It may be recalled that the conditions that trigger a pattern failure were discussed along with the pattern concerned. Objectivity while defining the patterns helps in clearly defining the failure criteria as well. A Failure or negation of a pattern is a significant piece of information that should not be ignored. Negation of bullish pattern is bearish event and that of bearish pattern is bullish event. Pattern failure, irrespective of it happening immediately or later, is an important piece of information from the analysis perspective.

Figure 2.8.1 is a daily 0.25% × 3 P&F chart of Tata Motors.

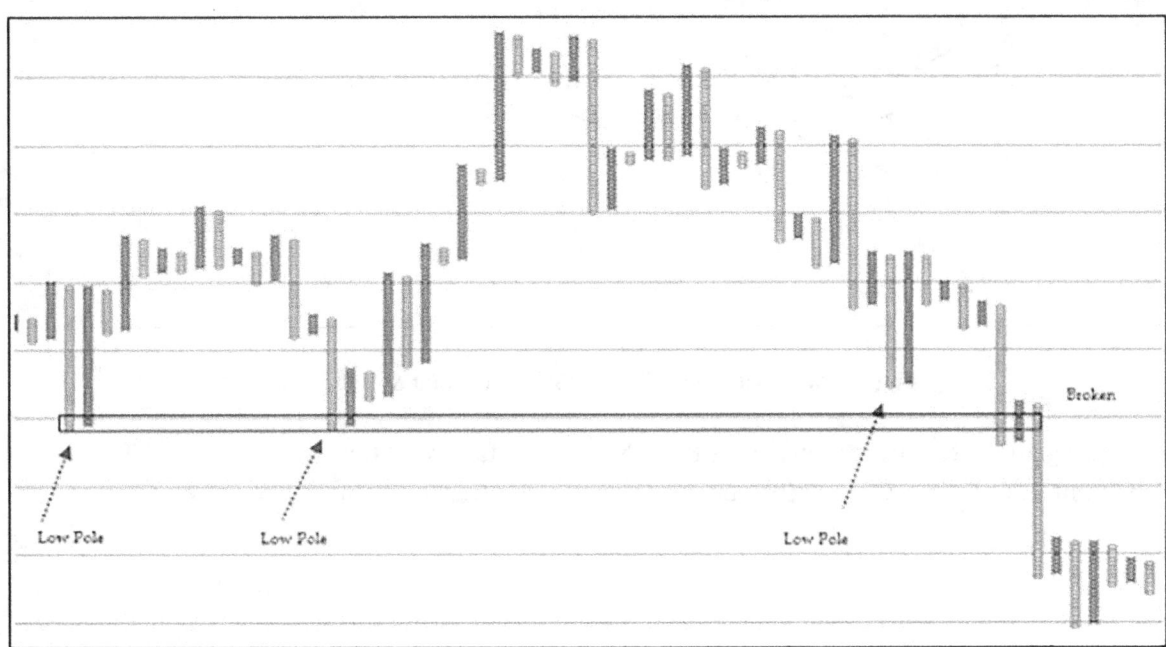

Tata Motors 0.25% x 3 cl Point & Figure chart

Figure 2.8.1: Tata Motors daily 0.25% × 3 cl Point & Figure chart

Three Low Poles can be seen around same levels. The first two witnessed the Follow-through and the third did not, which eventually resulted in failure. This is a strong sign of the underlying weakness.

Bull traps and High Poles are often found in Uptrend, which gets invalidated when the uptrend is strong. The failure of a pattern is an indication of the strength of the underlying trend. A pattern failure can also turn out to be an early sign of weakening of the underlying trend that can eventually result in a trend reversal.

We discussed that traps in the direction of trend are good setups. Traps against the trend when failed are equally good setups. In other words, Bull Trap in Uptrend when fails, or Bear Trap in Downtrend when fails add to the strength of the trend. Negation or Failure of a bearish pattern in Uptrend and bullish pattern in Downtrend is a strong pattern in the direction of the trend. As per my experience, Trap and Pole failure are very useful setups in strong and established trends.

Observe the Bata India P&F chart shown in Figure 2.8.2.

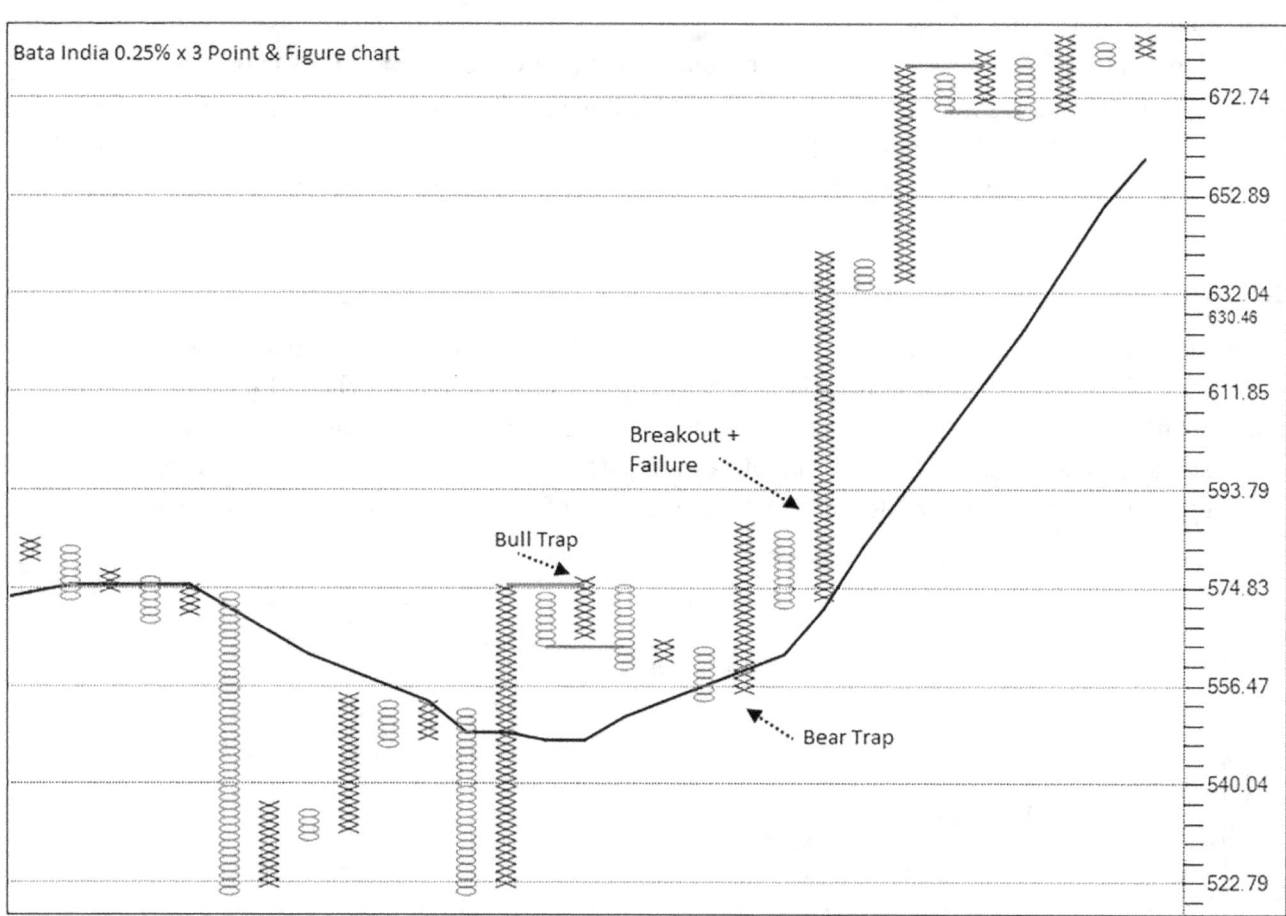

Figure 2.8.2: Bata India daily 0.25% × 3 cl Point & Figure chart

Price going above top price of previous Bull Trap shows failure of bearish pattern in Uptrend, which is a bullish event. Look at the Grasim P&F charts shown in Figures 2.8.3 and 2.8.4.

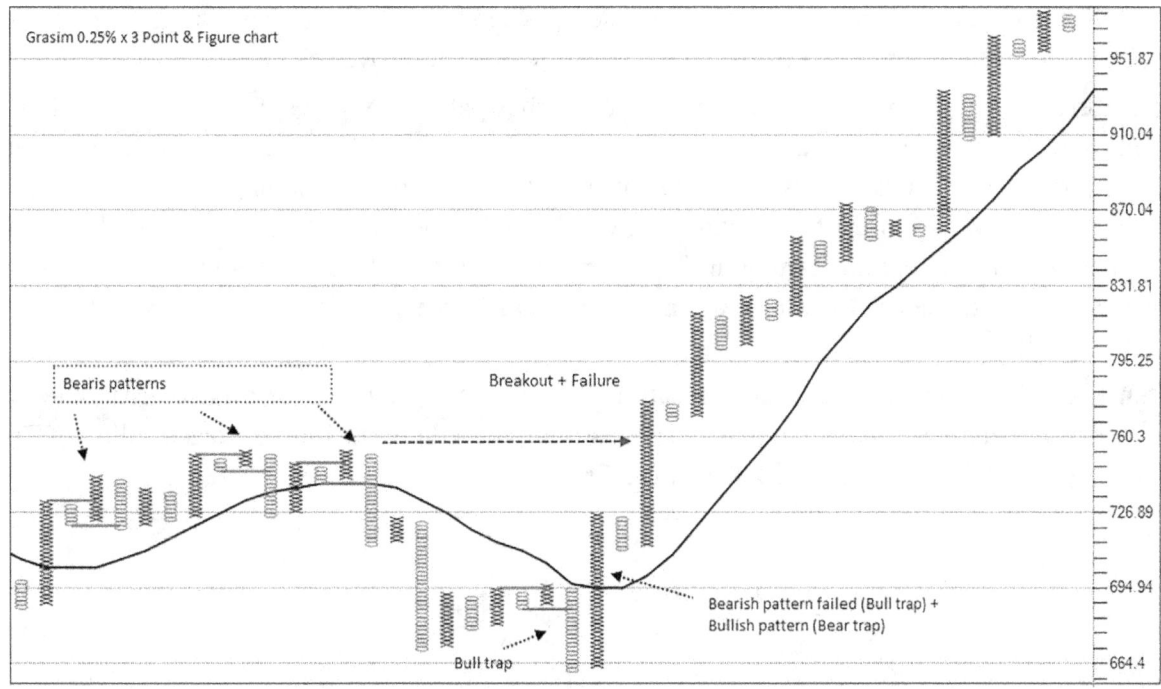

Figure 2.8.3: Grasim daily 0.25% × 3 cl Point & Figure chart

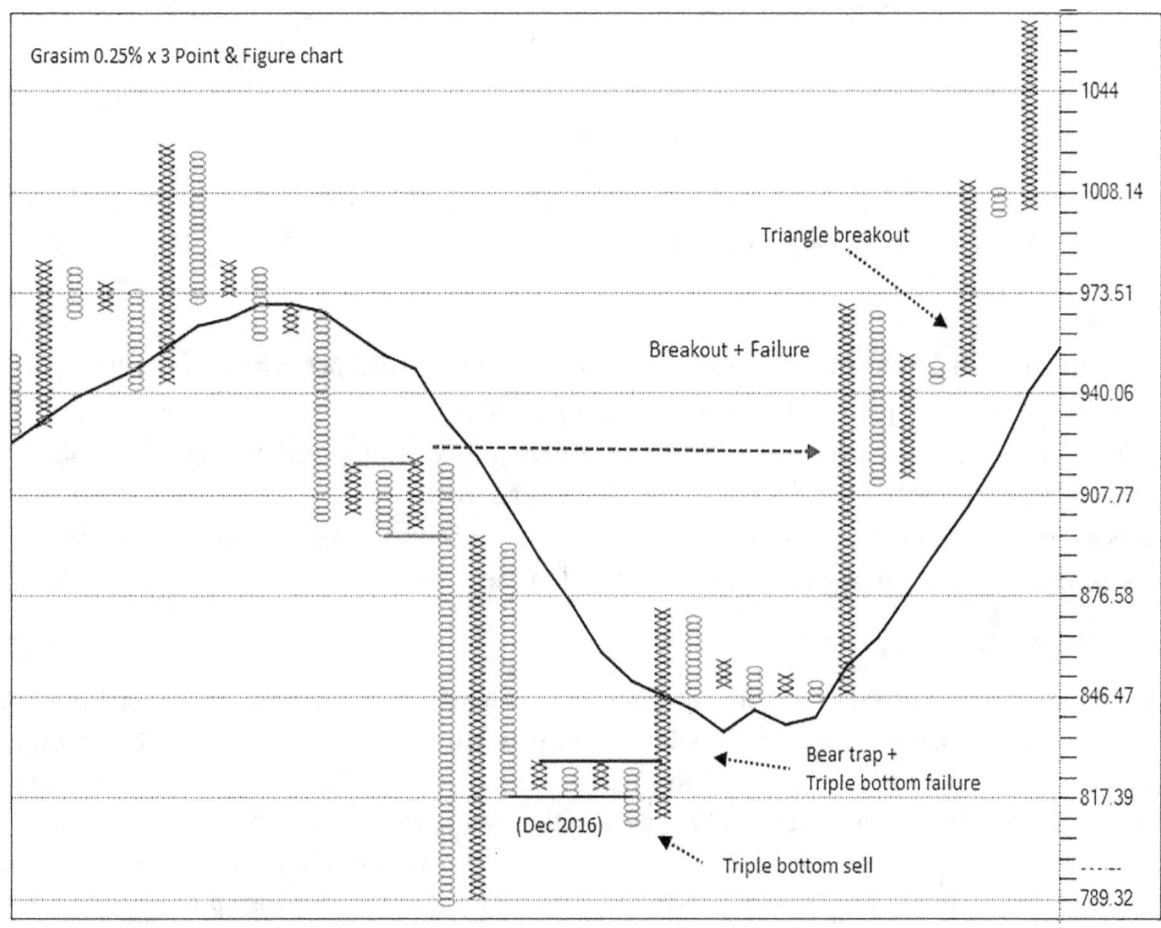

Figure 2.8.4: Grasim daily 0.25% × 3 cl Point & Figure chart

Arrow in both the charts shows the strength of setup when there is a price breakout pattern along with failure of another side. A setup that has failure as an ingredient, improves chances of success.

If a pattern fails in the immediate column, then another pattern emerges. Failure of basic signals is a Trap. Failure of 100% Pole is also a Trap. Failure of Trap is a Broadening formation. Failure of Bullish–Bearish pattern reversed is also a Broadening formation. Failure of Broadening formation is a Double Broadening formation. Failure of one pattern gives birth to another, which is one of the important ingredients of the multi-column formation that makes them noticeable. They comprise both, failure and breakout. Note that these are the cases when patterns fail in the immediate column, but they can fail eventually as well.

Often a first breakout from converging pattern like triangle proves to be a false breakout; trade in reverse direction is a breakout pattern that has failure as an ingredient. In simple words, failure of Triangle is an equally profitable pattern. Image 2.8.1 shows Triangle failure.

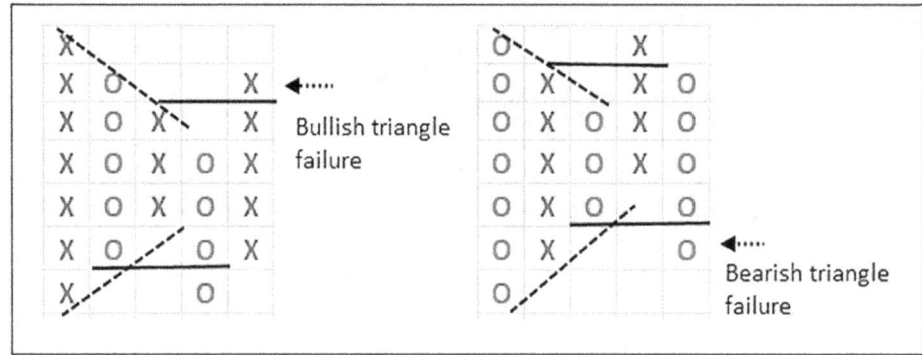

Image 2.8.1: Triangle failure pattern

If you notice, bullish Triangle failure is nothing but a triangle pattern, followed by a Bear Trap and bearish triangle failure is a triangle pattern followed by a bull trap.

Summary

- ➤ Failure of bearish pattern is a bullish event and failure of bullish pattern is a bearish event.
- ➤ Pay attention when price invalidates the previous pattern.
- ➤ Overcoming the defeat or ability to bounce back proves the strength; chances of success are significantly improved when a setup has failure as an ingredient.

Charts shown in this book are from TradePoint software which has ready-made scanners for all time frames of all the patterns and other methods discussed in the book.

2.9: PATTERN FOLLOWING

Patterns that we have discussed can help us in analyzing the markets and instruments. A trading approach can also be developed using them, which is known as pattern following. Take a trade based on bullish pattern and exit when bearish formation is formed, or take a short position based on bearish formation and exit when a bullish pattern is formed. We can shortlist candidates to trade based on our own analysis or even based on information from some trusted sources. But instead of blindly taking trades in them, it would be prudent to trade if there is some recognizable P&F pattern in those instruments. The advantage of using pattern-based approach is the objectivity when it comes to determining entry, exit and failure levels. With this, we trade and follow patterns, and utilize all other things as complementary tools.

For this approach, prepare a list of patterns that you are most comfortable with and follow them on charts. Remembering major patterns only will also suffice; the rest will come handy eventually.

For analysis, if you are new to the subject, begin with practicing basic and major patterns and gradually move to the other sections of this chapter. P&F patterns are specific and objective in nature and hence can be practiced easily. Ignore unaffordable signals and wait for Continuation or Follow-through patterns. Follow-through coming after Double pattern or Triple pattern (Pattern retest) is a powerful setup.

From the analysis perspective, major formations complement each other: Triple Tops and Bottoms are support–resistance breakout patterns; Traps are patterns showing breakout and failure in the same setup; Triangles are converging patterns; Broadening shows expanding price formation and 100% Pole shows vertical reversal.

Profit booking upon column reversal can also be initiated if boxes in the column exceed a particular number. And trade can be re-initiated upon Fresh signal. There can be many such ideas that will come to mind when formations are being practiced. You can indulge in a lot of such experiments, as long as you know when to exit a trade and keep the potential loss to the minimum. Pattern following imbibes art of booking the losses, which makes one the winner in the long run.

There is an element of bullishness when the trend is down, but the price is not making any significant downside progress. Failures of bearish patterns are early signals of reversal of Downtrend. 'X' at same level is a traditional Double Top formation and 'O' at same level is traditional Double Bottom formation, which reflects support or resistances at previous major point. It is also possible that swing failure pattern in lower box-value or time-frame chart is a trap or weak breakout on a higher box-value chart.

Patterns and Follow-through can be traded by defining position-sizing rules. For instance, an initial position may be taken when a major pattern is completed and positions may be scaled-in either on a Follow-through signal or a column reversal. These rules will ensure that the losses are at a minimum when the pattern fails while the reward is significant when the pattern works and the price gets into a trending mode. Follow-through formation is more important for bearish trades.

The behavior of every stock and instrument is different. Triple Tops work very well on several instruments and you won't find many Triangles on them. Few work very well after Triangles and don't see much of Follow-through after major patterns. Knowing your instrument is very important. Not all setups work effectively in every instrument and few setups work very well on a particular instrument – this is not only about P&F. Knowing the instrument through setup gives a better idea about its behavior.

Long–Short

The undertone of market is always bullish because upside is infinite and downside is limited to zero. Markets go up in the longer run; hence, returns from bullish setups look more attractive than from bearish setups; 50 to 100 are 100% returns and 100 to 50 are 50%. It is as simple as that.

This is very relevant especially with index where the downside is limited in comparison stocks. For this reason, nature and treatment of bullish and bearish setups should be quite different. Success ratio of bullish setup over a longer period of time is more. An up move in price is typically gradual, while the fall is relatively steep. It is said that bulls climb the stairs and bears use the elevator. Hence, bearish trades on lower box-values tend to work better. Follow-through and confirmation are more important for bearish reversal formations. Bearish patterns in the Downtrend are more effective and produce quick returns.

This is my understanding of market derived from experiencing them over a period on various time frames. Exactly opposite, what works for long doesn't work for short.

Long-Only Approach

If one is particularly bullish on a stock, one can just follow bullish basic signals on it and ignore bearish signals. Short patterns can be traded in derivative segments only and need more trading engagement. Short-term investors may want to follow long-only approach with objective setups, which can be a very sensible and safe way of investing. The long-only approach is to trade only bullish patterns and ignore bearish patterns. One will remain invested when equities are performing and exit when there are signs of weakness. This remains true for all types of market.

"I am frequently asked, how long should I hold the stock? Other questions are "should I hold the stock for long term or medium term? Such questions are meaningless as the price action should dictate the holding time period. Stocks don't run based on our definition of time horizon. We have recently been in a multi-year bull market and it is therefore natural to hear about multi-bagger stocks. But the examples of stocks that have been big losers are seldom publicized. Not every cricketer becomes Sachin Tendulkar, in spite of being as talented. Markets are dynamic and they change without serving notice. An investor can hold on to a stock for many years if there is potential and when it is performing. He can book profits or switch to better investments when there is a change in scenario. A sensible idea is to design objective setups and follow them; let price prompt us instead of imposing our opinions on it. This is discussed further in Chapter 8 on investing and relative strength analysis.

Pattern Following

I have seen many accurate and brilliant predictions. There are great minds who can foresee things based on a variety of methods and their experience. They should be listened to always and followed but it is not prudent to blame them when they go wrong. Trade execution and management should always be under our control.

Adopting an objective, pattern-based trading approach is the best way of dealing with the different types of analysis, emotions and assumptions.

We can't have cosmic knowledge so to speak, but following P&F patterns can help to avoid the stress of wanting it. The key is to find the confluence zone and then wait for a low-risk entry after a pattern confirmation. So if a friend asks you to buy something based on whatever news, just consider the friend as a scanner that identifies the instrument for you. Trade the patterns in the chart and you end up making money when the information you get is correct and you get out early with minimal loss if the information turns out to be false. Most importantly, you don't need to ask them what to do next. To my mind, 'Should I take this Double Top Buy?' is a better question than 'Should I buy here?' A pattern comes with rules and it helps in taking decisions. It effectively controls the issue of overtrading which is one of main problems that affect trading performance & profitability. We learned that P&F charts do not plot unwarranted data; hence, large amount of price data is compressed and captured in a few columns. Not every column generates signal, hence trades based on it get reduced further. Then again, not every signal is a fresh signal or a specific pattern. Hence, pattern trading is a perfect way to address the issue of overtrading."and also achieving better profitability.

One may prefer to focus on three to four setups that one understands well and ignore the rest. Along with the patterns, the use of a few other tools or indicators can result in a well-defined trading setup. One can certainly benefit by executing it, and most importantly by ignoring the rest.

Continuation patterns are much more powerful than reversal formations. Even the basic method of following patterns filtered by trend is a profitable strategy. Let's move to the next part where we will learn techniques of analyzing trend and counts.

Chapter 3

ANALYSIS

We discussed about various Point & Figure patterns in the earlier chapters. Trades should be taken based on their occurrence. Techniques of analyzing them by applying various tools are explained in this chapter, which shall help in filtering the patterns and defining the setups.

3.1: MINI TOPS AND MINI BOTTOMS

Tops and Bottoms are very easy to identify on any given chart because they are the past events. They can be spotted using P&F charts also, as shown in chart in Image 3.1.1.

Image 3.1.1: Major Tops and Bottoms

Tops at pattern A and C and bottom at point B are marked in the above chart, which are undisputable. These are called major Tops and Bottoms because they are followed by serious price reversals. We can spot and perform various analyses on them. They can become significant reference points for future as well. People also use various mathematical calculations to the important tops and bottom price levels to arrive at targets/projections.

If you notice the chart, within these major Tops and Bottoms, there are many that have seen significant Follow-through and worked as important reference points going forward. They are temporary halts but may turn out to be the major reversal points as well. There is a method in Point & Figure chart that helps us identify important reference levels and potential major Tops and Bottoms. It is known as Mini Top–Mini Bottoms, which is a very important concept to know not only from trading perspective but also to learn various tools of analysis that we are going to discuss further.

Bottom–Top

Before we discuss Mini Bottom and Mini Top, let's understand definition of bottom and top. Have a look at Image 3.1.2. Is it a Bottom?

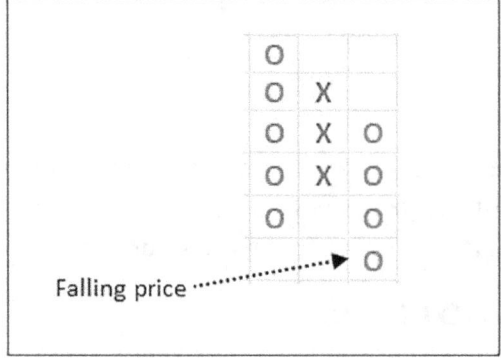

Image 3.1.2: Falling price

It is a lowest point of three columns but it can't be called a bottom because price is still falling. We can mark a bottom there only if price turns up and generates a Buy signal. (See Image 3.1.3)

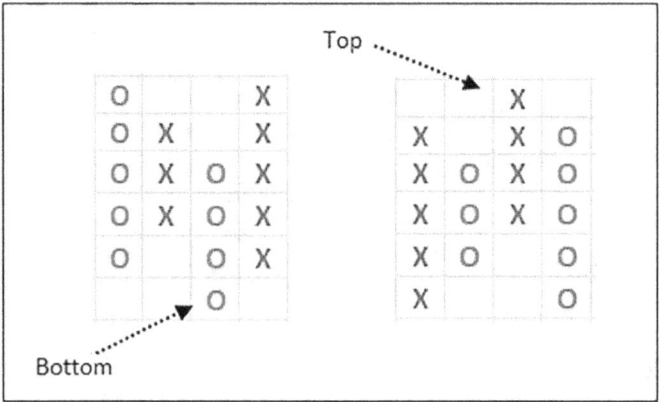

Image 3.1.3: Bottom and Top

Similarly, Sell signal occurring after Buy signal marks the Top at high price of 'X'. It is not necessary that Buy or Sell signal should occur in immediate column; they can come later also but Top or Bottom is marked only upon their occurrence.

The definition of Mini Bottom and Mini Top is given below; a stepwise explanation that follows will help you understand them better.

Mini Bottom and Mini Top

In an uptrend, the first condition for the Mini Bottom is a Double Bottom Sell pattern, followed by a Double Top Buy pattern. The second requirement or condition is that the Double Bottom Sell pattern that occurred in this instance should not be lower than the most recent "Mini Bottom."pattern. It might seem a bit complex in the beginning. But once you understand the logic and have a look at the examples, the concept should be very easy to grasp and internalize.

The conditions are just the opposite while identifying Mini Tops

Remember, a Bottom is marked when Sell pattern turns to Buy pattern and a Top is marked when Buy pattern turns to Sell pattern.

A Mini Bottom is marked once Mini Top gets broken and a Mini Top is marked once Mini Bottom gets broken. Hence, at any given point, either Mini Top or Mini Bottom will be active on a chart. If you have understood the definition, it is an objective technique of marking higher lows and lower highs. Let me explain it stepwise with examples.

1	2	3	4	5	6	7	8	9	10	11	12	13	14	15
														X
												X		X
										X		X	O	X
						X		X		X	O	X	O	X
				X	O	X	O	X	O	X	O	X	O	
		X			X	O	X	O	X	O	X	O		
X		X	O	X	O			O	X	O				
X	O	X	O	X			O							
X	O	X	O											
	O													

Image 3.1.4: Mini Bottom and Mini Top

Image 3.1.4 is a P&F chart showing rising prices. Assume that this is a beginning of a chart. There is a bottom at column 2 and price has marked Fresh Double Top Buy at column 3. There are Continuation Double Top Buy signals at column 5 and 7 but without any Sell signal in between. A Double Bottom Sell signal is triggered in column 8, which is a Sell signal in an uptrend. After this sell signal, there was a buy signal in column no. 11. This sequence of a Double Bottom Sell, followed by a Double Top buy is the first requirement or condition for identifying Mini Bottom. Notice that when the sell signal was triggered, price did not fall below the prior bottom, which is the low of column no. 2. This takes care of the second condition mentioned earlier for identifying Mini Bottom. Now that the twin conditions mentioned above is validated, the low at column 8 qualifies as a valid Mini Bottom. Once the Mini Bottom is formed, it will remain relevant until broken. Column 13 and 15 are Continuation Double Top Buy patterns. Notice that a Mini Bottom got marked when Buy signal was formed at column 11 and not before that.

15	16	17	18	19	20	21	22	23	24	25	26	27	28	29	30
									X		X				
						X		X		X	O	X	O	X	
						X	O	X	O	X	O	X	O	X	O
				X				X	O	X	O	X	O		O
		X		X	O	X	O		O			O			O
X		X	O	X	O	X			O						O
X	O	X	O	X	O				O						O
X	O	X	O	X											O
X	O		O	X											O
X		O													O

Image 3.1.5: Mini Bottom and Mini Top

Image 3.1.5 is the continuation of the previous chart. Continuation Buy signal is marked at column 17. Double Bottom Sell signal occurred at column 18, which is immediately followed by Double Top Buy at column 19. The Sell signal did not breach the Mini Bottom at column 8 and turned to Buy again. Hence, bottom of column 18 is a Mini Bottom. There is another Continuation Buy at column 21. Column 24 marks another Double Bottom Sell signal that was followed by a Double Top Buy signal at column 25. Price did not go below bottom of column 18, which is the previous Mini Bottom; hence, low of column 24 is new Mini Bottom. Price witnessed Double Bottom Sell signal at column 28. It turned to 'X' at column 29 but did not generate the Buy signal; hence, bottom of column 28 is not a Mini Bottom, though it is above previous Mini Bottom. A Sell signal is generated in column 30 and price went below Mini Bottom at column 24; hence, the Mini Bottom stands broken now. Mini Top is marked the moment Mini Bottom gets broken. Mini Top is marked in the chart at the top of column 27, being the highest box-price between breakout column and previous Mini Bottom. The trend turns bearish as the Mini Bottom is breached. The bearish trend will be in force until the price moves above a prior Mini Top.

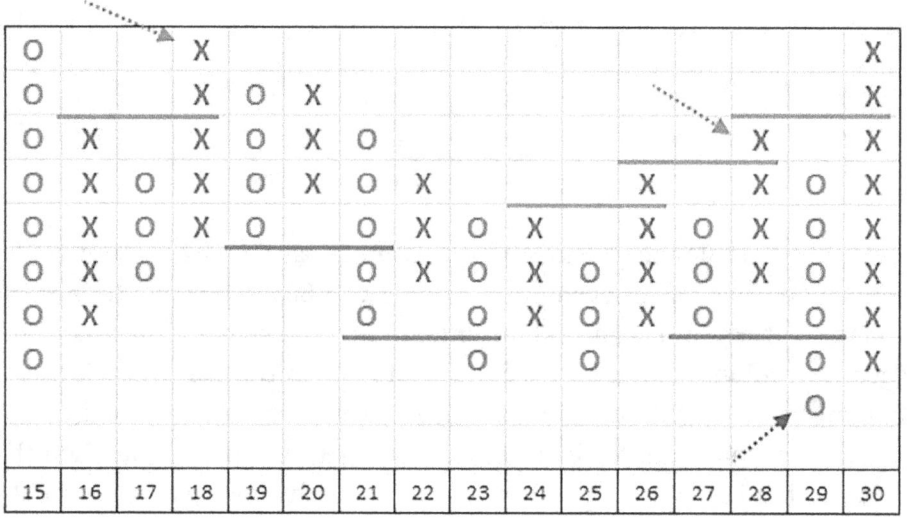

Image 3.1.6: Mini Bottom and Mini Top

Image 3.1.6 continues the chart further. Double Top Buy signal is marked at column 18. But price did not go above high of column 27 and reversed to Sell signal at column 21. Hence, top of column 18 is Mini Top. There are Continuation Sell signals at columns 21 and 23, followed by consecutive Double Top Buy signals at columns 26 and 28 that indicate price attempted to rise but failed to go above Mini Top at column 18. It turned to column of 'O' and formed Double Bottom Sell signal at column 29; hence, top of column 28 qualifies as Mini Top. Price turns to 'X' at 30 and forms Double Top Buy, which is also above the top of previous Mini Top at column 28. A Mini Top is broken; hence, bottom of column 29 qualifies as Mini Bottom.

The Mini Tops and Bottoms can also qualify as Major Tops and Bottoms. The method like all other techniques of P&F is completely objective. It is a technique of trailing Bottoms when prices are rising and trailing Tops when they are falling. Price will be in an uptrend as long as the most recent Mini Bottom is not breached. Similarly, a downtrend will be in force until the price moves above the most recent Mini Top. It becomes a technique of defining the trend by trailing the Top and Bottoms. Understand that Mini Bottom is marked when buy signal is generated and Mini Top is marked when sell signal is triggered. In a way, this is a method of marking the rising bottoms and falling tops, but made objective with P&F.

Mini Bottoms and Mini Tops are often a Trap pattern or a variation of it. A Mini Bottom may or may not be a Bear Trap, but a Bear Trap in Uptrend will always be a Mini Bottom. Similarly, Bull traps in

Downtrend form Mini Tops. Hence, Traps in the direction of the trend will always qualify as Mini Top or Mini Bottom.

When you come across any P&F chart, mark Major Top or Bottom visible on it and start marking Mini Tops or Bottoms. Figure 3.1.1 is a chart of Arvind between July and December 2015 plotted with 1-point box-value of hourly closing prices. The markings of Tops and Bottoms are shown in the chart as per the method discussed above.

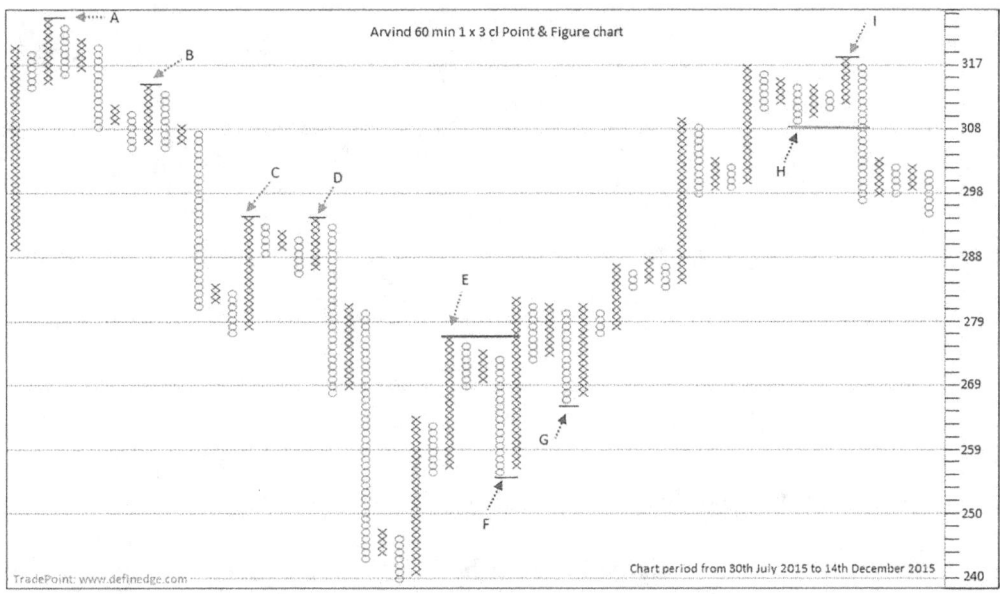

Figure 3.1.1: Arvind 60 min interval 1 × 3 cl Point & Figure chart

Downtrend that begins at point A, trails down with Mini Tops till Point E, which was breached and marked Mini Bottom at point F. Mini Top at point I is marked when Mini Bottom at point H is broken.

Figure 3.1.2 is a 1% × 3 P&F chart of daily prices of Aban. Uptrend that commenced after forming Bottom at point A is trailed up till point F, which is the last Mini Bottom of the trend. It got broken, which resulted in a reversal of the Uptrend and in a Mini Top at point G. The Downtrend is trailed with Mini Tops shown in the chart till point L.

Figure 3.1.2: Aban daily 1% × 3 cl Point & Figure chart

The method can be applied on all box-values and time frames. It is also useful during Sideways market where some frequent Tops–Bottoms are marked around the same zone, but it reduces noise to a larger extent. Figure 3.1.3 is a daily 0.50% × 3 P&F chart of Reliance Industries between August 2012 and April 2014. Mini Tops and Mini Bottoms are marked in the extended period of horizontal trend.

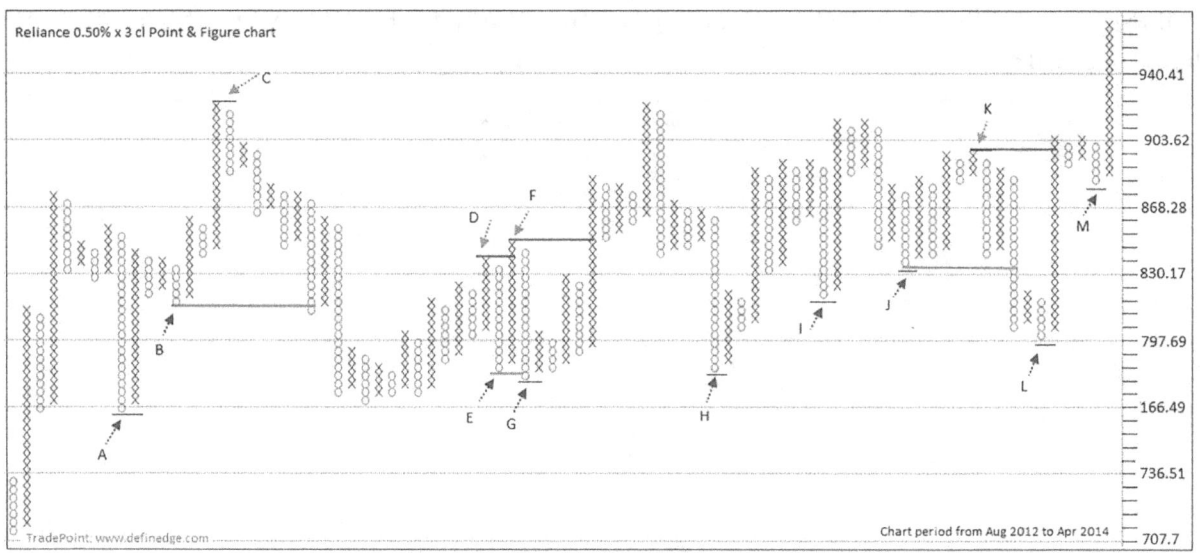

Figure 3.1.3: Reliance daily 0.50% × 3 cl Point & Figure chart

Markings in the chart above are relatively more because trend is flat but confusion over trend is removed to a large extent.

After forming the Mini Bottom in Uptrend, it may happen that two consecutive columns of 'O' are at the same level and a Sell signal is therefore not generated. The price can then turn around and trigger a Buy signal. Mini Bottom should be marked at such instances too even though a sell signal was not generated. The logic here is that the prior low box-price was tested is a valid reason to mark the low as Mini Bottom. Similarly, Mini Top should be marked even if price comes at previous 'X' and fails to generate Buy signal. The latter column should be treated as Top or Bottom. (See Image 3.1.7)

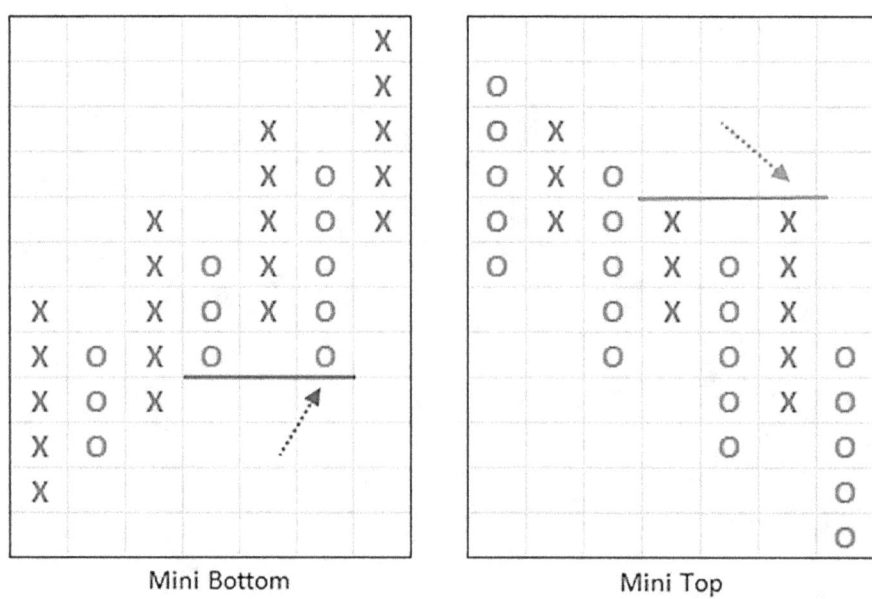

Image 3.1.7: Mini Bottom and Mini Top

Figure 3.1.4 is a 1% × 3 daily chart of Arvind.

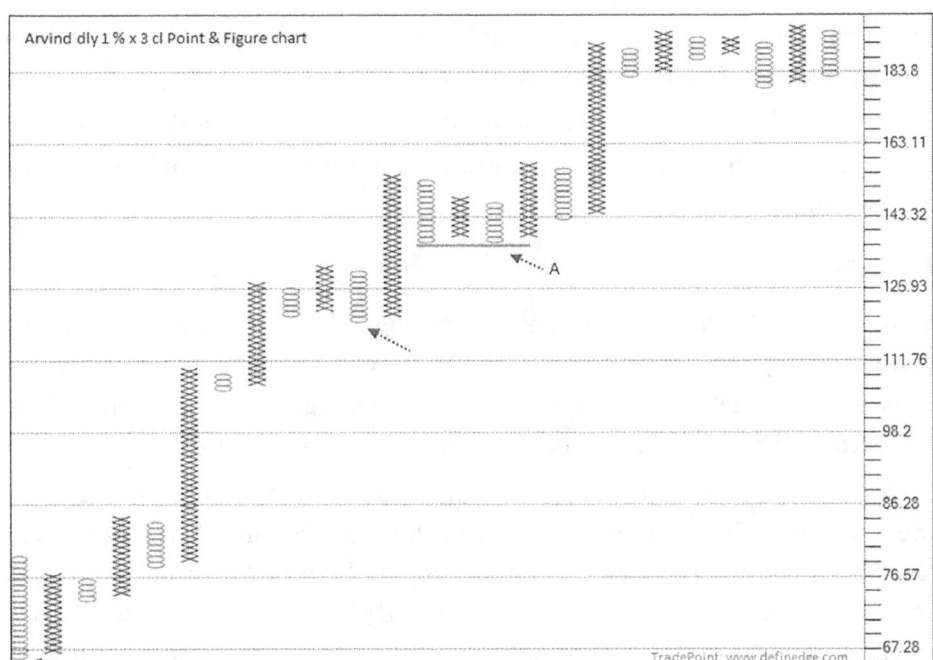

Figure 3.1.4: Arvind daily 1% × 3 cl Point & Figure chart

Even though a Double Bottom Sell pattern was not triggered at Point A, it should still be considered as a valid Mini Bottom because the low of the two columns of 'O' were at the same level.

Identifying Mini Tops and Mini Bottoms is a very useful method of riding the trend. It can also become a well-defined trading method. Long trades can be trailed up until a Mini Bottom gets broken and short positions can be ridden until Mini Top is breached.

The technique of marking Mini Tops and Mini Bottoms is simple but it needs a little practice to get better at identifying it. The chart to mark Mini Tops and Mini Bottoms is given below. Understanding this method is essential before reading the next sections. Figure 3.1.5 is the daily closing price chart of Bajaj Auto plotted using 0.25% × 3 parameters. Mark Mini Tops and Mini Bottoms in the chart as per method discussed above. We will discuss the chart during our next discussion on trend line.

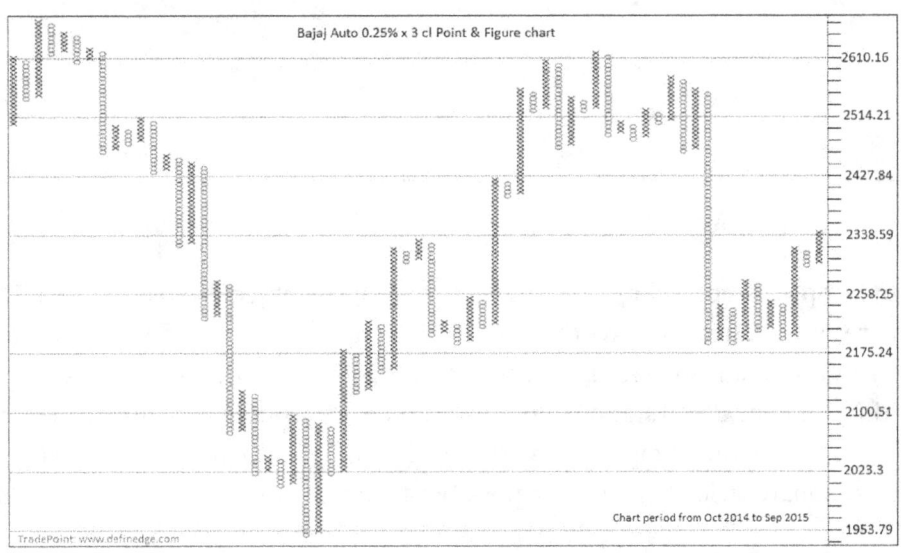

Figure 3.1.5: Bajaj Auto daily 0.25% × 3 cl Point & Figure chart

Summary

- ⅄ Sell pattern turned to Buy in Uptrend completes Mini Bottom and Buy pattern turned to Sell in Downtrend forms Mini Top.
- ⅄ Mini Tops and Mini Bottoms are a method of marking higher low and lower high, made objective.
- ⅄ Riding trend with the help of Mini Tops and Mini Bottoms is a simple yet beautiful method of trading or investing.

3.2: TREND LINES

Trend line is a most basic and widely used tool of identifying trends. We often plot it on usual price–time charts by connecting two highs or lows. Bullish line is drawn by connecting two lows and bearish line is drawn by connecting two high points. Upward line shows higher low formation that reflects rising demand and downward lines show falling peaks that display Downtrend.

These are called subjective trend lines because minimum two points are required to draw the line and the two points are chosen by the user and slope of the line depends on the points chosen. They can be drawn on Point & Figure charts as well by connecting the high or low points of two columns. Figure 3.2.1 shows the subjective trend lines on a P&F chart of HDFC. Line A and D are bullish lines drawn by connecting the bottom points of two columns of 'O'. Line B and C are bearish lines drawn by connecting the peak points of two columns of 'X'. Slope or angle of these lines can be steep or flattish, which depends on the points elected to draw them.

Figure 3.2.1: HDFC daily 0.50% × 3 cl Point & Figure chart

The unique and popular method of P&F charts is 45-degree objective trend lines. Unlike subjective lines, two points are not needed to draw the objective trend line. Just one point is required to draw it because angle of the line is always 45-degrees. Before discussing the points or columns from which these lines should be drawn, understand their importance. A 45-degree line can be drawn only when there is a perfect square; meaning height and width of the box are equal. Unlike usual charts, P&F charts are plotted on fixed square grid; hence, it is possible to draw 45-degree trend lines on these charts. (See Image 3.2.1)

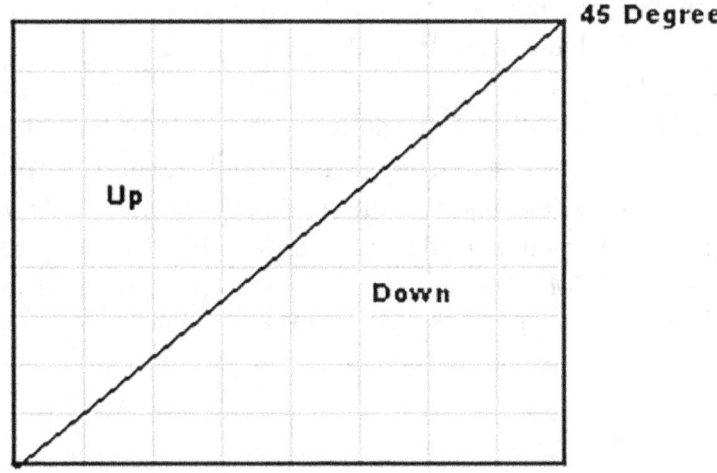

Image 3.2.1: A 45-degree line

The plotting on square grid gives the advantage of objective lines to P&F charts. These lines are more relevant not only because of their fixed angle but also due to their importance from a mathematical perspective. Image 3.2.2 shows two charts showing upward and downward 45-degree lines.

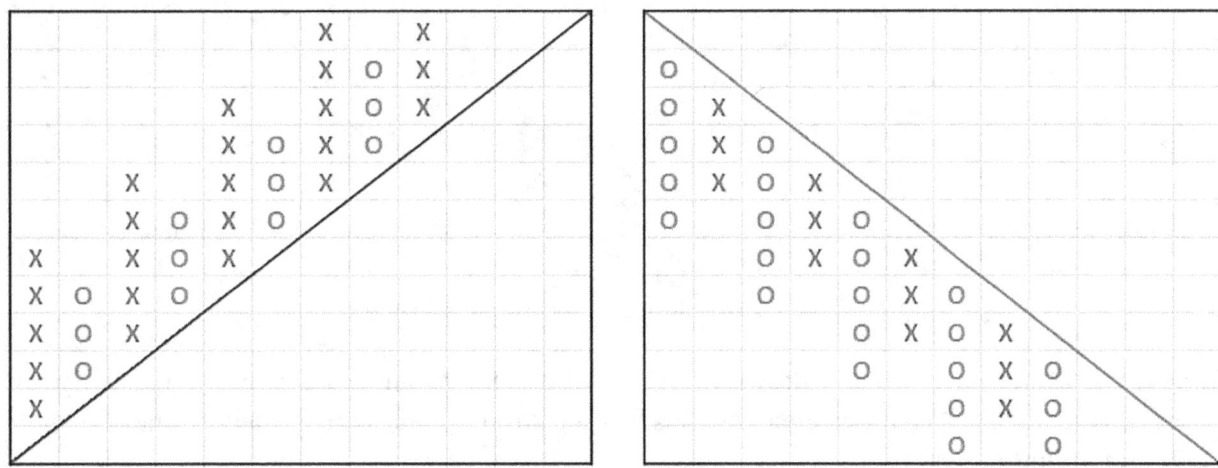

Image 3.2.2: Bullish and bearish 45-degree lines

Note in the image shown above that every new column of 'X' has to go above previous column of 'X' to maintain the 45-degree line. Not only that, the rise has to be at least two boxes more after breakout from previous column of 'X'. Similarly, every column of 'O' has to fall at least two boxes more after breakout from previous column of 'O' to maintain 45-degree bearish line. So it can be said that each column should rise by a minimum one box more to maintain the bullish 45-degree line. It should be maintained on an average basis, so large columns will offset the requirement for falling columns and take the price away from trend line, but pace needs to be maintained to ensure that trend line remains intact. Hence, rises should be more than falls for price to maintain bullish 45-degree line and falls should be more than rises to keep bearish 45-degree line intact –This helps in clear definition and identification of the underlying trend. The 45-degree Downtrend lines are also referred to as 135 degree lines, which is a 45-degree angle turned upside down (180 − 45 = 135). But for simplicity, we will refer both the lines as 45-degree lines. A 45-degree trend line plotted from column of 'O' moving upwards is a bullish line and line plotted from column of 'X' moving downward is a bearish line.

We just need one point to draw the 45-degree line because the slope of the line is already fixed, but it shouldn't be drawn from any column arbitrarily. Major peaks and troughs are the points from which we should plot these lines. If the price rises more than it falls from the important Bottom, it is a sign that Uptrend from that Bottom is strong and the Uptrend is intact. Similarly, bearishness remains in force as long as the price trades below the down-sloping 45-degree trend line drawn from a major or significant high. The traditional technique is to draw just one line at a time. Hence, if 45-degree bullish line is active, bearish line is not drawn and the moment bullish line gets broken, bearish line becomes active. So it means that there will always be one line plotted at any point in time as price is either in Uptrend (above trend line) or Downtrend (below trend line). Refer Figure 3.2.2 shown below.

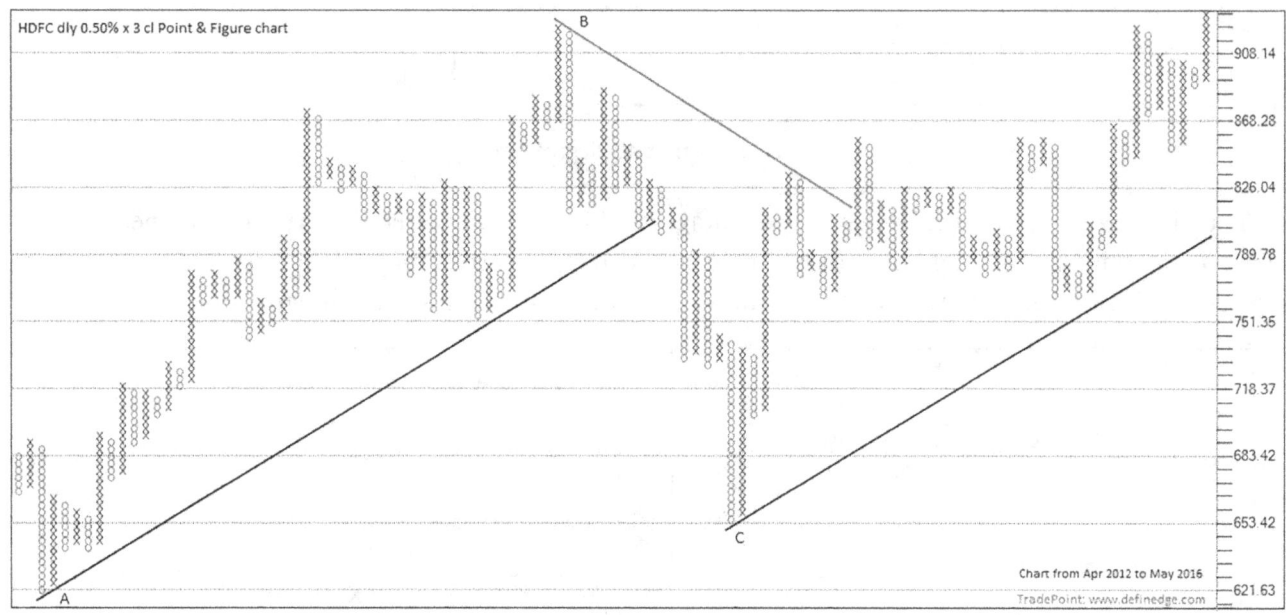

Figure 3.2.2: HDFC daily 0.50% × 3 cl Point & Figure chart

Line A is a 45-degree bullish line drawn from the Bottom. Bearish line is drawn at point B once line A gets broken. Bullish line C is drawn once line B is broken. All these lines are 45-degree lines drawn from Major Tops and Bottoms.

The 45-degree trend lines drawn from important peaks and troughs are very effective and usually respected by the prices. A P&F analyst should always plot it from important peaks and troughs of the chart. Understand that the breach of bullish line indicates that the Bottom from which the line is plotted has become weak and breach of bearish line indicates that the Top from which the line has been plotted has become weak. It informs us that price has failed to maintain the pace or strength of the Major Top or Bottom.

Apart from major peaks and troughs, 45-degree lines can also be plotted from Mini Tops and Mini Bottoms. Bullish 45-degree trend lines can be drawn from all Mini Bottoms and bearish 45-degree lines are drawn from Mini Tops. I would only stick to these rules to draw the 45-degree trend lines; hence, it becomes a complete objective technique where angle of plotting and rules to plot them are certain.

Figure 3.2.3 is a daily 0.50% × 3 P&F chart of Aban that explains the method of plotting the 45-degree trend lines.

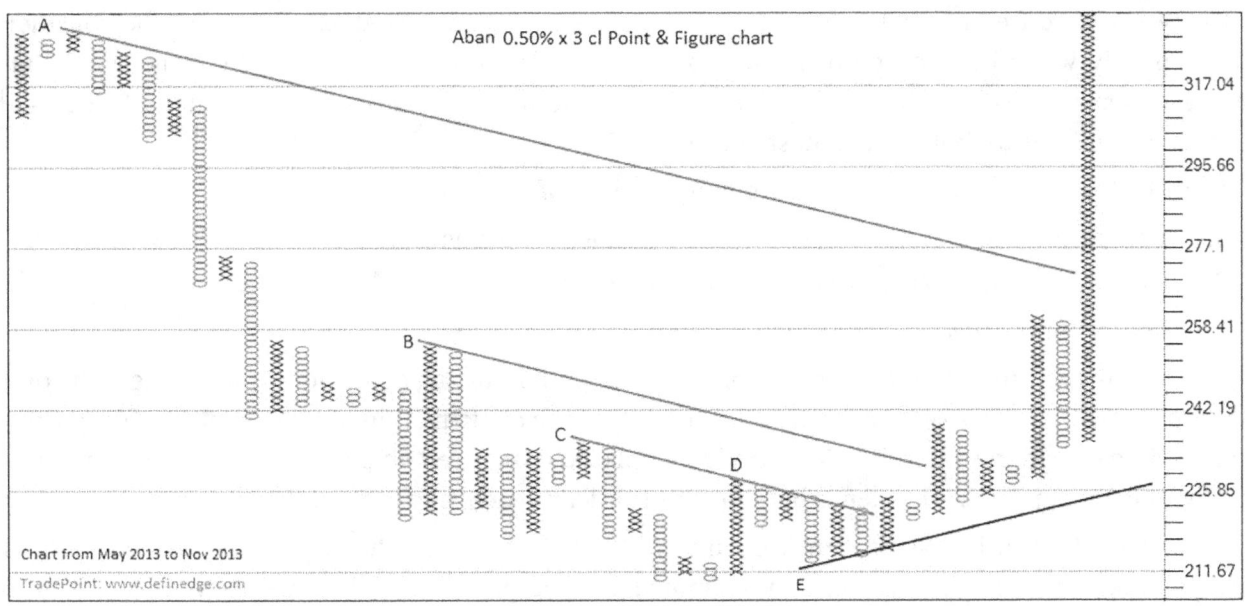

Figure 3.2.3: Aban daily 0.50% × 3 cl Point & Figure chart

Lines A, B, C and D are bearish 45-degree lines drawn from all Mini Tops of the chart. Bullish 45-degree line is drawn once line D is broken. Bullish 45-degree line E was drawn from the last Mini Bottom. It is obvious that a breakout of 45-degree lines will occur earlier than the breach of Mini Tops and Bottoms.

Figure 3.2.4 is the next picture of the same chart. Lines F, G, H and I, shown in the chart, are 45-degree bullish lines drawn from all Mini Bottoms. The strength of these Bottoms remains intact unless the objective line drawn from them gets broken.

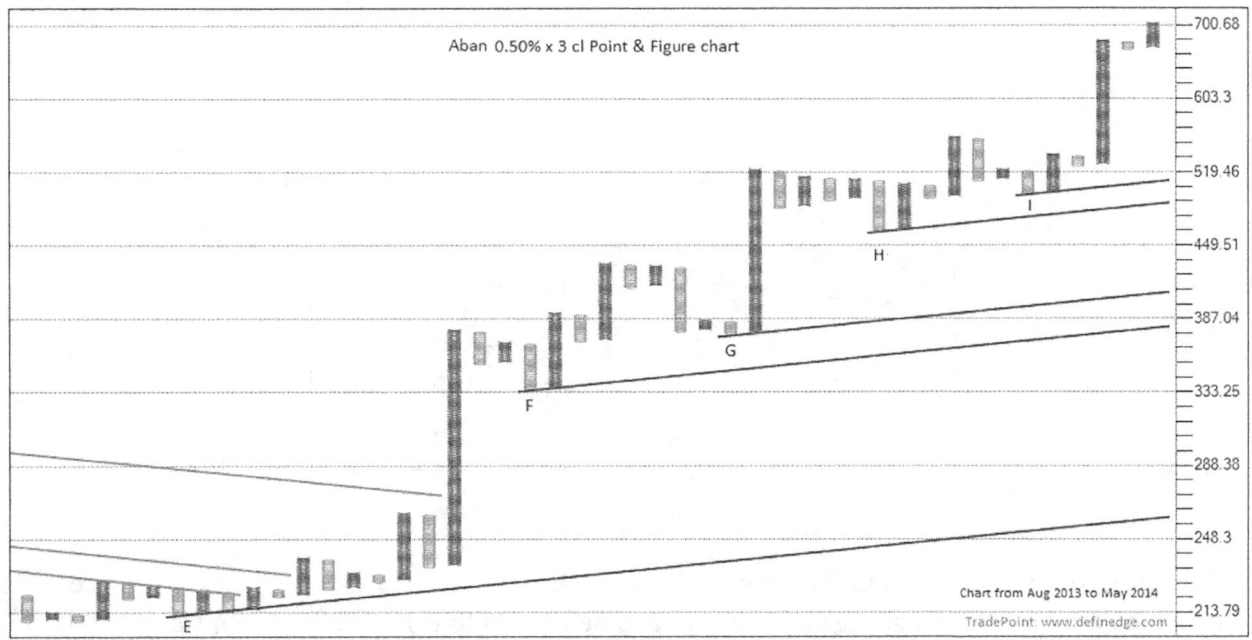

Figure 3.2.4: Aban daily 0.50% × 3 cl Point & Figure chart

Note:

The slope of 45-degree line shown in the charts don't look like 45-degree angles because they are adjusted for the gap between two columns and vertically compressed for better visualization of the charts.

There can be different ways in which trend line breach is considered as valid. It can be considered as broken only when Double Top or Double Bottom signals are formed beyond the trend lines. But at times, initial breach also provides important information to which price reacts immediately. There can be different approaches to deal with it; most keep it flexible.

Broadly, there can be three ways of deciding a breach of the trend line:

1. Basic patterns above/below trend line to consider breach as valid
2. Even one box above/below is a breach of trend line
3. Next column as test of trend line

All of them are valid, but following one principle helps in reducing confusion while taking decisions in real time. As per first approach, one can prefer to wait for the confirmation of Buy or Sell signal after trend line breach to consider it as a valid. Fresh trades are placed only based on patterns. There is less confusion with the second approach – broken is broken. The third approach is explained below.

Consider a bullish line as broken if column of 'O' falls below it. But if price regains strength and bounces back above broken line in the next immediate column of 'X', then draw the new line from the new Bottom marked by the column of 'O'. Keep the bearish line tentative till then and remove it if price bounces immediately.

If price recovered immediately in the next column, then it proves strength of the trend line. Plot new line if price regains the territory immediately, so the trend is considered as reinstated with new column. Hence, the next column is always a test of the breach or breakout, whether it is sustained or proved false. Refer Image 3.2.3.

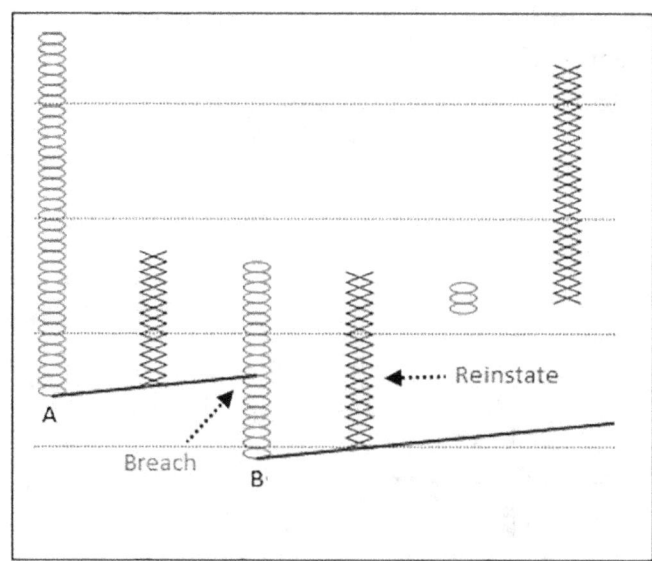

Image 3.2.3: Trend line breach

The bullish trend line drawn in the above image is broken but price again moved inside the trend line in the next column. So trend has regained control and new trend line should be drawn from new Bottom which is at point B. And that should be referred to for further analysis. Vice versa rules are applied for bearish trend lines.

Similarly, treat the breach as valid when column of 'X' rises above bearish line, but draw new line from new column of 'X' if price falls below the trend line in the next immediate column. So, direction of the trend line remains intact with this approach but it is drawn from new column. This eliminates subjectivity while plotting the lines on the chart and makes the trend identification method simple and well defined.

Figure 3.2.5 is a daily 0.50% × 3 P&F chart of Axis bank showing the method discussed above.

Figure 3.2.5: Axis bank daily 0.50% × 3 cl Point & Figure chart

Trend line A is initial 45-degree bullish line. Bullish line B is drawn from Mini Bottom that trails up the Bottom. It got breached but immediately regained at point C from which new bullish line is drawn. Bearish line from point D is drawn once bullish line C was broken. Price attempted breach of line D but reversed immediately in the next column; hence, new bearish line E is drawn from the column that attempted the breakout. Bullish line F is drawn from Mini Bottom that broke eventually, which gave early indication of weakness in the structure. Points G, H, I and J are bearish 45-degree lines drawn from Mini Tops that trailed the downward trend.

From the trading perspective, waiting for confirmation of new column can prove devastating. If price breaks the bullish trend line, then long position should be liquidated and new signal should be awaited. If there is immediate recovery in price after the breach of a trend line in the previous column, the trade can then be reinstated.

It is important to understand that one trend line will always remain active on any P&F chart, either bullish line or bearish line. Hence, any P&F chart will either be in Uptrend or Downtrend at any point in time. Trends being trailed via trend lines are a unique feature of P&F charts.

There are four major methods of using these 45-degree objective lines on charts:

1. Trend Identification

We discussed trend identification and riding technique using Mini Bottoms and Mini Tops in an earlier section. There is a trend reversal when a previous Mini Top or Bottom is breached. We have discussed how 45-degree lines can be plotted at all Mini Tops and Bottoms. Trend can be ridden using them in a similar manner. An Uptrend remains intact unless price falls below bullish line drawn from Mini Bottom and a Downtrend remains intact until price goes above 45-degree trend line drawn from Mini Top. A new line is drawn as soon as new Mini Top or Mini Bottom is formed.

Below are charts that were shown in the section on Mini Tops and Bottoms. Same charts are shown applying 45-degree lines on them as per method discussed above.

Figure 3.2.6: Aban daily 1% × 3 cl Point & Figure chart

Figure 3.2.6 shows P&F chart of Aban with 45-degree lines drawn from all the Mini Tops and Mini Bottoms. We get the early indication of weakness of Tops or Bottoms with the help of trend lines. A trend reversal happens only when the bullish 45-degree line gets broken. The technique is very effective when it comes to riding the trends.

Figure 3.2.7 is the chart of Bajaj Auto that was given previously for exercise. Objective trend lines from all the Mini Top and Mini Bottoms are marked on the chart.

Figure 3.2.7: Bajaj Auto daily 0.25% × 3 cl Point & Figure chart

Point A is where bearish 45-degree trend line was breached, indicating a reversal of the Downtrend. Point B is where trend turned to down when the price fell below the bullish trend line drawn from Mini Bottom. Point C is where Downtrend ended with the breach of bearish trend line.

2. Patterns with Trend Line

If trend can be defined via 45-degree lines, then pattern filtration becomes easy. If trend is up, look for bullish patterns and when it is down, look for bearish patterns. Even basic signals like Double Top and Double Bottom formation can be filtered via trend. We discussed the method to trade these basic signals in Chapter 1; they can be filtered based on 45-degree lines. This is explained in simple words, as follows:

- ⌃ Trade long when Double Top Buy gets formed above trend line.
- ⌃ Exit long trades when Double Bottom Sell signal is formed.
- ⌃ Trade short when Double Bottom Sell signal appears below trend line.
- ⌃ Cover short trades when Double Top Buy signal is formed.

In brief, don't trade short when price is above trend line and avoid long trades when price is below the trend line. Most people are not SAR (Stop and Reverse) traders; hence, trend identification is important for them.

Figure 3.2.8 is the same Bajaj Auto chart that we discussed earlier. Patterns are shown along with trend line on the chart.

Figure 3.2.8: Bajaj Auto daily 0.25% × 3 cl Point & Figure chart

All patterns highlighted in the above chart represent Fresh basic signals. Fresh Sell signals below bearish line and Fresh Buy signals above bullish line are marked on the chart. Pattern A is a Fresh Sell signal. Pattern B is a Bull Trap, which is also a Fresh Sell signal. Pattern C is Bearish Broadening formation. Pattern D is Double Top Buy after Low Pole when trend turned up. Pattern E is Bear Trap in Uptrend. Pattern F is Double Top Buy after Low Pole (Follow-through) that was immediately followed by High Pole. Pattern G is Bear Trap. Pattern H is failure of Low Pole formation and also a Follow-through to 100% Pole appearing along with breach of bullish trend line. Pattern I is a Triangle breakout. The Triangle failed in the immediate column that breached the Downtrend line. Pattern J is a Buy signal above trend line and also a Follow-through to the Bear Trap and Triangle failure patterns.

We discussed earlier that poles can also be used for exiting the trades especially when it comes to system trading. They are also important reference points from the analysis perspective.

Figure 3.2.9 is a P&F chart of Arvind that we discussed in the Mini Top and Bottom section. It is a three-box reversal hourly chart plotted using closing prices with absolute box-value of 1-rupee.

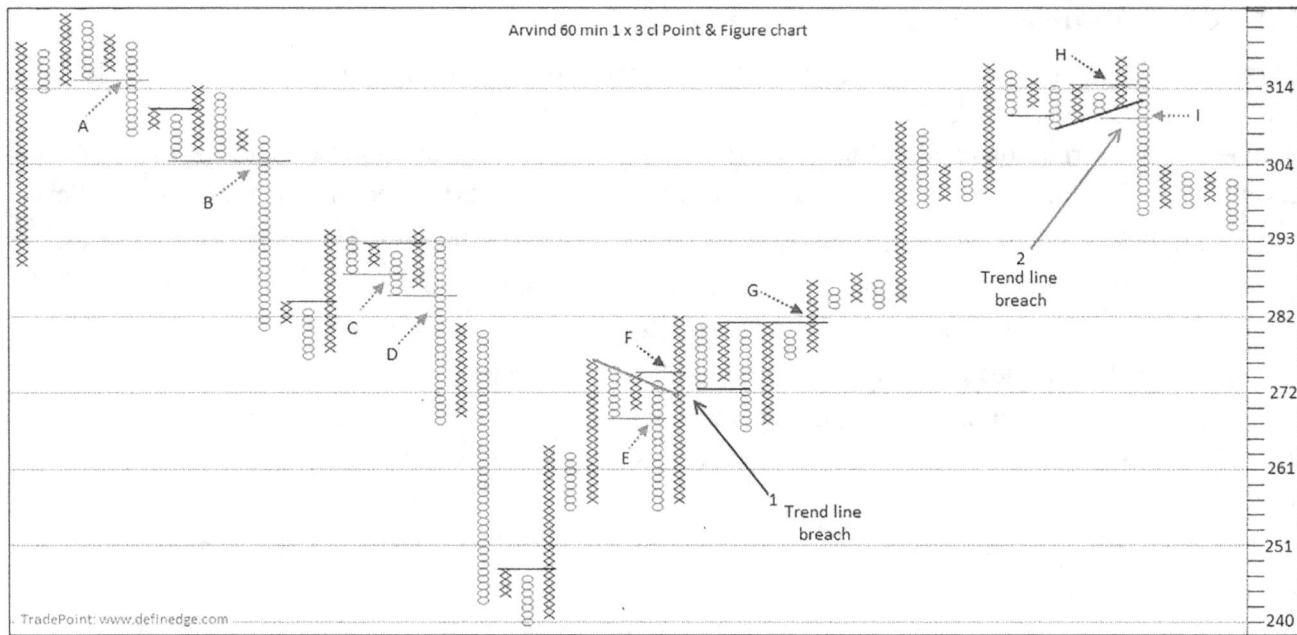

Figure 3.2.9: Arvind 60 min interval 1 × 3 cl Point & Figure chart

There are only two trend lines shown in the chart which are broken lines. Trend line 1 was broken and indicated that the trend has turned up. Trend line 2 was broken, indicating the beginning of a Downtrend. All signals marked in the chart are Fresh signals.

Pattern A is Fresh signal and also a Triangle breakout. Pattern B is Triple Bottom Sell signal below the bearish trend line. Pattern C is Fresh signal and six-column Trap that reversed to Buy in the immediate column. Pattern D is Bearish Broadening formation. Pattern E is bearish three-column Triangle breakout but immediately followed by Low Pole and then bullish 100% Pole appearing above bullish trend line at pattern F. Pattern G is Triple Top Buy pattern above bullish trend line. Pattern H is Fresh Buy signal that got reversed immediately to complete a Bull Trap at pattern I.

Trading the patterns in the direction of the trend improves the trading performance significantly. The advantage with pattern trading is that it has clear rules for entry and exit.

3. Support–Resistance & Pullback

The 45-degree trend lines prove to be very important support and resistance lines. Price tends to bounce from these lines, which displays strength of the Top or Bottom from which they are plotted. Patterns around trend lines should be monitored, which gives opportunity to trade the bounce. Refer Image 3.2.4.

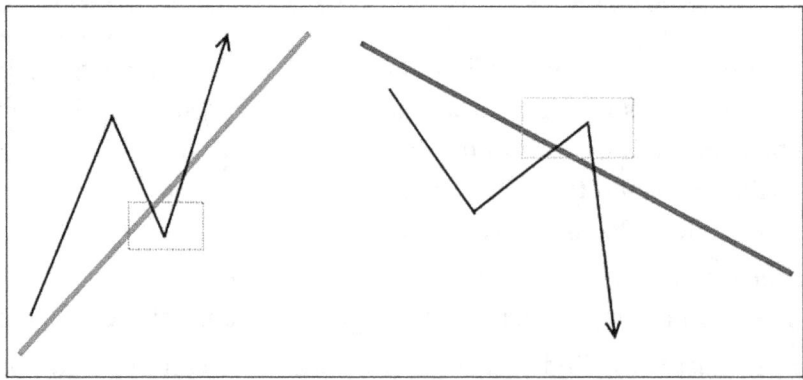

Image 3.2.4: Flirting with trend line

134

See 1% × 3 P&F chart of Dr. Reddy shown in Figure 3.2.10.

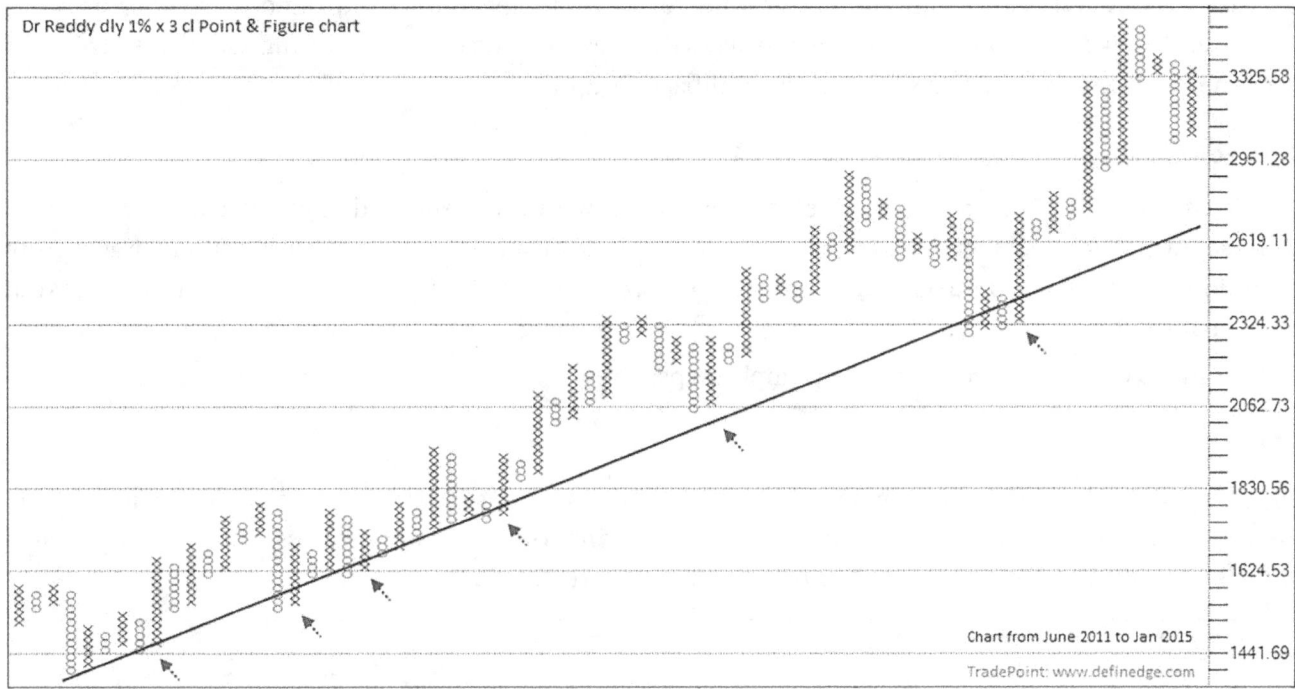

Figure 3.2.10: Dr. Reddy daily 1% × 3 cl Point & Figure chart

The above chart shows numerous opportunities that patterns near trend lines were generated. A bullish formation after a breach of the bullish trend line or bearish pattern after flirting around bearish trend lines are effective pullback setups and often provide trading opportunities during strong trends.

Figure 3.2.11 is a daily 1% × 3 chart of Reliance Capital showing price flirting near 45-degree lines.

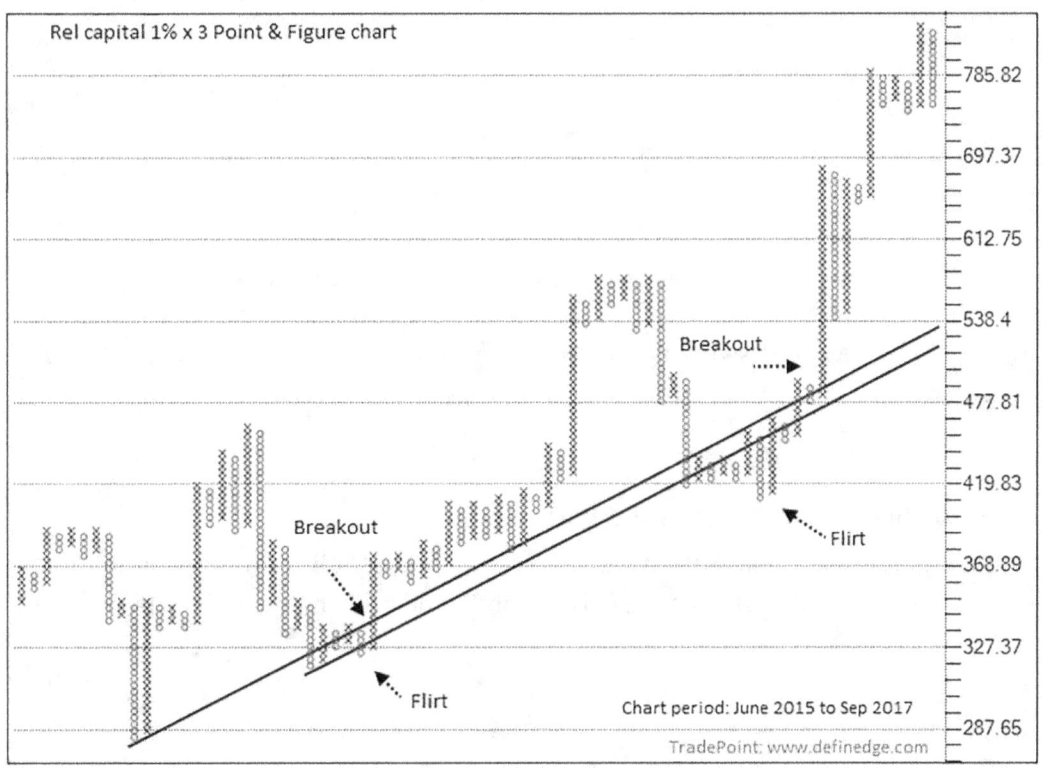

Figure 3.2.11: Reliance Capital daily 1% × 3 cl Point & Figure chart

The 45-degree lines along with patterns can help in ascertaining price supports and resistances. Angle of these lines is certain, they are not flat or non-trending and hence flirting around these lines provides nice pullback trading opportunities. When price witnesses some retracement during established trends, a pattern near trend line becomes an effective pullback setup.

4. Breakout

We discussed that 45-degree trend lines can be trailed with the trend and it can become an effective trend identification technique. If the price is in an Uptrend (trading above bullish trend line drawn from Mini Bottom), then the 45-degree lines drawn from Tops during the Uptrend can be used as a breakout confirmation tool.

Let me explain the concept in three simple steps.

Step 1

Open any Point & Figure chart, and spot the major or significant Tops and Bottoms that can be easily identified. It should be a very simple task as we are looking for Tops and Bottoms that are clearly visible and identifiable. Refer chart of Tata Motors shown in Figure 3.2.12.

Figure 3.2.12: Tata Motors daily 1% × 3 cl Point & Figure chart

Points A, B & C are the major swing points in the above chart. Point A and C are Major Bottoms and point B a Major Top.

Step 2

Plot 45-degree trend line from these Tops and Bottoms.

In the TradePoint software, select the 45-degree trend line and click on that column to draw the line; bearish line will be drawn from the top of the column of 'X' and bullish line will be drawn from the bottom of 'O'.

Figure 3.2.13: Tata Motors daily 1% × 3 cl Point & Figure chart

Bullish lines are drawn from points A and C and bearish line is drawn from point B as shown in the Figure 3.2.13.

Breakout is a point where price has crossed the trend line. It shows that the top or bottom from which it has been broken is weakened for the reasons we discussed earlier in the chapter. In an Uptrend, it would be logical to expect the price to breakout above the down-sloping lines. This is a sort of confirmatory mechanism. The same logic applies in a Downtrend too. Price in a Downtrend will often breach the upsloping trend lines drawn off recent lows.

Figure 3.2.14 is a chart of BHEL showing 45-degree trend lines drawn from important Tops and Bottoms.

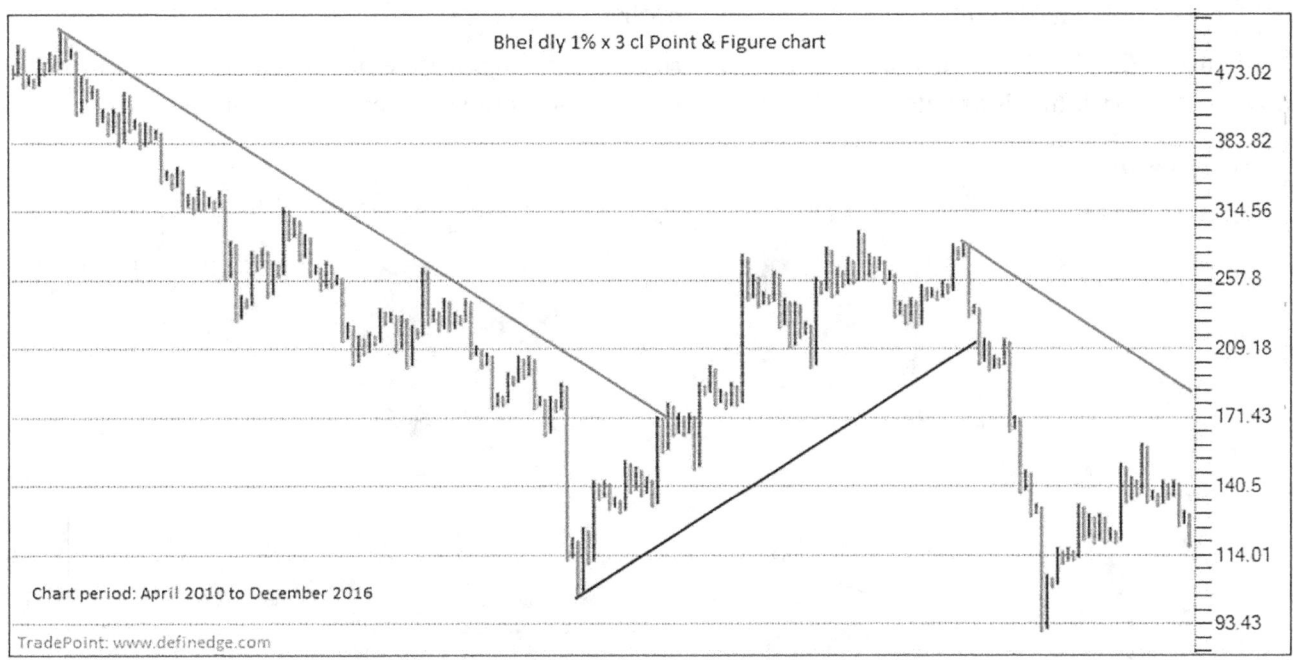

Figure 3.2.14: BHEL daily 1% × 3 cl Point & Figure chart

Step 3

When a trend line is broken, refer to the patterns to identify the trading opportunity. Even the basic P&F patterns will suffice.

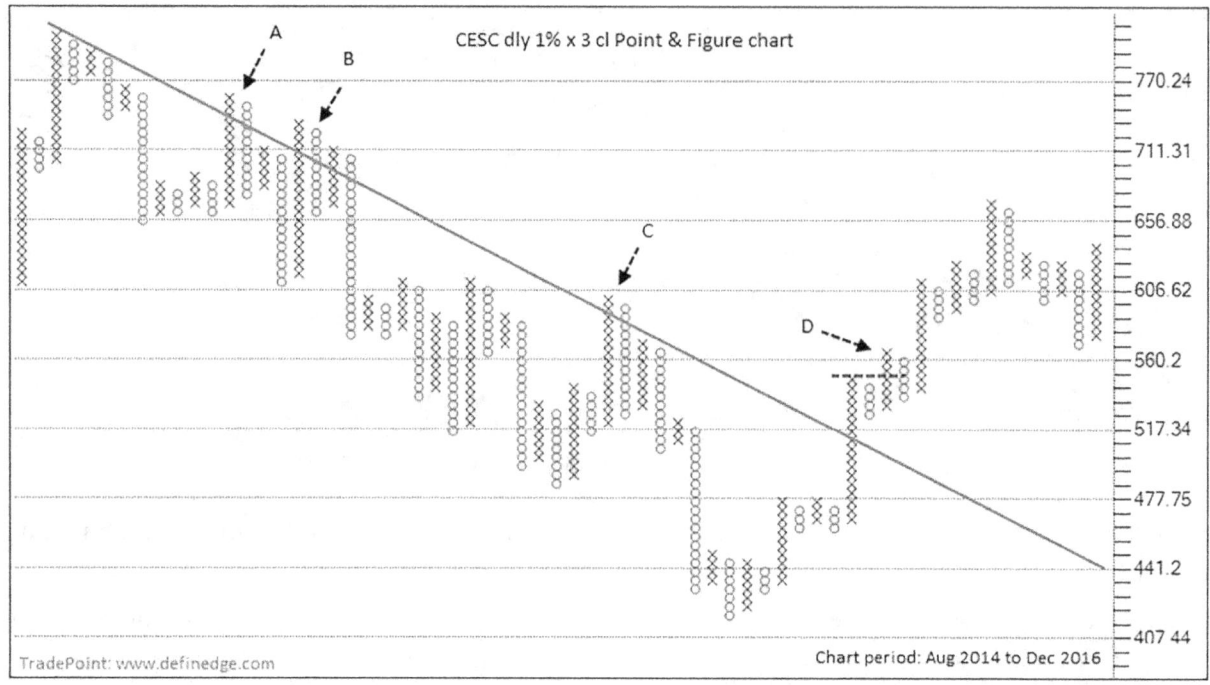

Figure 3.2.15: CESC daily 1% × 3 cl Point & Figure chart

Have a look at the chart of CESC shown in Figure 3.2.15. Point A is when price has crossed above trend line but there was not even a basic Buy signal thereafter. The breach at Point B also failed to generate any bullish pattern. Similar story at Point C. Point D is where basic bullish signal was triggered above the trend line; hence, it becomes an important marker and confirms trend reversal.

Figure 3.2.16 is a P&F chart of Federal bank. Price sustained above the bullish trend line for about 40 months. A bearish line is drawn from significant Top that shows the breakout along with pattern.

Figure 3.2.16: Federal bank daily 1% × 3 cl Point & Figure chart

The method is applicable on all time frames, instruments and box-values. Figure 3.2.17 is a chart of Andhra bank showing bearish trend line and pattern breakout on a 0.25% chart.

Figure 3.2.17: Andhra bank daily 0.25% × 3 cl Point & Figure chart

With this method, we are playing 45-degree trend line breaks. The trend line breakout will be more significant the longer and the more tested the trend line is. If there was a vertical move before breaching the line, there may be some exhaustion in the short term; pattern will help in filtration. Formations such as a Trap or other major patterns make it a more logical and productive setup. Figures 3.2.18 and 3.2.19 are daily charts of PEL and CESC, respectively, showing 45-degree line breakouts along with major patterns.

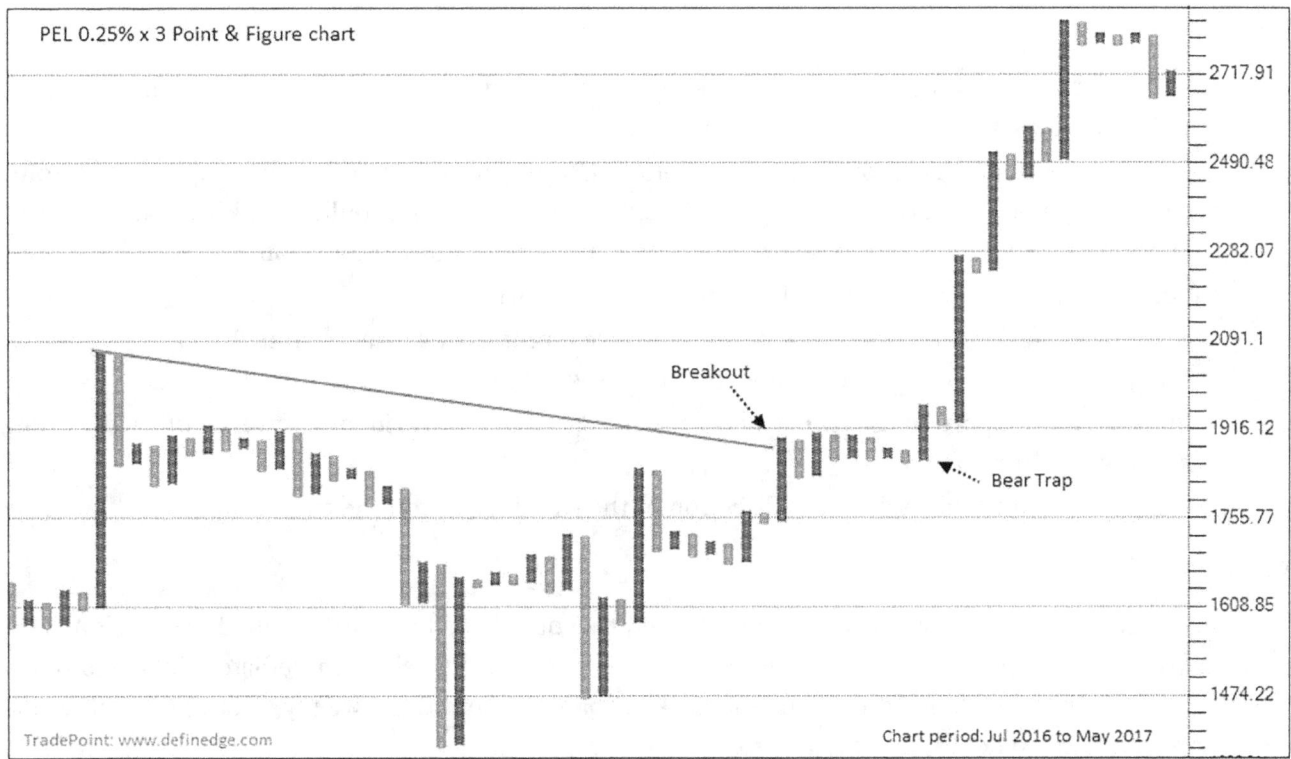

Figure 3.2.18: PEL daily 0.25% × 3 cl Point & Figure chart

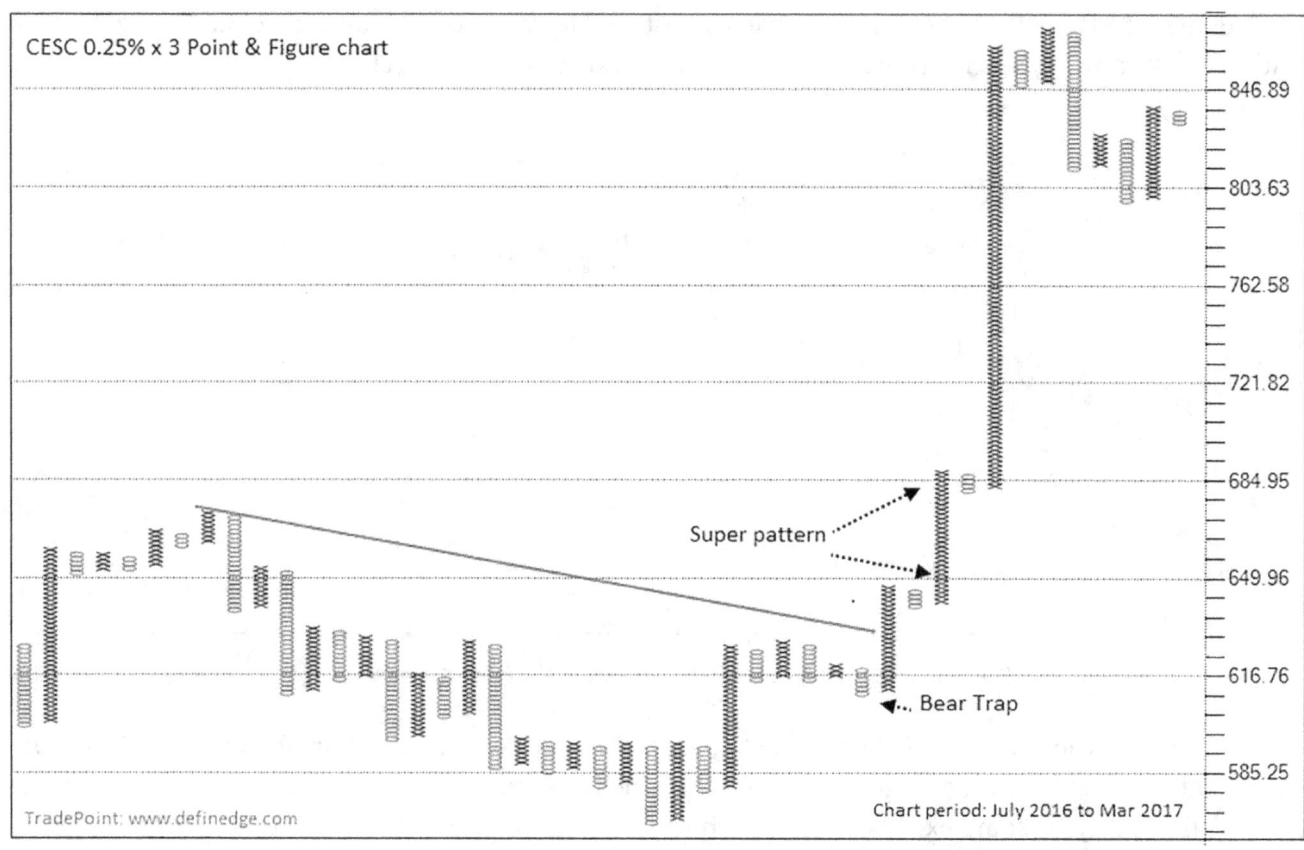

Figure 3.2.19: CESC daily 0.25% × 3 cl Point & Figure chart

Summary

▲ Angle of the 45-degree lines is pre-fixed and hence they are known as objective lines. Unlike subjective lines, they need just one point to draw.

▲ A 45-degree trend line should always be plotted from important and major Tops and Bottoms whenever you come across a P&F chart. It demarcates the chart in bullish and bearish zones and tells you more about the strength or weakness of important Tops and Bottoms.

▲ Plot them from last Mini Top or Mini Bottom of the chart.

▲ Strength of the pattern remains valid unless negated; breach of 45-degree line drawn from the Top or Bottom of the pattern is early indication of the weakness.

▲ There are four important usages of trend lines on P&F charts: trend identification, pattern filtration, pullback and breakout.

▲ Strategy of trading patterns in the direction of the trend has stood the test of time.

3.3: COUNTS

If you meet any market participant, you will often find two questions that can be called the stock market anthem: *kya lagta hai?* (How do you see market?) and the question that shall immediately follow is *kahan tak?* (How far?) Once we identify the trend or breakout pattern, next thing we try to do is to apply some projection technique to determine the target for the move.

Projection or targets is very important when it comes to subjective analysis. System traders react to setups and trade them. They are price followers and exit the trade when price generates the Sell signal. They don't need targets. It is jokingly said that there are only two things possible with a target: either price will exceed or fall short of it. But analysis is performed to form a view or to guess what will happen next. There are several methods of deriving targets from the pattern. The usual method that people follow to calculate target is to measure the height of the pattern and add or subtract it from breakout levels. Fibonacci extension numbers are also useful for such kind of projections.

Count in P&F is a price projection technique. There are two types: horizontal counts and vertical counts. They are applied based on the structure and nature of the formation before breakout. Let us begin the discussion with horizontal counts.

Horizontal Counts

Horizontal count is the oldest method of applying counts on P&F charts. It is applied when the pattern is horizontal in nature before breakout or there is a base creation formation. It is quite similar to the traditional method of extending the width of the pattern to derive the target levels. As the name indicates, count is taken by projecting width of the horizontal pattern to the direction of the breakout.

It is required to identify horizontal formation before taking the count from it. A horizontal pattern can broadly be defined as a pattern that develops between two parallel horizontal lines that display accumulation or distribution phase. There is subjectivity in doing that, but the pattern should have consolidating columns in between. It can be an 'M' or a 'W' type of pattern that shows consolidation between two legs. There are multiple methods of taking horizontal counts, which you can find in old literature on P&F. I am focusing on the best and the most applicable one.

Entry and exit columns need to be defined while determining a horizontal pattern. Entry column is entry into the pattern (not trade) and exit column is exit from the pattern. Exit column must rise above highest 'X' in the pattern so that there is clear setup of price consolidation between entry and exit columns. (See Image 3.3.1)

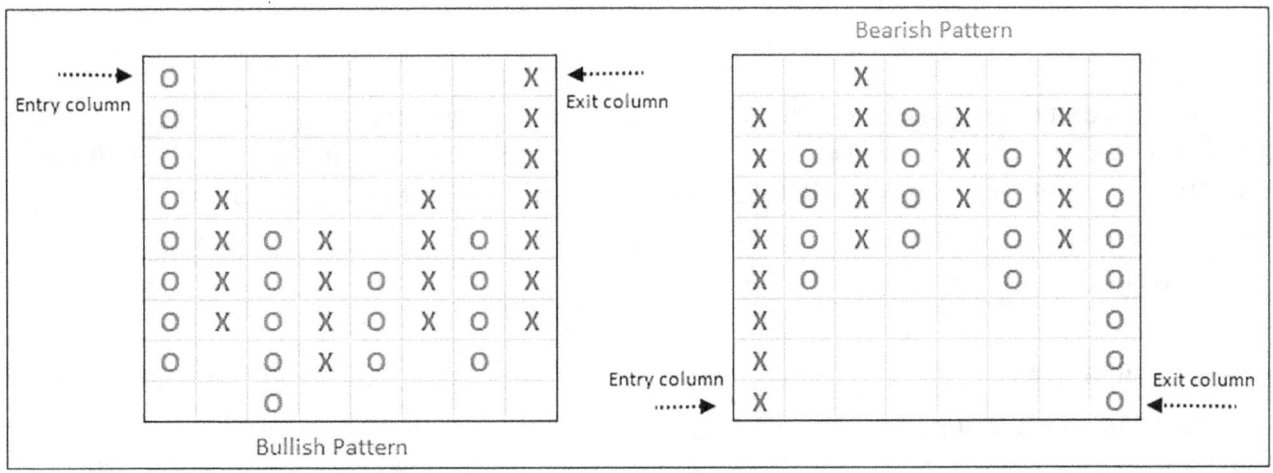

Image 3.3.1: Horizontal pattern

There are many methods of taking horizontal counts and some brilliant research has happened around this. Below is the calculation which is common and more useful.

Formula

Bullish Horizontal count = Bottom of the pattern + (Width of the pattern x Box-value x Reversal value)

Bearish Horizontal count = Top of the pattern − (Width of the pattern x Box-value x Reversal value)

Width of the pattern is the number of columns in the formation. It is multiplied by the box-value and reversal value. The result is added to the Bottom box-price of the pattern to arrive at bullish count and deducted from the Top box-price of the pattern to calculate bearish count.

Bottom box-price of bullish formation is box-price of lowest 'O' of the pattern and Top box-price of bearish pattern is box-price of highest 'X' of the pattern. The number of columns to determine width should include entry and exit columns.

Image 3.3.2 explains the calculation of horizontal count from a consolidating pattern.

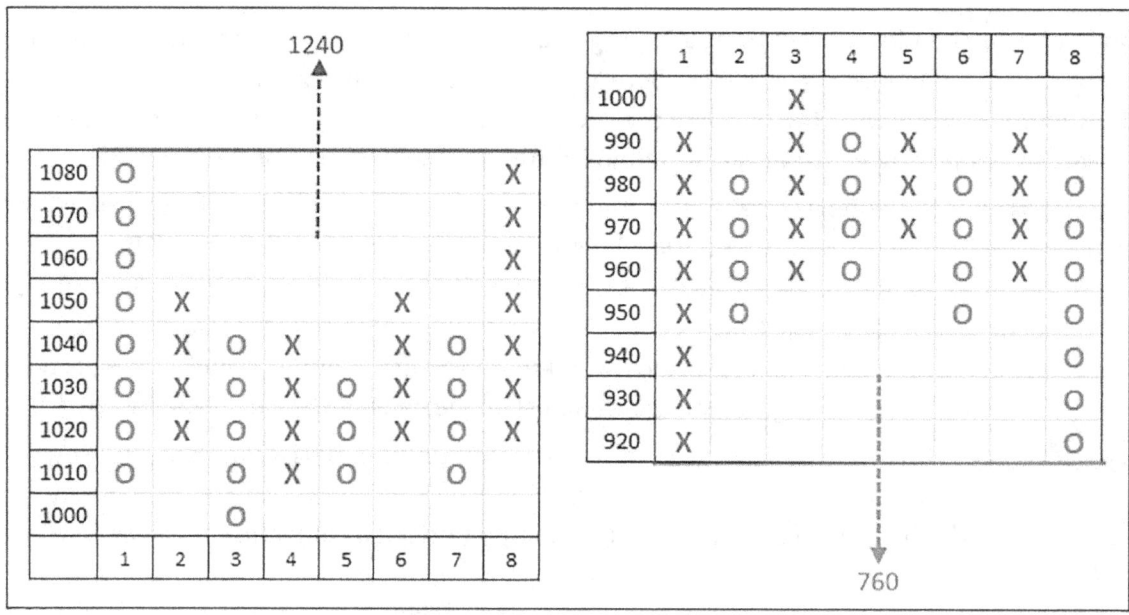

Image 3.3.2: Horizontal counts

Image above shows a bullish and bearish horizontal formation with width size of eight columns. Box-value of the chart is 10 and reversal value is 3. The Bottom of the first chart in the image is 1000 and the Top of the second chart in the image is 1000. Below is the calculation of both the counts as per method discussed above.

Bullish Horizontal count:

8 × 10 × 3 = 240

240 + 1000 = 1240

Bearish Horizontal count:

8 × 10 × 3 = 240

1000 − 240 = 760

A bullish count of 1240 and bearish count of 760 arrived as per above calculation is shown in the chart.

Figure 3.3.1 is the 30 × 3 P&F chart of daily prices of Nifty. There is a 16-column horizontal formation with clear entry and exit columns. The Bottom box-price of the formation is 2550. The target of 3990 shown in the chart can be calculated as per formula shown above.

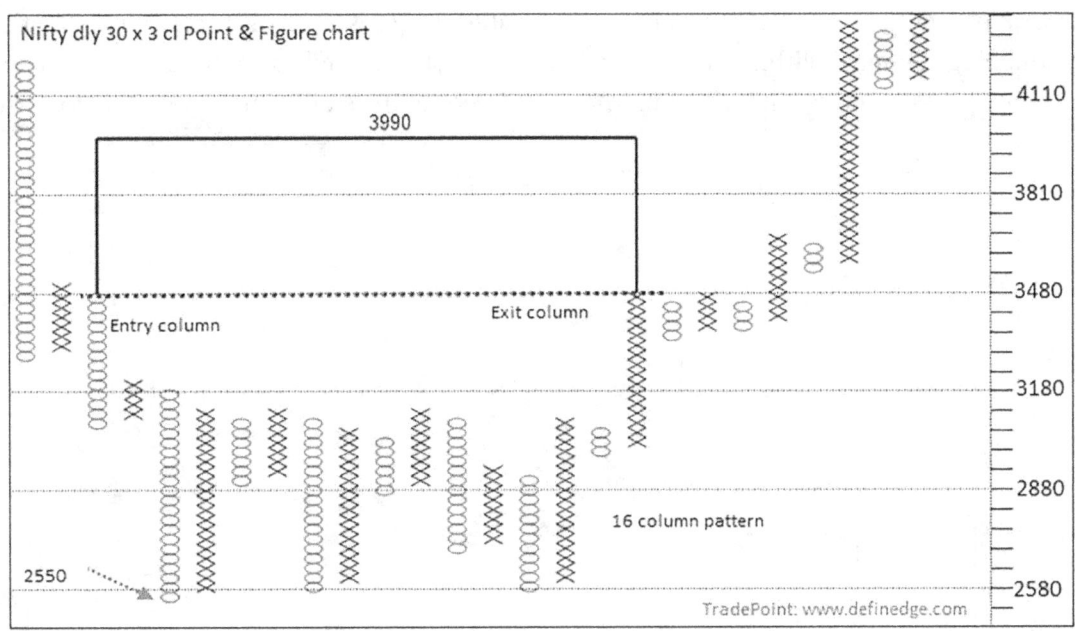

Figure 3.3.1: Nifty daily 30 × 3 cl Point & Figure chart

There can be a smaller horizontal formation within a larger one. If chart shown above is observed carefully, a 16-column formation has an 8-column consolidation formation within the larger 20-column consolidation. They are also valid patterns and qualify for applying horizontal counts. Hence, multiple counts can be taken from the same pattern that can be considered as count 1, count 2 and so on.

Figure 3.3.2 shows the same Nifty chart with multiple horizontal formations. There are patterns within patterns with different widths, but they all qualify for counts. Horizontal counts from each of them are shown on the chart.

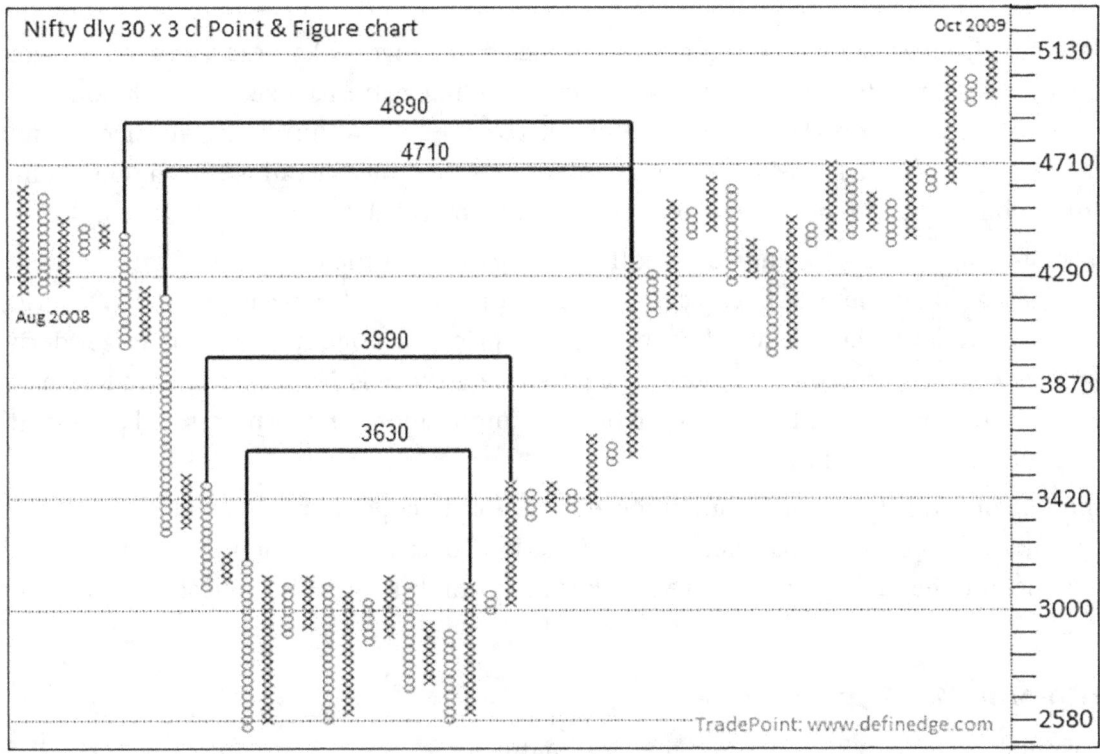

Figure 3.3.2: Nifty daily 30 × 3 cl Point & Figure chart

Figure 3.3.3 is a daily 1% × 3 P&F chart of JP Associates. There is a larger horizontal formation shown with entry and exit columns, within which there are smaller horizontal formations as well. The multiple downside counts arrived with such kind of method can become the significant reference points in future.

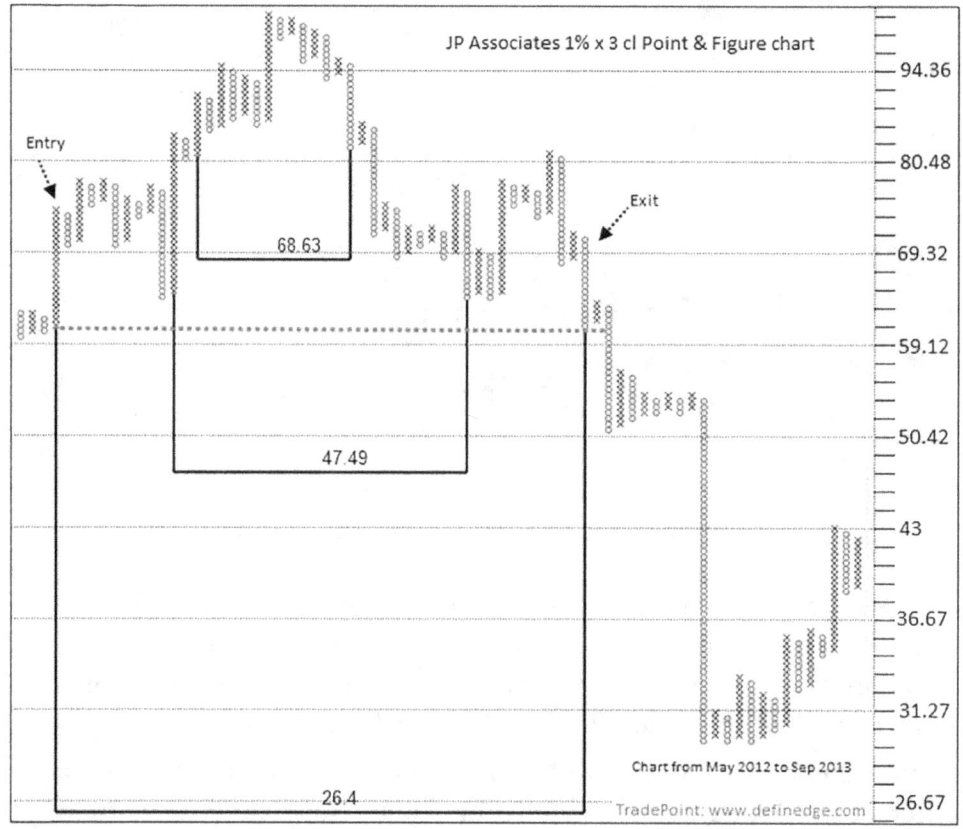

Figure 3.3.3: JP Associates daily 1% × 3 cl Point & Figure chart

The larger width horizontal formation shown in the chart above looks like Head & Shoulders pattern. Horizontal patterns are often H&S, Cup-handle or rounding patterns like accumulation–distribution patterns from which horizontal count can be calculated. These Western price formations are clearly visible on P&F charts as well. Noiseless manner of plotting is the added advantage of finding them on these charts. Horizontal counts can be applied to them to derive their P&F targets.

Horizontal count method extends the width of the pattern in the direction of the breakout. If base is strong, meaning that if some serious accumulation or distribution has occurred, then the price should be able to accelerate up to the calculated count or target price. Can one trade for the target derived from these methods with stop based on pattern negation? The answer is No. From the trading perspective, I recommend trading patterns only. Counts can become important reference points and provide direction. Patterns are guides that help in trading them.

The method of taking horizontal count is more applicable to larger box-values and patterns with larger width. It cannot be applied to small horizontal formations because extension of width from bottom of them will fall within the pattern itself. I have tweaked the formula to make it applicable on small horizontal formations.

Horizontal Count – Aggressive

Small horizontal patterns will not throw up meaningful projection if the width is projected from the bottom of the pattern. And I always felt there is usefulness in deriving horizontal counts even from small formations. To find a solution, a small tweak was considered in the formula. Instead of adding to the bottom of the formation to arrive at bullish count, it is added to the breakout level for generating the count. It shows comparatively aggressive counts and hence the name.

Small horizontal formations are basically the patterns that consolidate between five and eight columns. There can be Traps, Triangles, Broadening formations or their variations. Width of such patterns can be extended further to take a count after breakout. This method plots aggressive counts but suits the smaller width formation where usual horizontal count is not useful.

The logic behind adding it to breakout level is that the thrust can result in quick move, which should achieve 100% of entire width. This is an idea derived from traditional price projection methods. Below are the charts showing counts from such small horizontal formations.

Figure 3.3.4 is the chart of daily prices of Financial Technology plotted with 1% × 3 parameters.

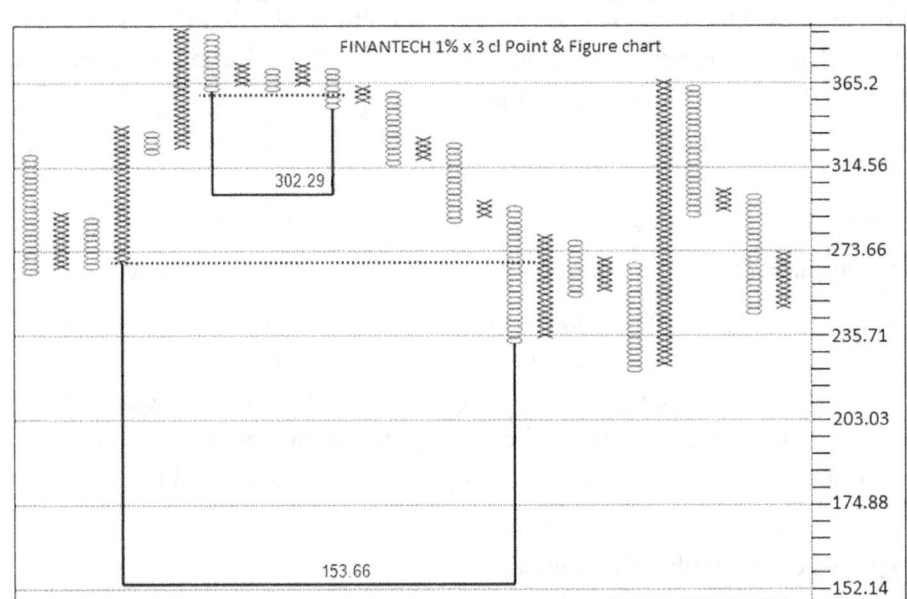

Figure 3.3.4: Finan tech daily 1% × 3 cl Point & Figure chart

Horizontal count – aggressive is applied on both the patterns shown in the chart. The horizontal pattern shown in the chat is significant. But, the breakout from the pattern is too far away from the Top or Bottom. The usual horizontal count target will not be useful or significant in such cases.

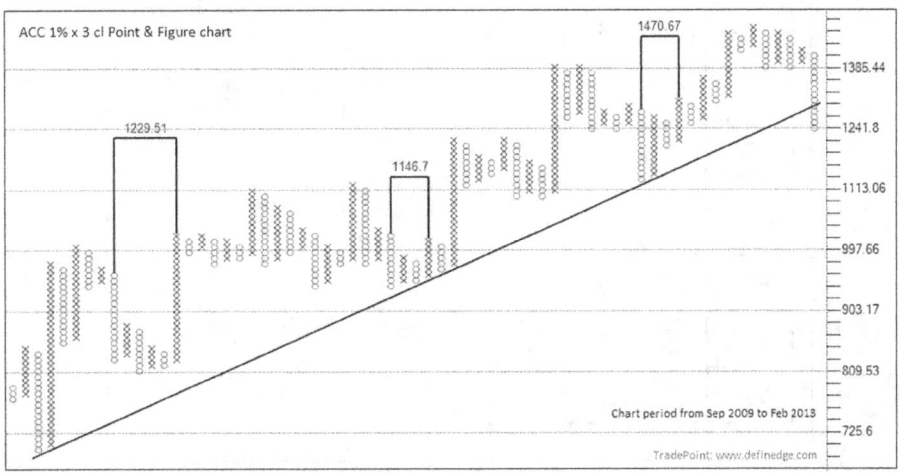

Figure 3.3.5: ACC daily 1% × 3 cl Point & Figure chart

Figure 3.3.5 is a 1% × 3 chart of ACC. Aggressive horizontal method of counting is applied to small formations that occurred above bullish trend line.

This counting method should be applied only when the width is small and there is a breakout. It should usually be more than a four-column formation. Ideal is a seven to eight column setup having a formation of Follow-through or pattern failure within it. Breakout after such kind a scenario is more effective. The method is very useful when applied on small patterns using large box-values.

Bullish horizontal counts remain valid so long as the Bottom of the formation is not broken and Bearish horizontal counts remain valid so long as the Top of the formation is not taken out.

Vertical Counts

This is my favorite method of taking the counts, mainly because it is objective in nature. Vertical counts are a method of projecting targets from single P&F column. A column of 'X' is always projected toward upside and a column of 'O' will always be projected toward downside. The column selection is not subjective and the formula for calculating the projection is detailed below.

Formula

Bullish Vertical count = Bottom of the pattern + (Length of the pattern × Box-value × Reversal value)

Bearish Vertical count = Top of the pattern – (Length of the pattern × Box-value × Reversal value)

Bullish count is always taken from the column of 'X' and Bearish count is always taken from column of 'O'. Length of the pattern is number of boxes in the column. It is multiplied by the box-value and reversal value and added to the bottom of the pattern to arrive at bullish count. It is deducted from the top of the pattern to arrive at bearish count. Bottom of the pattern is the bottom price of previous column of 'O' in case of bullish count. And Top of the pattern is Top price of previous column of 'X' in case of bearish count.

Image 3.3.3 explains the formula discussed above.

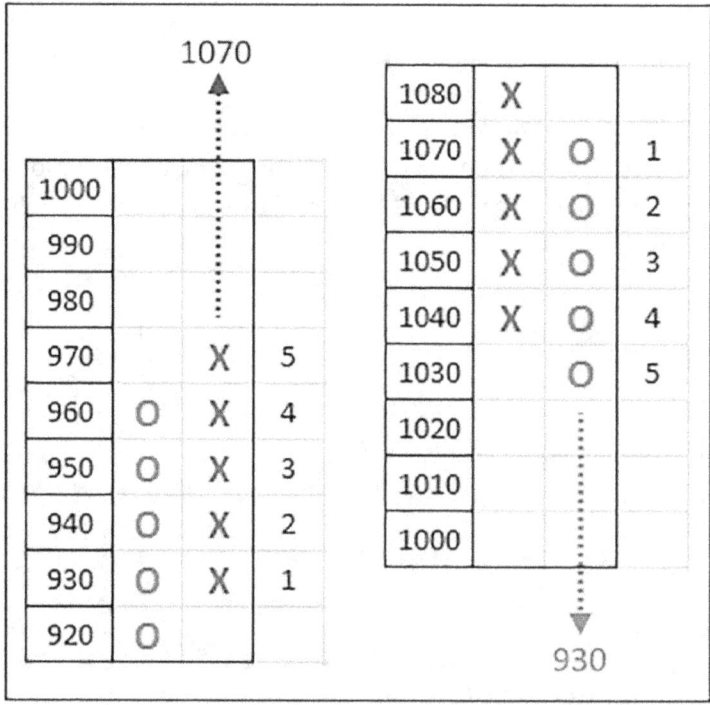

Image 3.3.3: Vertical counts

Length of both the columns from which count is taken is 5, that is, the number of boxes in the column. The Bottom of the first pattern is 920, which is the Bottom price of its previous column of 'O'. The Top of the second pattern is 1080, being the top box-price of its previous column of 'X'. The charts are plotted with 10 × 3 parameters. The calculation of both the counts is given below.

Bullish Vertical count

5 × 10 × 3 = 150 (Length of the pattern × Box-value × Reversal value)

150 + 920 = 1070

Bearish Vertical count

5 × 10 × 3 = 150

1080 − 150 = 930

This is how we can project the column of 'X' higher and column of 'O' lower. But the projection cannot be taken from every column. There are rules to define the column that qualifies for calculating vertical counts. It is basically applied to the column occurring after a significant Top or Bottom. A column of 'X' coming after Bottom should be projected higher and a column of 'O' coming after Top should be projected lower (see Image 3.3.4).

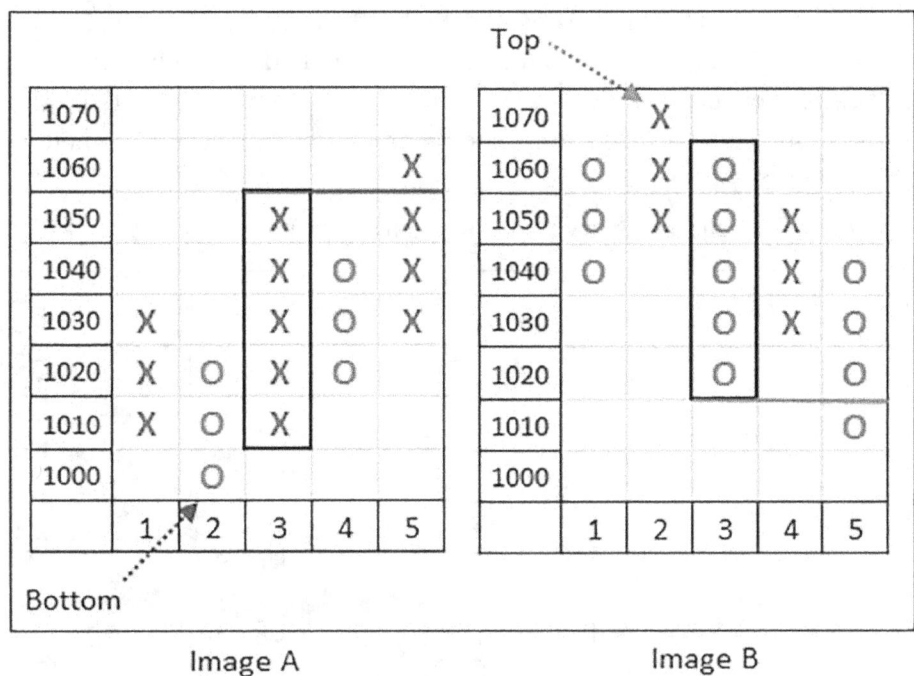

Image 3.3.4: Bottom and Top

Bottom of the bullish formation shown in the first figure is 1000, being the Bottom box-price of column 2. Bullish vertical count is applied from the column of 'X' at 3 coming after forming the Bottom. Top of the bearish pattern in the second figure is 1070, being the Top box-price of column 2. The bearish vertical count is calculated using the column of 'O' at 3, and is deducted from the top of the previous column high at 1070.

Every vertical count has two stages: Establishment and Activation. Upside count gets activated when high of the column from which count is established is broken by one of the subsequent columns. The breakout need not be in the immediate column but could occur in any of the subsequent columns. The only condition is that the recent low of the pattern must not be breached before the breakout happens.

Similarly, downside count gets activated when Low of the column from which count is taken is broken without the price going above the Top of the pattern.

Refer to the first figure in Image 3.3.4 again. Column 3 qualifies for calculating the vertical count and the high of this column is 1050. The count is an established count initially; it gets activated when any subsequent column of 'X' goes above 1050, which is the top or the high price of the column 3. It happened at column 5 in the image shown above. It becomes Double Top Buy formation because the Top price of the column gets broken in the immediate column, but it may not happen always. The breakout above the high price of the qualifying column can happen in any subsequent columns as well. The only condition is that the bottom of the pattern, 1000 in this example, should not be breached.

Refer the second figure in Image 3.3.4; Bottom price of the column 3 from which bearish count is applied is 1020. The count gets activated when this bottom gets broken subsequently, which happened at column 5. The breakout is valid if it happens before breaching the Top of the pattern, which is at 1070.

Only activated counts are important and valid. Established but nonactivated counts should be removed from the chart. In fact, they should not be plotted or calculated in the first place.

Vertical counts are applied from the columns appearing after significant Tops and Bottoms. The Activation stage confirms the strength of the first leg and makes it a valid case for calculating targets.

Counts should be applied from Major Tops and Bottoms. They can be calculated from Mini Tops and Mini Bottoms as well. Bullish vertical count should be applied from column of 'X' that occurred after Mini Bottom. Bearish vertical count should be applied from column of 'O' that occurred after Mini Top. Hence, columns from which vertical counts should be plotted are clearly defined, which makes the method completely objective.

Figure 3.3.6 is a 10 × 3 P&F chart of Nifty plotted on daily closing prices.

Figure 3.3.6: Nifty daily 10 × 3 cl Point & Figure chart

All bullish counts shown in the chart are plotted from the column of 'X' formed after Bottoms/Mini Bottom that got activated subsequently. Figure 3.3.7 is a daily 0.25% × 3 P&F chart of Andhra bank. All vertical counts shown in the chart are active counts.

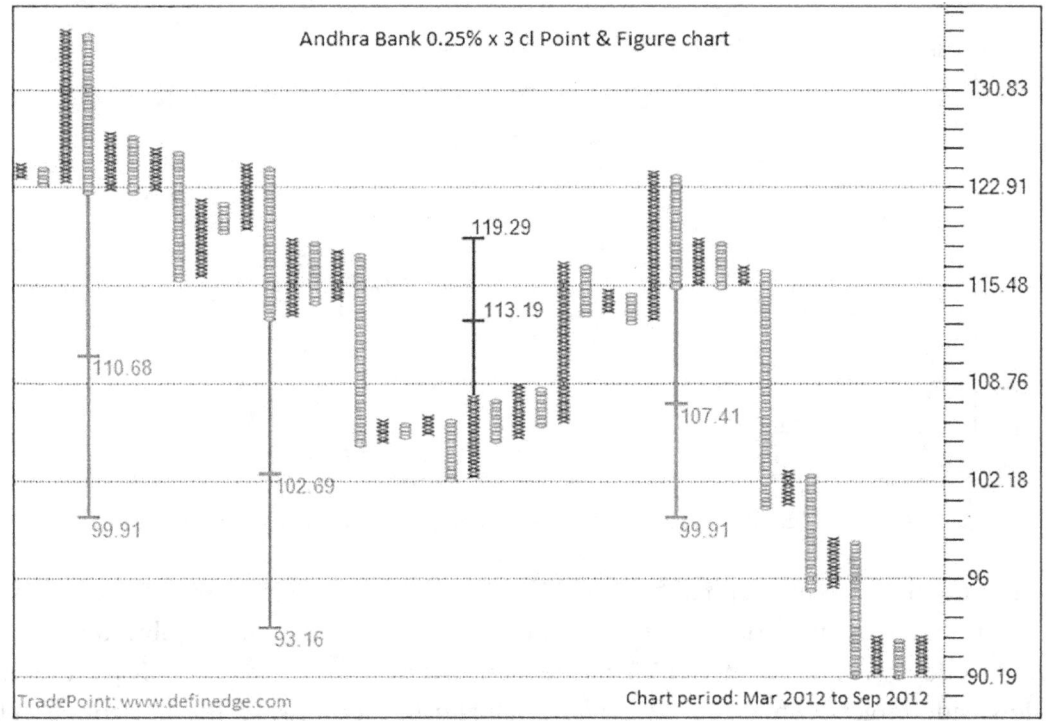

Figure 3.3.7: Andhra bank daily 0.25% × 3 cl Point & Figure chart

Apart from plotting trend lines Mini Top and Mini Bottom may be used to calculate vertical counts too. Vertical counts extend the first leg after forming important peak or trough; hence, the count is derived based on strength of the first leg and activation stage ensures that there is Follow-through. The counts in the direction of the trend are stronger counts and have higher probability of being achieved. Counts against the trend are less relevant unless there is a trend reversal.

Figure 3.3.8 is the same Bajaj Auto chart that we used during the discussion on Mini Top and Bottoms and 45-degree trend lines. The same chart with trend line and vertical counts is featured below.

Figure 3.3.8: Bajaj Auto daily 0.25% × 3 cl Point & Figure chart

Figure 3.3.9 is a P&F chart of BHEL plotted using 0.25% box-value on closing prices of every minute.

Figure 3.3.9: BHEL-I futures 1 min interval 0.25% × 3 cl Point & Figure chart

Downside vertical counts are applied from all Mini Tops in the chart. Bearish horizontal count is also plotted from horizontal ranging price action seen at the Top, which suggests distribution. The horizontal count projected a downside target of 134.75. Subsequent counts taken from Mini Tops resulted in fresh successive downside targets, while the price was gradually headed toward the horizontal count target price of 134.75. The trend lines from Mini Tops confirm the Downtrend and help in riding the trend, using these targets as a guidepost. Patterns A and B are downside breakouts after Triangle. Patterns C and D are Bull traps in the Downtrend.

This makes the entire setup well defined and objective in nature. We have discussed clear and objective ways to identify trend, various methods to ride the trend, identify Mini Tops and Bottoms, patterns in the direction of the trend and calculating counts or targets. All these aspects can be easily implemented in any given P&F. They can be applied on all instruments, box-values and time frames. Practice is what is required for successful execution.

All bullish active counts are valid unless the Bottom from which they are calculated is broken and all bearish active counts are valid unless the Top from which they are calculated is broken. The terminology along with a brief explanation with regard to counts is as follows:

Negation of counts: If bottom of column from which upside count is taken gets broken, then the upside counts gets negated; vice versa for negation of downside counts.

Closed counts: Counts which are achieved are known as closed counts.

Open counts: Counts that are neither achieved nor negated are known as open counts.

Counter-trend counts: Counts against the direction of the trend.

The P&F counts are reliable targets in most cases. They can certainly be important reference points for future. Patterns in direction of active counts should be the focus point for traders. Look for positive counts when price is above 45-degree trend line and look for negative counts when price is below 45-degree trend line. Open counts should be kept in screen and closed or negated should be removed. Sometimes multiple counts get opened on both the sides, which happens usually during the period of consolidation. Keep referring to valid and active counts until there is a breakout, resulting in the invalidation of the counts in one direction.

Note that 'X' or 'O' occurring at same level are considered as Mini Tops and Mini Bottoms; hence, counts and trend line from those points should always be plotted.

Vertical counts can also be plotted from significant columns or from next column if qualified column is small, or a column that displays breakout from horizontal base, etc. I have kept things simple and objective, which according to me is best. Variations and experiments can be done after gaining experience and practicing the basic things.

Give more preference to vertical counts, practice them to begin with. Plot counts in the direction of the trend line whenever they get activated. At times, the column qualified for applying the vertical count happens to be very long. It shows targets that are too far from current levels, which looks fascinating but is not of much use. Though people like to see or publish charts showing huge targets, they have very little practical value.

To keep the things relevant, the technique mentioned below should be used to plot counts when column is long.

Vertical Count – Conservative

Unusual targets get displayed from long columns, which are often the exaggerated counts having limited use from the trading perspective. This also happens when counts are applied on higher box-values.

Hence, I prefer taking vertical count – conservative from such columns. The conservative count is calculated by tweaking one parameter in the formula that is used in the usual vertical count. Two-thirds of the reversal value is used for multiplication instead of full reversal value, all other things remaining the same. So it provides a lower and conservative count compared to the one derived from the usual formula.

Figure 3.3.10 is a 1% × 3 P&F chart of daily closing prices of HDIL showing vertical count – conservative applied from the column of 'X'.

Figure 3.3.10: HDIL daily 1% × 3 cl Point & Figure chart

To decide if a column is long or not, is quite subjective in nature and depends on the box-value. Conservative vertical counts are basically equal extension of the column. It is a sensible approach to apply this conservative method for counter-trend counts. It is not that counts derived from the usual method are non-achievable. The best method is to plot both the counts and treat them as Target 1 and Target 2.

Figure 3.3.11 is a 0.50% × 3 P&F chart of Auro Pharma.

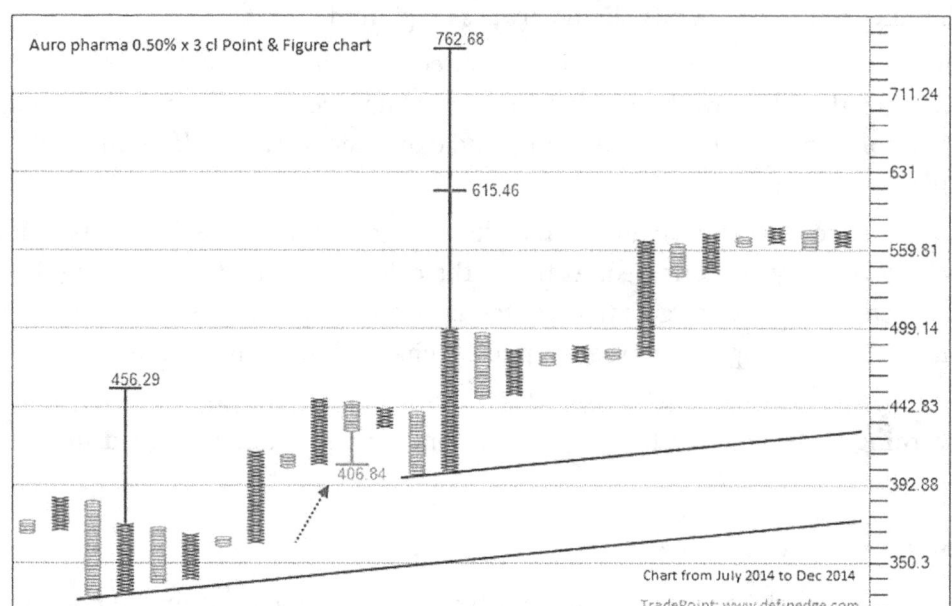

Figure 3.3.11: Auro Pharma daily 0.50% × 3 cl Point & Figure chart

Downside count shown by arrow in the chart is against the trend; hence, vertical count – long is applied. Both the counts are applied from the bullish column that appeared after Mini Bottom. They are treated as first and second target derived from the column.

Vertical count – conservative and count-clusters are more reliable and high-probability targets. When different counts form a confluence at a price zone, it is called a clustered-count area.

Figure 3.3.12 is chart of Bharat Finance showing count cluster where there is sort of confluence between the first count and second count plotted from two different columns.

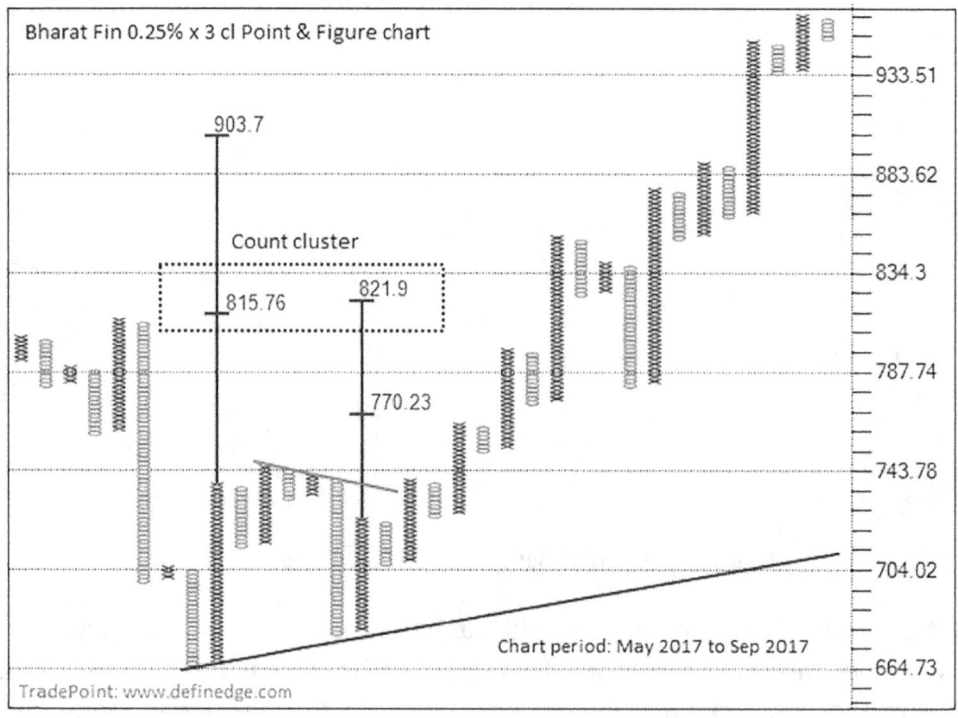

Figure 3.3.12: Bharat Finance daily 0.25% × 3 cl Point & Figure chart

Andhra bank chart discussed earlier is featured again in Figure 3.3.13 with both the counts applied.

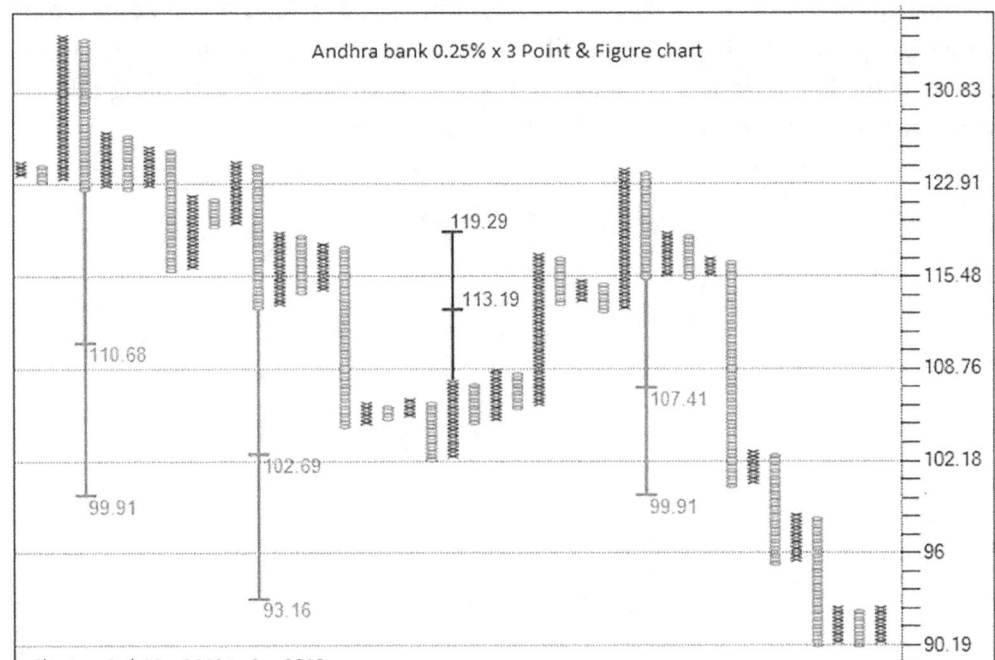

Figure 3.3.13: Andhra bank daily 0.25% × 3 cl Point & Figure chart

The benefit of conservative count can be observed in the chart shown above. Price achieved bearish conservative count at 102.69, turned positive, generating bullish counts which were achieved. Eventually, second bearish counts were also achieved. Notice the count cluster near 100 that was achieved.

Apart from using vertical count as a potential target, it can also be viewed as a technique to gauge the state or strength of the trend. When new bullish counts get activated, which are higher than previous open bullish counts, then the probability of achieving the previous open counts is higher. Negation of bullish count in an Uptrend and a bearish count in Downtrend are early indications of a trend reversal.

Combination of patterns, 45-degree lines and counts are traditional Point & Figure techniques. When all are in sync, it is a clear chart and should be traded. Inconsistencies should be ignored. The concepts discussed till now are more than sufficient to trade any type of instrument, box-value and time frame.

Summary

- ⅄ Horizontal and aggressive horizontal counts are subjective methods of projection.
- ⅄ Vertical counts should be plotted from Major Top or Bottom and Mini Top or Bottom.
- ⅄ Conservative counts should be used for counter-trend counts.
- ⅄ Only open counts should be kept on the chart.
- ⅄ Conservative vertical counts and count cluster indicate reliable targets.
- ⅄ Trade clear charts where count, trend line and patterns are in sync.

3.4: ANCHOR POINT

Anchor point is the most amazing and underused tool in the Point & Figure world. Anchor point is the most logical area of demand and supply where indecision or confusion is seen among market participants. It is the battlefield of Bulls and Bears where the fight had been most indecisive. Eventually one side will get dominant, but it can certainly work as a reference area when revisited by the price.

Anchor point can be defined as an area where price has traded the most between two points. It is the most filled row that indicates the level where most action has been seen between two reference points. Image 3.4.1 shows the pattern with number of filled boxes in each row, shown at the right-most column. The row highlighted in the chart has 20 filled boxes which is the highest among all rows. This most populated row is defined as an Anchor point of the formation.

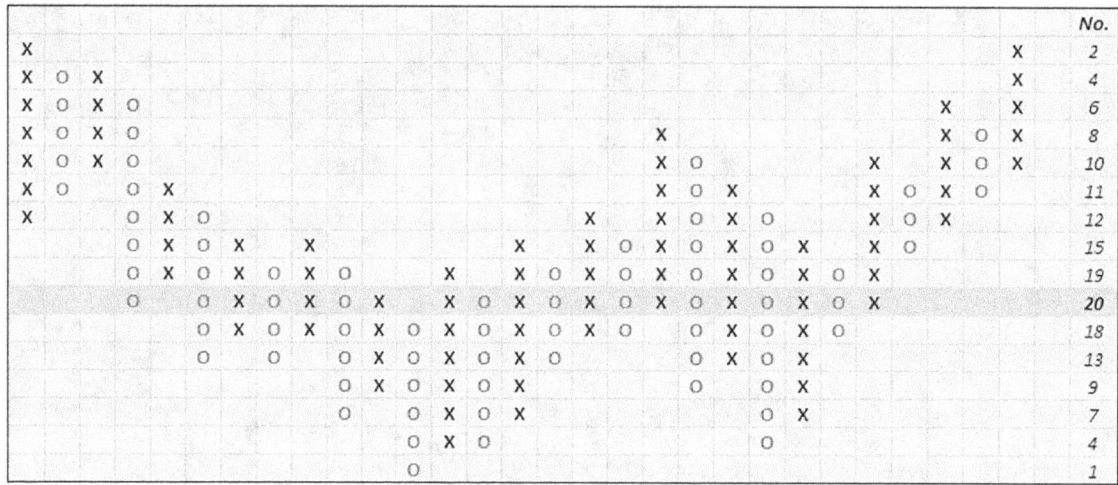

Image 3.4.1: Most filled row

Anchor point is shown by horizontal line extended to the right, representing the most populated row.

Anchor point is basically a concept borrowed from one-box reversal charts and is used to identify the base of a horizontal pattern. But the tool is useful in many ways. Anchor point displays the actual spots where there was a tug of war between Bulls and Bears and hence they become important reference areas. Setups occurring near these areas would turn out to be wonderful trading opportunities.

The Anchor point is always calculated between two columns. The software automatically captures the Anchor point based on the columns chosen by the user. Anchor point is the most active or most populated row between two columns chosen by the user. It can be plotted on horizontal formation to seek the reference level of entire pattern.

Image 3.4.2 shows the Anchor point plotted on the horizontal pattern.

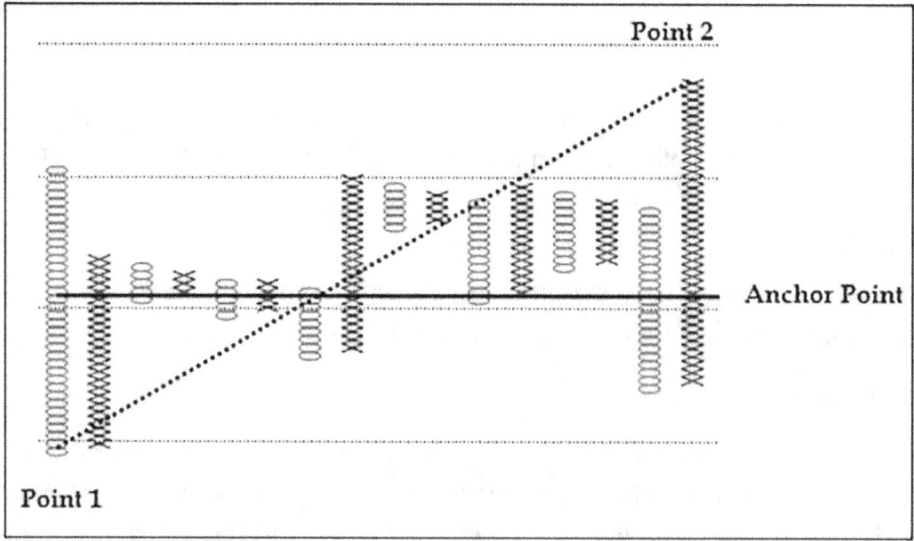

Image 3.4.2: Anchor point

A horizontal line shown in the chart shows the area where most number of boxes is recorded between Point 1 and Point 2.

Image 3.4.3 is a 10 × 3 Figure chart of Bank Nifty shown with Anchor point

												18210	
												18200	18200
18190												18190	18190
18180	18180											18180	18180
18170	18170											18170	18170
18160	18160									18160		18160	18160
18150	18150	18150								18150	18150	18150	18150
18140	18140	18140	18140	18140		18140				18140	18140	18140	18140
18130	18130	18130	18130	18130	18130	18130				18130	18130		18130
18120	18120	18120	18120	18120	18120	18120		18120		18120			
18110	18110	18110	18110		18110	18110		18110	18110	18110			
18100					18100	18100		18100	18100	18100			
18090						18090	18090	18090	18090				
18080						18080	18080	18080	18080				
18070						18070	18070	18070	18070				
18060						18060		18060					
18050													

Image 3.4.3: Anchor point

Level of 18130 is important because it is most traded price in the entire formation. To word it differently, Anchor point is the row which is most populated between the two chosen columns. The level has been important for various market participants and hence, can be helpful information when it is revisited in future. Viewing on figure chart helps in understanding its usefulness.

Multiple rows that are close to each other can also qualify as Anchor points if they have equal number of populated rows. More than one row that qualifies as anchor column will result in the completion of an Anchor point zone.

Figure 3.4.1 is a 0.25% × 3 P&F chart of Nifty showing Anchor point plotted from horizontal formation that occurred during late 2014 and early 2015. There are multiple rows with equal number of price points, resulting in an Anchor point zone.

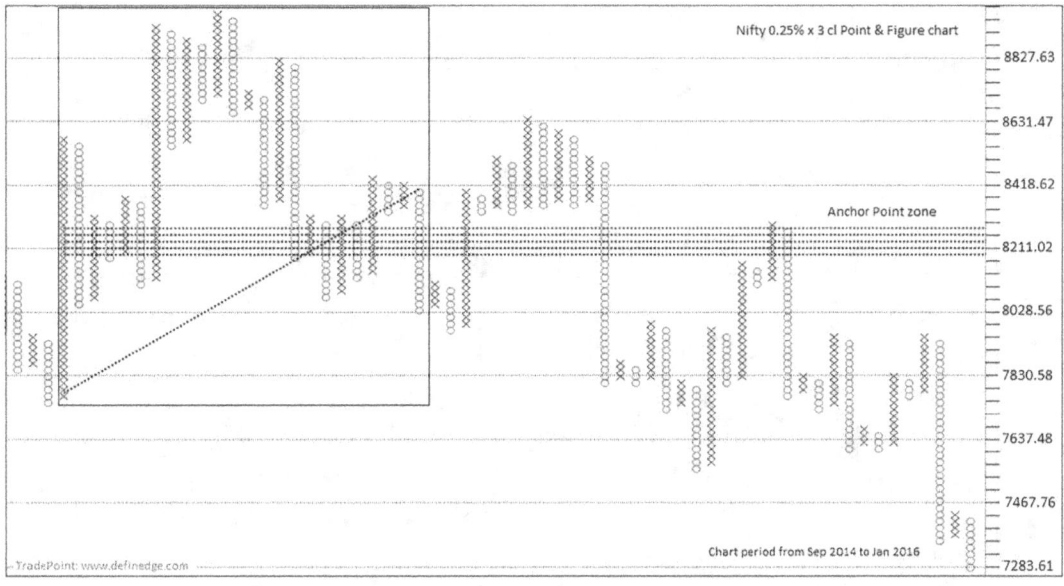

Figure 3.4.1: Nifty daily 0.25% × 3 cl Point & Figure chart

Draw Anchor point when the horizontal setup is seen, as shown in the chart above. Another way is to draw it from important Tops and Bottoms. Draw them from Major Tops and Bottoms to seek major price reference levels. It is like plotting the traditional Fibonacci retracements. My experience has been that the level derived from Major Top and Bottom points usually gets respected on a revisit.

Image 3.4.4 shows the Anchor point of area between Bottom at Point 1 to Top at Point 2.

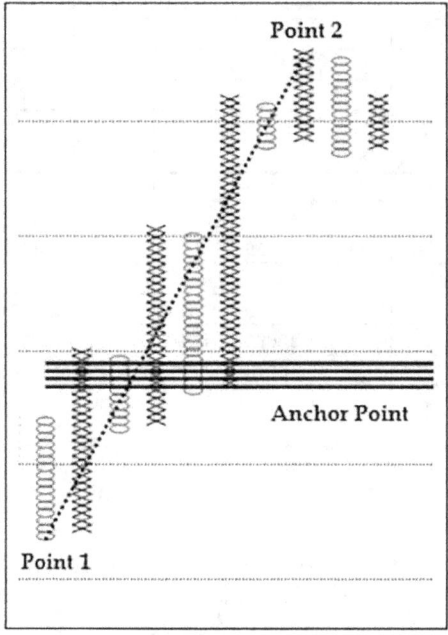

Image 3.4.4: Anchor point from bottom to top

It can be drawn from Mini Top or Bottoms as well, but they should not be very close to each other. Roughly, there should be a difference of at least seven to eight columns between them to ensure that they are not part of the same pattern. Understand that Anchor point will get plotted only when there is a column consolidation in between. Figure 3.4.2 is a 0.25% × 3 P&F chart of HDFC Bank. Anchor point is plotted by connecting Points A and B, which are significant swing points and not close to each other.

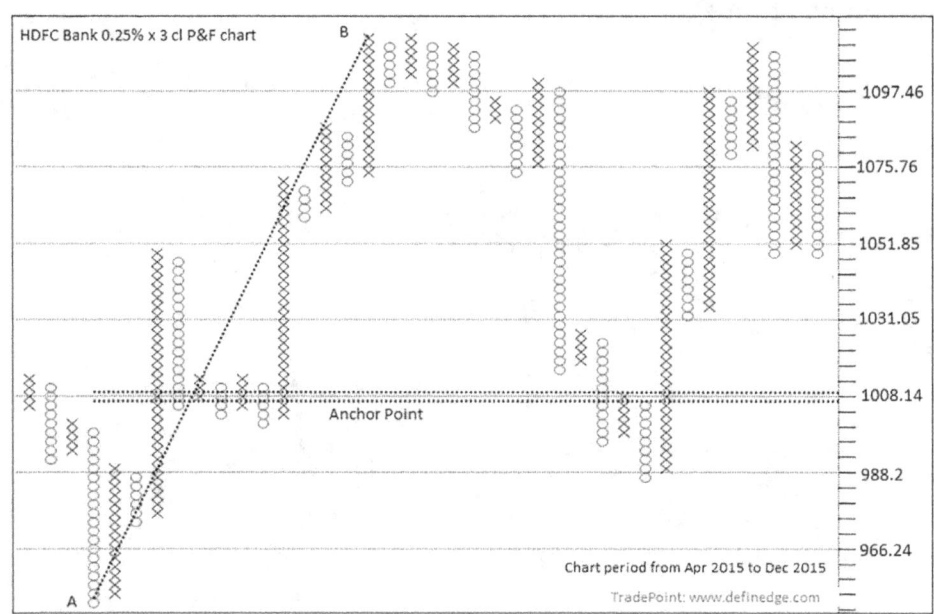

Figure 3.4.2: HDFC bank daily 0.25% × 3 cl Point & Figure chart

Anchor points work as reference level when price revisits it. It is a most logical method to identify support or resistance levels. Look for tradable pattern when price reaches the Anchor point level. Bullish pattern at Anchor point support level or bearish pattern at Anchor point resistance level generates effective mean reversion or pullback trading setup. Remember, a trade cannot be placed unless there is a pattern (see Image 3.4.5).

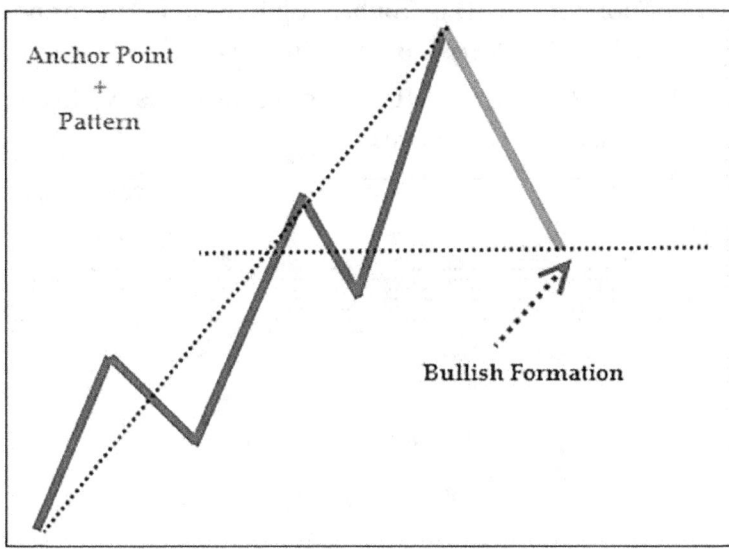

Image 3.4.5: Anchor point plus pattern

Anchor point is the most logical reference level because it is where participants have been most active in the past. Demand-supply proposition may get affected when price retests the same level on multiple occasions.

It is also possible that Anchor point is not respected at all. That is why patterns are more important. A break of support or resistance is equally important information that will be confirmed by patterns.

Figure 3.4.3 is 0.50% × 3 P&F chart of Heromotoco.

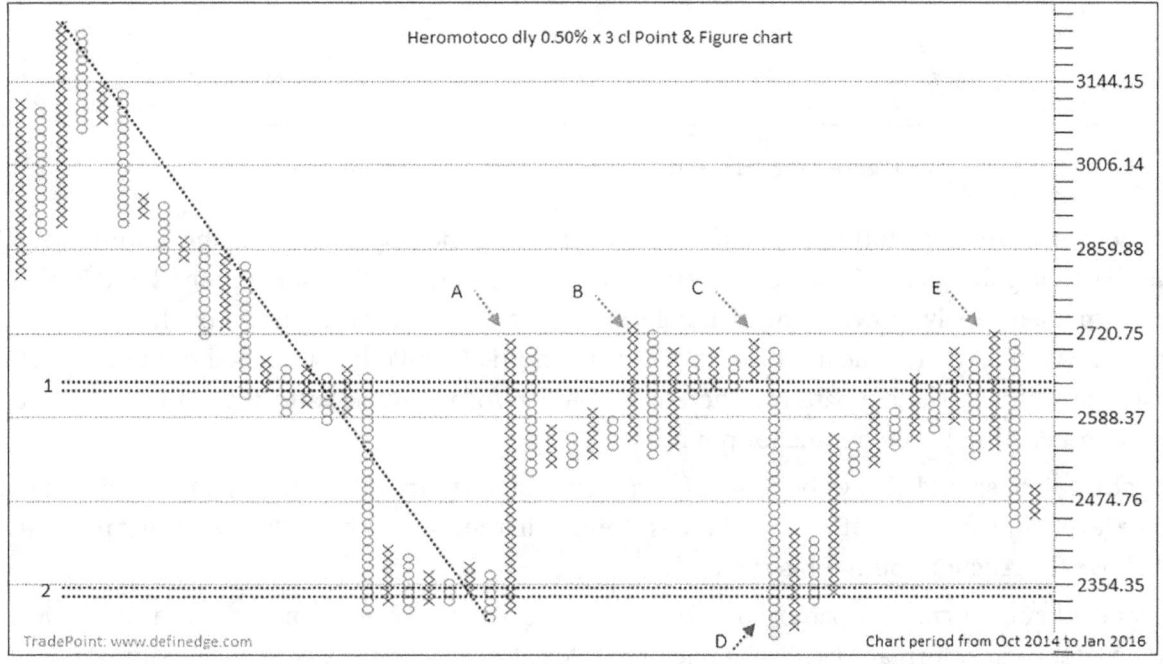

Figure 3.4.3: Heromotoco daily 0.50% × 3 cl Point & Figure chart

The Anchor point in the chart is plotted by connecting two important swing points. Two Anchor point zones marked in the chart as 1 and 2 were plotted because two different zones qualified as Anchor points as they had the same number of populated rows in each of them. Price had to contend with supply at Anchor point 1 and demand at Anchor point 2. There is no bearish pattern at spot A. Spot B is bearish 100% Pole, which saw Follow-through at spot C, which is also a Bull Trap that resulted in sharp fall to the support level placed at Anchor point 2. Spot D is Double Top Buy from Anchor point support level, which is also a bullish Double pattern. Spot E is Bearish Broadening reversal and a bearish Double pattern.

Figure 3.4.4 is the 0.25% × 3 P&F chart of HDFC plotted using daily closing prices. Anchor points shown in the chart are drawn from two swing moves.

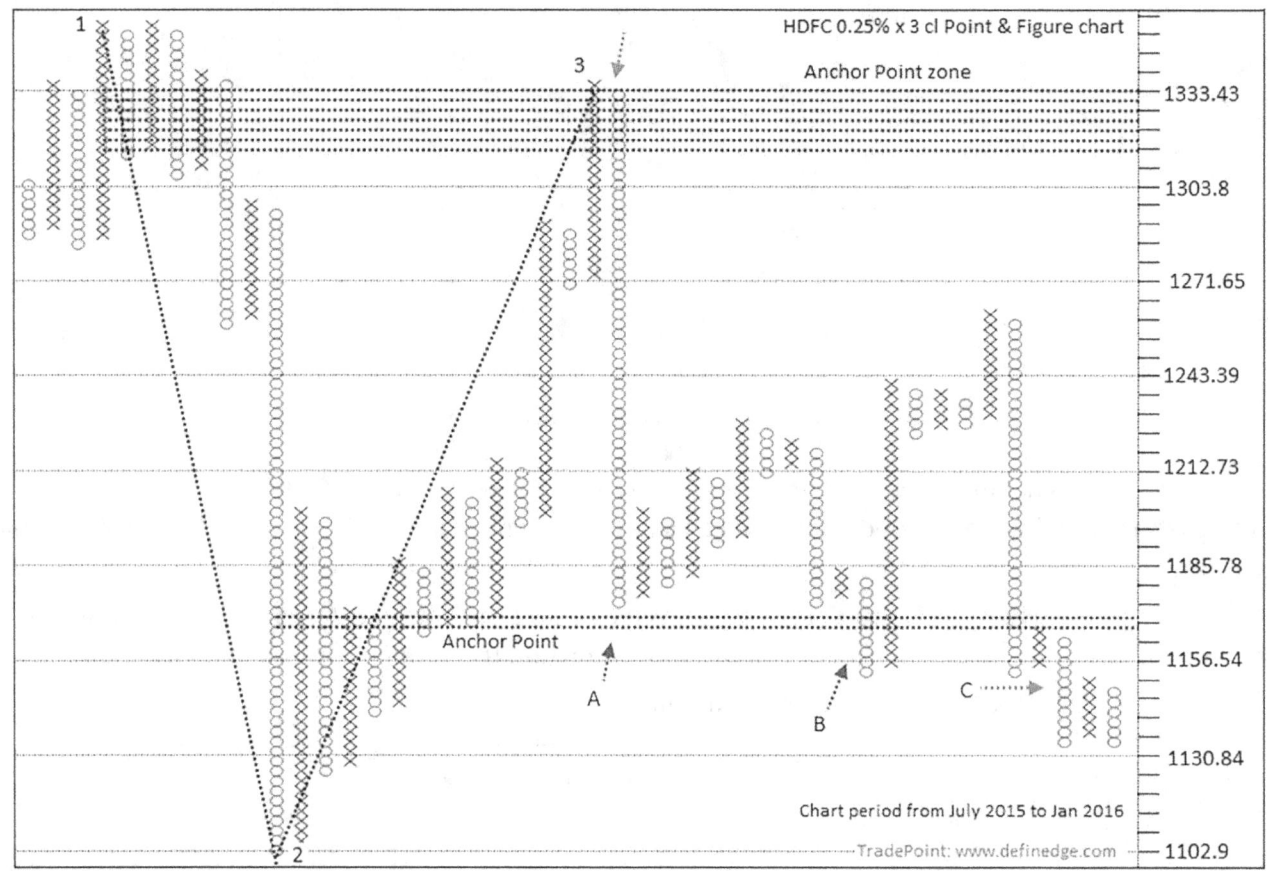

Figure 3.4.4: HDFC daily 0.25% × 3 cl Point & Figure chart

Anchor point zone is plotted in the chart by connecting the Top at point 1 and Bottom at point 2. Another Anchor point shown in the chart was formed by connecting Bottom at point 2 and Top at point 3. Price witnessed supply shown by bearish Pole when Anchor point was revisited by the price at point 3. Pattern A is Double Top Buy near Anchor point. Pattern B is Low Pole that turned to bullish 100% Pole, which is also a bullish Double pattern. There is no bullish formation at pattern C; in fact, it is a bearish Double Bottom Sell signal below anchor point.

Anchor points should always be drawn from major and important swing points to know the crucial reference levels and to seek confluence. There is strength in the base of the bullish pattern if price manages to stay above the Anchor point of that pattern.

If some other confirmatory pattern occurs near Anchor point, it can become a significant indication of reversal. Pattern retest formations like Double or Triple patterns forming at Anchor point make it a logical trading setup. Figure 3.4.5 is a 0.25% × 3 P&F chart of Bank Nifty is an interesting case-study.

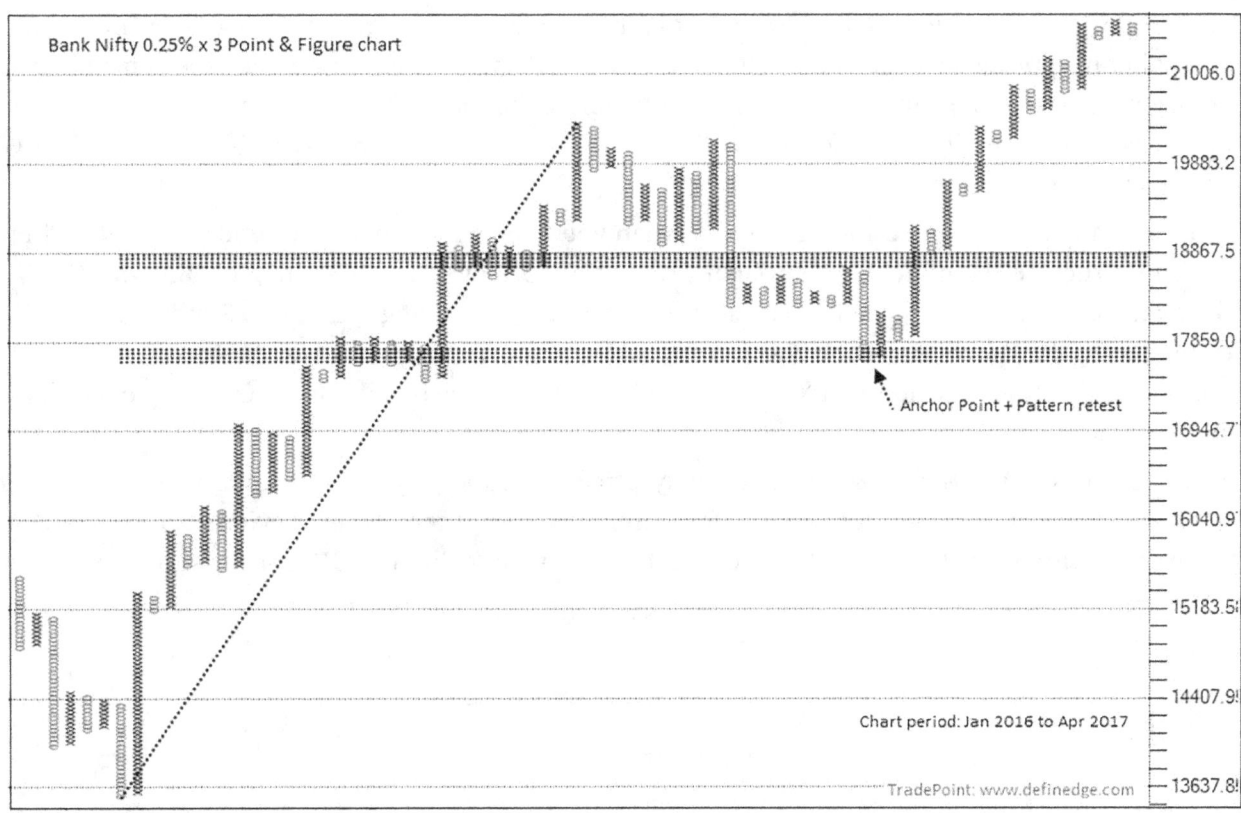

Figure 3.4.5: Bank Nifty daily 0.25% × 3 cl Point & Figure chart

A strong trend is usually followed by consolidation. When price revisits the most active area of the trend, it is often followed by sharp pullback rally. It can also become a classic case of pattern retest at Anchor points. Follow-through coming at Anchor points or any other confirmation from indicators or other tools, improve the odds of success of the trade setup.

Summary

- ⅄ Anchor point can be plotted from the horizontal formation to know the reference point of the pattern.
- ⅄ It can be plotted from significant Top and Bottom to see where price traded most during the move.
- ⅄ They are expected to act as significant reference points when price revisits.
- ⅄ Pattern retest at Anchor points is a useful setup and indicates significant reversal.

3.5: SUPPORT–RESISTANCE

Finding support and resistance on charts is a conventional method of analysis and well known among chart practitioners. Support is the area where demand is expected to exceed the supply; hence, price should stop falling at those levels. Similarly, resistance is the level where supply is likely to exceed demand; hence, the up move may come to a halt. There are many methods of finding these areas. We discussed 45-degree lines and Anchor point as tools to identify supports and resistances on Point & Figure charts. Let's discuss the other methods of analyzing supports and resistances.

Anchor Columns

Anchor column is another gift from P&F to the world of technical analysis. The concept of anchor column is simple, yet most amazing. A long column in a P&F chart is called an anchor column. Remember, P&F

columns represent a trending move. A long column represents strong trend backed by momentum. Anchor columns typically change the look of the charts and display the levels at which the demand-supply equation got skewed in one direction. It is difficult to define number of boxes required to call it an anchor column because it depends on the box-value. But, any column that looks relatively long on the chart will qualify as an anchor column.

You can immediately notice anchor column when you open a P&F chart as it tends to standout in the entire price structure. Trend remains strong if price sustains above the low of long column of 'X'. When a bullish anchor column is violated, it is a strong sign of an impending weakness. Similarly, it's bullish development if price moves above the high price of a bearish anchor column. Always remember, low price of column 'X' is Bottom of column of 'O' preceding it and high price of column of 'O' is Top of column of 'X' preceding it.

Figure 3.5.1 is a 0.25% × 3 P&F chart of daily prices of Apollo Tyre. Horizontal lines from anchor columns are shown in the chart for observation. Support line is drawn from previous column of 'O' for bullish anchor column and Resistance line is drawn from previous column of 'X' for bearish anchor column.

Figure 3.5.1: Apollo Tyre daily 0.25% × 3 cl Point & Figure chart

Anchor column can also result in a near-term exhaustion in prices. Traders can take profit on a column reversal after the anchor column and wait for the next signal to reinstate fresh trading positions.

Large columns are catalysts; they change the look of the chart. They indicate strength of the trend; they act as important trend markers. When price is in an Uptrend, anchor column of 'X' represents bullish sentiment and momentum behind the Uptrend. It provides confidence to ride the trend and trade the continuation patterns. Anchor column of 'O' in an Uptrend is a warning sign for the bulls and indicates weakness in the Uptrend. Follow-though to anchor column is an important trading setup.

Previous Peaks and Troughs

Previous Tops and Bottoms are important reference points. It is an effective method of identifying support or resistance levels and the same concept can be used in P&F charts too.

If price had faced resistance at a particular level, there is a high probability that the level will again act as resistance on a revisit later. It gets more interesting when market is overbought or when broader market trend looks overstretched when such a revisit of old resistance or support zone happens.

Figure 3.5.2 is a 0.25% × 3 P&F chart of Dr. Reddy.

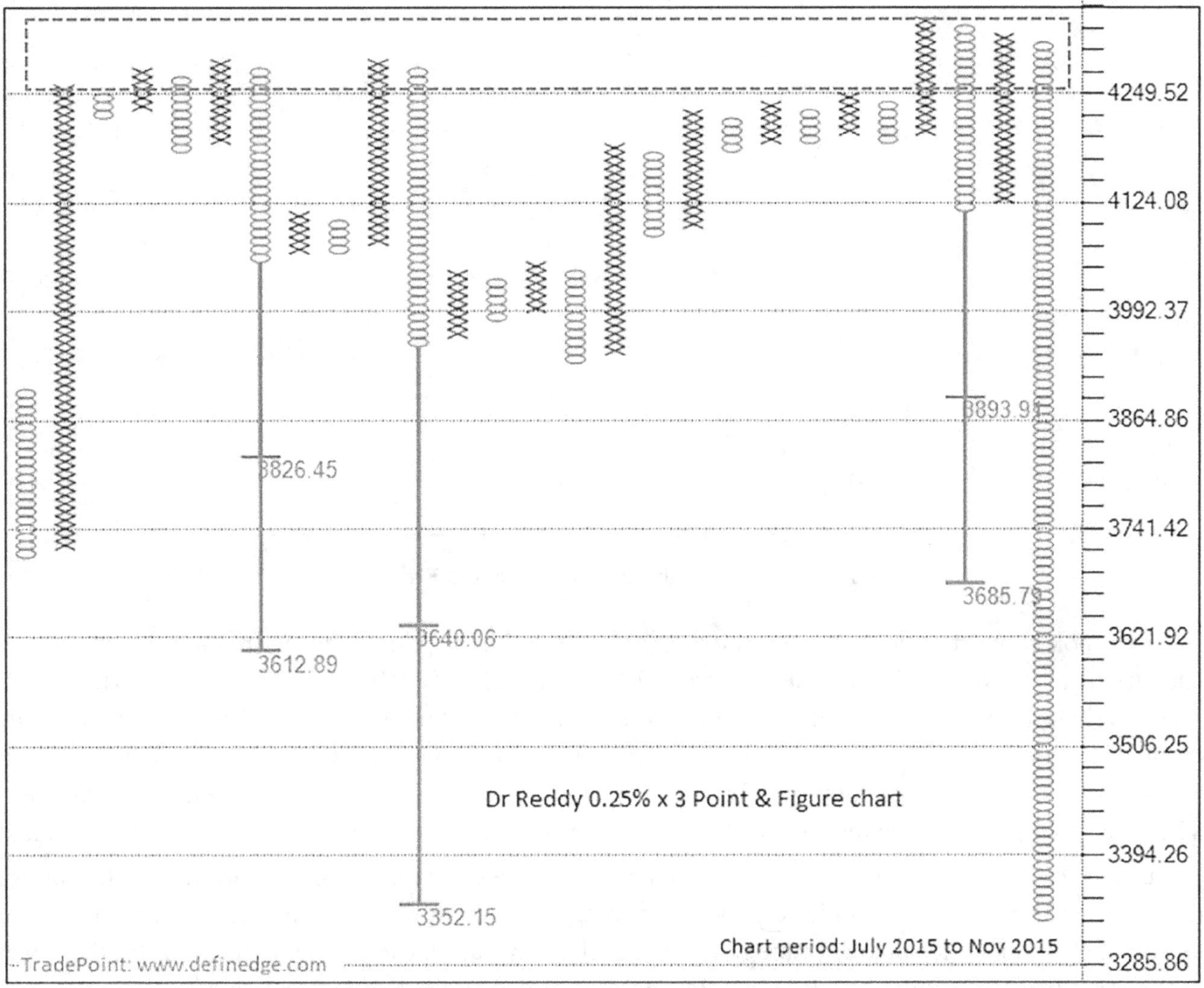

Figure 3.5.2: Dr. Reddy daily 0.25% × 3 cl Point & Figure chart

Price turned lower frequently from the same supply zone and there were numerous bearish patterns around them in the chart shown above. The nature of patterns and the frequency of their occurrences will depend on the box-value chosen. Vertical count at pattern 1 can be referred to when pattern 2 was completed at same level. Notice that pattern shown in the Figure 3.5.2 is a bearish triple pattern formation.

Polarity Principle

The polarity principle is very popular in the conventional time-based charts. The concept of prior support, when broken, turning into resistance or vice versa is the essence of the polarity principle. It is also applicable on P&F charts. Though it can be viewed on all box-values and time frames, it can be better analyzed using higher box-value charts to know the important reference points from the broader market perspective.

Figure 3.5.3 is a 0.50% × 3 P&F chart of Nifty.

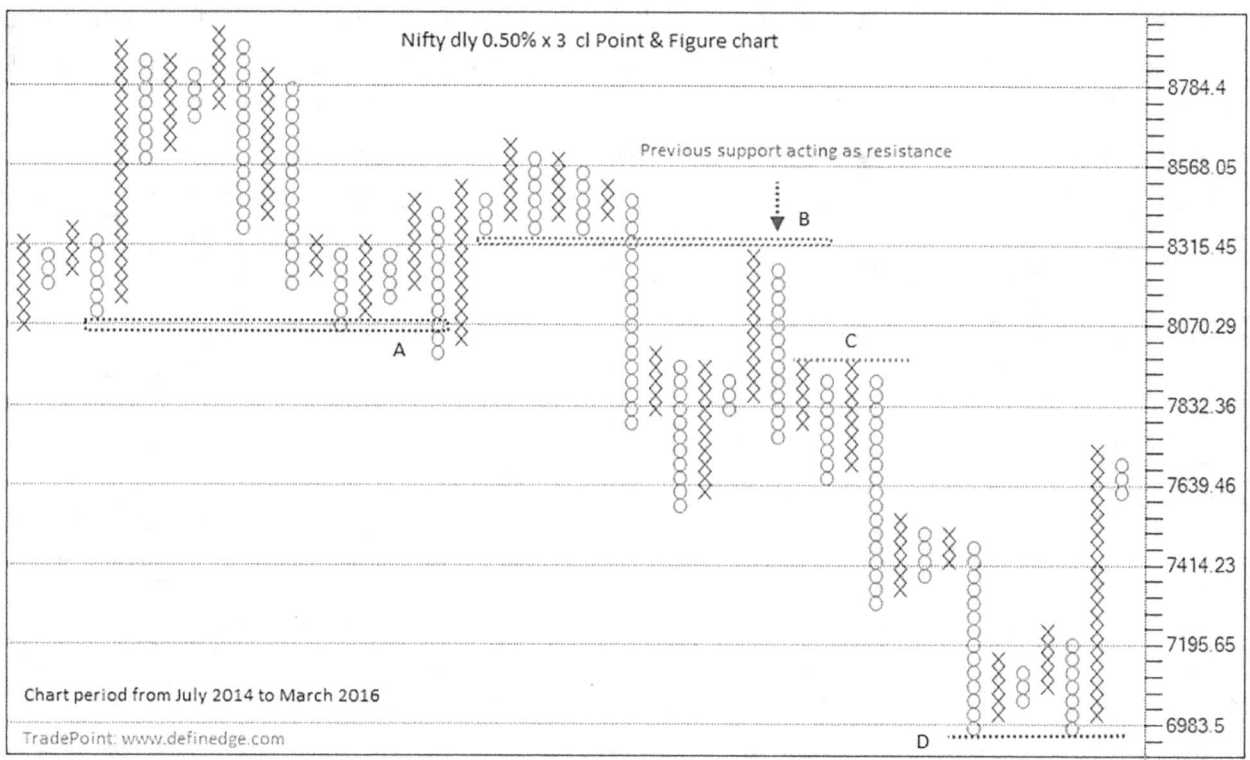

Figure 3.5.3: Nifty daily 0.50% × 3 cl Point & Figure chart

Price took support at previous demand area at point A. The support seen by frequent column of 'O' that turned to Quadruple Sell signal became resistance at point B. Being aware of the important price levels can help in curbing the excitement. Point C is point of resistance and point D is support shown by multiple columns witnessing column reversal at the same price zone. A retest to the breakout is always an interesting opportunity. A support, when broken, would act as a resistance in strong trending markets. Whenever a support or resistance is broken and changes polarity, it is a strong sign of a trend reversal.

Such kind of information gathered from higher box-value charts becomes important for all types of traders. Even the short-term trader can decide strategy looking at the reference level from the higher box-value charts. Pattern on lower time frame or lower box-value charts can be referred for trading them along with other confirmatory tools. A simple column reversal on the higher box-value charts might have produced some significant multi-column setup on other charts. The Figure 3.5.3 chart of Nifty above shows resistance and support patterns at point C and D, respectively; there can be a pattern retest on lower box-value charts at those points.

Fibonacci Retracement and Extensions

There is much written about Fibonacci series. Though its relevance in markets can be debated, but those who believe in it can use it in P&F charts too.

What Is a Fibonacci Series?

The Fibonacci sequence is named after Italian Mathematician Leonardo Pisa, known as Fibonacci. He introduced the sequence to the Western world in the 12th century. It is said that this sequence has been described earlier as Virahanka numbers in Indian mathematics.

The Fibonacci sequence is a series of numbers, as follows:

0, 1, 1, 2, 3, 5, 8, 13, 21, 34, 55, 89, 144, 233, 377 ...

Each number in the sequence is simply the sum of the two numbers before it. For example, 2 is arrived at by adding the two numbers before it (1 + 1). Similarly, 3 is nothing but the sum of the two numbers before it (2 +1) and so on.

Fibonacci numbers are treated as nature's number because it is said that they are found in the arrangement of leaves in plants or florets in a flower, etc.

There are many natural things where this ratio is not found, and even if found, it is not necessary that it would be applicable to markets. I am mentioning it only to be aware that it is not a magical ratio. However, setups can be designed using it.

Fibonacci Ratios

If one number of the series is divided by the number that follows it, the ratio will be 61.8%, which is also referred to as the Golden ratio. If one number in the series is divided by the number after the next one in the sequence, the ratio we get is 38.20%. Similarly, every number in the sequence is 23.60% of the number after the next two numbers in the sequence. Have a look at the excel sheet shown in Image 3.5.1.

Fibonnaci sequence	Ratio with next number	Ratio with number after next	Ratio with number aftertwo
0			
1	100.00%	50.00%	33.33%
1	50.00%	33.33%	20.00%
2	66.67%	40.00%	25.00%
3	60.00%	37.50%	23.08%
5	62.50%	38.46%	23.81%
8	61.54%	38.10%	23.53%
13	61.90%	38.24%	23.64%
21	61.76%	38.18%	23.60%
34	61.82%	38.20%	23.61%
55	61.80%	38.19%	23.61%
89	61.81%	38.20%	23.61%
144	61.80%	38.20%	23.61%
233	61.80%	38.20%	23.61%
377	61.80%	38.20%	23.61%
610	61.80%	38.20%	23.61%
987	61.80%	38.20%	23.61%
1597	61.80%	38.20%	23.61%
2584	61.80%	38.20%	23.61%
4181			
6765			
10946			

Image 3.5.1: Fibonacci calculation in excel

Generally, 23.60%, 38.20%, 50%, 61.80% and 78.60% are treated as key Fibonacci ratios.

Actually, the 50% level has nothing to do with the Fibonacci sequence but traders use this level because of the tendency of price to reverse at the midpoint of a move.

How to Apply Fibonacci on Charts

Traders who prefer to initiate trades at the support or resistance levels, find Fibonacci ratios a useful companion.

Below are the steps to follow:

Step 1

Find a swing or a trend and mark the Tops and Bottoms of that swing or move on the chart. If it is an up move, point A will be the called the Bottom of the move and point B the Top. For a down move, point A will be the top and point B the bottom.

Step 2

Calculate the distance between two points and apply Fibonacci ratio to the distance to project price retracement.

For example, if point A is 100 and point B is 200 in an up move, the method to calculate 50% retracement is as follows:

Distance = Point B - Point A = 200 − 100 = 100 points

50% Retracement = 50% x Distance = 50% × 100 points = 50 points

Retracement price = Point B - Retracement amount = 200 − 50 = 150

All ratios are calculated in a similar manner. For the bearish retracement, price is added to point A. Though the software will automatically calculate those retracement levels, it is always better to know the calculation behind it.

Image 3.5.2 is a picture showing retracement to bullish price move from point A to B.

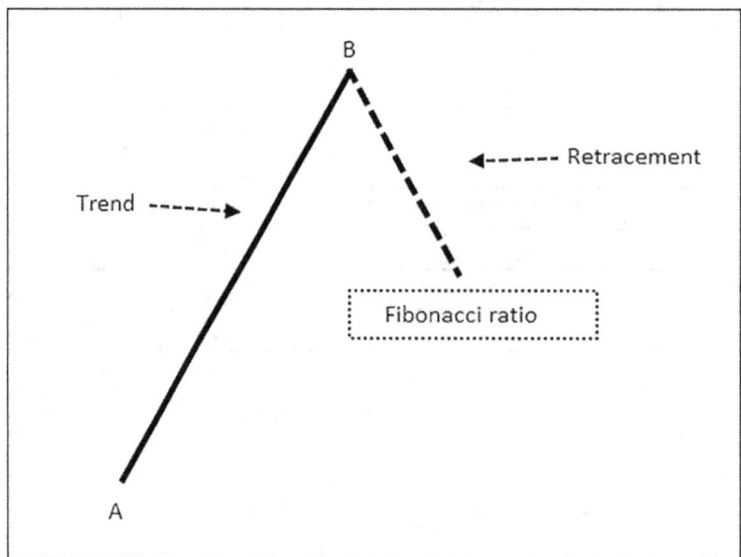

Image 3.5.2: Fib retracement of bullish move

Image 3.5.3 shows retracement to bearish price move from point A to B.

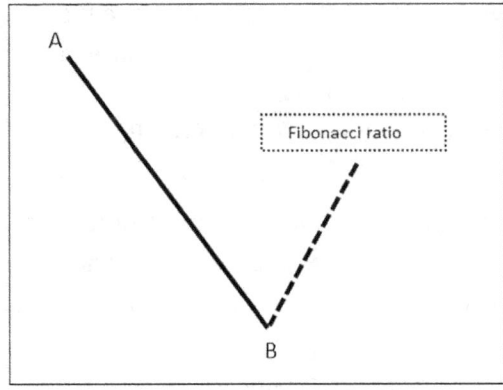

Image 3.5.3: Fib retracement of bearish move

Price correction to the strong move is the logical scenario to enter the trade. The risk is usually low and there is a sense of comfort of not buying at high or selling at low price points.

The Fibonacci ratio is a mathematical calculation to identify retracement points. Strong price trends witness retracement up to 23. 6% to 38.2%. There may be deeper price corrections up to 61.80–78.60% levels too.

How to Apply Fibonacci on P&F Charts

We can apply Fibonacci retracement to P&F charts as well – by connecting Top and Bottom of the price columns. We don't know whether the price will halt at 23.60% or 38.20% or if it will get into a deeper correction. Chances are that the price may choose to ignore all retracement levels and get into a sharp counter-trend move. Therefore, it makes little sense to take trading decisions based on retracement levels alone. It is always advisable to use other confirmatory tools to trade those levels.

Knowledge of Point and Figure formations can be very helpful for those interested in taking trades off those retracement levels. It can help in eliminating guesswork about which retracement level will be respected by the price. Have a look at the daily 0.25% × 3 SBI chart in Figure 3.5.4, which shows the Fibonacci price retracement to the bullish move from point A to B.

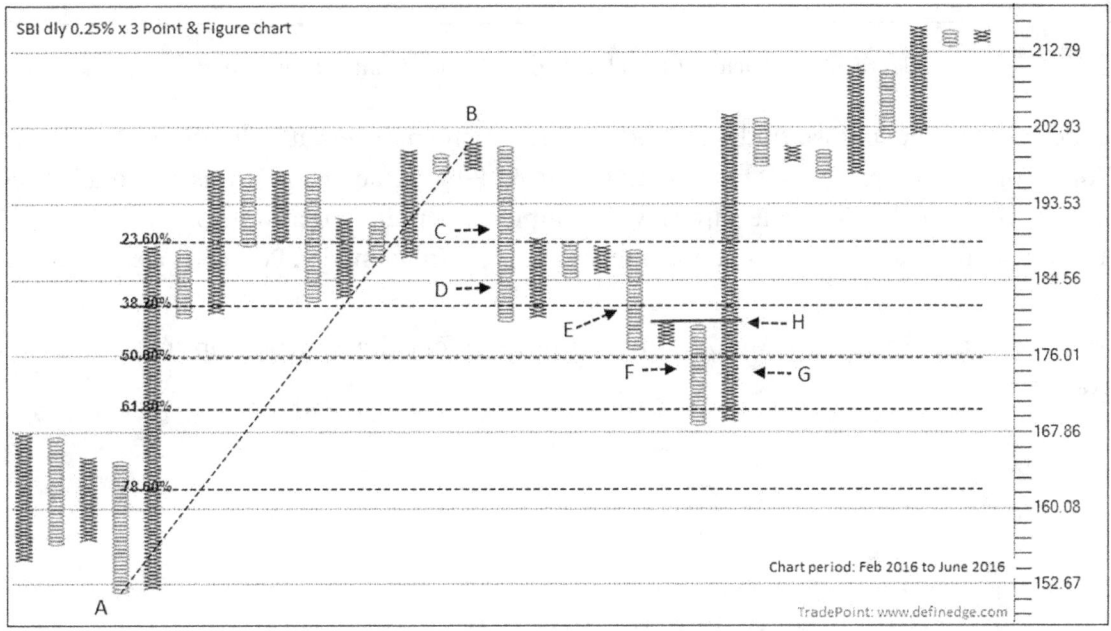

Figure 3.5.4: SBI daily 0.25% × 3 cl Point & Figure chart

Fibonacci retracement is drawn from the low at point A to the high at point B to look for bullish trades at the retracement levels. Price did not generate any bullish pattern at points C, D, E and F which were 23.6%, 38.2% and 50% retracement of the A-B swing. A Low Pole pattern occurred at point G, which coincides with the 61.8% retracement of A-B swing. The Low Pole turned out to be a bullish 100% Pole at point H.

Using P&F patterns along with Fibonacci ratios is a more objective way to initiate trades. Instead of speculating on which retracement level will be respected by the price, the trader can associate it with P&F formations and wait for price to suggest when to initiate the trade. It can help in improving the odds of trading success.

Figure 3.5.5 is a daily 0.25% × 3 P&F chart of Reliance Capital.

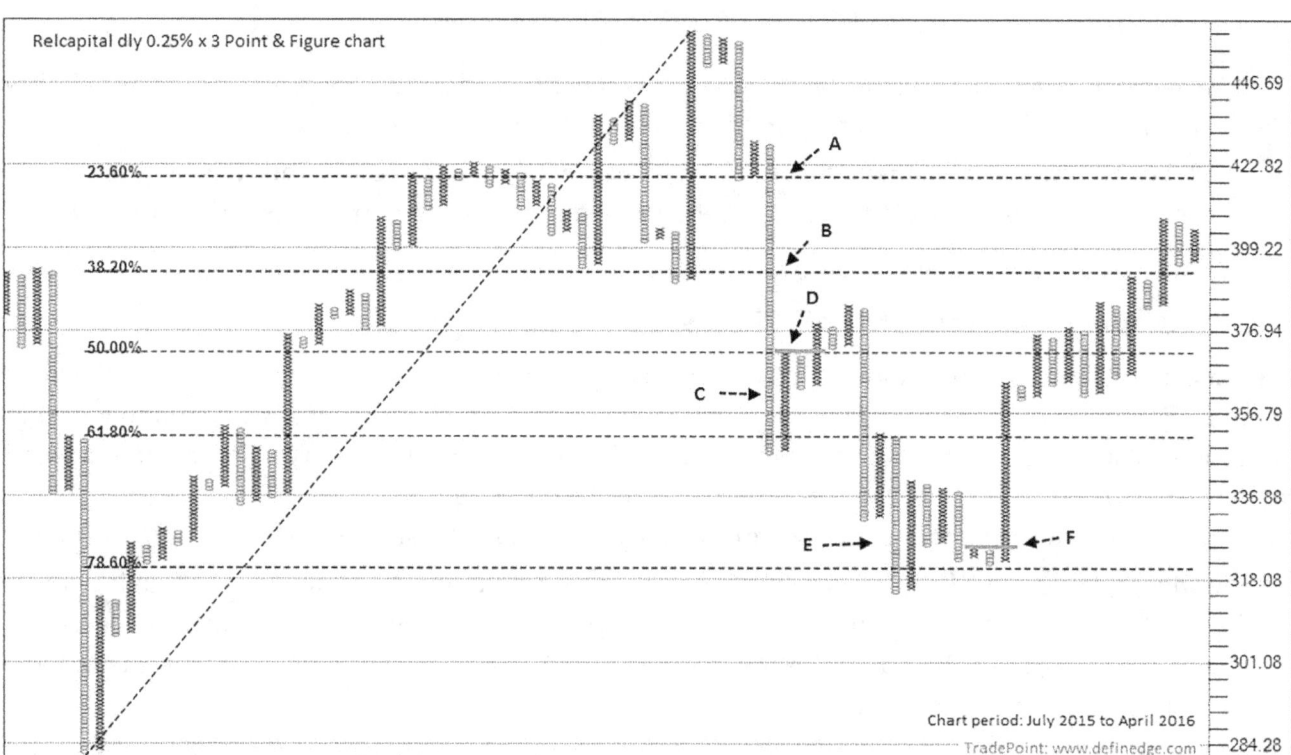

Figure 3.5.5: Reliance Capital daily 0.25% × 3 cl Point & Figure chart

Price did not generate bullish trades at Fibonacci retracement levels at points A, B and C. It triggered Double Top Buy pattern at price D after correcting up to 61.80% retracement. It was eventually followed by Double Bottom Sell signal. A low Pole pattern was completed at point E that was followed by an affordable Double Top Buy pattern at the 78.60% retracement at point F. Incidentally, Point F is also a bullish Double pattern!

Figure 3.5.6 is a chart of Tata Motors showing retracement drawn from top to bottom to look for bearish trades.

Figure 3.5.6: Tata Motors daily 0.25% × 3 cl Point & Figure chart

Price did not generate any bearish pattern while it was a correction to the previous bearish move until point A. Thus, we come to know that 38.20% retracement level is being respected by the price. Note that it generated bull trap formation while falling below 23.60% retracement level at point B.

Have a look at an interesting chart of Tata Steel (see Figure 3.5.7).

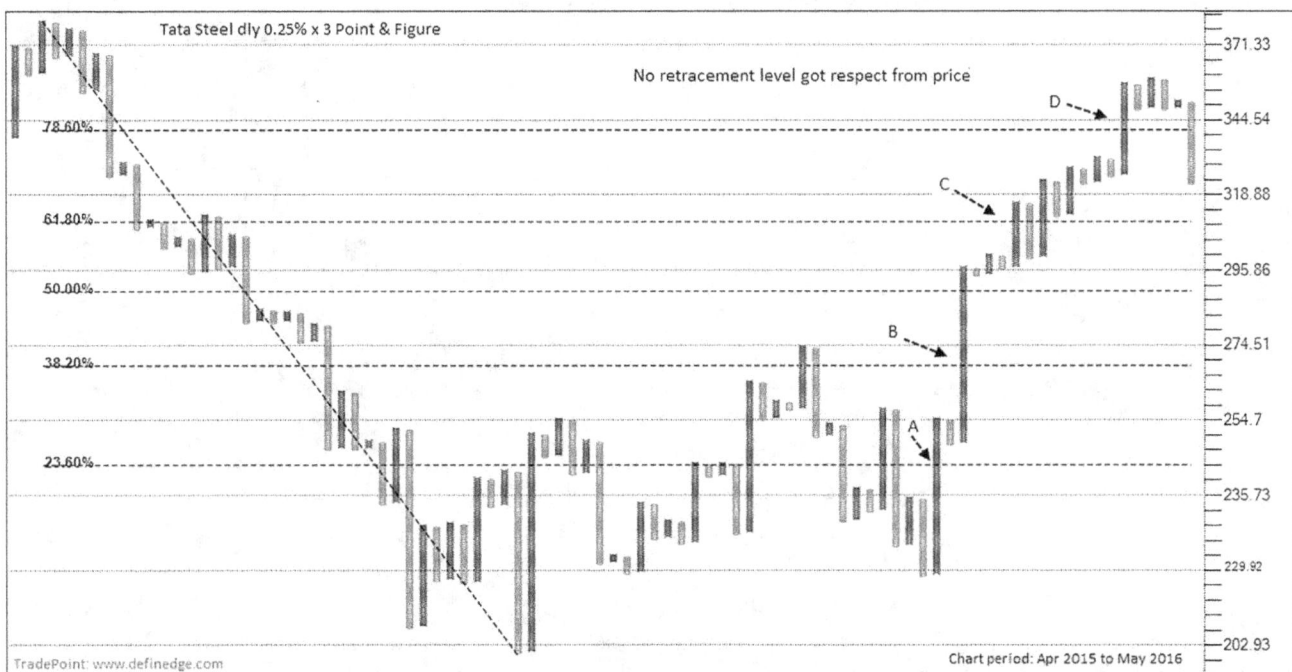

Figure 3.5.7: Tata Steel daily 0.25% × 3 cl Point & Figure chart

There were no bearish patterns at points A, B, C & D in the above chart. The use of P&F patterns in conjunction with Fibonacci retracement levels will help eliminate a lot of unproductive trades, which is after all one of the key ingredients to achieve higher returns in trading. The underlying strength of P&F methodology is objectiveness and elimination of noise. These two are key ingredients that determine the profitability of a trader.

Remember, with this methodology, though Fibonacci retracements are a major part of the setup, what we trade is a P&F pattern and the trade should be exited if the pattern fails. Pattern following approach has the advantage of knowing the risk while taking the trade. Fibonacci clusters and extensions can also be traded along with patterns in the same manner.

I strongly believe that the usage P&F patterns can complement Fibonacci retracement study. Decide a tool or method that you would want to trade and stick to it. Remember, the key to trading success lies in deciding things that one should not do.

45-Degree Channel Lines

Drawing channels is the popular approach in the traditional method of technical analysis. We draw parallel lines to the subjective trend lines to plot the price channel. This trend channel is used to identify the significant reversal or breakout points that can be traded. Trend channels can also be drawn in the Point & Figure charts. A trend channel using 45-degree trend lines can be used in Point & Figure charts.

We typically draw a bearish 45-degree line from the top of a column of 'X'. A parallel line to this bearish trend line same can be drawn from a column of 'O' of a Mini Bottom to complete the downward channel. Similarly, parallel line to a bullish 45-degree trend line can be drawn from the top of the column of 'X' that qualifies as a Mini Top. This will complete a bullish trend channel. Important feature is that the slope of the channel line is also 45-degrees.

Look at 1% × 3 P&F chart of Hind Petro shown in Figure 3.5.8.

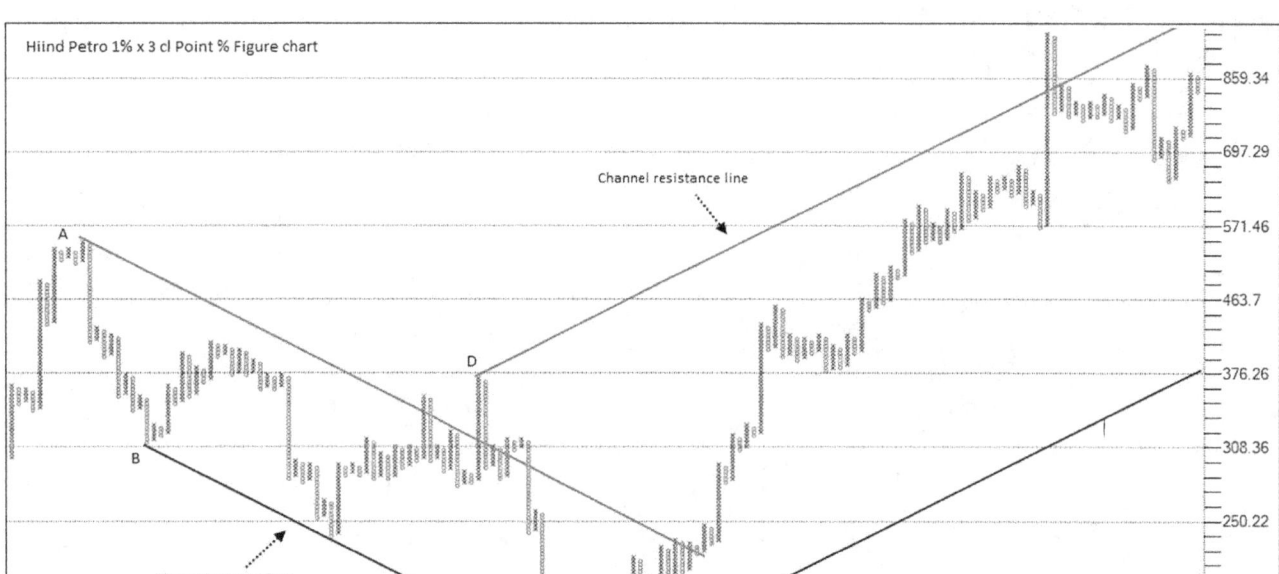

Figure 3.5.8: Hind Petro daily 0.25% × 3 cl Point & Figure chart

Bearish 45-degree line is drawn from point A. Down-sloping 45-degree line is drawn parallel to it from the Mini Bottom at point B. It creates a 45-degree channel and price is typically expected to take support at the lower channel line. Bullish 45-degree trend line is drawn from point C once price breaches the downward channel. An up sloping 45-degree line parallel to trend line C, is drawn from point D, which creates a trend channel. This parallel line is expected to act as a point of resistance going forward.

Objective channel lines are drawn from Mini Tops and Mini Bottoms only. And remember, though price is expected to face support or resistance at these channel lines, trades must be initiated only if there are supportive P&F patterns. Bullish pattern at lower channel line and bearish pattern at upper channel line create trading setups with an attractive risk–reward ratio.

Channel lines are also known as support and resistance lines. A parallel line drawn to bearish 45-degree line is support line and a parallel line drawn to bullish 45-degree line is known as resistance line. It is not important to remember these names. An understanding that a parallel line is expected to work as support or resistance is more essential than remembering names.

Channeling is an age-old and time-tested technique and it is equally effective in P&F charts. 45-degree lines and channel lines should always be applied on log charts, especially when plotted using end-of-the-day prices. They are more effective on three-box reversal charts. Objective rules of plotting and predefined slope separates P&F channeling technique from the conventional methods.

The support–resistance analysis should not be overdone and should be considered only if it is confirmed by P&F patterns. Most of us are guilty of predicting tops at every resistance in an uptrend. Similarly, in a downtrend, we are preoccupied with identifying the next support level. Shouldn't it be otherwise? Will it not be more logical to buy at support in an uptrend and sell at resistance in a downtrend?

The X and O at the same level patterns, which were discussed earlier, are a good proxy for identifying supports and resistances. Trend lines, indicators and Anchor point methods of identifying support–resistance levels were also discussed in prior chapters. Patterns such as Traps and Poles found at significant support–resistance levels provide strong confirmation of demand/supply and qualify as excellent trading setups.

Summary

- ⌁ Anchor column is a catalyst and a significant reference point in any price chart.
- ⌁ Previous peaks and troughs, and polarity principle work equally well on P&F charts.
- ⌁ P&F patterns along with Fibonacci retracement increase the odds of success in a trade.
- ⌁ 45-degree channel lines are important support–resistance lines.
- ⌁ Buy at support when trend is up; Sell at resistance when trend is down.

3.6: VOLUME

It is also possible to plot volume on P&F charts, but the method of plotting them is different. Volume is shown as a histogram below the P&F charts but they are calculated only when a box is printed in the P&F column. So, volume during insignificant price moves will be ignored. Usual method of reading volume can be applied on P&F charts as well.

Figure 3.6.1 is a chart of Biocon plotted along with P&F volume bars.

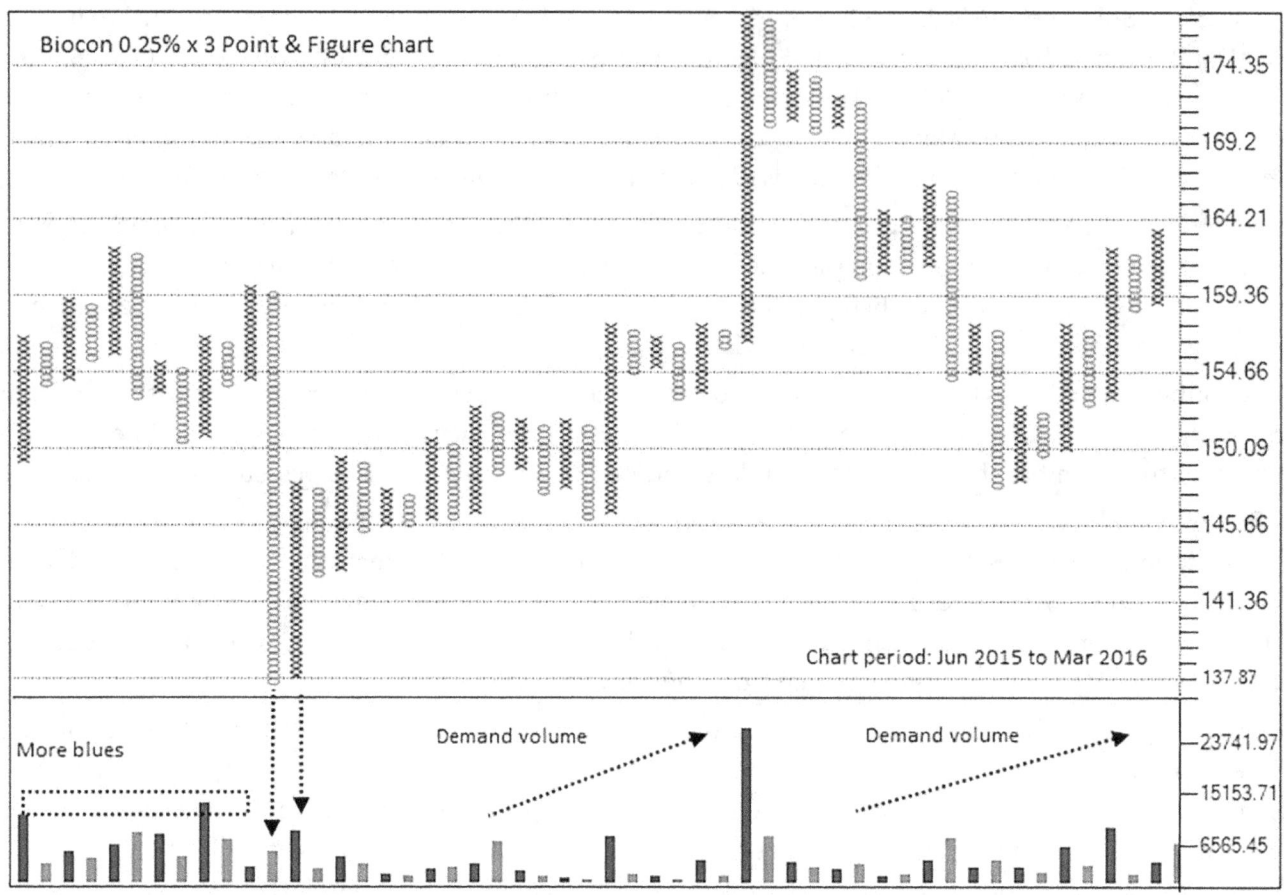

Figure 3.6.1: Biocon daily 0.25% × 3 cl Point & Figure chart

The first arrow going down in the above chart shows a long column of 'O' with a relatively less trading volume. In contrast, the volume in the next column of 'X' was much higher, though it was smaller in length compared to previous column of 'O'. The time period captured in both the columns was almost the same. This was a sign that the bulls were more active in column of 'X' which had higher volume. While the price was consolidating in a large trading range, more bullish volume bars were visible even though there were a series of sell signals in between. After this consolidation, the stock rallied to 400 in a year's time.

Climax

Buying and Selling climax formations indicate impending trend reversal, or indication of significant change in demand-supply equation.

P&F selling climax can be defined as follows:

- ⅄ Trend is down.
- ⅄ Anchor column of 'O' is immediately followed by Anchor column of 'X'.
- ⅄ Volume of column in 'X' is higher than volume in column of 'O'.
- ⅄ Follow-through.

Figure 3.6.2 is the chart of Yes bank showing selling climax formation explained above.

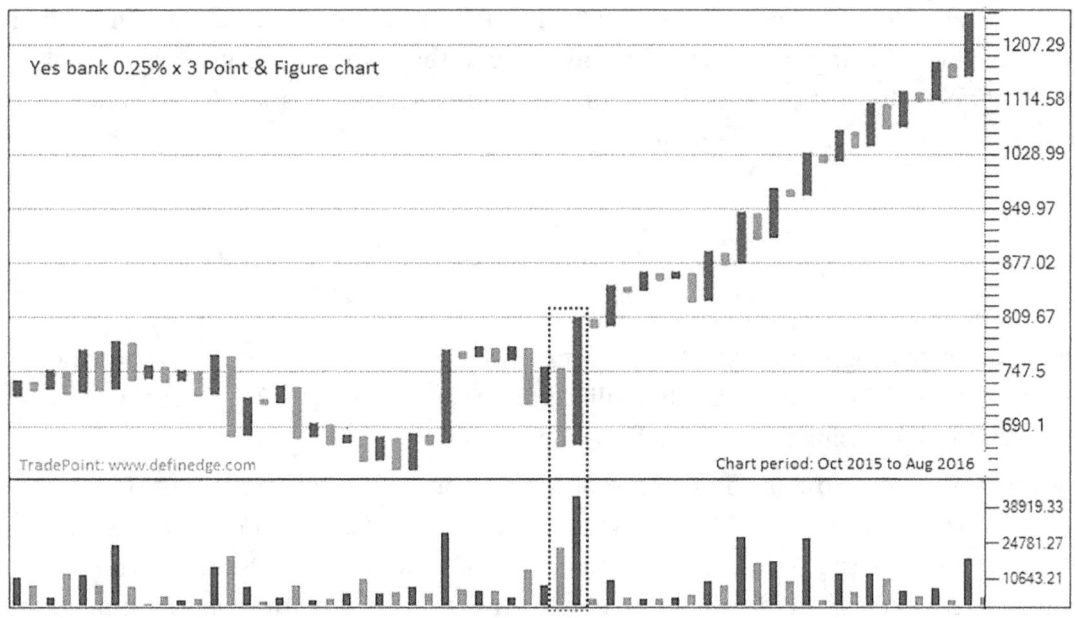

Figure 3.6.2: Yes bank daily 0.25% × 3 cl Point & Figure chart

P&F buying climax can be defined as follows:

⌄ Trend is up.

⌄ Anchor column of 'X' is immediately followed by Anchor column of 'O'.

⌄ Volume in column of 'O' is higher than volume in column of 'X'.

⌄ Follow-through.

Figure 3.6.3 is the chart of Dr. Reddy showing buying climax formations.

Figure 3.6.3: Dr. Reddy daily 0.25% × 3 cl Point & Figure chart

The unique method of plotting volume on P&F makes the volume analysis more meaningful in P&F charts. It can indicate demand volume and supply volume that can complement price analysis because trader can effectively filter the patterns based on the volume characteristics. It adds another dimension while using trend line, count and price patterns in a Point & Figure charts.

3.7: ABC

"Know the rules well, so you can break them effectively"

– Dalai Lama XIV

Once the basic concepts are mastered, it becomes far easier to tweak them to suit personal requirements. Trend lines, counts and P&F patterns can be utilized to design various trading setups. Here is an example of one such setup defined using a combination of these tools.

ABC setup explained below is an outcome of a lot of practice and research on P&F charts. It is an impressive setup which consists of a long column, a 45-degree trend line and vertical count. This pattern has turned out to be very successful over a long period of time, especially in lower box-values such as 0.25% in the daily time frame. Remember, it is an exclusive setup, where the rules relating to the columns that qualify for calculating counts and drawing 45-degree trend lines are not followed. In other words, we can calculate targets using vertical counts from the ABC pattern.

Bullish ABC: You may recall that a long column of 'X' or 'O' is defined as an anchor column. When an anchor column of 'X' is followed by corrective or consolidating columns, plot a down-sloping 45-degree bearish trend line and calculate the bullish vertical count from the anchor column. The chances of the vertical count target being achieved are very high when a subsequent column of 'X' breaks out above the down-sloping 45-degree trend line. The setup remains valid, unless bottom of the anchor column is broken.

I like keeping the terminology simple. It helps in remembering the setup easily. The alphabet A in ABC pattern stands for anchor column, B for breakout and C for count. A few examples will make the ABC pattern recognition simpler.

Figure 3.7.1 is a 0.25% × 3 P&F chart of Siemens showing ABC formation.

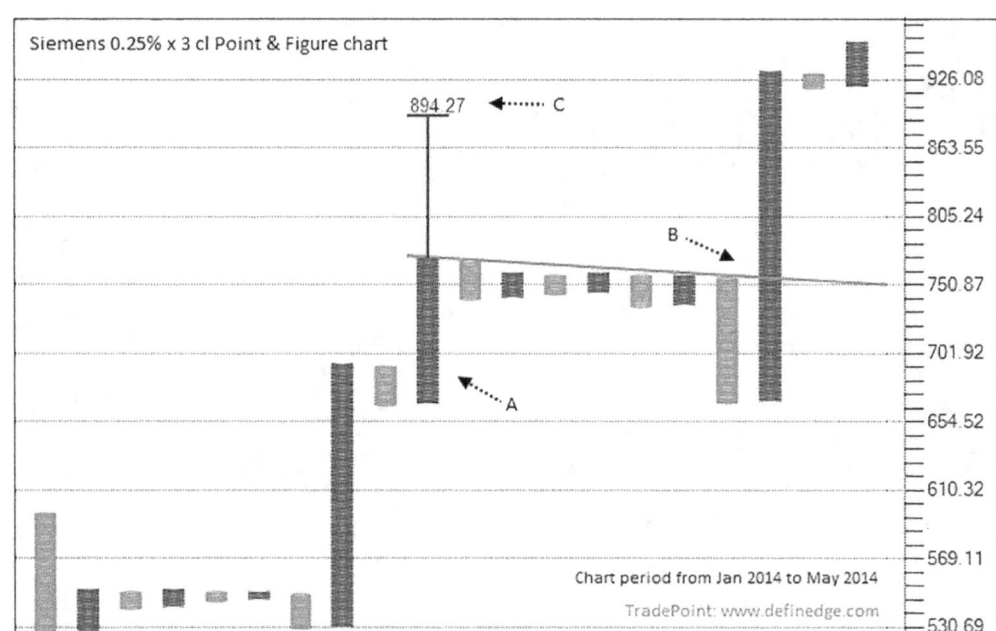

Figure 3.7.1: Siemens daily 0.25% × 3 cl Point & Figure chart

Point A is a long column of 'X', also known as an anchor column. It is followed by consolidation that did not go below Bottom of the anchor column. Point B is where the price breached the bearish 45-degree trend line drawn from the high of the anchor column. Point C is vertical count plotted from the anchor column, which is the target for the setup.

The setup remains valid, unless the bottom of point A is breached. As long as the ABC setup is valid, re-entry may be considered upon second breakout if the first breakout fails. ABC is a framework and one can use patterns to initiate trades. Always think in terms of affordability and entry–exit rules.

Figure 3.7.2 is another example of bullish ABC setup in the 0.50% × 3 P&F chart of IRB.

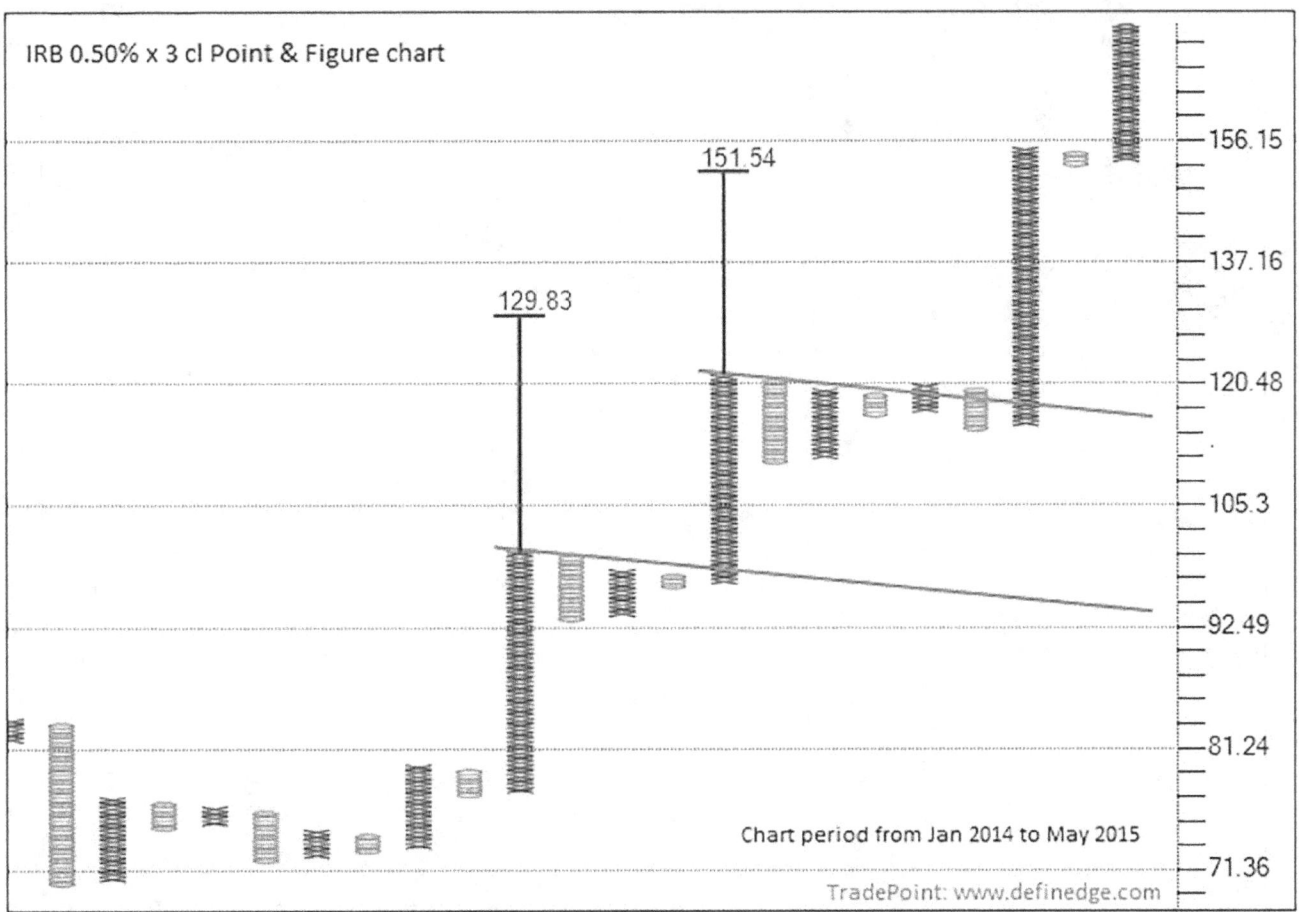

Figure 3.7.2: IRB daily 0.50% × 3 cl Point & Figure chart

Notice in the chart above that it was a four-column Triangle when first ABC was formed and Bear Trap when second ABC breakout happened.

ABC is useful especially in trending scenarios and improves the odds of a trade turning into a winner. The ABC setup is a blend of a pullback setup, breakout and Follow-through. Breach of 45-degree line plotted from anchor column indicates strength of the column and breakout after the retracement. The entry, exit and target criteria are clearly defined in the ABC setup, which also facilitates objective risk–reward calculation.

Let's now look at the Bearish ABC setup, wherein the rules are just the reverse compared to the bullish variant.

Bearish ABC setup: Anchor column of 'O' is followed by consolidating columns. Plot an upsloping 45-degree trend line and calculate the bearish vertical count from the anchor column. The pattern is complete when a subsequent column of 'O' breaks the upsloping trend line. The target calculated using the vertical count has a very high probability of success. The setup remains valid unless top of the anchor column of 'O' gets broken.

Figure 3.7.3 is a 0.25% × 3 P&F chart of TCS showing Bearish ABC setup.

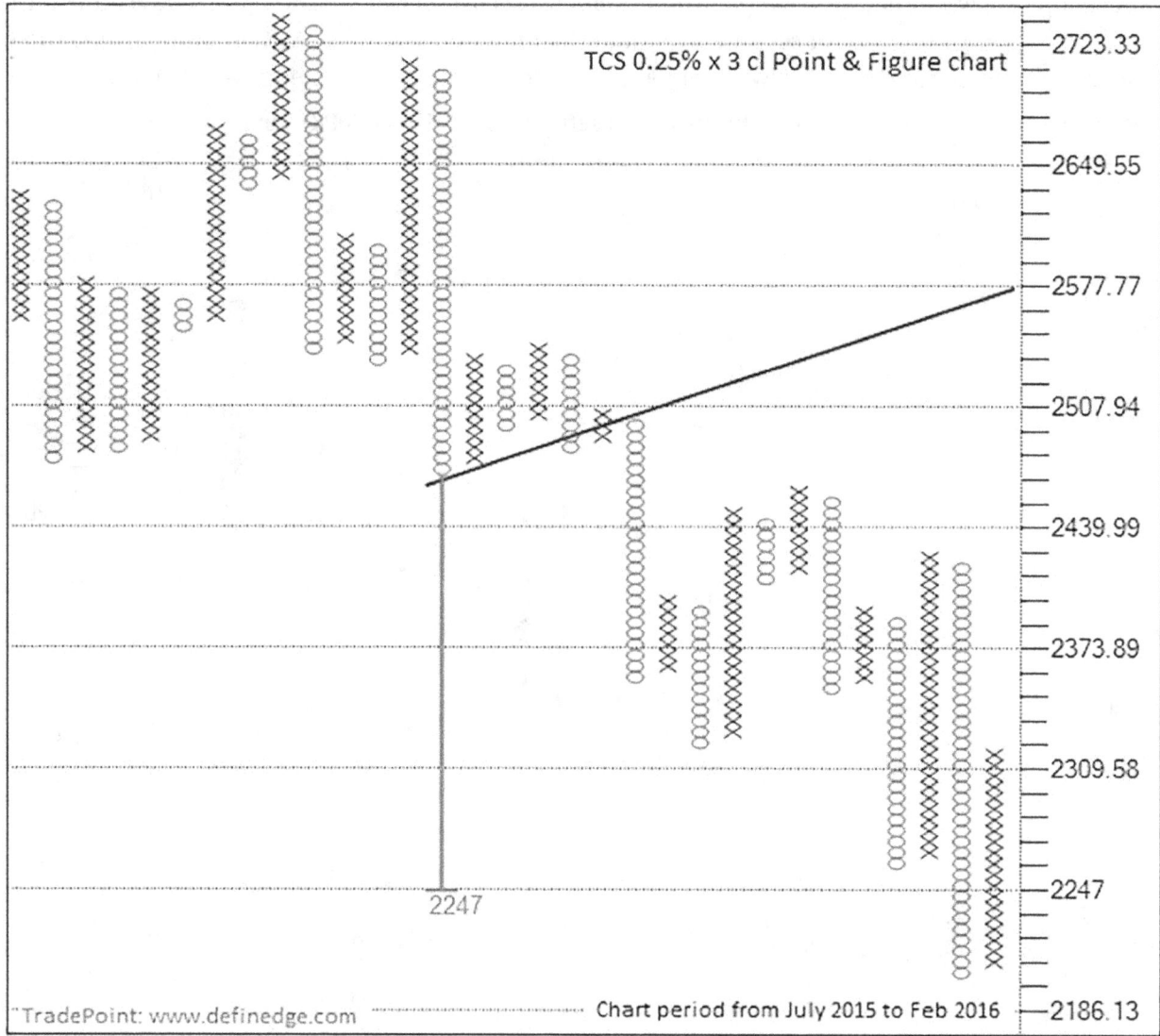

Figure 3.7.3: TCS daily 0.25% × 3 cl Point & Figure chart

ABC setups don't occur very frequently because price usually does not correct for more than two to three P&F columns after anchor column. Both vertical counts can also be used as target 1 and 2 for such setups. It is advisable to use the conservative vertical count to ensure higher win ratio, especially for bearish trades.

ABC setup is applicable on all time frames. Figure 3.7.4 is a 0.15% × 3 P&F chart of Hindalco futures plotted using the closing prices of every minute that has a Bearish ABC setup.

Figure 3.7.4: Hincaldo futures 1 min interval 0.15% × 3 cl Point & Figure chart

It is similar to the flag patterns we analyse on usual price–time charts; the essence is same but the introduction of the 45-degree line to judge the consolidation helps in timing the trade better. Vertical counts and patterns are other P&F tools that come in handy while executing the trade and calculating targets & exit criteria.

This is one of my most favorite setups for momentum trading. I hope this prompts you to explore more ideas using the array of tools & patterns in the P&F world; most of the practitioners till now have used it in the traditional way. So, get more creative and you can come with fresh methods, setups and approach to suit your personal trading style.

3.8: P&F TWEEZERS

I have borrowed the word Tweezer from Steve Nisson's popular and wonderful book *Japanese Candlestick Charting Techniques*. He has described the Tweezer Candlestick pattern in his book. Though there is no similarity in the two patterns, I recalled that pattern while working on Tweezers, hence the name.

Though they look simple, P&F Tweezers are an outcome of a reverse-engineering process. A few charts always catch the eye and there is something that we like about them; our subconscious mind remembers images and perhaps it is something that it likes about a chart because it has seen a few patterns occurring time and again. I mark such charts and try to come up with a trading setup using the common thread across them. This process has resulted in a few good discoveries; Tweezer is one such price pattern.

Have a look at the pattern shown in Image 3.8.1. It is a simple horizontal pattern indicating accumulation or distribution that we usually analyse on the time-based charts. It shows us that a base is created before price changes direction.

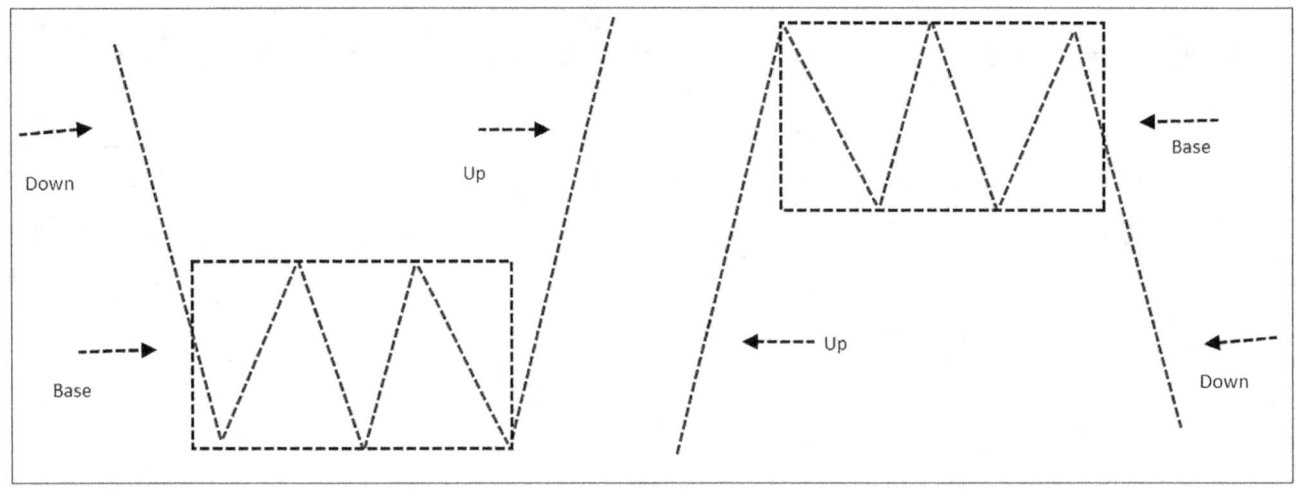

Image 3.8.1: Accumulation–distribution patterns

The same formation can also be designed on P&F charts. Have a look at Image 3.8.2.

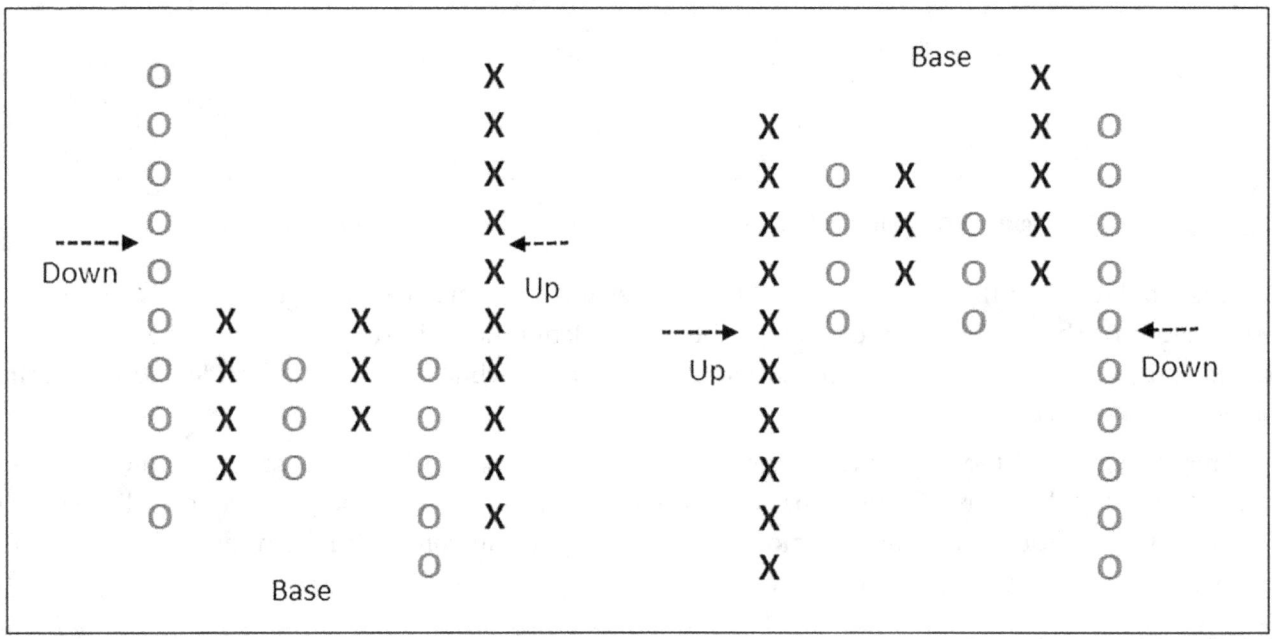

Image 3.8.2: Accumulation–distribution patterns on P&F

There is a price consolidation pattern between two columns. For the bullish pattern, column of 'O' is entry into the pattern and column of 'X' is exit from the pattern. Similarly, for bearish pattern, entry column should be column of 'X' and exit column should be of 'O'.

Horizontal pattern between the columns could be any pattern. I scanned and studies several charts and back-tested them to identify the rules for trading this pattern.

The first rule is that entry and exit columns of Tweezer should be anchor columns and the second anchor column should be within the range of the first anchor column. Second, there should be a consolidation of at least two columns between the two anchor columns. But these are non-active Tweezers from a trading perspective; they get activated upon a Follow-through signal. Bullish Tweezer becomes active when price moves above the high price of column of 'X' that completed the pattern. A bearish Tweezer gets active when price goes below the low price of column of 'O' that completes the pattern. (See Image 3.8.3)

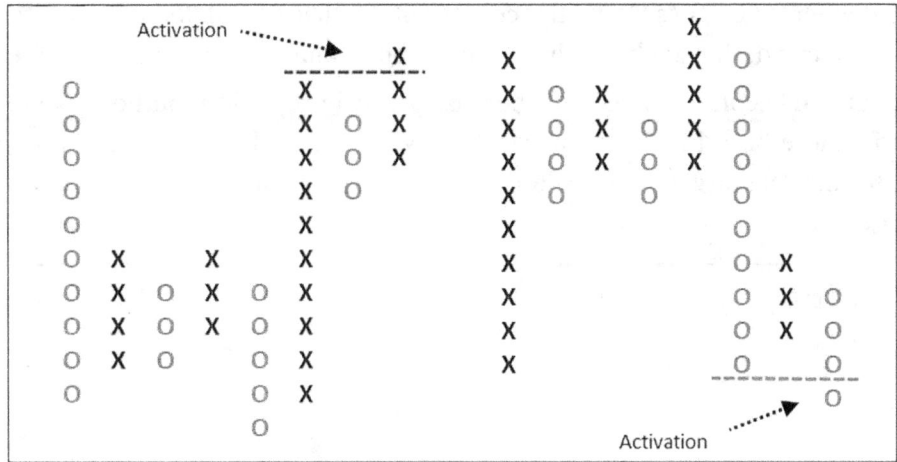

Image 3.8.3: P&F Tweezers

Activation can happen in the next immediate column or few columns later. But price shouldn't fall below the Bottom of the bullish pattern or the Top of the bearish pattern before activation.

To begin with, I recommend this pattern on 1% (medium term) box-value. If consolidation between the columns is not more than that of six columns, the pattern is strong.

Have a look at Figure 3.8.1, which shows the chart of Axis bank showing the Tweezer formation.

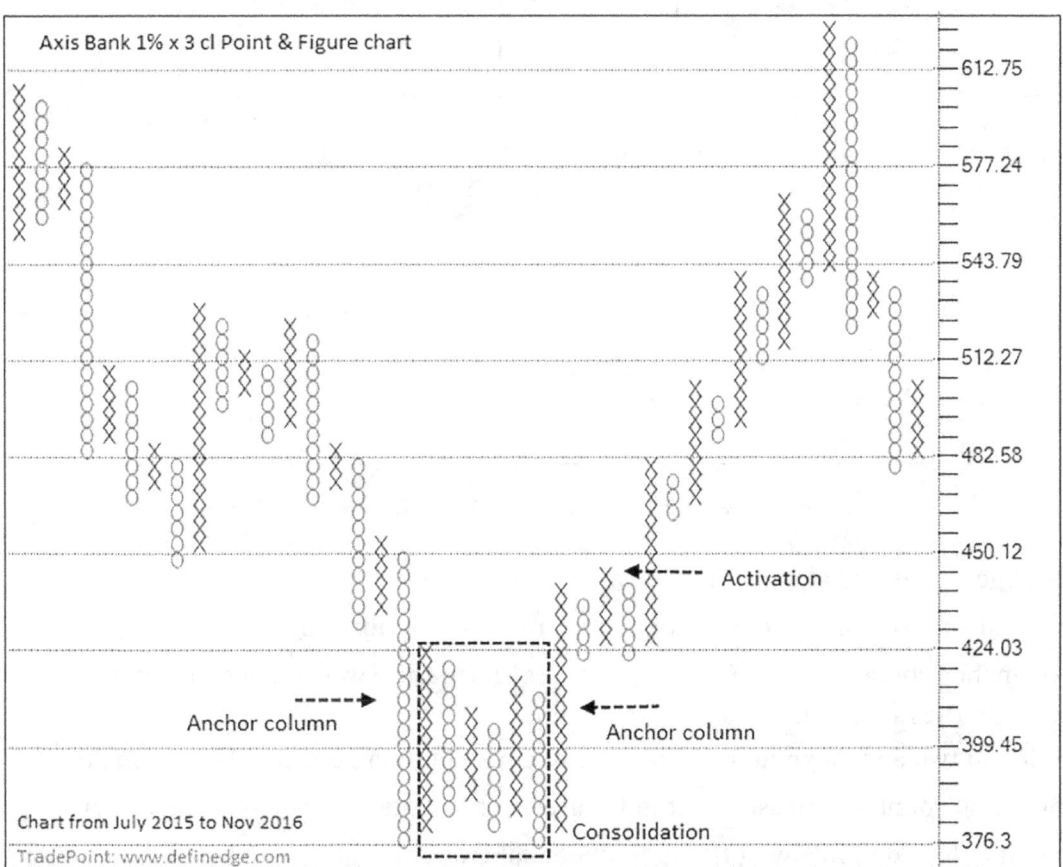

Figure 3.8.1: Axis bank daily 1% × 3 cl Point & Figure chart

Notice that the columns marked by arrows on the chart are the entry and exit anchor columns. There is a six-column consolidation pattern between them and the bullish Tweezer pattern gets activated in the subsequent column when price goes above the column of 'X' that completed the Tweezer. For simplicity and to begin with, one can define anchor column on 1% box-value as a column with at least ten boxes.

This way, the pattern becomes objective. There is a logical projection method also in the P&F arsenal that can be used in these base breakout formations. We can use the "aggressive horizontal counts."in Tweezer patterns to calculate targets. Have a look at the same chart of Axis bank along with counts, shown in Figure 3.8.2.

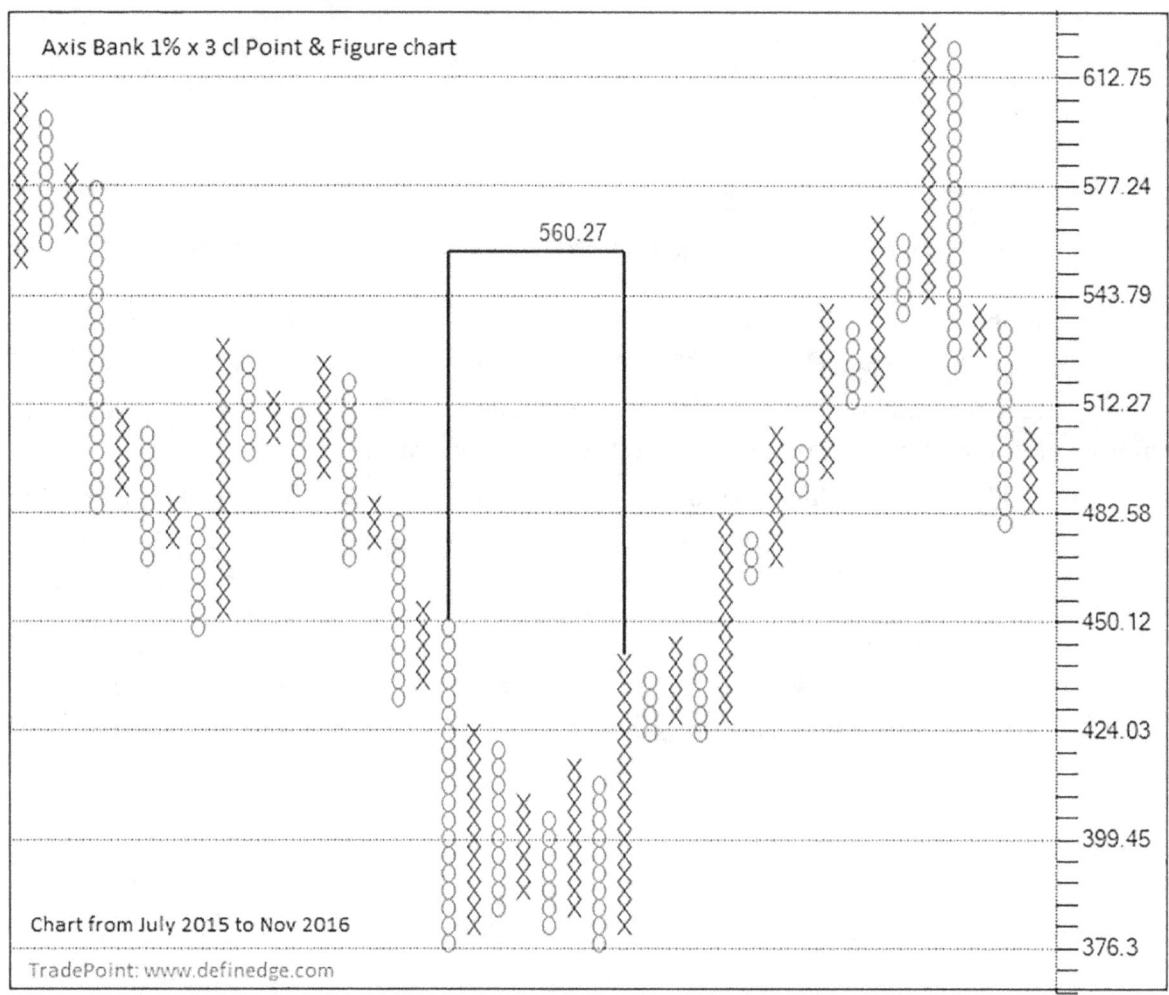

Figure 3.8.2: Axis bank daily 1% × 3 cl Point & Figure chart

The count gets activated along with Tweezer.

The following is a summary of Tweezer pattern rules on 1% box-value:

1. Two anchor columns (not less than ten boxes) form the Tweezer. Second anchor column should be within the range of the first anchor column.

2. Minimum two and maximum six columns of consolidation between the two anchor columns.

3. Horizontal count – aggressive method is used to calculate targets from the pattern.

4. A column breakout in any of the subsequent columns, activates the Tweezer and the count.

5. It fails or gets negated when Bottom of bullish pattern or Top of bearish pattern is broken.

The Tweezer formation captures the shift in the demand-supply equation. The second anchor column is a signal that one side has claimed control and the Follow-through reaffirms their strength.

Figure 3.8.3 is a chart of Bharat Forge showing the Tweezer formation.

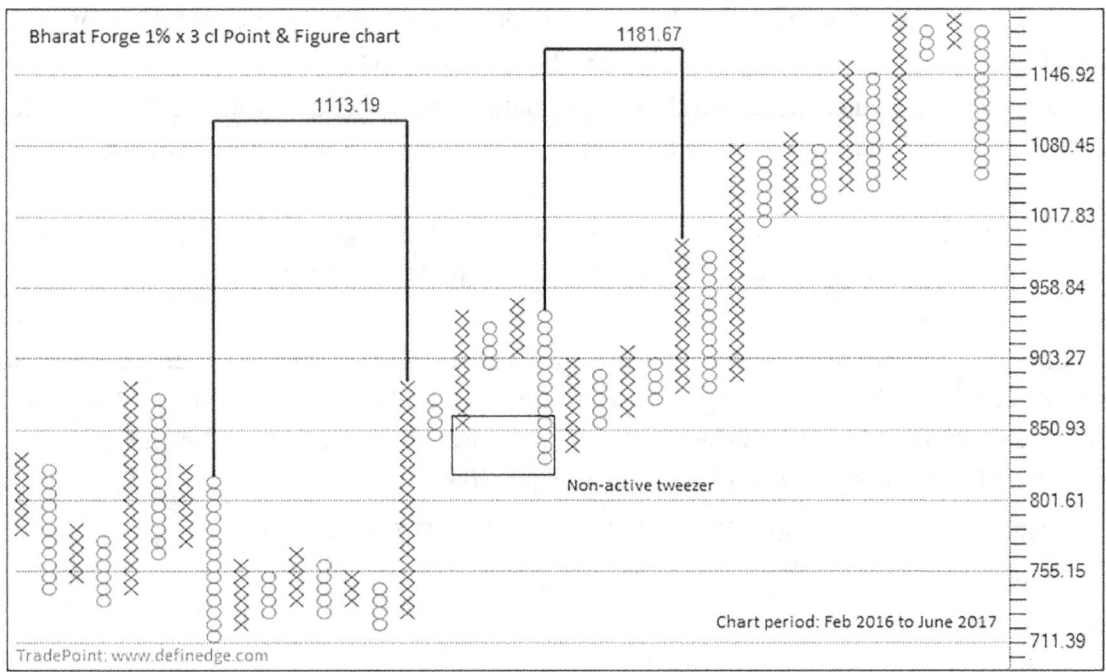

Figure 3.8.3: Bharat Forge daily 1% × 3 cl Point & Figure chart

A nonactivated bearish Tweezer is shown in the above chart. Remember, only active Tweezers are valid and should be traded. Never pre-empt the pattern because you will find many Tweezers and apparently good-looking formations that do not get active or become active later. So, it is always advisable to wait for the confirmation of the pattern completion before initiating trades

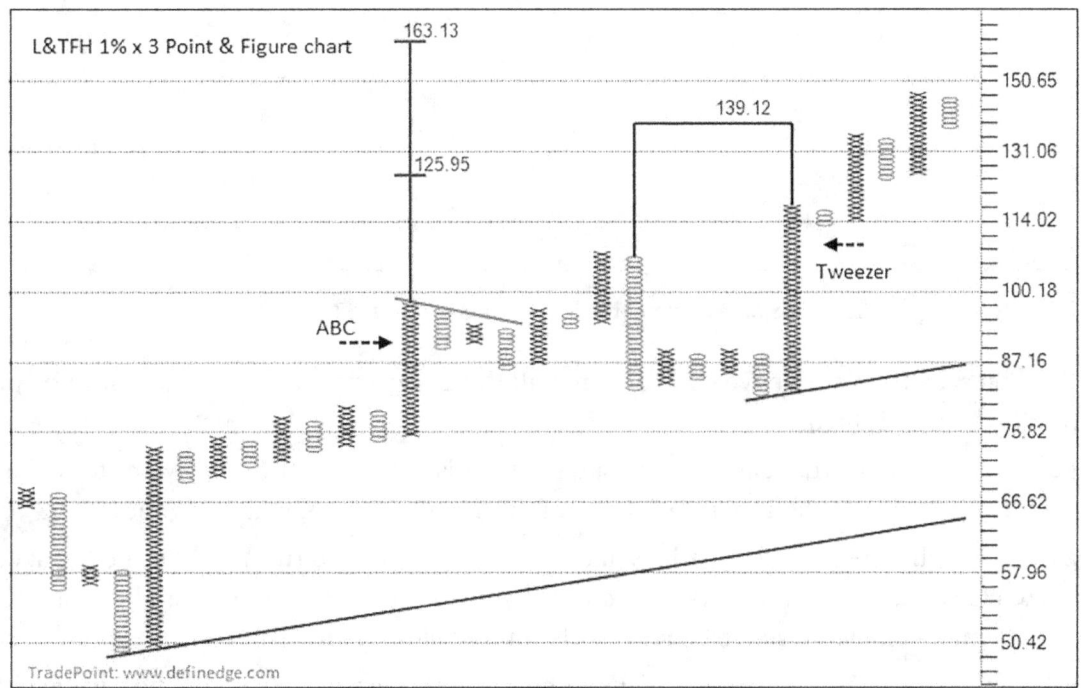

Figure 3.8.4: L&TFH daily 1% × 3 cl Point & Figure chart

A bullish ABC pattern and 45-degree upsloping trend lines from Mini Bottoms are also shown in the above chart Figure 3.8.4. A bullish Tweezer pattern is also highlighted. Notice that Follow-through that activates bullish Tweezer pattern is also a Super pattern in this instance.

One can also trade basic signal after the Tweezer pattern and ignore the targets. From the trading perspective, below are the possible ways to handle Tweezer patterns:

1. Trade it as per the rules discussed above. Calculate the initial risk measuring the failure level from entry and the reward shown by the horizontal count. If risk–reward ratio is favorable, then initiate the trade.

2. Trade basic signals or any other pattern after the completion of the Tweezer pattern. Keep Tweezer as a part of confirmation and take trades using P&F patterns. With this approach, you look at the overall chart structure and take trades.

3. Identify candidates where Tweezer pattern is activated and trade them on your preferred box-value, time frame or method. For example, you can find a candidate with Tweezer on 1% box-value and Super pattern on 0.25% box-value. You can trade that Super pattern on lower box-value and the trade will have a higher probability of turning profitable.

Figure 3.8.5 is a chart of Andhra bank showing different active Tweezers.

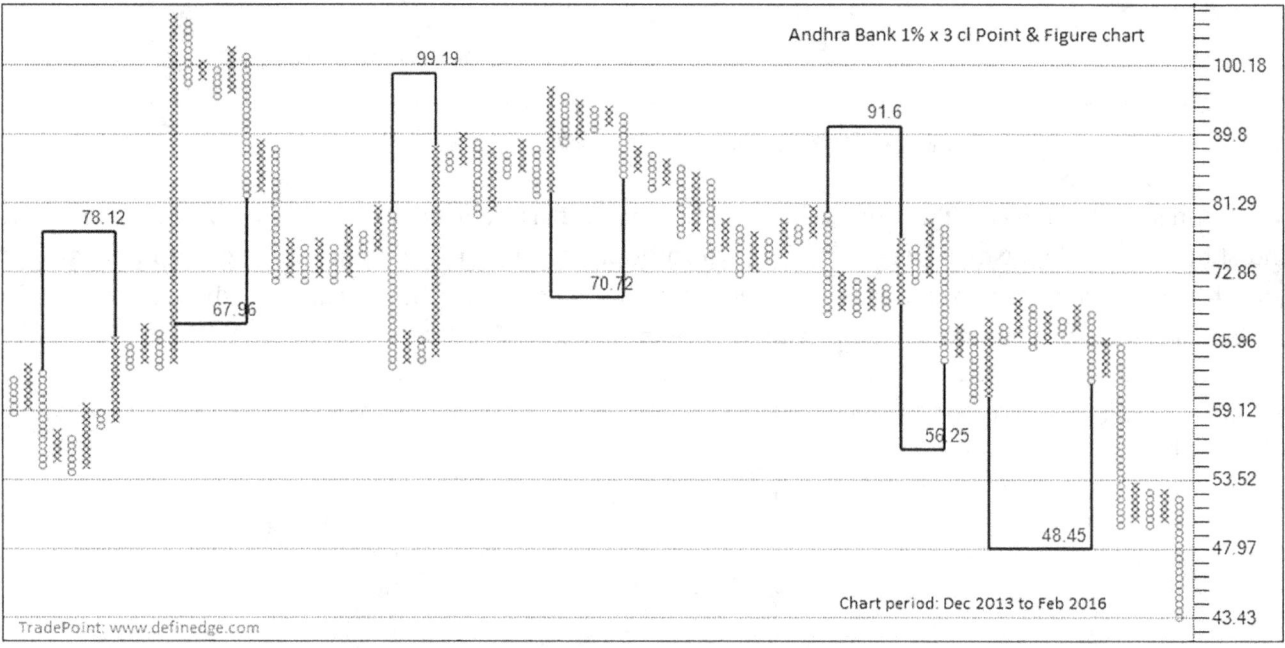

Figure 3.8.5: Andhra bank daily 1% × 3 cl Point & Figure chart

It can be observed from the above chart that not all the Tweezer patterns turned out to be profitable, but the overall win ratio is high.

There can be more rules that can be associated with this pattern, but I don't want to make it sound complicated. People will have their own variations of dealing with them, which is good.

Tweezers are applicable on all box-values and time frames, but the rules need to be tweaked a bit in lower box-size charts. In the 0.25% box-value chart, the consolidation columns can be up to 10 and the anchor column length should be above 20 boxes. The other rules are unchanged.

Figure 3.8.6 is a chart of Asian Paints, showing the Tweezer pattern on a 0.25% box-value chart.

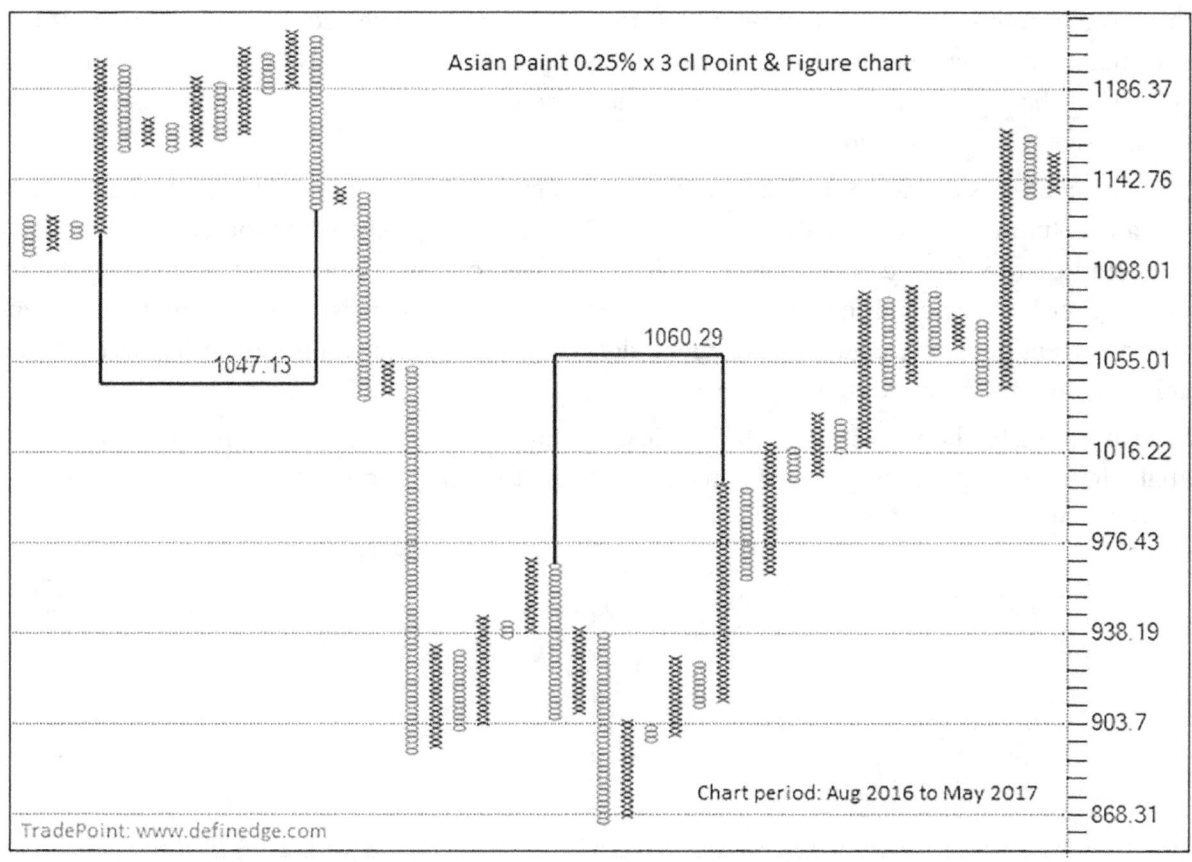

Figure 3.8.6: Asian Paints daily 0.25% × 3 cl Point & Figure chart

There can be Tweezers within the Tweezer; all of them are valid as long as they comply with the rules.

3.9: ANCHOR TOPS AND ANCHOR BOTTOMS

This is a method that helps us in identifying if significant Top or Bottom has been formed. Have a look at 1% box-value chart of Bharat Forge, shown in Figure 3.9.1.

Figure 3.9.1: Bharat Forge daily 1% × 3 cl Point & Figure chart

There is a corrective move when the overall trend is up. Stock price corrected for about 18 months and price bounced in between, but there was no Follow-through to it and the bounce did not sustain. Long columns of 'X' that appeared during the Downtrend were immediately followed by bearish patterns and resulted in price falling to new lows.

Point A is a 20-box anchor column formed during August 2016, which marked the highest number of boxes in any column of 'X' in the entire Downtrend. This is a strong signal that something significant has happened and that bulls have taken control. Price witnessed consolidation post the anchor column and formed a higher low and a subsequent Follow-through Buy signal. This is when the anchor Bottom gets marked and strength of that column gains more significance. The formation indicates that correction is probably over and price can reach higher levels.

We can calculate the target using the vertical count from the anchor column to judge the upside potential. Figure 3.9.2 is a chart of ICICI bank highlighting the same setup.

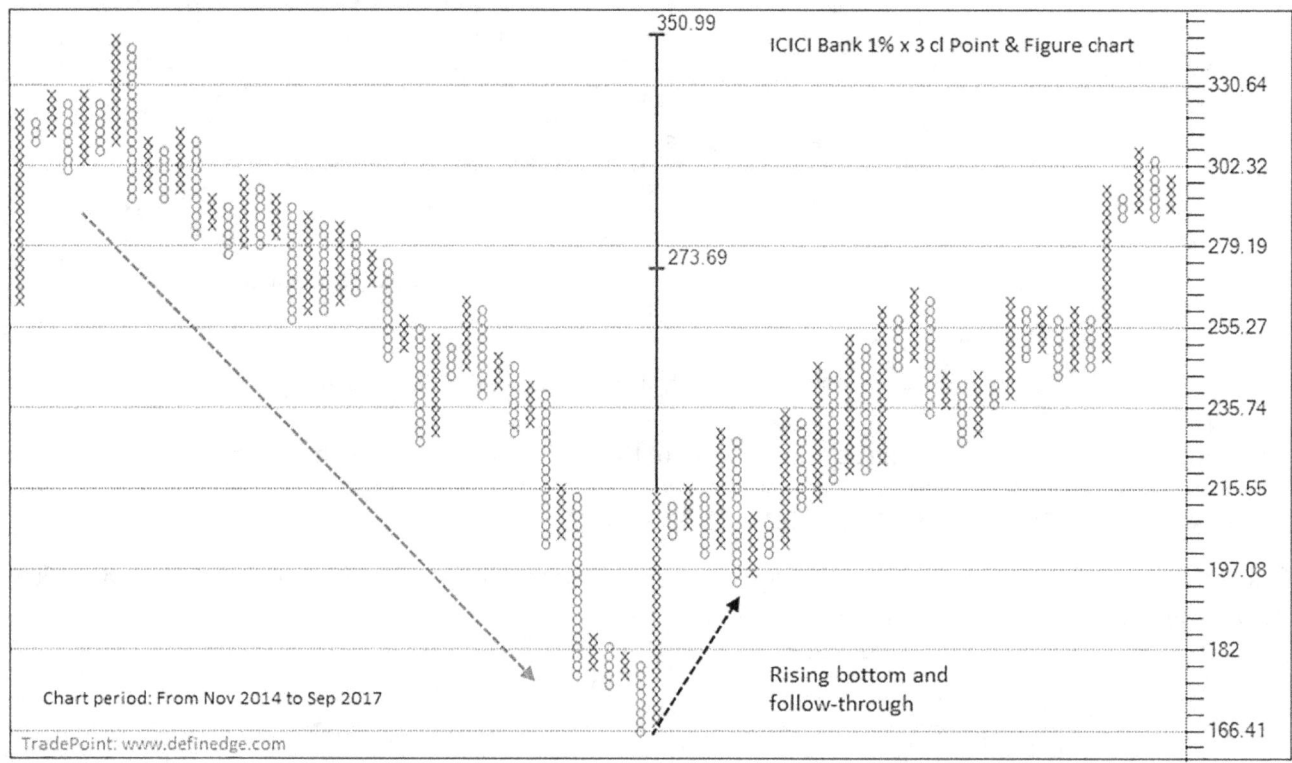

Figure 3.9.2: ICICI bank daily 1% × 3 cl Point & Figure chart

Anchor column Follow-through after Downtrend is the underlying concept behind the pattern. The consolidation and rising bottom pattern are confirmatory signs.

Anchor Top–Bottom pattern fails if Top of bullish anchor column or Bottom of bearish column gets broken. Price may not move immediately, or may even fail, but this formation is logical and the risk–reward is typically very attractive. This pattern provides significant information about the change of in the demand-supply equation which can be traded on different time frames as per the style and preference. For example, one can trade bullish formations on lower box-value chart when this setup is spotted on a higher box-value chart. See the chart of Ashok Leyland shown in Figure 3.9.3.

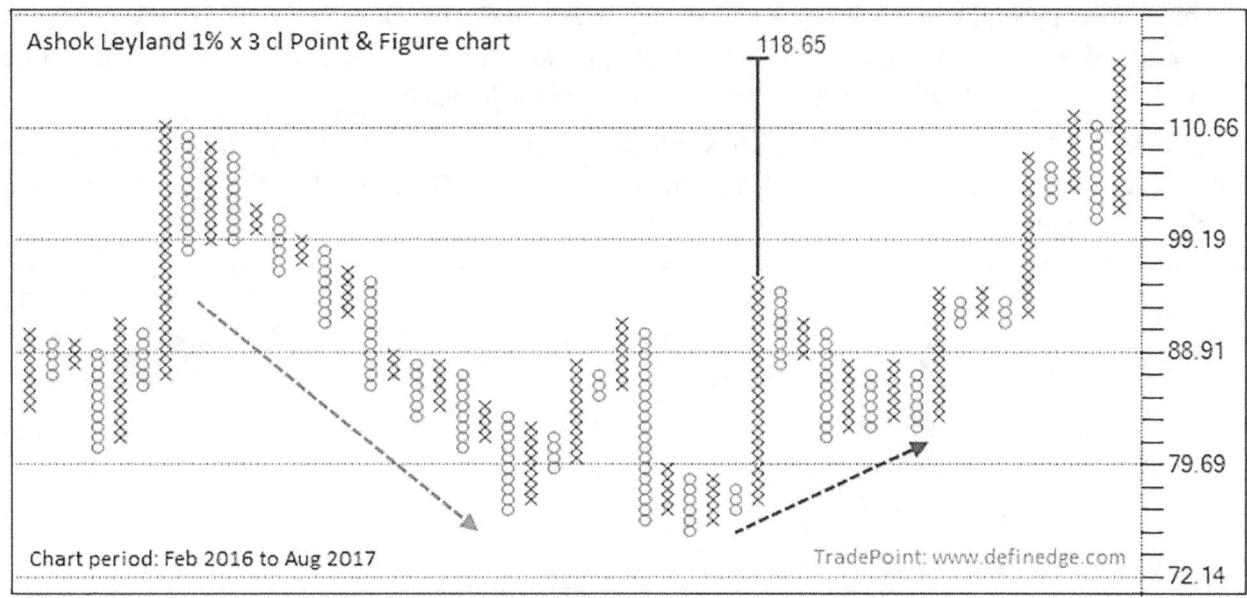

Figure 3.9.3: Ashok Leyland daily 1% × 3 cl Point & Figure chart

Anchor bottom is found on 1% box-value chart around 93. Bullish patterns can be traded on lower box-value charts of the same instrument. Figure 3.9.4 is a 0.25% box-value chart of Ashok Leyland showing 45-degree lines, breakout and counts.

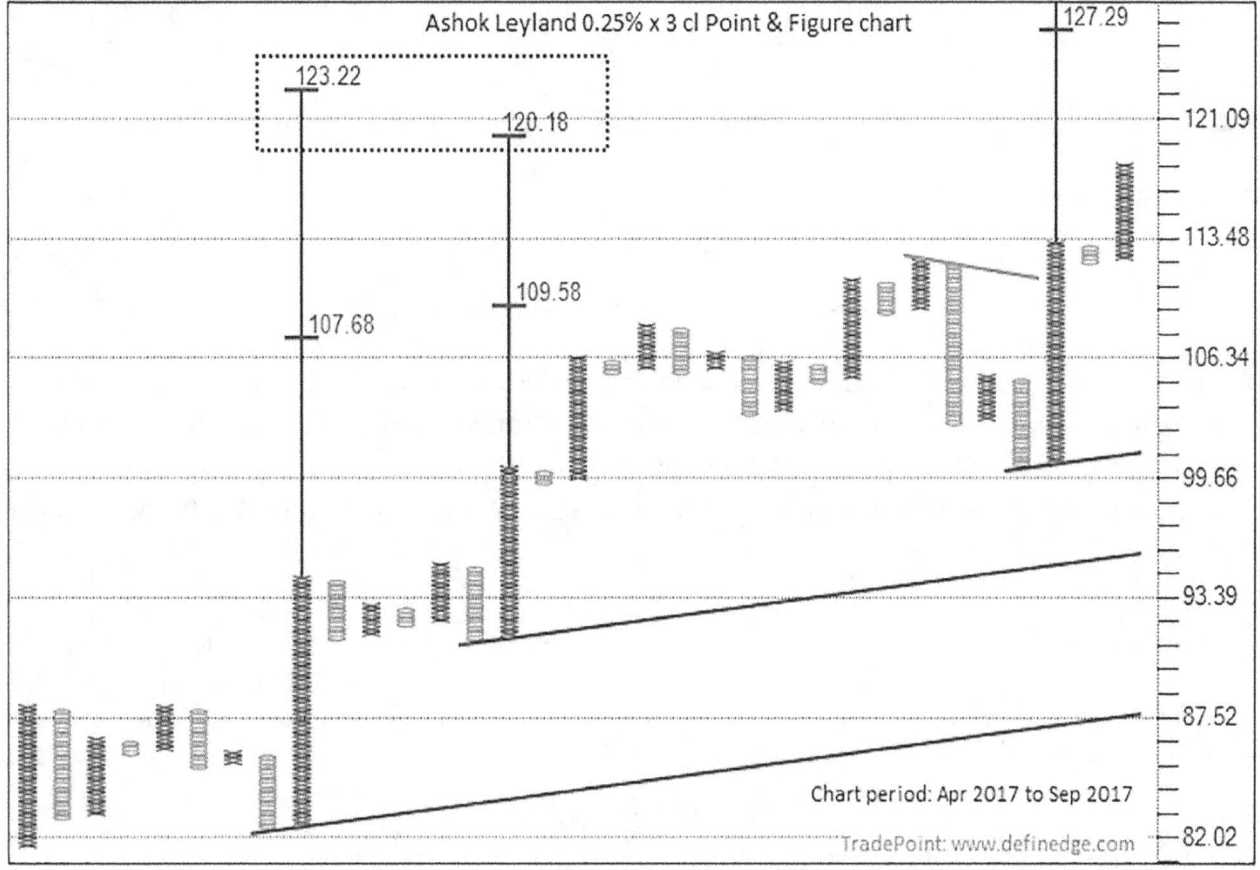

Figure 3.9.4: Ashok Leyland daily 0.25% × 3 cl Point & Figure chart

There are many bullish formations seen on the above chart that offered trades with an affordable risk–reward for short-term traders. It is a sensible approach for short-term trader to hunt for bullish trades when there are indications that medium-term Bottom is in place.

The reverse is applicable for Anchor Tops. Anchor column in Uptrend, followed by Lower Top and Follow-through breakout, indicates that significant Top is in place. Have a look at the 1% × 3 Sun Pharma chart shown in Figure 3.9.5.

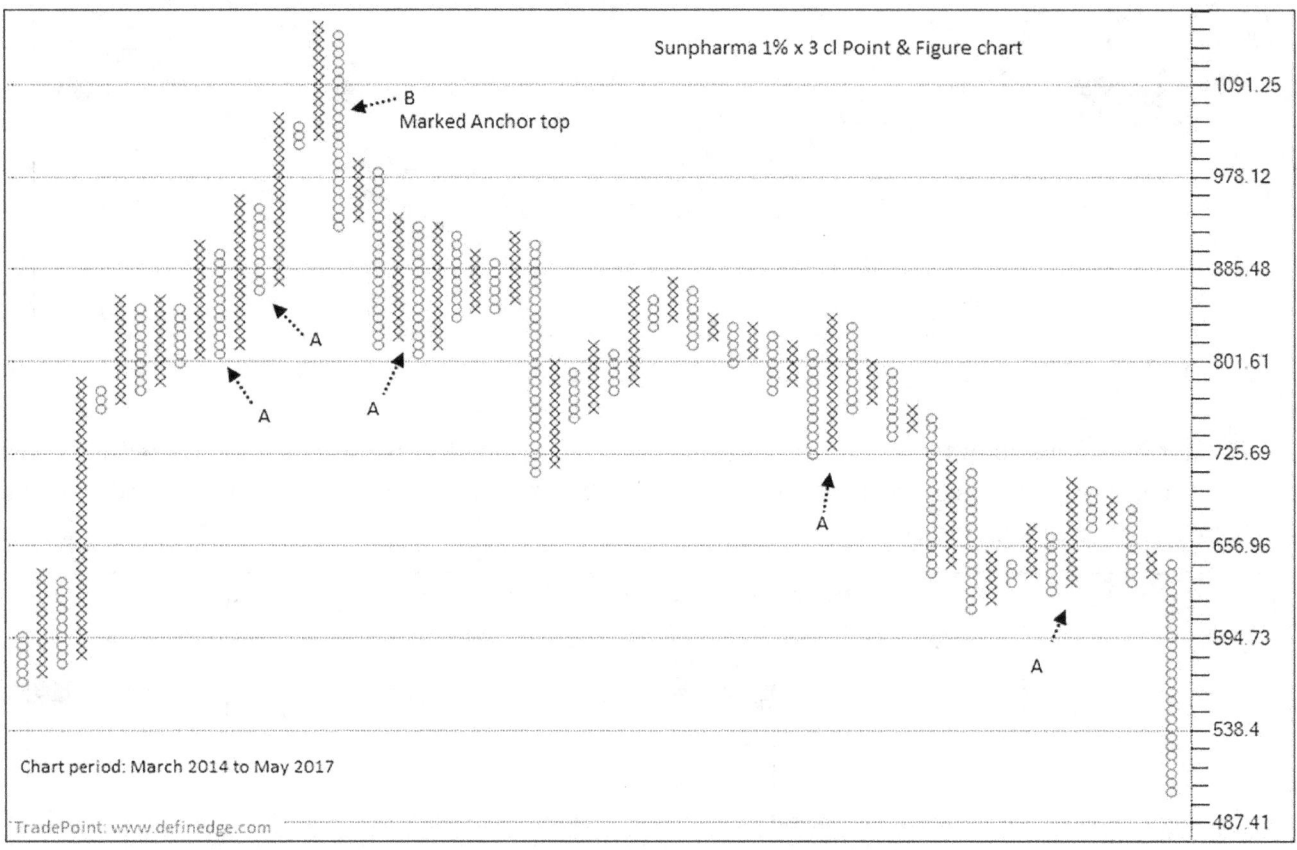

Figure 3.9.5: Sun Pharma daily 1% × 3 cl Point & Figure chart

All arrows marked A on the chart are anchor column against the trend that did not see Follow-through. The arrow marked as B is an anchor column that had a Follow-through and a lower high was also completed thereafter. This effectively makes the recent top, an anchor Top.

For Anchor top, lower box-value such as 0.25% is also useful. Have a look at the HDIL chart in Figure 3.9.6.

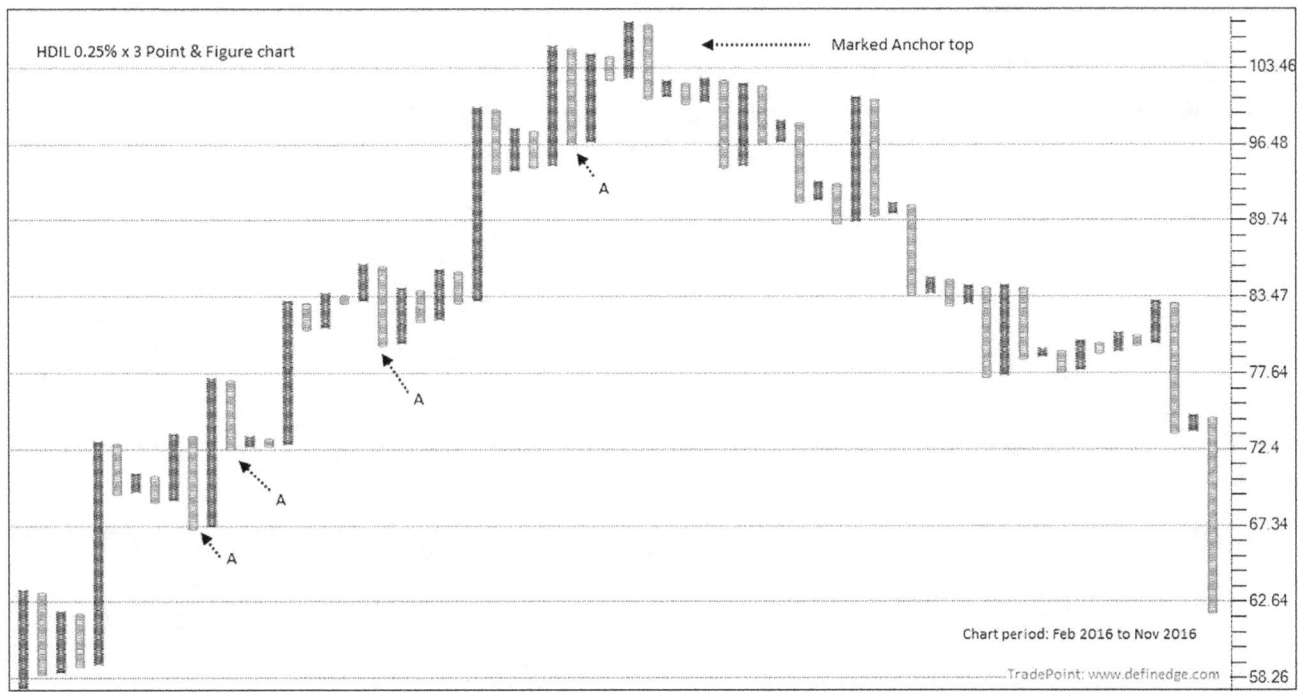

Figure 3.9.6: HDIL daily 0.25% × 3 cl Point & Figure chart

Arrows marked A in the chart above are bearish anchor column that did not see any Follow-through. Arrow B witnessed Follow-through and a consolidation thereafter, followed by a lower Top.

The pause in terms of consolidation and lower Top or Bottom that occurs after the rebellious anchor column is at the heart of this strategy. Continuation signals post that, offer highly profitable trades.

Chapter 4

INDICATORS

I was of the opinion initially that indicators are not required on Point & Figure charts. Price is a leading indicator and there is already a noise removal mechanism that is in-built in P&F charts. My thought was that more lines or indicators on P&F charts will only complicate the issue. But, I soon realized that indicators can be effectively utilized to design objective systems in P&F charts. They are also helpful to identify trend and instruments that should not be traded and the patterns that should be ignored. As we discussed during the chapter on analysis, every basic P&F pattern cannot be traded but their objectivity and noiselessness is still a big advantage. Indicators can complement them and help in filtering the setups that can increase the odds of success in trading.

There are so many indicators we plot on the usual bar and candlestick charts and all of them can be plotted in Point & Figure charts as well. Their formula remains the same but the logic changes, because a P&F column is not a bar or candle that represent a particular time period. There is a difference between 10 candles and 10 columns. 10 candles on a daily chart will consist of the prices of 10 days, but 10 columns of P&F represent 10 trends consisting of the prices of a minimum 10 days.

This makes indicators on P&F charts quite interesting. P&F setups can be designed with a combination of indicators or they can also be filtered by using indicators. Few indicators are explained in this section to help you understand the idea and logic of their application on P&F charts. Any type indicator can be plotted in the same manner and usual methods of reading them are applicable in P&F charts. I have avoided discussion about the formula and basic explanations because they are very popular indicators and tons of literature is available online about them.

Let us begin with most basic indicator we know.

4.1: MOVING AVERAGES

Gilbert Foster is said to have invented method of applying Moving averages on Point & Figure charts during 1960s. Moving average is the most basic indicator that we use in all types of charts. It can be applied on Point & Figure charts too. A 10-day Moving average on bar or candlestick chart calculates average price of the last 10 prices, usually the closing price. It can be calculated on open, high or low prices also but with one given price point. Same way Moving average of last 10 Point & Figure columns can also be plotted by using one price from every column.

There are two methods to pick single price from the column:

1. Mid-price method

This is a traditional method and widely used. Average price or mid-price of every column is a proxy price considered for calculating the moving average. Below is the formula:

Mid-price of every column: (High price of the column + Low price of the column)/2

180			X	
170			X	O
160	X		X	O
150	X	O	X	O
140	X	O	X	
130	X	O	X	
120	X	O	X	
110	X	O		
100	X			
	1	2	3	4

Moving Average plotted
by connecting mid prices

Image 4.1.1: Moving average calculation

Image above shows 1 column simple moving average plotted by connecting the mid-price of every column. Mid-price of the first column is 130 as per formula shown above. Mid-price of second column is also 130. Flat line is drawn showing the moving average on these columns. Mid-price of the third column is 150 and fourth column is 160. All these prices are connected to draw the one column moving average line. It is worth noting that fourth column is of 'O' that shows a downward price move but moving average went up because the mid-price of the column was higher than its previous column.

Moving average for any parameter can be calculated in the same manner. First plotting price of a 10 column moving average will be calculated based on the average price of last 10 columns' mid-price. New column will come with new mid-price. Moving average will be calculated in the usual manner only by taking new price in account and dropping the first price of the series.

Note that with mid-price moving average method, for price to go above 1 period moving average requires mid-price of that column to be above mid-price of its previous column. Hence, with this method, mid-price of a column should be above moving average to call it a breakout. High of the column of 'X' above moving average is not a breakout but the mid-price of that column should be above the moving average to qualify as a valid breakout. Same way, mid-price of the column of 'O' should be below moving average line to call it a valid negative breakout below the moving average line.

Below is the Nifty bank 0.50% × 3 P&F chart showing the 5 column moving average plotted with mid-price method.

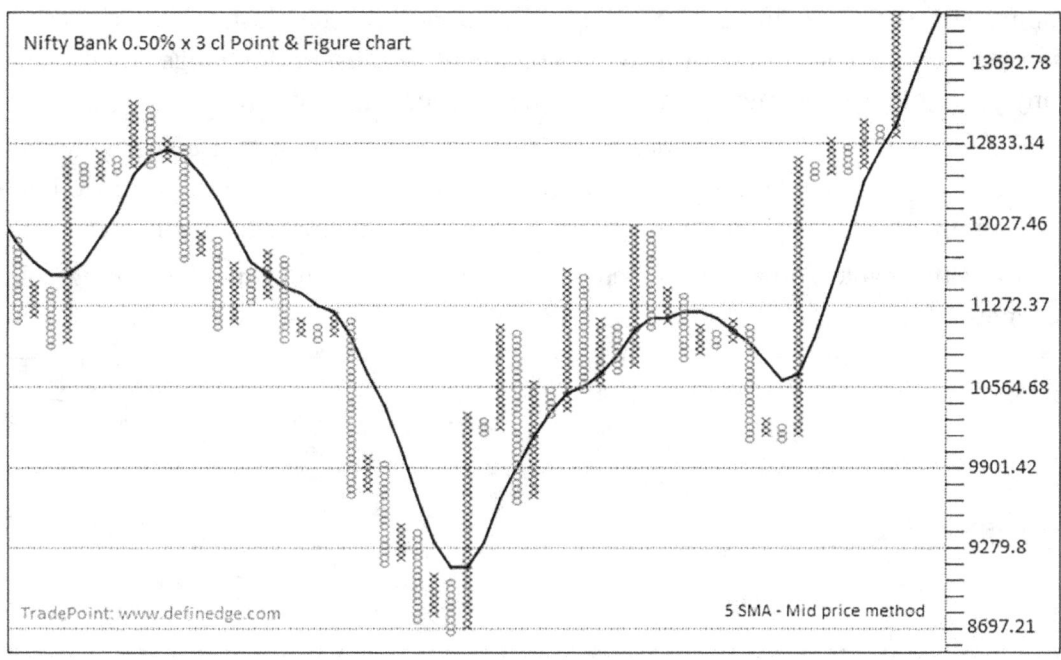

Figure 4.1.1: Nifty bank daily 0.50% × 3 cl Point & Figure chart

2. Closing price method

Another method is to consider closing price of the column as a proxy price of that column. Don't let the name confuse you, the closing price of column of 'X' is high price of that column and need not be the actual closing price on any given day. Similarly, closing price of column of 'O' is low price of that column. This is relatively simple method to understand.

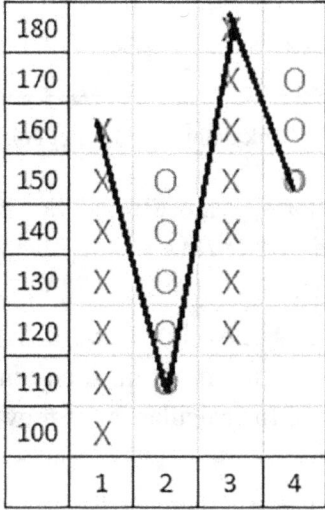

Moving average plotted
by connecting the closing
prices of a column

Image 4.1.2: Moving average calculation

Image above shows the moving average plotted by connecting the closing prices of every column, that is high price of column of 'X' and low price of column of 'O'. Rest of the things remain same, moving average of any parameter can be calculated in the same manner using this method.

With closing price method, it is not necessary that the mid-price of that column should be above moving average to qualify as a valid breakout. A column of 'X' going above the average line is a valid breakout and column of 'O' going below the moving average is valid downside breakout.

Below is the Nifty bank 0.50% × 3 P&F chart showing the 5 column moving average plotted with closing price method.

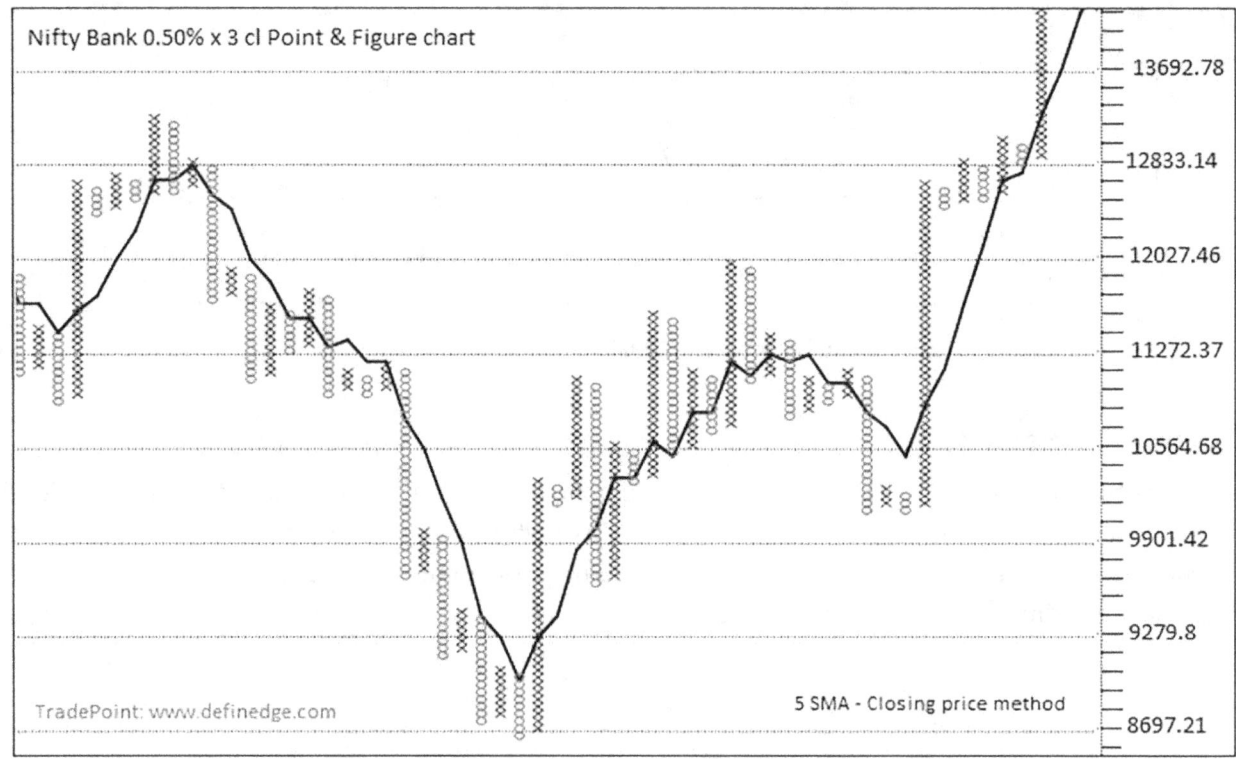

Figure 4.1.2: Nifty bank daily 0.50% × 3 cl Point & Figure chart

Both these moving averages can be plotted using Simple Moving Average (SMA), Exponential Moving Average (EMA), Weighted Moving Average (WMA), Adaptive Moving Average (AMA) or any other method of calculating the moving average.

Calculation of moving average remains same on P&F charts but they are different in nature. A column represents a trend and don't occur at fixed time interval. A column may consist of many days or months or quarters and will produce just one price for calculation of moving average. So a 10 column average on P&F chart is average price of last 10 swings.

P&F chart connected with 1 SMA using closing price method was shown in the chapter x. The obvious question by now is which method should be used. Both are good if the plotting is understood. Look at the figure below showing below 10 column Moving average plotted using both the methods. Blue line is the moving average plotted with average price method and Red line is one plotted with closing price method.

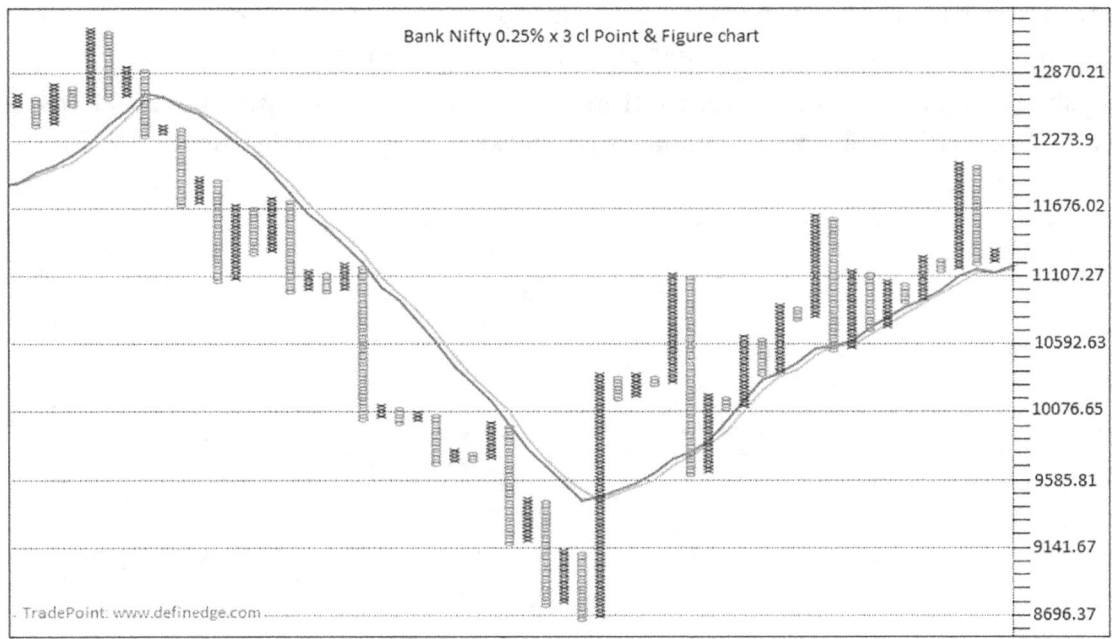

Figure 4.1.3: Nifty bank daily 0.25% × 3 cl Point & Figure chart

There is not much of a difference between them when the parameter used is not small. However, a moving average with closing price method would be preferred because it doesn't require the mid-price of column to be above the moving average to indicate a valid breakout. This makes it simple to comprehend and use the crossovers effectively.

All methods of reading moving averages are applicable to Point & Figure charts too. A 45-degree trend line is a far superior method for trend identification and no other indicator is required if one understands the 45-degree trend line. But moving average can act as an effective substitute for 45-degree lines for the purposes of trend identification. Moving average can also be useful while designing the systems and back-testing the occurrences. In this way, all usages of a 45-degree trend lines that we discussed in prior chapters are applicable to moving averages. Hence, trend can be trailed using moving average line, patterns can be filtered using moving averages and pull-backs to average line can be traded with relevant patterns.

With moving average, Uptrend can be defined as price trading above the moving average and Downtrend as price positioned below moving average. So if we replace 45-degree lines with moving average, basic system with trend filtration rules are as follows:

⯅ Trade long when Double Top Buy pattern is triggered above the moving average line.

⯅ Exit long trades when Double Bottom Sell signal is formed.

⯅ Trade short when Double Bottom Sell signal is triggered below the moving average line.

⯅ Cover short trades when a Double Top Buy signal is formed.

Moving average and price crossover is a traditional technique which is simple and successful that has stood the test of time. The major problem with this technique on time-based charts is the whipsaws during the sideways move. That problem is effectively dealt with, in P&F charts. The P&F charts by default filters out most of the noise, resulting in fewer columns during the sideways period. The moving average will therefore remain flat during such phase. Trades are placed based on patterns instead of crossover that will generate far lesser trades and hence fewer whipsaws. The whipsaws will be far lesser and the trending phase will not be missed out due the breakout technique inherent in the P&F methodology.

Figure shown below is 1% × 3 P&F chart of Aban plotted with daily closing prices. Plotted on it is a 20-column average with closing price method. Fresh Buy signals above average line and Fresh Sell signals below average line are shown in the chart.

Figure 4.1.4: Aban daily 1% × 3 cl Point & Figure chart

The moving average is in sync with the price swings during this phase. Below is the 15 years chart from June 2001 to Jan 2016 of Aban with same parameters to visualize the effectiveness of the moving average.

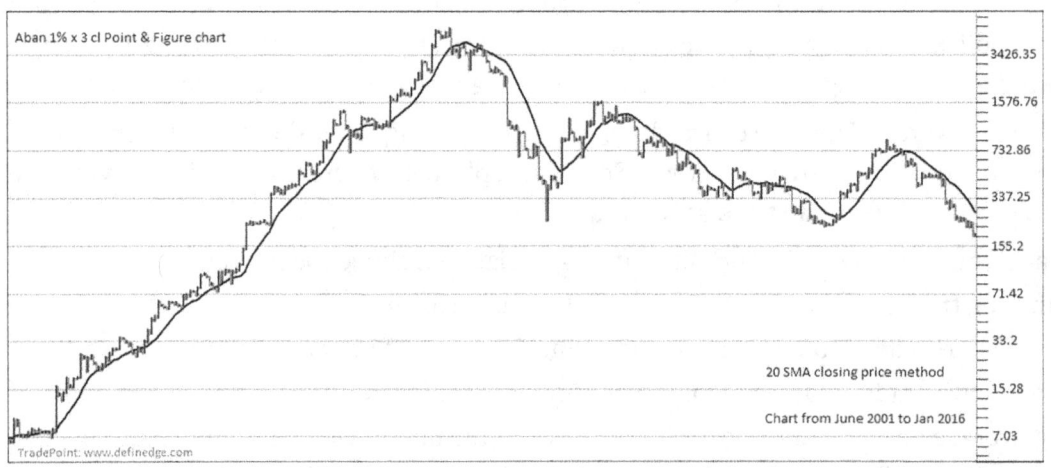

Figure 4.1.5: Aban daily 1% × 3 cl Point & Figure chart

You will notice in the chart above that simple crossover of averages along with pattern confirmation could be an effective trading technique.

Various systems can be designed using moving average and P&F patterns. One can also explore the use of exponential or weighted averages in P&F charts. Normally a 10- or a 20-column average suits all timeframes and box-values. It can also be easily back-tested and optimized for every instrument before using it. Exit can be applied based on penetration of average line as well.

Moving average in trending markets act as an excellent tool to identify pullback trade setups. Bullish Poles and Bear traps and its variations that touch the moving average line indicate rejection of price at the moving average line and prove the strength of the average line. It indicates that correction is complete and that the price is set to resume the earlier trend. Image below shows the bullish and bearish pullback setup with the help of moving average line.

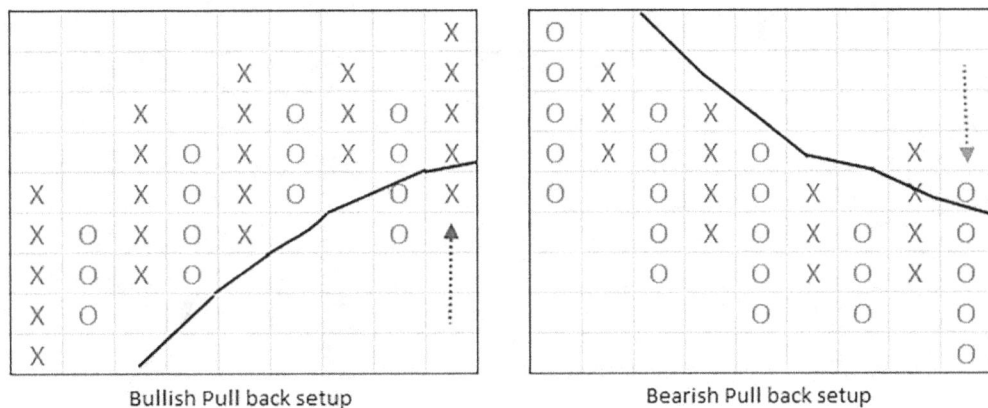

Image 4.1.3: Moving average pullback

Below is 0.50% × 3 P&F chart of SKS micro-plotted using daily closing prices.

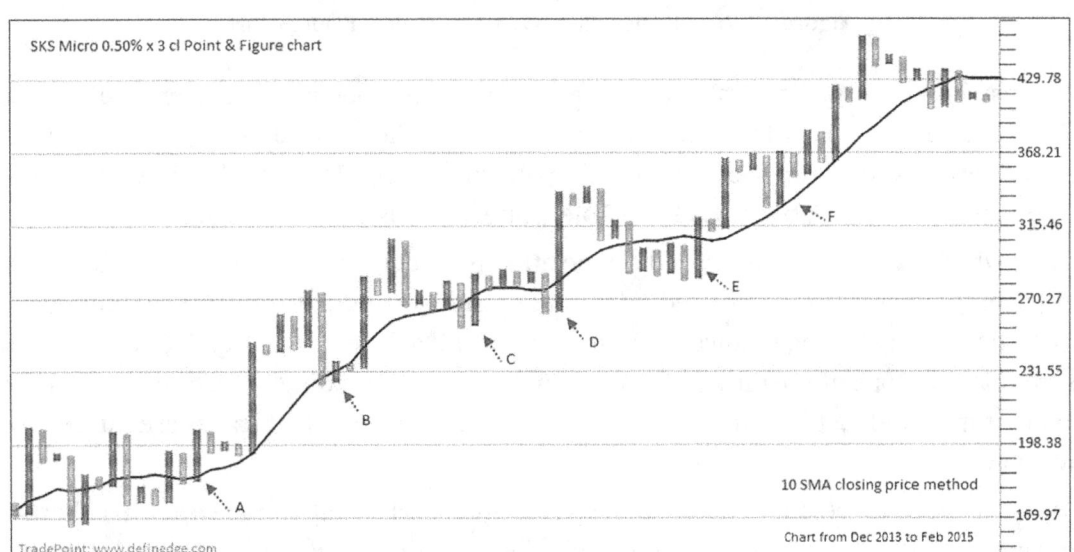

Figure 4.1.6: SKS micro daily 0.50% × 3 cl Point & Figure chart

All arrows in chart indicate bullish patterns that occurred near the moving average line. Pattern A is negation of the High Pole pattern. Pattern B is an affordable Double Top Buy taking support at the moving average line. Pattern C is bullish Broadening formation. Pattern D is 100% Pole and also a Bear Trap. Pattern E is Bullish Double Broadening formation. Pattern F is 100% Pole near the average line.

People tend to focus on the support level in a Downtrend and resistance in an Uptrend but it should be the other way around. The best advantage of identifying support level in Uptrend is that it provides an opportunity to go along and participate in the trend with a better risk–reward proposition. Appearance of bullish pattern makes it a powerful trading set up. Same way knowing resistance in a Downtrend confirmed by bearish setup is the opportunity to trade short. Pattern confirmation is the key, because it offers a with clear entry and exit norms.

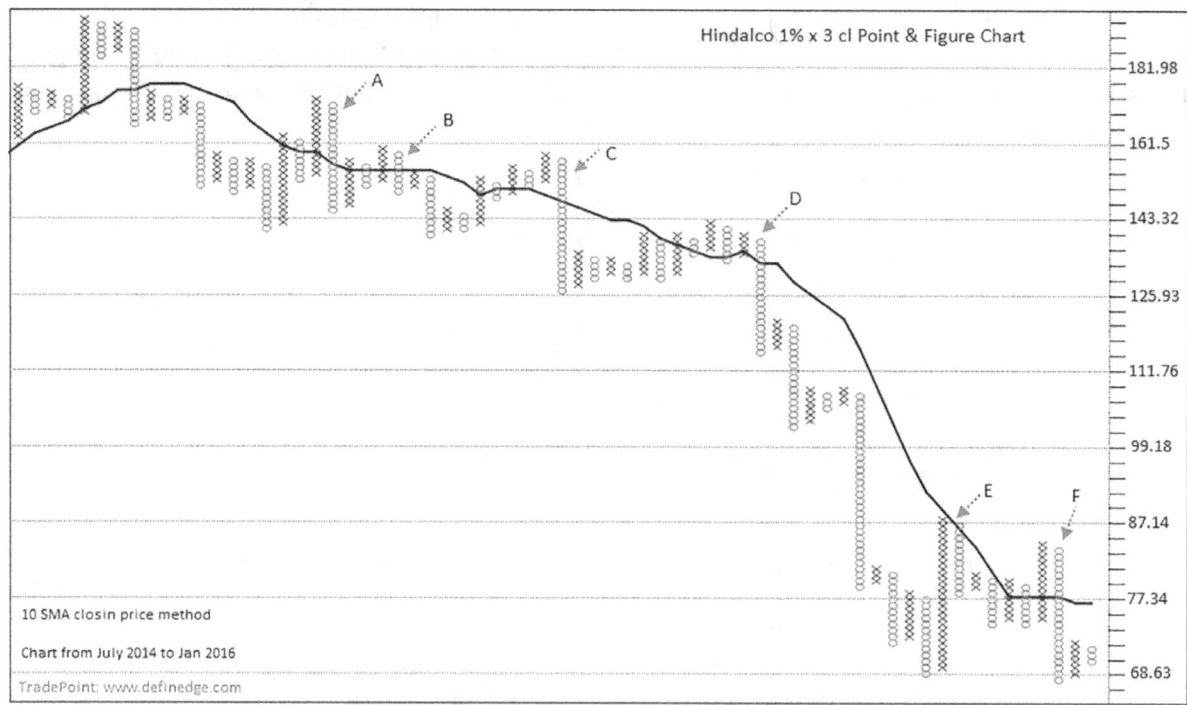

Figure 4.1.7: Hindalco daily 1% × 3 cl Point & Figure chart

All patterns shown in the chart above are bearish patterns touching the average line. Pattern A is Bearish 100% pole. Pattern B is Bull Trap, which is also a Follow-through to pole at point A. Pattern C is Bullish pattern reversed and bearish Double pattern. Pattern D is Double Bottom Sell which is a Follow-through to Bull Trap. Pattern E is High Pole. Pattern F is Bearish 100% Pole.

When and which pattern must be traded can be effectively determined using trend identification filter like moving average. For setup based trading, pullback and flirting patterns are the best opportunities to trade with the moving average indicator. Remember, pullback setup is effective in established trends hence ensure that the slope of the moving average line is rising for trading bullish setups and falling while using bearish setups. Trading performance will be improved considerably if trades are filtered by the slope of the moving average line.

Many studies are conducted for choosing the parameter for moving average on usual charts. Different parameters suit to different instruments. Thankfully there are limited choices with P&F. Broadly 5, 10, 15, 20 or 30 column averages can be used. Back-testing and optimization techniques can help in identifying the right parameter for an instrument. One can also use Fib numbers as moving average length. Start with 10 or 20. One of them will typically suffice. I am a fan of simple and round numbers but odd or middle numbers can be used as an alternative. It also depends on the behavior of the instrument, some works well with 20 and some with 15. Most importantly, parameter should be used based on the setup you want to trade. If you are trading a system for price average crossover then begin with applying 20 because it may suit more. If you are looking for pullback setup then 10 would be better number to begin with.

Double and triple moving average crossover reading can be applied on Point & Figure charts for trend filtration. But besides that, there is one more interesting observation when triple moving average is applied on a P&F chart. Below is a 0.25% × 3 P&F chart of Star shown along with 10,15,20 column simple moving average.

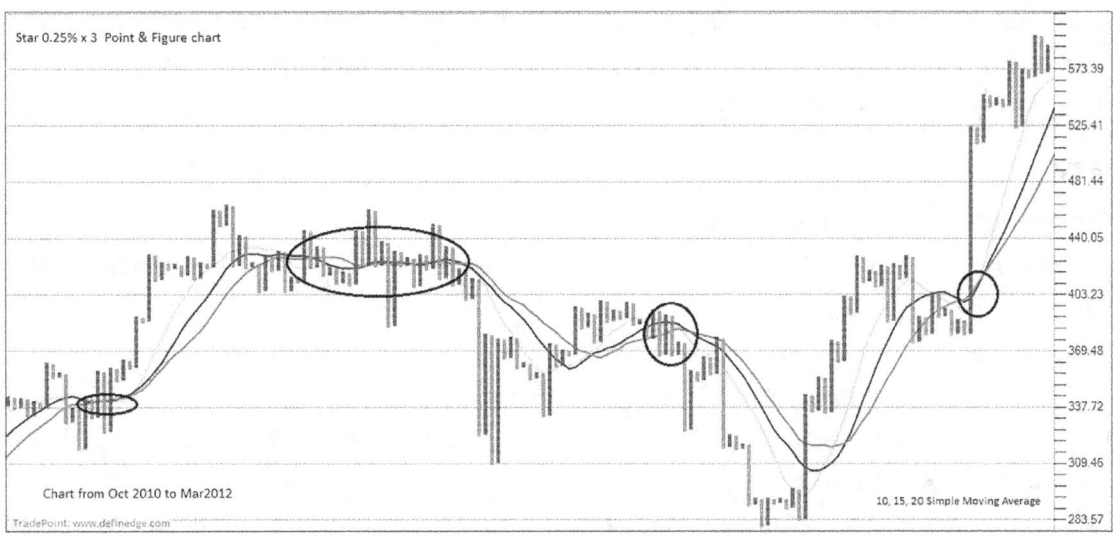

Figure 4.1.8: Star daily 0.25% × 3 cl Point & Figure chart

Circled area is an area of convergence. Three averages coming close to each other is a convergence that shows the consolidation phase. On P&F chart, convergence indicates a period of consolidation post which a breakout and a trending move is expected. The basic signal after convergence will indicate the direction of the breakout

Triple moving average configuration of short-term moving average positioned above the medium and the medium above the long term, works well on P&F charts too. I recommend 10, 15 and 20 moving averages for the same, only on a lower box-value charts such as 0.25% (Refer slot 1 charts from the chapter on box-value). Trade patterns during such cases and ignore when averages are in converging mode. It helps in trading clear charts and avoiding stocks which are in consolidation/confusing zone.

Adaptive moving average (AMA) is a type of moving average developed by Perry Kaufman that takes care of the market noise. It uses the smoothing constant (SC) and Efficiency Ratio (ER) to calculate the moving average, which results in the average line that goes flat when the trend is not strong. Rising and Falling lines indicate a trending phase. Setups can be developed based on the slope of the line. Parameter should be lower when plotted using the closing method but they nicely complement the P&F setups basically because of its nature of going flat during uncertain times. Below is 0.50% × 3 P&F chart of Nifty bank along with 20-column AMA applied on them. Arrow marks show the pullback setups.

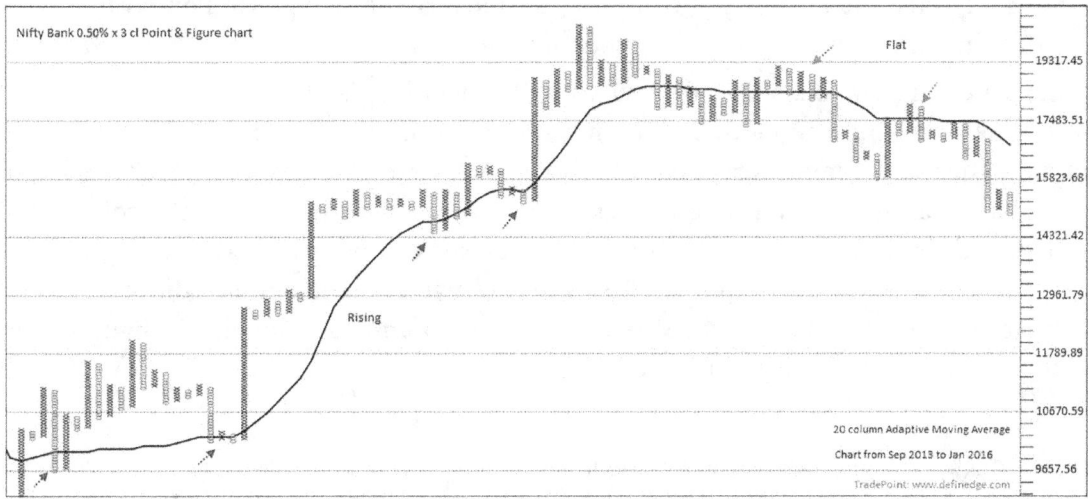

Figure 4.1.9: Nifty bank daily 0.50% × 3 cl Point & Figure chart

Idea of averages on P&F charts was a great invention indeed that has opened opportunities to explore these charts in many ways. Apply them and have a feel. You may find many other ways to utilize them. It can also be used along with Bollinger bands which is our next discussion.

Summary

- ⅄ Concept of moving average on P&F is fascinating.
- ⅄ Trend is bullish when price is above average line and bearish when it is below average line.
- ⅄ Patterns can be filtered with the moving average line.
- ⅄ Trade pullback setups to moving averages.
- ⅄ Trend can be ridden using 10 or 20 column moving average line.
- ⅄ Different systems can be designed with P&F patterns and single moving average, or double–triple moving average crossovers.
- ⅄ Triple moving average convergence and P&F pattern breakout indicate significant price consolidation breakout.

4.2: BOLLINGER BANDS®

Bollinger Bands® is a wonderful invention of John Bollinger in the field of Technical analysis. It is the best channel indicator available out there.

Advanced Indicators such as Bollinger Bands on Point & Figure charts were first used by Jeremy du Plessis in his book *The Definitive Guide to Point and Figure*[1].

Bollinger bands are standard deviation bands calculated from a moving average. Normally two standard deviation bands above and below moving average are plotted on the chart. Since we can plot moving average on P&F charts, it is also possible to plot Bollinger bands alongside. If we plot 10-column average with 2 standard deviation Bollinger bands on P&F charts, then three channel lines or bands will appear on the chart. Middle band is moving average line, Upper and lower band are 2-standard deviation lines above and below middle band, respectively. The bands adjust with the volatility and contain majority of price action within them. There are many ways of using the bands. The book *Bollinger on Bollinger Bands*, authored by John Bollinger, is a must-read to understand Bollinger bands in detail.

The major difference of using them on P&F is that here the standard deviation is calculated from average of columns, not price bars. We discussed that moving averages on P&F can be plotted using two methods, mid-price and closing price. Bollinger bands can be also plotted on both the methods of plotting average line; the difference needs to be understood.

Below are 10-column with 2 standard deviation Bollinger bands plotted on a P&F chart using mid-price method. Because they are plotted using mid-price method, the upper band gets breached only when mid-value of the column rises above the band. A simple crossover of 'X' above band is not a breach of the band. Similarly, lower band gets broken only when mid-value of the column falls below the lower band. All breaches of upper and lower bands shown by arrows are invalid except the one shown by red arrow at the end, simply because the mid-value of the column did not cross above or below the band to call it a valid breach. Mid-value of the column is below lower band in case of last breach on the chart that makes it a valid breakout.

---

* Bollinger Bands® is a registered trademark of John Bollinger.

1. The Definitive Guide to Point and Figure: *A comprehensive Guide to the Theory and Practical Use of the Point and Figure Charting Method,* Petersfield: Harriman House Publishing, 2006.

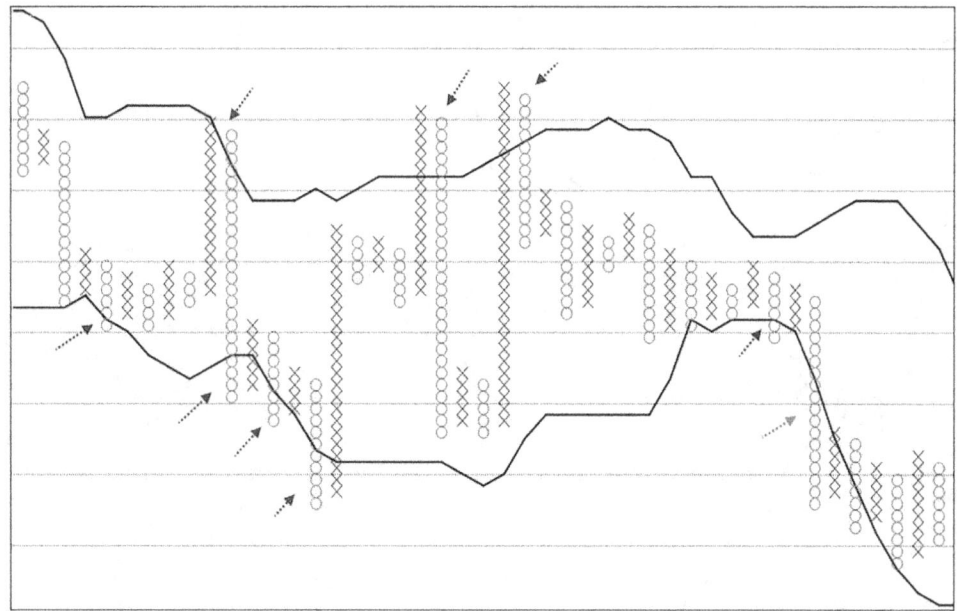

Image 4.2.1: Mid-price method Bollinger bands on P&F

Below is same chart plotted with 1 column simple moving average line using mid-price method shown with red color that display the mid-value of every column. It can be seen that the average remained well within bands during entire period except during the last breach when it fell below the lower band.

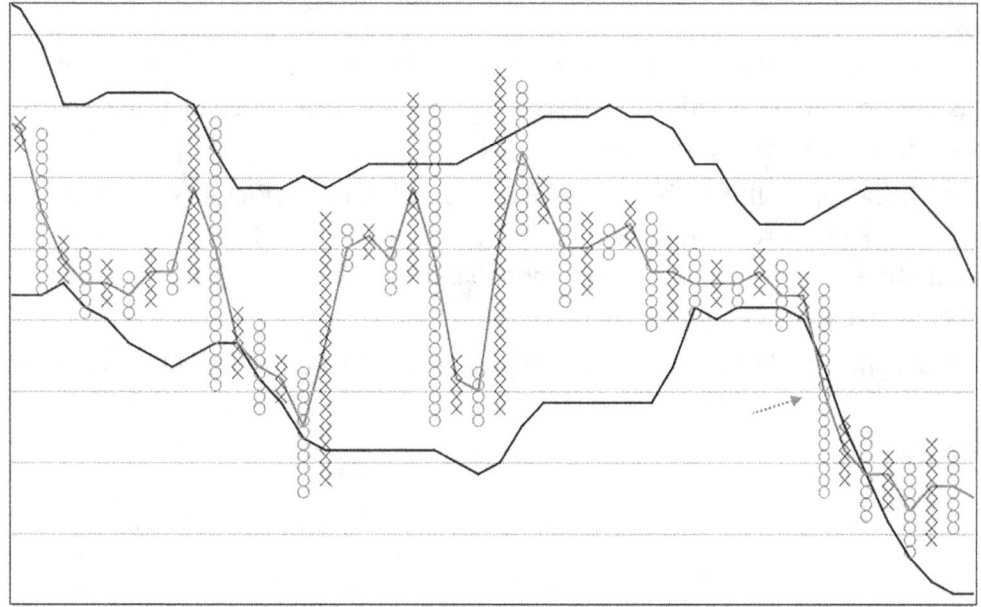

Image 4.2.2: Mid-price method Bollinger bands on P&F

Chart below shows the Bollinger bands plotted with closing price method on the same chart. It is not required for mid-value of the column to be above or below bands to call it a valid breach with this method.

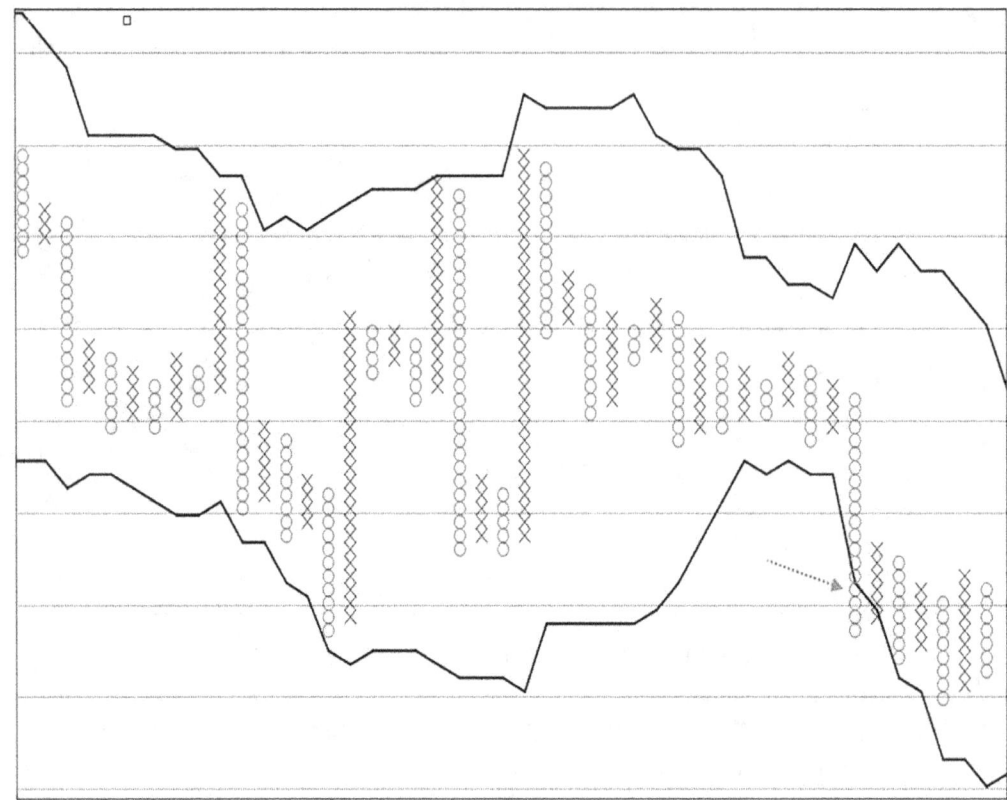

Image 4.2.3: Closing price method Bollinger bands on P&F

Breach is very simple to view with closing price method but bands are very wide and difference between both is visible. Though Bands plotted with this method easily display price excursions, the ones plotted with the mid-price methods are more effective and useful.

All methods of reading Bollinger bands are also applicable on P&F charts. 10 column bands with 2 standard deviations are preferred parameters on Point & Figure charts. Bollinger bands and P&F Patterns complement each other. The main utilization of these bands on P&F charts is that it can help in identifying instances of when to avoid breakout patterns.

Below is a figure showing Bollinger bands plotted on P&F chart but X and O are removed from it.

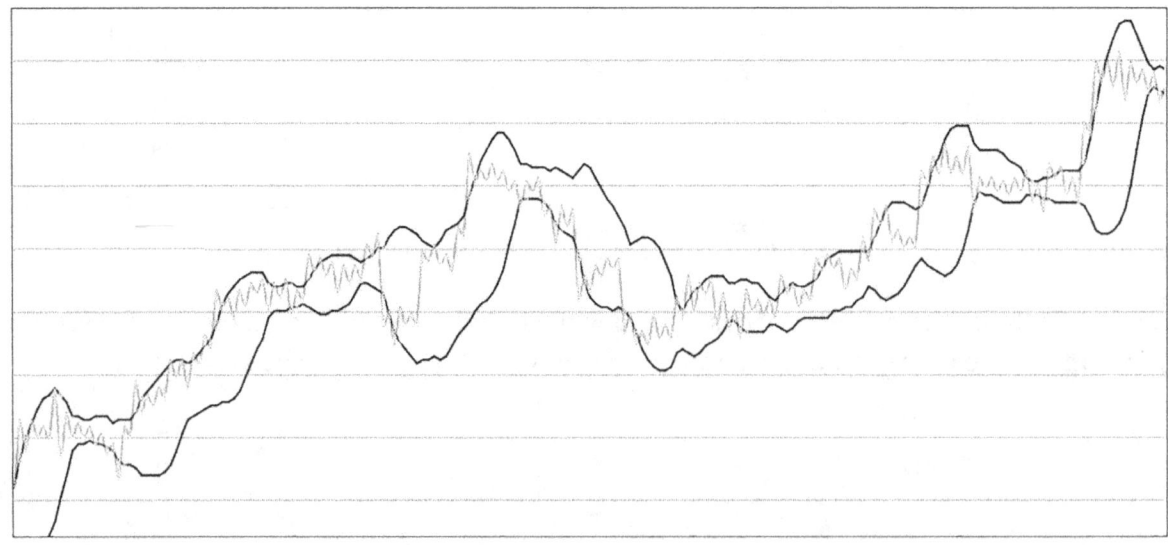

Image 4.2.4: Bollinger bands on P&F swings

Apart from all popular methods of reading of Bollinger bands, I found behavior of bands quite intriguing and useful when applied on P&F charts.

Broadly there are four types of band behavior that can be distinguished. Flat bands, Narrow bands, Trending bands and expanding bands as shown in image below.

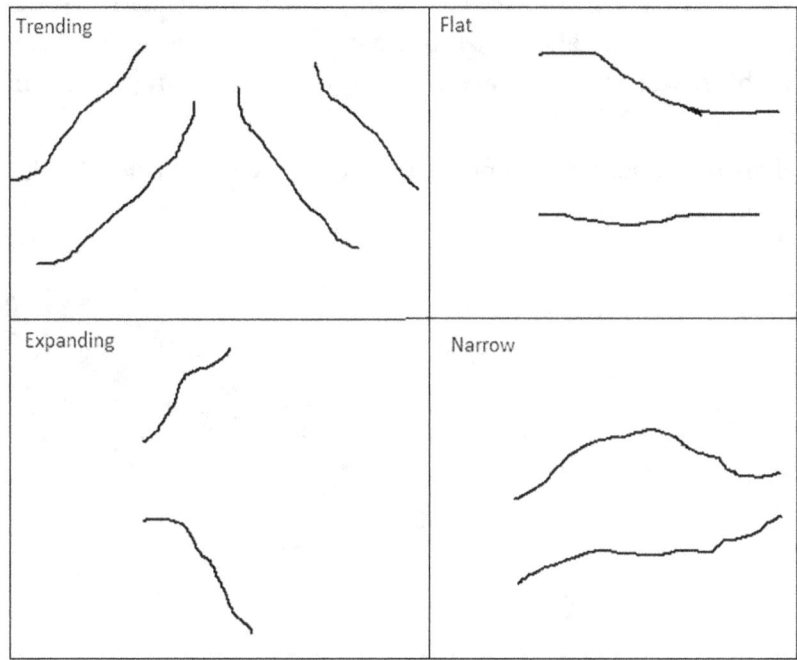

Image 4.2.5: Bollinger band shapes

Below is the explanation in brief and how P&F patterns can be filtered based on it

Flat Bands

When both the bands are moving flat, it indicates consolidation and hence breakout patterns should not be traded unless the band moves.

Narrow Bands

Narrow bands represent price squeeze. It would typically be followed by a trending move but signals should not be pre-empted. Breakout patterns should be avoided until band moves or widens as you never know how long will it take for the breakout. Take trades based on Follow-through signals as the first breakout after the tight consolidation often proves to be false.

Trending Bands

When both the bands are rising or falling then they are known as trending bands. Positive breakouts should be traded in up trending bands and negative breakout in Downtrending bands, also known as walking the bands. It is a nice pullback system when bands are rising and price comes to lower band and triggers some bullish formation. Same way, a bearish formation at upper band is effective when bands are trending down.

Expanding Bands

Bands are called expanding when upper band is rising and lower band is falling. They are often followed by trending bands and should be referred for continuation signals. Bearish reversal formation at upper band

and bullish reversal formation at lower band when they are expanding, is an interesting reversal setup especially if there is a follow-through.

The behavior explained above for pattern filtration is very effective for short-term trading. It is said that 70% of days are non-trending and remain Sideways. Flat and narrow bands during such sessions can filter out many breakout trades and helps avoid getting whipsawed during non-trending phases. Bearish pattern near upper band and bullish pattern at lower band when bands are not trending can be a useful trade setup. A trending band will typically have a series of continuation pattern that can just be ridden using P&F signals.

Below is 1% × 3 chart of Ajanta Pharma plotted with daily closing prices with 10,2 Bollinger bands with mid-price method applied on them.

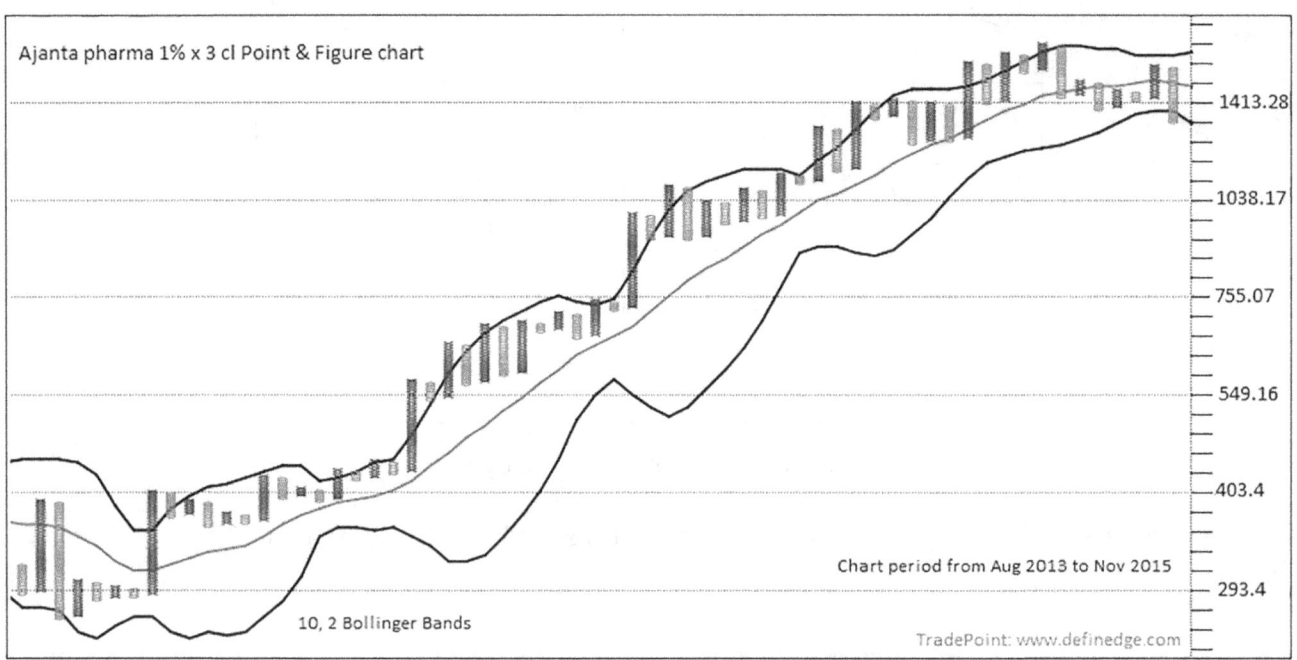

Figure 4.2.1: Ajanta Pharma daily 1% × 3 cl Point & Figure chart

Price touched lower band during August 2013 that did not happen again until November 2015. Walking the bands would have been effective strategy during this period. No bearish pattern occurred during the period that witnessed a Follow-through.

There is a benefit of plotting the bands using the mid-price method. The patterns that occur near band extremes, even though their mid-values might not have broken the band, show the failed attempt of breakout by the price. Such reversal formations are more interesting when bands are not trending. Such formations cannot be seen with bands plotted using closing price method because bands are placed wide and price don't interact with them frequently.

When bands are trending on higher time frames or box-values, pullback setups on lower box-value charts are effective. Band squeeze is typically followed by a trend or expansion and price patterns can offer a clue about the breakout direction. Bands work as support or resistance when they are flat. Bear Trap or pole especially when there is also a pattern retest formation at band extremes are effective setups. Follow-through setups are more effective when bands are not flat. Patterns at band extremes can be traded based on the shape of the bands.

Figure below is 0.25% × 3 P&F chart of Amararajabat plotted using daily closing prices.

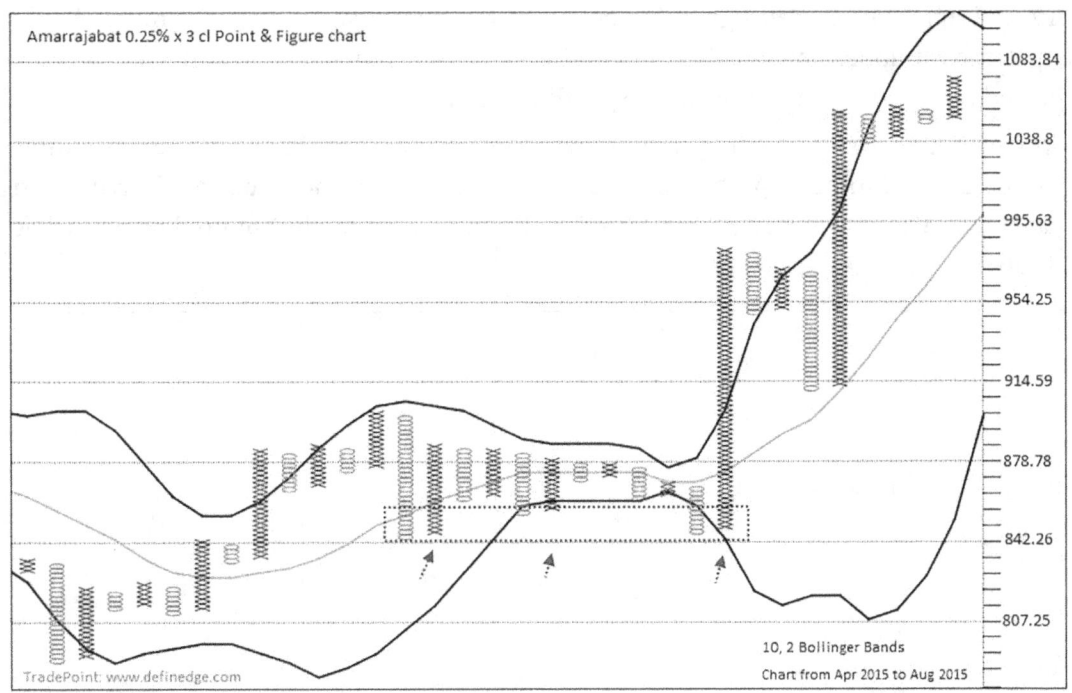

Figure 4.2.2: Amararajabat daily 0.25% × 3 cl Point & Figure chart

Arrow shows pattern retest formation with series of Low Poles that occurred around same levels. Third occurrence of pole at lower band was followed by expanding bands and the pattern turned out to be a bullish 100% Pole.

Notice patterns after the breakout in the chart, price correction to the Uptrend formed pullback setup with low pole at the moving average.

Figure shown below is 0.25% × 3 P&F chart of SBI plotted with closing prices.

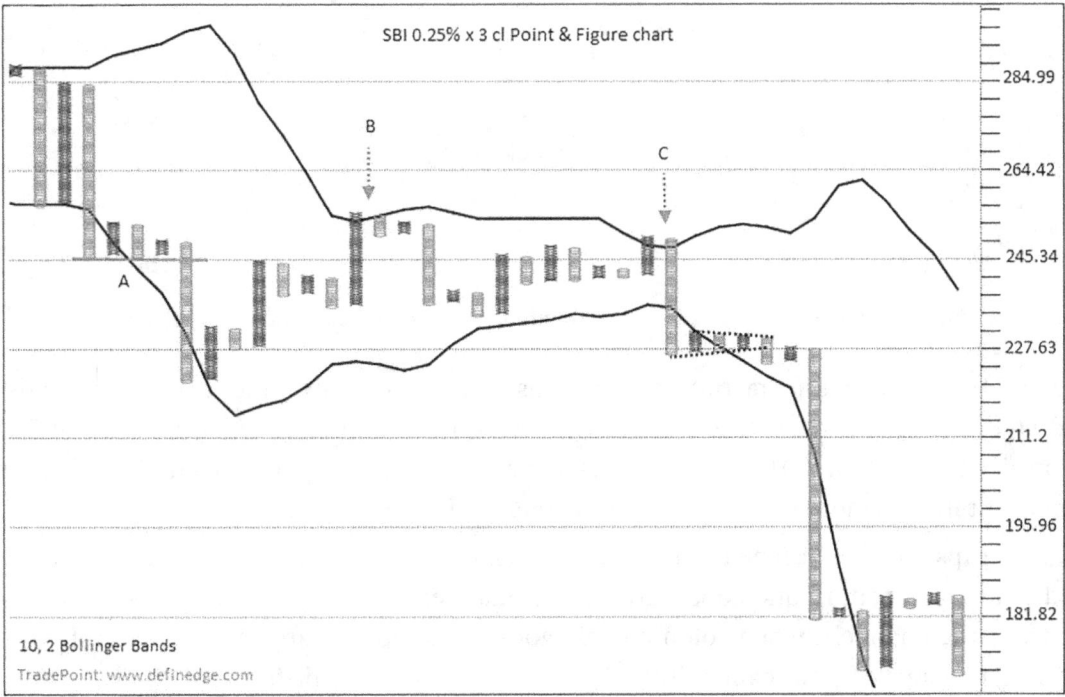

Figure 4.2.3: SBI daily 0.25% × 3 cl Point & Figure chart

Pattern A is Triple Bottom Sell signal that occurred while the bands were expanding. Pattern B and C are bearish patterns at upper band during converging or non-trending bands. Pattern C is Bearish Double Pattern followed by Triangle formation and expanding bands.

When broader markets are trading in a Sideways mode or when bands are not trending, the band extremes can be utilized to book profits or exiting the trades. This goes well for short-term traders and time interval charts. Figure shown below is 10 × 3 P&F chart of Bank Nifty plotted using the closing price of every minute.

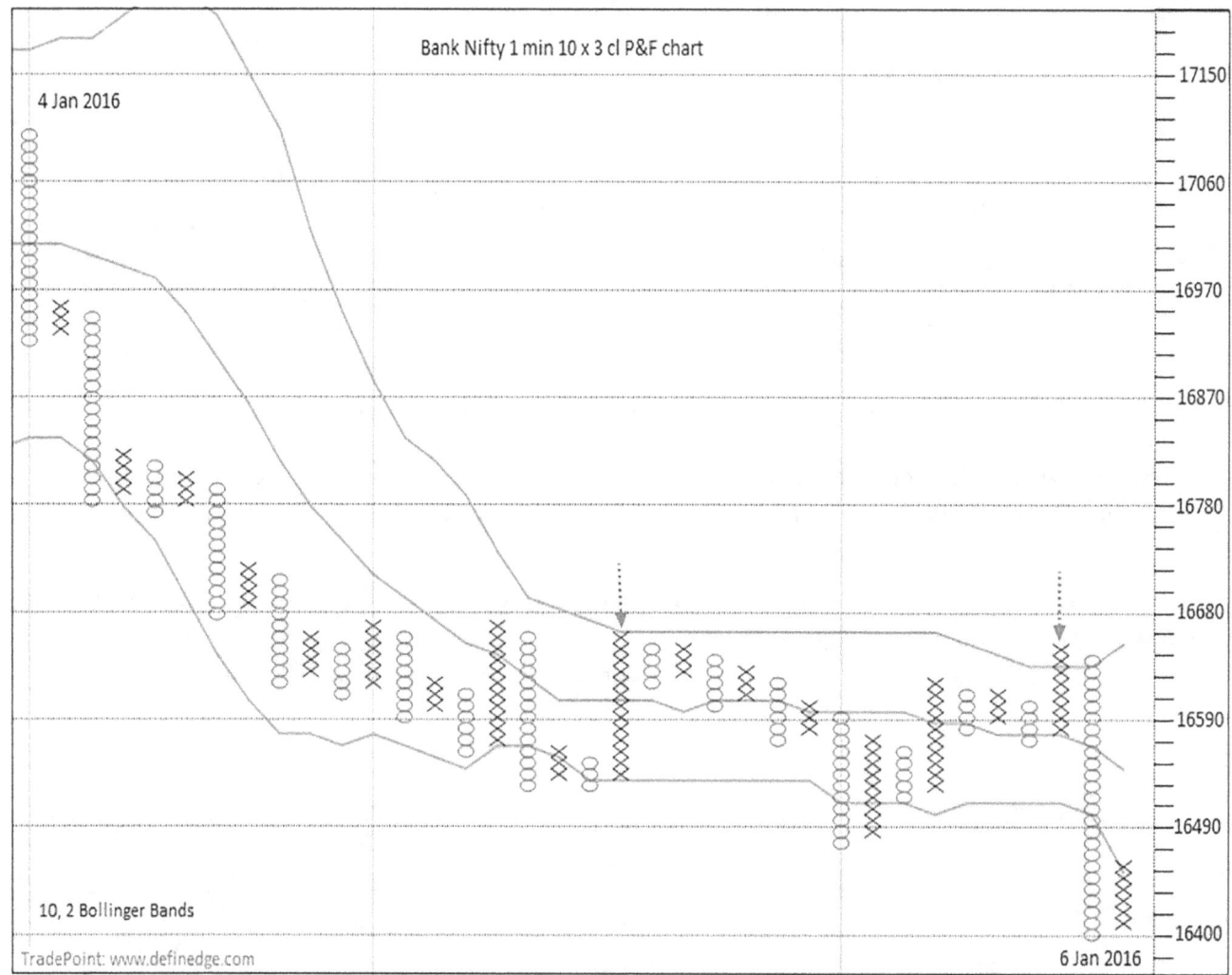

Figure 4.2.4: Bank Nifty-I futures one min interval 10 × 3 cl Point & Figure chart

During the time of above formation, pattern was bearish on daily time frame and bands on them were trending down. As can be seen on the chart, Bands are trending down with series of P&F bearish continuation signals on 4th Jan 2016. Later, bearish formations at flat upper bands indicated resistance and proved important information when context in the higher time frame is known.

Different setups can be designed with price and channel indicators. Consecutive buy signal above upper band is a bullish pattern and consecutive sell signal below lower band is bearish. There is another method to trade the channels, when column of 'X' goes above upper band, should be broken by another column of 'X' going above upper band within 5 columns to call it a bullish setup. Similarly, the low price of a column of 'O' going below lower band should be broken within next 5 columns with breach of lower band to call it a bearish setup.

Band Squeeze

Difference between bands can be plotted as indicator to find out when the bands are contracting. We can anticipate breakout during such cases but we don't know about the direction and how long will it take to materialize. With P&F, job becomes much easier especially with the knowledge of follow-through.

Below is a chart of DLF plotted with indicator showing difference between two bands to show the area where bands are narrow.

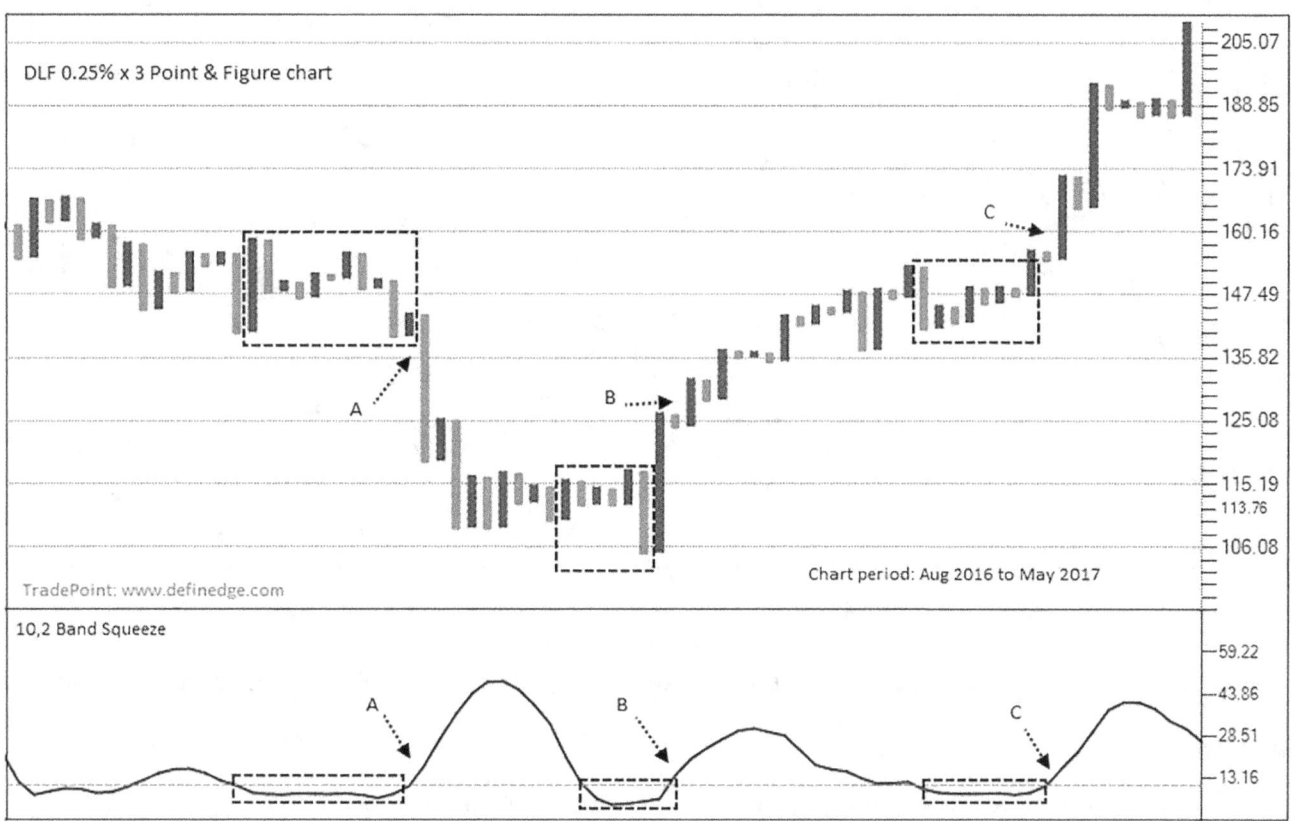

Figure 4.2.5: DLF daily 0.25% × 3 cl Point & Figure chart

Observe how both complement each other. Point A shows indicator coming out from narrow zone, next follow-through Double Bottom Sell signal provide affordable bet. P&F patterns during the time it was in narrow zone could have been avoided. Point B is where indicator came out from exhaustion zone and Follow-through bullish signal gave affordable trading opportunity. Point C is another move indicated by bands where bullish P&F signal could have been traded.

Relative High-Relative Low

Even Relative High and Relative Low can be easily defined using P&F formations. A column of X goes above upper band and subsequent column of 'X' remaining below upper band is a Relative High. Same way a column of 'O' goes below lower band and a subsequent column of 'O' remaining above lower band is known as Relative Low. Relative High displays weakness of high because it fell short of touching the upper band. Similarly, Relative Low indicates weakness of the low. Basic signal coming after them is a tradable setup; it becomes more interesting when it is also a reversal formation like pole. Relative Low are more reliable than Relative high.

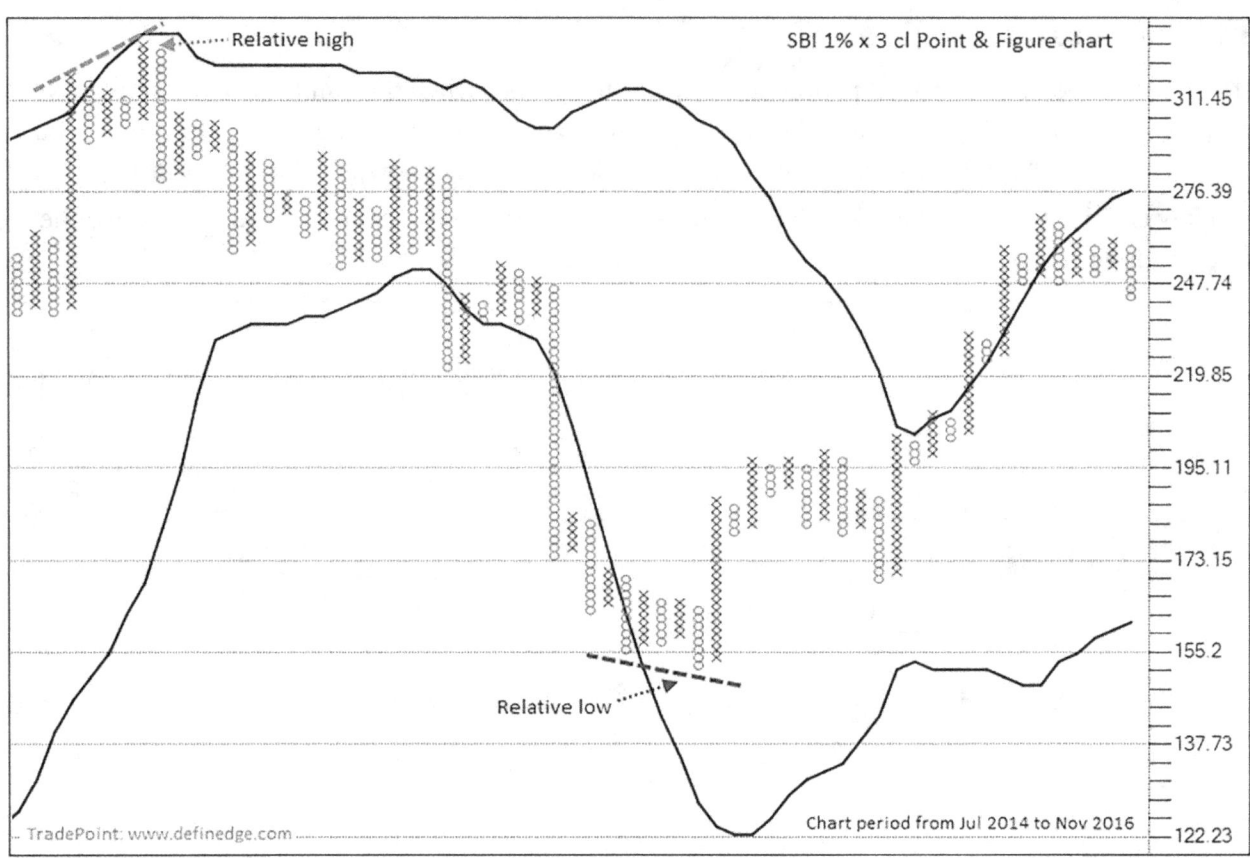

Figure 4.2.6: SBI daily 1% × 3 cl Point & Figure chart

I have consistently experienced the usefulness of Bollinger bands on P&F on time interval charts.

Summary

- ⮝ All methods of reading Bollinger bands are also applicable on P&F charts.
- ⮝ Trading strategy can be designed based on shape of the bands.
- ⮝ Pattern retest at band extremes is a significant setup.
- ⮝ Patterns like traps, poles or weak breakouts at band extremes are useful setups.
- ⮝ Bullish pattern at lower band when higher time-frame trend is bullish and bearish pattern at higher band when higher time-frame trend is bearish are productive setups.
- ⮝ Walking the bands with P&F basic patterns, avoiding patterns when bands are flat, squeeze, and trading reversals at band extremes when price is in horizontal trend are important benefits of Bollinger bands on P&F charts.
- ⮝ Narrow bands breakout and P&F Follow-through signals make a nice trading setup.

4.3: RSI

Developed by J. Welles Wilder, Relative Strength Index (RSI) is perhaps most popular and widely used indicator. It is also possible to plot it on P&F charts. Formula remains the same but the underlying logic differs.

Below is the formula of Relative Strength Index:

RSI = 100 − 100/(1 + RS)

Where RS = Average gain/Average loss

A 14-day RSI is widely used setting to plot RSI that takes closing prices of the last 14 sessions into account. It is a momentum oscillator that moves between 0 and 100. If an instrument has had more positive changes then RSI would be higher and if it had more negative changes then RSI would be lower, level of equilibrium is 50. RSI on P&F charts would get plotted based on 14 columns, instead of 14 days. So RSI on P&F measures the magnitude of rising columns versus losing columns. Higher RSI suggests strength and lower RSI shows weakness.

All types of analysis such as overbought–oversold zones, mid-value crossovers, Divergences, trend lines and range rules are applicable on P&F charts also, but trades on P&F charts are placed based on the P&F pattern. This way, trades get filtered & become more productive. Sticking to the same parameter of 14 is fine. It doesn't make much difference when we use some other number around that. A 7-period RSI, which is half of the standard parameter of 14, is effective on P&F charts, especially for short-term analysis. The behavior remains the same, irrespective of whether we plot it using closing price method or mid-price method, though the latter will display smooth curves.

Below is 0.25% × 3 P&F chart of M&M plotted using daily closing prices.

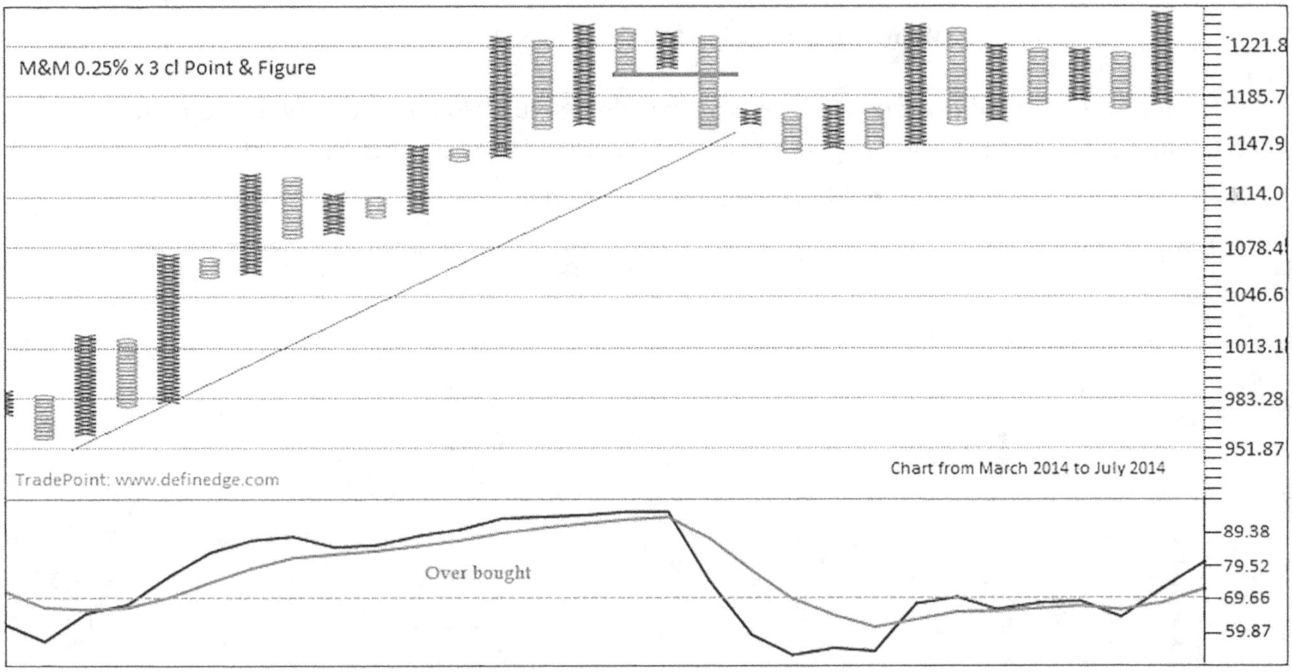

Figure 4.3.1: M&M daily 0.25% × 3 cl Point & Figure chart

RSI remained in overbought territory for a considerable time but pattern turned bearish much later, which indicated sell signal.

Divergence on RSI is the most useful technique on P&F charts. Negative divergence occurs when price makes new high but the indicator does not. Positive divergence occurs when price makes a new low but indicator does not. P&F technique help determine the trend and effectively ride it. I often felt the need of something that can indicate weakness of 'X' or strength of 'O'. Divergences can help to some extent in doing that. Bullish breakout when there is negative divergence or bearish breakout when positive divergence indicates weakness of breakout. The beauty of using it along with P&F charts is that both perfectly complement each other. Wait for negative divergence to be followed by bearish pattern to trade it. Similarly, positive divergence followed by or along with bullish pattern is an effective trading setup.

Below is 0.25% × 3 P&F chart of LT showing bullish and bearish divergences.

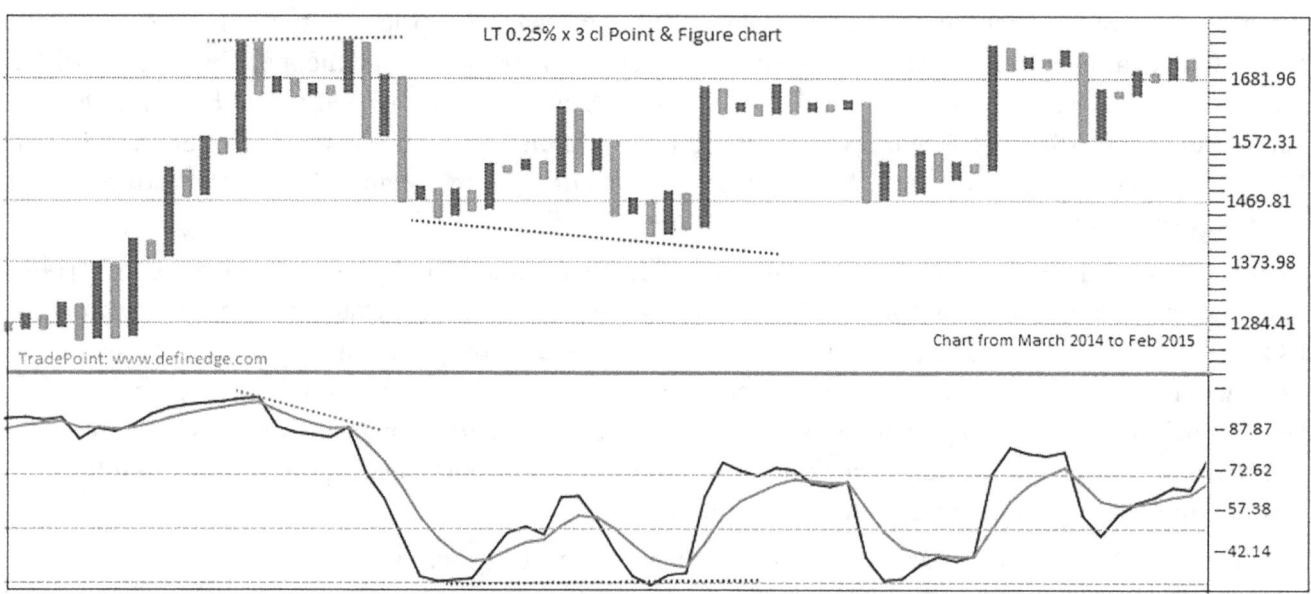

Figure 4.3.2: LT daily 0.25% × 3 cl Point & Figure chart

Pattern retest with indicator divergence is an excellent setup. Note that divergence is confirmed only when column gets locked. A column gets locked when column reversal occurs.

Below is 0.25% × 3 P&F chart of Mindtree plotted using daily closing prices.

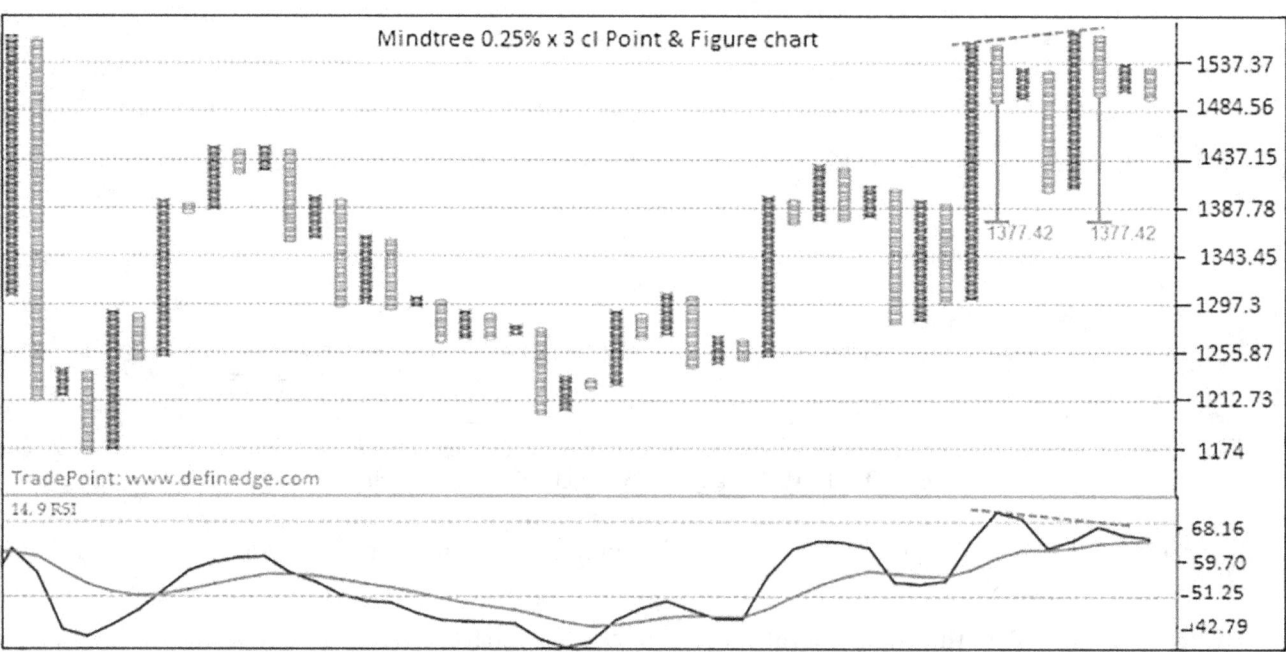

Figure 4.3.3: Mindtree daily 0.25% × 3 cl Point & Figure chart

New high made by the column of 'X' did not correspond to a similar high in RSI, resulting in a negative divergence that indicated weakness in the price. Follow-through is seen and both the counts are pointing at the same level. The sell signal is affordable and there are multiple reasons to take it. The active counts shown on the charts were eventually achieved.

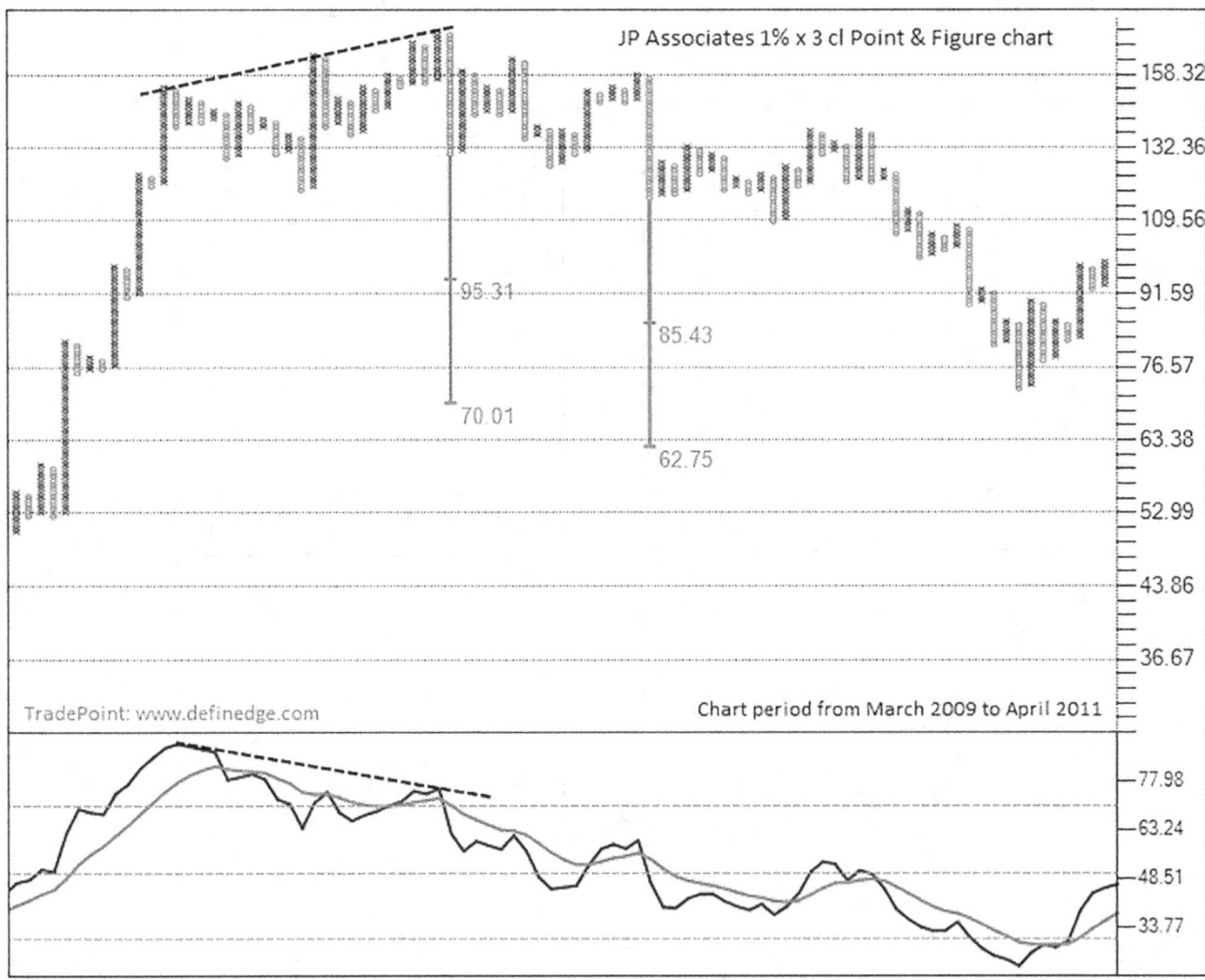

Figure 4.3.4: Jp associate daily 1% × 3 cl Point & Figure chart

Figure shown above is 1% × 3 chart of JP Associates. Weakness of the high marked by the patterns that correspond with negative divergence in RSI is highlighted in the chart. Formation on 1% box-value chart hinted the potential downside. Bearish formations and open bearish counts represent interesting trading opportunities. Price cracked down later and fell to much lower levels. Study of formations on higher box-values can help trader to know what to expect in the lower box-value chart formations.

Oversold indicator with positive divergence and bullish pattern or overbought indicator with negative divergence and bearish pattern makes the setup logical and affordable for entry having all ingredients of an efficient setup.

Trap–Divergence

There is an interesting observation. Trap formations can be filtered based on RSI divergences. Have a look at image shown below.

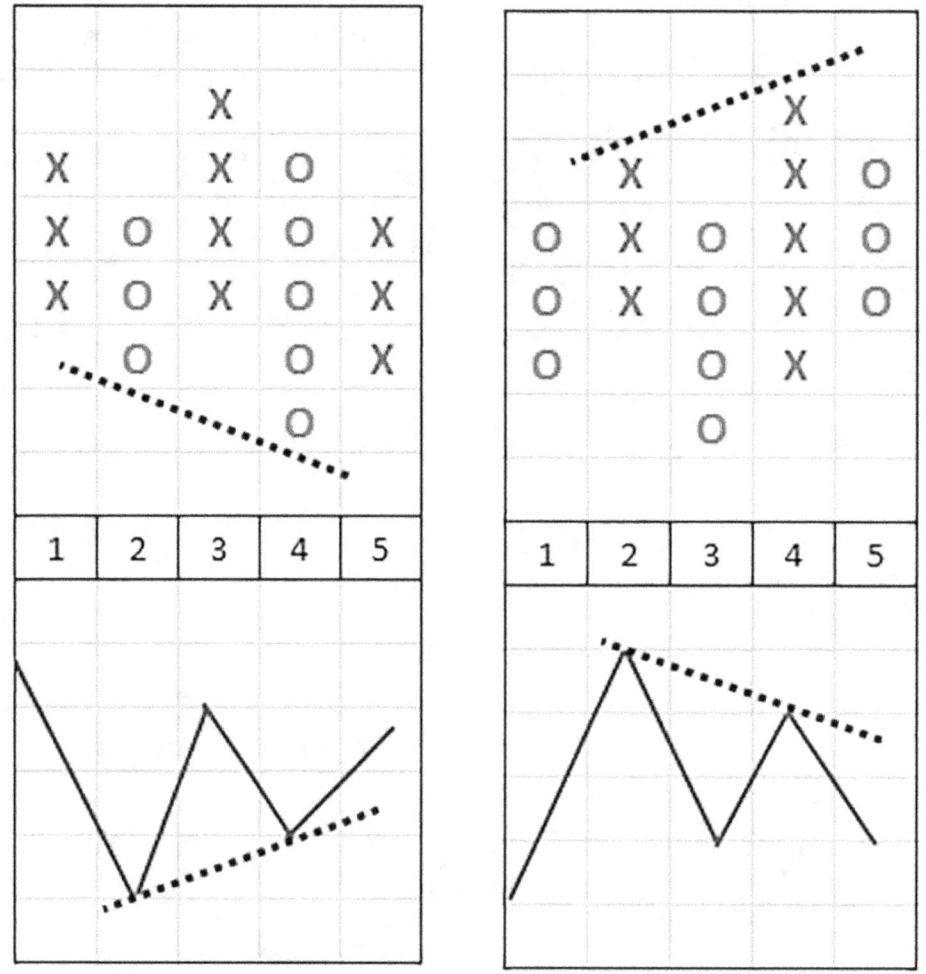

Bull Trap with Positive Divergence   Bear Trap with Negative Divergence

Image 4.3.1: Trap pattern with divergence

Pattern at image XA is a Bull Trap that got formed at column 4. When column of 'O' at 4 fell below its previous column of 'O' and made new low, RSI produced positive divergence by not falling below the prior low. Note that the RSI reading at column 4 gets fixed only when the column is complete and is followed by 'X' at column 5. Hence it becomes a 5 column setup that shows Bull Trap with positive divergence. Similarly, image XB shows Bear Trap formation with negative divergence in RSI.

Trap pattern with divergence make it a less reliable pattern and chances of a failure are high. They can be avoided or need further investigation. It is a wonderful opportunity when such formations are seen in the Traps occurred against the trend. A column reversal or Follow-through becomes powerful and affordable setup in such cases.

Figure shown below is 1% × 3 P&F chart of Tata Motors plotted using daily closing prices.

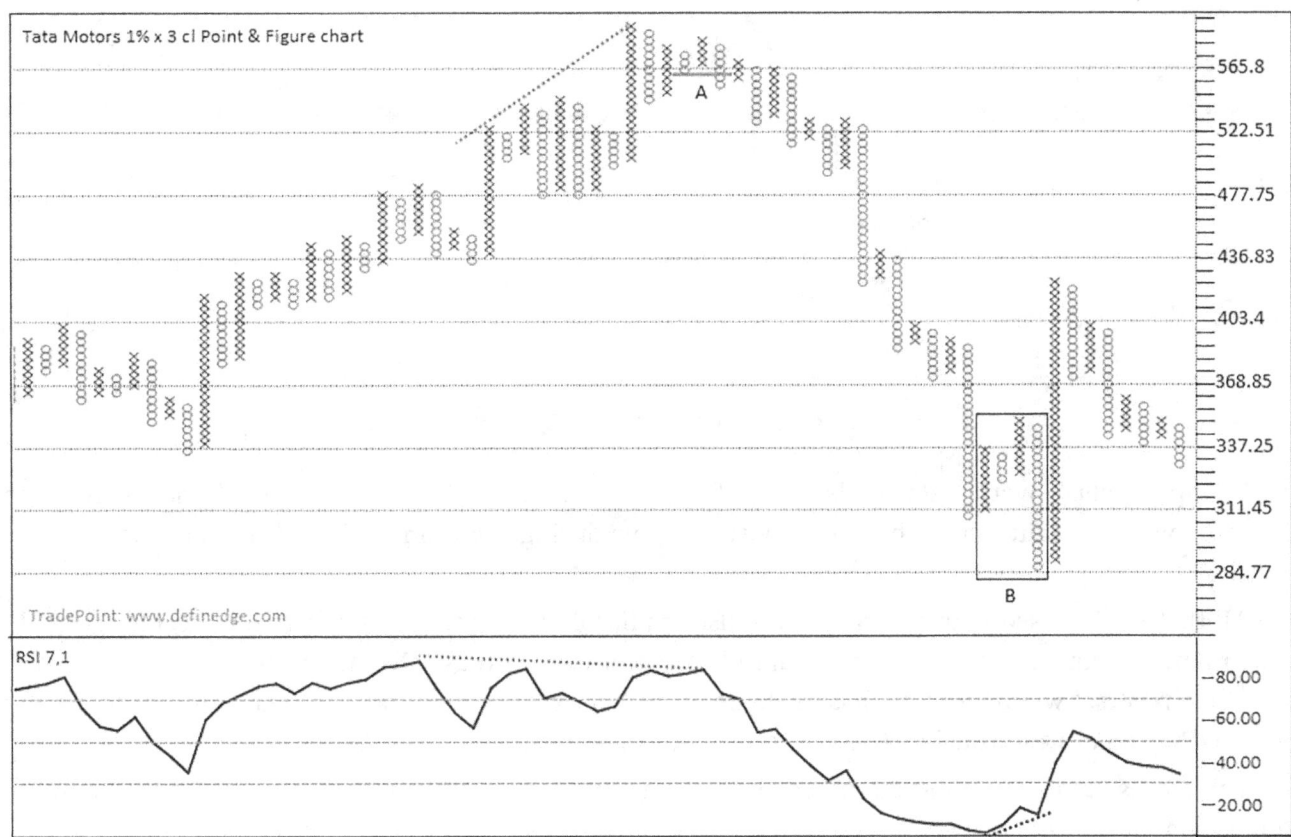

Figure 4.3.5: Tata Motors daily 1% × 3 cl Point & Figure chart

Pattern A is a bearish formation after a negative divergence. It is a Bull Trap that occurred after a High Pole that makes the entire setup effective. Pattern B is Bull Trap in downtrend but there is positive divergence in RSI hence it could be avoided.

These types of setups can be scanned and would be helpful for short-term trading as well. They are relatively rare but work effectively. It helps filter out trap patterns that may be avoided or need follow-through to trade. This formation is often seen during important top–bottoms but it is not necessary to have it always, and there is no reason to skip Traps with the trend because there was no divergence.

P&F technique should be followed to ride the trend and derive targets after entry based on this setup. The divergence is useful for short-term trading when found in lower box-values and provides significant information from a medium-term perspective when found in higher box-value charts.

There are numerous possibilities of designing systems because P&F is a charting technique like bar or candlestick charts. For example, when RSI above 50 on higher box-value chart, trade double moving average crossover on lower box-value chart and trail the trend with the help of moving average line. This is just a simple concept that I have illustrated and you can explore more such possibilities.

Box-Values – RSI Cluster

The best sell signals to take on lower box-value charts are when the sell signal happens after RSI has reached overbought zone in multiple box-values. Similarly, the best buy signals on lower box-value charts are the ones occurring after the RSI has reached oversold zone in multiple box-values. It is similar to signals occurring after a cluster of multi-period price cycle extremes. Below is the chart of Arvind on various box-values along with RSI.

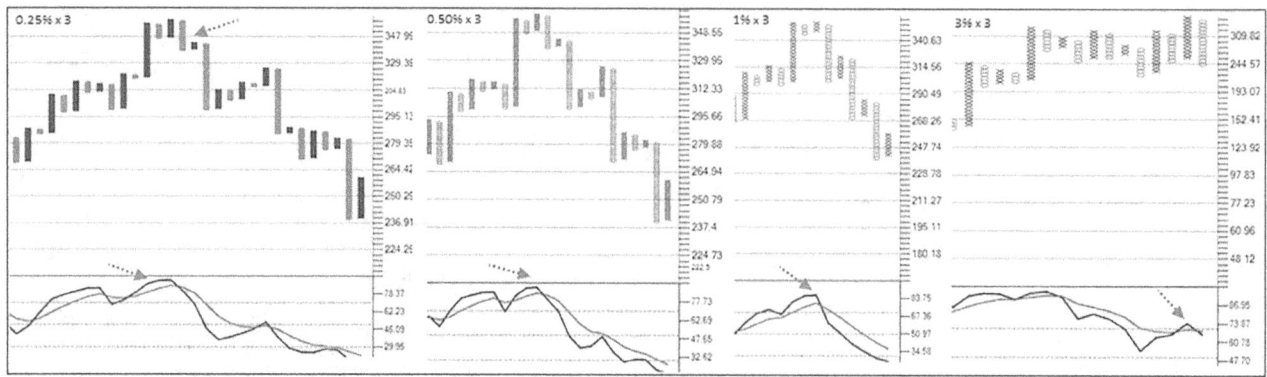

Figure 4.3.6: Arvind daily Point & Figure chart charts

RSI approached overbought levels on all the box-values. The Sell signal that would normally occur first on lower box-value charts becomes most effective during such times. Vice versa is applied for Buy signals.

All that is discussed with divergences is also applicable to positive and negative indicator reversals. When indicator makes new high but column has not, it is known as a Negative reversal. It is known as a Positive reversal when indicator has made new low but price column has not. They are also known as hidden divergences and equally effective setups on P&F as well.

The charts reading method discussed above using the RSI indicator may be applied using any other momentum indicator.

Summary

- ↖ All methods of reading RSI like extreme, mid-value crossover, overbought–oversold, RSI and average line crossover, divergences, positive-negative reversals, trend line breaks on RSI or range rules are also applicable on P&F charts.
- ↖ RSI Divergences helps in analyzing strength of 'O' and weakness of 'X'.
- ↖ RSI divergences along with pattern retest are high-probability reversal setups.
- ↖ RSI cluster on different box-values indicate significant price reversal.

4.4: ADX

ADX is another popular indicator developed by J. Welles Wilder that evaluates strength of the trend. It fluctuates between 0 and 100 and displays strength of the current trend, whether it is up or down. Three lines are plotted below the price chart, which are the components of the ADX indicator. DMI+ and DMI-lines of the indicator display trends and ADX line display strength of the trend.

There are multiple uses of this indicator but it is widely used to gauge the strength of the underlying trend. ADX can also be plotted on Point & Figure charts and the usual interpretation is equally relevant in P&F charts too.

But it is important to understand ATR before discussing ADX. Directional movement indicators (DMIs) which are major constituents of ADX divide the trend by volatility indicator known as ATR. A 14 day ATR is an average of true range of an instrument over 14 days of prices. True range on bar or candlestick chart is calculated on as follows:

True Range = Max [(high – low), abs (high – previous close), abs (low – previous close)]

Difference between high and low is the range of a bar or candle. True range compares the length with previous closing price in order accommodate the gaps. Same formula can be applied to calculate true range on P&F charts to calculate ATR. P&F column display high and low value of the column which is range of that particular move. High price of the column is its closing price when it is a column of 'X', and low price is its closing price when it is a column of 'O'. So we get True range of a column as shown in the image below.

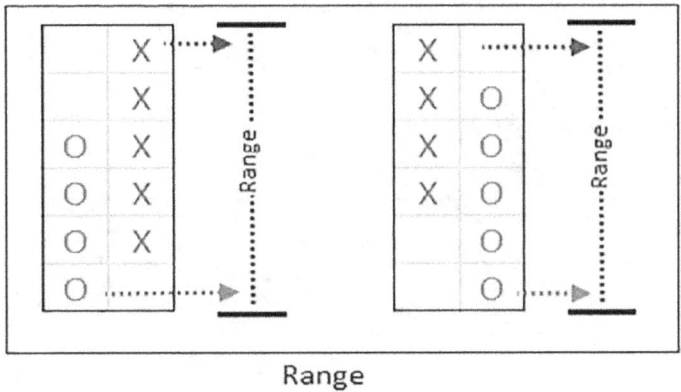

Range

Image 4.4.1: Range calculation in P&F

Hence it is possible to calculate ATR using same formula. The closing price of the column is used for calculating ADX. It can also be calculated using the mid-price method instead of closing price. But plotting it with closing price method is more reliable approach though not much difference is seen between values when larger parameters are used.

ATR in itself is an effective volatility indicator. When plotted in a P&F chart, ADX displays volatility of P&F columns. There are methods to design systems using ATR values and multiples of it, which is possible with P&F methodology as well.

ATR plotted with above method is taken into account for calculating Directional movement index (DMI) and Average Directional index (ADX) indicators. When DMI+ is above DMI- indicator, it is treated as a bullish zone and DMI- below DMI+ is treated as a bearish zone. Their crossovers are also a trading signal. Rising ADX line indicates that the underlying trend is strong. A rising ADX line does not necessarily indicate that the trend is bullish. In essence, ADX can trend up irrespective of the direction of the underlying trend. When DMIs are in bullish zone, a rising ADX will display the strength of the uptrend, and the same when DMIs are in bearish zone will capture the strength in the downtrend. ADX below 20 indicate lack of strength in the existing trend, be it up or down.

ADX above 20 indicate strength in the trend and that is where setups can be traded. When column of 'X' is dominating in bullish DMI zone and ADX is also rising above 20 then it is a market phase to trade bullish formations and ignore the bearish ones. Similarly, dominating column of 'O's in bearish DMI zone and rising ADX suggest that bearish patterns are to be traded and the bullish ones ignored. Bullish or bearish zones, when ADX displays a dull phase, are the markets or instruments to be avoided for trading.

Normally, ADX going above 40 is considered as exhaustion. With P&F, it easily goes up to the 50 mark. It can be treated as a warning sign when that happens. P&F patterns would typically provide early clue before the ADX reverses.

Figure shown below is 0.25% × 3 P&F chart of Reliance infra with ADX indicator plotted below it.

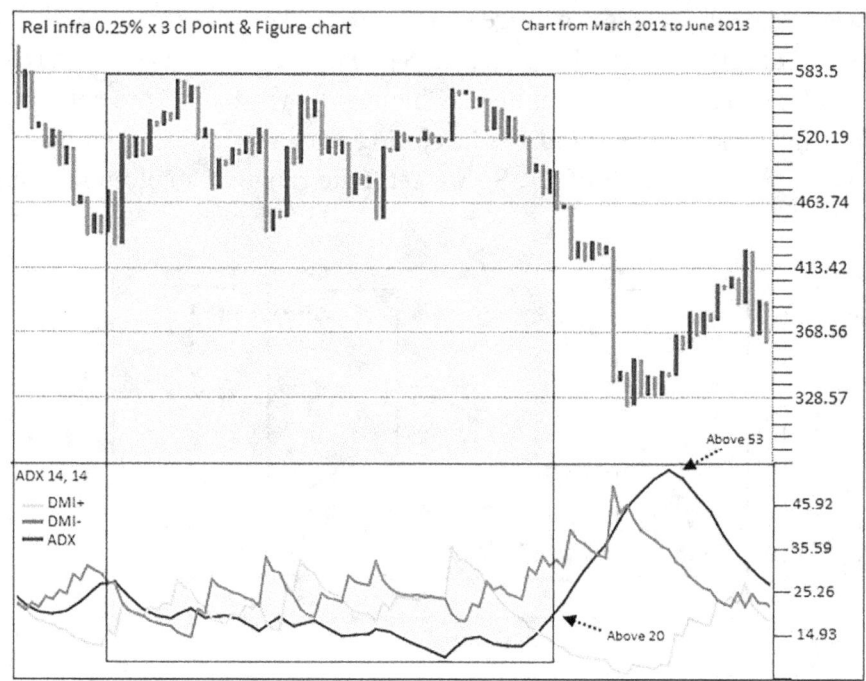

Figure 4.4.1: Reliance infra daily 0.25% × 3 cl Point & Figure chart

Green line is DMI+ line, Red is DMI- line and the blue one is ADX line. Box drawn on the chart shows the price formation when DMIs are in the congestion zone and ADX is below 20. ADX went above 20 with bearish price formation and negative DMI zone that display strength in the downtrend. Price fell with bearish continuation patterns. Indicator went above 50 that indicated exhaustion where bearish signals should be avoided even though trend is down.

Reversal signals being formed typically when the distance between the two DMIs is wide and ADX is in exhaustion zone, becomes interesting. Pullback and Follow-through P&F patterns work very well during established trends; ADX is useful in identifying the same.

Figure shown below is the 30 min chart of Nifty futures plotted with 5 × 3 parameters along with ADX indicator.

Figure 4.4.2: Nifty-I futures 30 min interval 5 × 3 cl Point & Figure chart

Horizontal line in ADX indicator is drawn at the level 20. Arrow shows breakout of ADX indicator with clear DMI signals indicating established downtrend. Negative setups like Bull traps, bearish pullback and Follow-through look effective during such phase. Another arrow shows exhausted ADX line where continuation patterns are to be avoided.

So, a complete system is offered by ADX on P&F: Trade bullish P&F signals when DMI+ is above DMI- and ADX line is above 20. Trade bearish P&F signals when DMI- is above DMI+ and ADX line is above 20.

ADX is useful for short-term trading as well. Those instruments where there is no clear trend may be avoided until the price gets into a strong trending mode. The DMI lines that are bunched up close to each other or when the ADX line is not rising typically indicate a dull phase. Instruments displaying such ADX characteristic may be avoided from trading perspective.

Figure shown below is 0.15% x3 P&F chart of Yes bank plotted using closing prices of every minute.

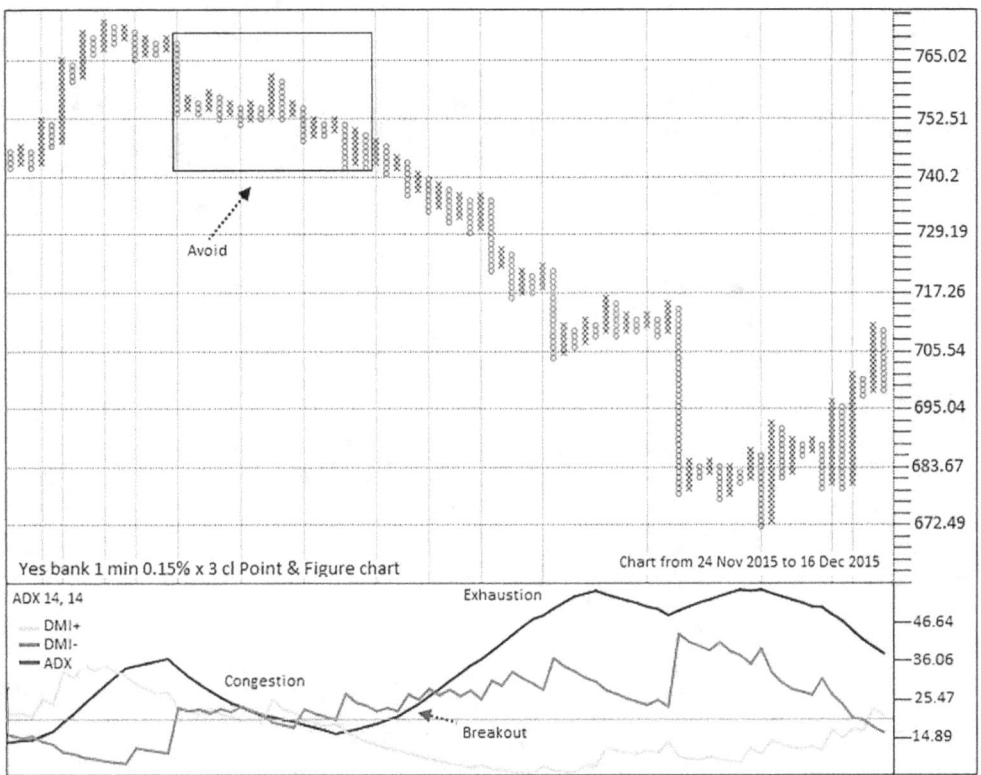

Figure 4.4.3: Yes bank 1 min interval 0.15% × 3 cl Point & Figure chart

Arrows on the chart shows the setups & days that can be avoided for trading due to non-confirmation by the ADX. It is most important for a trader to know when not to trade.

ADX is an effective tool in P&F charts and, applicable on all box-values and time frames. Remember, pattern should be the leading method with above technique and indicator should be used for confirmation, it should not be the other way around.

How about plotting ADX line indicator as a P&F chart? Column of 'X' in that case would indicate trending phase and column of 'O' would suggest staying away!

A lot can be written about ATR and ADX or other indicators on P&F. The purpose here is to explain the availability and utility of these indicators on Point & Figure charts. Do explore them.

Summary

- ⚊ ADX line below 20 indicate dull phase, and above 50 indicate exhaustion.
- ⚊ Positive DMI crossover + adx line above 20 + bullish pattern = bullish setup.
- ⚊ Negative DMI crossover + adx line above 20 + bearish pattern = bearish setup.
- ⚊ Trade charts where ADX is clear, that is, all three lines are apart from each other.

It would be repetitive to discuss or show charts using more indicators. But all indicators are applicable on all box-values and time frames on P&F charts and all methods of reading them are also applicable in P&F charts. Vertical plotting is the advantage and patterns complement them in P&F charts. In all cases, patterns are to be traded with its rules. Below is a P&F chart of Century textile plotted along with MACD and Ichimoku (calculated on P&F) for your observation.

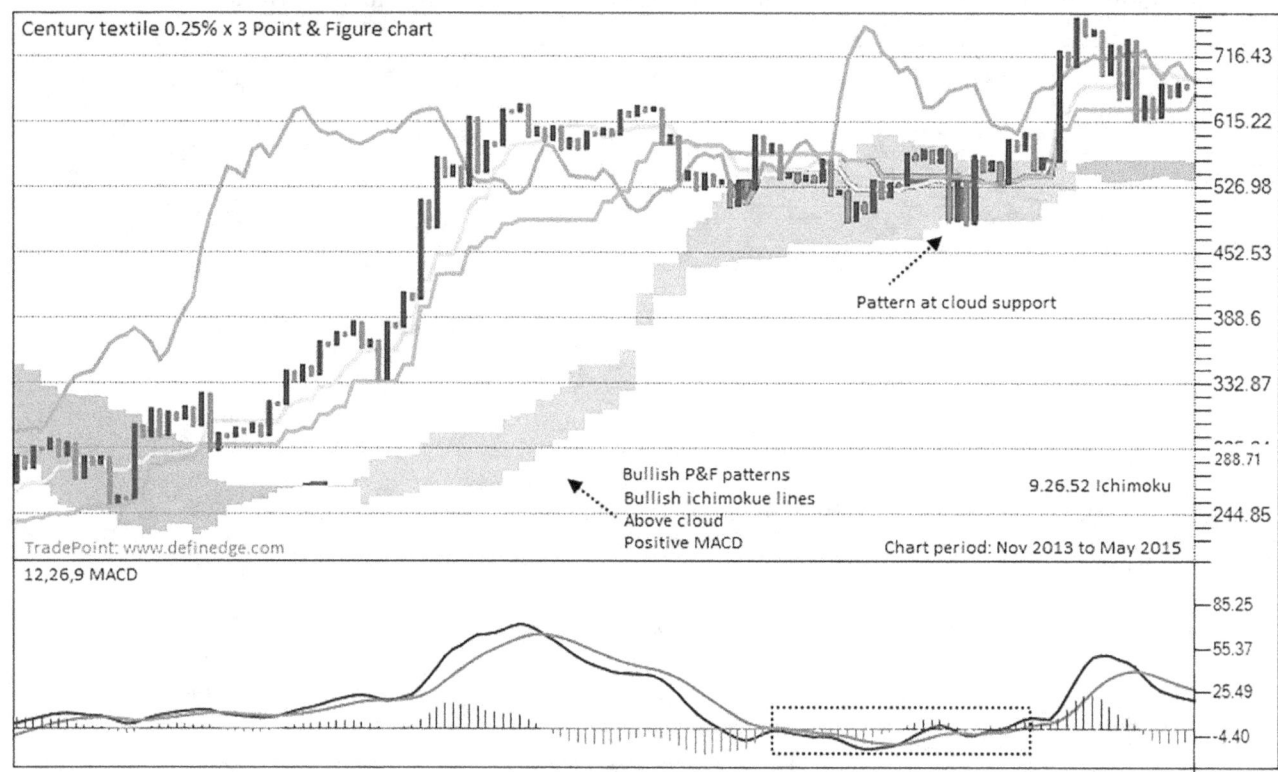

Figure 4.4.4: Century textile daily 0.25% × 3 cl Point & Figure chart

Explore your favorite indicators on P&F, and take advantage of strength of both the worlds.

But discussion on indicator doesn't end here.

4.5: P&F INDICATORS

We discussed popular indicators and their application on P&F charts. But P&F is a charting system and it can have its own unique set of indicators as well. The indicators can be built using the unique features associated with the P&F charts. Unlike usual charts, P&F charts do not move horizontally and one of their main features is that they produce boxes when price fulfill certain criteria. We can count number of boxes in every column. A large column is one having relatively more number of boxes, which in turn represents a strong move.

Cycle of expansion and contraction in markets is a well-known concept. It is logical that price will produce more boxes during strong trends and fewer boxes during the congestion. Number of boxes can also be plotted as an indicator that will display count of boxes in the setup or pattern. The indicator is named as XO indicator that counts total number of boxes whether 'X' or 'O' during the period. For example, a 20 column indicator will show total number of boxes during last 20 columns.

Below is 30 min interval 10x3 P&F chart of Nifty futures along with 20 column XO counts plotted as an indicator.

Figure 4.5.1: Nifty-I futreus 30 min interval 10 × 3 cl Point & Figure chart

Rising line shows that number of boxes are increasing hence strong trend and falling line suggests consolidation.

This can also help us estimate the price volatility. Breakout patterns should be avoided during congestion period. Indicator falling below previous lows displays strong congestion that should be followed by expansion. As always, use the P&F patterns as your guide to initiate trades.

A P&F chart is bullish when 'X' are dominating and vice versa. A reversal can change the column but may remain temporary and the trend will typically resume if it is strong enough. It is logical to say that a bull phase should produce more boxes of 'X's than 'O's and a bear phase should produce more boxes of 'O's than 'X'. This gives birth to 'XO' indicator producing two lines below the P&F chart. Below is the formula of 20-column 'XO' indicator:

X: Total number of boxes in the column of X during last 20 columns

O: Total number of boxes in the column of O during last 20 columns

Parameter 20 is an example and not a recommendation. It can be plotted using any other number. It's a simple formula that plots total of 'X's and 'O's during the period. Typically even number should be used to keep number of columns equal for 'X' and 'O' during the period. Below is the same 10x3 P&F chart of Nifty futures plotted on 30 min time frame along with 'XO' indicator below it.

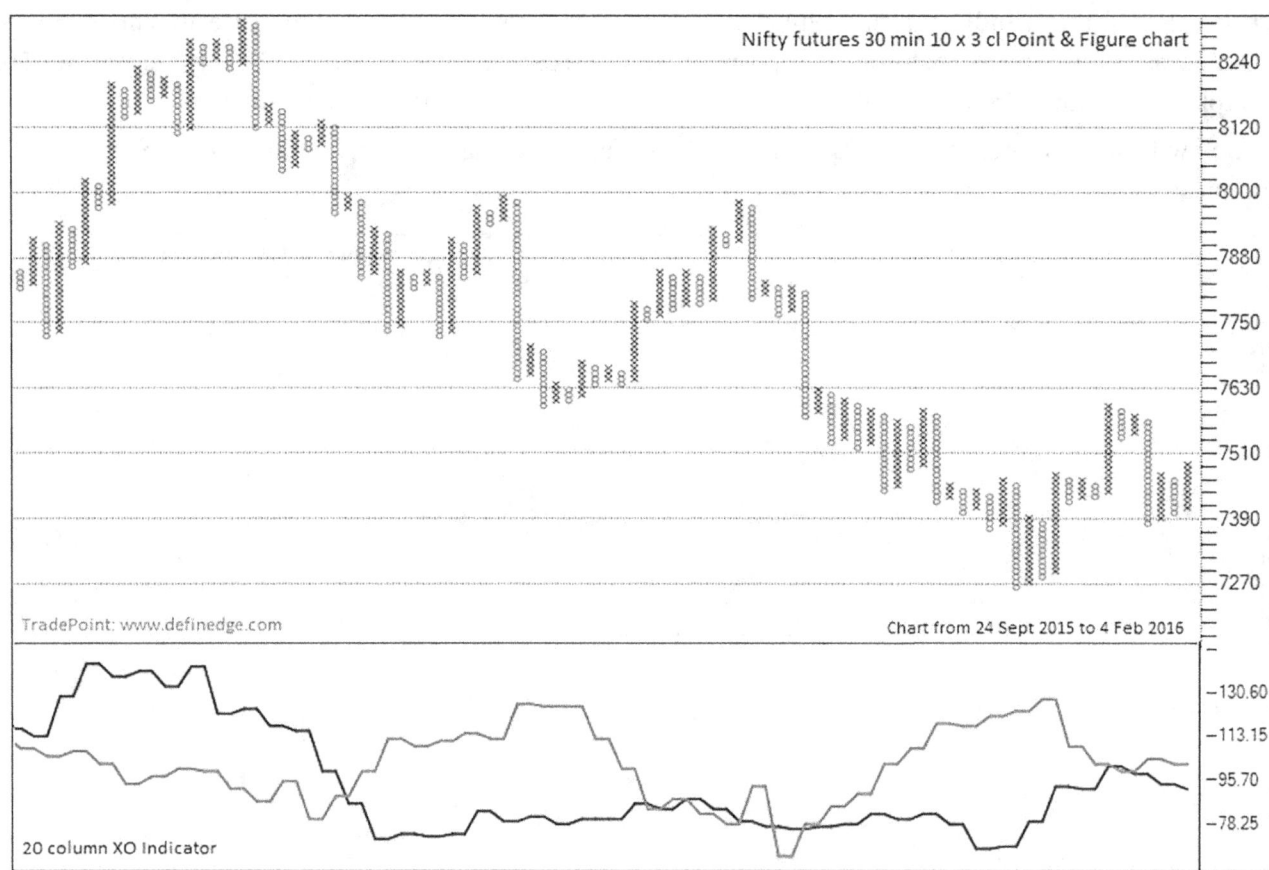

Figure 4.5.2: Nifty-I futures 30 min interval 10 × 3 cl Point & Figure chart

Blue line in the chart above is the bullish line that shows total boxes of 'X' and Red line is bearish line showing the total boxes of 'O's that occurred during the period. It is a crossover indicator that shows dominance of 'X's or 'O's. Bullish line crossing bearish line shows that there are more number of 'X's in comparison to the 'O's, indicating bullish undertone. Similarly, bearish line crossing bullish line suggests that number of 'O's have outnumbered the number of 'X's, indicating a bearish undertone.

It is truly a sensible indicator that shows clear picture where one side has gained control over the other. As we discussed earlier it can help us in ascertaining the setups that can be traded. Patterns and pullback setups in the direction of the trend is always an effective strategy. The trend is established when distance between the lines widen and it is a congestion when they converge. This leads to idea of defining the bullish and bearish zone that can be displayed when this indicator is plotted in histogram mode.

Below is the formula for plotting XO indicator in histogram style named as XO zone.

XO zone = Number of 'X' boxes – Number of 'O' boxes

The indicator will oscillate around zero line and can become negative also. It will show positive value when number of boxes of 'X' are higher than 'O' and turn to negative value when they go lower than number of boxes of 'O' during the period. Below is the same 30 min and 10x3 P&F chart of Nifty futures along with XO zone below it.

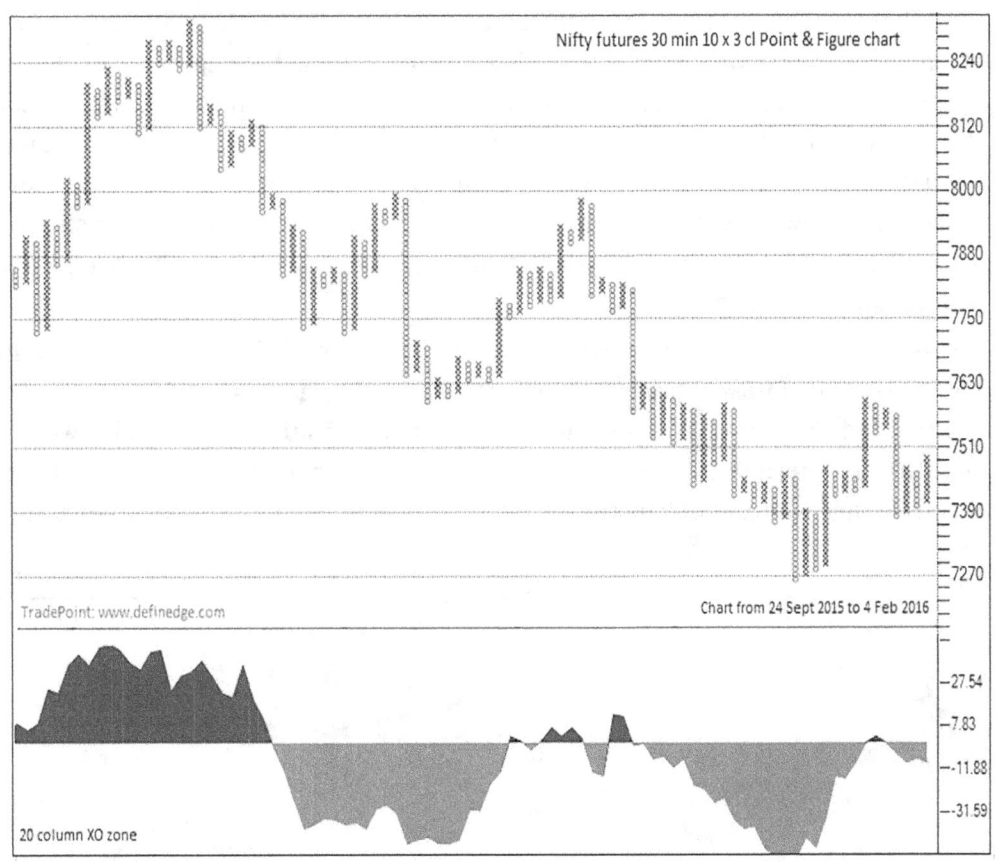

Figure 4.5.3: Nifty-I futures 30 min interval 10 × 3 cl Point & Figure chart

It is called a zone because it displays positive and negative zones clearly. Positive zone is when net 'X' count is positive or above zero and negative zone is when it falls below zero. Another usefulness of indicator is the congestion zone that they display when they hover around zero line. The breakout from zero line along with pattern confirmation creates a great trading setup. Below is a 1% × 3 Point & Figure chart of PNB plotted with XO zone below it.

Figure 4.5.4: PNB daily 1% × 3 cl Point & Figure chart

The indicator shows clear demarcation between bullish and bearish dominating boxes on the chart. The breakout from equilibrium along with bearish Triangle breakout at the beginning of chart was followed by a strong downtrend in price. Pattern A is Triple Bottom Sell in a bearish zone. Pattern B is High Pole in bearish zone that failed and did not have a Follow-through. Pattern C is series inside columns broken out when zone turned bullish. Pattern D is Bull Trap in bullish zone that should have been ignored. Pattern E is Double Top Buy after a Low pole in bull zone. Pattern F and G are Low Poles in bearish zone that should have been ignored. Pattern H is Bearish 100% pole and pattern I is a Bull Trap, both appearing in bearish zone makes them reliable trade setups.

XO zone crossover can be traded as well. Meaning, trade bullish pattern post bullish XO zone crossover and bearish pattern post bearish XO zone crossover. Methods of analyzing a typical histogram are applicable to this indicator also. Equilibrium in this indicator indicate balance between 'X's and 'O's that shows congestion and periods having no clear trend. Lengthy bars, where the histogram gets farther away from the middle line, indicate exhaustion. Falling bullish zone and rising bearish zone also indicate weakening trend.

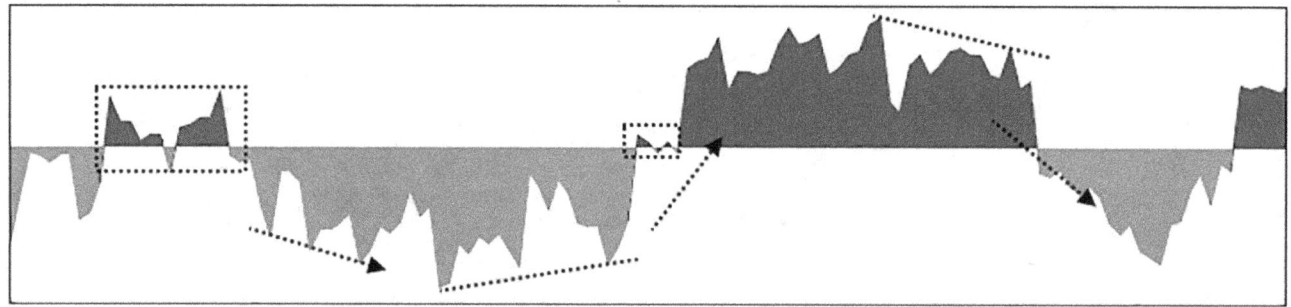

Image 4.5.1: XO zone indicator anlaysis

Summary

- ⮝ XO indicators are simple, yet very logical to gauge strength of the trend.
- ⮝ They use the best strength of P&F charts and display clear trends.
- ⮝ Trade long when 'X' is dominating and look for shorts when 'O' takes the control – XO indicators helps in identifying such phases.

Perfect Indicator

There is an obvious question which might have popped-up in your mind: Which indicator works best in P&F charts? Unfortunately, there is nothing best or worst in the market. The method of reading and utilizing each indicator has been discussed thoroughly. Use what you are comfortable with and what suits you most. Indicators have got their own important features to explore, for example, averages are simple trend identification technique, RSI shows divergence, Bands have different shapes, ADX has strength indicator line, etc.

One may not be comfortable with an indicator or tool or method, however popular it may be. There is no perfect system or indicator that exists and there is no perfect methodology to trade the markets. An amazing method or system for someone can prove disastrous for another.

Like sports, every trader has his own instinct and style. A trader needs to understand what suits him most. Which indicator he is comfortable with, that his eyes love to see and that he can interpret easily. It boils down to the question of developing a trust in an indicator and to trade logically using them. Following a pattern or an indicator just because some expert is recommending it, is not a sensible approach. Money can't be made on borrowed ideas; having conviction is of utmost importance. Your own tweaked rules and patterns may work wonders for you, they have a better chance of being successful than Googled-ideas!!

There is an incident to talk about here. Couple of guys came to me after my seminar on P&F and told me that they are beginners but found the things interesting and asked me to guide. I was thinking something since morning, hence asked them about one thing that they understood very well in the seminar. They said they are amazed with triangle pattern and completely clear with it. I asked them to view 500 charts and look for only the Triangle pattern in them and come back within a week. I had little hope that they will be seen again. I warned them about trading it because I have a secret to share about trading this pattern and it will change their life completely. Both came back, shared some successful observations, which was expected! I told them to view triangles more during next one week, and this time make a note of all the charts.

I asked them to view more charts when they came back and the trouble could be sensed from their facial expressions. They asked me the reason for the exercise and explained me that they understand triangles very well now and they felt little reason to review it any further. They explained that they have even back-tested it on many instruments and it is a wonderful pattern. I had to play the 'secret' game again. One of them came back with more notes, the other guy disappeared. More discussions and meetings happened thereafter. The discussions were again Triangle-pattern-centric. I gave him the task of looking at a list of stocks to view triangles on various time frames. The process continued and over a period, he viewed thousands of charts only for triangles. Next time, he told me that he can't really express or formulate, but there are certain situations when triangles work well!

He was astonished when I told him that no man on the planet has probably viewed as many charts as him, looking only for P&F triangles. I asked him to continue this process. I told him, "There will be masters of the game out there, but you will trade this formation best and probably understand it more than anybody else." Now, he focuses primarily on the Triangle pattern and trades them across different time frames and instruments. He achieved that 'noiselessness' in trading by practicing one price setup consistently. It's his perseverance that has made him achieve it. The Bruce Lee quote has really inspired me since the beginning, which says, "I don't fear a man who has practiced 10,000 kicks but I fear a man who has practiced one kick 10,000 times."

People say that knowledge is wisdom, and that has the edge that can make you different from others. But I think that knowledge is fine – it can certainly make you a good speaker or trainer. But it is practice that will make you a good trader. There is no magic in any tool, and there is one in every tool. It is purposeful practice that makes one develop expertise in any endeavor. It is not okay to be good at something; the objective must be to excel at something.

Chapter 5

PARAMETERS

After understanding the techniques of identifying patterns and analyzing P&F charts, the important question that will pop up is: how do we determine the basic parameters to construct a P&F chart? Because, the analysis and various P&F patterns and setups depend on the parameters we choose to construct the chart.

Below are the parameters that one must decide before plotting a P&F chart:

- ⬈ Box-value
- ⬈ Construction scale – absolute or log
- ⬈ Time frame – daily or any other intraday time interval
- ⬈ Type of the chart – closing price or High–Low
- ⬈ Reversal value – between 1 and 5

An introduction to these parameters was given in Chapter 1. But we can take it further since you know P&F better now. All these parameters are discussed in detail in this section so that you can choose the settings that are ideal for your style of trading or investment.

5.1 BOX-VALUE

Learning the patterns and other methods of analysis gives one a better understanding of the box-value. Therefore, we discuss about box-values now, after explaining the patterns & formations. Whenever we decide to plot a P&F chart, determining the box-value is important. Every aspect relating to the box-value decision is discussed in this chapter.

Box-values vary with time frames; the same box-value cannot be used for a daily and intraday chart. Log box-value is recommended when a daily P&F chart is plotted. Though the default reversal value is three box, other reversal values are also discussed in the next chapter.

Let us begin the discussion with how to determine a log box-value when a three-box reversal P&F chart is plotted using daily closing prices.

Log box-values are a brilliant invention that have not only simplified the subject but also made it practically more effective. Box-values can simply be classified as per time horizon of a trader or investor. A short-term trader may use a lower box-value, while the long-term trader can settle for a higher box-value because trades and patterns appear more frequently on the lower box-value charts. The following guidelines may also be considered:

- ⬈ Use 0.25% box-value for short-term investment.
- ⬈ Use 1% box-value for medium-term investment.
- ⬈ Use 3% box-value or above for long-term investment.

These are not rigid rules but guidelines to begin with. One can use 1.25% instead of 1 or 0.75% or even something like 1.10% for that matter. Round numbers are mentioned for simplicity, it is more about having a general idea to reduce the confusion. It is classified in a simple manner so that we can corroborate it with the daily, weekly or monthly time frames in time-based charts. There is more to understand about box-values.

Every box-value provides some useful information for traders across all time horizons. While every technique and setup that we have discussed is equally applicable to all box-values, there are certain aspects that should be kept in mind while deciding the box-value.

Look at the chart shown below of Axis bank plotted with 0.25% box-value. A few setups are shown in the boxes and explained in the image.

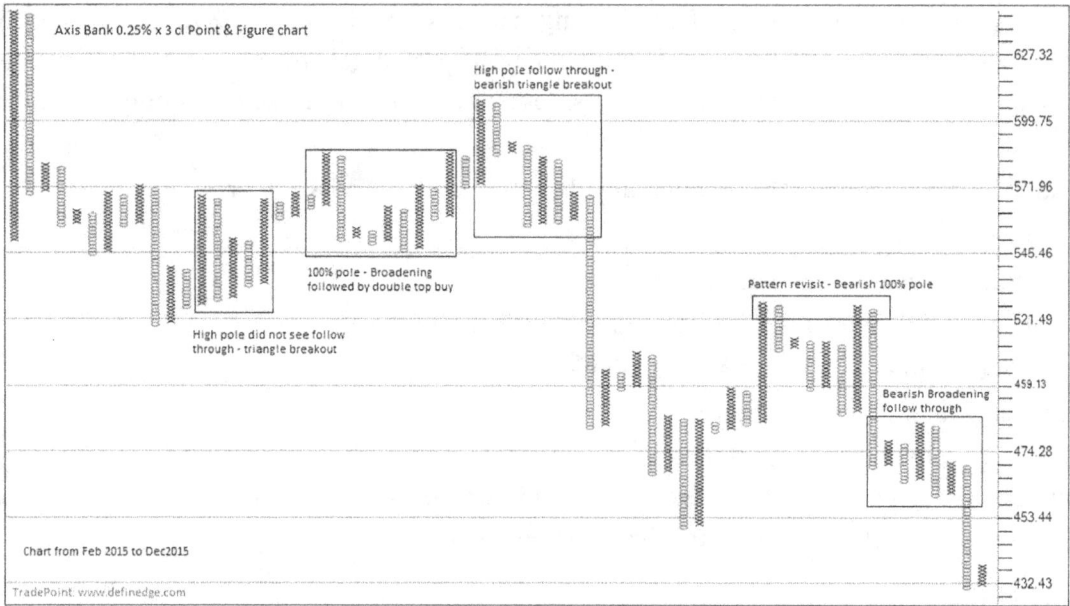

Figure 5.1.1: Axis bank daily 0.25% × 3 cl Point & Figure chart

The setups are more about combination of patterns. Same chart and setups are shown in the chart below plotted with 0.50% box-value.

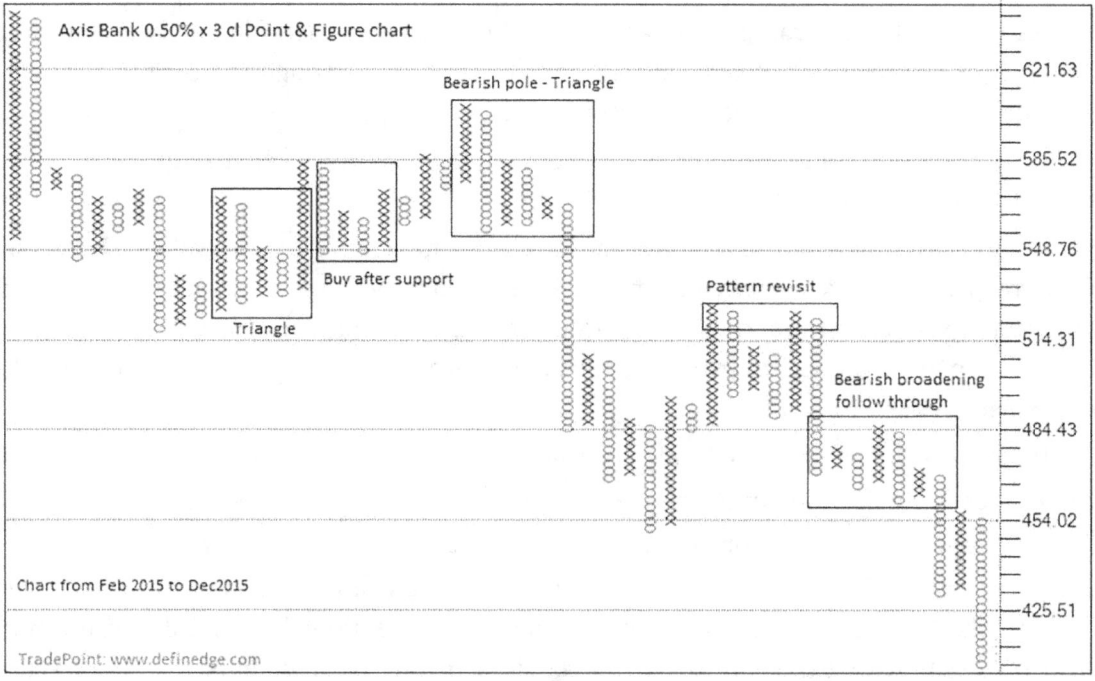

Figure 5.1.2: Axis bank daily 0.50% × 3 cl Point & Figure chart

You must have noticed that when the box-value is higher, the number of columns gets reduced in the chart. Also notice that similar types of setups are visible in both charts. The combination of patterns portrays a detailed view of the price behavior in a lower box-value chart. Below is the same chart plotted with 1% box-value.

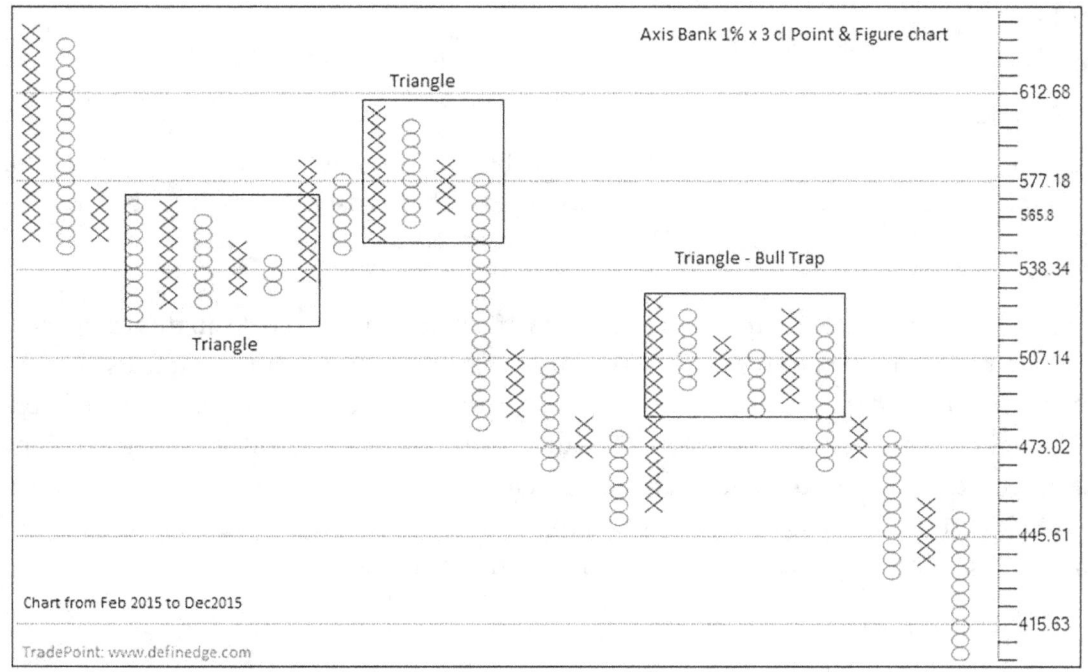

Figure 5.1.3: Axis bank daily 1% × 3 cl Point & Figure chart

Notice that there are far fewer columns in this 1% box-value chart. A few of the setups that were visible in the lower box-value charts are not seen in this chart as the number of columns are compressed because of the bigger box-size. It would be interesting to see what happens when box-value is increased further. Below are the charts for the same period plotted with 1.5%, 2%, 3% and 5% box-values, respectively.

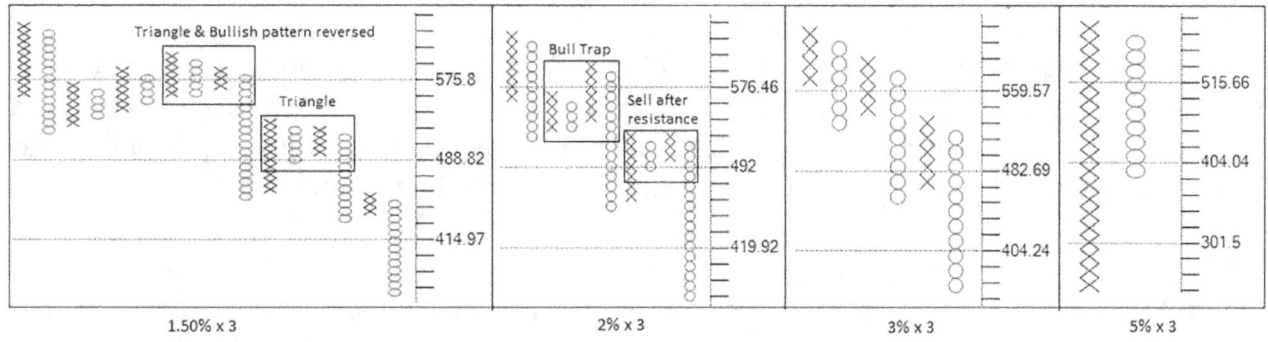

Figure 5.1.4: Axis bank daily Point & Figure charts

It is apparent that the columns get compressed even further as the box-size increases. The patterns visible in 1.5% and 2% box-value charts span across 3–5 columns at best. These patterns, however, morph into a basic sell signals in the 3% box-value chart. And, the number of columns gets reduced more drastically in the 5% box-value chart where just a High Pole pattern or falling column of 'O' is visible.

One can easily observe that the behavior of setups and patterns change as we increase the box-value. A trader can analyse the price structure by looking at the different setups by plotting multiple P&F charts with different box-values. Let us categorize the box-values into different slots as per the nature of the formations that typically occur in each chart. The following are the slots describing the box-values on a daily time frame using closing prices:

Slot 1: 0.25– 1%

Slot 2: 1–3%

Slot 3: 3–5%

Slot 4: 5% and above

Certainly, we can apply all patterns & methods in all box-values. But there are certain unique attributes of each box-value that should be understood. Let us explore the characteristics of each slot.

Slot 1

The price action will be captured across more numbers of columns of 'X' and 'O' in this category compared to others. Combination of patterns, Follow-through, variations and pattern retests are a common occurrence in this slot and they turn out to be effective setups to trade. All indicator-related observations are applicable for charts in this slot. Just the 3–5 column patterns alone are not sufficient and confirmation from other methods is required while dealing with charts in this slot. ABC setup, volume climax and indicators work better while the column reversal pattern has little relevance. Mini Top, Mini Bottoms, objective trend lines and counts are more important on these charts.

Slot 2

The 3–7 column P&F patterns, which we discussed in the earlier chapters, are more relevant and important for the charts in this slot. Structures are clear and the basic signals are more relevant. Column reversal is also an important piece of information. Multi-column breakouts like Triple Top–Triple bottoms formations have more significance here. Anchor top–bottoms, tweezers also work better. Indicator and other methods of analysis like trend lines and counts are equally relevant. Use the conservative vertical counts for the charts in this slot.

Slot 3

The number of columns of 'X' and 'O' are far fewer in the charts from this slot and the setups are clearer. Overall structure and price performance of a chart can be analyzed quickly. Basic breakout patterns and 3 to 5 column P&F patterns are more relevant. Column Reversal follow-through setup is an important piece of information too. Indicators and other tools are, however, not much relevant.

Slot 4

Support–Resistance ('X' or 'O' at same level), weak breakouts and column reversal signals are more important patterns for the charts in this slot. Realize that each column of 'X' or 'O' by themselves represent a big trending move. Indicators and Follow-through signals are not relevant.

Remember, the higher the box-value, greater is the significance of the column reversal pattern. Understanding box-values based on the relevant setups helps understand the utility of each box-value. A 3–5 column formation showing support and resistance needs more confirmation if visible in lower box-value charts such as slot 1. But they have far more significance when they occur in high box-value charts such as slot 3 or above. They indicate that price is at significant support or resistance. The support or resistance or weak breakout setup on higher box-value charts such as slot 3 or 4 is significant information even for a short-term trader, as it helps in identifying trade setups on a lower box-value chart to initiate trades.

Similarly, a multi-column horizontal formation of lower box-value charts displays the base building or accumulation–distribution formations that are important for even a long-term trader to know. The same formations in a higher box-value chart will come across as a simple 3–5 column patterns. Multi-column formations should be referred in slot 1 charts and affordable patterns looked for to fine-tune the entries.

The column reversal pattern is not significant or relevant to view in slot 1 charts, but they can be very useful in higher box-value charts. Their importance increases with the box-value. As the number of columns in the chart is comparatively less and compressed in larger degree box-value charts, patterns such as Low Pole or Follow-through signals are relatively infrequent in higher box-value charts.

So different box-values are important and provide useful information and it is important to know how to read them. Trading methods such as Mini Top–Mini Bottom or 45-degree trend lines are more relevant in slot 1 and slot 2 categories. The basic signals in large box-value charts or column reversal in lower box-value charts are not too relevant from a trade decision-making perspective. Supports-Resistances can be easily viewed on higher box-value charts, which can be useful for all types of traders. A single column or appearance of 'X' or 'O' becomes more important and captures the trend when charts are plotted using high box-values such as 5% or 10%. The confluence of patterns on multiple box-values can help traders of all time frames and prove valuable from the trading perspective. This confluence of patterns across different box-sizes is called a "pattern cluster."

Have a look at the Tata Motor charts plotted with 1% and 0.25% box-values featured below. The support shown by a column of 'O' at same box-value in slot 2 chart comes across as a pattern retest formation in slot 1 chart. Entry can be refined using this kind of background information.

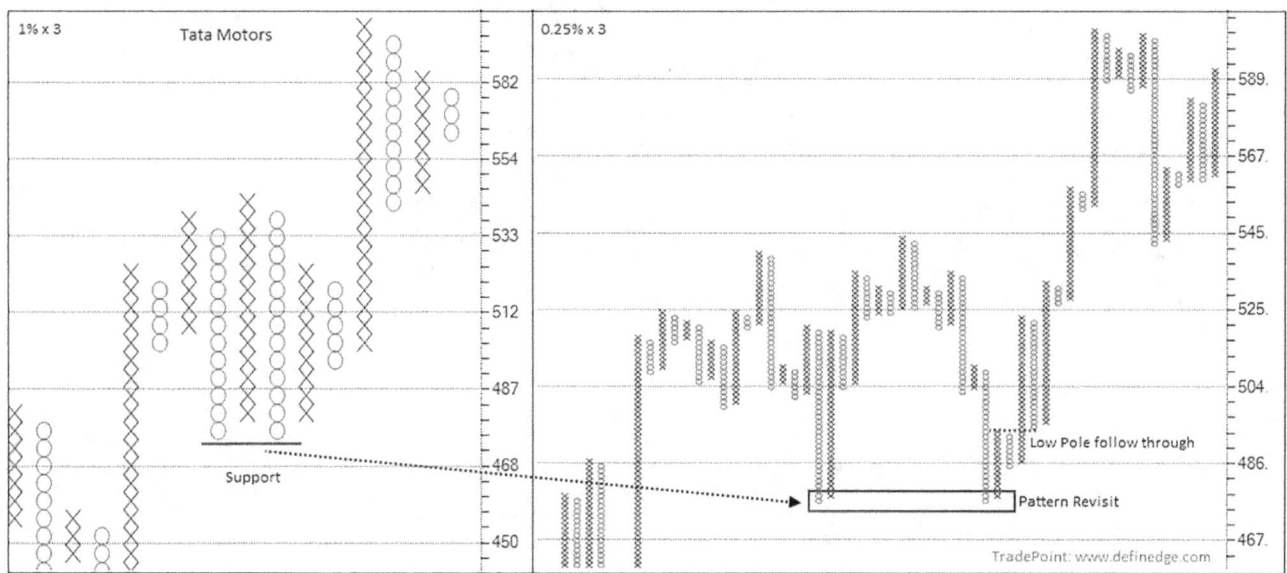

Figure 5.1.5: Tata Motors daily Point & Figure charts

There are patterns inside patterns, which is popularly known as market fractals. For example, 'X' or 'O' at same level, or weak breakouts can come across as pattern retest in lower box-value charts. Look at P&F charts shown below of PNB plotted using 0.25% and 3%, respectively.

Figure 5.1.6: PNB daily 0.25% × 3 cl Point & Figure chart

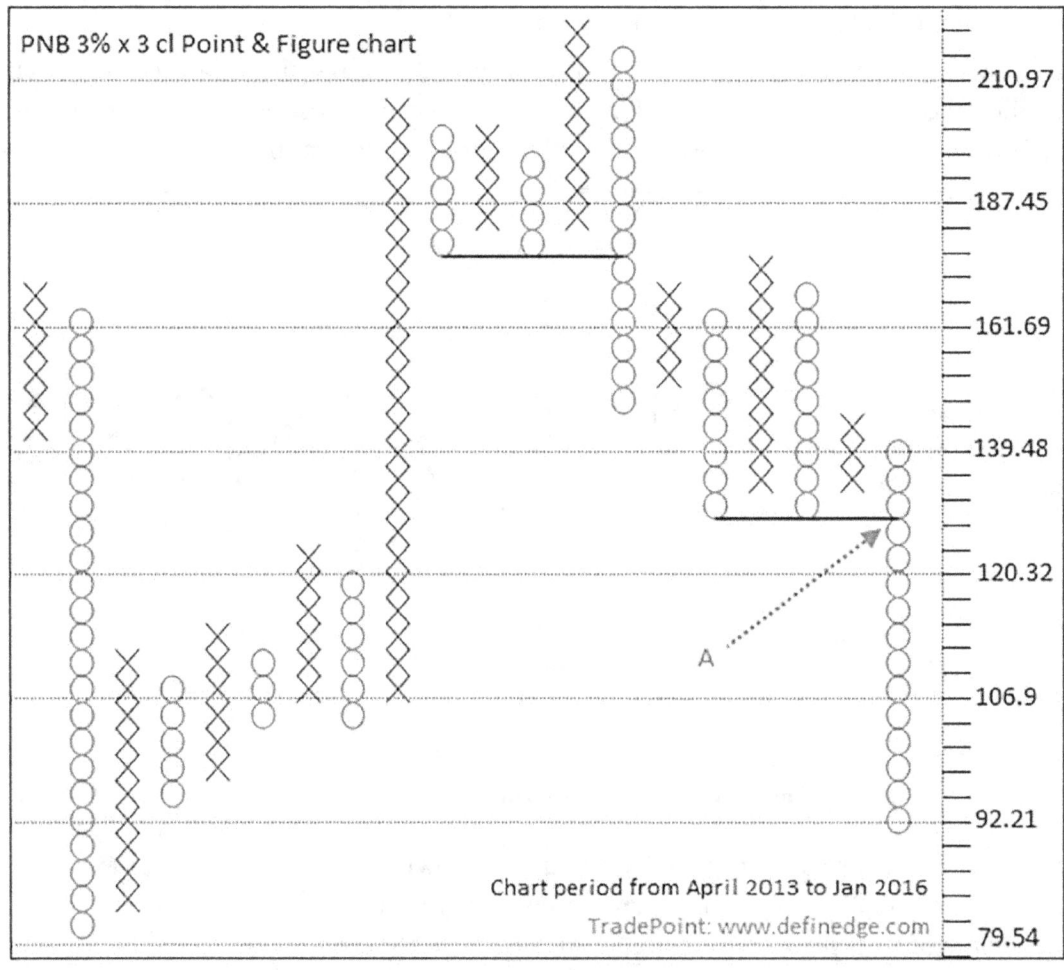

Figure 5.1.7: PNB daily 3% × 3 cl Point & Figure chart

Point A is multi-column breakout bearish formation in 0.25% box-value chart shown in Figure 5.1.6. This pattern is compressed and morphs as a Triple Bottom Sell pattern in the higher box-value chart displayed in Figure 5.1.7.

The best approach is to be aware of the patterns in the higher box-value charts and trade continuation patterns on the lower box-value charts. The idea is to trade pull-backs in lower box-value charts that are in the direction of higher box-value charts. This ensures that we are trading in sync with the trend in the higher time frame or higher box-value charts.

I am often confronted with the question, whether a pattern is profitable and about their performance across various box-values. Remember that the patterns are a by-product of the box-values we use. One can adopt a top-down approach while analyzing the price setup.

It may surprise you but even very high box-values like 8–10% are effective. We get to know about overall price performance and behavior of the instrument at a glance. Below is the chart of daily P&F chart of Wock Pharma plotted with 10% × 3 parameters.

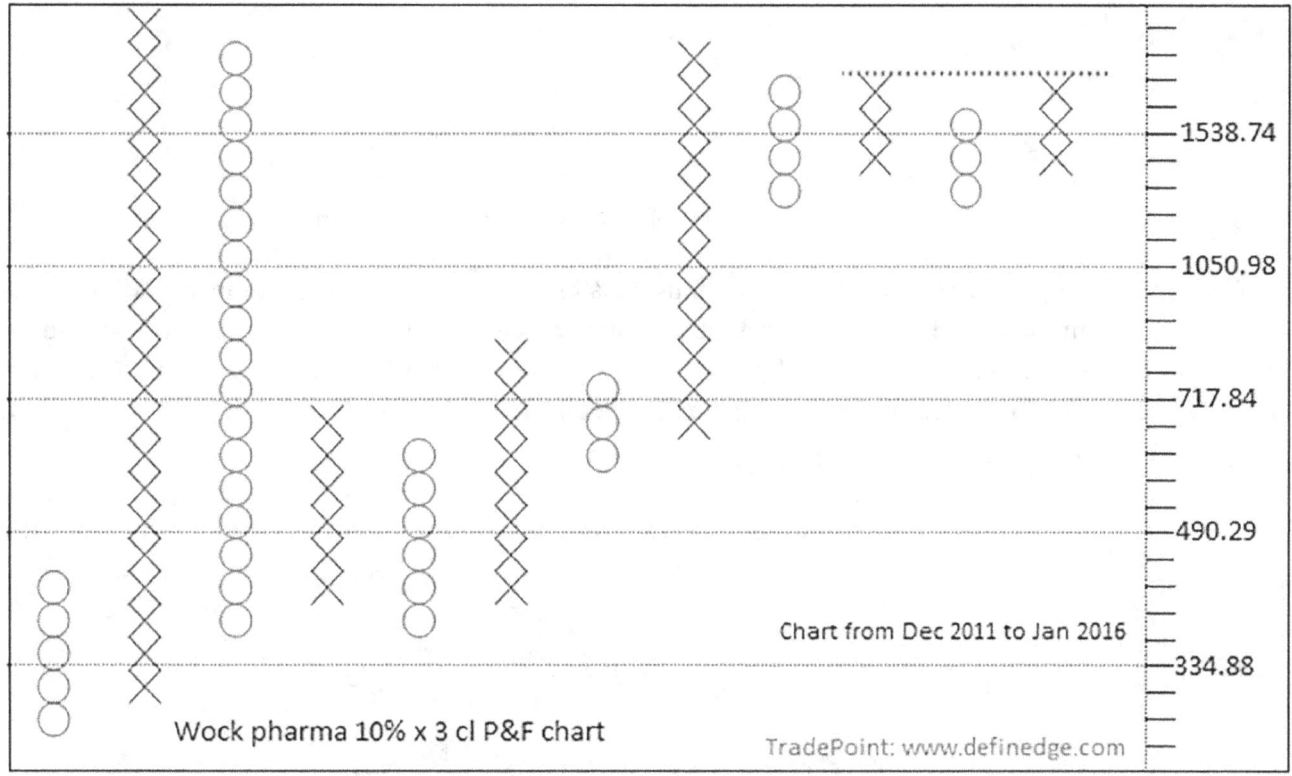

Figure 5.1.8: Wock Pharma daily 10% × 3 cl Point & Figure chart

The chart captures more than 4 years of price action. What is of relevance here is that the entire price action is compressed into a few columns of 'X' & 'O' in the above chart. This falls into slot-4 box-value category chart where column reversal and every single column of 'X' or 'O' are extremely important. Notice that in the last column, the 'X' is at the same level as the previous one, indicating resistance. It is also at a zone where the column flipped from 'X' to 'O' frequently. Realize that it takes a 30% move to trigger a column reversal in this chart. A study of the lower box-value charts will provide confirmation on whether the' X' at the same level does in fact indicate resistance.

Below is 3% × 3 chart of Wock Pharma of the same period.

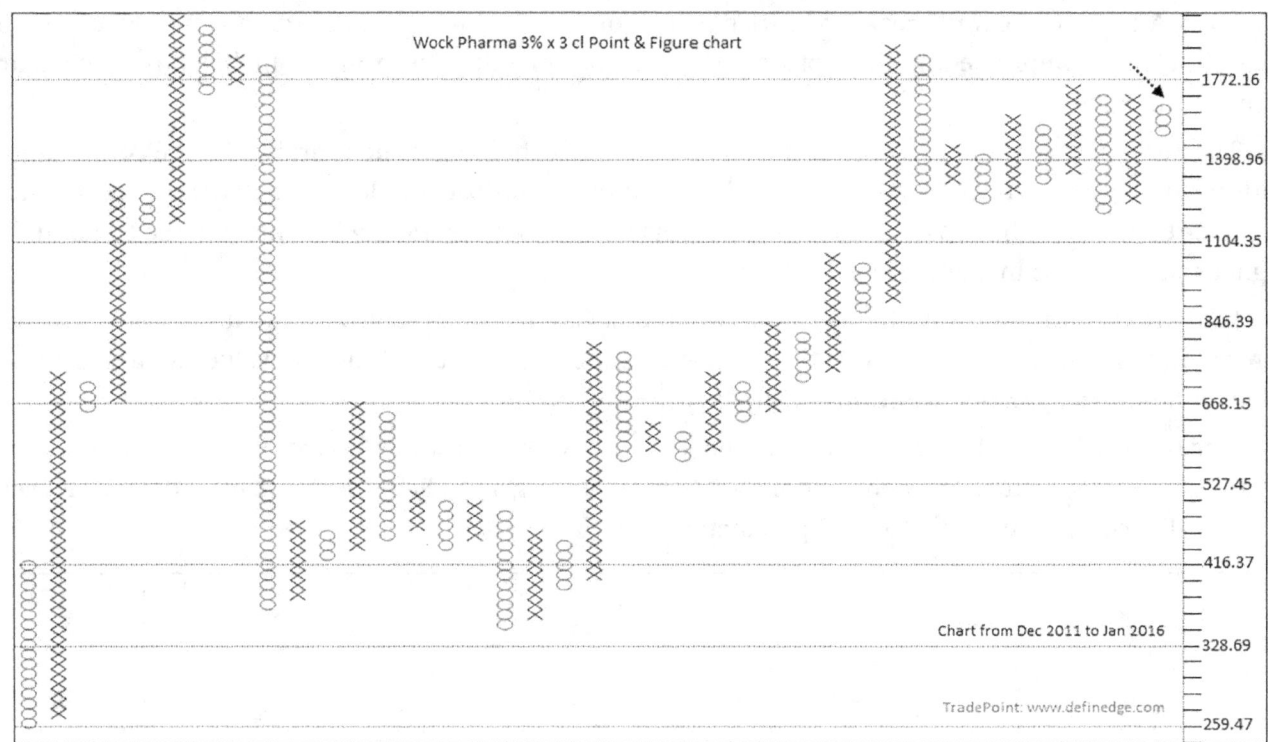

Figure 5.1.9: Wock Pharma daily 3% × 3 cl Point & Figure chart

The same time period covered in the previous 10% chart is displayed in the above 3% box-value chart. The arrow in the chart indicates a negative column reversal after the Bull Trap pattern. The column reversal is a Follow-through pattern after the Bear Trap pattern which has bearish implications. Recall that column reversals are an important piece of information to take note of in the charts falling in this category.

Figure 5.1.10 is the Wock Pharma chart plotted with 1% box-value.

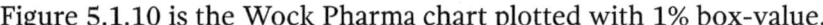

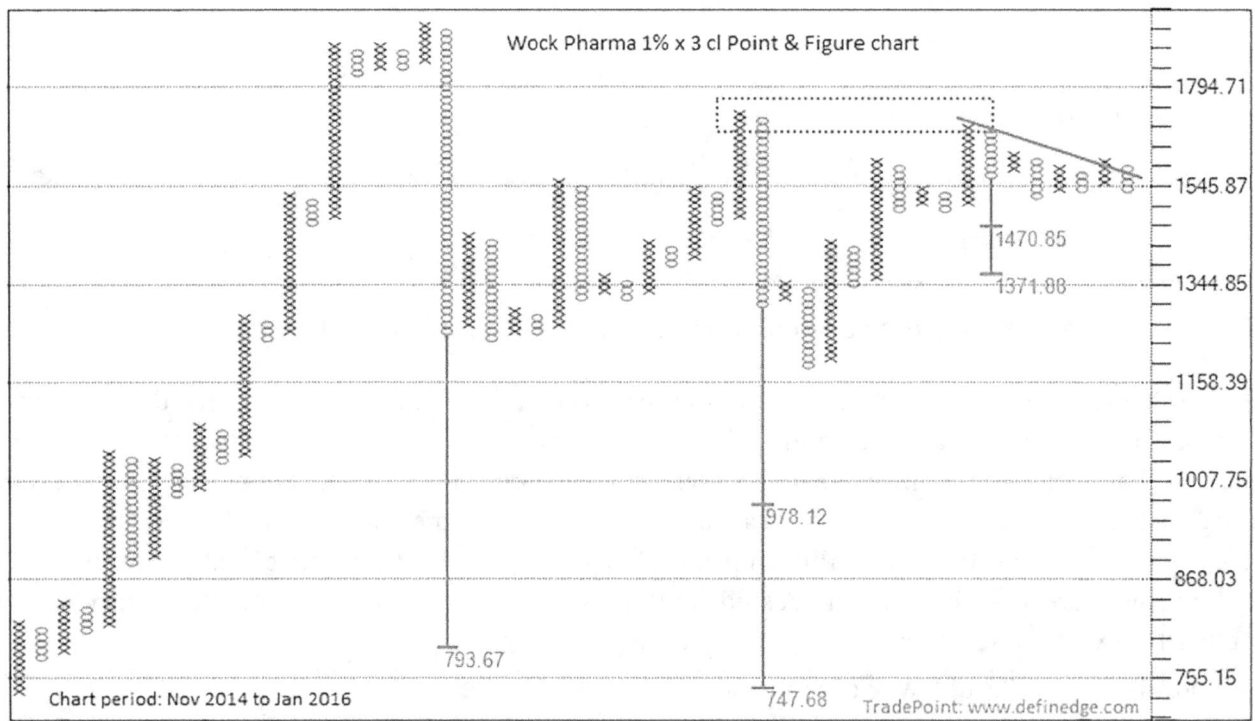

Figure 5.1.10: Wock pharma daily 1% × 3 cl Point & Figure chart

Setup on this chart is negative because of a Sell signal below the trend line and bearish counts that were active. Bearish double pattern and a Follow-through to it are also visible in this chart. The Follow-through to High Pole is also active.

Figure 5.1.11 is the 0.25% × 3 P&F chart of the same stock.

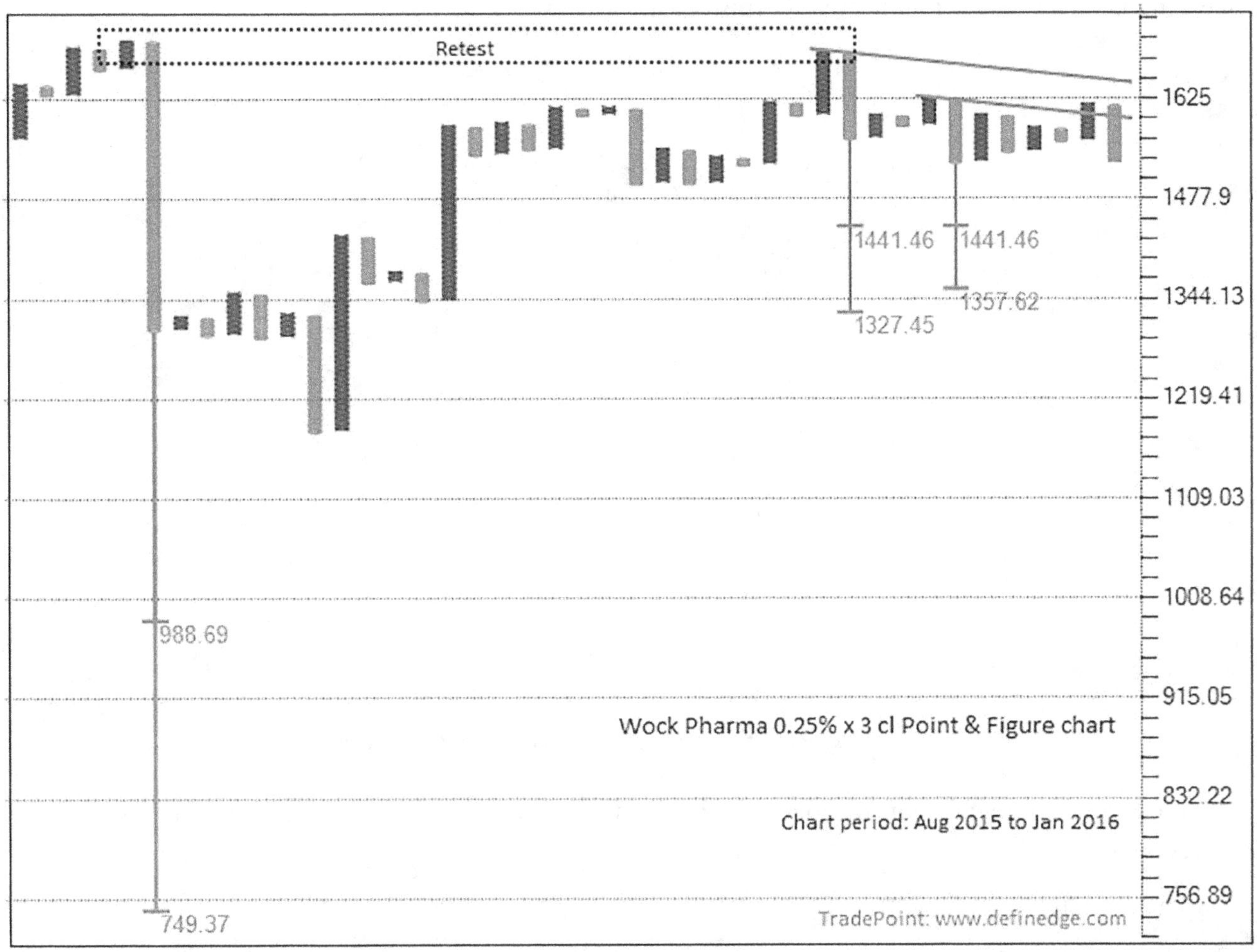

Figure 5.1.11: Wock Pharma daily 0.25% × 3 cl Point & Figure chart

Bearish formations such as Traps and Poles are seen around the same level. Bearish pattern retest, and bearish counts are active and the recent formation is a Bull Trap and a bearish Triangle failure pattern below the bearish trend line. Interestingly, all counts shown in the chart were achieved later.

Reading the patterns in different box-value charts helps in understanding the context and overall price structure. A simple bearish setup seen in a higher box-value chart helped in fine-tuning the entry using lower box-value chart in this Wock Pharma example. This kind of a top-down approach is important for all types of traders and investors. The Wock Pharma stock cracked below 900 in the month of Feb 2016 and fell below 650 in Dec 2016.

A 3–5 column setup on the higher box-value chart can be traded when there is a bullish setup or pullback on the lower box-value chart. Higher box-value charts generate clear setups but they lag at times and they do not offer affordable trade entries as the stop-loss is invariably too wide. The multi-column formations are more relevant and visible in lower box-value charts. These patterns can be fine-tuned while considering a trade entry. The trades are also more affordable in the lower box-value as the stop-loss is not as wide as in higher box-value charts. It makes a lot of sense to take trades off lower box-value charts when there is a confirmation from the higher box-values.

Have a look at 0.25% × 3 chart of Bajaj Auto shown in Figure 5.1.12. Observe the bigger picture and try to visualize what could be the pattern of this chart in a higher box-value. Notice that the price is converging from a broader perspective in this chart.

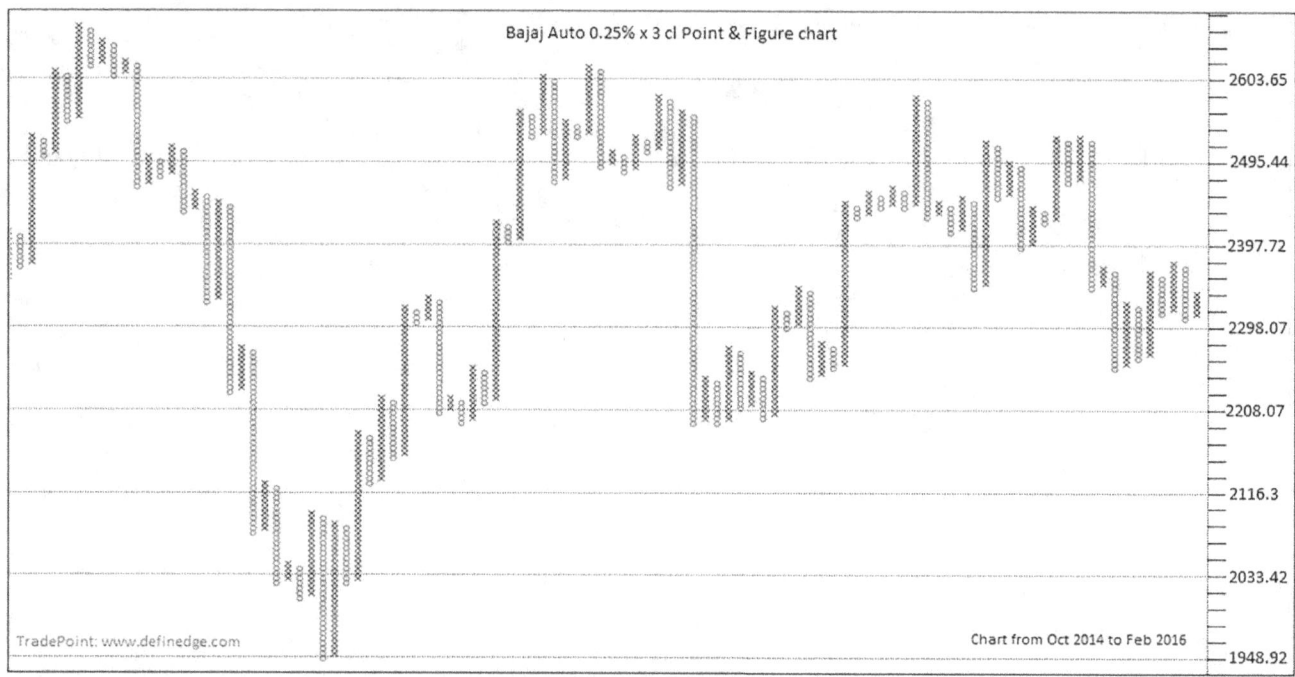

Figure 5.1.12: Bajaj Auto daily 0.25% × 3 cl Point & Figure chart

Figure 5.1.13 is the chart of 3% box-value of the same period. A triangle or series of inside columns can be seen.

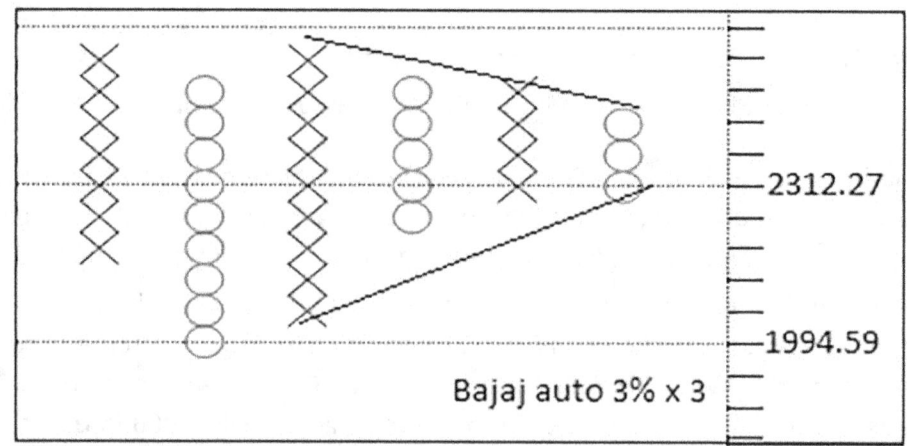

Figure 5.1.13: Bajaj Auto daily 3% × 3 cl Point & Figure chart

It could work the other way around too. If you come across a triangular formation on the higher box-value charts, then you can visualize the setup in lower box-value chart. Am sure you are familiar with how to deal with triangles from a trading perspective. Knowledge of converging formation on higher degree helps in trading the setups in at lower time frame or lower box-value charts. With practice, it would be possible to visualize setups on other slot charts by looking at a pattern in any given chart. And eventually a formation seen in one or two box-values will tell you the overall story.

Always start off with a chart from slot 4 box-value while looking at a chart of an instrument for the first time. Switch to lower box-sizes after getting a broad perspective from slot 4 charts to 3Simple formations in higher box-values translate into multi-column setups on lower box-values, which helps to analyse the entire price action of any instrument.

The above slots or categories are applicable to stocks. It is, however, inappropriate to plot stocks and indices with the same parameters, simply because stock and index are different in terms of their underlying volatility. An index captures the price of many stocks. Typically, stocks can easily see a daily movement of 5–10%, which however is very rare for an index. A stock can get delisted if the company goes bankrupt, but an index will seldom fall to zero unless the stock exchange itself fails.

 The box-value slots for indices are mentioned below:

Slot 1: 0.10– 0.25%

Slot 2: 0.25–1%

Slot 3: 1–2%

Slot 4: 2% and above

Reading of slots remains the same with index as well. Figure 5.1.14 presents 2% and 1% box-value charts of Nifty, respectively.

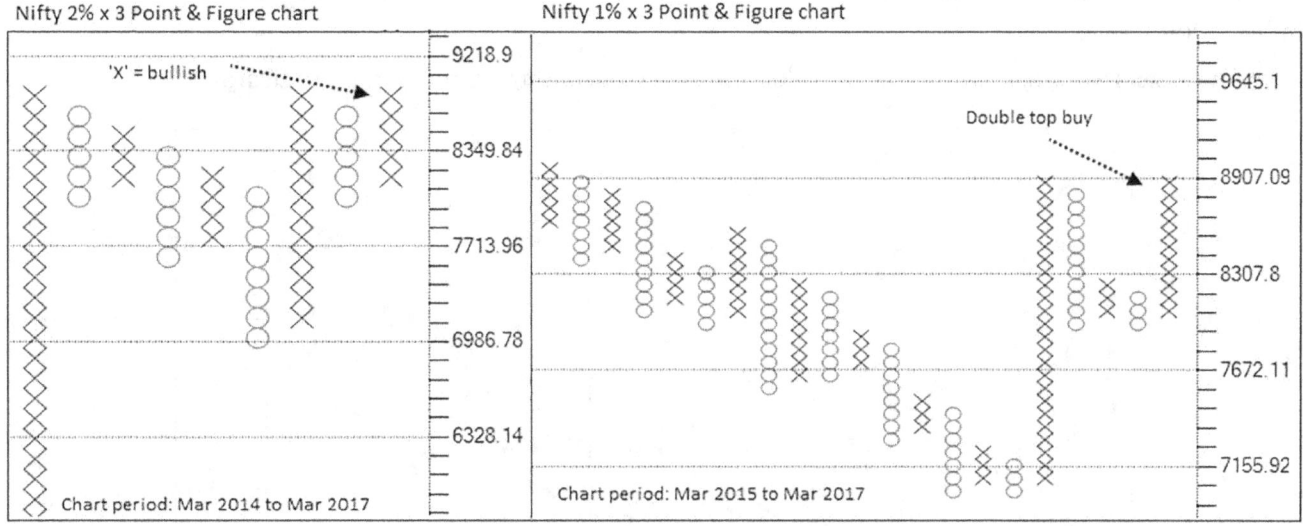

Figure 5.1.14: Nifty daily Point & Figure charts

Last column is of 'X' in 2% chart suggesting that the trend is bullish. Question might arise if it is at resistance when we look at left. This is when a look at the lower box-size charts will provide more clarity. There is clear bullish Double Top Buy signal after support in 1% box-value chart; hence, the undertone is bullish.

Figure 5.1.15 is the chart plotted with 0.25% box-value.

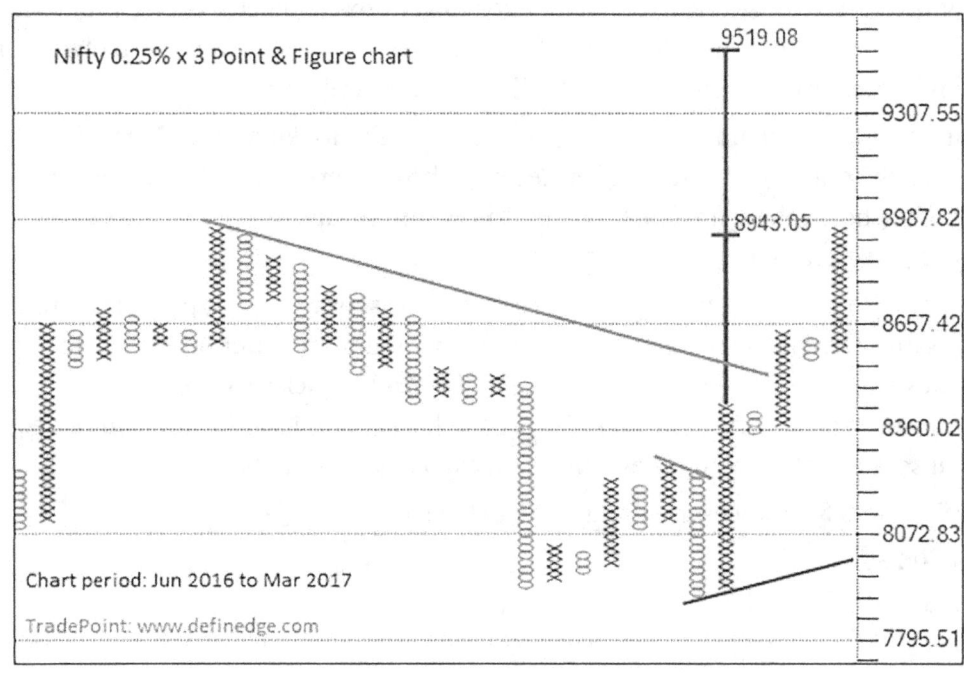

Figure 5.1.15: Nifty daily 0.25% × 3 cl Point & Figure chart

Price is trading above the bullish 45-degree line and there is also a breakout above the bearish 45-degree line drawn from an important top. The bullish vertical counts are open, and the last signal is bullish Double Top Buy.

Figure 5.1.16 is the chart plotted with 0.10% box-value along with XO zone indicator.

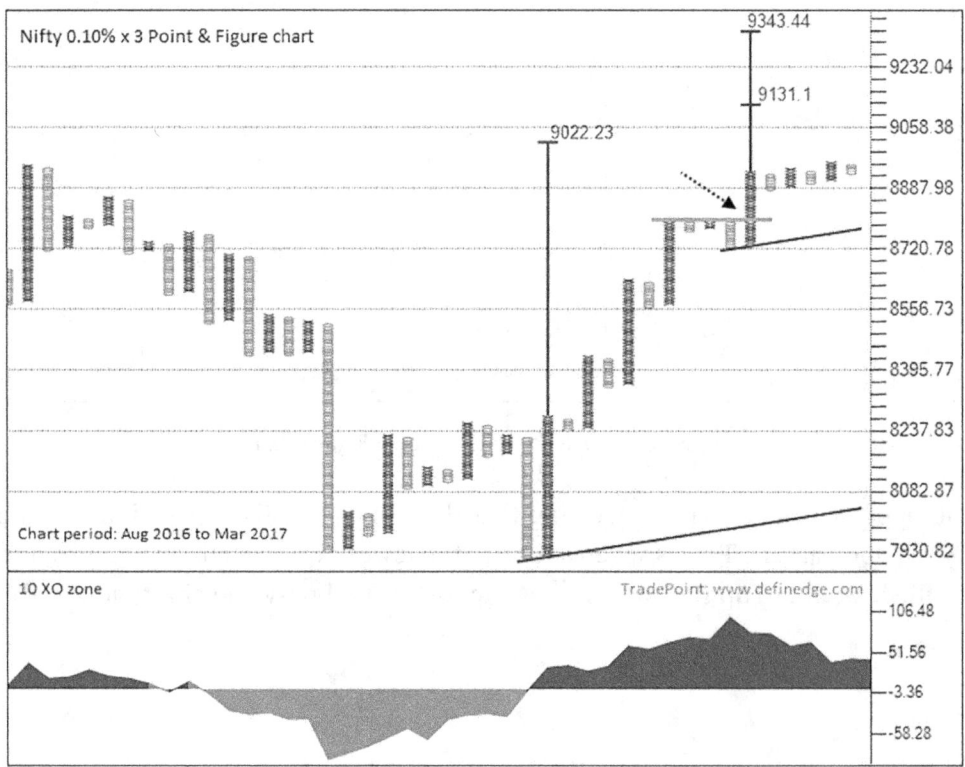

Figure 5.1.16: Nifty daily 0.10% × 3 cl Point & Figure chart

One can easily spot the bullish XO zone, price trading well above bullish 45-degree lines, Mini Bottom is in place and bullish vertical counts are open. The arrow in the chart highlights the bullish Triple Top pattern along with a Bear Trap pattern.

Combination of patterns is the key. Frequent Low Poles that occurred at same level show strong demand and High Poles at same price level represent strong supply zone. Combination is more powerful than the basic patterns, particularly for slot 1 box-value charts.

Setup, trend and counts may vary as per the box-value. Different box-values may lead to different targets and a question may arise about which counts are more reliable. All counts are valid unless negated. Counts in the direction of the trend should be given preference. Plot the charts with different box-values to seek target confluence. But don't use higher box-size charts just to arrive at bigger counts or targets. Avoid the big number fantasy. Consider one at a time and refer to the nearer-counts first. The conservative vertical counts may be used on higher box-value charts and when counter-trend counts are being plotted.

We discussed the typical nature of box-value of every slot. When different box-value charts are in sync, it is a scenario that one should not miss. Bullish setup and Uptrend in slot 3–4 charts with pullback in slot 1–2 charts is a great pullback setup.

Because of log box-values, same rules are applicable to all instruments. Some tweaking may however require as per the volatility of the instrument. Absolute box-value as per slots can also be used if an instrument is being traded consistently. I have tracked Nifty for several years with a 10-point absolute box-value.

Figure 5.1.17 is the 10 × 3 P&F chart of Nifty plotted with daily closing prices.

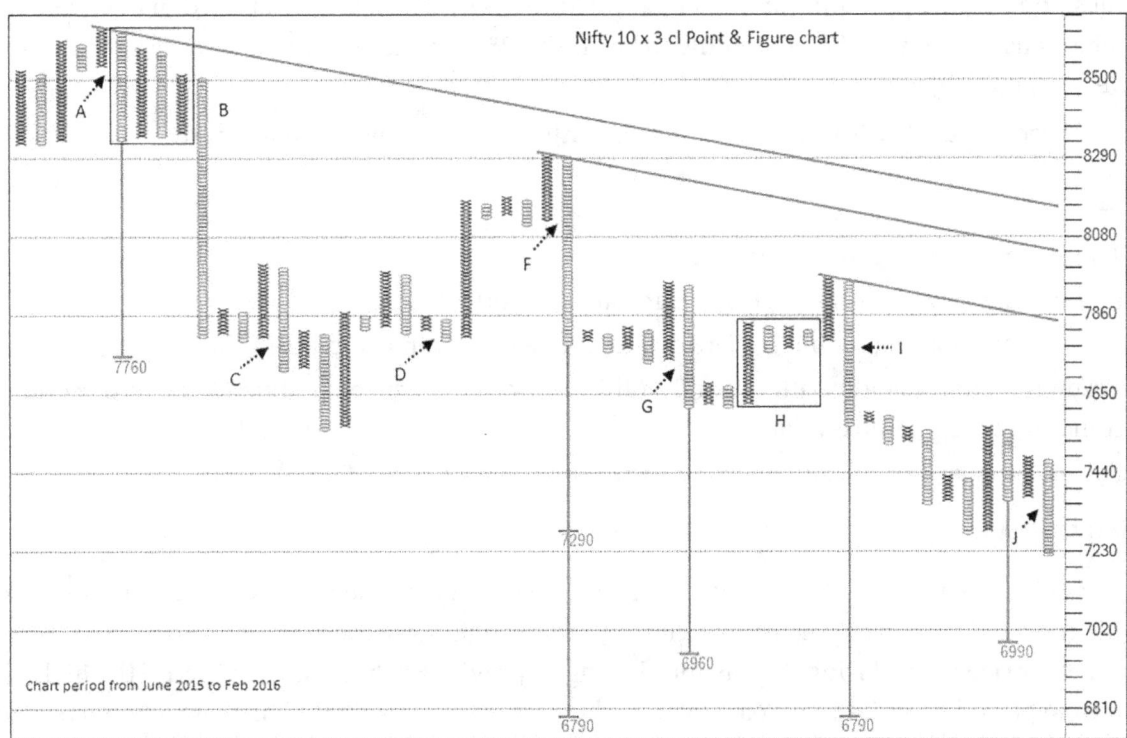

Figure 5.1.17: Nifty daily 10 × 3 cl Point & Figure chart

Pattern A is a Bull Trap followed by Triangle at pattern B. Pattern C is Bearish Broadening formation followed by sell signal. Pattern D is Follow-through sell signal to the High Pole, which was invalidated in the next column. Pattern F and G are bearish 100% Poles and Mini Tops. Pattern H is a Triangle that failed at pattern I with a pole formation. Pattern J is Double Bottom Sell signal after a High Pole.

It is pertinent to mention that the simple signals in higher box-value are far more reliable and profitable though they might lag. Different types of indicators can be plotted and used effectively in the lower box-value charts. For example, a triple moving average crossover method can be traded in the lower box-value when it is in sync with the higher box-value charts.

Box-values and slots are not rigid numbers and may be tweaked to suit one's preference or the behavior of an instrument. Also remember that you may want to analyse formations on various box-values, but trades should be consistently initiated in just one box-value. The general rules described above will be helpful to make a beginning. Columns are relatively long when lower box-values are used. When long column of 'X's and 'O's are visible, it is a pointer that either the box-size must be increased or a lower time-frame chart might be more appropriate from a trading perspective. For mid-cap stocks, the 1% and 3% box-values are more relevant.

Lower time-frame box-values would be different from daily time frame. It should typically be half of the box-values that we discussed above. Detail explanation is given in the chapter on time interval charts.

The important takeaway is that using multiple box-values provides an edge. We discussed about separate treatment to long and short setups in the pattern segment. Box-value is an effective tool to achieve it. Just increase the box-value while considering long positions and reduce the box-size when look for shorting opportunity in stocks. Higher box-value charts need only a periodical viewing as they do not move as swiftly as lower box-value charts. The box-value distinctions are general guidelines to begin with. When you open the chart, you would invariably get a feel about which box-value is appropriate for the given instrument and what patterns should be referred to in a given box-value.

All these box-values are applicable on charts plotted with daily price data. I don't see any point in plotting charts using the weekly or monthly price in the P&F charts. We can always tweak the box-value to achieve the same objective.

The next section deals with the charts plotted with the High–Low price method.

Summary

- ⋏ There are 4 slots of box-values.
- ⋏ Pattern cluster and a top-down approach are very effective.
- ⋏ Analyse multiple charts but initiate trades in one time frame and box-value.
- ⋏ Trade the continuation patterns and pull-backs in the lower box-value chart, in direction of the trend in the higher box-value chart.
- ⋏ For mid-cap stocks, 1% and 3% are effective box-values.

5.2: HIGH–LOW CHARTS

It must be obvious by now that P&F charts can be plotted with just one price. Charts plotted with closing prices will generate patterns based on the closing price. High–Low method of plotting considers either the high or low price made during the day for plotting. If previous column is of 'X' and if the high price for the given time period qualifies to plot a new box, then a new 'X' gets plotted and the low price is ignored. If previous column is of 'O' and price falls further, new 'O' gets plotted and the high price is ignored. This method is effective but there is a problem. We don't know whether high has occurred first or the low on a given day. Price can go high during the day and qualify for new 'X', but it can go below the required level of reversal during the same day. As per the rules, low price will be ignored for plotting on that day though it may have triggered the exit level. Such instances are, however, not too frequent. Otherwise, it is an effective method particularly for short-term traders because it is possible to take decisions in real time and there is no need to wait for the closing price. This approach is useful in instances when intraday time interval charts are used.

High–Low method plot more columns compared to the closing price method. Therefore, the number of columns is higher and the chart gets wider in nature, warranting the use of a higher box-value to deal with it. Basic signals alone are not sufficient in these charts. All methods and techniques that we have discussed earlier are not equally applicable to these charts. The box-value slots that we discussed for closing price method are not applicable to High–Low method. Below are the slots for High–Low method charts.

Slot 1: 0.5–1.5%

Slot 2: 1.5–3%

Slot 3: 3–6%

Slot 4: 6% and above

The nature & behavior of these charts is quite different. Columns are relatively longer; hence, the pole pattern is not as significant in these charts. The instances of Poles and Broadening patterns are much higher in these charts. Combination of patterns and 7–9 column formations are more relevant than the usual setups. Catapult, Triple Top–Triple Bottom formations and their variations are also frequently seen in these charts. The use of indicators for trend filtration and their divergences with price are more significant. Pattern retest and multi-column breakout are effective setups in this method. Bullish pattern reversed and Bearish pattern reversed appear more frequently and the ones in the direction of the trend are reliable patterns to trade. The 45-degree lines appear relatively steep because of the horizontal nature of the chart. Columns are long, hence, the use of conservative vertical count or horizontal counts are more relevant.

Figure 5.2.1 is 6% × 3 P&F chart of BHEL plotted using High–Low method. The last column is of 'O', which displays Downtrend. Supports and Resistance indicated by boxes occurring at the same level are shown in the chart.

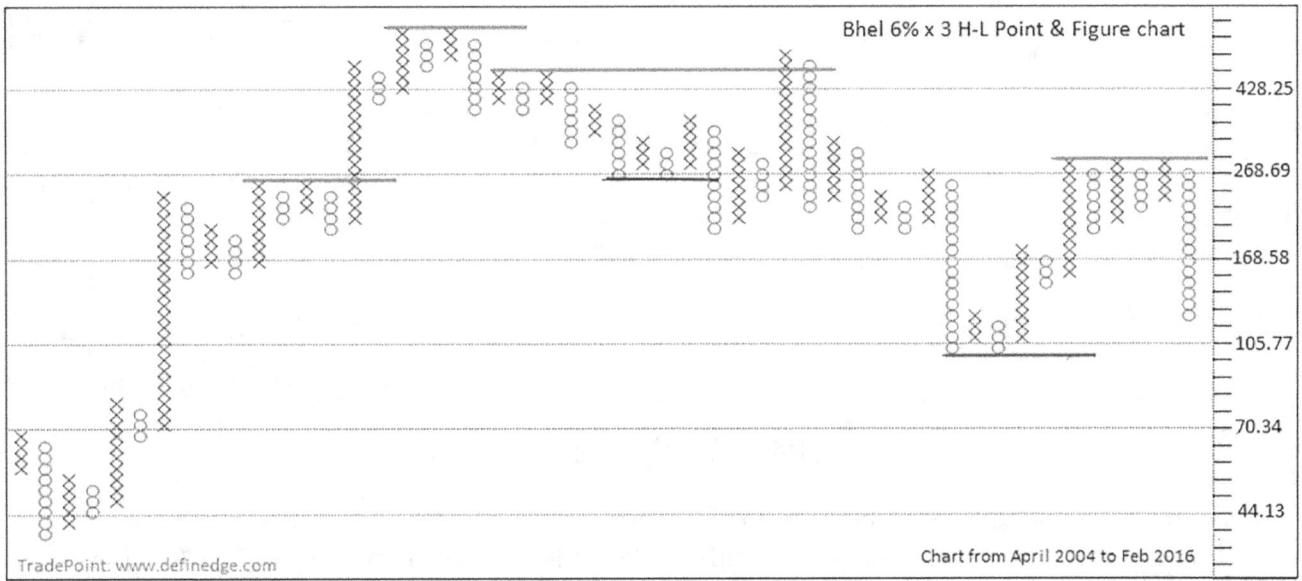

Figure 5.2.1: Bhel daily 6% × 3 H-L Point & Figure chart

Below is the same chart plotted with 3% box-value.

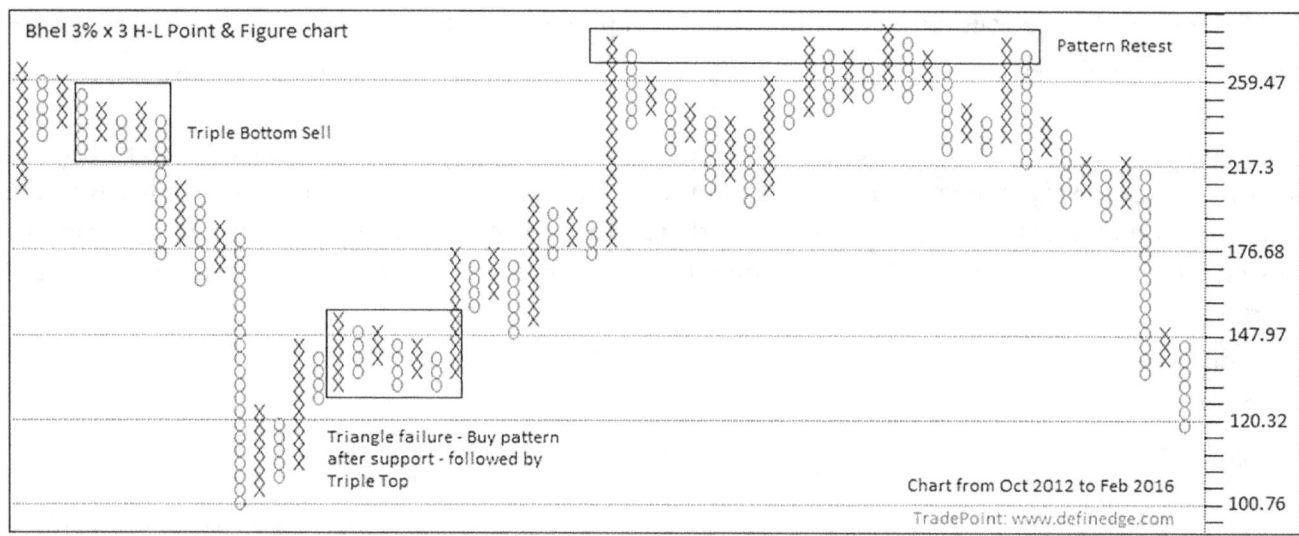

Figure 5.2.2: Bhel daily 3% × 3 H-L Point & Figure chart

Pattern combinations are shown in the chart. A Triple Bottom Sell and its Follow-through is highlighted by the box drawn around them. Pattern Retest with Triple Bottom Sell occurred during Aug 2015, followed by significant fall in prices.

The formations shown in the chart above are useful but realize that the box-value is high. We can focus on multi-column setup while studying the lower box-values charts. Figure 5.2.3 is the same chart plotted with 1.5% box-value.

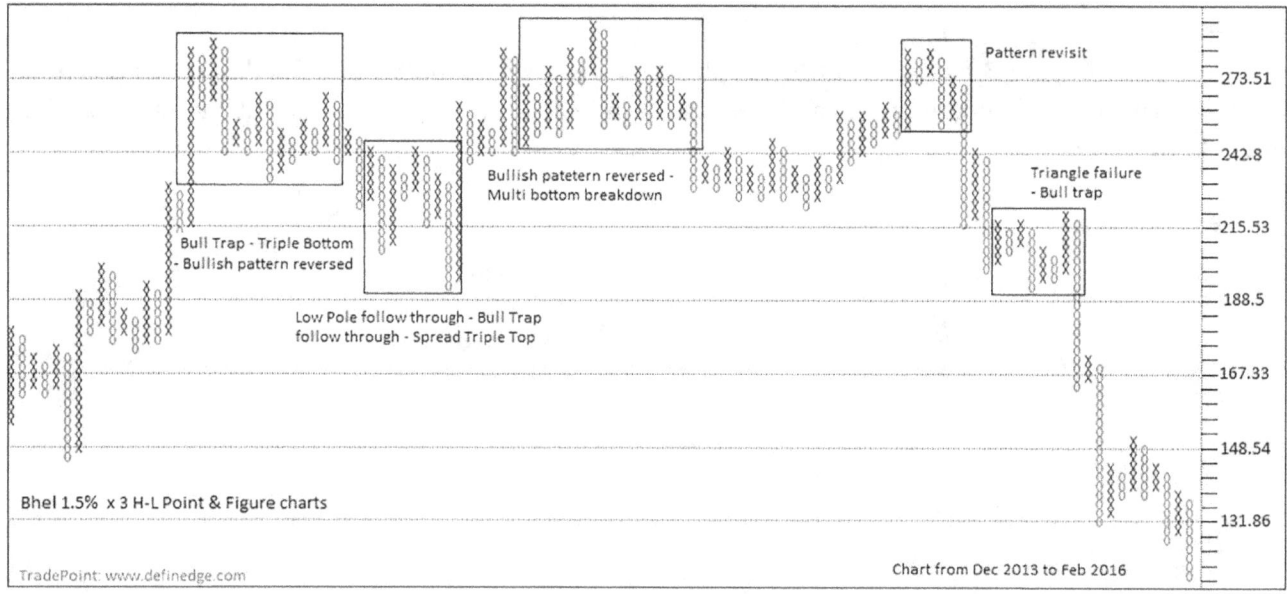

Figure 5.2.3: BHEL daily 1.5% × 3 H-L Point & Figure chart

The prominent setups are highlighted in the charts. It can be observed that columns are relatively longer when charts are plotted using this method. Below is same chart plotted with 0.50% box-value, multi-column formations are highlighted in the chart.

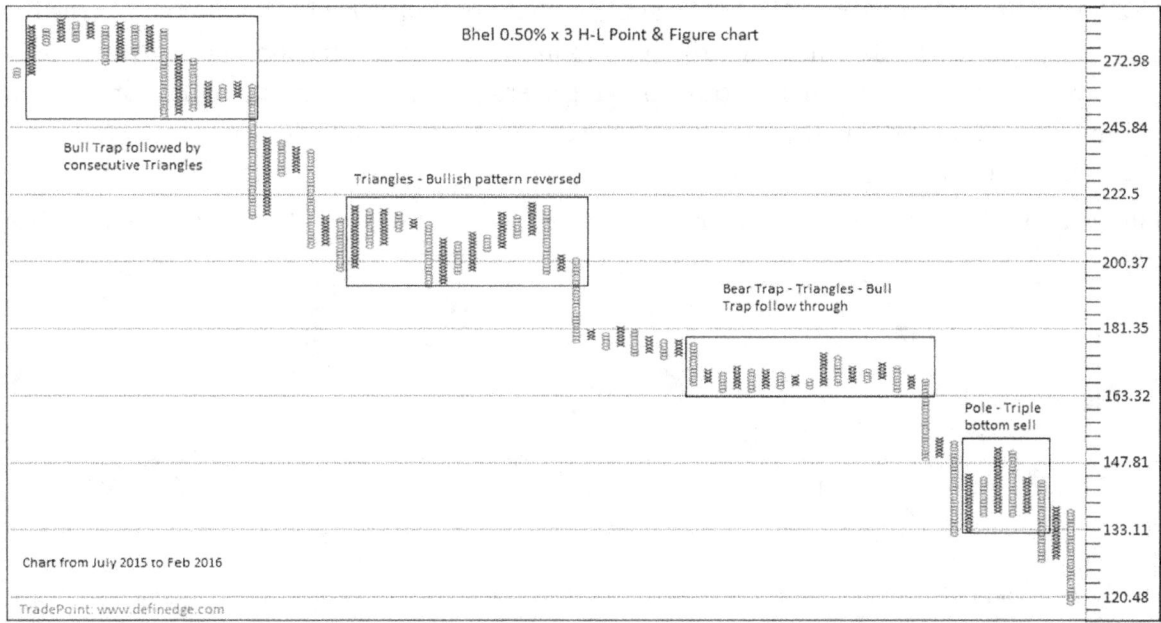

Figure 5.2.4: Bhel daily 0.50% × 3 H-L Point & Figure chart

Box-values of each slot will be changed for index. It should typically be twice the box-value used in the closing price methods. Pattern cluster occurring in multiple box-values can be traded effectively using this method as well. Behavior of an instrument and overall context are better understood by multi-time-frame analysis.

Remember, you can't trade simple Double Top or Double Bottoms on High–Low charts, multi-column breakout patterns are more relevant on them. Apply subjective tools and indicators on them for better analysis and simple execution. Methods like triple moving average crossover and other indicators can be easily traded on these charts.

Figure 5.2.5 is a 3% × 3 P&F chart of Kajariacer plotted on daily price data, using the High–Low method.

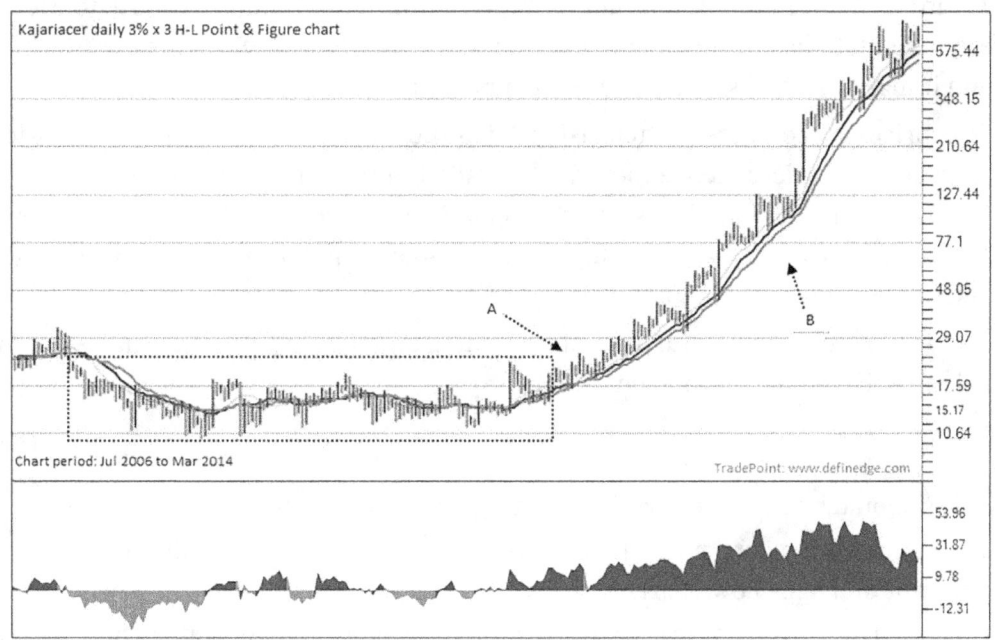

Figure 5.2.5: Kajariacer daily 3% × 3 H-L Point & Figure chart

The above chart features 10, 15 & 20 SMA along with 20-period XO zone. Point A shows the breakout from a 3-year price consolidation. It is a rounding bottom breakout after long period of triple moving average convergence. Point B is when all three moving averages start trending up with short-term average above the medium term and the medium term above the long term along with a positive XO zone. This is a very bullish configuration.

Figure 5.2.6 is 1% × 3 H-L chart of LT plotted with 10, 15, 20 SMA, 20 XO zone and 14 period ADX.

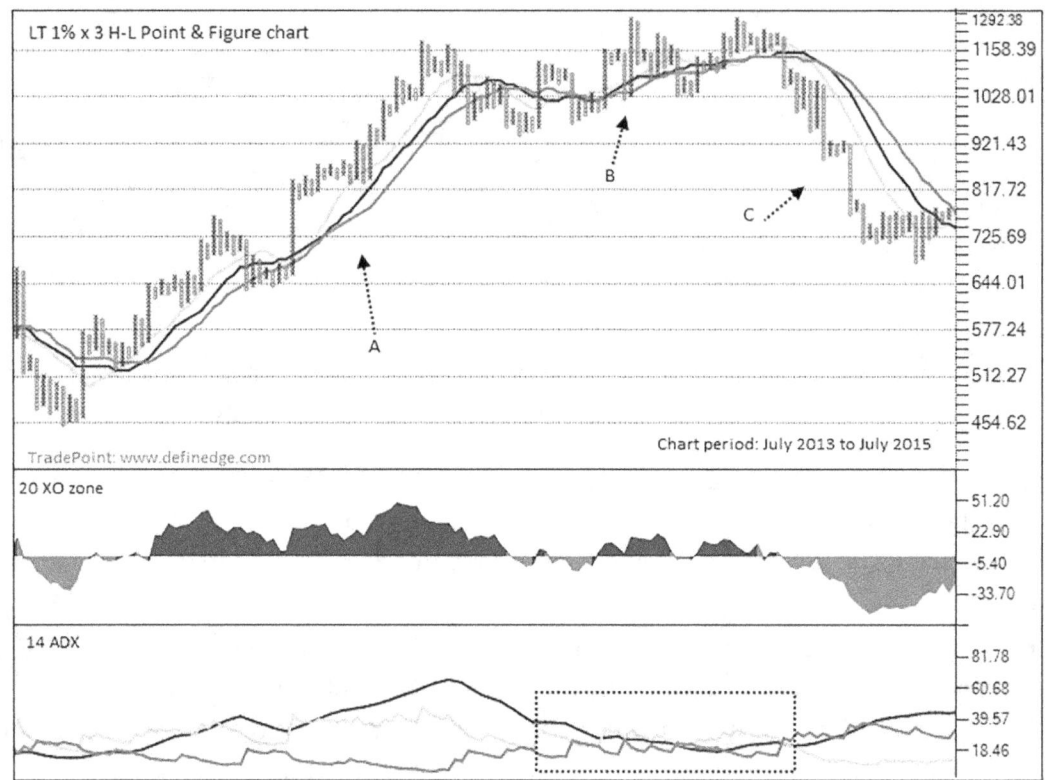

Figure 5.2.6: LT daily 1% × 3 H-L Point & Figure chart

Notice behavior of ADX. I call it a *khichadi* ADX, where three ADX lines are close to each other. Point A and C represent market phase when moving averages, XO zone and ADX point toward the presence of a clear trend and it makes a lot of sense to trade such phases.

High or Low prices of columns plotted using High–Low method will display box-prices recorded based on the high and low prices, hence they can be traded in real time. The use of harmonic patterns is quite popular in the candle and bar charts and they can be effectively used in the High–Low P&F charts too. Subjective chart patterns such as rounding Top/Bottoms, Cup & Handle and Head & Shoulders can be easily spotted in these charts.

High–Low charting method is useful for system trading and intraday traders. High–low chart can also be referred to along with closing method chart.

Summary

- ➤ Box-values should be increased while analyzing High–Low charts.
- ➤ Simple P&F formations are not applicable on them. Complex and multi-column formations are more relevant on High–Low charts.
- ➤ Traditional patterns of technical analysis, subjective lines and Indicators help in implementing them better.

5.3: CLOSING OR HIGH–LOW

The next obvious question would be: Which method should be used, closing or High–Low? Both come with their own set of issues and advantages. A chart plotted with closing prices mark the column at end of the day, hence signals appear late but the charts plotted with High–Low price produce more columns of 'X' and 'O'.

This is an issue with all the charts, not only P&F. The question is similar to whether one should use a line chart or a bar chart. A bar or candle gets locked at end of the day but most of the indicators are calculated on the closing prices. Any trading decision taken in between is based on assumption or pre-emption. End-of-the-day or positional trading systems are usually traded based on the closing prices.

Closing Price Method

Setups are clear and the charts are relatively noise-free when plotted with closing prices. This is perhaps the reason why Charles Dow, John Murphy and many others prefer line charts over bar charts. Charles Dow considered the daily close as the most significant price and relied exclusively on them. The usual line chart that plots only closing prices is one of the oldest and most important methods of plotting the prices. Also, as Murphy* argues, "Many chartists believe that because the closing price is the most critical price of the trading day, a line chart is more valid measure of price activity." P&F charts filter noise from usual line charts and allow us to define setups using combination of columns.

But it is normally felt that trading based on a closing method is practically difficult, especially on daily time frame, because the column gets locked only at the end of the day and breakout that we see on the chart during the day might not be valid until the closing price is known. The same problem is prevalent in candlestick charts too. The candles seen during the day might change based on the closing price. This is a typical problem faced by people trading end-of-the-day chart systems based on any charting method. There are several ways to deal with this issue.

1. Wait for the closing price of the day and ignore the intraday moves. If the closing price turns out to be so high that the risk becomes unaffordable, then ignore the trade and wait for the next opportunity.
2. Initiate the trade the next day when the breakout is confirmed by the closing price of the previous day. If the price opens higher, which makes the initial risk unaffordable, then just ignore the trade. This is the safest method with the lowest impact cost.
3. Many of the times, price moves significantly on same day itself. Entry can be made upon breakout in real time, and exit the trade if the closing price is below the box-price requirement. The cost of doing it should get offset normally due to the profits made in the process over time. Another way to handle this is by taking the trades in the last hour of trading. This minimizes the impact cost to a large extent.
4. For positional traders, this issue can be dealt using position-sizing rules. Initiate a portion of the budgeted quantity during the day and add more when the breakout is confirmed while closing. I strongly believe this as the best approach for momentum traders.
5. For an active trader, this method is most suited. Shift to lower time-frame charts once breakout has happened on daily charts. Trade it as per the formations during the day on lower time interval chart, and get back to daily chart at end of the day. If breakout is sustained, shift to end-of-the-day charts. Impact cost is minimum with this because there will also be profits made on lower time-frame charts by following this.

*Murphy, John J. Technical Analysis of the Financial Markets: A Comprehensive Guide to Trading Methods and Applications. New York: New York Institute of Finance, 1999, P. 36.

Select a method that suits you most and, more importantly, follow that consistently.

For exiting the position, do it based on the box-price requirement even in real time and reinstate the position if closing price doesn't meet the exit price requirement. The debit occurred in the books during the process is the impact cost that would get offset over a period due to the cost saved with the same exercise.

Things are quite simple for positional and long-term traders because they use higher box-values where the issue is not much relevant. Momentum traders using lower box-value charts should also use time interval charts and trades can be placed based on the setup in them where the issue can be minimized. The patterns on closing price charts are much clearer and more reliable and I recommend using this method to plot charts for trading.

High–Low

The advantage of High–low charts is that they help in taking real-time trading decisions. One need not wait for closing to happen before initiating the trade. If previous column is of 'X', and if box-price requirement to qualify for a new 'X' is met during the day, then plotting will remain same till end of the day. So, a decision can be taken confidently in real time. This method is more suitable to someone trading an instrument on a consistent basis or following a system-based approach to trading. It is possible that 'X' plotted in bullish column will remain same for the day even if price has turned down and the reversal criteria are met because the low price is not considered as the price in a column of X. But, such situations are relatively uncommon and they typically occur when the breakout and reversal happen on the same day. One can exit when reversal criteria are met and wait for the next signal to deal with it; expenses that occur in the process are the impact cost, which is comparatively low.

One can also use both the High–Low method and closing method in conjunction. Setups in the closing price charts may be traded during the day as per the levels in the High–Low charts. For momentum and derivative traders, instead of using High–Low method on daily prices, it is better to shift to time interval charts. The next section discusses the same.

5.4: TIME INTERVAL CHARTS

Time interval charts are the ones plotted on any time frame lesser than daily. P&F charts can be plotted using the price from any time interval such as hourly, 30 min, 15 min and so on. They can even be plotted using tick-by-tick prices, which is the origin of P&F charts but they are best used with time interval charts. The user can decide the preferred time interval to plot the chart but one-minute price is probably the best. People prefer an hourly or 15 min interval charts for momentum trading in the time-based charts but the scenario is different with respect to P&F charts. Unlike the usual charts, one minute is a very dynamic time frame on Point & Figure charts. Instead of increasing the time interval, box-value can be increased in the chart plotted with 1 min price. Varying the box-value on the same time frame can help in varying the noise or quantum of information that is captured in the chart.

Every technique that we have discussed is applicable on time interval P&F charts but the slots of box-values are different. Normally, it should be half of what we discussed for the daily time frame. Below are the slots for P&F chart plotted on time interval charts:

Slot 1: 0.05–0.20%

Slot 2: 0.20– 0.4%

Slot 3: 0.4–1%

Slot 4: 1% and above

The 3–4 column setups is more relevant in the higher box-value charts. Pattern combinations and follow-through setups are effective in the lower box-value charts.

Below is the 0.25% × 3 P&F chart of PNB plotted on daily time frame. It would be the box-value a short-term trader would refer to before drilling down to the lower time frame.

Figure 5.4.1: PNB daily 0.25% × 3 cl Point & Figure chart

Pattern combinations are more relevant in the chart shown in Figure 5.4.1. The chart covering the same period is displayed with different box-values based on the 1 min price. Figure 5.4.2 is a 1.5% box-value chart for the same period plotted with closing prices of every minute.

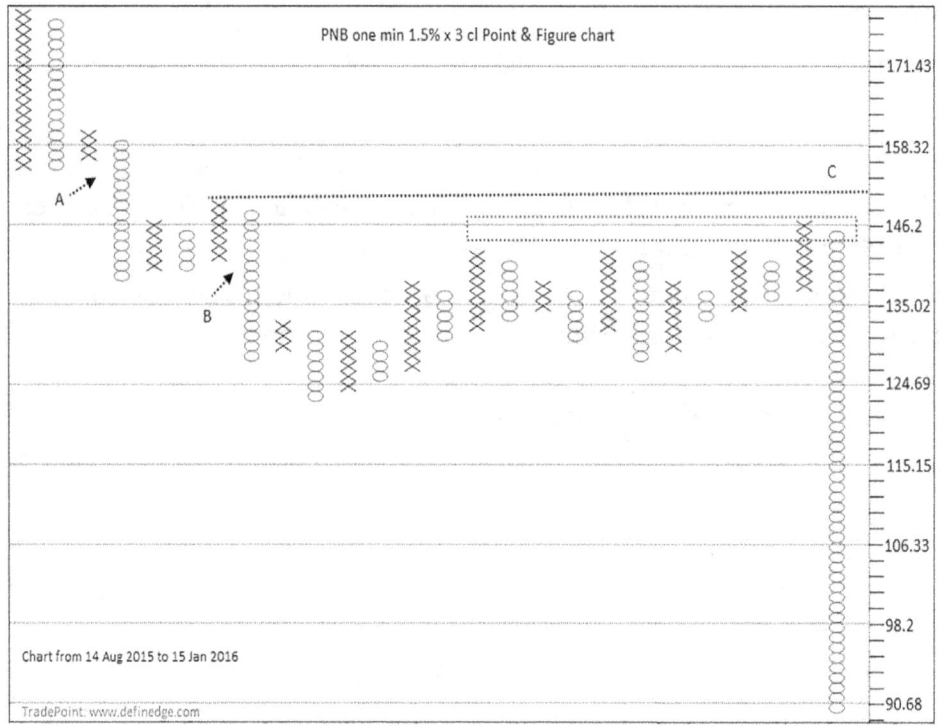

Figure 5.4.2: PNB 1 min interval 1.5% × 3 cl Point & Figure chart

It is fascinating to see a five-month price action using a 1 min interval price being captured in a few columns. Pattern A is Double Bottom Sell signal after a High Pole. Pattern B is a Bull Trap in the direction of the trend. Pattern C is Pattern Retest formation with bearish 100% Pole and bullish pattern reversed in the direction of the trend. As the noise is removed to a big extent, it is a useful time frame even for positional trader. Long column of 'O' in the above chart shows a price move in the same direction for several days. Continuation signals in lower box-values during such period can be effective trade signals for short-term traders.

Figure 5.4.3 is the same chart plotted with 0.15% box-value along with Bollinger bands plotted using mid-price method.

Figure 5.4.3: PNB 1 min interval 0.15% × 3 cl Point & Figure chart

Vertical lines are day-separating lines to observe intraday price moves. The 45-degree trend lines and vertical counts are plotted from Mini Tops. This box-value will be ideal for very short-term or intraday traders. Information derived from higher box-values helps in identifying the instruments that are in a strong trending phase. The price action of entire day is captured in a few columns of 'X' and 'O'. There are also fewer signals triggered in such charts. Columns will be lesser with clear setups during trending days. Box-value can be reduced further to generate more trading signals.

P&F is adept at portraying charts using the one-minute price. Though there is an option to use hourly or 30 mins or any other time interval price data, I believe increasing the box-value on 1 min time frame is a better strategy because it minimizes the impact cost significantly. You essentially get to look at the bigger picture on a lower frequency. A 15 min candle gets locked at the end of 15 min; it can fluctuate wildly in between, which might increase the impact cost. The same applies to P&F as well. Nonetheless, hourly and such other time frames can also be effectively used.

Below are P&F chart of Bharti Airtel shown for three different time frames. The image below shows chart of daily and hourly time frames.

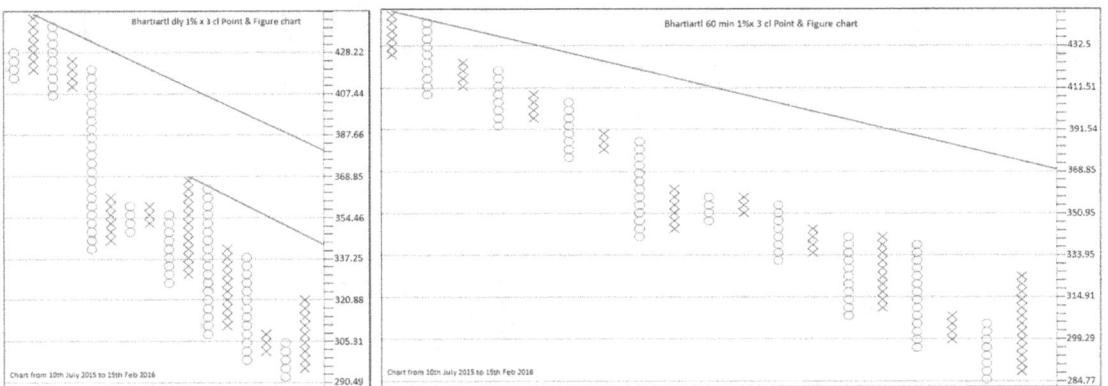

Figure 5.4.4: Bharti Airtel daily and 60 min interval Point & Figure charts

Figure below shows chart of 1 min time interval during this time period.

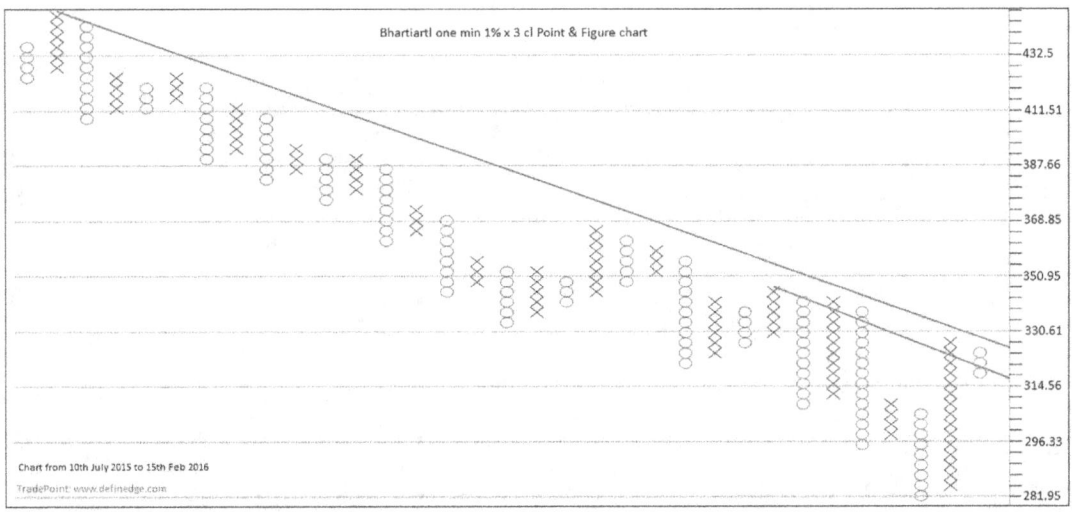

Figure 5.4.5: Bhartiartl 1 min interval 1% × 3 cl Point & Figure chart

Notice the difference between hourly and 1 min time frame chart with the same box-value. Patterns in the 1 min time frame provide nice momentum trading opportunities. It will also have a lot of opportunities to initiate trades on pull-backs.

Another thing to notice in the above charts is that the price in all the charts was trading below the 45-degree line, which shows that the trends across multiple time frames were in sync. Patterns in the direction of trend, when multiple time-frame trends are in sync, are very profitable. The price trading above or below 45-degree trend line across different box-values is important information.

For indices, 0.05%, 0.15%, 0.25% and 0.50% box-values can be used for time interval charts. Absolute box-values are recommended in time interval charts; particularly if an instrument is traded on consistent basis, it is useful to remember levels and track the setups.

Below is the chart of Nifty with absolute 25 boxes plotted using closing prices of every minute.

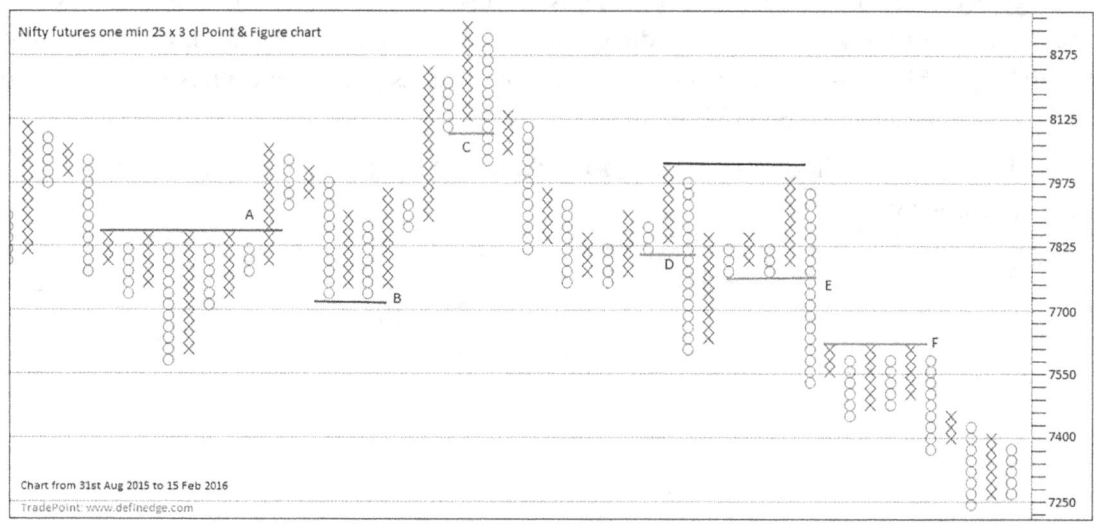

Figure 5.4.6: Nifty-I futures 1 min interval 25 × 3 cl Point & Figure chart

Pattern A is multi-column breakout formation. Pattern B is support taken by price at pattern retest. Pattern C is a Bull Trap that witnessed Follow-through. Pattern D is bearish pole and bullish pattern reversed. Pattern E is Triple Bottom Sell signal at pattern retest. Pattern F displays strong resistance by the price, followed by Sell signal.

Figure 5.4.7 is a 5 × 3 chart of Nifty.

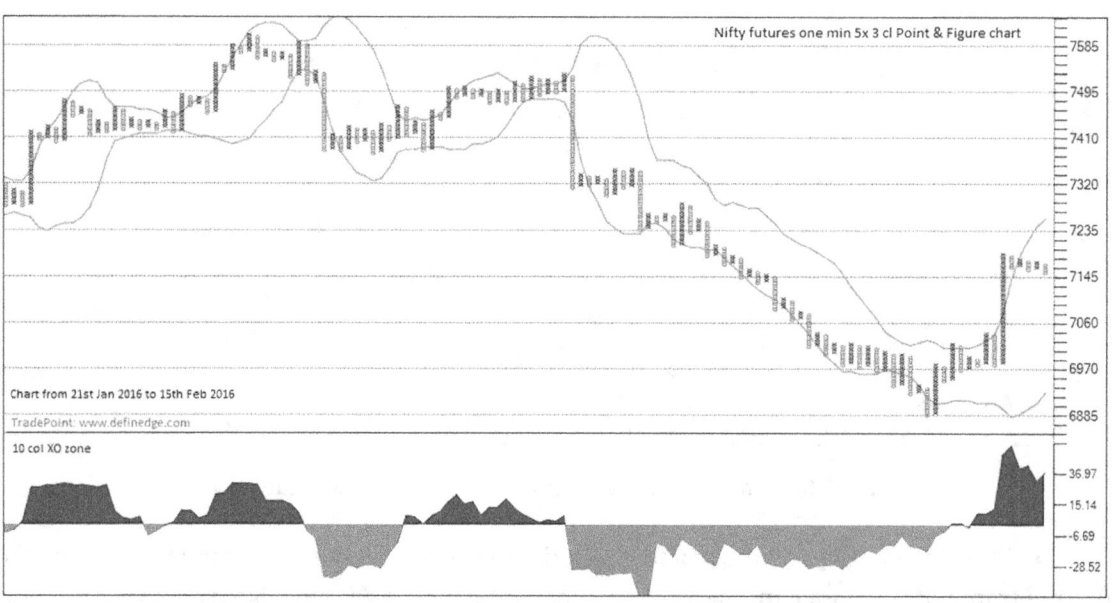

Figure 5.4.7: Nifty-I futures one min interval 5 × 3 cl Point & Figure chart

Head and Shoulder price formation is visible on the chart shown above. Technique of Bollinger bands and XO zone on P&F charts is particularly useful for very short-term trading like intraday.

Box-value can be reduced further for intraday trading, which will generate more columns and hence more trade signals. Using objective setups are very helpful to manage the trade and risk.

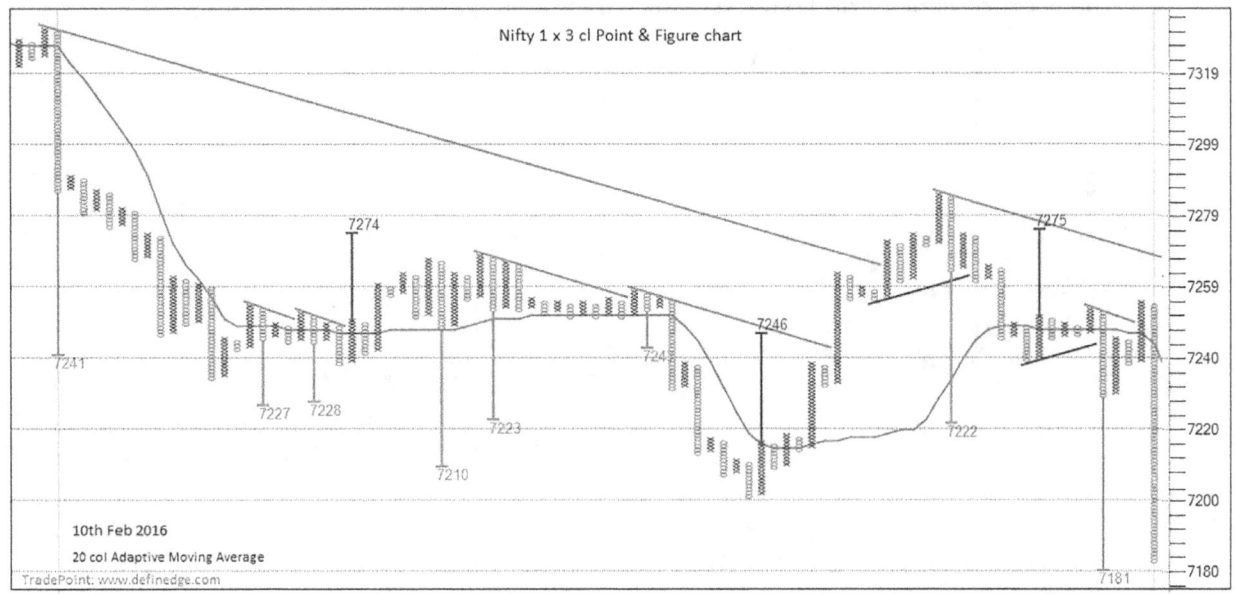

Figure 5.4.8: Nifty 1 min interval 1 × 3 cl Point & Figure chart

Figure above captures the price movement of Nifty for a single day plotted using 1-point absolute box-value. There are fewer columns plotted where the price movement is lackluster. The trading gets simple and trend riding becomes far easier when price is in a trending mode during the day.

Below is the chart of Bank Nifty plotted using 0.25% box-value using closing price of every minute.

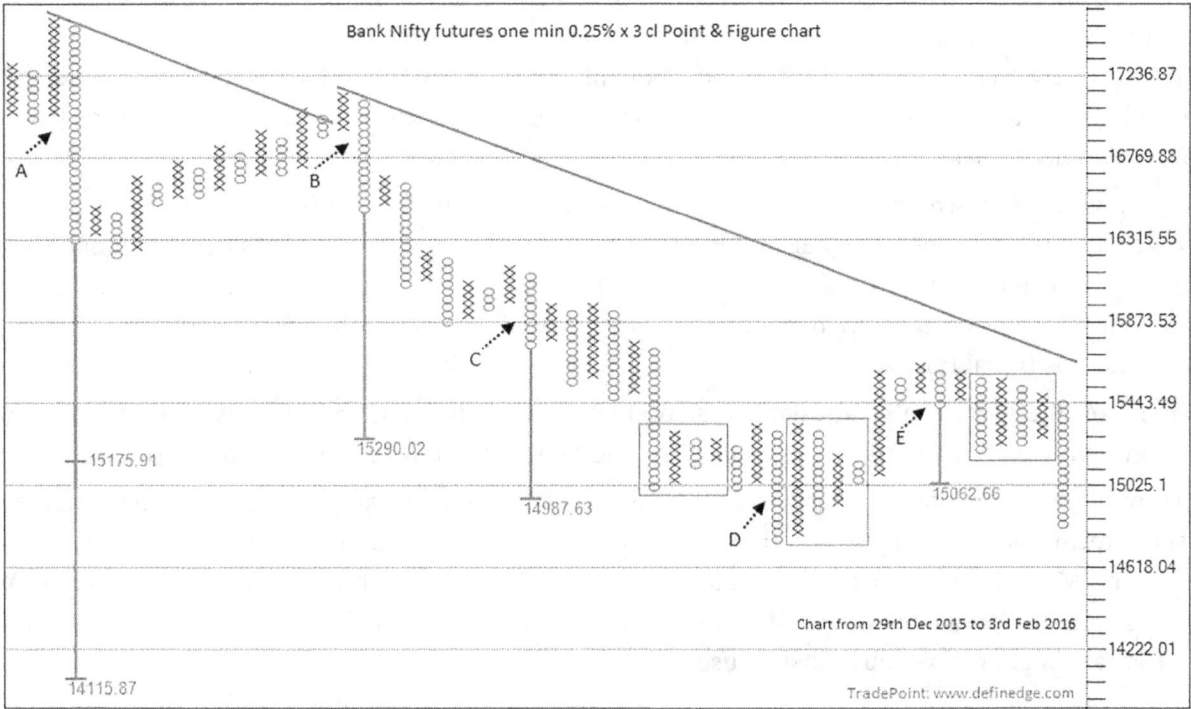

Figure 5.4.9: Bank Nifty-I futures 1 min interval 0.25% × 3 cl Point & Figure chart

Pattern A is a Bull Trap that activated lower count. Pattern B is bullish pattern reversed and a Mini Top. Pattern C is Mini Top, which is also a Bull Trap in Downtrend. Pattern D is Bearish Broadening formation followed by a Triangle (Diamond). Pattern E is a Bull Trap that locked another Mini Top, which was followed by another Triangle.

Below is the chart of same period plotted using 0.15% box-value along with Bollinger bands.

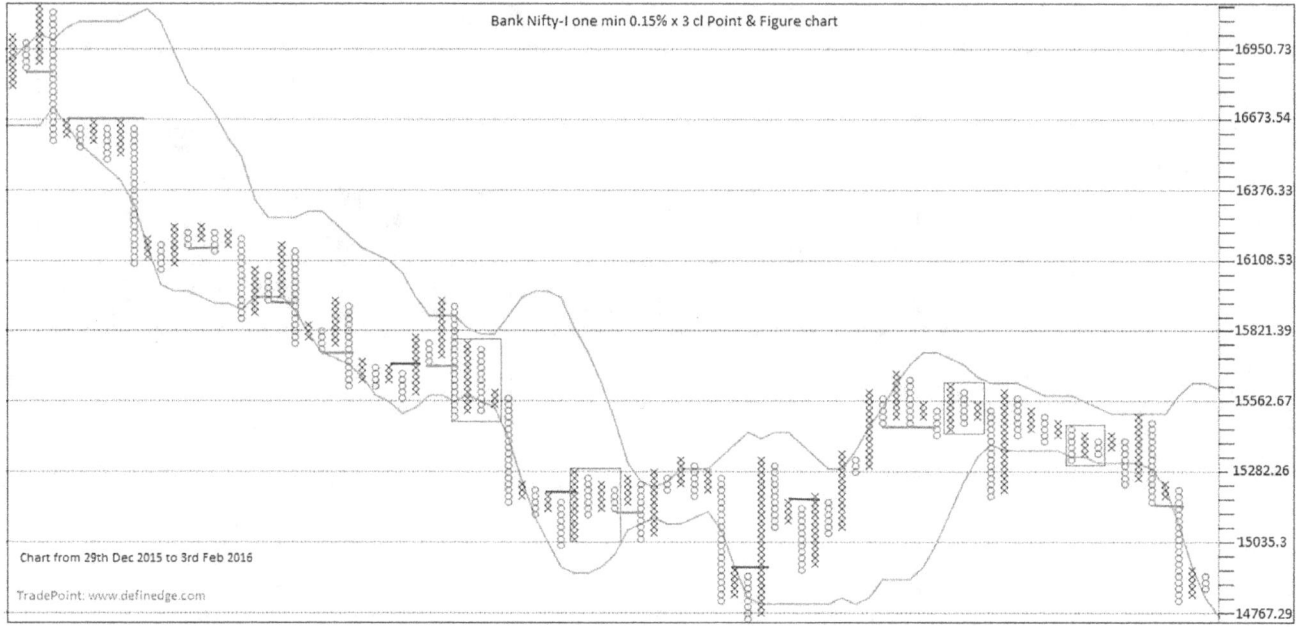

Figure 5.4.10: Bank Nifty-I futures 1 min interval 0.15% × 3 cl Point & Figure chart

Patterns are marked on the charts which can be effectively implemented along with Bollinger bands.

Bollinger bands are very useful, particularly for intraday traders. Narrow bands filter the setups during range-bound markets and work as reference levels in a trending scenario. Pattern at upper band when price is in Downtrend and pattern at lower band when it is in Uptrend are wonderful pullback setups that can be effectively traded. When the trend in the daily chart is up, buying setups at lower band in time interval charts, is an effective strategy and vice versa. Flat bands are very helpful to identify instances when one should not trade.

Gap up and gap down openings are challenges for traders which can result in long columns on time interval charts. If price opens higher and if risk is not affordable, wait for a fresh entry signal. Column reversal setups can be of help for affordable entry during such times. A trading position should be exited immediately if the price gaps open against you. This is why the position sizing should be different for intraday and positional trades.

High–Low method can also be used in case of time interval charts but box-values need to be increased, for reasons explained earlier. It can be a useful method when it comes to automation or trading systems.

I recommend time interval charts to active intraday traders, especially in the derivatives segment. A very short-term trader can begin with 0.15% box-value on 1 min time frame for stocks and adjust it as per requirement. Momentum or positional traders can use a 1% box-value on daily and 1 min time frame as well. These are just broad guidelines. If you see very long columns in a chart, the behavior of instrument indicates that a higher box-value must be used.

Summary

- ⅄ One-minute time interval should be preferred over others.
- ⅄ Unlike usual charts, 1 min is a dynamic time frame on P&F charts.
- ⅄ Increase the box-value for momentum trades; decrease it for very short-term trades like intraday or scalping strategies.
- ⅄ Absolute box-value charts can be used on this time frame if an instrument is being traded consistently.

5.5: OTHER METHODS OF PLOTTING

ATR-Based Box-Values

We discussed Average True Range (ATR) in the chapter on indicators. There is a method of plotting P&F charts using the ATR values. With this approach, Average True Range of any instrument is calculated on bar charts, and a P&F chart is plotted with that ATR-based box-value. For ATR, 14 is a popular parameter. For example, suppose the 14-day ATR of Nifty is 50, then the ATR-based P&F chart of Nifty will be plotted with a 50-point absolute box-value. ATR is a volatility-based indicator. Hence, this way, box-value of the chart is based on the current volatility of the instrument. It is, however, better to plot percentage ATR when this method is followed. Meaning, in the above example, if price of Nifty is 5000, then 1% log box-value chart (ATR value of 50 divided by current price of 5000) can be used to plot instead of 50-point absolute box-value, so that past P&F patterns become relevant for the analysis.

All the methods and analyses discussed in the book are applicable on charts plotted using ATR values as well. The method is fine if one wants to scan for the P&F pattern and trade it using other techniques. There is an issue if one wants to trade P&F chart with ATR value on consistent basis. When ATR value changes, the chart itself will change. So the pattern that was visible in a chart earlier might just vanish because of the change in the box-size. Hence, it is difficult to trade ATR-based charts on a consistent basis.

Point & Figure charts are plotted using one price only. We have discussed the methods of plotting using closing price or High–Low prices. The other methods of plotting P&F charts are explained below.

HLC Method

This is a technique of plotting P&F chart using high or low price but validating them with closing price. Rules of plotting them are explained below.

On High–Low charts:

If Last Column Is of 'X'

- ⅄ If close is meeting the requirement to plot new 'X', consider high price for plotting.
- ⅄ If close is not meeting the requirement to plot new 'X', don't plot 'X' and check low price.
- ⅄ If close is qualifying the column reversal requirement, consider low price for plotting 'O'.
- ⅄ If close is not qualifying for column reversal requirement, plot nothing.

If Last Column is of 'O'

- ⅄ If close is meeting the requirement to plot new 'O', consider low price for plotting.
- ⅄ If close is not meeting the requirement to plot new 'O', don't plot 'O' and check high price.
- ⅄ If close is qualifying the column reversal requirement, consider high price for plotting 'X'.
- ⅄ If close is not qualifying for column reversal requirement, plot nothing.

In brief, if high price is meeting the requirement to plot new 'X' but did not sustain till closing, then it will not get plotted. And if low price of column reversal requirement is met but did not sustain till closing, then plotting will not happen.

Sustenance till closing is the key element in this method. It is a nice combination of High–Low and closing method.

There is another method that considers OHLC prices and allows plotting of P&F charts with two prices. P&F charts can be plotted with typical price (High + Low + Close) as well, it is good for exploring the analysis but difficult to take trades based on it. A P&F chart of open instead of close can also be experimented. There may be other methods as well, but all of them come with their pros and cons. One may wish to plot charts using any of them, but understand the method before doing it. Not a single chart in the book is plotted with other than traditional methods, to avoid complications. It is not that one method will generate more profitability than others; it is the understanding of their nature and method of trading them that will lead to success. The key is to keep things simple.

We discussed the implications of different box-sizes using the 3-box reversal method. In the next section, we will look at the charts plotted with different reversal values.

Gaps

Many analysts and experts believe that non-displaying of gaps is a distinct disadvantage of P&F charts. I fail to understand this logic. Gaps are in any case irrelevant for the intraday trader. For positional traders or investors, the issue of gaps is prevalent while using traditional time-based charts too. We can't really do much about it and we don't know about their occurrence beforehand. Gaps occurring in favor of the trading position will be most welcome. The trade must be exited immediately if there is a gap occurring against the current trading position. If it is about analyzing gaps, then we have got usual charts to do that better, we don't need P&F for that. It doesn't display gaps, which I think should be fine.

Summary

- ⅄ ATR-based charts can be helpful if one just wants to scan the stocks for patterns.
- ⅄ Log box-value charts are far more dynamic and relevant for advanced P&F analysis.
- ⅄ Low–High, HLC, OHLC, etc., are other methods of plotting P&F charts.
- ⅄ Understanding of what is being used is more important. Traditional P&F methods of plotting are simple yet powerful.

Chapter 6

OTHER REVERSAL VALUE CHARTS

6.1: ASYMMETRIC CHARTS

This chapter will help you understand other facets of the Point and Figure charting method. The charts we have discussed so far are based on the three-box reversal. It is the most popular and traditional manner of plotting the P&F charts. Number 3 has a lot of significance in the world of technical analysis. But the question as to why three and why not any other number is quite natural.

P&F charts can be plotted with other reversal values as well. A chart plotted with one-box reversal value is discussed in the next chapter. By using a higher reversal value, we ensure that the continuation is easier than reversal and there should be a strong reason or an extra force behind price to trigger a reversal.

Apart from 1 and 3, the two-box and five-box reversal charts are commonly used. Values more than 5 are not very common, but things applicable to five-box charts are applicable to them as well.

Most of the things that we discussed about the three-box are applicable to the two-box and five-box reversal charts. But, it is important to understand their characteristics; five-box reversal charts are quite conservative, whereas two-box charts are very aggressive.

Two-Box Charts

Two-box charts have the flavor of aggression of one-box reversal charts and the smoothness of three-box reversal charts. All patterns discussed in the three-box charts are valid on the two-box charts as well. It is obvious that they will have more columns than three-box charts. Trend lines and counts are also equally applicable, but because these charts are more horizontal than the three-box charts, the 45-degree trend lines will be breached more frequently. There is no need of conservative vertical count method on these charts because lesser reversal values tend to shorten the length of the columns, resulting in an automatic conservative count. Using the usual vertical count target is a major feature of two-box reversal charts. They are very effective on these charts and have higher probability of being achieved. If length of the column is similar, conservative counts on three-box charts and usual counts on two-box charts will show the same target.

Below is 0.25% × 3 P&F chart of Bank Nifty plotted using daily closing prices shown with objective trend lines and counts.

Figure 6.1.1: Bank Nifty daily 0.25% × 3 cl Point & Figure chart

Below is the same chart plotted with two-box reversal value.

Figure 6.1.2: Bank Nifty daily 0.25% × 2 cl Point & Figure chart

Observe the trend lines, counts and patterns in the above chart. The counts are more effective and patterns offer a relatively lower-risk trade entry. Most of the patterns seen on three-box charts are visible in two-box reversal charts as well but there will be more Triangles than Poles due to their inherent horizontal nature. Follow-through patterns are equally effective on them.

It is interesting to point out that the popular Japanese charting method - Renko chart – is similar to the two-box reversal P&F charts. All techniques that we have discussed so far are applicable on these charts also, so I am avoiding repetition. The number of columns of X & O will be more, compared to the three-box reversal charts; hence, breakout will happen early but there will be more such occurrences than the three-box reversal charts.

Entry can be made more affordable by using two-box reversal charts. Hence, if an instrument is in a strong trending phase, then two-box charts will produce more continuation patterns than three-box charts for one to take advantage of. Continuation patterns are far more powerful than the reversals.

Below is 1% × 2 P&F chart of Bata India plotted with daily closing prices.

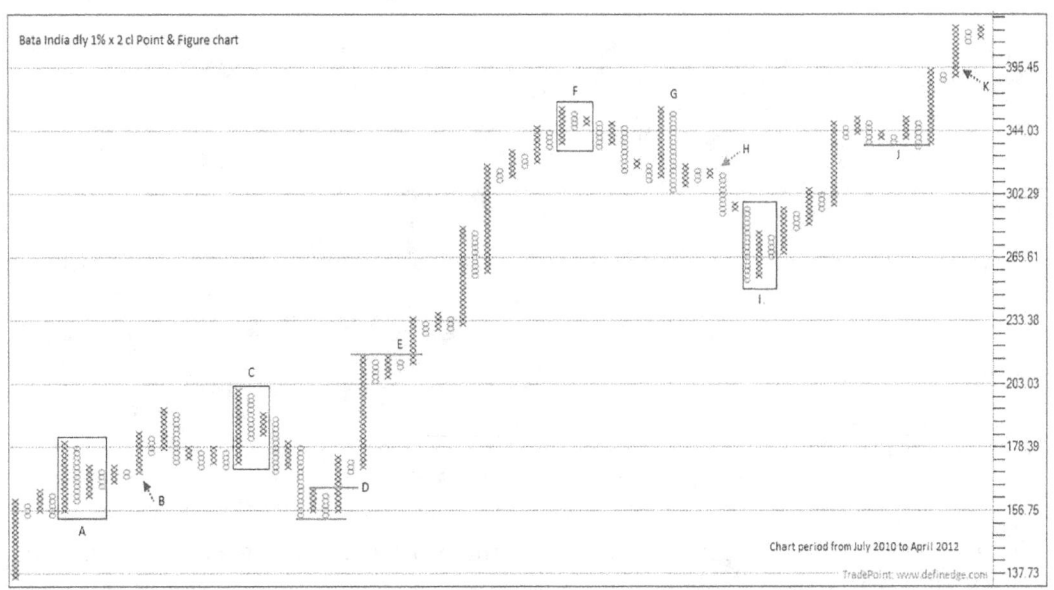

Figure 6.1.3: Bata India daily 1% × 2 cl Point & Figure chart

Pattern A is a four-column Triangle followed by a Double Top Buy signal at point B. Pattern C is a Triangle followed by negative breakout. Pattern D is a Buy signal after support and also a bullish Double pattern. Pattern E is a Triple Top Buy; it is a two-box Buy signal as well, meaning prior column is of two boxes and hence offers a low-risk entry. Understand that pattern E would not be visible in three-box chart because any reversal below three-box will not get plotted there. Pattern F is a Triangle with two-box Sell signal; hence, this pattern would not be visible on three-box charts. Pattern G is a High Pole formation and also a bearish Double pattern confirming the supply zone. Pattern H is a two-box Sell signal and also a Triangle breakout. Pattern I is a Triangle having Low Pole within that, followed by bullish breakout. Pattern J is a Triple Bottom Sell signal that failed. Pattern K is a two-box Buy signal following a Bear Trap.

Two-box charts will plot more columns, resulting in some extra noise during horizontal trends, but there will be more effective trades and counts during the trending phase. Patterns, analysis and rules of validation remain same with these charts. You may need to increase the parameter for the indicators in a few cases, simply because the two-box reversal charts are wider than three-box ones.

Five-Box Charts

Five-box reversal charts provide a higher weightage to the reversal. They are slow-moving charts compared to other reversal value charts for the obvious reason that they need a five-box move for a reversal to happen. Hence, they are compressed charts having fewer columns and therefore lesser trades. Stop is comparatively wide for setups on these charts, but failure rate is lower, and a trend can be ridden very effectively. Conservative vertical count and horizontal count should be applied on these charts. Remember that the normal vertical counts will typically throw up exaggerated targets.

Below is same chart of Bank Nifty that we discussed earlier, plotted with five-box reversal value and shown with trend lines and counts.

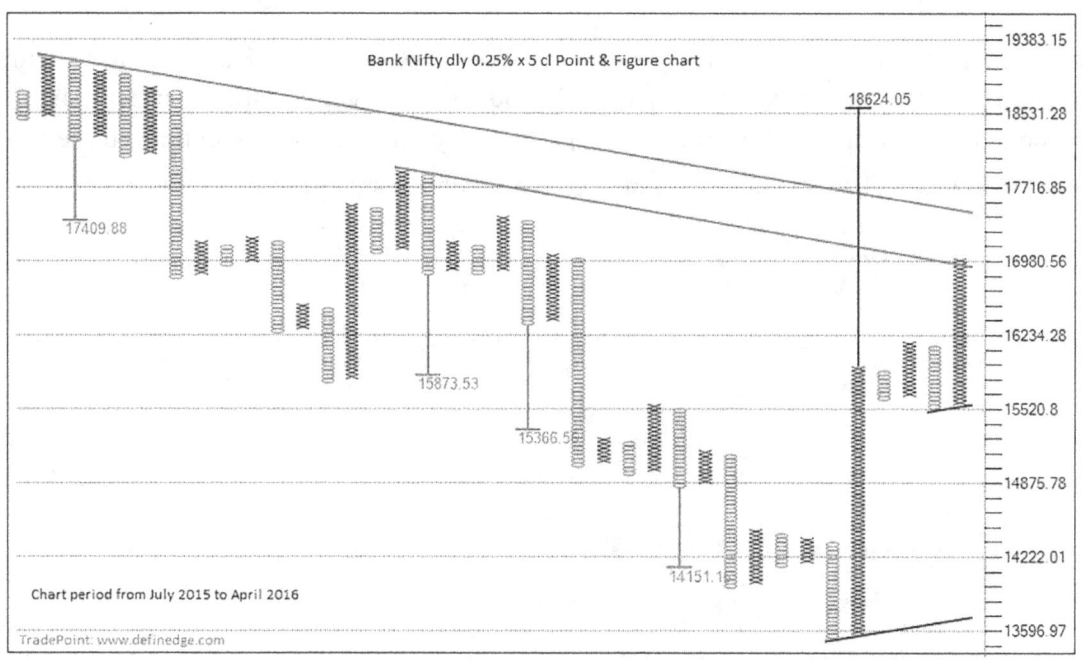

Figure 6.1.4: Bank Nifty daily 0.25% × 5 cl Point & Figure chart

Notice that there are far fewer signals compared to the other charts. Conservative vertical counts look effective and practical. Below is the same chart where usual vertical counts are applied.

Figure 6.1.5: Bank Nifty daily 0.25% × 5 cl Point & Figure chart

The above chart is to demonstrate that usual counts are not relevant on these charts. They are fancy to plot and might help one get some attention in the social media. But it is of no relevance when it comes to trading.

As the number of columns is reduced to a significant extent, there is a bigger element of noise reduction in the charts. The five-box reversal charts are more suited to positional traders and investors who focus on riding the trends.

Patterns and their rules are equally applicable on these charts but due to their compressed nature, Poles and Traps will be seen more than Triangles.

Figure below is a 5 × 5 P&F chart of Nifty plotted on closing prices of every minute.

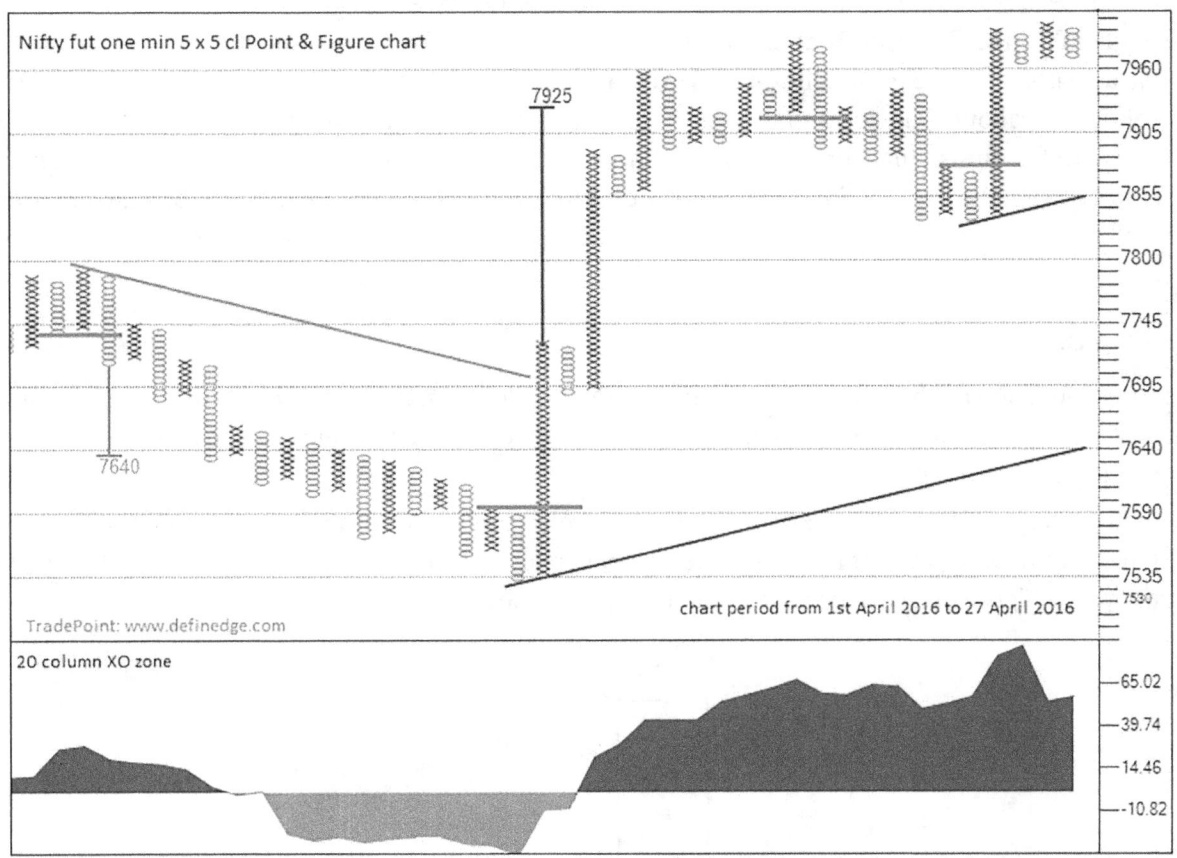

Figure 6.1.6: Nifty-I futures 1 min interval 5 × 5 cl Point & Figure chart

The above chart shows 20 column XO zone indicator, 45-degree trend lines and Fresh basic signals. Fewer Fresh signals offer far less trading opportunities than other charts, though the initial risk is higher.

You may or may not trade these charts, but knowing them will only help you get a better understanding of the Point & Figure method. The next section discusses the technique of using one-box reversal charts.

Summary

- ⌁ Two-box reversal charts are more aggressive and five-box reversal charts are conservative.
- ⌁ All methods discussed so far are applicable on them as well, but it is important to know their nature and difference compared to three-box reversal charts.

6.2: ONE-BOX REVERSAL CHARTS

One-box reversal P&F charting method is also known as a Wyckoff method, named after the late Wall Street legend Richard D. Wyckoff. It is the original P&F method of plotting the charts. We discussed the construction of one-box reversal P&F charts in Chapter 1. Recall that the reversal value is '1'; hence, column is changed even if price is reversed by one box instead of three. Hence, there are more numbers of columns in one-box charts compared to any other P&F chart and therefore these charts have their own place of importance.

It is interesting to know that all the three-box P&F patterns and most of the techniques that we have discussed are not applicable for one-box reversal charts, basically because they don't have asymmetric filter. They don't necessarily reverse by three boxes before resumption of the trend to call it an effective breakout. Due to more number of columns of 'X' and 'O', these charts are wider than any other P&F chart and hence 45-degree lines and vertical counts are not used in these charts.

Usual Double Top Buy and Double Bottom Sell are not valid signals in one-box reversal charts. When these basic patterns appear on three-box reversal chart, formation on one-box chart will be that of multi-column breakout. The continuation patterns on these charts are called semi-catapults and reversal formations are fulcrums. But I am avoiding that nomenclature here to avoid complication. I will keep the discussion restricted to the major points that underline the usefulness of the one-box reversal charts. There are three important features of one-box reversal charts that differentiate them from other reversal charts.

1. One Step Back

The expression One-step back was invented by Jeremy du Plessis in his book The Definitive Guide to Point and Figure[1]. It is the most important feature of one-box reversal charts. Below is the stepwise explanation of One Step Back formation.

One-box chart flips to a new column even if there is a reversal of one box. Meaning, column of 'X' will flip to column of 'O' even if there is a one-box reversal. You may recall that we discussed it during the construction of Figure chart in chapter 1. See Image 6.2.1 shown below.

180		
170		
160		
150	X	
140	X	O
130	X	
120	X	
110	X	
100		
	1	2

Image 6.2.1: One-box Point & Figure

Column of 'X' turned to column of 'O' in the image shown above because price dropped from 150 to 140. It has not gone below 130, so another box is not marked. If the price resumes the uptrend and moves past 150, then the column needs to be changed to 'X' marked at 150.

---

1 The Definitive Guide to Point and Figure: *A comprehensive Guide to the Theory and Practical Use of the Point and Figure Charting Method,* Petersfield: Harriman House Publishing, 2006.

	1	2	3
180			
170			
160			
150	X		X
140	X	O	
130	X		
120	X		
110	X		
100			

Image 6.2.2: One-box Point & Figure

Price went above 150 again without falling below 130; hence, column needs to be changed to 'X'. When column reversal happens after marking just one box in a column, then both the columns are merged together, which looks like the image shown below.

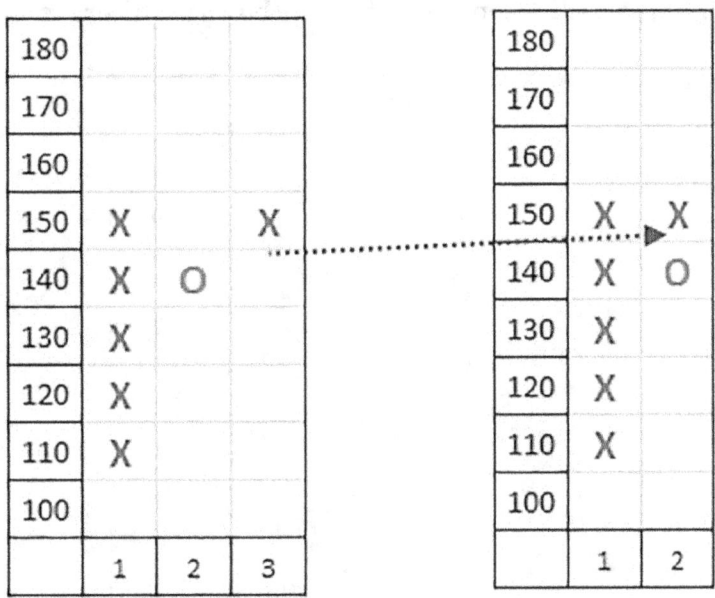

Image 6.2.3: One-box Point & Figure

Whenever a reversal happens after marking just one box of 'O', the column will be merged to subsequent column of 'X'. So the column of 'X' can have single 'O' in the bottom. Similarly, whenever reversal happens after marking just one box of 'X', it is merged with subsequent column of 'O'. So a column of 'O' may have single 'X' at the top of it. Refer image shown below.

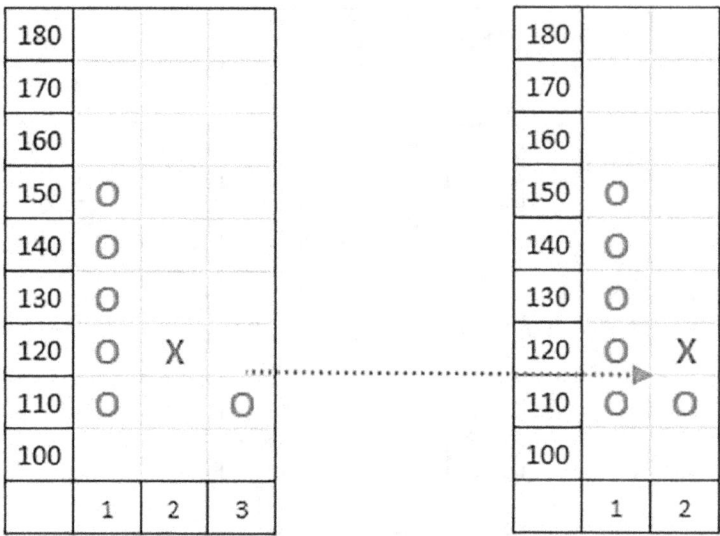

Image 6.2.4: One-box Point & Figure

Columns are merged in case of reversal after single marking only. If two boxes are formed in a column before they get reversed, then they are not to be merged. So, any column of one-box P&F chart will have minimum two boxes in it. And a merged column of 'X' cannot have more than one box of 'O' at the bottom of it or merged column of 'O' cannot have more than one box of 'X' at the top of it.

So, unlike other reversal charts, one-box P&F column can have 'X' and 'O' in the same column. This formation is known as One Step Back. It represents just one box back before resumption of the trend.

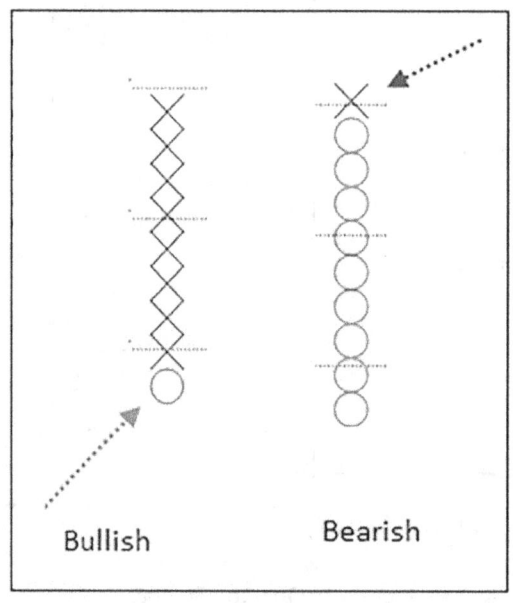

One Step Back

Image 6.2.5: One Step Back

Bullish One Step Back (OSB) happens when the second box appears as 'X' and bearish OSB gets is identified when the second box appears as 'O'.

Three-box reversal charts will not change the column before it is reversed by three boxes, so the OSB formation will not be visible in them. In fact, any reversal below three boxes will not be marked in them. Image below shows the reversals that will not be seen on three-box reversal charts.

	X			X			X
	X			X			X
X	X		X	X		X	X	X
X	O		X	O	X		X	O	O
X			X	O			X
X			X				X

Image 6.2.6: One-box Point & Figure

First chart in Image 6.2.6 is bullish OSB, second chart is two-box chart Double Top Buy signal and third chart is two bullish OSBs in a row. Vice versa is for bearish patterns, which cannot be seen on three-box reversal charts.

OSB is a useful tool particularly in strong trending markets. Price produces large columns during trending scenarios. It retraces by one box in between and resumes the trend again. Bullish OSB after long column of 'X' provides opportunity to trade in the direction of trend because it shows that bulls stepped in immediately and correction could last just one box. We will not get this information in three-box reversal chart. Similarly, bearish OSB after long column of 'O' provides opportunity in the direction of the bearish trend.

Figure shown below displays the three-box and one-box reversal charts of Bank India plotted with 1% box-value. Two large columns of 'O's in three-box reversal chart generated bearish OSB formations in one-box reversal charts between October 2015 and January 2016.

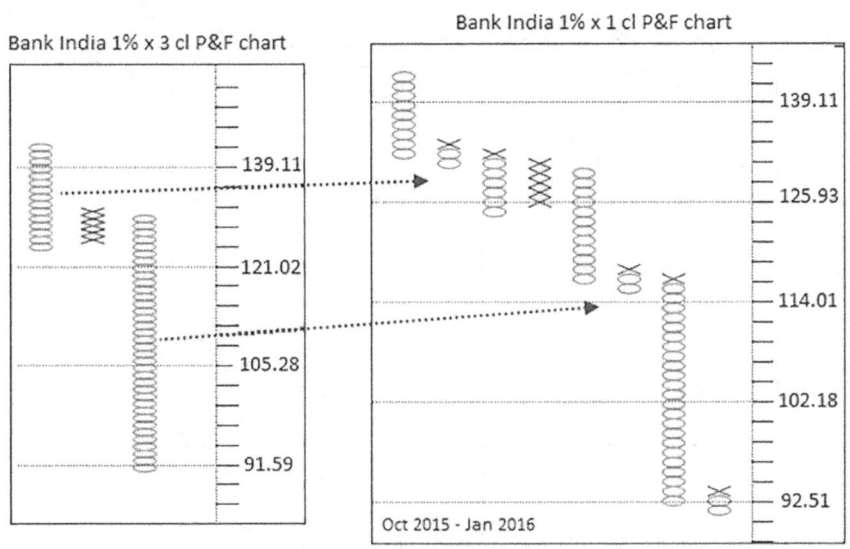

Figure 6.2.1: Bank India one-box reversal Point & Figure charts

OSBs can be traded during strong trends and when there is an anchor column formed in the direction of the trend. OSB is a useful formation for short-term traders when a strong trend is in place. It can be traded with a stop of just two boxes. Figure below is one-box reversal daily chart of Auro Pharma plotted with 1% box-value. Arrow shows the columns, which are One Step Back patterns in the column of 'X'.

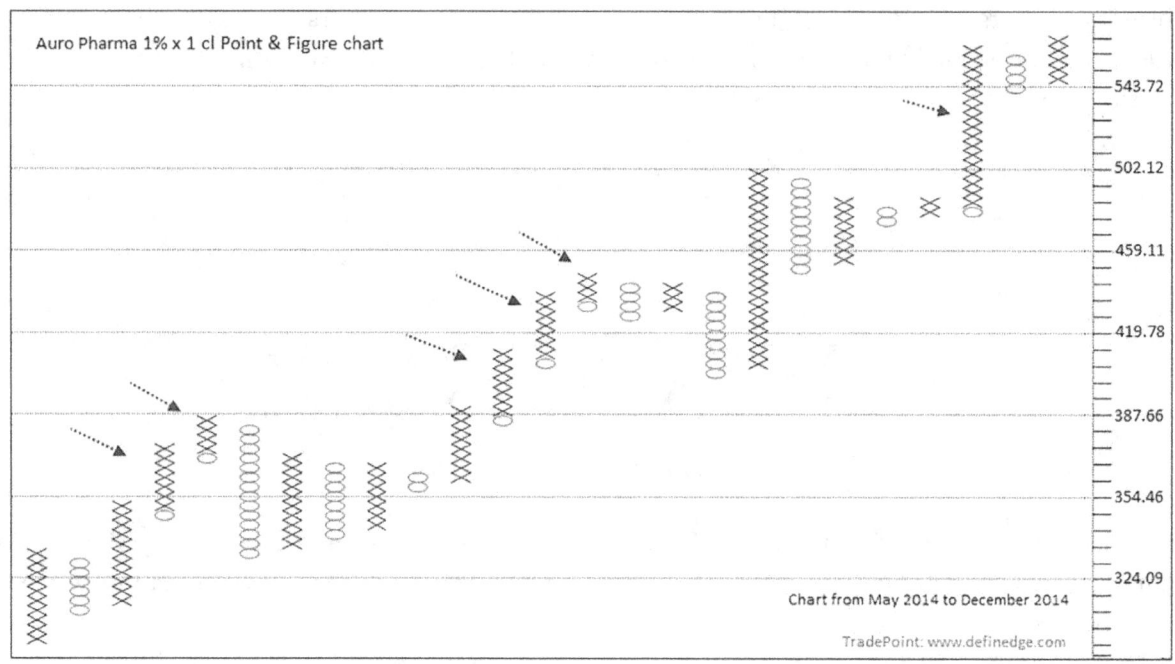

Figure 6.2.2: Auro Pharma daily 1% × 1 cl Point & Figure chart

The box that formed OSB pattern is important because it shows the price that was rejected. Hence, OSBs are important reference levels. Price violating or going below bullish OSB is bearish signal and a breakout above a bearish OSB is a bullish formation.

At times, price immediately changes the direction after forming OSB. So there will be just two boxes in a column, one is 'X' and another is of 'O'. See image shown below.

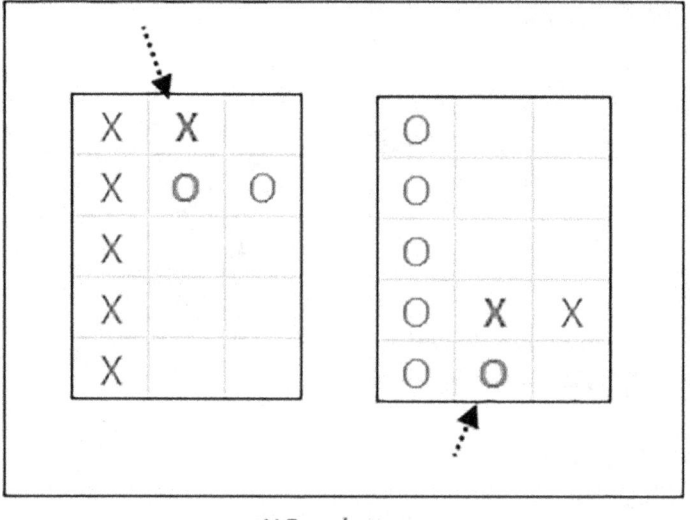

XO column

Image 6.2.7: XO column

I call them XO columns. They display price congestion and indecision. Series of XO column display serious congestion and breakout in either direction can turn out to be a profitable trade.

Below is one-box reversal 1 min P&F chart of Nifty plotted using 0.25% box-value.

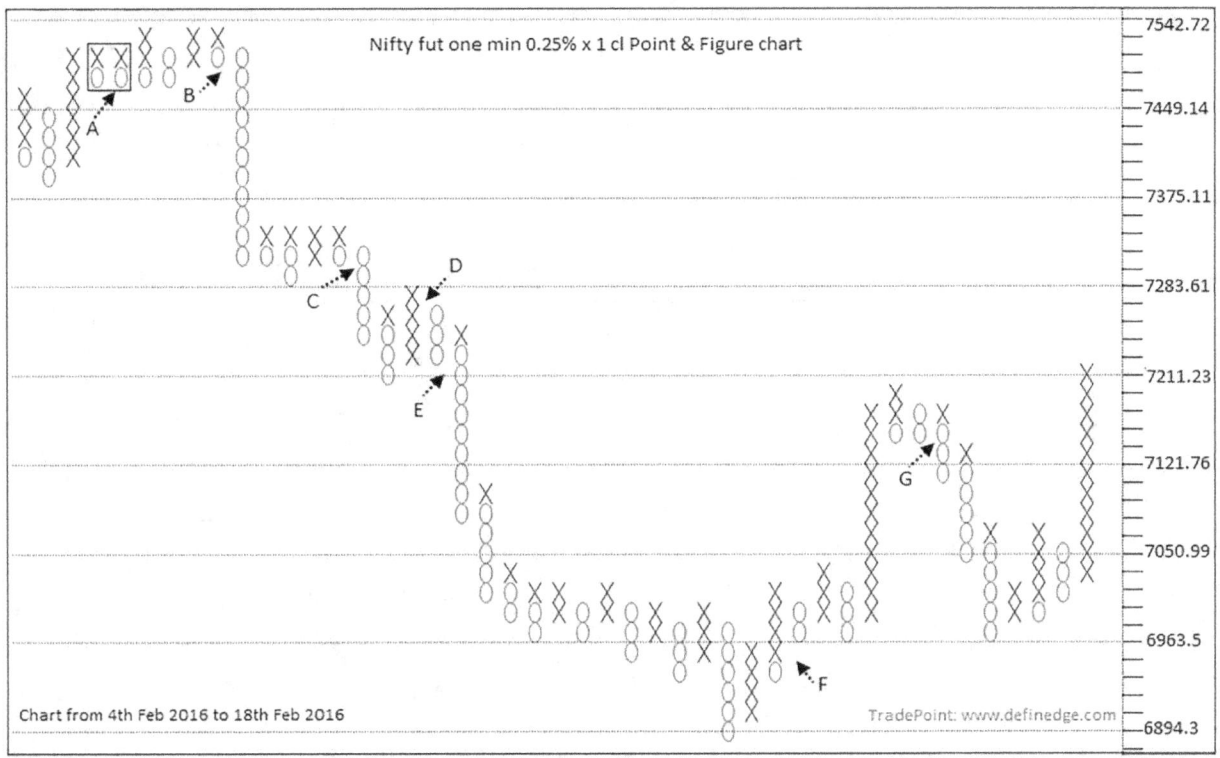

Figure 6.2.3: Nifty-I futures 1 min interval 0.25% × 1 cl Point & Figure chart

Pattern A is consecutive XO columns. Pattern B is bearish breakout of congestion pattern that includes series of XO columns. Pattern C is a breakout from XO columns as well. Pattern D violates bearish OSB of its previous column but price reversed immediately and produced bearish OSB at pattern E which is followed by a series of bearish OSBs. Pattern F is bullish OSB. Pattern G violates bullish OSB of congestion formation prior to it.

2. Horizontal Count

Another tool that can be used in the one-box chart is the method of plotting horizontal counts on these charts. One-box is the traditional P&F charting technique and formula of count is quite different from three-box horizontal counts. The horizontal count in one-box reversal chart is calculated from horizontal formation or congestion patterns. The difference is instead of adding it to the bottom or deducting from top, the anchor point is used to calculate the targets. It can show the count at both the sides because breakout direction from the congestion formation is initially unknown. The count on other side is removed once the direction of the breakout is confirmed.

Below is the formula for Horizontal counts on one-box charts:

Bullish count = Anchor point of the pattern + (Width of the pattern × Box-value × Reversal value)

Bearish count = Anchor point of the pattern − (Width of the pattern × Box-value × Reversal value)

You may recall the discussion on Anchor Point in an earlier chapter. Anchor points are nothing but the most active or populated row in the congestion pattern. Width is the number of columns in the pattern. Image below shows the plotting of Horizontal count on one-box charts.

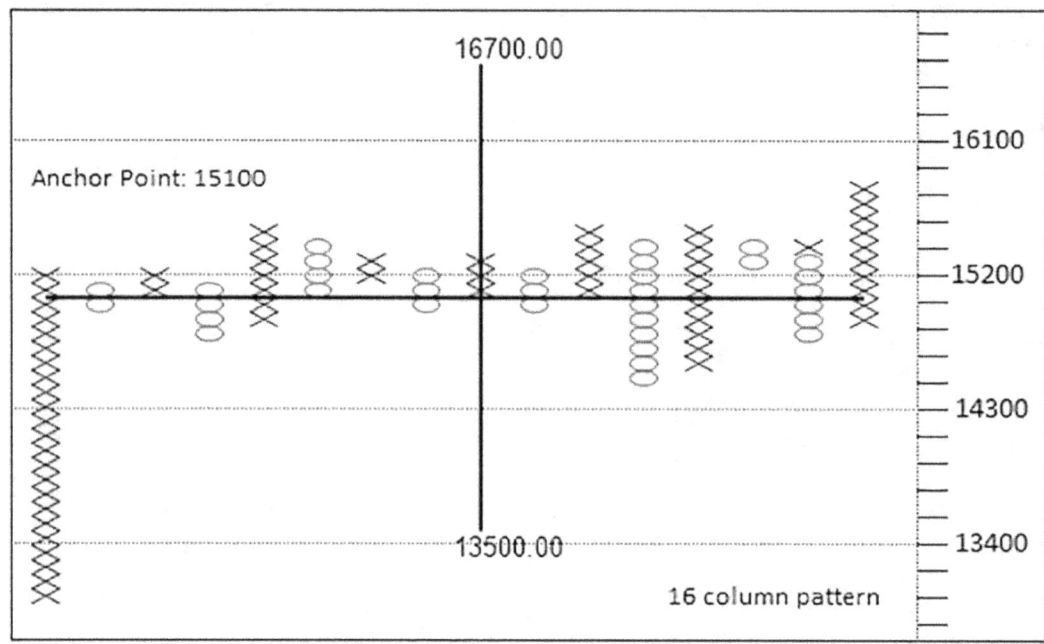

Image 6.2.8: One-box horizontal count

Horizontal counts are taken from consolidating formations. There will more instances of horizontal patterns in one-box charts than any other reversal value charts. One-box P&F charts are an effective tool for congestion pattern analysis or fulcrum analysis. Fulcrum is basically a horizontal or congestion formation.

Figure shown below is 1% × 1 P&F chart of SKS micro-plotted on daily closing prices. A consolidation phase is seen after nice Uptrend and the count in both directions is captured on the chart. These targets act as a reference point in case of breakout in either direction. Normally, a non-trending or contracting phase should be followed by expansion. Counts of both sides are shown in the chart because there is no clue on direction of breakout.

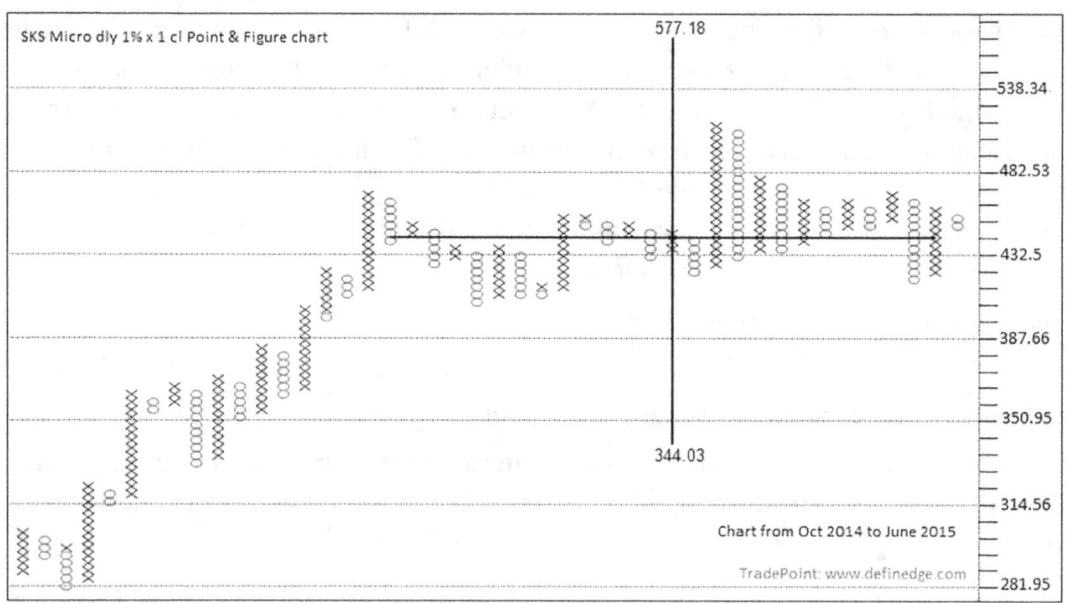

Figure 6.2.4: SKS micro daily 1% × 1 cl Point & Figure chart

Figure below shows same chart after few days. The bearish count is removed from the chart because of the upside breakout.

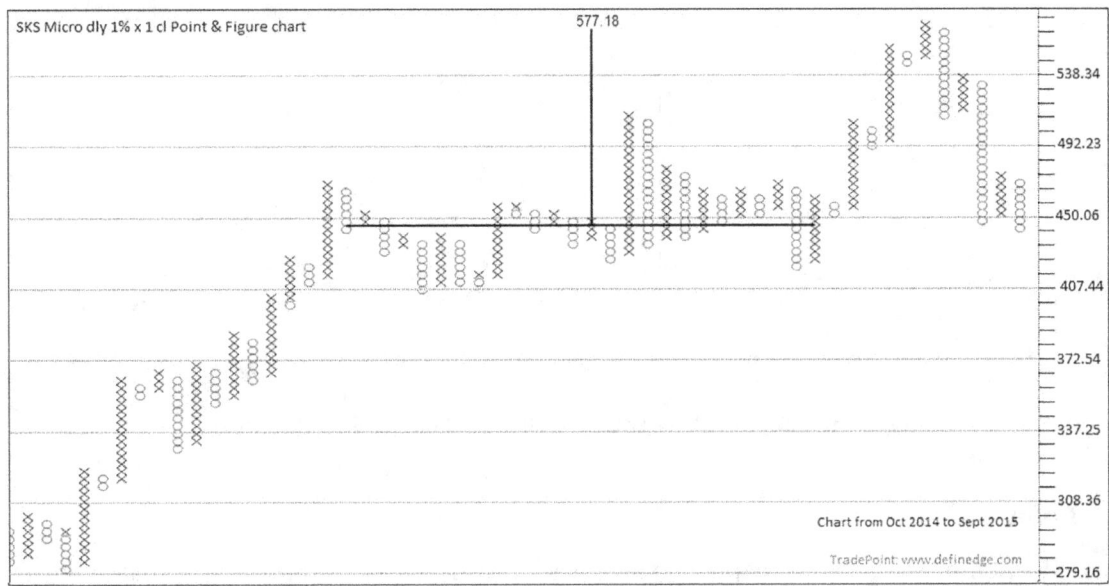

Figure 6.2.5: SKS micro daily 1% × 1 cl Point & Figure chart

Width of the pattern is subjective, but it is a useful method during the periods of congestion. A breakout happens when the high or low price of the horizontal pattern is breached. Have a look at the horizontal counts from the congestion formations in the Rcom chart below.

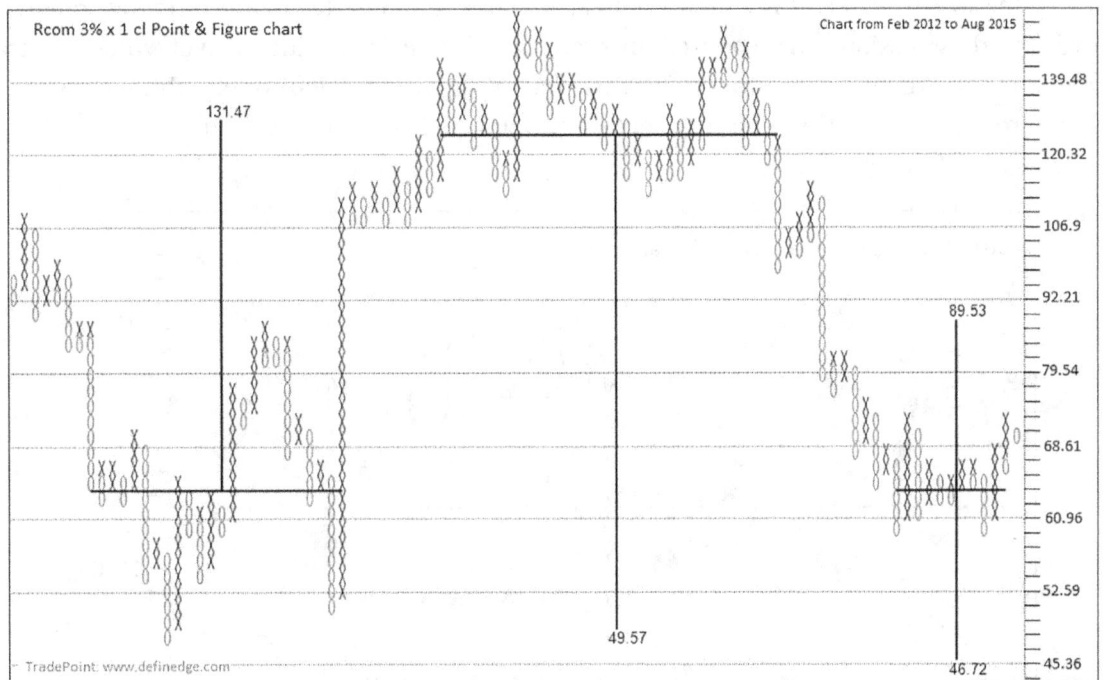

Figure 6.2.6: Rcom daily 3% × 1 cl Point & Figure chart

As the direction of the breakout in last formation is not known, the counts on both sides are displayed. Figure shown below is 100 × 1 P&F chart of Bank Nifty showing the bearish count from the congestion formation.

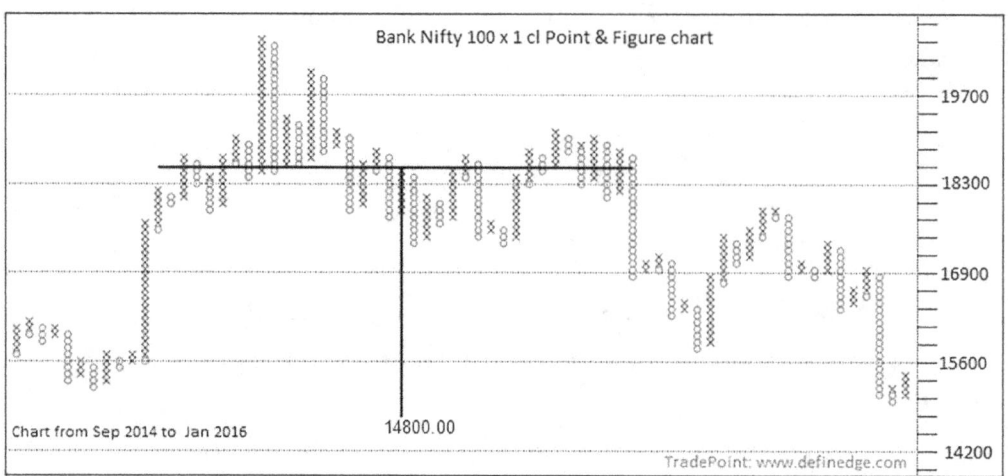

Figure 6.2.7: Bank Nifty daily 100 × 1 cl Point & Figure chart

3. Anchor Point

We discussed Anchor point in the chapter on analysis. It is a row that is filled or populated with the most number of boxes in the pattern or a level where most of the action has taken place. It is basically a one-box reversal chart tool which evaluates the strength of the pattern by analyzing its base and is utilized for calculating the horizontal counts.

We discussed the usefulness of Anchor points on three-box reversal charts and they are applicable to one-box charts too. But the best utilization of Anchor point is in applying them on time interval charts and 1 min time frame in particular. It is a great tool particularly for short-term and intraday traders. Anchor point of every trading session can be plotted on 1 min time frame. It provides a level which was traded the most during the day. Anchor point drawn for a particular day is extended to its right, which can become important reference level for the sessions thereafter. Below is 5 × 1 Point & Figure chart of Nifty plotted with closing prices of every minute.

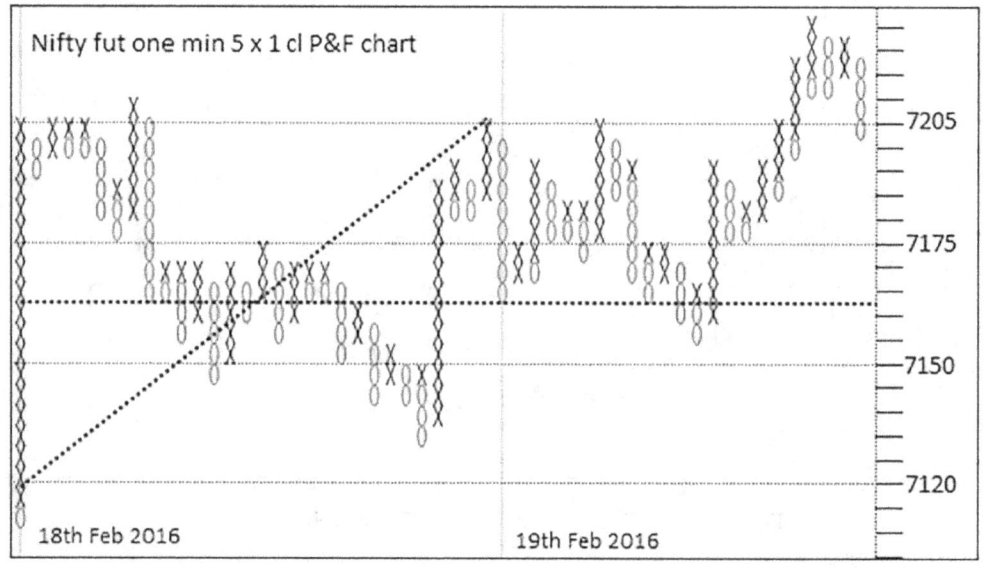

Figure 6.2.8: Nifty-I futures 1 min interval 5 × 1 cl Point & Figure chart

Anchor point is drawn across the entire price move of first session and extended to its right. It becomes reference level for the next session to monitor price formation when price reaches that level. It can act as a significant support or resistance level for the coming sessions. Logically, anchor points display the price area where most of the action has taken place. It displays the most active price level in a day, which has a strong potential to act as support or resistance when revisited.

Anchor point of last few sessions can be plotted on the chart for reference. Box-value needs to be quite low when used for this method. It may not help in analyzing the patterns but reason for using lower values is that it considers most of the price move to plot the anchor point. I prefer using five- and ten box-values for Nifty and Bank Nifty, respectively.

Most of the time markets remain in bracketed trend. Support and resistance derived from Anchor point prove effective during such times. They are also useful when important Tops and Bottoms are revisited by the prices.

Below is 10 × 1 Bank Nifty chart plotted on closing prices of every minute. Vertical line shows sessions from which Anchor point is drawn.

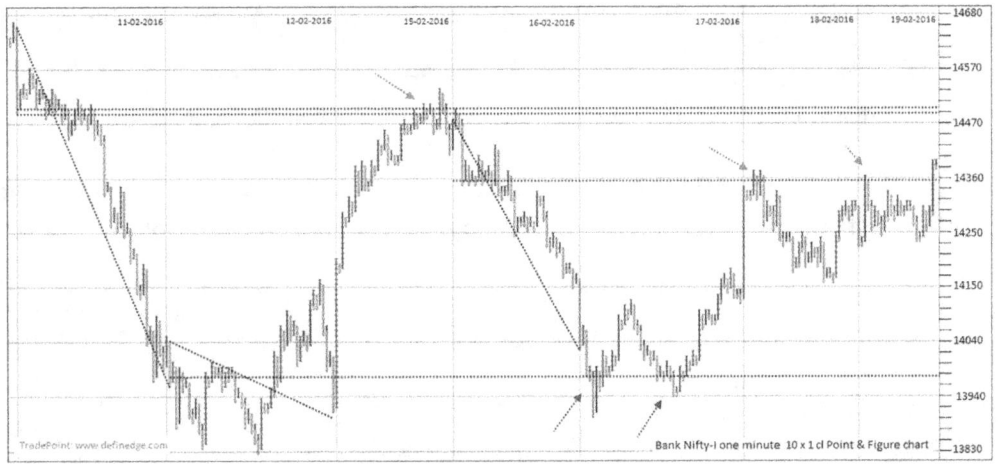

Figure 6.2.9: Bank Nifty-I futures 1 min interval 10 × 1 cl Point & Figure chart

Anchor points of three trading sessions are plotted in the above chart. Anchor point plotted on 11th Feb worked as resistance when price revisited that level on 15th Feb. The Anchor point of 12th Feb worked as support on a revisit on 17th Feb. Anchor point of 16th Feb worked as resistance on 18th and 19th Feb.

Charts shown below are Nifty 5 × 1 chart plotted on 1 min time frame that shows Anchor point acting as an effective reference point in subsequent sessions.

Figure 6.2.10: Nifty-I futures 1 min interval 5 × 1 cl Point & Figure chart

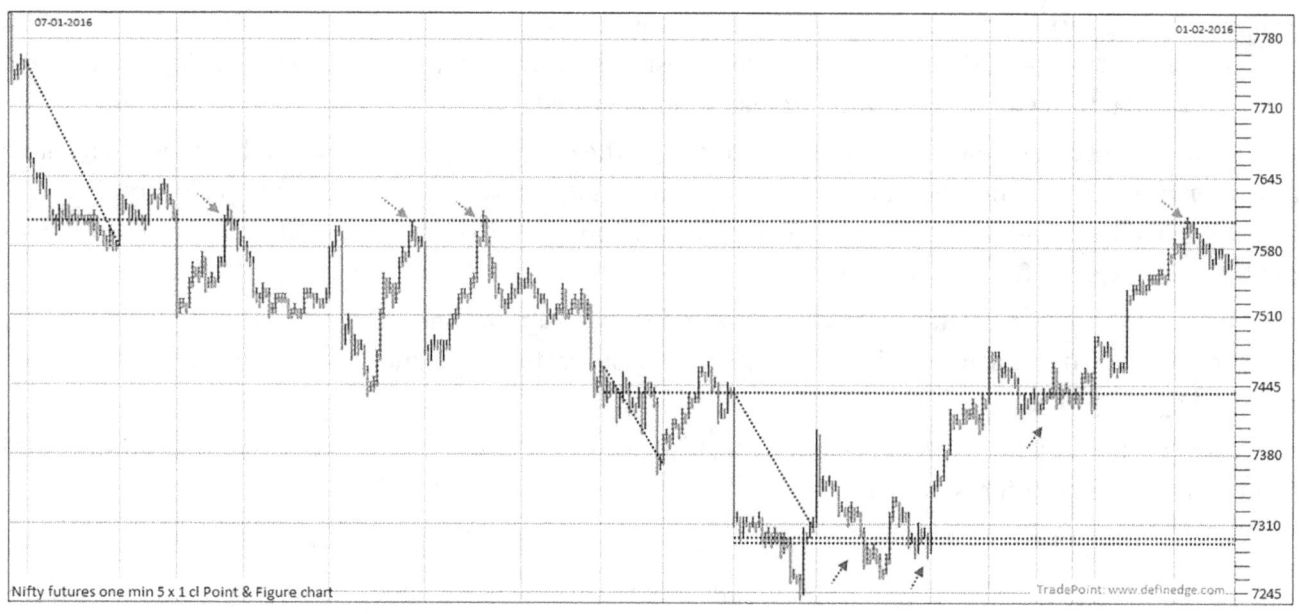

Figure 6.2.11: Nifty-I futures 1 min interval 5 × 1 cl Point & Figure chart

It can be very useful when tracked on indices. But the method is equally relevant when applied to stocks or any other instrument. Below is 0.25% × 1 chart of Reliance Capital plotted on 1 min interval prices.

Figure 6.2.12: Reliance Capital-I futures 1 min interval 0.25% × 1 cl Point & Figure chart

There are numerous examples to shows its usefulness. When there is a congestion day, a horizontal count can be applied from Anchor point of the day that shows counts of both the side. One of the counts gets activated upon breakout and the count should be removed when the breakout happens. Below is the 5 × 1 Nifty chart plotted using prices of every minute.

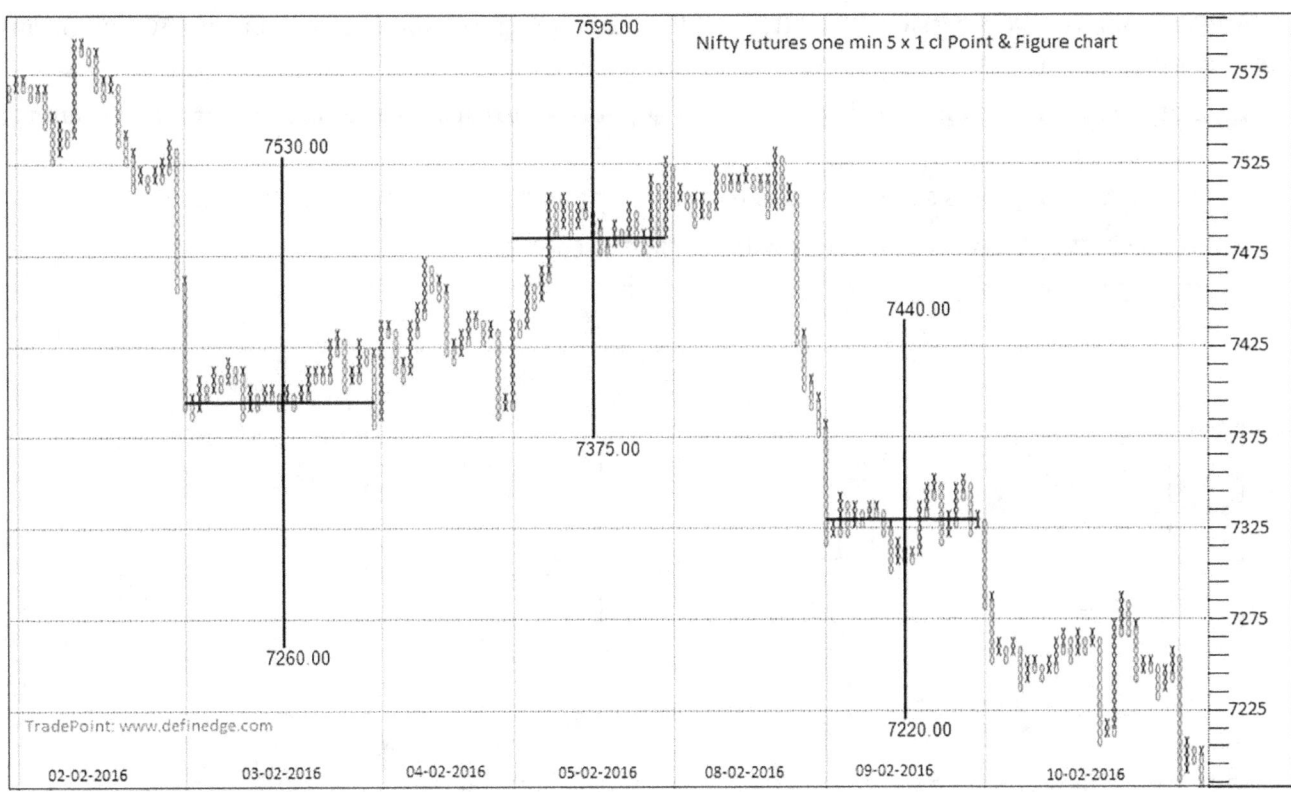

Figure 6.2.13: Nifty-I futures 1 min interval 5 × 1 cl Point & Figure chart

Intraday horizontal counts are the levels to refer in coming sessions in case of breakout. Sequence of Sideways sessions may be followed by a trending phase. The projections from the trendless sessions can be used to calculate targets are reference levels when the breakout and trending phase get underway.

Have a look at the 5 × 1 intraday chart of Nifty shown below.

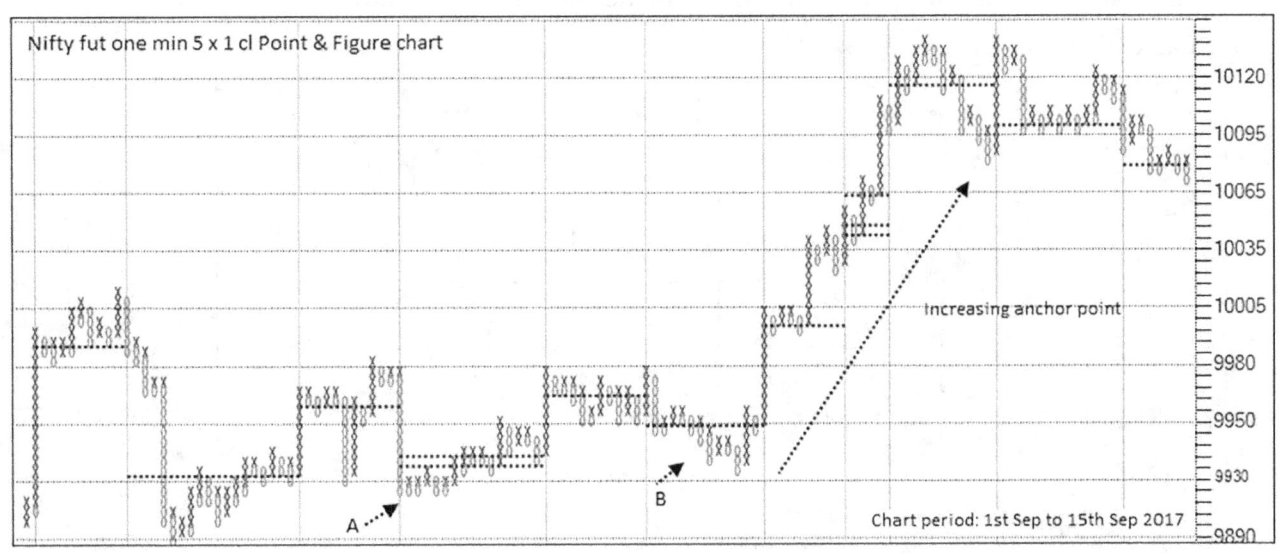

Figure 6.2.14: Nifty-I futures 1 min interval 5 × 1 cl Point & Figure chart

Anchor points of every session are plotted; I call them running Anchor points. There are two important interpretations based on it:

1. They act as important reference levels for support and resistances going forward. See points A and B.

2. Rising Anchor points show that base is increasing and there is strong trend in place.

See same chart of Nifty plotted below with horizontal counts.

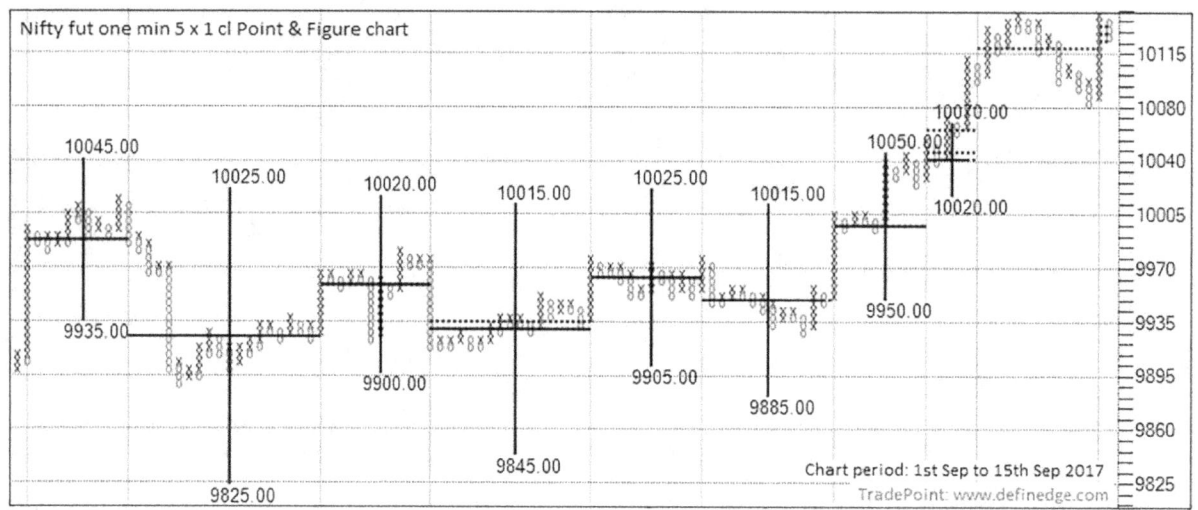

Figure 6.2.15: Nifty-I futures 1 min interval 5 × 1 cl Point & Figure chart

These are running horizontal counts that show important counts that are open on both sides. A target cluster can be easily identified while using running Anchor point analysis explained above. With this method, it indicates exhaustion of Downtrend when down side counts are not being achieved. Similarly, when upside counts are not achieved in an uptrend, it is a sign that the bulls are exhausted. Usually, during strong trends accompanied by open counts have a higher probability of getting achieved.

See Bank Nifty chart shown below.

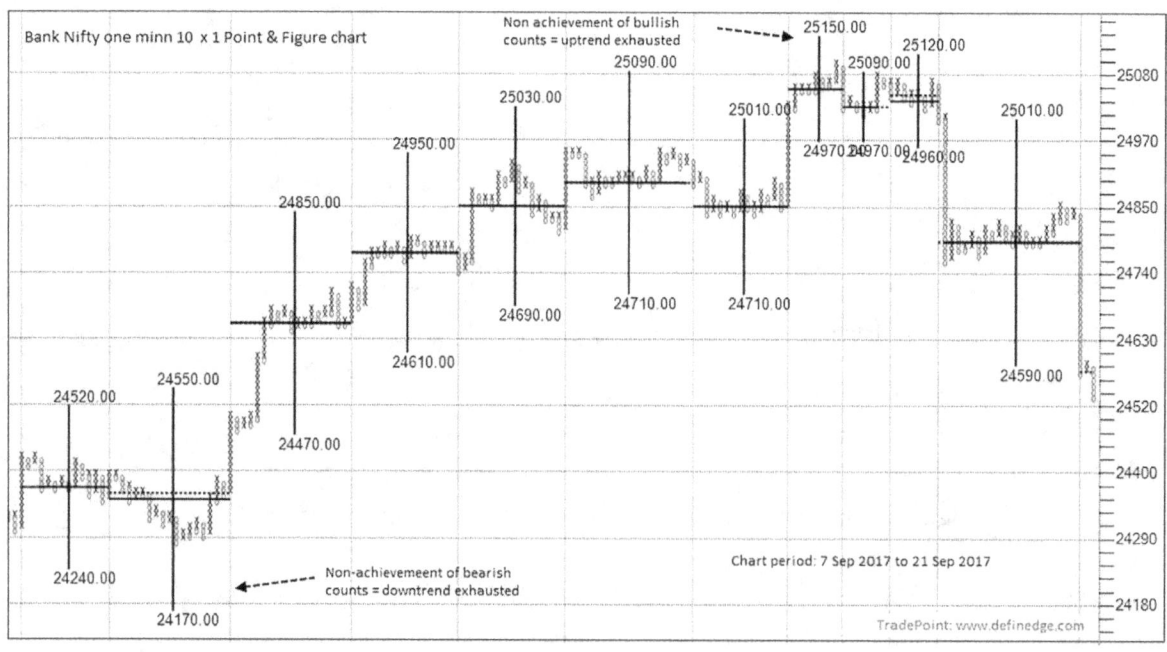

Figure 6.2.16: Bank Nifty-I futures 1 min interval 10 × 1 cl Point & Figure chart

It was non-achievement of downside counts and non-achievement of upside counts that indicated that there is exhaustion and other direction count can be referred.

Box-Value and Indicators

Typically, box-value for one-box reversal charts must be higher than the usual charts, especially when OSBs and XO column patterns are used. But lower box-value is required when intraday anchor point method is the focus. Multi-column breakouts or breakouts from well-tested 'X's and 'O's are important patterns on these charts.

Indicators and their interpretation in one-box charts remain the same but the parameter needs to be tweaked/increased in a few cases. Below is the P&F chart of CEAT ltd on 1 min time frame plotted with 0.50% × 1 parameters.

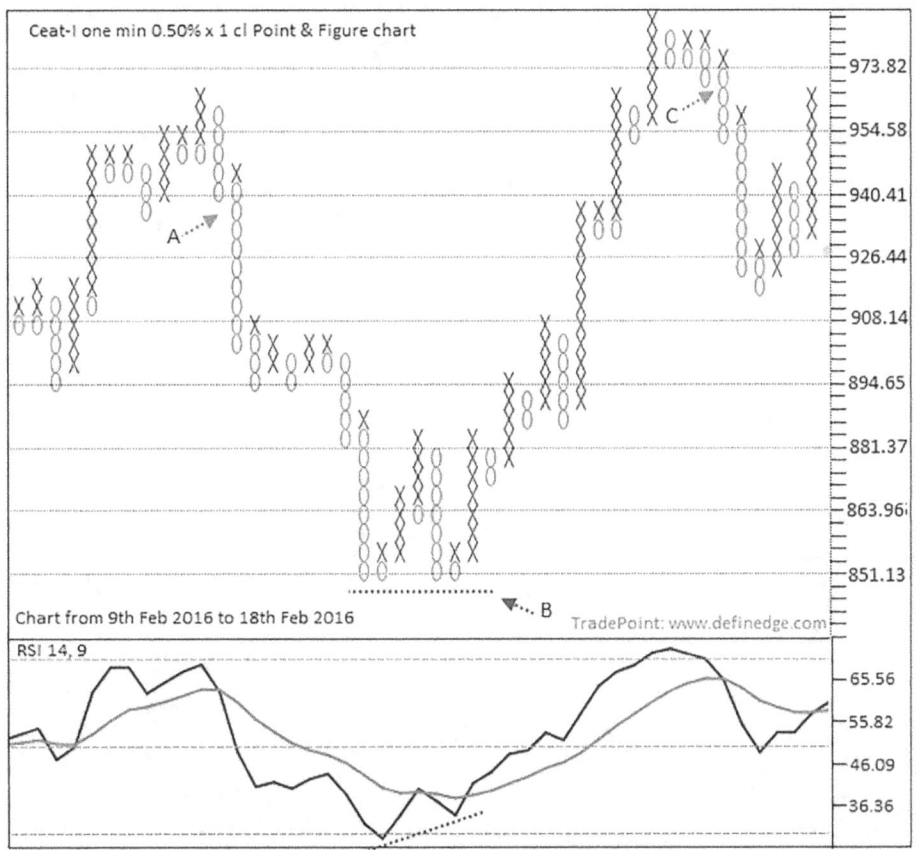

Figure 6.2.17: CEAT-I futures 1 min interval 0.50% × 1 cl Point & Figure chart

Pattern A is bearish OSB along with RSI that turned down after not so positive confirmation to the new high made by the price. There is also a series of XO columns in the congestion formation. Pattern B is where price rallied after XO column at multiple support area and positive divergence in RSI. Pattern C is bearish OSB after RSI turned down from overbought zone and XO columns are visible too.

All other indicators can also be plotted on these charts. It is natural to sense that the noise level is more in one-box chart. But once three-box charts are practiced well, one-box charts are handy.

You may or may not plot other reversal value charts, but know them well, their strengths and drawbacks. Knowing the tools more may help you to design and tweak your trading setups. For example, you may decide that once a trending move is spotted, trades can be taken on a One Step Back. It is also equally logical to switch to a higher reversal value chart in a volatile market condition.

Summary

- ⅄ One-box reversal chart is a complete charting method.
- ⅄ Tools and method of reading them are different from asymmetric P&F charts.
- ⅄ OSB, horizontal count and Anchor point are most useful tools of one-box chart analysis.
- ⅄ Running Anchor points and horizontal counts are applicable on intraday time interval charts. They make a complete setup for short-term trading.

Chapter 7

MATRIX AND SYSTEMS

7.1: P&F MATRIX

We have discussed basic P&F patterns. It is possible to run the scanner to shortlist stocks which have generated Double Top Buy or Double Bottom Sell signal on a given day. But, how about scanning for a pattern on multiple box-values and ranking them based on some scoring methodology?

The Point & Figure performance matrix evaluates the chart pattern in each instrument across different box-values and ranks them based on the total score. The TradePoint software has this feature to calculate the P&F Performance Matrix. It is an effective tool to view and understand the overall market performance at a glance.

A Bear Trap on 0.25% box-value may be a bullish formation on higher box-value, which adds to the strength of the pattern, whereas a bullish setup on lower box-value but bearish on higher box-value indicates that there is a weakness. Scoring based on patterns across multiple box-values helps in identifying the stocks with setups that are in sync across different box-values.

The objectivity associated with the P&F methodology enables an effective way of assigning scores based on various patterns. Below is the method of scoring followed for Point & Figure Performance Matrix.

If there is a Double Top Buy and column is also 'X', it is a strong formation; hence, score given to such pattern is 2. But if column has turned to 'O' after buy signal but not generated a sell signal, it becomes a weak formation; hence, score given in such situation is 1. Refer image shown below.

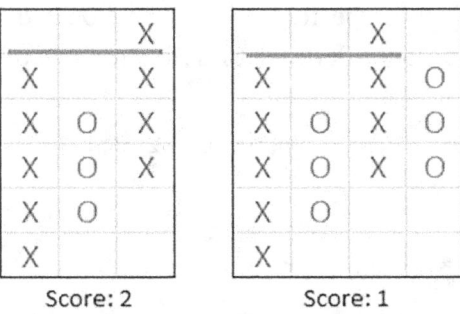

Score: 2   Score: 1

Image 7.1.1: Matrix score

If there is Double Bottom Sell signal and column is also of 'O', it is a weak structure; hence, score assigned is -2. But if there is a column of 'X' after Double Bottom Sell signal that has not yet generated a buy signal, then score is -1.

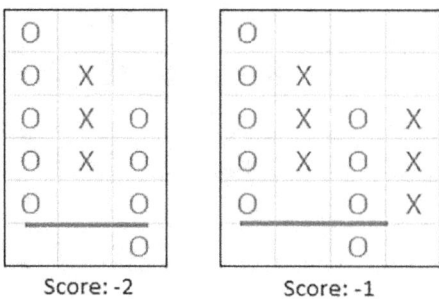

Score: -2   Score: -1

Image 7.1.2: Matrix score

But if there is no Buy or Sell pattern on the chart, then score given is 0.

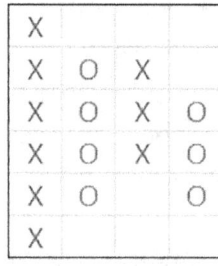

Score: 0

Image 7.1.3: Matrix score

Hence every stock can be scored based on the recent pattern as per the method explained above. Maximum score is 2 and the minimum is -2. It will be zero if there is no signal. Matrix calculates score on four different box-values and aggregates them. Stocks are ranked based on the total aggregate score. If signals are Double Top Buy along with column of 'X' on all four box-values, then the maximum score of 8 will be assigned, indicating strong bullish trend across box-sizes. If pattern is Double Bottom Sell signal on all four box-values, then score is -8, which is the lowest possible score, suggesting bearish structure.

It is a very useful tool to analyse the performance of all stocks of a group or sector at a glance. The Box-values for the analysis will be user-defined to suit personal preference. Read the discussion on box-value for further information.

Below is the Point & Figure performance matrix on 0.25%, 0.50%, 1% and 1.5% box-values, based on the scoring method discussed above.

Scrip	0.25%	0.5%	0.75%	1%	Score
Nifty Consumption	2	2	2	2	8
Nifty Pharma	2	2	2	2	8
Nifty Metal	2	2	2	2	8
Nifty MNC	2	2	2	2	8
Nifty Energy	1	2	2	2	7
Nifty Fin Service	2	0	0	0	2
Nifty 50	2	0	0	0	2
Nifty FMCG	1	0	0	0	1
Nifty IT	0	-2	0	0	-2
Nifty PSU Bank	-1	-2	-2	-2	-7
Nifty Serv Sector	-2	-2	-2	-2	-8

Image 7.1.4: Nifty all sectors Matrix score chart

It can be seen from the image above that price patterns of Consumption, Pharma, Metal and MNC are bullish across the box-values, whereas Service sector and PSU banks seem to be under pressure. Further analysis can be performed on individual charts of sectors or Relative strength charts, which we will discuss in Chapter 8.

Similarly, stocks from a sector or group can also be viewed in the matrix format. Below is the image showing Performance Matrix of all stocks from the Nifty Metal index sector on 0.25%, 0.50%, 0.75% and 1% box-values.

Script	0.25%	0.5%	0.75%	1%	Score
WELCORP	2	2	2	2	8
NATIONALUM	2	2	2	2	8
HINDALCO	2	2	2	2	8
JSWSTEEL	2	2	2	2	8
TATASTEEL	2	0	2	2	6
JINDALSAW	1	1	1	1	4
JINDALSTEL	0	0	2	2	4
SAIL	0	0	2	2	4
VEDL	0	2	0	0	2
COALINDIA	2	2	-1	-1	2
ORISSAMINE	1	0	0	0	1
BHUSANSTL	0	0	0	0	0
NMDC	-2	-2	-2	1	-5

Image 7.1.5: Nifty metal index Matrix score chart

A list of performing and non-performing stocks can easily be identified using this objective method. Individual analysis of stocks can be performed thereafter. Box-values shown in the example can be varied to suit the user.

Score greater than 6 indicates bullish trend and below -6 indicates bearishness. Stocks with maximum score display strength and also a possible exhaustion. Matrix also calculates the breadth based on the scoring of the stocks of a particualr group or Nifty 50 stocks. Percentage of stocks above or below 0 in the group works as breadth indicator. If more number of stocks are in uptrend, it is a sign of underlying strength, but it is also a signal to be cautious about creating fresh positions.

A score of zero on all box-values indicates a tight consolidation phase. Expansion or a strong trending phase is expected after such a tight congestion. Hence, such stocks should be analyzed further. Score will be zero if there is a Triangle or series of inside columns in a box-value.

Formations on multiple box-values give an idea about price structure. Matrix is a very useful tool and helps us assess the performance of all stocks at a glance across different time frames or box-size. Remember, it is not an alternative or proxy for individual stock analysis. Trades cannot be placed on the basis of matrix and individual patterns should be studied for the same.

Summary

- Matrix is an advanced method of technical analysis that scores a chart based on the patterns.
- It calculates the total score of patterns across different box-values.
- 8 and -8 are maximum readings. They indicate trend or exhaustion. 0 indicates congestion.

7.2: SYSTEM DESIGN

The discussion in this section will be of interest particularly to the people who are thinkers and prefer to design systems. We know that every P&F pattern is a combination of columns. A pattern or system can be designed by defining the columns and combinations.

A column represents a trend. The major ingredient of a column is the number of boxes in it and the relation with its previous column. A simple Double Top Buy is a three-column formation where the most recent column is above the previous column of 'X'. If we number the columns starting from right to left, meaning that most recent column is 0 (zero), then Double Top Buy occurs when the high of the box-price of column 0 moves above the high of the box-price of column 2. Refer image shown below.

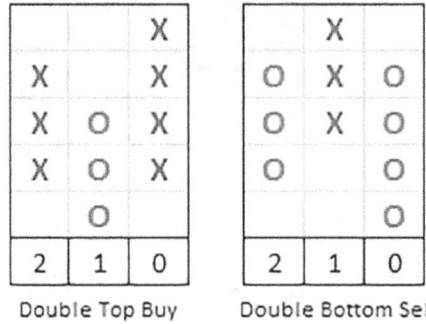

Double Top Buy   Double Bottom Sell

Image 7.2.1: Double Top Buy and Double Bottom Sell

Same way, Double Bottom Sell signal is where low price of column 0 is lesser than low price of column 2. This is the basic P&F formation. Ask yourself if any other pattern can be defined objectively in a similar manner?

Can you design a Triple Top or Triple Bottom pattern? Or, what if you need to define a column where there is no Buy or Sell pattern has been triggered?

It can be done as follows:

High price of column 0 < High price of column 2

    and

Low price of column 0 > Low price of column 2

By doing this, we can know the column where Buy signal is not yet triggered and we also know the level at which it will happen. A list of stocks with levels can be prepared in advance by designing and scanning this condition.

We can define the setups further. For example, if you want to scan for buy setups with minimum reversal after the signal, then you can define the buy signal as shown above and insert another condition to define the number of boxes in column number 1. It can be kept at the minimum for identifying more affordable trade setup. This will be 2 in case of two-box reversal charts, 3 in case of three-box reversal charts and so on. So, a list of stocks can be generated where Buy and Sell signals have been triggered with minimum reversal.

If you want to identify candidates where a Buy setup has traveled minimum five boxes after breakout, then condition "number of boxes after breakout signal."needs to be defined. The logical operands such as 'And', 'Or' and 'Not' kind of conditions can be utilized to define the relationship between two or more columns.

For instance, think of a Triple Top Buy or Triple Bottom Sell as five-column pattern. Breakout has happened at column 0; one can tweak the rules of column 2 or 4 to define variations. A Pole is a four-column pattern. Question can come to mind, why five boxes after breakout and why not seven or three or any other number for that matter? And why 50% retracement and what about 61.80% or 38.20% or any other number? It can certainly be designed. Below is the example of a High Pole with seven-column requirement and 61.80% retracement.

High price of column 1 > High price of column 3

   and

Minimum number of boxes after breakout in column 1 are 7

   and

Retracement to previous column at column 0 is 61.80%

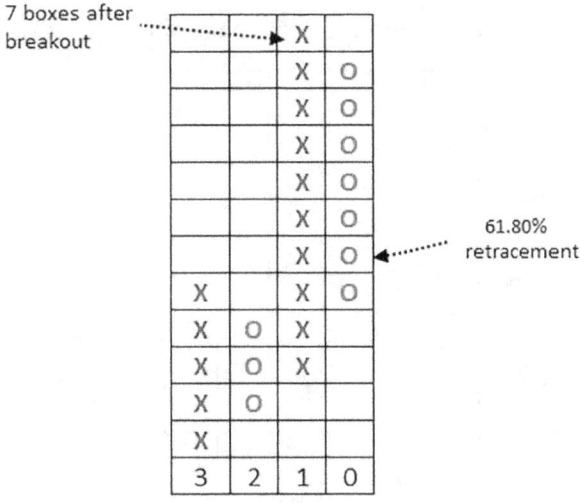

Image 7.2.2: Seven-box and 61.80% Pole

A Bull Trap is a four-column setup, defined as Double Bottom Sell signal at column 0 and Double Top Buy pattern at column 1. Similarly, Bear Trap can be defined as Double Top Buy signal at column 0 and Double Bottom Sell at column 1. Follow-through formations are defined as basic signal after major patterns such as Poles, Traps or Broadenings.

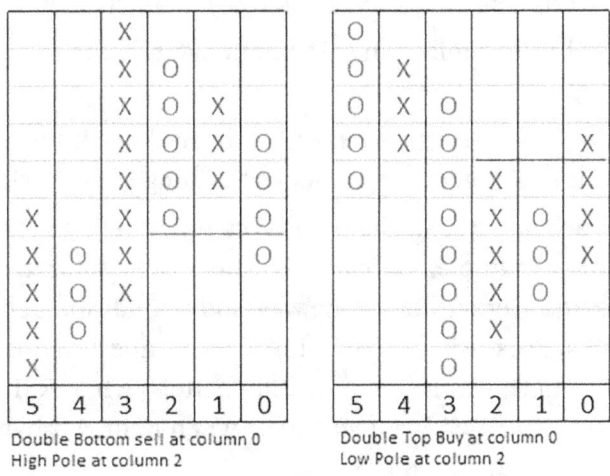

Image 7.2.3: Pole Follow-through

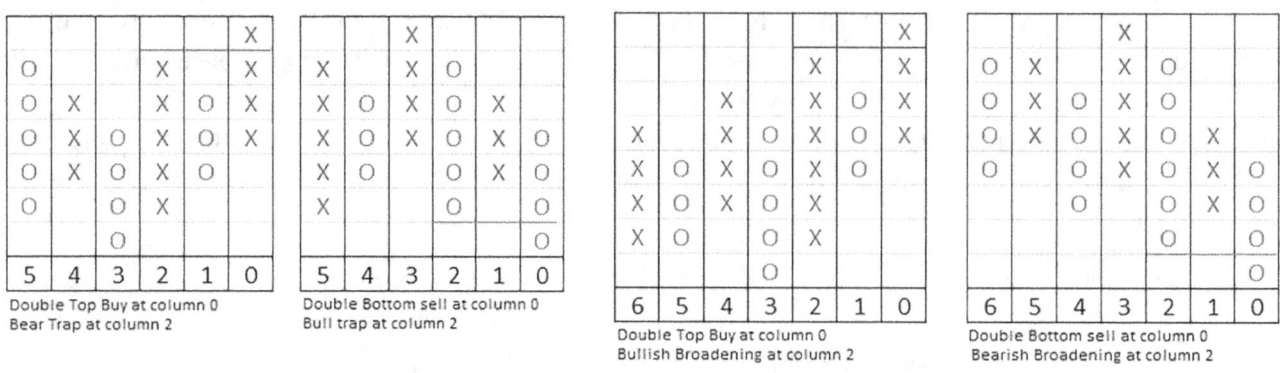

Image 7.2.4: Trap and Broadening Follow-through

A three- or four-column Triangle is defined as a series of inside columns. Breakout after Triangle and even failure like head fake can easily be defined. Refer image shown below.

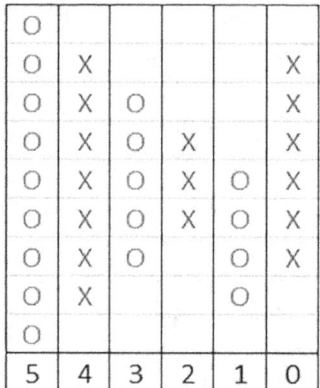

Triangle at column 2
Double Bottom sell at column 1
Doouble Top buy at column 0

Image 7.2.5: Triangle failure

These formations are already built into the TradePoint software, but knowing the logic will make you design better and more advanced systems. A column reversal can also be utilized instead of basic signals. How about variation of Traps? I am sure you will easily be able to define it by now. The software provides ready to use features but designing a system on your own will make you enjoy P&F more.

Any other pattern can also be customized in this manner. All that is required is the ability to observe and be creative.

The advantage of designing is that it can be easily compared, back-tested and analyzed for the past performance. It can also be scanned to get a list of stocks fulfilling the criteria.

Indicators are important part of system design. The combination of patterns and indicators can create interesting setups or systems. For example, a Double Top Buy can be filtered by adding another condition that column 0 is above the moving average line. Same way, add a condition of below average line at column 0 to filter Double Bottom Sell signals using the moving average line. Any other indicator instead of the moving average can also be used in a similar manner. Buy pattern when RSI is above 50 or when MACD is positive or when RSI is below 30 or CCI is above 100 or when Bollinger bands are rising or falling, etc., are examples of systems that can be designed.

I know you might be thinking why am I explaining all these when software gives it ready-made. We are not programmers, we are traders, and that's precisely the reason why I am explaining all these. It doesn't require any programming or coding skills to design a system. All that is required is a simple logic that only a trader can know. There are many software sellers selling their magical indicators and it is easy to fall prey to them thinking that the smart Buy-Sell signals that they generate can help make tons of money. Never ever trade any system, unless you are aware of all its ingredients well so that you understand its behavior.

This knowledge has helped me design so many patterns on my own. We keep coming across new things and if we can learn to make it objective we can make best use of the varied knowledge base or information. Let me give you an example. Three advancing soldiers and three black crows are popular candlestick formations that suggest exhaustion. Three consecutive bullish or bearish candles define this candlestick setup. Similarly, three consecutive trends can be defined in P&F that suggests some exhaustion in the near term. Image 7.2.6 shows the three consecutive columns without a reversal signal in between.

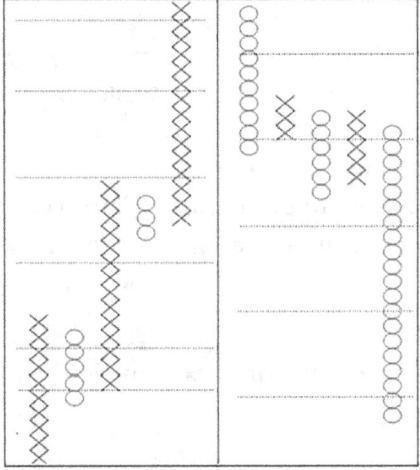

Three consecutive columns

Image 7.2.6: Soldiers and crows

Columns 0, 2 and 4 should have Buy signals and 1 and 3 shouldn't have signals to define bullish three-consecutive trend setup. Sell signal in columns 0, 2 and 4 and absence of Buy signal in column 1 and 3 define bearish three-consecutive column setup.

Any price setup that one comes across can be designed if it can be clearly defined. Take the Wolfe wave pattern for instance. Wolfe wave, which is named after Bill Wolfe and Brian Wolfe, is a five-wave pattern where the fourth wave enters into the territory of the first wave. It can be designed using P&F columns as shown below.

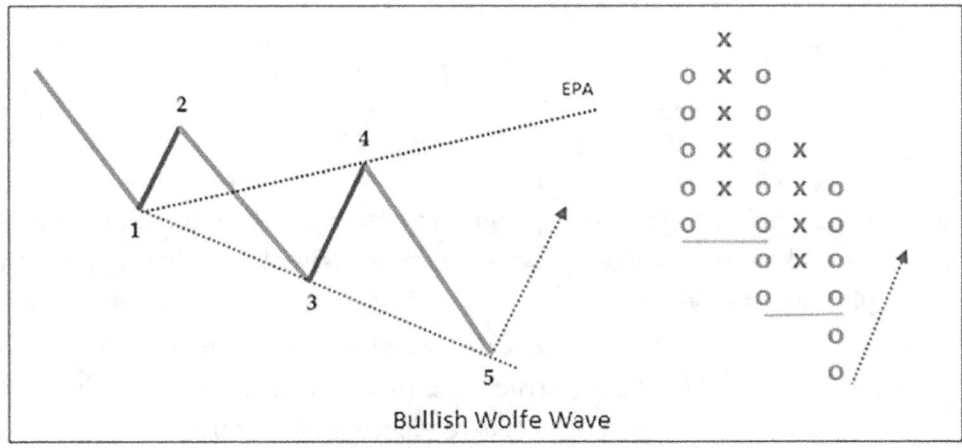

Bullish Wolfe Wave

Image 7.2.7: Bullish Wolfe Wave

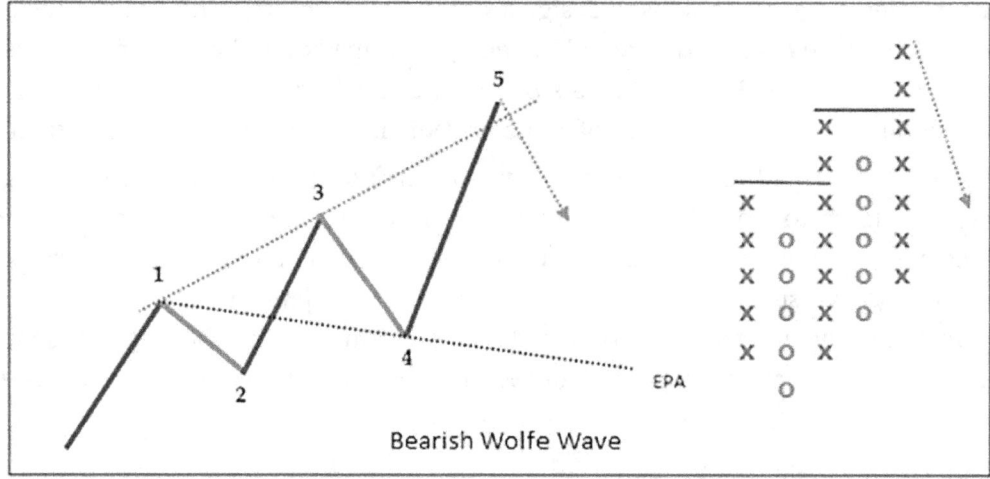

Image 7.2.8: Bearish Wolfe Wave

It doesn't capture all Wolfe waves and they are not valid at all times. It is difficult to define such type of pattern completely, but it can help one to get the list of probable candidates to verify it with pattern rules. I borrowed this knowledge from Wolfe waves and designed P&F WW formation. If you apply your mind, a Wolfe wave formation is nothing but a variation of bullish pattern reversed and bearish pattern reversed.

Let me give you some homework. See harmonic patterns in the image shown below.

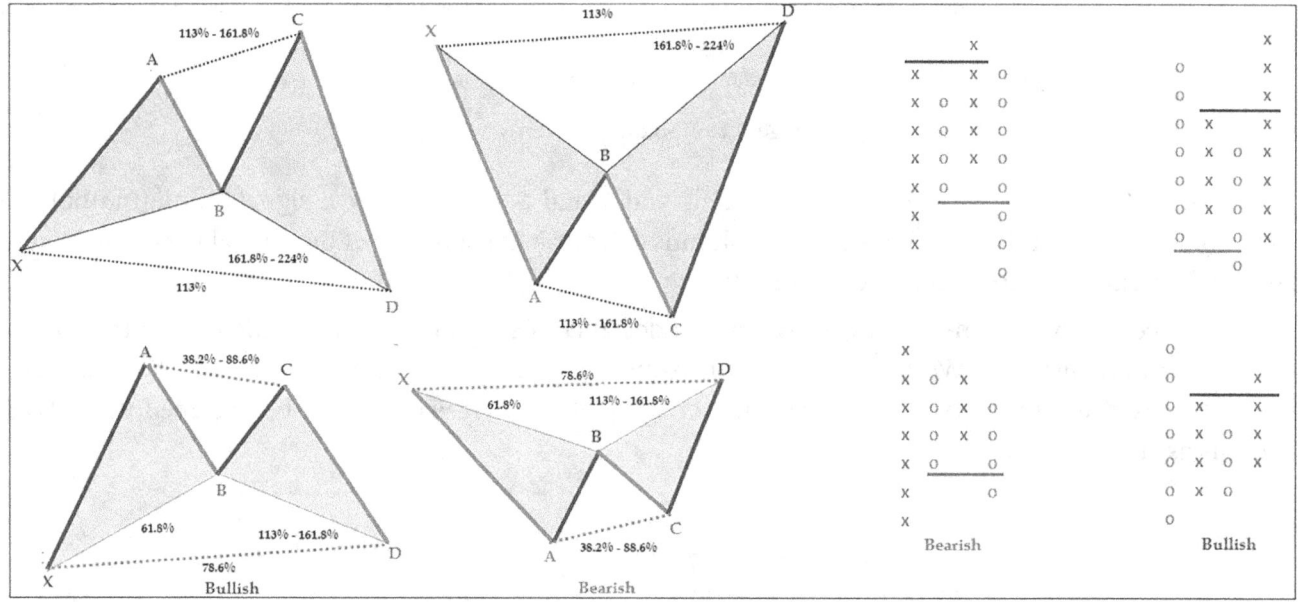

Image 7.2.9: Harmonic patterns

Can this be designed on P&F? Harmonic patters are reversal formations and can complement a price-following technique like P&F. The key is to view them on higher box-value charts such as slot 3 or 4 using the High–Low plotting method.

They are not exactly Harmonic or Wolfe wave patterns and purpose of showing them is to demonstrate the possibilities of designing any kind of price structures. However, trades can be initiated based on P&F patterns when a Wolfe waves or Harmonic patterns are identified in the usual candlestick or bar charts. They tend to complement each other.

The possibilities are infinite. Any price behavior that one observes, or imagines can be designed, tested and scanned. Another advantage is that you spend time thinking about your observations so that you can design them and make it objective to the most possible extent. Celebrate the power of your imagination.

Summary

- ⅄ P&F has given us opportunity to distribute price moves into boxes, which can be measured, defined and designed.
- ⅄ Any observation can be made objective using P&F.

Chapter 8

RELATIVE STRENGTH

The concept of Relative Strength is very popular and although much written about, it is truly under-utilized by market participants. It is a very simple and effective method of measuring performance of an instrument. Don't confuse it with RSI indicator due to similarity in name; they are entirely different concepts.

Whether it is investing, position trading, short-term trading or even intraday trading, strength analysis is the most important for all types of traders and it can improve the performance of their trading methods significantly.

Ratio Chart

If we divide the price of one instrument with that of another, what we get is a ratio of those two instruments. For example, if Bank Nifty is trading at 20000 and Nifty at 10000, if we divide the former by latter, we get a ratio of 2. It is the ratio of one price to another for that particular period. This way, the ratio of two instruments can be derived on regular basis and plotted on a chart. It will look similar to usual line chart plotted by connecting two prices.

Figure shown below is the daily Ratio chart of Bank Nifty to Nifty.

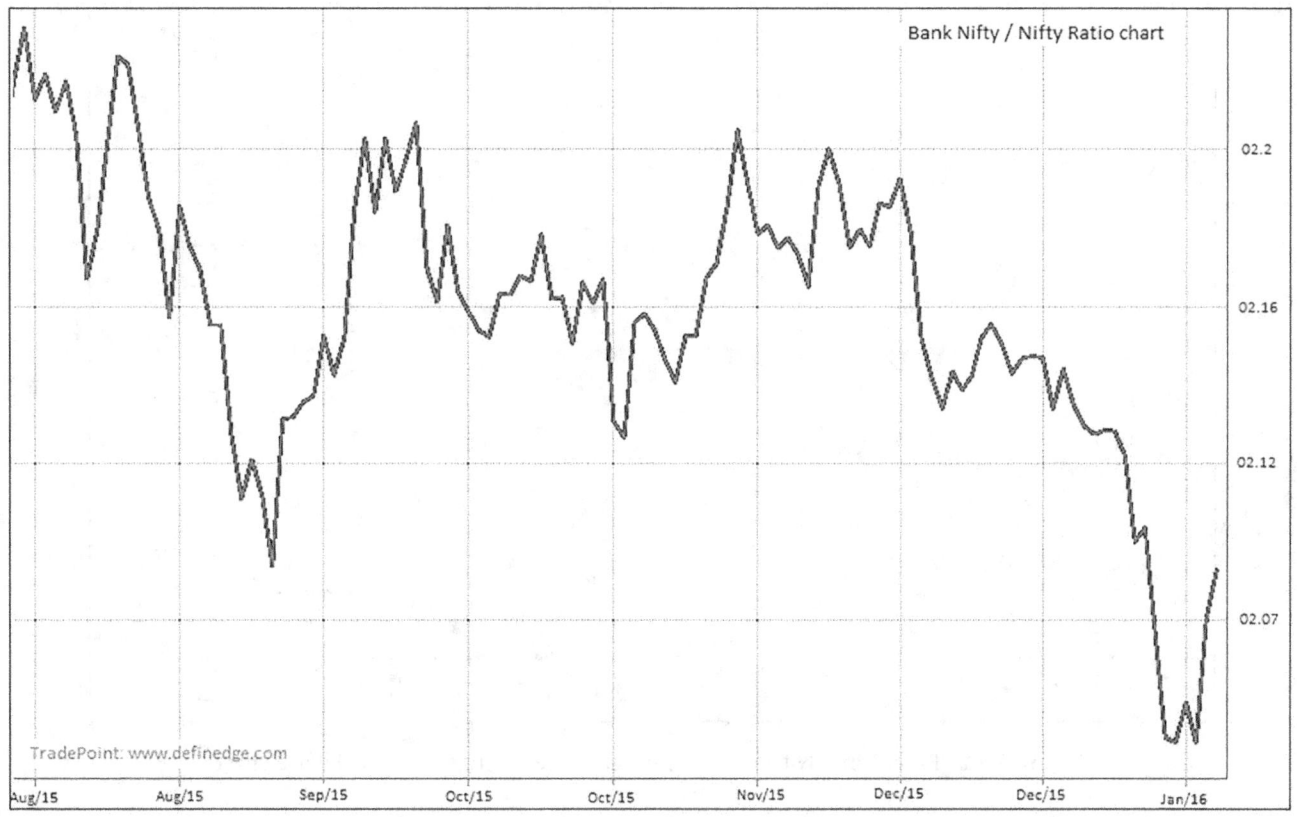

Figure 8.1.1: Bank Nifty/Nifty daily Ratio chart

The ratio line shown in the chart can also be analyzed the way we do price, but understand what it represents. The rising or falling lines are not showing the trend of the price, but of the ratio line.

For ratio line to go up, instrument used in the numerator will have to produce a bigger reading than the denominator. Hence, rising ratio line indicates that numerator is outperforming the denominator and falling ratio line indicates that it is underperforming denominator. Note that outperformance doesn't necessarily mean that numerator is rising and denominator is falling. It is just outperformance when former is rising more than latter or falling less than it.

The ratio of two instruments may remain in a range over a period of time. Mean reversion techniques can be effectively implemented in such scenarios. But this way, we can easily analyse the performance of one instrument with another. The concept is fascinating.

P&F Relative Strength

The ratio chart shown above can be plotted with Point & Figure construction method as well. The formula of P&F Relative strength charts is as follows:

P&F Relative Strength = (Scrip 1/Scrip 2) × 100

All methods and patterns that we have discussed till now are applicable to the P&F relative strength chart also.

Below is Bank Nifty/Nifty 50 Relative strength chart plotted using 1% × 3 parameters.

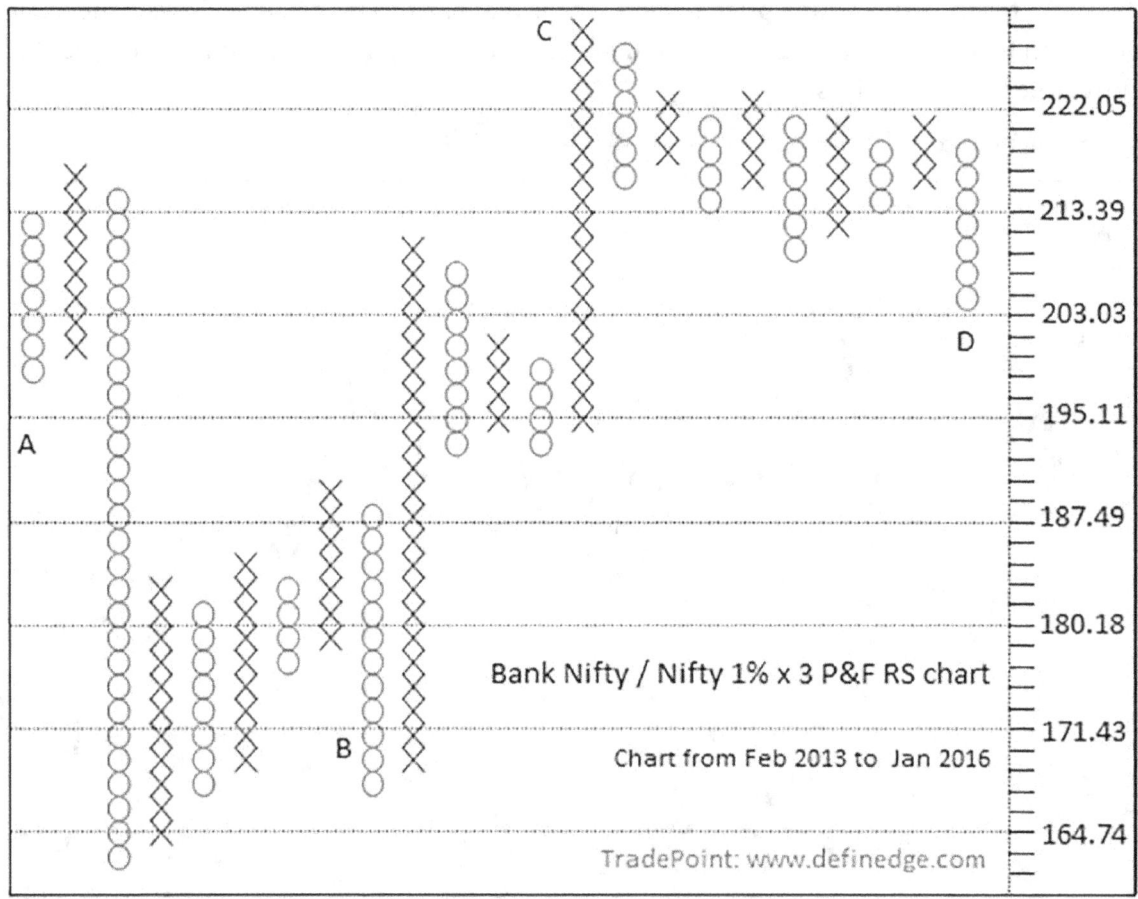

Figure 8.1.2: Bank Nifty/Nifty 1% × 3 daily Relative Strength Point & Figure chart

Above chart shows the performance of Bank Nifty against Nifty for about 3 years. A to B represents the performance in the year 2013, B to C is 2014 and C to D captures 2015.

Now that we have a ratio in the P&F format, all methods applicable to P&F charts to perform price analysis can also be used on RS charts for performance strength analysis.

There are three distinct uses of a P&F Relative Strength chart.

1. Identify Strength and Weakness

It is always advisable to get rid of underperformers from the portfolio and ride the strength. Strong stocks become stronger in Uptrend as trend matures and resume the trend soon after corrections. Weak counters will be beaten hard during corrective phases making the portfolio bleed and underperform the overall market. A strength-centric portfolio would deliver better returns over a period.

If denominator in a Relative Strength chart is a broader market index such as the Nifty 50, then the chart will show the performance of numerator instrument against it. Numerator can be an individual stock or sector or any other instrument for that matter.

Let me explain to you the importance of Relative Strength. Indian markets have witnessed a massive rally after the NDA government came into power in May 2014. Nifty gained by ~18% from April 2014 to December 2015. Many stocks witnessed sensational runs and outperformed the broader markets significantly during this period. But there were weak or underperforming stocks and sectors too. Many stocks have fallen by more than 50–60% during this period. The likes of Cairn, Aban and JP Associates are a few names in this category. This happens during every up and downtrend. Stocks behave according to the macro- and micro-factors associated with the company and the sector. The focus should be on riding the strengths and discarding the weaknesses. It is said that stocks must be treated like employees, fire them if they don't perform!

A. Top-Down Approach

Every P&F technique that we have discussed including trend lines and counts is applicable on Relative Strength charts also to analyse the strong-performing stocks and sectors against the benchmark. They can be traded based on the setups of their individual charts. Bullish setup of strong RS charts and Bearish setup of weak RS charts add another dimension to the pattern trading.

Trend and patterns of Point & Figure charts help in analyzing these charts. Below are the box-value slots for P&F Relative strength charts:

Slot 1: 0.25–0.50%

Slot 2: 0.50–1%

Slot 3: 1–2%

Slot 4: 2% and above

The method of reading box-values in each slot remains same. The trend that column displays is more important in slot 3 & slot 4 charts and combination of patterns becomes more important in slot 1 & 2 charts.

Sector performance can be compared against the broader market index to assess their relative performance. Figure shown below is daily 0.50% × 3 P&F Relative Strength chart of Pharma index against Nifty.

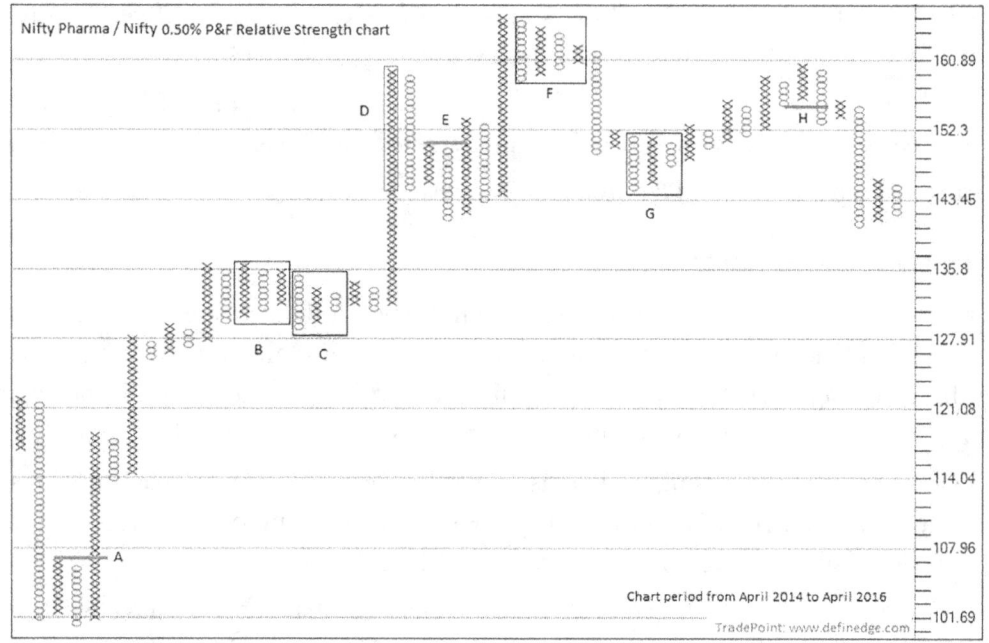

Figure 8.1.3: Nifty Pharma/Nifty 0.50% × 3 daily Relative Strength Point & Figure chart

Pattern A is Bear Trap. Pattern B is two consecutive Triangles that display prolonged congestion. Pattern D is High Pole, followed by Bear Trap at pattern E. Pattern F is another Triangle at the top. Pattern G is a Triangle and bullish Double pattern followed by rising ratio. Pattern H is timely occurrence of bullish pattern reversed.

So we read it as a price chart and find opportunities based on patterns, but here we analyse the strength. The patterns on Sector RS charts tell us about the performance of the sector against the benchmark. Bullish patterns indicate outperformance and bearish patterns suggest weakness or underperformance.

Below is the same chart plotted with 1% and 1.5% box-value.

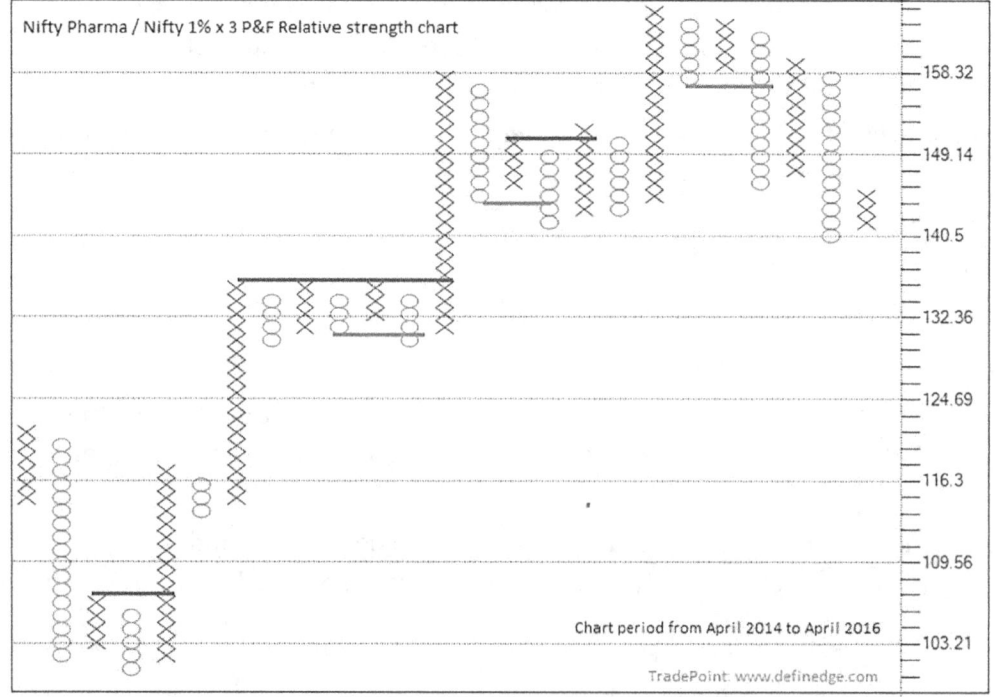

Figure 8.1.4: Nifty Pharma/Nifty 1% × 3 daily Relative Strength Point & Figure chart

Only basic formations are marked. It is to demonstrate what kind of information to study from charts of different slots. Even a column reversal becomes important in this chart. 45-degree trend lines can also be applied on it. Figure shown below is the same chart plotted with 1.50% box-value.

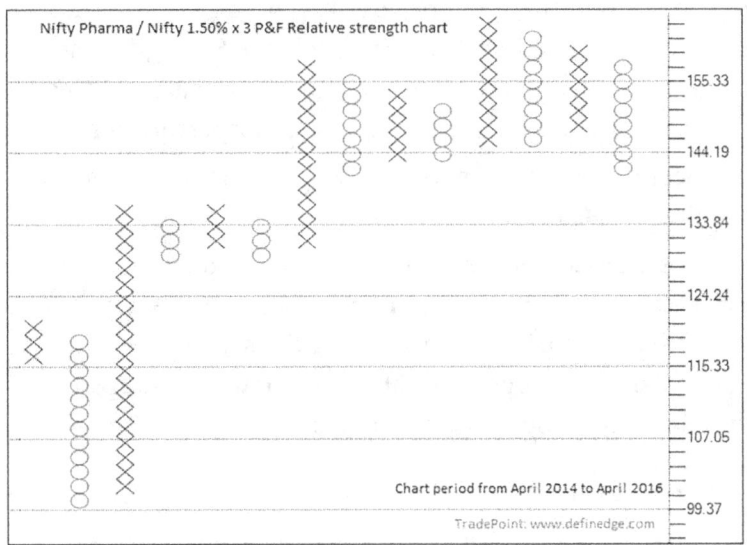

Figure 8.1.5: Nifty Pharma/Nifty 1.50% × 3 daily Point & Figure Relative Strength chart

A trend or strength can be known by the column analysis itself. By looking at various charts, the view and strength analysis for long term, medium term, short term, etc., can be performed.

Sector performance analysis gives an idea of sectors that are performing and underperforming across various time horizons. Once the interesting opportunities in sectors are found, performance of the sectors ingredients can be analyzed in a similar manner. You need to increase the box-values in each slot when stocks are viewed.

Below are the 1.5% × 3 P&F Relative Strength charts of the stocks from the Pharma sector plotted against the Nifty Pharma index during the same period.

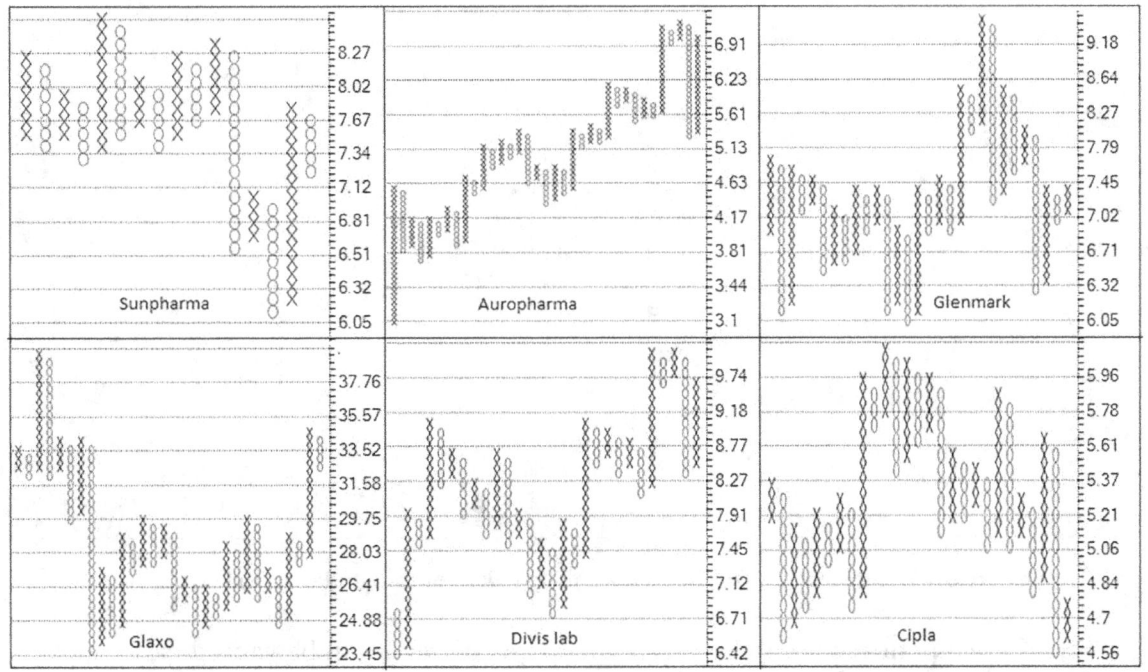

Figure 8.1.6: Pharma stocks/Nifty Pharma Relative Strength Point & Figure charts

The performance of stocks against the Pharma index can easily be observed on the charts shown above. As can be seen in the RS chart of Pharma against Nifty, the sector outperformed the broader market index till September 2015, which is the earlier period of the chart. The above image displays the stocks that outperformed the sector during the same period. It can be seen that Auro Pharma, Divis Labs and Glenmark were among leaders. The left side of Pharma Relative Strength chart indicates weakness and it can be seen from the image above that Sun Pharma and Glaxo are currently leading that fall. So this way, you get to know of the stocks which are outperforming in an outperforming sector!

Top-down approach = Sector to Broader market index -> Stocks to outperforming sector -> Individual P&F analysis of leaders of the outperforming sectors.

If I go to lower box-values, 45-degree trend line breakout and anchor columns would provide some early signs. The Pharma sector is shown as an example; these factors are applicable to any sector. The formations in the Relative Strength charts help in knowing the state of the markets and the outperforming industries. You may wish to select just one box-value and view the setups on it accordingly. P&F chart removes noise of the ratio lines and produces clear setups.

B. Against Broader Market Index

Sector analysis gives idea about general trend and the trending industries. Strong stocks in those sectors can be identified by plotting RS charts of stocks against the sector index and broader market index Nifty or Sensex.

Stocks in the same manner can be viewed against Nifty as well, to analyse the strength of the stocks against broader market index.

Figure 8.1.7 is a 1% × 3 P&F Relative Strength chart of Tata Steel against Nifty.

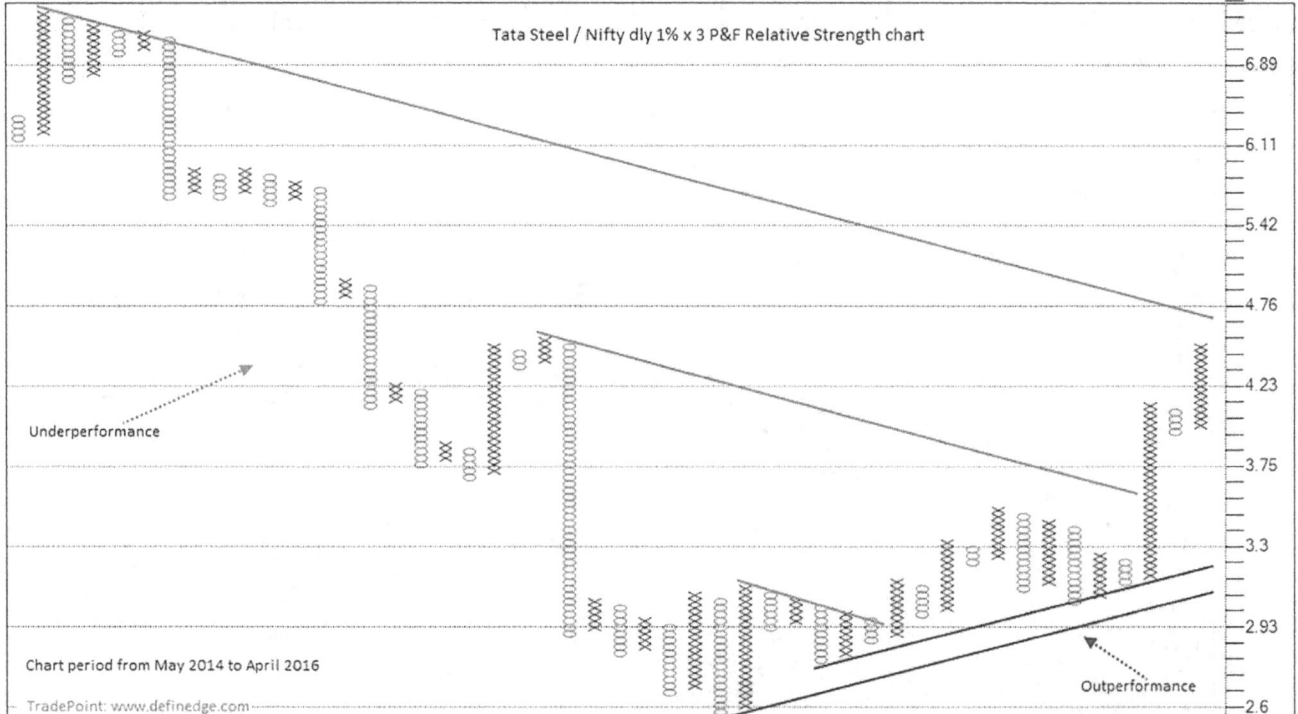

Figure 8.1.7: Tata Steel/Nifty daily 1% × 3 daily Relative Strength Point & Figure chart

The story of price performance of Tata Steel of couple of years can be gauged easily looking at the chart shown above.

45-degree lines and anchor column are nice tools to analyse the Relative Strength chart. They provide some early signs of strength or weakness in the price. Follow-through to anchor columns is a sensible approach, hence setups like Anchor Tops and Bottoms, ABC and Super Pattern work well on RS charts as well.

Observe 1% × 3 RS P&F chart of Maruti/Nifty.

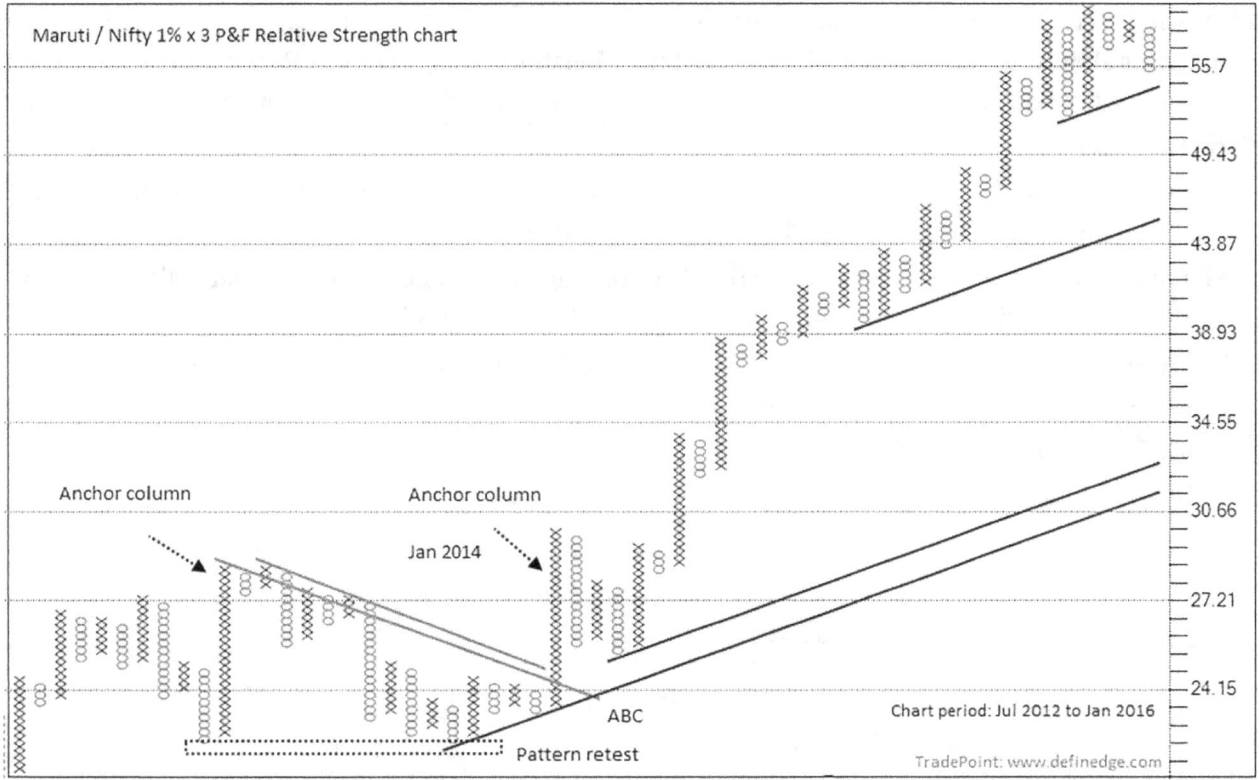

Figure 8.1.8: Maruti/Nifty daily 1% × 3 daily Relative Strength Point & Figure chart

The anchor columns indicate the strength in the counter. Pattern retest, ABC and 45-degree lines from Mini Bottoms are patterns that help us know the strength in the stock. Price of stock increased more than five times in the next 3 years.

The strength of the stock is known better when markets correct. Stocks that show relative strength when the markets correct, tend to do well when markets recover. One should always embrace corrections and pull-backs because a buy signal in RS charts when markets are in corrective mode indicates potential upside in the stocks when the trend resumes.

Henceforth, make it a point to check the relative strength chart of stock against Nifty before buying it. Ignoring the bullish formations of a stock chart during its period of underperformance and looking for it when it is outperforming the broader market is a logical and effective approach. Trade the formations of the individual charts in the direction of the Relative Strength chart. Price breakouts coupled with Relative Strength breakouts are the key to identifying potential out-performers.

In the same way, weakness can also be analyzed and traded. Shorting the weak counters is more profitable when broader market corrects. It will offer better risk–reward trades than shorting the stronger counters. Pattern studies of individual stocks certainly play an important role. Remember, trades are placed based on study of the individual charts. Relative Strength helps in finding where to fish.

Trading based on Relative Strength chart is altogether a different technique, as explained below.

2. Pair Trading

Relative Strength chart is plotted with ratio line of two instruments. Both the instruments need to be traded if one wants to trade Relative Strength chart patterns and formations.

A Double Top Buy or appearance of 'X' in P&F RS chart indicates that numerator price is performing better than denominator. Hence, both the instruments are traded simultaneously in opposite directions to trade these charts. If the bullish signal of this chart has to be traded, then numerator should be bought and denominator should be shorted. This is how we buy a Relative Strength chart. When a Relative Strength chart produces bearish setup, it can be sold by trading short the numerator instrument and trading long the denominator.

The approach is also known as pair trading where two stocks are traded simultaneously. Relative Strength chart is one of the best methods to initiate pair trades.

All techniques of trading and analyzing the P&F chart are applicable to P&F RS charts also but the pair is traded instead of a single instrument. Note that a pair should always be value-neutral.

Figure shown below is daily 1% × 3 P&F Relative Strength chart of BPCL against ONGC.

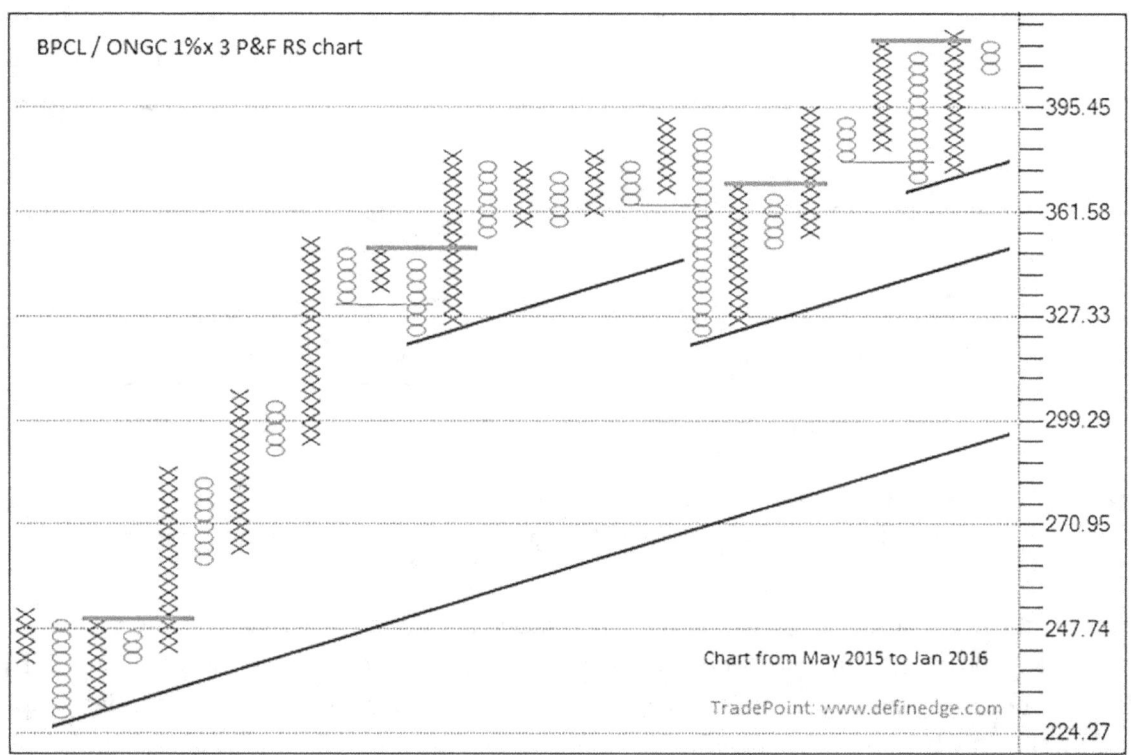

Figure 8.1.9: BPCL/ONGC daily 1% × 3 Relative Strength Point & Figure chart

Chart is in Uptrend, as shown by 45-degree lines. Fresh Double Top signals are marked in the chart. Buy signal above trend line is a bullish signal that can be traded by buying BPCL and selling ONGC. The trade shall remain open unless Sell signal is triggered in the chart.

Displayed below is the daily 3% × 3 P&F Relative Strength chart of Dr. Reddy versus Auro Pharma.

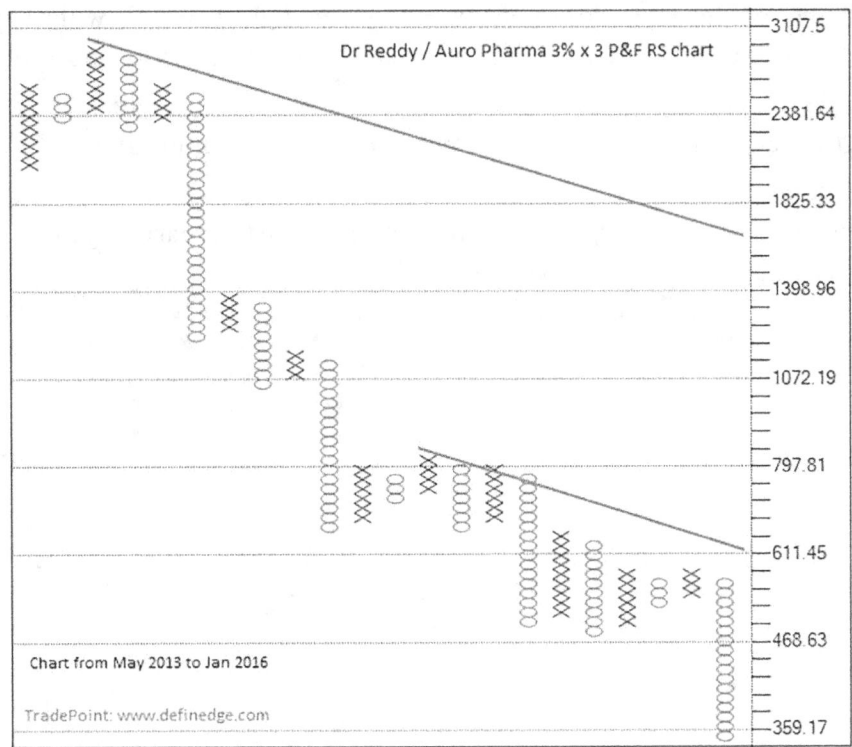

Figure 8.1.10: Dr. Reddy/Auro Pharma daily 3% × 3 Relative Strength Point & Figure chart

The above chart indicates underperformance of Dr. Reddy in relation to Auro Pharma since May 2013. There are two Fresh Sell signals besides long anchor columns in Downtrend. The numerator in this chart – Dr. Reddy should be sold and Auro Pharma, the denominator should be bought when a sell signal is triggered in the chart. Both stocks were in Uptrend during the maximum part of the chart period but returns of Auro Pharma were significantly higher than that of Dr. Reddy showing clear outperformance.

Now, when Auro Pharma was numerator, the stock has really performed. Below is the same chart with reverse sequence: Auro Pharma is numerator and Dr. Reddy is denominator.

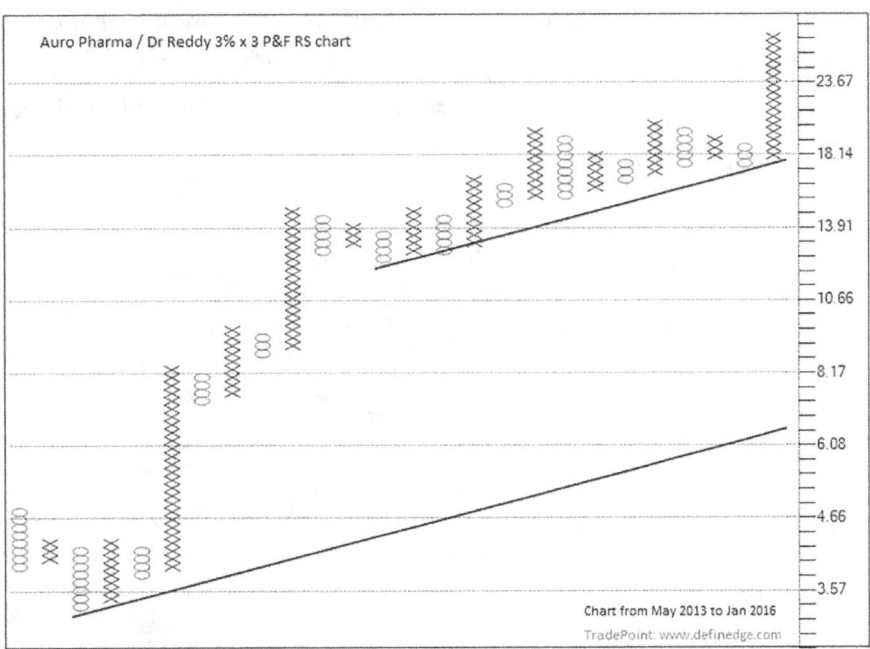

Figure 8.1.11: Auro Pharma/Dr. Reddy daily 3% × 3 Relative Strength Point & Figure chart

Chart is bullish and is an exact opposite of the earlier one. Bullish signals will be traded here, which is executed by trading long in Auro Pharma, being numerator, and taking short positions in Dr. Reddy. So the trades remain same.

Relative Strength chart turns bullish when numerator is outperforming and bearish when numerator starts underperforming.

Figure shown below is daily 1% × 3 P&F Relative Strength chart of Maruti against Tata Motors shown with trend lines and counts.

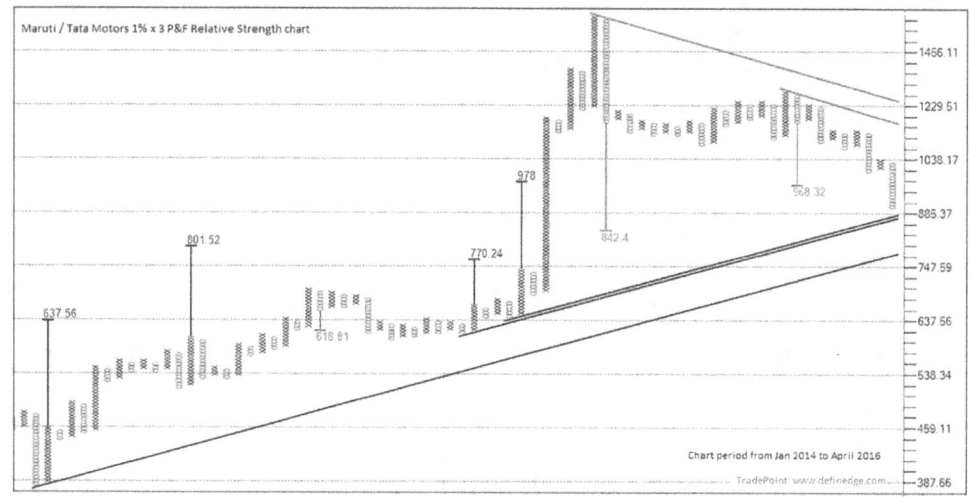

Figure 8.1.12: Maruti/Tata Motors daily 1% × 3 Relative Strength Point & Figure chart

P&F count is an effective tool to be applied on Relative Strength charts for pair trading.

3. Inter-Market Analysis

The relationship between various asset classes such as Bonds, Stocks, Commodities and Currency is very well explained by John Murphy in his seminal work, "Inter-market analysis." It's a wonderful book and is a must-read to understand the inter-relationship of global market behavior and the impact of changes in interest rate and inflation on them. He plotted ratio charts of two instruments to understand the behavior. It is possible to do it using P&F charts as well and perhaps in a better manner.

Figure shown below is 1% × 3 RS P&F chart of FMCG sector index chart plotted against Metal index.

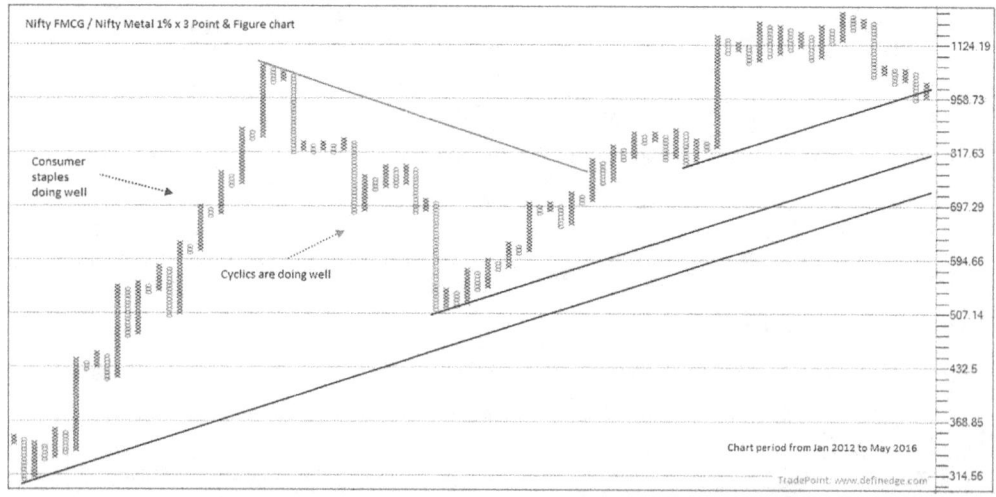

Figure 8.1.13: Nifty FMCG/Nifty Metal daily 1% × 3 Relative Strength Point & Figure chart

Rising prices and bullish formations above bullish trend line suggest that consumer staples are doing better than the cyclical metal sector stocks. Falling prices indicate that one should shift focus to the cyclical sector, which would improve the performance of the portfolio.

Figure shown below is 3% × 3 RS P&F chart of MCX Gold chart plotted against Nifty 50.

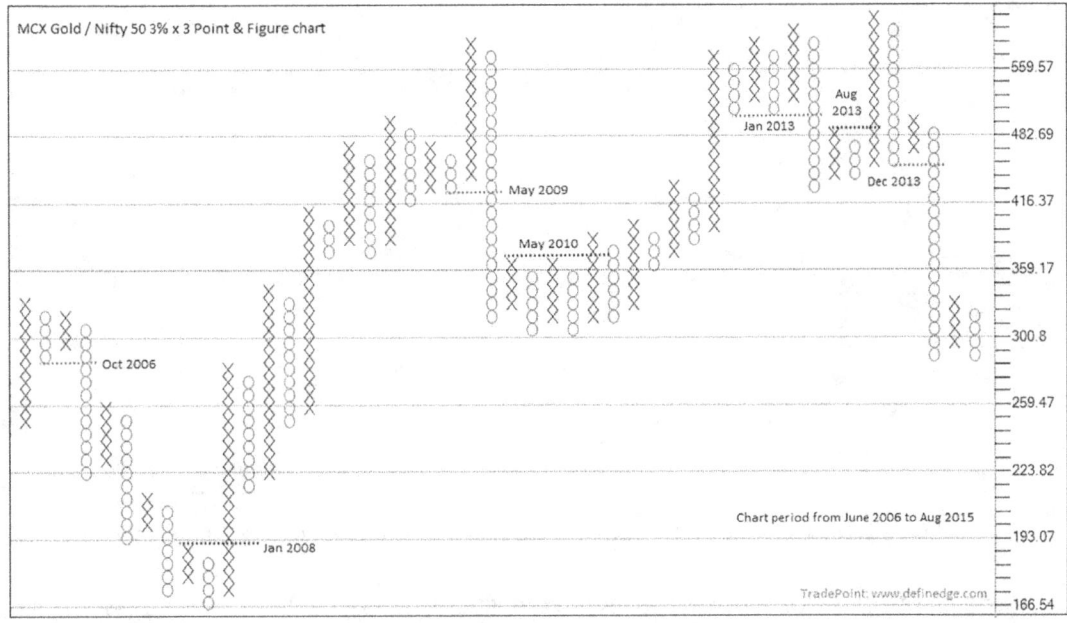

Figure 8.1.14: MCX Gold/Nifty daily 3% × 3 Relative Strength Point & Figure chart

Date and patterns are displayed in the chart. Bullish formations suggest that yellow metal is doing better than Nifty and bearish formations indicate that equities are a better place to be.

Figure 8.1.15 is a 2% × 3 RS P&F chart of Nifty 50 index plotted against Nasdaq 100. Observe P&F formations during all three phases shown in the performance chart.

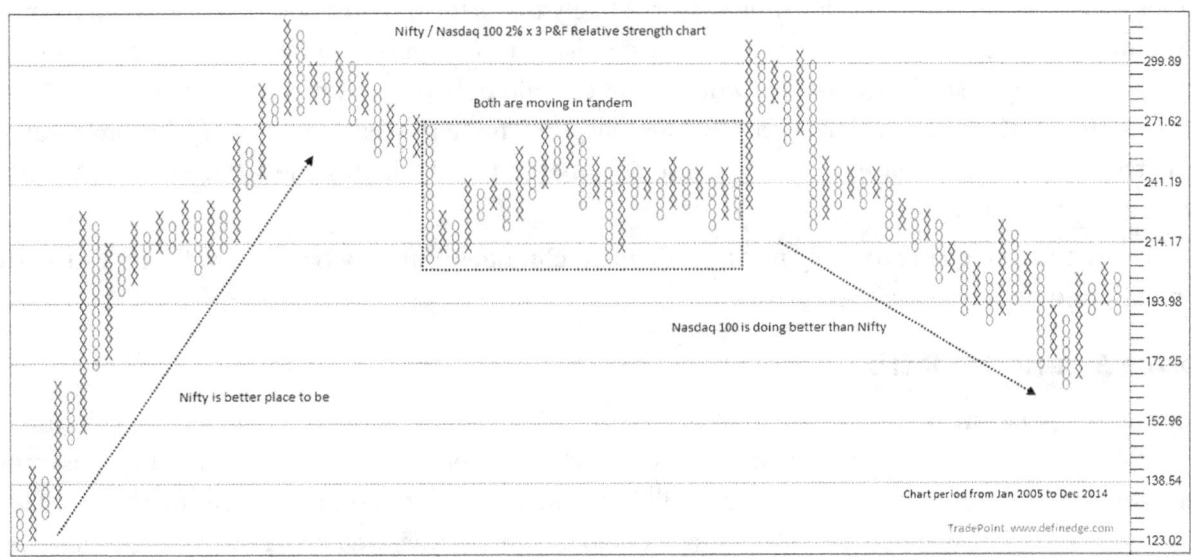

Figure 8.1.15: Nifty/Nasdaq 100 daily 2% × 3 Relative Strength Point & Figure chart

Figure 8.1.16 is a 2% × 3 RS P&F chart of Gold plotted against USDINR.

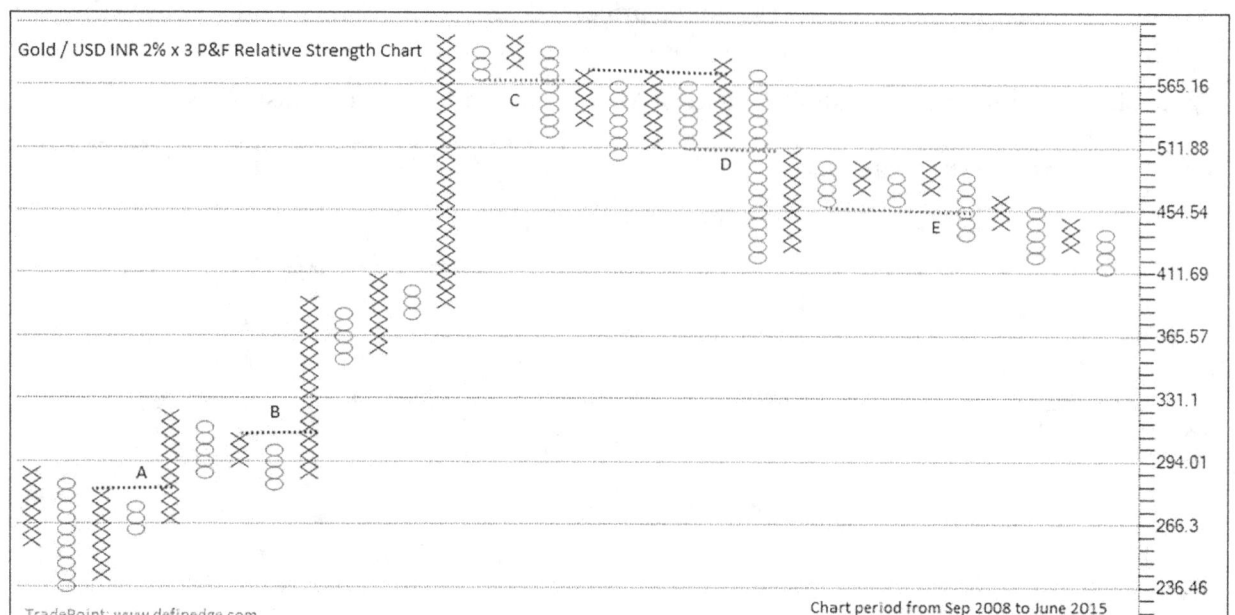

Figure 8.1.16: Gold/USD INR daily 2% × 3 Relative Strength Point & Figure chart

Pattern A is a Fresh Buy formation that occurred during early 2009. Pattern B is a Bear Trap and Triangle failure formation. Pattern C is a Fresh Sell signal triggered in September 2011, suggesting that the currency is getting stronger than the metal. Pattern D is a Bull Trap and failure of Triple Top Buy formation. Pattern E is a bearish continuation Triple Bottom Sell signal.

P&F analysis on RS charts can prove very effective method of analyzing the flow of money. Chart of any asset class against another can be plotted to see which asset class is moving and where the economy is heading.

Stock elected from strong-performing sector is likely to perform better compared to stock from weak sector. Similarly, stock of underperforming sector is likely to fall more and better shorted as opposed to the one from strong or stable sector. One would want to build portfolio in Uptrending market, but it would be better if the portfolio consists of stocks that are outperforming the markets, and quickly shy away from underperforming stocks. Relative strength is the best method of evaluating the strength or weakness and to stay with the leaders.

Ratios are the best charts to apply mean reversion techniques. But they trend as well, and P&F patterns are a most useful tool to trade their breakouts.

Relative Strength Matrix

We discussed performance matrix and the method of assigning scores in the earlier section. The performance matrix captures the performance of individual stocks or a index or any other instrument. Relative strength performance matrix can be built in a similar manner to score patterns on the RS charts, as depicted by the table in Figure 8.1.17. These matrix tables can be generated using the TradePoint software.

Scrip	0.25%	0.5%	0.75%	1%	Score
GAIL	2	2	2	2	8
YESBANK	2	2	2	2	8
DRREDDY	2	2	2	2	8
HDFCBANK	2	2	2	2	8
HINDUNILVR	1	2	2	2	7
BAJAJ-AUTO	2	0	0	0	2
BOSCHLTD	0	-2	0	0	-2
M&M	-1	-2	-2	-2	-7
IOC	-2	-2	-2	-2	-8
ICICIBANK	-2	-2	-2	-2	-8
BHARTIARTL	-2	-2	-2	-2	-8

Figure 8.1.17: Relative strength matrix chart

A group of stocks forming part of an index or sector can be benchmarked against another instrument, Nifty in this example. The relative performance is assessed across different box-values and entire performance can be viewed at a glance in the above matrix table. To keep it simple, don't invest in stocks that have a score less than 0.

Summary

- ⅄ P&F chart removes noise of the ratio lines and produces clear setups.
- ⅄ P&F methods applicable for price analysis are also applicable on RS charts for strength analysis.
- ⅄ Top-down approach is the sensible way of finding out stocks that are leading the outperforming sectors.
- ⅄ 45-degree lines and Anchor column are very useful tools on RS charts.
- ⅄ Price breakouts coupled with Relative Strength breakouts are potential out-performers.
- ⅄ Inter-market analysis and pair trading are made very effective with P&F RS charts.
- ⅄ Stock against broader market index should be viewed before individual analysis. Dump what is bearish on RS chart.

Chapter 9

BACK-TESTING

The biggest advantage of Point and Figure patterns is that they are objective in nature. Hence, they can be easily back-tested to analyse past performance, but the task is not very easy, given the multiple parameters to plot in P&F charts. This chapter deals with these difficulties and we test the P&F patterns from different perspectives.

P&F charts are mainly plotted using two methods: closing price and High–Low price. There are 3-box reversal charts and other charts. This section is divided into four parts. The first deals with the closing price method; second with the High–Low method; third with other reversal values and the fourth section talks about testing on Nifty.

The testing essentially gives us a general idea about past performance. Realize that the markets are so dynamic that time there could always be some element that can ruin even well-tested setups. Back-testing is a tool to develop our market understanding. Analyzing the past occurrences can improve our understanding of setups and market behavior. More importantly, back-testing gives us the much needed conviction and confidence in using the patterns and the method.

The approach I am adopting here is to test the performance of patterns. They are not trading systems; hence, slippages or any other charges are not considered while testing, so the numbers are gross. A period of 20 years starting from 1st January 1996 to 31st December 2015 or listing date, whichever is earlier, is considered for testing the setups. The back-testing was conducted over the universe of 500 stocks forming part of the Nifty-500 index as on 31st December 2015. It is the largest group available in National Stock Exchange and includes most of the stocks of different groups and sizes so that we can have a sufficiently large and diverse sample size. Bullish and Bearish patterns are shown separately so that both can be analyzed independently. Open trades are not considered for tests.

The following columns are presented in the back-testing tables.

Occurrence: Number of times pattern has occurred. It can vary as per the exit criteria defined.

Average return: Gain or loss generated per occurrence.

Risk–reward ratio: Average profit of all successful trades divided by average loss of all failed trades. It shows the reward generated against the risk of 1 point or 1-rupee.

Success ratio: Ratio of occurrences that resulted in a positive outcome. It is also known as gain–loss ratio or hit ratio.

Expectancy: While performing tests on pattern occurrence, success rate alone is not sufficient to evaluate. A pattern can have lesser winning rate but be more rewarding over a period due to higher risk–reward rate. Hence, outcomes must be evaluated based on expectancy; its formula is as follows:

Expectancy: (Success Ratio x Risk–Reward Ratio) - Failure Ratio

The failure ratio is the percentage of occurrences that resulted in negative outcome. Expectancy basically indicates whether a strategy is profitable or not. In simple words, if the success rate of any strategy is 80% but risk–reward is 0.20, then it is not a profitable strategy, simply because 0.20 paise is made 8 times and 1 rupee is lost twice, which will generate negative expectancy. So success rate alone or risk–reward for that matter is not sufficient to analyse the performance. Positive expectancy helps in identifying workable strategies.

9.1: CLOSE-ONLY METHOD

Before we analyse the testing results, it is important to understand that for back-testing with closing price method, the box-price that qualifies the pattern is considered as an entry price. It may differ from actual price because it gets updated at the end of the day and it also doesn't take gaps into the account. So the results derived from testing may vary from actual trading results. This should be kept in mind while analyzing the test results and hence they should be taken with a pinch of salt. But testing helps us in gaining broader perspective about the performance of various patterns.

Let's begin with basic Point & Figure strategy. Table 9.1.1 shows back-testing numbers of basic bullish strategy, which is defined as Double Top Buy as an entry pattern and Double Bottom Sell as the exit formation. There are various box-values with which P&F charts can be plotted. Ten different box-values were considered, which were round numbers and sufficient to provide a broad idea. As stated earlier, testing is conducted on 500 stocks over 20 years of daily closing prices.

Table 9.1.1: Back-tested numbers of P&F bullish basic strategy on Nifty 500 stocks over 20 years of daily closing prices

Chart Parameter	Average Occurrence	Average Return	Risk-Reward Ratio	Success Ratio	Expectancy
0.25% x 3	133.92	6.47%	5.44	54.29%	2.50
0.50% x 3	92.94	7.91%	4.99	53.02%	2.18
0.75% x 3	68.34	9.58%	4.87	52.16%	2.06
1.00% x 3	52.67	11.45%	4.90	51.45%	2.03
1.25% x 3	41.81	13.51%	5.03	50.53%	2.05
1.50% x 3	34.28	15.64%	5.11	49.87%	2.05
1.75% x 3	28.54	18.66%	5.42	49.14%	2.15
2.00% x 3	24.16	22.09%	5.92	48.28%	2.34
3.00% x 3	13.55	41.08%	7.73	47.36%	3.13
5.00% x 3	6.34	97.43%	10.86	50.19%	4.95

Entry pattern: Double Top Buy
Exit pattern: Double Bottom Sell

Average occurrence is the average number of times the pattern has occurred over 500 stocks. Average return per occurrence increases with an increase in the box-value. This highlights the importance of simple breakouts on higher box-value charts. Expectancy is positive across the box-values, indicating the significance of consistently following the breakout strategy.

Table 9.1.2 shows the testing result of Bearish basic P&F strategy, meaning Double Bottom Sell as an entry pattern and Double Top Buy as exit formation.

Table 9.1.2: Back-tested numbers of P&F bullish basic strategy on Nifty 500 stocks over 20 years of daily closing prices

Chart Parameter	Average Occurrence	Average Return	Risk-Reward Ratio	Success Ratio	Expectancy
0.25% x 3	134.15	3.34%	3.59	50.39%	1.31
0.50% x 3	93.04	3.39%	3.06	47.58%	0.93
0.75% x 3	68.37	3.39%	2.72	46.02%	0.71
1.00% x 3	52.68	3.29%	2.47	44.78%	0.55
1.25% x 3	41.82	3.11%	2.29	43.77%	0.44
1.50% x 3	34.20	2.82%	2.15	42.61%	0.34
1.75% x 3	28.54	2.57%	2.01	42.31%	0.27
2.00% x 3	24.18	2.32%	1.91	41.86%	0.22
3.00% x 3	13.63	1.09%	1.64	40.60%	0.07
5.00% x 3	6.46	-2.29%	1.32	39.33%	-0.09

Entry pattern: Double Bottom Sell
Exit pattern: Double Top Buy

Though most of the box-values display positive expectancy, short setups are not as effective especially in higher box-value charts. This is because the inherent nature of the market is bullish and India has not seen a long-term structural bear market during the testing period of 20 years. It highlights that using exactly the opposite of what works for longs may not necessarily work for shorts. The numbers also suggest that bearish patterns on higher box-values are quite lagging; trader should prefer lower box-values while considering bearish setups. There is another reason for lackluster performance of bearish trades on higher box-values which is that the stock's downside is capped at zero which is the maximum possible outcome in a short trade. So, return-wise performance may not be as impressive compared to bullish trades.

Poles are reversal formations and can be utilized as an exit pattern. Table 9.1.3 presents the results to analyse when pole formation is considered as an alternative exit pattern to basic signals.

Table 9.1.3: Back-tested numbers of P&F basic strategies when Pole is applied as alternate exit on Nifty 500 stocks over 20 years of daily closing prices

Chart Parameter	Average Occurrence	Average Return	Risk-Reward Ratio	Success Ratio	Expectancy
0.25% x 3	168.86	5.65%	5.50	66.08%	3.30
0.50% x 3	117.01	6.68%	4.64	62.79%	2.54
0.75% x 3	85.76	7.87%	4.30	60.78%	2.22
1.00% x 3	66.07	9.12%	4.13	59.44%	2.05
1.25% x 3	52.47	10.47%	4.10	58.19%	1.97
1.50% x 3	42.82	11.87%	4.12	56.90%	1.91
1.75% x 3	35.69	13.62%	4.22	55.92%	1.92
2.00% x 3	30.07	15.97%	4.53	55.24%	2.05
3.00% x 3	16.84	28.35%	5.44	54.51%	2.51
5.00% x 3	7.92	54.78%	6.58	55.96%	3.24

Long Entry pattern: Double Top Buy
Long Exit pattern: Double Bottom Sell or High pole

Chart Parameter	Average Occurrence	Average Return	Risk-Reward Ratio	Success Ratio	Expectancy
0.25% x 3	164.51	3.48%	3.87	61.97%	2.02
0.50% x 3	112.65	3.58%	3.10	56.61%	1.32
0.75% x 3	81.59	3.68%	2.72	53.73%	1.00
1.00% x 3	62.20	3.70%	2.45	51.87%	0.79
1.25% x 3	49.10	3.68%	2.27	50.36%	0.65
1.50% x 3	39.78	3.59%	2.12	49.12%	0.53
1.75% x 3	33.10	3.45%	1.99	48.12%	0.44
2.00% x 3	27.92	3.30%	1.87	47.69%	0.37
3.00% x 3	15.84	2.33%	1.54	46.06%	0.17
5.00% x 3	7.31	-0.18%	1.27	43.72%	-0.01

Short Entry pattern: Double Bottom Sell
Short Exit pattern: Double Top Buy or Low Pole

Hit ratio improves when Poles are used as exit criteria. It increases the number of trades but also improves the average return per occurrence; therefore, it is effective especially for bearish setups. Thus, Low Pole as an exit tool for short trades should prove an effective method.

Using High Pole or low pole as an exit criteria along with any trend filtration tool would yield much better performance of these basic patterns. This is just an idea to explore further.

Column reversal is the most basic P&F formation. A question that would come to mind is: Can't a trader follow a simple strategy of trading upon column reversal? It may be difficult to implement such a strategy on lower box-values due to higher impact cost. But it is feasible on higher box-values.

Table 9.1.4 shows the test conducted for column reversal trading strategy. Box-values above 1% are displayed because of better feasibility.

Table 9.1.4: Back-tested numbers of P&F column reversal strategy on Nifty 500 stocks over 20 years of daily closing prices

Chart Parameter	Average Occurrence	Average Return	Risk-Reward Ratio	Success Ratio	Expectancy
1.00% x 3	232.35	5.82%	6.47	60.62%	3.53
1.25% x 3	186.89	6.24%	5.98	57.57%	3.02
1.50% x 3	153.95	6.69%	5.59	55.56%	2.66
1.75% x 3	129.28	7.15%	5.35	54.14%	2.44
2.00% x 3	110.10	7.65%	5.19	52.80%	2.27
3.00% x 3	64.12	10.31%	5.11	50.26%	2.07
5.00% x 3	30.53	17.47%	5.71	46.22%	2.10

Long Entry pattern: Positive Column Reversal
Long Exit pattern: Negative Column Reversal

Chart Parameter	Average Occurrence	Average Return	Risk-Reward Ratio	Success Ratio	Expectancy
1.00% x 3	232.48	3.88%	4.68	57.94%	2.29
1.25% x 3	187.08	3.87%	4.17	54.38%	1.81
1.50% x 3	154.15	3.84%	3.76	51.91%	1.47
1.75% x 3	129.48	3.80%	3.48	49.81%	1.23
2.00% x 3	110.31	3.74%	3.25	48.16%	1.05
3.00% x 3	64.39	3.54%	2.68	44.52%	0.64
5.00% x 3	30.74	2.48%	2.13	40.22%	0.26

Short Entry pattern: Negative Column Reversal
Short Exit pattern: Positive Column Reversal

Tests of bearish setups would improve if trend filtration is applied along with column reversal.

Pattern Performance

Below is the pie chart showing the occurrences of all P&F patterns except basic signals during the period of 20 years.

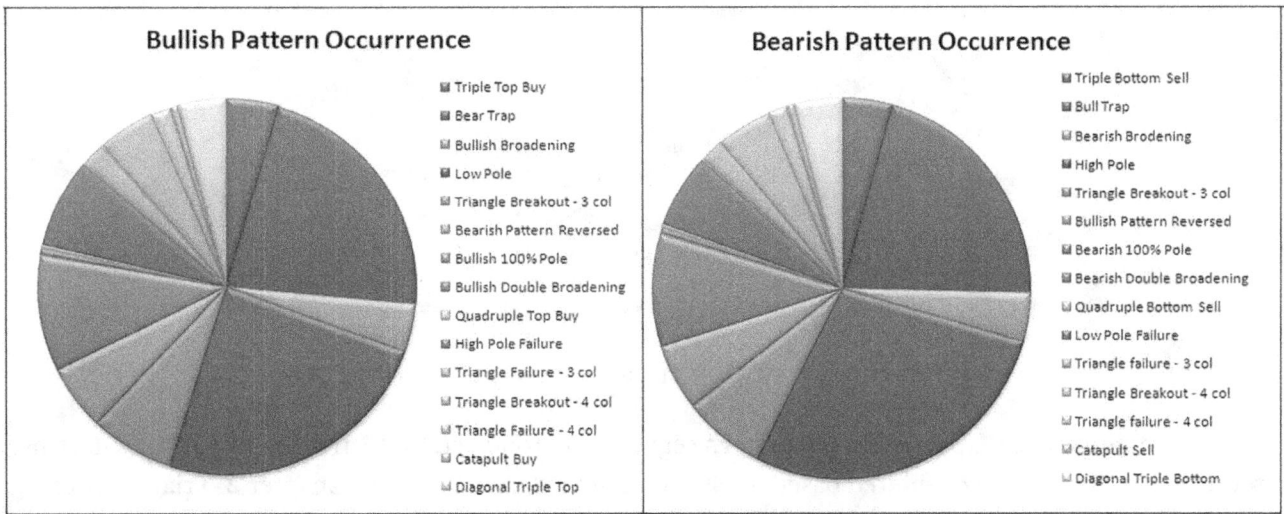

Image 9.1.1: Bullish and Bearish pattern occurrence pie chart

The chart shows that Traps and Poles are patterns that have a higher frequency of occurrence. I have considered all the major patterns that we have discussed in the pattern segment. Failure of Triangle and Pole is also considered simply because, as mentioned in the pattern segment, failure is a pattern and immediate failure of one pattern becomes another pattern. The pattern chart shown below can be referred to refresh your understanding of each pattern.

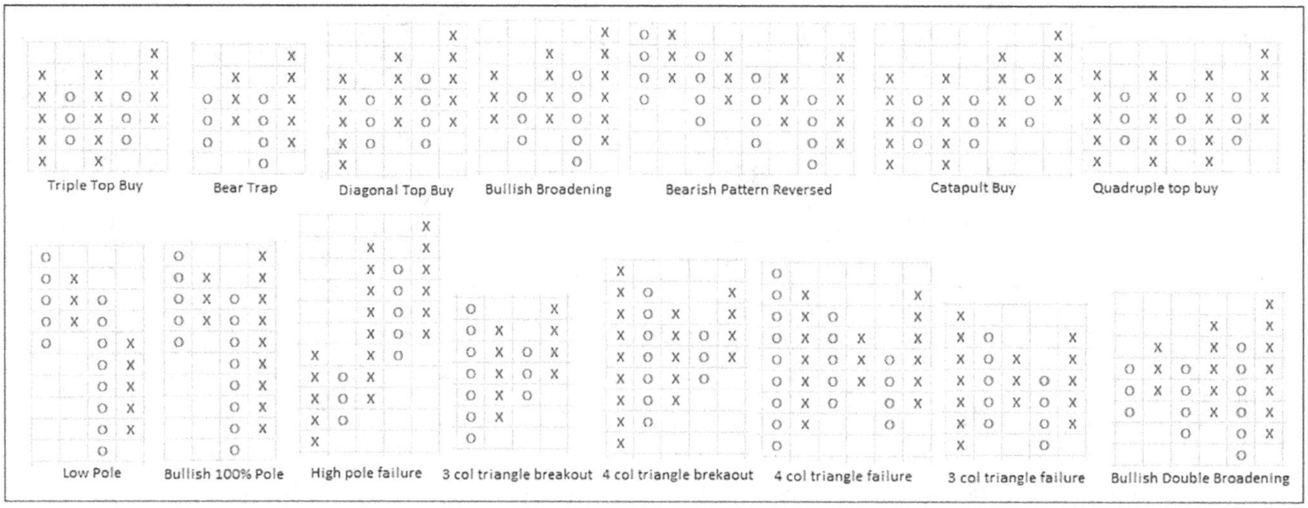

Image 9.1.2: Picture of bullish patterns shown in back-testing table

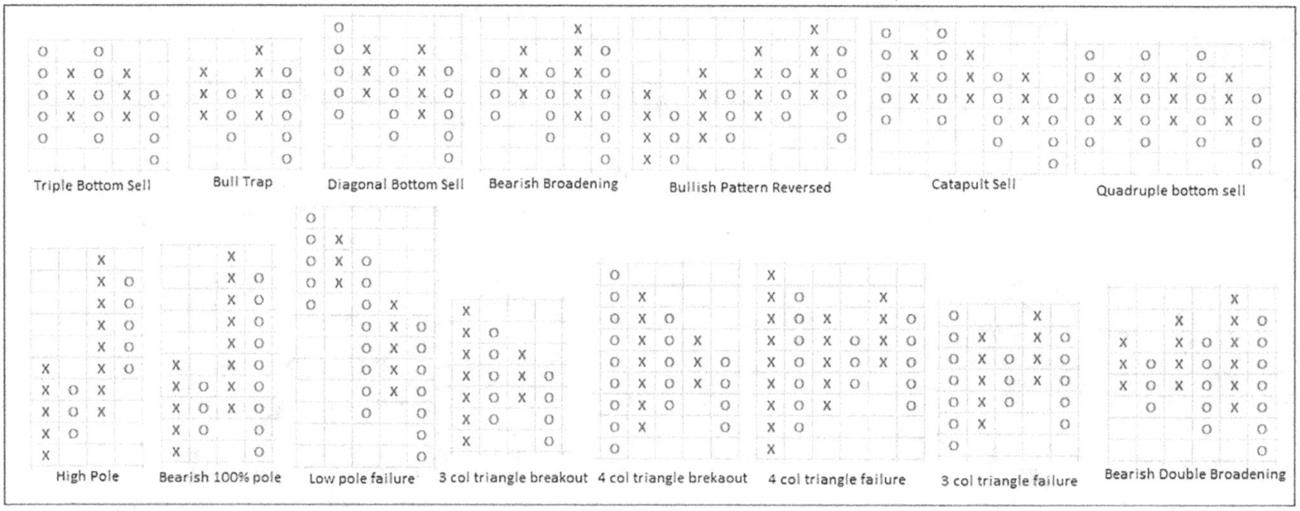

Image 9.1.3: Picture of bearish patterns shown in back-testing table

Pattern failure rules explained in the pattern segment are followed for testing them. For back-testing, a three-column Triangle is considered based on 50% column rule, explained in Chapter 2. Triangle breakout in subsequent column is also considered for testing. Sell signal after triangle breakout is considered as Triangle failure, which is also an entry signal.

The work on P&F would be incomplete without presenting the test results of patterns. But it is not an easy task, because there are multiple box-values and it is practically quite difficult to present the results spanning so many tables, showing the test results of each pattern. Moreover, it would be impossible to analyse so many tables. But it is important to test them on different box-values to analyse the consistency of pattern performance. So, for longs trades, each pattern is tested over eight different box-values: 0.25%, 0.50%, 0.75%, 1%, 1.25%, 1.50%, 1.75% and 2% on daily time-frame charts of Nifty 500 group of stocks. Based on the learning from the earlier testing that bearish trades should not be taken on higher box-values, for short trades, only the first four box-values have been considered for test purposes. This way, sample size becomes significant to analyse the results. Average numbers of testing across the box-values are shown in the tables and total occurrences in all the box-values put together are presented. The average of profitable trades are divided by the average of losing trades to calculate the risk–reward ratio. Importantly, average box return is shown in the tables to remain relevant and consistent across the box-value. Meaning, if average box return is 10, it has produced 2.5% average return on 0.25% box-value chart and 10% on 1% box-value chart.

For testing, the entry points are patterns shown in the above images. But testing can be conducted based on exit criteria. Table 9.1.5 shows the performance of bullish patterns when exit criterion is basic P&F Double Bottom Sell signal.

Table 9.1.5: Back-tested numbers of bullish P&F patterns on Nifty 500 stocks over 20 years of daily closing prices with Double Bottom Sell as exit criteria

Pattern	Total Occurrence	Average box return	Risk-Reward Ratio	Success Ratio	Expectancy
Triangle Breakout - 4 col	27467	13.46	6.18	51.13%	2.67
Quadruple Top Buy	1789	14.32	5.45	54.61%	2.53
Triangle Breakout - 3 col	40172	13.66	5.55	51.75%	2.39
Triple Top Buy	25703	13.44	5.33	52.72%	2.34
Catapult Buy	3972	12.73	5.18	53.68%	2.32
Diagonal Triple Top	22528	12.35	5.45	51.30%	2.31
Bullish Broadening	25024	16.83	4.58	57.81%	2.23
Bullish Double Broadening	3565	17.27	4.42	58.01%	2.14
Bear Trap	132708	14.55	4.56	54.49%	2.03
High Pole Failure	40982	13.96	4.24	57.12%	1.99
Triangle Failure - 3 col	13392	13.50	4.42	54.49%	1.95
Low Pole	146647	12.62	4.80	50.52%	1.93
Triangle Failure - 4 col	10372	12.54	4.37	52.91%	1.84
Bullish 100% Pole	60372	14.87	3.99	55.99%	1.79
Bearish Pattern Reversed	33784	13.00	4.26	52.36%	1.76

Patterns are shown in order of efficiency. What is important to observe in the above table is the positive expectancy in all the patterns. Bullish Broadening, Double Broadening and 100% Pole have produced maximum average return boxes.

Table 9.1.6 shows test results of bearish P&F formations.

Table 9.1.6: Back-tested numbers of bearish P&F patterns on Nifty 500 stocks over 20 years of daily closing prices with Double Bottom Sell as exit criteria

Pattern	Total Occurrence	Average box return	Risk-Reward Ratio	Success Ratio	Expectancy
Triangle Breakout - 4 col	20117	7.64	3.94	45.66%	1.25
Diagonal Triple Bottom	13753	6.94	3.48	44.99%	1.01
Catapult Sell	2235	7.93	3.29	46.94%	1.01
Triangle Breakout - 3 col	26782	6.95	3.26	46.09%	0.96
Quadruple Bottom Sell	1056	7.20	3.11	46.59%	0.92
Triangle failure - 4 col	7542	7.29	2.77	50.01%	0.88
Triangle failure - 3 col	8517	7.70	2.70	50.68%	0.87
Low Pole Failure	26939	8.27	2.54	52.67%	0.86
Triple Bottom Sell	15737	6.79	2.95	46.89%	0.85
High Pole	126661	6.61	2.75	48.04%	0.80
Bearish Broadening	18742	7.83	2.35	52.93%	0.78
Bull Trap	90926	7.10	2.49	50.30%	0.76
Bearish 100% Pole	46561	7.53	2.24	53.42%	0.73
Bearish Double Broadening	2670	7.10	2.18	53.30%	0.69
Bullish Pattern Reversed	24471	5.99	2.36	48.40%	0.63

Bearish breakout formations generate positive expectancy as well when they are exited based on Double Top Buy pattern. Numbers would improve further if Low Pole is included as an alternate exit method. Low Pole failure, Catapult Sell and Bearish Broadening have produced maximum average returns.

Note that, in this testing process, if the same pattern occurs when the earlier one is still active/open, then the recent occurrence is not considered for testing. The objective is to conduct the test across a significant sample size to assess their performance.

Pattern remains valid unless it gets negated. Usually, a pattern should be tested based on its performance of achieving certain target without being negated. So, profit stop is another method of testing the patterns; it is practically very difficult to test it in P&F method. For example, if 10% profit stop is determined as an exit criterion; it has got different relevance with box-value of 0.25% and that of 2%. The solution is that instead of making it as 10%, 10-box can be used as a profit stop to test the pattern. So if box-value is 1%, profit stop is 10% and if box-value is 0.50%, the profit stop will be 5%.

Table 9.1.7 shows the pattern performance numbers when 10-box profit stop or pattern negation, whichever comes early, is defined as exit criteria. With this method, we have put a limit on profits so risk–reward is going to be affected. Hence, the patterns are sorted based on success ratio with this method and expectancy is shown for observation.

Table 9.1.7: Back-tested numbers of bullish P&F patterns on Nifty 500 stocks over 20 years of daily closing prices with 10-box profit or pattern negation as exit criteria

Pattern	Total Occurrence	Average box return	Risk-Reward Ratio	Expectancy	Success Ratio
Bullish 100% Pole	58903	2.25	0.50	0.15	77.11%
Bullish Double Broadening	3558	3.35	0.57	0.20	76.59%
Bullish Broadening	24587	3.72	0.70	0.27	74.63%
Catapult Buy	3936	3.83	0.80	0.32	73.02%
High Pole Failure	44105	3.67	0.79	0.30	72.87%
Bear Trap	123349	3.11	0.80	0.26	70.02%
Triangle Failure - 3 col	13640	3.29	0.89	0.31	69.38%
Triangle Failure - 4 col	10348	2.99	0.86	0.27	68.61%
Bearish Pattern Reversed	33601	2.48	0.76	0.20	68.25%
Diagonal Triple Top	22948	3.39	0.95	0.32	67.90%
Quadruple Top Buy	1789	3.97	1.16	0.46	67.75%
Triple Top Buy	25683	3.46	1.04	0.36	66.78%
Low Pole	143281	2.57	0.94	0.26	65.00%
Triangle Breakout - 4 col	29596	3.66	1.44	0.53	62.64%
Triangle Breakout - 3 col	42155	3.27	1.32	0.45	62.37%

Success ratio column shows percentage of times patterns hit the profit stop without getting negated. Expectancy is positive across the formations. You can see impact on risk–reward because of limiting the profits, thought win ratio is reasonable. Triple, Quadruple Top and Triangle breakouts scored high on the expectancy parameter. Table below shows results of bearish P&F formations applied with 10-box criterion as profit stop.

Table 9.1.8: Back-tested numbers of bearish P&F patterns on Nifty 500 stocks over 20 years of daily closing prices with 10-box profit or pattern negation as exit criteria

Pattern	Total Occurrence	Average box return	Risk-Reward Ratio	Expectancy	Success Ratio
Bearish Double Broadening	2661	0.93	0.46	0.04	71.40%
Bearish 100% Pole	45081	0.80	0.47	0.04	70.92%
Bearish Broadening	18381	1.34	0.53	0.07	69.98%
Low Pole Failure	29089	1.66	0.58	0.10	69.67%
Bull Trap	84687	1.12	0.65	0.07	65.05%
Catapult Sell	2228	0.34	0.57	0.02	64.59%
Triangle failure - 4 col	7526	1.53	0.75	0.12	64.07%
Triangle failure - 3 col	8827	1.47	0.74	0.11	63.87%
Bullish Pattern Reversed	24334	0.59	0.65	0.03	62.47%
Diagonal Triple Bottom	13863	1.21	0.76	0.08	61.39%
Quadruple Bottom Sell	1055	1.40	0.81	0.10	60.66%
Triple Bottom Sell	15691	1.27	0.80	0.09	60.62%
High Pole	122847	1.18	0.82	0.10	60.31%
Triangle Breakout - 4 col	21518	2.66	1.30	0.32	57.62%
Triangle Breakout - 3 col	27812	1.87	1.13	0.21	56.62%

Triangles have performed well in this category too. Broadening pattern and 100% Pole have the maximum success ratio. Due to the limited downside, lower expectancy is expected on bearish setups when profit exit strategy is applied.

Ten-box is used as a round number for profit stop, just to provide a perspective; it can be tested with any other profit stop criterion. We considered pattern negation as an alternative exit in the above approach. But it may not be completely appropriate because the length of the pattern can be wide, making the initial risk unaffordable, which can logically skew the risk–reward ratio.

How about testing patterns from risk–reward perspective rather than the profit stop? Instead of taking a 10-box profit stop as an exit criterion, it can be correlated with the risk while initiating. Patterns can be tested based on risk–reward. So, if risk–reward task is 1:2, and if initial risk is 10-box, profit stop becomes 20-box. If initial risk is 5-box, profit stop becomes 10-box.

Table 9.1.9 shows the performance of bullish patterns with risk–reward as 2.

Table 9.1.9: Back-tested numbers of bullish P&F patterns on Nifty 500 stocks over 20 years of daily closing prices with 1:2 risk–reward or pattern negation as exit criteria

Pattern	Total Occurrence	Average box return	Risk-Reward Ratio	Expectancy	Success Ratio
Triangle Breakout - 4 col	29486	3.57	1.55	0.54	60.64%
Quadruple Top Buy	1774	5.95	1.80	0.65	59.02%
Triangle Breakout - 3 col	41670	3.96	1.61	0.51	57.95%
Catapult Buy	3842	9.44	1.92	0.69	57.94%
Triple Top Buy	24882	6.19	1.78	0.59	57.38%
High Pole Failure	40527	7.62	1.83	0.62	57.10%
Bullish Broadening	23143	9.14	1.91	0.65	56.65%
Diagonal Triple Top	22141	6.49	1.78	0.58	56.62%
Triangle Failure - 3 col	12962	6.32	1.74	0.54	56.42%
Triangle Failure - 4 col	10205	5.36	1.66	0.47	55.19%
Bullish Double Broadening	3494	9.58	1.87	0.58	55.12%
Bear Trap	106025	6.65	1.78	0.53	55.08%
Bullish 100% Pole	51908	8.76	1.86	0.54	53.77%
Low Pole	132416	4.29	1.69	0.43	53.11%
Bearish Pattern Reversed	32516	5.47	1.69	0.43	52.94%

It is apparent from the above table that exit based on risk–reward parameters (also known as R-Multiple by Van Tharp) should be preferred over arbitrary rules of booking profits.

Table 9.1.10 shows the performance of bearish patterns with risk–reward as 2.

Table 9.1.10: Back-tested numbers of bearish P&F patterns on Nifty 500 stocks over 20 years of daily closing prices with 1:2 risk–reward or pattern negation as exit criteria

Pattern	Total Occurrence	Average box return	Risk-Reward Ratio	Expectancy	Success Ratio
Triangle Breakout - 4 col	21360	2.92	1.53	0.37	54.07%
Triangle Breakout - 3 col	27246	2.65	1.59	0.26	48.66%
Triangle failure - 4 col	7392	2.43	1.60	0.16	44.75%
High Pole	105956	1.77	1.57	0.13	43.89%
Triangle failure - 3 col	8212	2.42	1.61	0.14	43.56%
Low Pole Failure	25308	2.79	1.64	0.15	43.50%
Quadruple Bottom Sell	1044	1.42	1.49	0.08	43.39%
Triple Bottom Sell	14862	1.87	1.57	0.10	42.92%
Diagonal Triple Bottom	13157	1.77	1.62	0.09	41.52%
Bull Trap	66449	1.31	1.59	0.06	41.03%
Bearish Broadening	16578	1.17	1.63	0.05	39.82%
Bullish Pattern Reversed	23189	0.52	1.57	0.02	39.66%
Bearish 100% Pole	36631	0.46	1.64	0.03	38.87%
Catapult Sell	2138	1.17	1.73	0.03	37.79%
Bearish Double Broadening	2586	-1.50	1.60	-0.07	35.92%

Many bearish patterns have posted negative returns. The major reason is the restriction on moving the stop-loss lower, especially when charts are plotted with higher box-values. Hence, it suggests that profit exit for bearish setups needs to be more aggressive.

The various methods of testing the patterns using multiple methods of exits were discussed to help readers gain a different perspective and flavor. The exit based on basic patterns shows better results mainly because of the trailing mechanism that helps riding strong trends.

Traps, Poles and Patterns reversed formation have higher occurrence; hence, filtration technique can improve their performance. We discussed the concept and importance of Follow-through. Table 9.1.11 shows the performance of basic patterns that occurred after major patterns that can help us to analyse if using such filters are worthwhile.

Table 9.1.11: Back-tested numbers of P&F follow-through patterns on Nifty 500 stocks over 20 years of daily closing prices with Double Bottom Sell as exit criteria

Double Top Buy followed after					
Pattern	Total Occurrence	Average box return	Risk-Reward Ratio	Success Ratio	Expectancy
100% Pole	27444	14.82	5.43	54.38%	2.50
Bullish Broadening	11658	14.21	5.33	55.02%	2.48
Bear Trap	60495	14.22	5.35	53.73%	2.41
Low Pole	65640	14.01	5.29	52.64%	2.31
Bearish Pattern Reversed	15478	13.44	5.26	51.32%	2.21

Double Bottom Sell followed after					
Pattern	Total Occurrence	Average box return	Risk-Reward Ratio	Success Ratio	Expectancy
100% Pole	21299	8.26	3.30	49.28%	1.12
Bearish Broadening	8355	8.03	3.23	48.75%	1.06
High Pole	56237	7.58	3.20	48.35%	1.03
Bull Trap	40243	7.81	3.21	48.25%	1.03
Bullish Pattern Reversed	10884	7.46	3.19	47.40%	0.99

Basic signals as exit criteria are shown in the table above. Risk–reward, hence efficiency, improves a lot when Follow-through signals are traded, especially for bearish setups.

For long trades, profit exit techniques improve the success rate significantly, but at the cost of a moderate risk–reward ratio. But, trades exited based on risk–reward method have yielded superior results. Riding method and exiting based on patterns can generate a lot of money because they deliver maximum returns during a trending phase.

Each method has its own pros and cons and one may adopt what suits one's personal preference. Techniques can be altered as per the market phases; profit stop or risk–reward technique may work better during non-trending phases or when markets are at extreme zones. Trailing the stop-loss to ride the trend is a very successful approach to trading, but very difficult to follow for most of traders. Psychologically, it is very difficult to sit on profitable trades and strangely enough holding on losers seems more comfortable task for traders. Beginners can start with profit booking methods, and gradually move toward trend-riding methods. For bearish trades, trend filtration and aggressive exit method seem to be important.

Performance of bearish setups would improve further if box-values used for testing are reduced to 2 from 4. Meaning, the lower the box-value, the better is the performance. Using the follow-through patterns for entry and exiting trades using pole as a criteria proves very effective for bearish strategies. This learning can help us in treating the bullish and bearish setups differently and adapt accordingly while dealing with them. This can help improve the overall profitability.

I decided to avoid optimization here. Obvious and round numbers are chosen to conduct the tests to help understand the basis and explore it further. There is an issue with respect to impact cost, but even factoring that, the methods listed above will turn out to be profitable. Analysis and experience can help better the performance. We discussed how we can design P&F setups in the chapter on system building; all such setups can be back-tested to analyse their past performance. Tables are presented to get an idea about conducting such back-tests. Different parameters and indicators can be applied which may improve the performance further. By using a trend filter tool, the number of trades will be reduced and the profitability will improve. But I am restricting the discussion to traditional P&F patterns here. It would turn out to be a very lengthy discussion if I get into a testing of trading systems on P&F; it may warrant a separate book to discuss it thoroughly.

The next section shows the tables capturing the results of the test conducted on charts plotted with the High–Low technique.

9.2: HIGH–LOW

Technique of plotting and analyzing High–Low charts were discussed in Chapter 5. High–low charts are horizontal in nature; hence, basic signals are not applicable on them. To avoid the presentation of unnecessary tables, we will move to testing the pattern performance based on profit exit methods because exit based on basic signals is not applicable on these charts. Box-values, stock group and method of testing are kept same.

Tables 9.2.1 and 9.2.2 show the performance of the pattern with the exit rule of 10-box in favor without negating the pattern.

Table 9.2.1: Back-tested numbers of bullish P&F patterns on Nifty 500 stocks over 20 years of daily High–Low prices with 10-box profit or pattern negation as exit criteria

Pattern	Total Occurrence	Average box return	Risk-Reward Ratio	Expectancy	Success Ratio
Bullish Double Broadening	8092	1.36	0.56	0.08	69.20%
Bullish 100% Pole	102970	0.50	0.51	0.02	68.02%
Bullish Broadening	49623	1.42	0.69	0.10	65.42%
High Pole Failure	98647	1.29	0.69	0.10	64.86%
Catapult Buy	17062	2.16	0.87	0.20	63.81%
Bear Trap	250784	0.97	0.79	0.08	60.37%
Triangle Failure - 3 col	52831	1.22	0.85	0.11	60.02%
Triangle Failure - 4 col	34660	0.88	0.80	0.08	59.91%
Low Pole	341918	1.13	0.87	0.11	59.56%
Diagonal Triple Top	65223	1.98	1.02	0.19	59.07%
Bearish Pattern Reversed	63435	0.46	0.78	0.04	58.35%
Triple Top Buy	78966	1.74	1.12	0.19	56.24%
Quadruple Top Buy	9223	1.78	1.24	0.22	54.38%
Triangle Breakout - 3 col	152160	1.29	1.18	0.16	53.20%
Triangle Breakout - 4 col	74724	1.37	1.22	0.18	53.20%

Table 9.2.2: Back-tested numbers of bearish P&F patterns on Nifty 500 stocks over 20 years of High–Low prices with 10-box profit or pattern negation as exit criteria

Pattern	Total Occurrence	Average box return	Risk-Reward Ratio	Expectancy	Success Ratio
Bearish 100% Pole	78165	-2.03	0.40	-0.09	65.24%
Bearish Double Broadening	5454	-2.48	0.40	-0.10	63.83%
Low Pole Failure	73952	-0.93	0.51	-0.05	62.82%
Bearish Broadening	37981	-1.59	0.49	-0.08	61.36%
High Pole	281582	0.04	0.72	0.00	57.93%
Catapult Sell	9963	-1.25	0.59	-0.08	57.51%
Bull Trap	157559	-1.49	0.58	-0.09	57.17%
Triangle failure - 3 col	32836	-1.16	0.64	-0.08	56.00%
Triangle failure - 4 col	25028	-1.06	0.67	-0.08	55.38%
Bullish Pattern Reversed	37207	-1.80	0.59	-0.12	55.30%
Diagonal Triple Bottom	37792	-0.98	0.77	-0.09	51.60%
Triple Bottom Sell	45046	-0.86	0.80	-0.09	50.54%
Triangle Breakout - 4 col	56630	0.11	1.02	0.00	49.59%
Triangle Breakout - 3 col	105704	-0.53	0.92	-0.06	48.86%
Quadruple Bottom Sell	5069	-0.45	0.90	-0.07	48.77%

Success ratio is better but risk–reward and expectancy are not very encouraging for bullish trades. Returns on bearish trades are negative. Let's see if there is any improvement when exit based on risk–reward ratio is implemented.

Tables 9.2.3 and 9.2.4 show the performance of patterns when risk–reward of 1:2 is applied as exit rule.

Table 9.2.3: Back-tested numbers of bullish P&F patterns on Nifty 500 stocks over 20 years of daily High–Low prices with 1:2 risk–reward or pattern negation as exit criteria

Pattern	Total Occurrence	Average box return	Risk-Reward Ratio	Expectancy	Success Ratio
Catapult Buy	16440	6.22	1.91	0.44	49.41%
Quadruple Top Buy	9165	3.52	1.73	0.32	48.25%
Diagonal Triple Top	61105	4.12	1.84	0.35	47.52%
Triple Top Buy	74963	3.48	1.79	0.31	46.98%
Bullish Double Broadening	7866	6.00	1.91	0.36	46.69%
Triangle Breakout - 4 col	73662	1.75	1.64	0.22	46.02%
Bullish Broadening	45661	4.52	1.87	0.30	45.41%
Triangle Breakout - 3 col	147022	1.86	1.66	0.20	45.09%
Triangle Failure - 3 col	50275	2.93	1.77	0.24	44.71%
High Pole Failure	84669	3.54	1.86	0.27	44.33%
Bear Trap	198226	3.01	1.83	0.22	43.20%
Triangle Failure - 4 col	27702	2.17	1.73	0.18	43.13%
Low Pole	286886	1.86	1.73	0.17	42.82%
Bullish 100% Pole	84325	3.93	1.92	0.22	41.66%
Bearish Pattern Reversed	60221	2.36	1.83	0.17	41.41%

Table 9.2.4: Back-tested numbers of bearish P&F patterns on Nifty 500 stocks over 20 years of daily High–Low prices with 1:2 risk–reward or pattern negation as exit criteria

Pattern	Total Occurrence	Average box return	Risk-Reward Ratio	Expectancy	Success Ratio
Triangle Breakout - 4 col	55153	0.02	1.69	-0.01	36.77%
Triangle Breakout - 3 col	99046	-1.15	1.67	-0.11	33.44%
High Pole	205911	-1.57	1.61	-0.11	34.10%
Quadruple Bottom Sell	4969	-1.54	1.62	-0.15	32.54%
Triple Bottom Sell	40749	-2.45	1.67	-0.17	31.05%
Triangle failure - 4 col	18781	-2.88	1.73	-0.17	30.28%
Low Pole Failure	56625	-3.60	1.74	-0.18	30.13%
Triangle failure - 3 col	30383	-3.34	1.71	-0.19	29.94%
Diagonal Triple Bottom	34452	-2.72	1.71	-0.19	29.84%
Catapult Sell	9347	-5.07	1.71	-0.23	28.53%
Bullish Pattern Reversed	34567	-4.60	1.69	-0.24	28.26%
Bull Trap	386581	-4.92	1.64	-0.24	28.68%
Bearish Broadening	31844	-5.79	1.71	-0.25	27.69%
Bearish 100% Pole	55790	-7.27	1.72	-0.28	26.43%
Bearish Double Broadening	5221	-8.64	1.60	-0.31	26.43%

The results of the bullish trades are much better, but the performance of bearish patterns is not encouraging; hence, they should be avoided on these charts. It is an important takeaway that back-testing must also throw up ideas about what should not be done.

Performance of bullish patterns will improve if higher box-values are used. Though positive expectancy of bullish setups with risk–reward as exit method makes them practically usable, it is advisable to trade based on charts plotted with the closing price method. The High–Low charts can be utilized to fine-tune entry in real time and the focus can then shift to charts plotted with closing prices.

Notice performance of bullish multi-column breakout formations in the table above. High–Low charts are comparatively wider in nature; hence, multi-column breakout strategies are more relevant on them. The Turtle type of multi-column breakout method that we discussed in Chapter 2 can be followed on High–Low charts for bullish setups. I tested a few combinations of them for bullish formations on different higher box-values from long-only approach; below is a summary of their back-tested numbers.

Table 9.2.5: Summary of back-tested numbers of bullish P&F multi-column patterns on 1.50%, 2%, 3% and 5% box-value charts of Nifty 500 group of stocks over 20 years of daily High–Low prices

Entry pattern	Exit pattern	Total Occurrence	Average box return	Risk-Reward Ratio	Success Ratio	Expectancy
20 'X' breakout	10 'O' breakdown	8630	39.80	8.47	49.83%	3.72
15 'X' breakout	10 'O' breakdown	9936	39.08	8.68	48.21%	3.67
15 'X' breakout	5 'O' breakdown	16305	17.93	5.81	46.71%	2.18
10 'X' breakout	5 'O' breakdown	19966	17.70	5.91	44.94%	2.11
10 'X' breakout	3 'O' breakdown	28902	7.77	4.20	43.20%	1.24
5 'X' breakout	3 'O' breakdown	41473	7.11	4.17	40.92%	1.12

Their performance is better than the usual patterns; hence if one wants to develop strategies on High–Low charts, they better be based on multi-column breakout setups. Subjective analysis and indicators can improve the performance of the setups in the High–Low charts. Methods such as moving average crossovers, convergence, etc., with an indicator-filter will improve the outcome rather than simple P&F formations on them.

9.3: OTHER REVERSAL VALUE BACK-TESTING

All testing results presented so far are on three-box reversal charts. Tables 9.3.1 and 9.3.2 show the performance of basic P&F strategy on two-box and five-box reversal charts.

Two-Box Charts

Table 9.3.1: Back-tested numbers of P&F basic strategy on two-box reversal charts on Nifty 500 stocks over 20 years of daily closing prices

Chart Parameter	Average Occurrence	Average Return	Risk-Reward Ratio	Success Ratio	Expectancy
0.25% x 2	148.05	6.16%	5.63	54.90%	2.64
0.50% x 2	111.47	7.11%	5.17	53.31%	2.29
0.75% x 2	86.44	8.25%	4.92	52.75%	2.12
1.00% x 2	69.27	9.48%	4.85	52.16%	2.05
1.25% x 2	56.72	10.83%	4.87	51.56%	2.03
1.50% x 2	47.60	12.29%	4.94	50.87%	2.02
1.75% x 2	40.48	13.71%	4.97	50.33%	2.01
2.00% x 2	34.95	15.57%	5.21	49.68%	2.09
3.00% x 2	21.34	25.59%	6.29	47.91%	2.49
5.00% x 2	10.16	54.54%	8.41	47.86%	3.51

Entry pattern: Double Top Buy
Exit pattern: Double Bottom Sell

Chart Parameter	Average Occurrence	Average Return	Risk-Reward Ratio	Success Ratio	Expectancy
0.25% x 2	148.29	3.33%	3.81	51.34%	1.47
0.50% x 2	111.65	3.36%	3.31	48.46%	1.09
0.75% x 2	86.54	3.39%	2.98	46.99%	0.87
1.00% x 2	69.27	3.38%	2.76	45.74%	0.72
1.25% x 2	56.74	3.33%	2.58	44.73%	0.60
1.50% x 2	47.60	3.20%	2.41	43.91%	0.50
1.75% x 2	40.51	3.01%	2.29	42.97%	0.41
2.00% x 2	34.91	2.91%	2.19	42.61%	0.36
3.00% x 2	21.38	1.99%	1.86	40.89%	0.17
5.00% x 2	10.38	-0.38%	1.55	38.43%	-0.02

Entry pattern: Double Bottom Sell
Exit pattern: Double Top Buy

Five-Box Charts

Table 9.3.2: Back-tested numbers of P&F basic strategy on five-box reversal charts on Nifty 500 stocks over 20 years of daily closing prices

Chart Parameter	Average Occurrence	Average Return	Risk-Reward Ratio	Success Ratio	Expectancy
0.25% x 5	110.05	7.17%	5.16	53.52%	2.30
0.50% x 5	67.55	9.66%	4.85	52.38%	2.06
0.75% x 5	45.91	12.63%	4.93	51.20%	2.04
1.00% x 5	33.50	16.04%	5.18	49.90%	2.08
1.25% x 5	25.51	21.03%	5.72	49.09%	2.30
1.50% x 5	20.01	27.03%	6.37	48.09%	2.54
1.75% x 5	16.12	33.30%	6.84	47.79%	2.75
2.00% x 5	13.21	42.77%	7.77	47.78%	3.19
3.00% x 5	7.12	88.87%	10.44	50.18%	4.74
5.00% x 5	3.31	194.96%	15.47	50.77%	7.36

Entry pattern: Double Top Buy
Exit pattern: Double Bottom Sell

Chart Parameter	Average Occurrence	Average Return	Risk-Reward Ratio	Success Ratio	Expectancy
0.25% x 5	110.21	3.36%	3.26	48.90%	1.08
0.50% x 5	67.57	3.39%	2.69	46.19%	0.70
0.75% x 5	45.90	3.20%	2.35	44.40%	0.49
1.00% x 5	33.56	2.82%	2.12	42.84%	0.34
1.25% x 5	25.55	2.54%	1.91	42.82%	0.25
1.50% x 5	20.02	1.98%	1.79	41.68%	0.16
1.75% x 5	16.15	1.44%	1.70	40.93%	0.11
2.00% x 5	13.33	0.96%	1.63	40.37%	0.06
3.00% x 5	7.28	-1.32%	1.39	39.53%	-0.06
5.00% x 5	3.45	-13.47%	0.87	36.39%	-0.32

Entry pattern: Double Bottom Sell
Exit pattern: Double Top Buy

The five-box reversal method comes across as more effective bullish strategy compared to three-box reversal while the two-box reversal charts looks interesting for bearish setups.

Open trades are not considered for calculation, which may have impacted the numbers of higher box-values. For example, Double Top Buy signal which came in Bajaj Auto at 284 in 3% × 5 chart during March 2009 did not generate Sell signal till 31st December 2015 when it was trading above 2500. But the trade is not considered for calculation as it is open till the end of the testing period.

9.4: NIFTY-50 INDEX

As discussed in the pattern segment, behavior of index is different than that of stock. It may be incorrect to assume that same kind of results would be generated when tests are conducted on an index such as Nifty-50. In this section, back-testing numbers of pattern performance on Nifty-50 index are presented.

Nifty is an actively traded instrument in the derivatives segment. Tables are presented in this section showing different tests on Nifty; it might help one analyse the numbers independently.

Testing is conducted on spot price of Nifty, and box-values starting from 0.15% are considered as we are discussing an index and not individual stocks. Table 9.4.1 shows the test results with basic Buy and Sell signals when traded on daily charts of Nifty.

Table 9.4.1: Back-tested numbers of P&F basic strategy on Nifty 50 index price over 20 years of daily closing prices

Chart Parameter	Average Occurrence	Average Return	Risk Reward Ratio	Success Ratio	Expectancy
0.15% x 3	196.00	3.22%	3.94	57.14%	1.83
0.25% x 3	150.00	3.52%	3.69	55.33%	1.60
0.50% x 3	93.00	4.65%	3.54	52.69%	1.39
0.75% x 3	58.00	6.62%	3.27	56.90%	1.43
1.00% x 3	49.00	6.16%	3.18	53.06%	1.22
1.25% x 3	38.00	7.21%	4.48	44.74%	1.45
1.50% x 3	28.00	11.04%	7.16	32.14%	1.62
1.75% x 3	19.00	16.74%	5.17	47.37%	1.92
2.00% x 3	17.00	17.22%	4.14	52.94%	1.72
3.00% x 3	7.00	39.60%	5.80	57.14%	2.89

Entry pattern: Double Top Buy
Exit pattern: Double Bottom Sell

Chart Parameter	Average Occurrence	Average Return	Risk Reward Ratio	Success Ratio	Expectancy
0.15% x 3	196.00	1.73%	3.24	50.00%	1.12
0.25% x 3	150.00	1.56%	2.60	47.33%	0.70
0.50% x 3	92.00	1.51%	2.30	45.65%	0.51
0.75% x 3	58.00	1.46%	1.91	46.55%	0.35
1.00% x 3	48.00	0.36%	1.69	39.58%	0.07
1.25% x 3	37.00	-0.07%	1.16	45.95%	-0.01
1.50% x 3	27.00	-0.80%	0.98	44.44%	-0.12
1.75% x 3	18.00	0.50%	1.80	38.89%	0.09
2.00% x 3	16.00	-1.09%	1.73	31.25%	-0.15
3.00% x 3	7.00	0.27%	2.58	28.57%	0.02

Entry pattern: Double Bottom Sell
Exit pattern: Double Top Buy

Bearish patterns in index are less profitable than the stocks, simply because chances of index falling to zero are far less than a stock falling to zero.

Pattern performance in index may vary when compared to stocks. To derive the average numbers for testing, patterns that occurred on 0.15%, 0.25%, 0.50%, 0.75%, 1%, 1.25%, 1.50% and 1.75% box-values of daily prices are considered for bullish patterns, and the first four box-values are considered for the bearish patterns.

Tables 9.4.2 and 9.4.3 show the performance of patterns on Nifty with exit based on basic patterns.

Table 9.4.2: Back-tested numbers of bullish P&F patterns on Nifty 50 index price over 20 years of daily closing prices with Double Bottom Sell as exit criteria

Pattern	Total Occurrence	Average box return	Risk-Reward Ratio	Success Ratio	Expectancy
Quadruple Top Buy	3	9.38	-	100.00%	-
Triangle Failure - 4 col	9	18.33	8.78	77.78%	6.60
Triangle Failure - 3 col	17	14.08	5.45	70.59%	3.55
Triple Top Buy	60	12.58	4.70	66.67%	2.80
Low Pole	386	10.68	4.24	53.63%	1.81
Diagonal Triple Top	51	7.32	3.54	58.82%	1.67
Bullish 100% Pole	181	12.02	3.02	62.98%	1.53
Bullish Broadening	87	8.80	3.54	55.17%	1.51
Bear Trap	367	10.30	3.21	56.95%	1.40
High Pole Failure	106	7.69	3.41	48.11%	1.12
Triangle Breakout - 3 col	77	4.73	2.76	49.35%	0.86
Bearish Pattern Reversed	115	6.13	2.24	53.04%	0.72
Triangle Breakout - 4 col	60	3.37	2.82	41.67%	0.59
Catapult Buy	7	-2.25	2.73	28.57%	0.07
Bullish Double Broadening	16	-0.22	1.05	43.75%	-0.10

Table 9.4.3: Back-tested numbers of bearish P&F patterns on Nifty 50 index price over 20 years of daily closing prices with Double Bottom Sell as exit criteria

Pattern	Total Occurrence	Average box return	Risk Reward Ratio	Success Ratio	Expectancy
Triangle Breakout - 4 col	26	11.87	3.94	65.39%	2.23
Quadruple Bottom Sell	7	41.52	2.61	71.43%	1.58
Diagonal Triple Bottom	36	7.31	4.58	44.44%	1.48
Triangle Breakout - 3 col	47	9.67	3.13	57.45%	1.37
Bullish Pattern Reversed	115	6.84	2.83	50.43%	0.93
High Pole	332	7.06	2.53	51.80%	0.83
Bearish 100% Pole	169	4.56	2.07	52.66%	0.62
Bull Trap	321	5.12	2.36	47.67%	0.60
Low Pole Failure	86	4.77	2.38	45.35%	0.53
Triangle failure - 4 col	31	5.52	2.11	48.39%	0.51
Bearish Broadening	60	2.46	1.97	45.00%	0.33
Triple Bottom Sell	39	3.32	1.86	43.59%	0.25
Bearish Double Broadening	15	0.78	2.63	33.33%	0.21
Triangle failure - 3 col	20	2.90	1.38	40.00%	-0.05
Catapult Sell	2	-8.08	-	0.00%	-

Triangle failure and multi-column breakout formations seem most successful patterns on daily chart of Nifty index. Four-column Triangle and multi-column Sell have been most successful bearish formations.

Notice that bullish pattern reversed have performed better than Bull Trap on these charts. Broadenings are not very profitable when applied to index. A few formations have fewer instances of occurrence. Tables 9.4.4 through 9.4.7 show the performance of patterns when profit exit strategies are applied.

Table 9.4.4: Back-tested numbers of bullish P&F patterns on Nifty 50 index price over 20 years of daily closing prices with 10-box profit or pattern negation as exit criteria

Pattern	Total Occurrence	Average box return	Risk-Reward Ratio	Expectancy	Success Ratio
Quadruple Top Buy	3	10.00	-	-	100.00%
Triangle Failure - 4 col	9	10.00	-	-	100.00%
Triangle Failure - 3 col	17	7.09	1.21	0.82	82.35%
Bullish 100% Pole	172	3.00	0.51	0.19	78.49%
Diagonal Triple Top	52	4.88	0.86	0.39	75.00%
Triple Top Buy	60	4.81	1.43	0.70	70.00%
Bullish Broadening	83	1.24	0.72	0.18	68.68%
Low Pole	376	2.79	0.88	0.28	68.35%
Bear Trap	377	1.83	0.68	0.14	67.91%
Bearish Pattern Reversed	114	0.98	0.60	0.07	66.67%
High Pole Failure	118	1.48	0.73	0.09	62.71%
Triangle Breakout - 3 col	77	2.79	1.19	0.37	62.34%
Triangle Breakout - 4 col	60	3.86	1.78	0.49	53.33%
Catapult Buy	7	0.04	0.61	-0.31	42.86%
Bullish Double Broadening	16	-9.56	0.26	-0.53	37.50%

Table 9.4.5: Back-tested numbers of bearish P&F patterns on Nifty 50 index price over 20 years of daily closing prices with 10-box profit or pattern negation as exit criteria

Pattern	Total Occurrence	Average box return	Risk-Reward Ratio	Expectancy	Success Ratio
Quadruple Bottom Sell	7	10.00	-	-	100.00%
Triangle Breakout - 4 col	28	5.39	1.13	0.68	78.57%
Bearish 100% Pole	163	0.84	0.46	0.09	74.85%
Bullish Pattern Reversed	114	3.54	0.77	0.27	71.93%
Bearish Double Broadening	14	14.19	0.84	0.31	71.43%
Bull Trap	330	2.04	0.64	0.16	70.91%
Bearish Broadening	58	1.74	0.60	0.10	68.96%
Diagonal Triple Bottom	36	2.25	0.56	0.04	66.67%
Triple Bottom Sell	41	2.37	1.12	0.39	65.85%
Triangle Breakout - 3 col	48	1.82	0.75	0.13	64.58%
Triangle failure - 4 col	31	-1.48	0.46	-0.06	64.52%
Low Pole Failure	95	1.24	0.74	0.10	63.16%
High Pole	328	1.65	0.83	0.15	63.11%
Triangle failure - 3 col	20	-1.75	0.37	-0.18	60.00%
Catapult Sell	2	-2.64	0.65	-0.17	50.00%

Table 9.4.6: Back-tested numbers of bullish P&F patterns on Nifty 50 index price over 20 years of daily closing prices with 1:2 risk–reward or pattern negation as exit criteria

Pattern	Total Occurrence	Average box return	Risk-Reward Ratio	Expectancy	Success Ratio
Triangle Failure - 3 col	17	10.29	2.72	1.63	70.59%
Triangle Failure - 4 col	9	15.24	5.05	3.03	66.67%
Triangle Breakout - 3 col	77	3.89	1.50	0.46	58.44%
Triple Top Buy	57	10.98	3.18	1.35	56.14%
Low Pole	330	5.35	1.87	0.56	54.24%
Diagonal Triple Top	49	5.53	1.86	0.52	53.06%
Triangle Breakout - 4 col	60	4.02	2.07	0.58	51.67%
Bullish 100% Pole	153	7.93	2.00	0.53	50.98%
Bear Trap	283	5.32	1.86	0.41	49.47%
Bearish Pattern Reversed	108	5.07	1.82	0.39	49.07%
Catapult Buy	7	19.21	2.05	0.31	42.86%
High Pole Failure	106	2.45	1.72	0.13	41.51%
Bullish Broadening	78	0.72	1.80	0.11	39.74%
Bullish Double Broadening	16	-14.46	0.81	-0.89	6.25%
Quadruple Top Buy	3	-13.19	-	-	0.00%

Table 9.4.7: Back-tested numbers of bearish P&F patterns on Nifty 50 index price over 20 years of daily closing prices with 1:2 risk–reward or pattern negation as exit criteria

Pattern	Total Occurrence	Average box return	Risk-Reward Ratio	Expectancy	Success Ratio
Quadruple Bottom Sell	7	20.17	-	-	100.00%
Triangle Breakout - 4 col	28	8.52	1.42	0.99	82.14%
Triangle Breakout - 3 col	48	4.55	1.06	0.33	64.58%
High Pole	312	3.43	1.44	0.30	53.20%
Triangle failure - 4 col	31	4.16	1.46	0.27	51.61%
Catapult Sell	2	21.34	3.79	1.40	50.00%
Triangle failure - 3 col	20	2.64	0.98	-0.01	50.00%
Diagonal Triple Bottom	35	9.75	1.77	0.35	48.57%
Triple Bottom Sell	39	3.09	2.17	0.46	46.15%
Bearish Double Broadening	14	1.61	1.62	0.12	42.86%
Bullish Pattern Reversed	106	3.57	1.86	0.21	42.45%
Low Pole Failure	78	5.91	2.25	0.38	42.31%
Bearish Broadening	48	7.32	2.28	0.37	41.66%
Bearish 100% Pole	133	3.12	2.06	0.24	40.60%
Bull Trap	227	2.96	2.08	0.21	39.21%

The above tables are presented for observation from various perspectives. Sequence of pattern mostly has remained the same.

Time Interval Testing

The testing we have conducted so far is based on the end-of-the-day prices. But as discussed earlier, P&F charts can be traded very effectively on time interval charts and that 1 min is the most dynamic time frame of P&F charts. Tests in this section are conducted on 1 min prices of Nifty over 5 years starting from 1st Jan 2011 to 31st December 2015.

Box-values 0.05%, 0.07%, 0.10%, 0.15%, 0.20%, 0.25%, 0.30% and 0.35% are tested for bullish patterns; the first four box-values are tested for bearish patterns. Tables 9.4.8 and 9.4.9 present the summarized performance of patterns on these box-values on 1 min time frame of Nifty spot prices.

Table 9.4.8: Back-tested numbers of bullish P&F patterns on 1 min time interval charts of Nifty 50 index price over 5 years of closing prices with Double Bottom Sell as exit criteria

Pattern	Total Occurrence	Average box return	Risk-Reward Ratio	Success Ratio	Expectancy
Quadruple Top Buy	78	13.89	4.72	56.41%	2.23
Triangle Breakout - 3 col	798	3.80	3.56	41.85%	0.91
Catapult Buy	128	2.99	2.96	47.65%	0.89
Diagonal Triple Top	574	3.26	3.10	43.20%	0.77
Triple Top Buy	733	3.82	3.10	41.88%	0.72
Bullish Double Broadening	43	3.29	1.73	60.47%	0.65
Low Pole	1435	2.75	2.88	41.39%	0.61
Bullish Broadening	380	2.14	2.47	45.79%	0.59
Bearish Pattern Reversed	501	2.68	2.89	39.32%	0.53
Bear Trap	2035	2.21	2.43	44.03%	0.51
Triangle Breakout - 4 col	291	1.91	3.16	35.74%	0.49
High Pole Failure	357	0.89	2.16	46.50%	0.47
Bullish 100% Pole	394	1.42	1.88	46.70%	0.34
Triangle Failure - 3 col	247	-0.16	1.73	48.18%	0.32
Triangle Failure - 4 col	82	-1.06	1.94	41.47%	0.22

Table 9.4.9: Back-tested numbers of bearish P&F patterns on 1 min time interval charts of Nifty 50 index price over 5 years of closing prices with Double Bottom Sell as exit criteria

Pattern	Total Occurrence	Average box return	Risk-Reward Ratio	Success Ratio	Expectancy
Triangle failure - 4 col	107	5.07	2.75	55.14%	1.07
Triangle failure - 3 col	247	4.45	2.81	50.61%	0.93
Triangle Breakout - 4 col	254	3.32	2.83	48.82%	0.87
Bearish 100% Pole	369	3.66	2.25	52.57%	0.71
Quadruple Bottom Sell	51	2.21	2.41	49.02%	0.67
Bull Trap	1868	3.35	2.54	47.16%	0.67
Diagonal Triple Bottom	595	2.48	2.68	44.37%	0.63
Bullish Pattern Reversed	423	3.15	2.58	44.68%	0.60
Bearish Broadening	326	3.07	2.24	48.77%	0.58
High Pole	1413	2.56	2.57	44.02%	0.57
Bearish Double Broadening	47	2.38	1.78	55.32%	0.54
Triangle Breakout - 3 col	697	1.93	2.61	40.89%	0.48
Triple Bottom Sell	645	1.86	2.46	42.32%	0.46
Low Pole Failure	283	1.12	2.04	43.11%	0.31
Catapult Sell	135	0.89	2.54	34.07%	0.21

Multi-column bullish formations and triangular formations have delivered better performance in the 1 min time interval Nifty chart. Few patterns have displayed better performance in Nifty than stocks. Study and testing makes us understand price behavior of different instruments and time frames.

9.5: Summary

Though details can be analyzed and observed from the given tables, it appears from overall testing that multi-column breakout, Triangular and Broadening formation across instruments and time frames have a definitive edge. Strategies can be designed based on these formations for better results.

Note that returns are shown in percentage terms and position-sizing rules are not applied to it. In simple words, they show the performance of a pattern with one quantity. The aim was to keep things simple to get an idea of the performance, and Nifty 500 group was elected to get a large and significant sample size to perform these back-tests. I did not delve into ranking of patterns or any such thing because it doesn't matter. Few numbers here and there can change the sequence; pattern is tradable if expectancy and average returns are positive. You are equipped with all the tables so that you can explore it further.

Remember, back-testing is certainly important, but it doesn't guarantee anything. It's a tool to understand the formation and its behavior during different market phases. No strategy is foolproof; we should expect difficult or underperforming period with any system but remember to stick to it to benefit from it over a period. If we change or tweak our method during difficult times, we might end up trading bad phases of the freshly chosen different method.

As said earlier, most obvious and rounded numbers are considered while conducting the tests because it is important to know the principles. Learning should be generic. It appears from the test results that long setups work well across box-values and even simple breakouts on higher box-values are significant and profitable. Short setups need a different treatment and it is advisable to spend a lot of time and energy on trend identification techniques. The performance of Bearish patterns is comparatively unimpressive because the overall trend has been bullish in Indian markets. The picture would be different if I show the performance in the year 2008 when all markets including India witnessed a big fall. It appears that using a wide stop would be suitable for bullish trades, but they have a higher failure ratio with bearish trades. Bearish trades on lower box-values have generated better performance. Follow-through signals have a better win ratio and they help in filtering premature breakouts. With the profit booking method, success ratio is improved but we compromise on risk–reward. Return wise, performance of patterns is better if stops are trailed instead of exiting on the achievement of a target. Nonetheless, approach can be varied as per the market phase but that involves subjective analysis. If the market phase can be determined, profit-based exit in Sideways or range-bound markets and trailing stop-loss method in trending markets can prove rewarding. The next chapter talks about the breadth indicator, which is one of the tools to identify market phase.

There is no guarantee that a system that delivers better back-testing results will help you trade effectively; it is important that you trade a system that suits your style and personality. Success ratio and risk–reward ratio have an inverse relationship. Aggressive profit booking may improve the win ratio of a system but it will affect the risk–reward. Hence, the system efficiency is lower in such cases. But I agree it is not an easy task to ride the trend, nor is it easy to operate with a moderate success ratio initially. But serious money can't be made unless one develops the method to ride trends by trailing stops accordingly. As a beginner, one can start with a profit booking approach and move eventually to trend-riding methods. Once your capital grows, it helps in handling psychological aspects of riding a trend in a more effective manner.

Instrument-wise testing can improve things further. I have observed that several setups work very well in specific instruments. For example, Triple Top Buy pattern has performed well in Jet Airways & Tata Steel stocks. A four-column Triangle breakout has performed well in stocks such as Fortis Healthcare and Nestle India. Every instrument has a unique characteristic and behavior that can be identified by back-testing the performance of various patterns in each instrument.

P&F patterns in this chapter were meticulously tested and have turned out to be very effective and profitable. One may want to apply exit based on Follow-through or based on any indicator and not simply on a basic Double Bottom Buy or Sell signal. I have restricted the back-testing to the traditional patterns because the discussion would get very lengthy if I include indicators.

All this testing is performed in TradePoint software. The user can design as well as test any type of system in any chart method including P&F using the TradePoint software. The framework is provided to test and develop new strategies and trading ideas for any financial market you wish to trade such as commodities and currencies.

Finally, the back-test results should not be blown out of proportion as it is conducted on past data. The market phases can change, and it can be a completely different scenario tomorrow. So, compare the current market conditions with the scenario that existed when the system performed well, to identify the potential to maximize profitable trades. Execution based on objective price formations will prevail and prove successful over a period.

Chapter 10

BREADTH

We have discussed various P&F formations and strategies to identify trend, and clear price patterns in a trending phase helps in riding those trends. But I noticed that when trend is strong and most of the stocks are flowing with it, new trades even in the direction of the trend don't prove profitable many of the times. This happens because overall market has reached a phase of exhaustion, often referred to as overbought or oversold zones. It is important to recognize such phases to improve the trading results. It is important to book profits periodically when a trend is not strong or there is broader consolidation happening. One of the methods is to use momentum indicators on the price chart of an index to identify the extreme zones. But that alone is not sufficient because it just measures price exhaustion of that instrument. There is a necessity to have a broader measure of exhaustion at a macro level.

It is often said that when you are right about the market, maximum number of people would tend to disagree with you. Stock or commodity market exists and functions because there are divergent opinions. Price shocks or surprises happen when there is consensus. I often felt the need of an indicator that gives an idea when there is a consensus in one direction. When news channels, magazines or analysts are confident about the price moving in a direction, it's often a reason to be cautious. Even while reading fundamental reports, one may notice too many analysts sounding bullish and confident about a target level, which again is a sign of complacency. It makes sense to get an idea of what most of the participants are doing, but it is practically impossible to read through the reports of all analysts. Given this backdrop, would it not be handy to have a scientific way to get an idea about such sentiment extremes?

Opinions of bench sitters are not of much importance. Trend of most of the stocks will be bullish when overall market trend is strong and up. But there comes the exhaustion when little fuel is left to keep the momentum progressing in the same direction. Taking long positions in such a scenario is not advisable even though the trend is up, and the chart is bullish.

Breadth indicators are very relevant in such instances. They evaluate the market sentiments by measuring the number of stocks above or below particular criteria. There are different types of breadth indicators available out there.

A. W. Cohen invented the first breadth indicator using P&F signals in 1955, which is known as bullish percent. P&F charts are objective and produce clear Buy-Sell signals. This unique feature of P&F chart was used to build a breadth indicator. A P&F chart is either bullish or bearish, there is no other possibility. The chart is bullish if the last signal is Double Top Buy and bearish when the last signal is a Double Bottom Sell. Bullish percent breadth indicator calculates the number stocks that are bullish in a group of stocks, and divides them by the total number of stocks in that group. Hence, a bullish percent indicator displays percentage of stocks having bullish signal in the group. So, if we build Nifty-50 bullish percent breadth indicator, it will calculate number of stocks in a Buy mode among the 50 stocks of Nifty and divide it by 50.

For example, if there are 25 bullish stocks in the Nifty-50 group on a particular day, the bullish percent reading for that day will be 50%. Everyday reading is plotted on the chart to build the bullish percent breadth indicator that oscillates between 0% and 100%. If last signal of all stocks of the group is a Double Top Buy, the indicator reading will be at the upper extreme of 100%, and if the chart is bearish for all stocks, the breadth indicator will be at the lower extreme of 0%.

DT-percent breadth indicator considers the number of stocks that has generated double-top buy signal in the last column. DT-Percent breadth indicator measures the number of stocks where the last column is Double-top buy signal and divides it by total number stocks in the group. Hence, it calculates ratio of stocks in the group which are in strong momentum.

Below is the DT-Percent indicator of Nifty-50 group of stocks that calculates the percentage of stocks trading in the Double top buy column on 0.25% × 3 P&F chart.

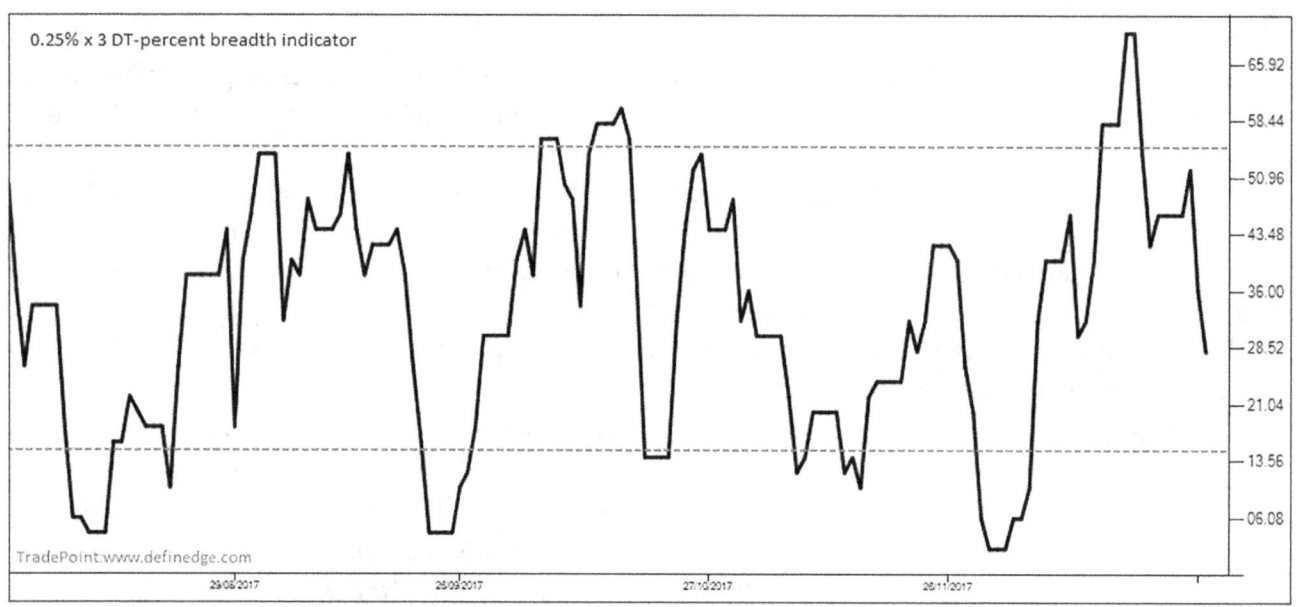

Figure 10.1.1: Nifty daily 0.25% × 3 cl DT-percent P&F Breadth chart

Breadth indicator in the chart shown above is plotted with 0.25% × 3 P&F charts. Meaning, it calculates the percentage of stocks trading in the double-top signal column on 0.25% × 3 individual P&F charts of the Nifty constituents. This indicator oscillates between 0 and 100. The indicator scans all the stocks in the group and therefore tells us about health of the overall market and state of the trend. When indicator shows a reading of 60%, it shows that 30 stocks out of the Nifty-50 universe are in column of 'X' where double-top buy pattern is triggered. This certainly happens when trend is up and strong, but it also indicates exhaustion or too much bullishness. Most of the individual charts will be in a bullish mode during such phases. Similarly, when the indicator drops below 20%, it suggests that 40 out of the 50 stocks forming part of the Nifty index are not in the column of double-top buy signal.

To keep it simple, market is in overbought zone when indicator is above 60% and oversold when it is below 20%. Overbought or oversold are extreme zones typically indicate exhaustion but not necessarily reversal.

It can be calculated on different box-values but remember it is calculated on a group of stocks and not on the index value. Hence, it gives us a true picture of the market sentiment. I can show you any number of examples when price keeps rising or falling without any indication of sentiment extreme in breadth; price oscillators would easily show overbought–oversold zones during such times. Hence, breadth is the most logical and useful indicator for sentiment analysis.

DT-percent is more aggressive in nature compared to the bullish percent indicator, but I find it very logical. A change of column gives an early sign about the change in sentiments. One can always choose to increase the box-value to adjust the frequency of the signals.

Below are the three major aspects to focus while interpreting the breadth indicator.

1. Breadth indicator pattern during extreme zones

A pattern in breadth indicator when it is in the extreme zone generates nice trading opportunity. Positive divergence in breadth indicator of Nifty-50 will occur when price makes new low and breadth is not at a new low. And negative divergence is marked when price makes new high but the indicator is unable to do so. Positive divergence at or near the oversold zone is considered bullish. A negative divergence at or near overbought zone is a sign of bearishness. Higher bottom in breadth indicator where previous bottom is in oversold zone or Lower top where previous top was at the overbought zone are the best readings of P&F DT-percent breadth indicator. Have a look at the image shown below.

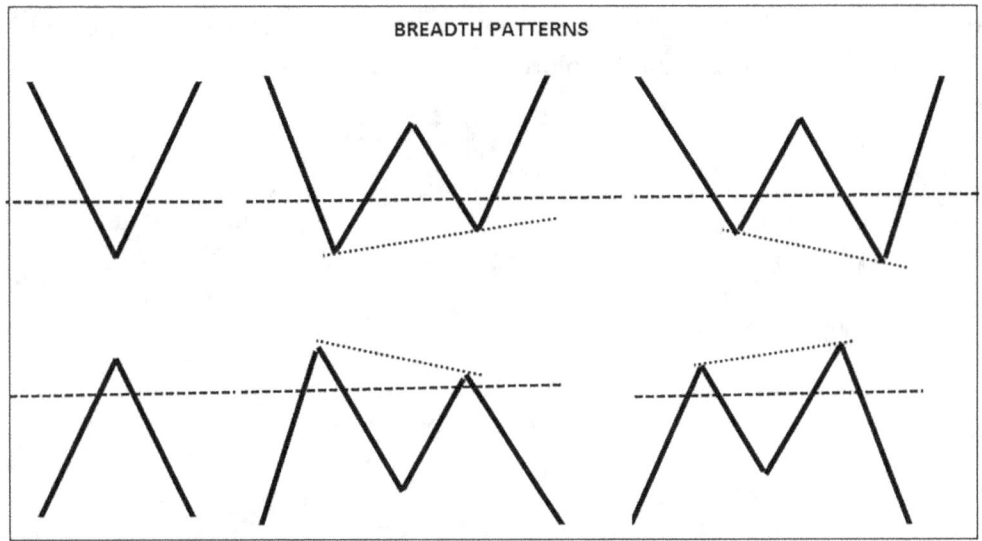

Image 10.1.1: Patterns on breadth chart

Below is the Nifty-50 0.25% × 3 DT-percent breadth indicator showing simple pattern analysis.

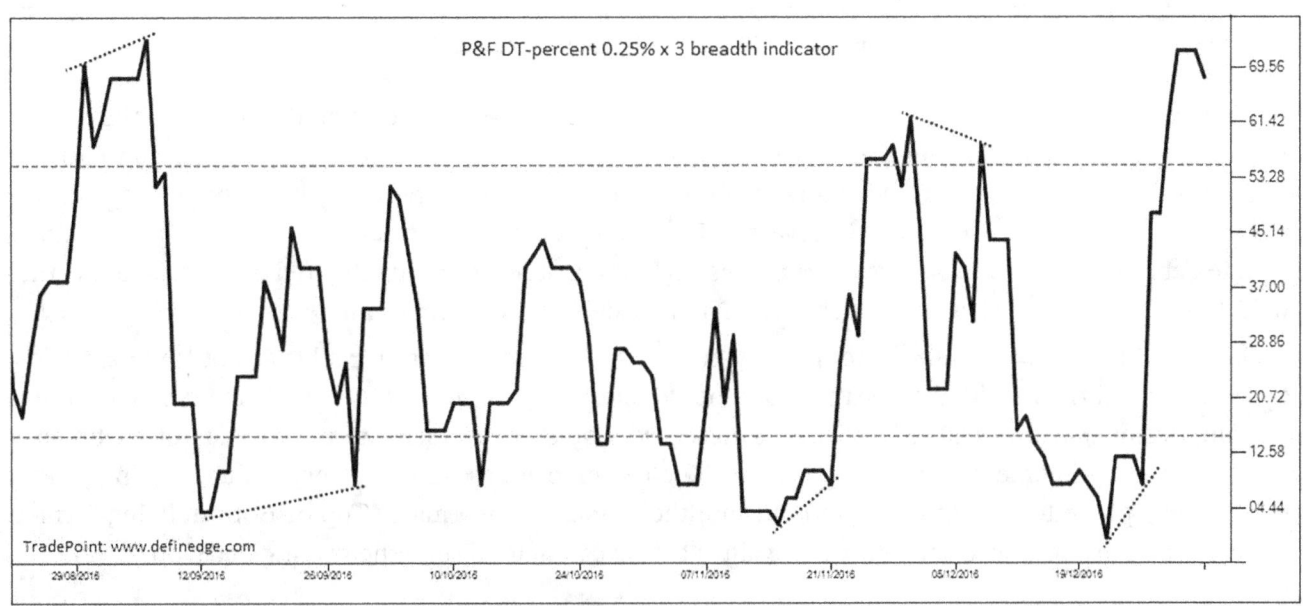

Figure 10.1.2: Nifty daily 0.25% × 3 cl DT-percent P&F Breadth chart

Price leaving oversold zone is when long trades have a better risk–reward and price leaving overbought zone is when the risk–reward for short trades is more favorable. But the breadth indicator alone is not sufficient; individual pattern of charts needs to confirm before a trade can be initiated.

How about this? For short trades, look for a sell signal in RS chart against Nifty when breadth is leaving overbought zone and there is bearish pattern in the stock. Similarly, look for long trades when there is a buy signal in RS chart against Nifty while the breadth is leaving the oversold zone and there is bullish pattern in the stock. Sounds complicated? Read it again and it will make sense!

2. Multi-breadth indicators to analyse price cycles and exhaustion

Breadth indicator can be plotted using different box-values. Lower box-values will be volatile and higher box-values will be relatively flat. Box-value of 0.25% is useful information for all kinds of traders. But one can track multiple breadth indicators to see if all price charts are indicating exhaustion. Major cyclical Tops and Bottoms get formed during such times. Observe Figure 10.1.3 showing breadth indicator of Nifty-50 for the period of around 15 months, plotted on four different box-values.

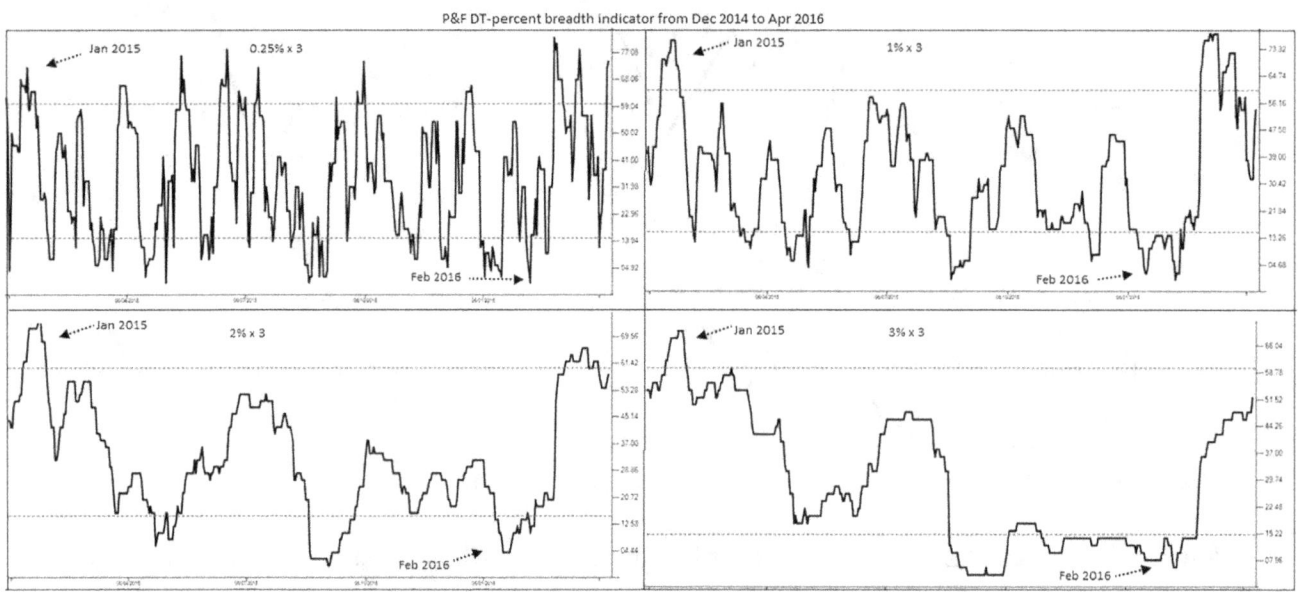

Figure 10.1.3: Nity P&F DT-percent breadth charts

Higher box-value indicators move at a slow pace and hence have a less-cluttered look. Lower box-value indicators oscillate smoothly but they are more aggressive and generate more signals compared to others. When multi-box-value breadth indicators are in sync and at an extreme zone, it is time to pay serious attention to the patterns that indicate reversal. For example, look what happened during late Jan 2015 and late February 2016 in the above charts. These specific instances are highlighted by arrows, indicating buying/selling extremes. Post these instances, Nifty made significant tops and bottoms respectively.

0.25% × 3 on Nifty is for short- to medium-term trend and is relevant for all types of traders. 1% × 3 shows medium-term breadth that the investors should monitor. The trend of the breadth indicator becomes more important aspect when the box-value is increased. Look for reversal patterns when multiple breadth indicators are in alignment at an extreme zone. The extreme zones on higher box-values are infrequent but they may prove to be significant and indicate the possibility of a major Top or Bottom being formed during such times. A look at the lower box-values charts can help to time the trading decision better.

3. Extreme zones and price setups

There are many possible rules that can be designed using breadth. The area of extreme zone which can be roughly defined as 60% and 20% in Nifty is very useful information. Market in this zone indicates exhaustion; hence, Fresh longs are better avoided when the indicator is above 60% and Fresh shorts may be avoided below 20%. Traders should remain cautious at breadth indicator extremes and reduce their position sizing during such periods. Leverage should be under control and allocation should be reduced; 10% and 70% readings are super extreme zones.

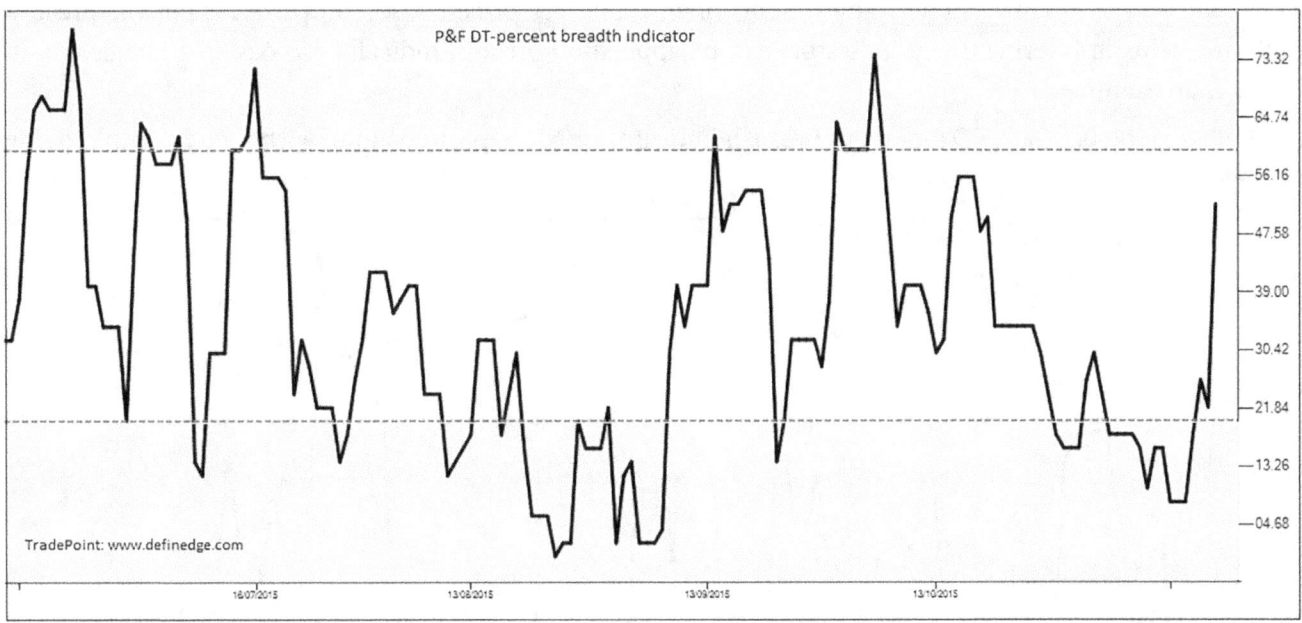

Figure 10.1.4: Nifty daily 0.25% × 3 cl DT-percent P&F Breadth chart

Instances when the momentum is strong will push the breadth to the extreme zone, it is a sign that the market should be given some breathing space. When the breadth indicator is at an overbought extreme, the risk–reward parameter is not typically in favor of the bulls. Hence, the position sizing should be reduced for Fresh longs. Same way, oversold breadth suggests that risk–reward for fresh shorts is not favorable. So, breadth tells us what not to do. Markets at an extreme zone may not necessarily reverse immediately. They can turn into a Sideways or volatile phase. It is therefore wise to step aside until the breadth extreme condition is resolved and it moves away from the extremes. I call it a yellow signal. We have three traffic signal rules in India, Green, Red and Yellow. Breadth in extreme zone is analogous to the yellow traffic signal in trading. One should slow down the accelerator and reduce the speed.

Breadth at extreme zone suggests unfavorable risk–reward metric for carrying forward positional trades. Wait for it to get back to neutral zone to initiate fresh trades. Remember, overbought or oversold breadth is not a proxy for market Tops and Bottoms. The breadth can remain at the overbought zones for a while during strong Uptrend and at oversold zones during strong Downtrend. They represent strong trends that can produce continuation patterns, hence current positions should be ridden as per the signals. There is no reason to exit the existing trades or investments when the breadth reaches the extreme zone. It is just that fresh trades should be curbed until the breadth returns to the neutral zone. Note that breadth is in neutral zone when it is not in extreme zone, meaning when it is between 60 and 20.

Breadth at an extreme zone indicates exhaustion which may be followed by a time correction, which typically happens during strong trends. A continuation breakout is often seen when breadth sustains in the extreme zone. Normally, there is a possibility of weak high or low getting formed in that zone before producing a reversal. During range-bound markets, bearish formation above 60 is weak and bullish pattern below 20 is strong. Wait for the Fresh formation. Pattern confirmation is more important signal to trade, never pre-empt and take the signal for granted.

Study of price trend can be helpful while reading breadth. Oversold DT-percent also indicates weakness because most of the stocks have changed column after breakout. Hence, it indicates caution and it is advisable to look for confirmation from other tools before taking contra-trend strategies.

Price patterns such as Pattern retest, indicator divergences or reversal patterns at Anchor point when breadth is in extreme zone are great mean reversion (reversal) setups. It can also help in generating list of stocks for trading on lower time frames. Remember, trades are placed based on patterns, but the breadth indicator helps in filtering them. Indicators can be applied on breadth indicators to design strategies on it. Below is an example.

Below is the 0.25% × 3 DT-percent breadth indicator of Nifty, plotted along with five-column moving average on it.

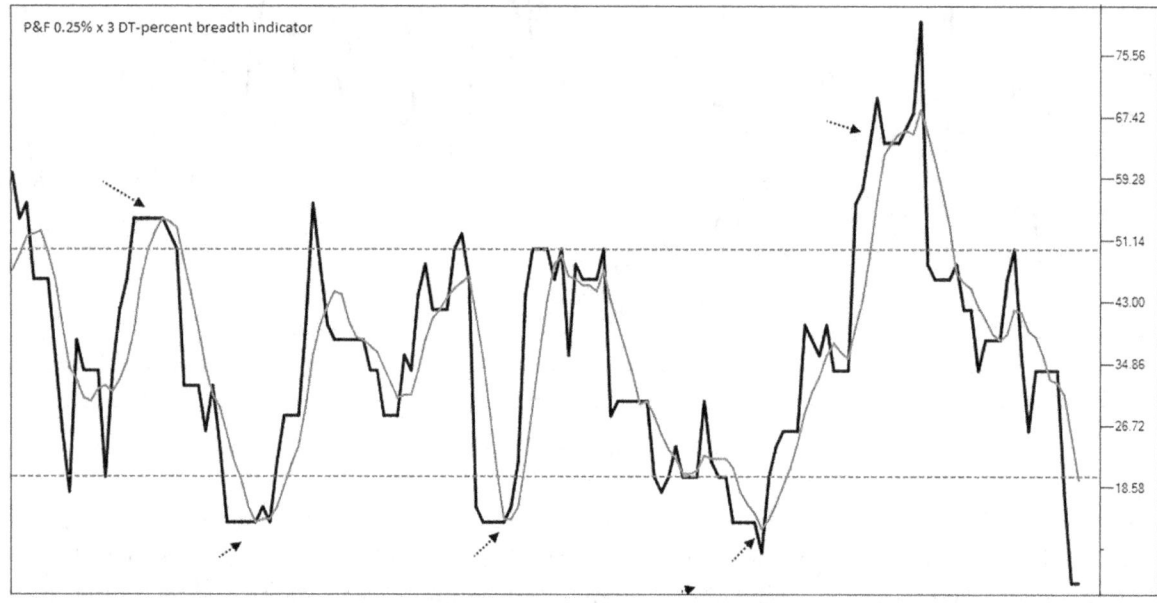

Figure 10.1.5: Nifty daily 0.25% × 3 cl DT-percent P&F Breadth chart plotted along with 5-column SMA

Above is an example of applying trend indicator on breadth. Bearish crossover once breadth line moves above 50 and bullish crossover below 20 are useful tools to apply contra –trend strategies.

Breadth can also help in designing exit strategies; aggressive profit booking techniques can be applied when it is in extreme zone and trends can be ridden with trailing stops when it is in neutral zone.

Let me show you an interesting chart. Have a look at 0.25% × 3 DT-percent breadth indicator chart of Nifty 50 during 2017.

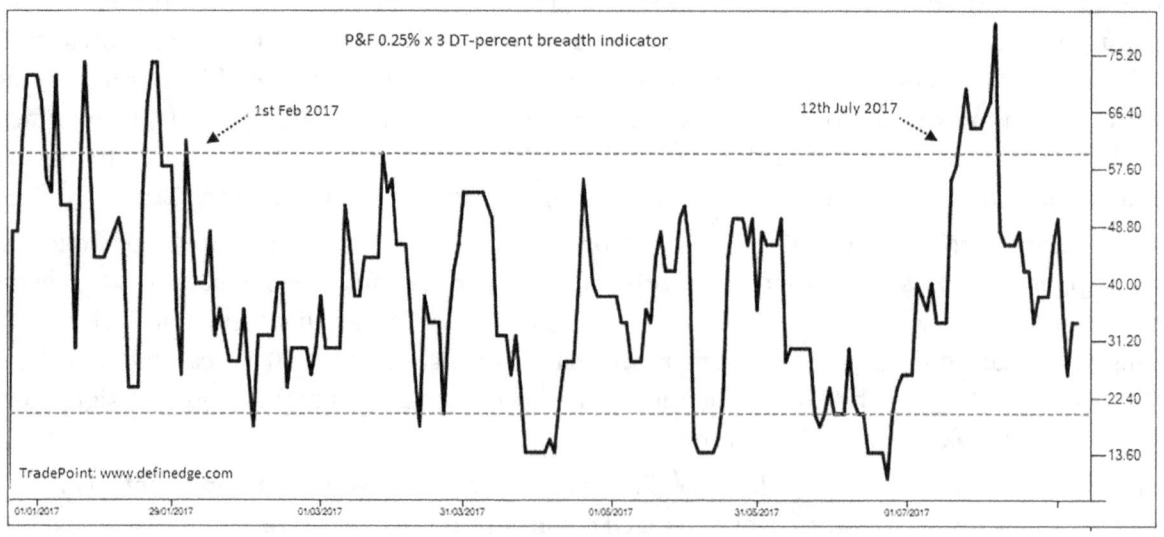

Figure 10.1.6: Nifty daily 0.25% × 3 cl DT-percent P&F Breadth chart

Breadth was in neutral zone for about six months and Nifty went from ~8600 to ~9800 during this period. It helps us in identifying strong trends and focusing on continuation breakouts during such phase and avoiding mean reversion techniques. Price oscillators would typically show overbought reading during such rally. The breadth considers the trend of all the group constituents and tracking it will help one assess the overall state of the market.

Remember these powerful rules with regards to breadth extreme zones. Oversold breadth during uptrend and Overbought breadth during downtrend provide wonderful mean-reversal trading opportunities.

Sectors & Stock Groups Breadth

We have seen breadth of Nifty-50, which should usually be followed to gauge the overall state of the market. Breadth indicator of sectors, other indices or group of stocks can be built in the similar manner.

Being cautious when there is euphoria associated with mid-caps and small caps can save one from getting stuck at the wrong levels. Figure 10.1.7 and 10.1.8 shows the 1% × 3, DT-percent breadth indicator chart of Nifty-500 and Nifty Mid-Small cap 400, respectively.

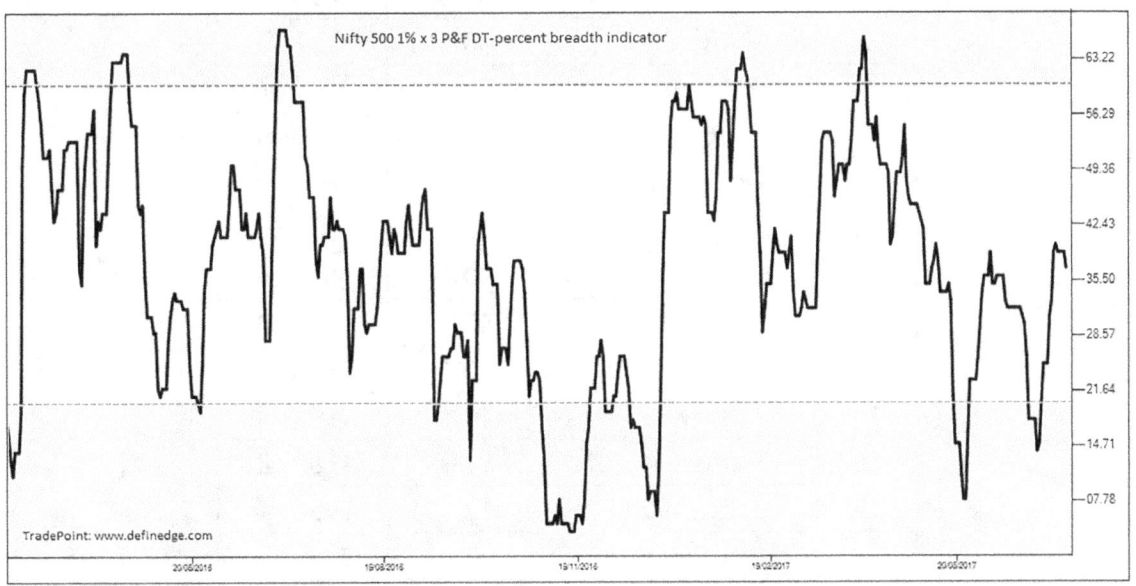

Figure 10.1.7: Nifty 500 daily 1% × 3 cl DT-percent P&F Breadth chart

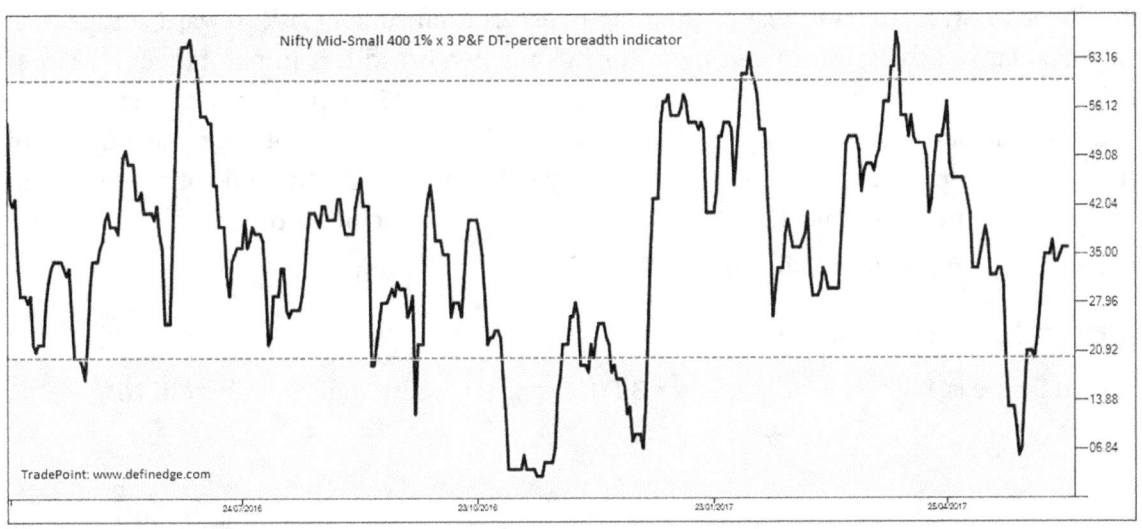

Figure 10.1.8: Nifty Mid-Small cap 400 daily 1% × 3 cl DT-percent P&F Breadth chart

All three approaches discussed can be observed on the above charts.

The representation would be better if there are more than 30 stocks in a group to build the breadth indicator. If there are fewer constituents the breadth indicator reaches extreme reading of 70–20% frequently. When multiple box-value breadth of a sector reaches extreme zone, it is a sign that a significant cyclical Top or Bottom is in the making.

Below is an example of a table showing breadth reading and comment against all sectors of Nifty.

Sr No.	Group / Sector	Breadth	Comment
1	Nifty Energy	80%	Extreme
2	Nifty IT	79%	Extreme
3	Nifty Commodities	56%	Neutral
4	Nifty Metal	56%	Neutral
5	Nifty Auto	56%	Neutral
6	Nifty Consumption	53%	Neutral
7	Nifty CPSE	50%	Neutral
8	Nifty Serv Sector	50%	Neutral
9	Nifty FMCG	50%	Neutral
10	Nifty Fin Service	40%	Neutral
11	Nifty Realty	40%	Neutral
12	Nifty Pvt Bank	40%	Neutral
13	Nifty Pharma	40%	Neutral
14	Nifty Infra	40%	Neutral
15	Nifty PSE	40%	Neutral
16	Nifty Bank	33%	Neutral
17	Nifty Media	12%	Extreme
18	Nifty PSU Bank	5%	Extreme

Figure 10.1.9: Nifty all sectors breadth indicator reading

Sector Relative Strength and Breadth can help to ascertain favorable risk–reward setups in a sector. Price and/or Relative Strength breakout in sector index when breadth is in neutral zone is an effective setup. When breadth of any sector is in extreme zone, look for the RS chart for indication of reversal – this could be one of the best reversal setups. One can also monitor the breadth of the personal portfolio on a regular basis or a group of interesting stocks to identify exhaustion. Breadth is one of the most important, logical and vital tool in any trading kit. The best part is that it complements other methods of analysis.

How about plotting breadth indicator as a P&F chart instead of line?

P&F of Breadth Indicator

Figure shown below is 1 × 3 P&F chart of 1% × 3 DT-Percent breadth indicator chart of Nifty-50.

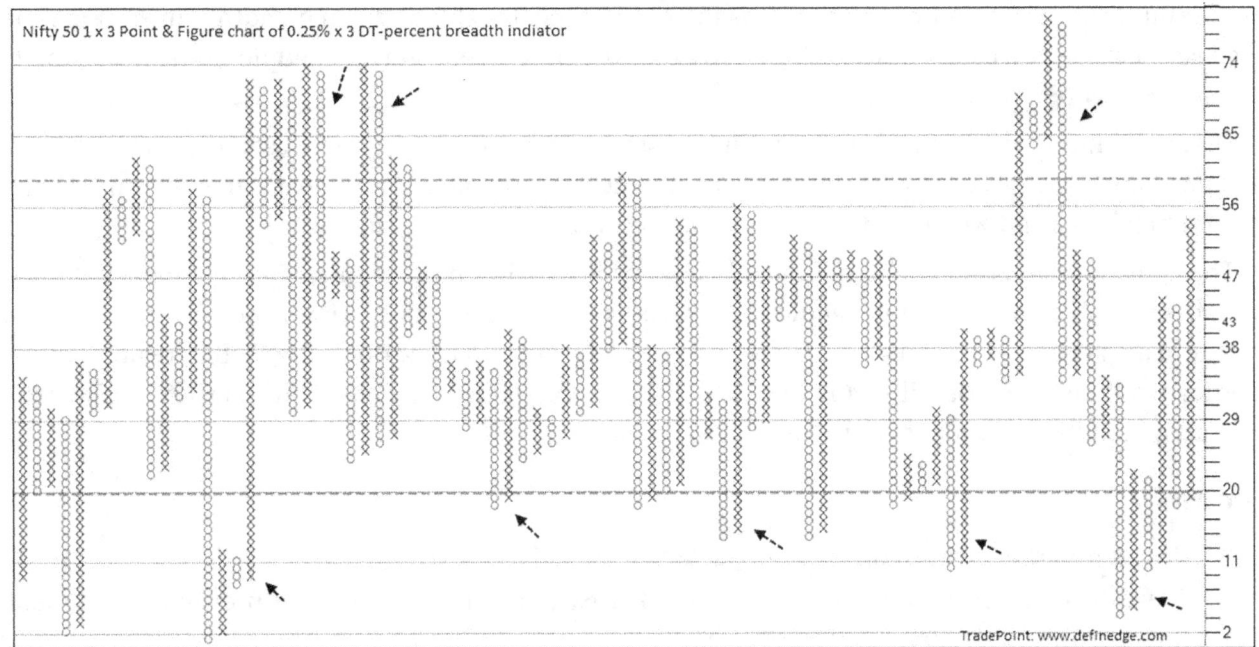

Figure 10.1.10: 1 × 3 P&F chart of Nifty daily 0.25 × 3 cl DT-percent P&F Breadth

The above P&F chart was plotted using absolute box-value 1, because it is an oscillator going to move within specific range; it is not a price range where log value is important. This can make all readings we discussed above very simple and objective. Follow pattern retest and breakouts during extreme zones. In fact, simple column reversal during extreme zones can be helpful because a price can remain there for a long time during strong trends. In simple words, we don't know how far the breadth can go after crossing 60 or going below 20, nor do we know how long it will remain at those extremes. A column reversal pattern will help in timely indication of an impending reversal and patterns will provide further confirmation. Bearish patterns on P&F chart of breadth are very helpful and turn out to be leading signals many of the times.

Breadth complements Point & Figure. We study strength and breakouts in P&F but breadth comes with controls that dramatically improve the profitability. It doesn't allow us to be complacent and it complements P&F breakout patterns. In cricketing analogy, a good batsman should know when to play offense and defense. The P&F patterns tell us how to hit; breadth helps us decide when to be aggressive and when the balls should be left alone and turn defensive.

Experienced traders use leverage to generate alpha. It is a skill, and it is important to understand when to utilize leverage. It is dangerous to remain over-positioned during overbought and euphoric phase and breadth indicator can help us identify such instances. Beginners should compulsorily avoid leverage. They should rather learn to be under-positioned, which will turn out to be to their biggest advantage.

Breadthastra

Astra is Sanskrit mean weapon. I gave this name to stress the powerful rule that has stood the test of time for me. I depend on the price breakout that occurs when breadth is in neutral zone (between 60 and 20). I have seen a high percentage of winning trades happen when the Nifty has active bullish counts, gives a pattern breakout while the breadth is in neutral zone. Same applies to negative breakouts and active bearish counts in downtrend when breadth is in neutral zone. Breakouts when breadth is in extreme zone are always a suspect. In cricketing analogy, look to score in singles and twos and do not look for the big shots when the breadth is at an extreme.

Many of times, significant breakouts are missed out by focusing on resistance, and significant resistances are overlooked by looking for breakouts.The breadth indicator is a method to identify when to focus on breakouts and when to look for reversal trades at resistance or support.

The above methods are applicable to bullish percent breadth indicator also. There are many breadth indicators available on usual bar or candlestick charts as well; stocks above-below average, new High–Low, number of advances and declines, etc. There are other P&F breadth indicators as well. But, realize that "All roads lead to Rome." So just follow any one of them but stick to the chosen one. I instantly fell in love with P&F-based breadth indicators because of their simplicity.

Summary

- ⅄ Broader market trend is the most important aspect of trading.
- ⅄ Breadth should be monitored by every market participant to be aware of prevailing sentiments; they perform well during strong trends.
- ⅄ Follow cautious approach when breadth reaches extreme zone.
- ⅄ Look for reversal patterns when multiple breadths coincide.
- ⅄ Pattern retest, indicator divergences or Anchor point support–resistance reversal formations when breadth is in extreme zone are great mean reversion setups.
- ⅄ Prefer breakouts when breadth is in neutral zone.
- ⅄ P&F chart of breadth indicator makes the job very easy and helps us in combining all the observations.

We have discussed all important aspects of P&F analysis. Take a pause and spend some time to ponder over the below-mentioned points.

- ⅄ Patterns: Basic, Major, other patterns, variations and failures
- ⅄ Analysis: Mini Top–Mini Bottoms, objective trend lines, Counts, Anchor point, Climax, Anchor Top–Bottoms, ABC and Tweezers
- ⅄ Indicators: Moving averages, Bollinger bands, RSI, ADX and XO zone
- ⅄ Parameters: Box-values, pattern cluster, High–Low charts, time interval charts
- ⅄ Other box-values: 2 box, 5 box and 1 box charts
- ⅄ Relative Strength: Identify out-performers and under-performers
- ⅄ Breadth: Identify phases of exhaustion or extremes

Before we take this further and discuss some more about trading, let's discuss some interesting aspects of P&F.

The purpose of the following chapter is to channelize your thoughts about various other possibilities. A few thought-provoking ideas are discussed in brief and explained via images.

Chapter 11

DYNAMIC POINT & FIGURE

11.1: P&F AND CANDLES

P&F techniques can be traded along with your current methods and systems. Candlestick formations are very popular and widely followed patterns. Point & Figure and Candlestick charts can be analyzed simultaneously to embrace the strength of each other. Below are some ideas.

Long P&F Columns

Long P&F column display trend, there could be a time consolidation in between that didn't qualify for the column reversal. Consider this example: A failure of the bearish candlestick pattern is a nice trading opportunity when the price is in a long column of X in the P&F chart. Refer image shown below.

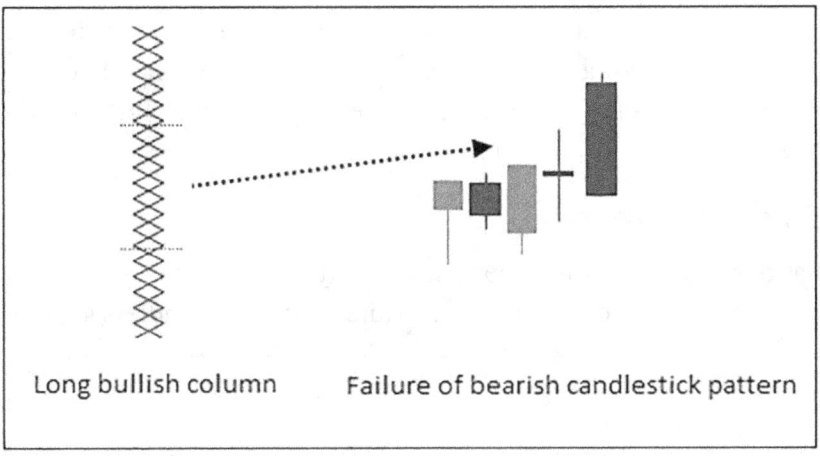

Image 11.1.1: P&F column and candlestick pattern

In the image shown above, hanging man and bearish engulfing failed when price went above the high of the red candle. One can trade it with stop based on candlestick formation. It is a simple yet powerful formation that traps the weak positions in the strong trend and provides fuel for the next move.

Similarly, bullish pattern failing when there is a large bearish P&F column is a bearish trading setup. There can be any candlestick reversal pattern such as Engulfing, Harami, Hammer, Doji, etc., for this setup which fails. Bearish candlestick pattern fails when price goes above the high of the pattern, and bullish candlestick pattern fails when price falls below the low price of the pattern.

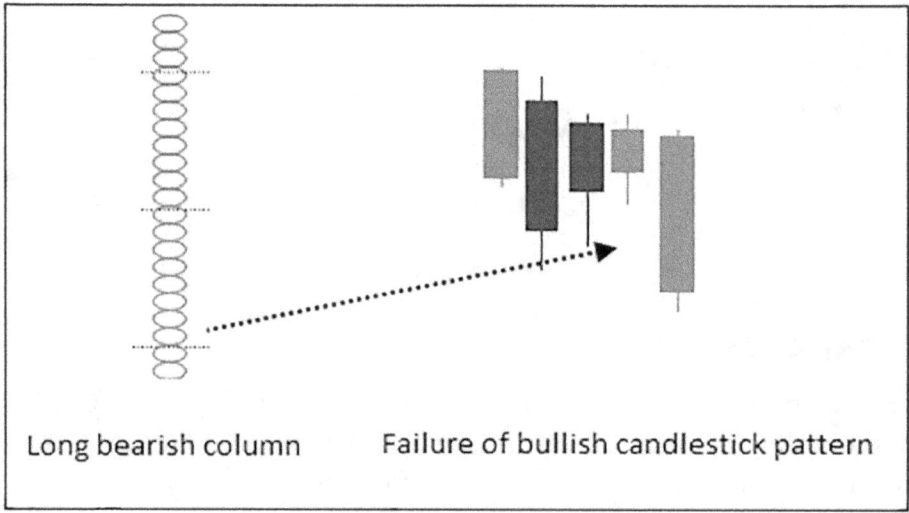

Image 11.1.2: P&F column and candlestick pattern

In the above image, bullish piercing and Harami candlestick patterns failed. Bearish trade can be taken with stop placed at top of the candle and bullish trade can be taken with stop placed at bottom of the candle that qualified the setup.

Of course, one can trade Continuation candlestick patterns as well during Anchor columns. But candlestick patterns we are referring to here are reversal patterns that failed during strong trends. Hence, this is a high-probability trade setup. These are examples where P&F and candlestick charts can complement each other.

Converging P&F Formations

Triangular P&F formations or series of inside columns display converging trend. Doji candlestick formation that suggests indecision, if occurred during the same time, indicates trendless state of the market.

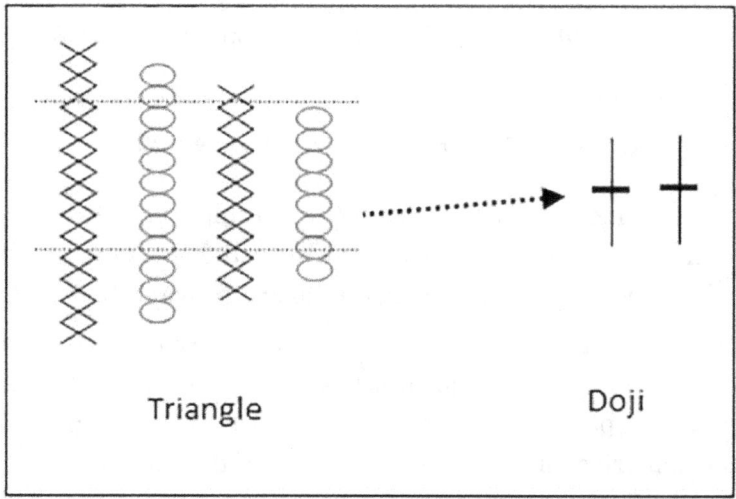

Image 11.1.3: P&F and candlestick pattern

It can be three- or four-column Triangle P&F formation and series of Doji candlestick formations or NR7 (Narrowest range in last 7 bars) that show serious congestion. This a strong signal of an impending breakout and a trending move. Breakouts in candlestick chart can also be traded in such cases as narrow range candles offer low-risk opportunities. Here, combination of both charts confirms the major congestion or squeeze in volatility.

Candlestick Reversal Formation

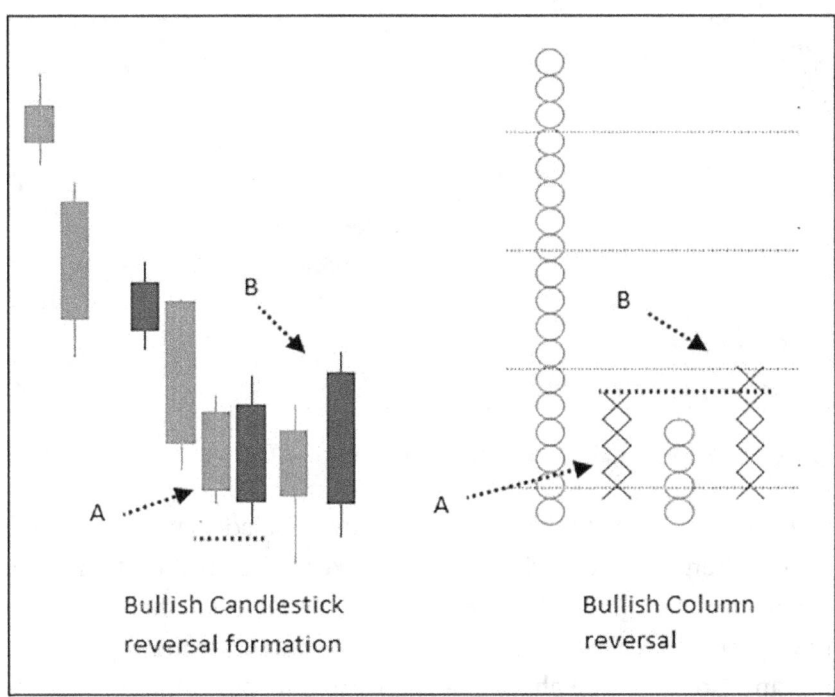

Image 11.1.4: Candlestick pattern and P&F chart

Have a look at the image shown above. Point A is bullish engulfing pattern that resulted in column reversal in P&F chart. As we know, a reversal candlestick formation indicates change in trend and not necessarily a reversal. In other words, it is possible that it is followed by the series of narrow candles instead of immediate breakout. The simple P&F formation can help in trading them. Point B is another bullish engulfing pattern that not only triggered a column reversal, but also ended up as a Double Top Buy pattern in the P&F chart. Reversal candlestick formations in such cases can be traded.

It is a method of waiting for swing breakout before acting on candlestick reversal patterns. At times, market goes Sideways after such reversal candlestick patterns or it may get failed as well. P&F patterns can act as a confirmatory tool which can improve the win ratio of trading candlestick reversals. If reversal is vertical, you'll have poles instead of basic signals. This way, I might be adding a bit of a lag to candlestick patterns, but they end up reducing the whips or false breaks.

P&F High–Low Traps and Candles

In High–Low P&F charts, a column flips from 'X' to 'O' only when a new high is not made during the day. It is turned to bullish only when new low is not made during the day. It is an important feature and filters many premature exits. While all examples shown above are equally applicable in the High–low P&F charts, below is an example of a pattern that occurred in both the charts.

Figure shown below is a Nifty daily candlestick chart and a High–Low P&F chart of the same period.

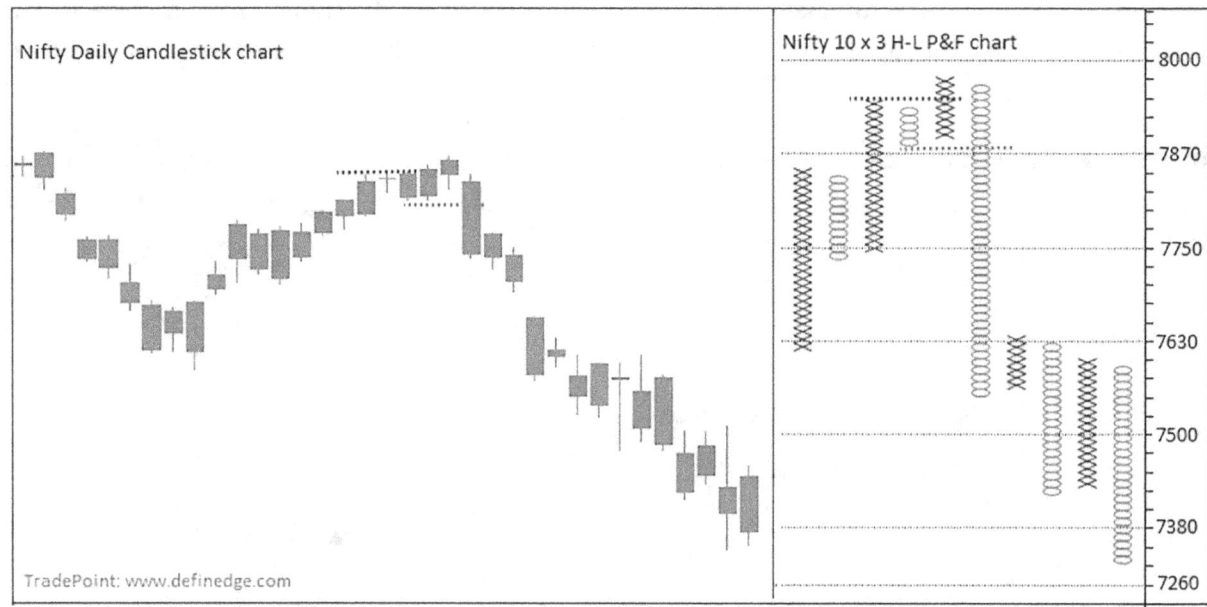

Figure 11.1.1: Nifty daily candlestick chart and 10 × 3 H-L Point & Figure chart

The Bull Trap P&F formation in the chart shown above is also marked on candlestick chart. Price made new high but failed when previous swing low got broken. The level that will trigger a P&F Bull Trap is clearly known, which can be helpful while trading even short-term candlestick patterns. It helps in knowing that bulls have become weak and continuation candlestick formations can be traded. Vice versa is applicable for Bear traps. Notice in the chart that there are only continuation bearish patterns post Bull Trap, whereas, there are many candlestick formations in between.

Knowledge of P&F formations and particularly traps can prove very useful information while trading candlestick formations.

Traditional Patterns

Below is the chart of Reliance Infra.

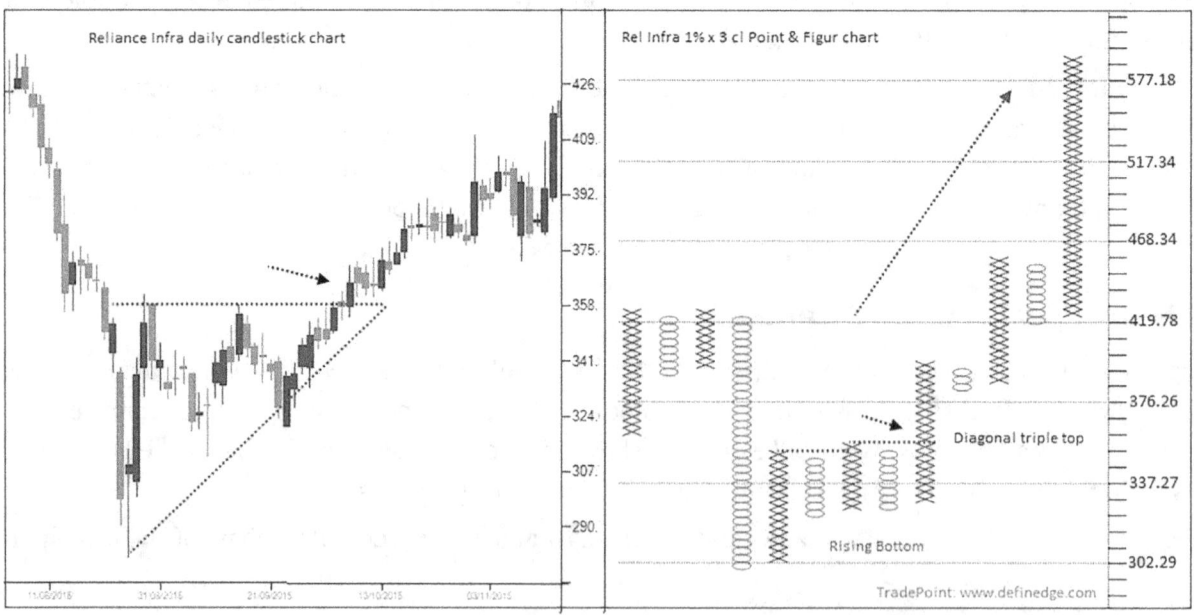

Figure 11.1.2: Reliance Infra daily candlestick chart and 1% × 3 cl Point & Figure chart

Ascending Triangle formation of usual charts is marked on the chart shown above. It was diagonal Triple Top at the same time on P&F charts. It is possible that one is not aware of such multi-column P&F patterns, but familiar with a significant pattern breakout on usual candlestick charts. In such a scenario, one can trade basic continuation P&F signals post the breakout in candlestick charts. This way one knows how to take advantage of such popular pattern breakouts by trading simple P&F signals. Observe that there was a low-risk trade after the diagonal pattern in the above chart. By the way, the Follow-through Buy after the diagonal pattern is also a super pattern. The above observation is applicable for all popular patterns such as H&S, cup and handle, rounding Tops–Bottoms, etc.

These are particularly useful information for short-term traders, but valid on every time frame. It is a sensible approach to pick the best of both worlds.

11.2: VOLUME INDICATOR P&F CHARTS

On Balance Volume, invented by Joseph Granville, is a most basic volume indicator. It adds the volume to the previous total when price rises, else it is deducted. OBV indicator calculated on usual charts when plotted using Point & Figure method becomes very simple to read due to the clear and objective formations.

The box-value of OBV should be kept between 0.15% and 0.25% even for long-term analysis. Figure shown below is the 0.25% × 3 Coal India price P&F chart shown along with its 0.25% × 3 OBV P&F chart during the same period. Note that value of OBV is divided by 1 lac for better visibility.

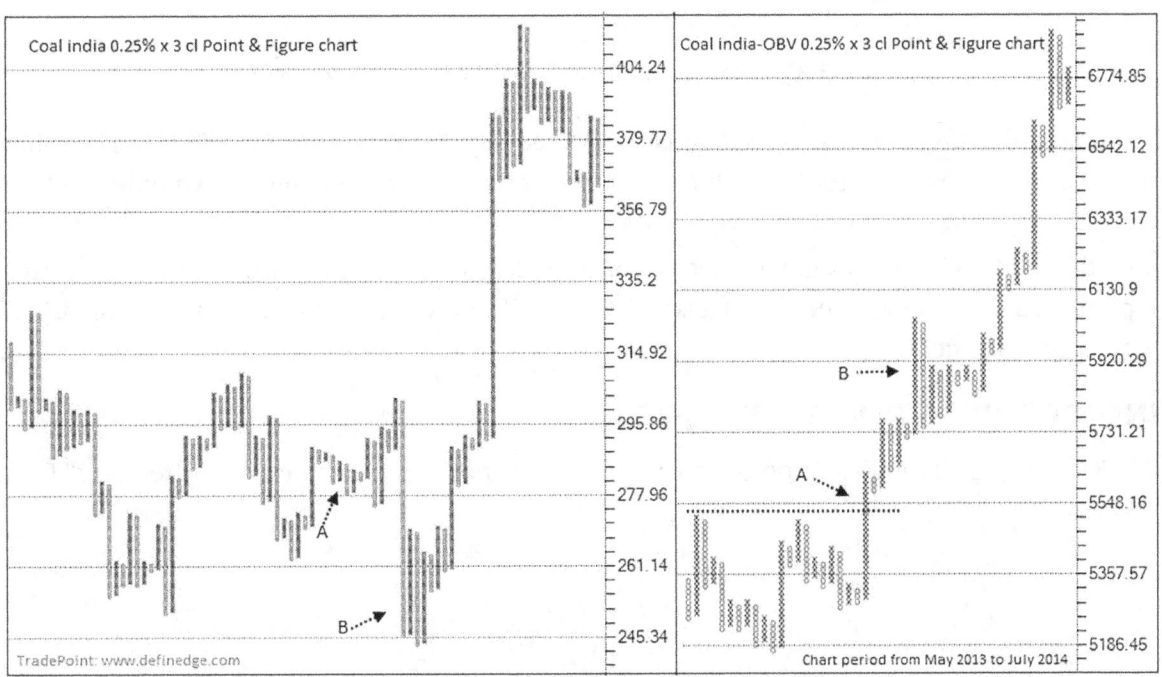

Figure 11.2.1: Coal India daily price and OBV 0.25% × 3 cl P&F chart.

Point A in price chart shows weakness while OBV indicator chart at the same time displayed multi-column breakout. Point B is where price witnesses large bearish column but OBV chart at the same time indicated lack of supply during the fall and showed continuation breakout columns.

Observe the smooth chart that OBV P&F shows. The column analysis and basic formations show the price and volume trend. Usual P&F chart will form a Double Bottom Sell pattern if price falls. If the fall in price is not accompanied by significant volume, the Sell signal then will not get marked on OBV charts. Same way, Double Top Buy pattern will not get marked on OBV chart unless the buying has happened on significant volume. They can significantly complement usual price P&F charts.

Strategy to trade OBV P&F charts is very simple; look for bullish price formations on price charts when OBV chart is bullish and look for bearish patterns on price chart when OBV chart is bearish.

Positive column reversals, pullback setups and bullish price patterns when OBV chart is bullish become interesting price and volume setup. By the same token, bearish patterns not accompanied by significant volume may be avoided. Have a look at below chart of IIFL.

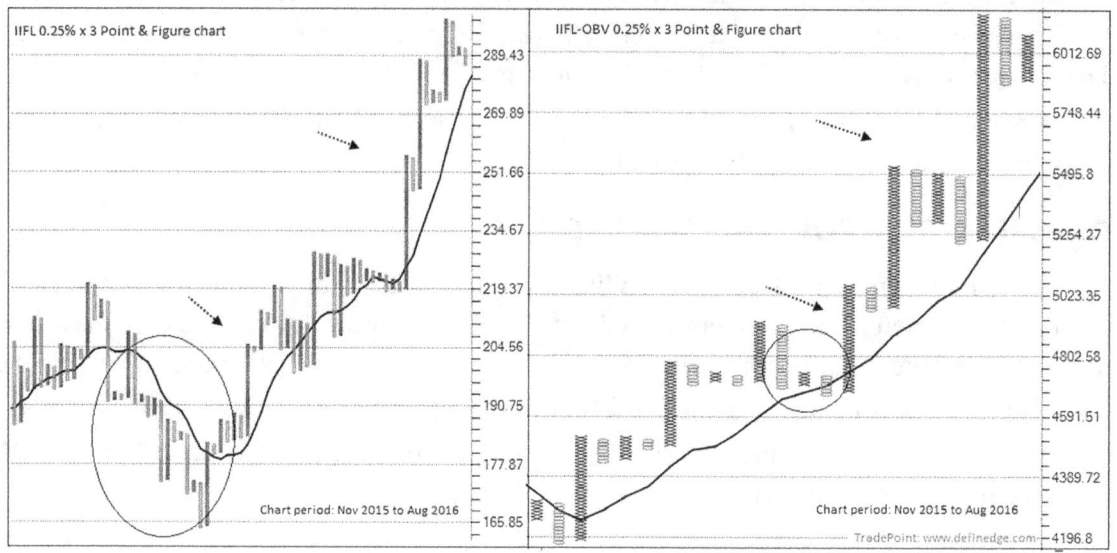

Figure 11.2.2: IIFL daily price and OBV 0.25% × 3 cl P&F chart.

Circled area on the chart shows that price corrected significantly but OBV chart was resilient and triggered Bear Trap. Arrows on the chart show that rise in price was accompanied by volume that translated into an Anchor column on OBV chart.

All methods of P&F analysis are applicable on P&F OBV chart as well. Other volume indicators can also be plotted in the same manner to analyse P&F chart if one wants to incorporate volume in P&F and analyse price-volume charts.

11.3: INDICATOR AS POINT & FIGURE

A 14-day RSI is a popular indicator on bar and candlestick charts. Same indicator plotted in P&F charts is featured below.

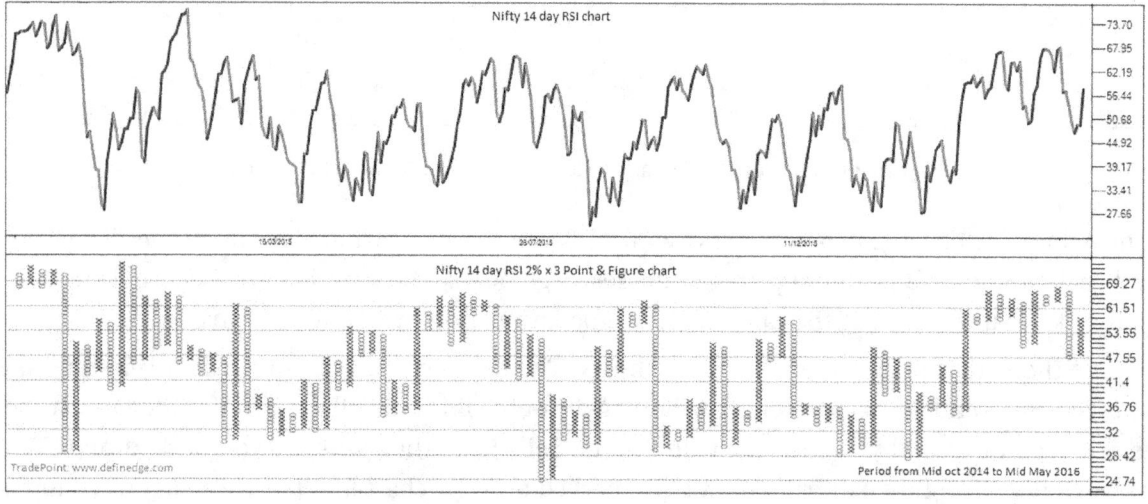

Figure 11.3.1: Nifty 14 day RSI line chart and 2% × 3 Point & Figure chart

This way, noise of RSI indicator can be removed and plotted for reading P&F patterns. Column reversals and basic formations can be useful indications to trade the underlying. Figure shown below is same RSI chart plotted using 1% box-value.

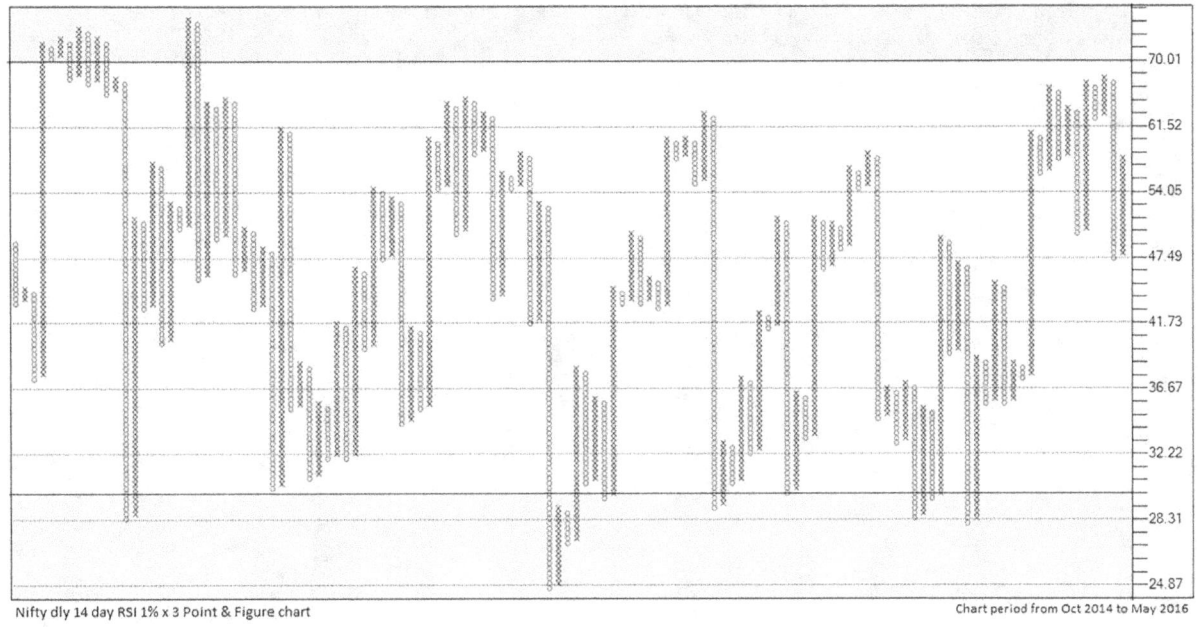

Nifty dly 14 day RSI 1% x 3 Point & Figure chart   Chart period from Oct 2014 to May 2016

Figure 11.3.2: Nifty 14 day RSI 1% × 3 Point & Figure chart

P&F pattern of RSI is a new dimension added to the usual analysis. Traps, Poles, Broadening, rising and falling Tops or Bottoms are patterns that help in trading RSI. Any indicator can be plotted using P&F method in the same manner, provided it doesn't get into the negative territory. Plotting a chart in P&F format results in significant value-addition to the usual analysis done on indicators.

Have a look at the daily candlestick chart of Bharti Airtel shown below.

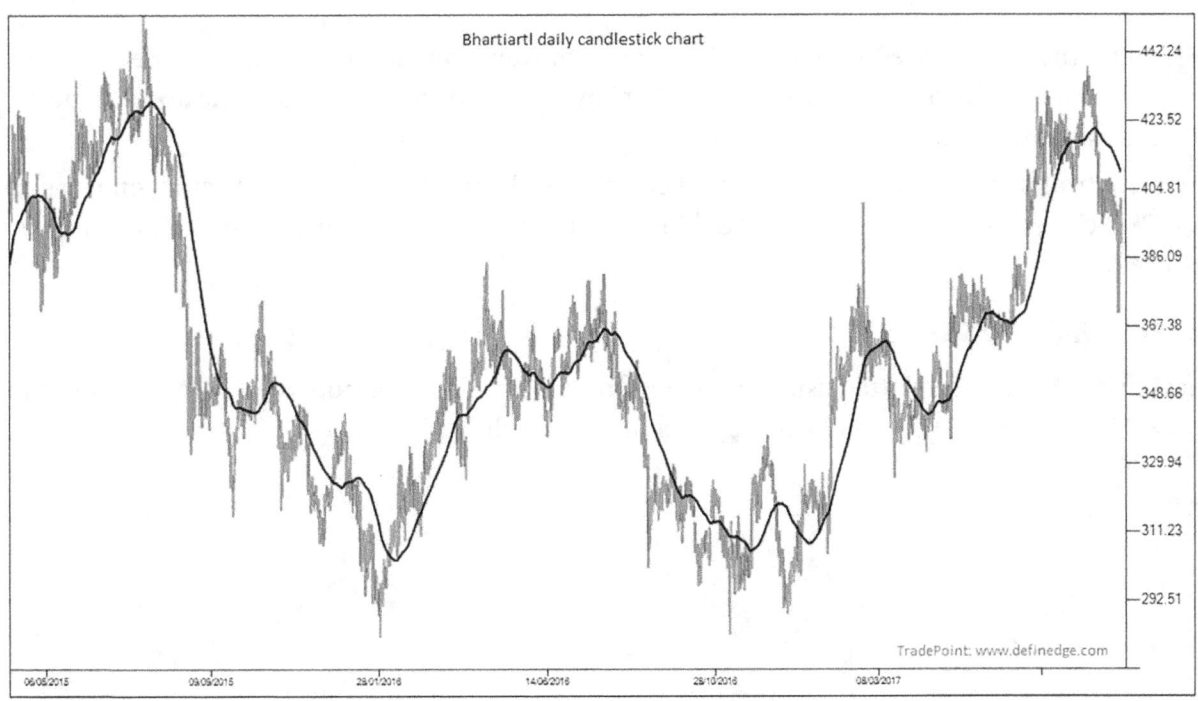

Bhartiartl daily candlestick chart

TradePoint: www.definedge.com

Figure 11.3.3: Bhartiartl daily candlestick chart

Twenty-day simple moving average is applied on the chart, which shows very smooth trend. How about applying that moving average as P&F? See below chart.

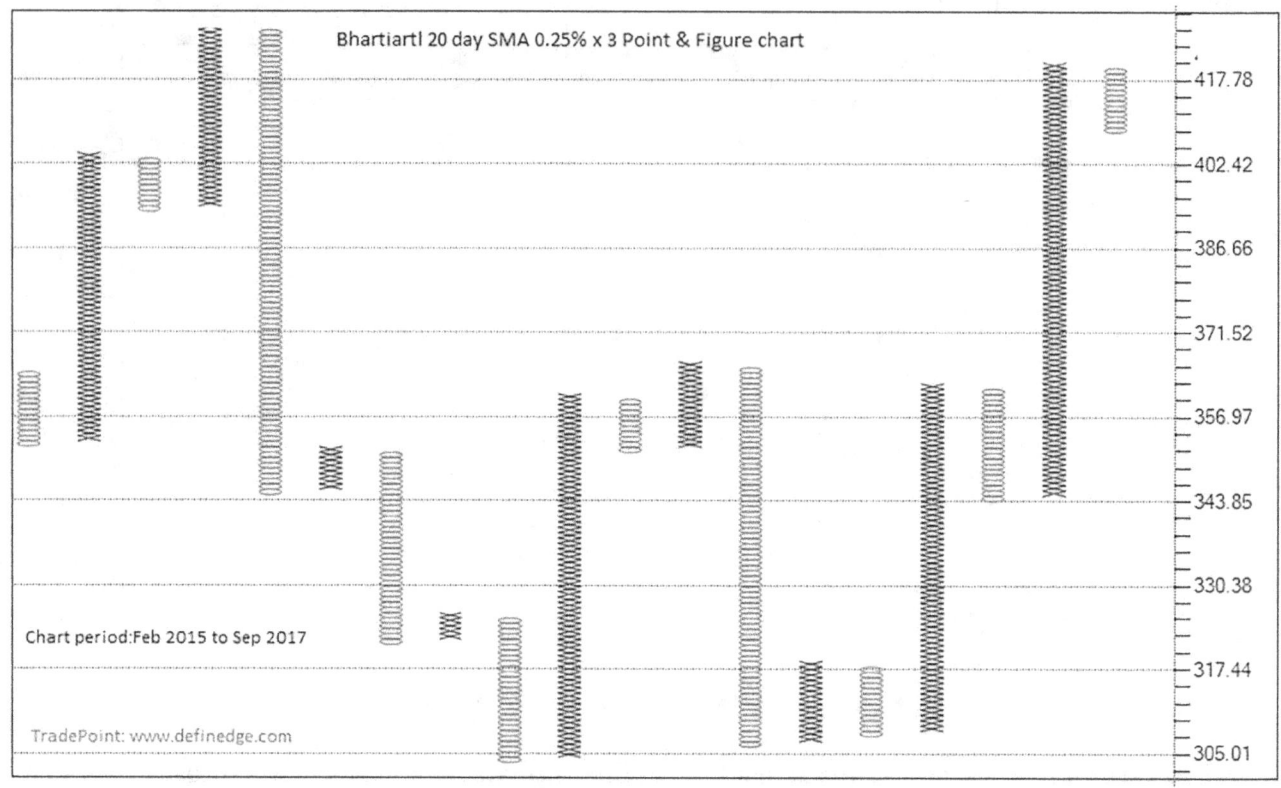

Figure 11.3.4: Bhartiartl 20 day SMA 0.25% × 3 Point & Figure chart

Above chart is of 2.5 year duration. This is the moving average plotted as P&F and notice how it captures the trend in a crisp and clear fashion. Column reversal and basic signals are very informative in this case.

Although there is no need of doing it, because such trend smoothening can be achieved simply by increasing the box-value on P&F charts. The chart above is just to showcase that indicators can be plotted as P&F to analyse the trend.

I am controlling my enthusiasm here and keeping the chapter brief. Many indicators on usual charts and on P&F charts can be plotted in the P&F format. It is not necessary, of course, but is a fun exercise nonetheless.

11.4: MUTUAL FUND P&F

Mutual Fund NAVs can be plotted using Point & Figure construction method as well. Figure shown below is a 2% × 3 P&F chart of HDFC Mid-cap Opportunities Growth fund.

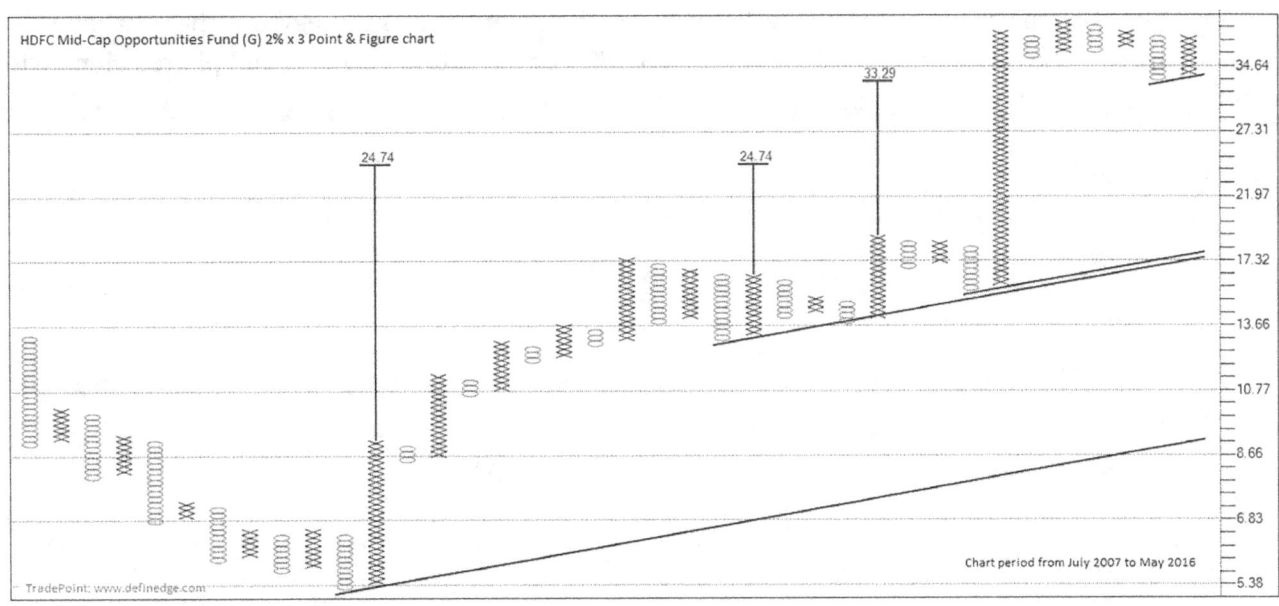

Figure 11.4.1: HDFC Mid-cap opportunities fund (G) 2% × 3 Point & Figure chart

Trend lines and counts on the chart are drawn from Mini Bottoms. It becomes simple to read and track Mutual Funds in this manner. The above chart captures about 9 years of data. Simple moving average indicator should also be sufficient to identify the trend.

Figure 11.4.2 shown below captures 14 years of data. It is a 2% × 3 P&F chart of HDFC Top 200 Growth fund plotted along with 20 column simple moving average indicator.

Figure 11.4.2: HDFC top 200 (G) 2% × 3 Point & Figure chart

P&F price patterns are equally applicable on these charts and tell us more about the sentiments of investor participants. Below is 2% × 3 P&F chart of HDFC Infrastructure Growth fund plotted along with 20-column simple moving average indicator.

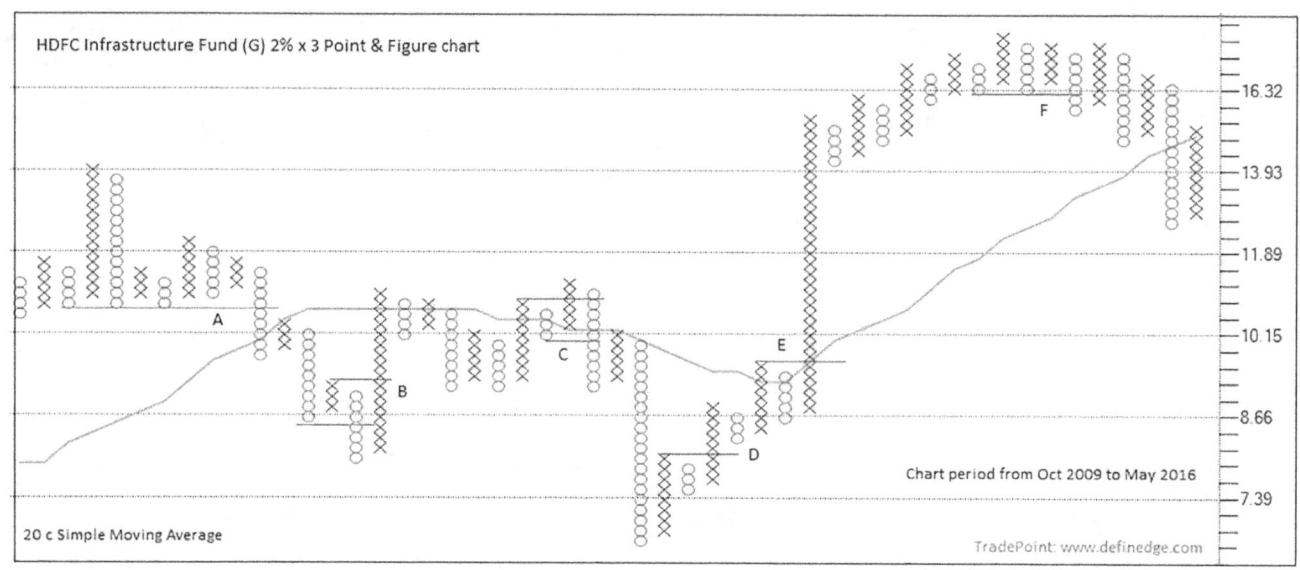

Figure 11.4.3: HDFC infrastructure fund (G) 2% × 3 Point & Figure chart

Pattern A is Multi-Bottom Sell formation. Pattern B is a Bear Trap though below moving average. Pattern C is a Bull Trap down crossing average line. Pattern D is bearish pattern that reversed followed by Buy signal above moving average at E. Pattern F is a Tripe Bottom Sell formation.

We usually view the table displaying the returns of Mutual Funds over a period of time to analyse their performance. Point & Figure Relative strength charts can be drawn to view the same. Figure below is 2% × 3 P&F chart of HDFC Mid-cap opportunities growth fund divided by Nifty. Rising columns in the chart shows outperformance and falling column suggests underperformance of the fund against market barometer.

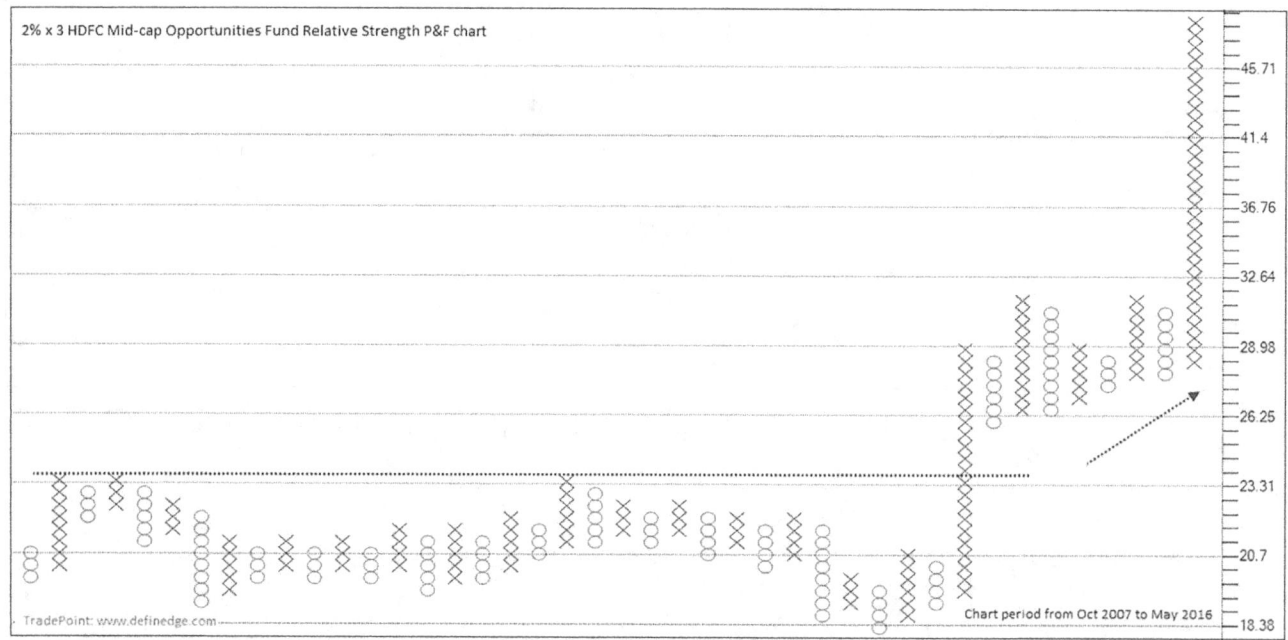

Figure 11.4.4: HDFC Mid-cap opportunities fund (G)/Nifty 2% × 3 Relative Strength Point & Figure chart

The breakout from large consolidation and series of bullish signal shows better performance of the Fund. Figure shown below is 2% × 3 P&F chart of HDFC Infrastructure growth fund divided by Nifty.

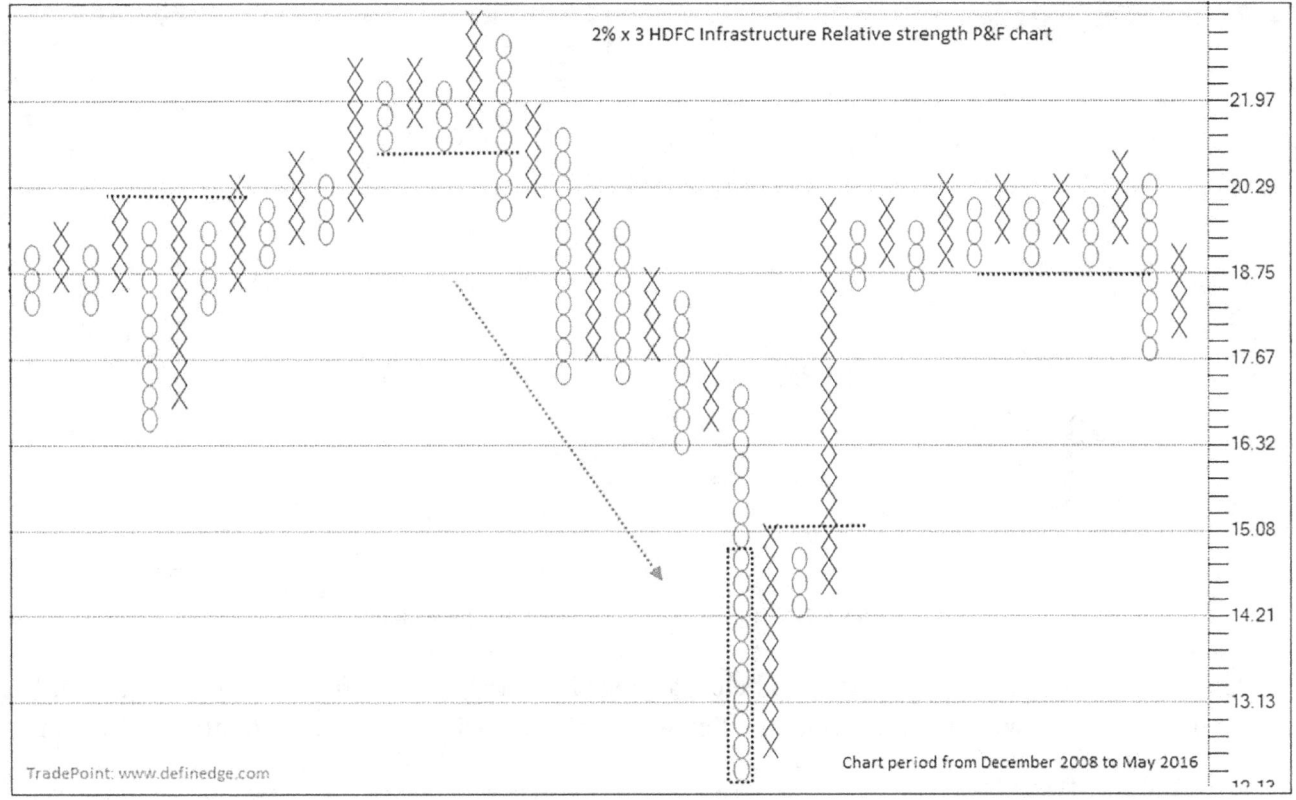

Figure 11.4.5: HDFC infrastructure fund (G)/Nifty 2% × 3 Relative Strength Point & Figure chart

Several patterns are marked on the chart. The series of Sell signal during 2010–2014 suggests underperformance of the Fund against Nifty.

Lower box-values can be referred to for short-term horizon. We discussed relative strength matrix in Chapter 8. Mutual fund performance matrix can be designed in the similar manner to rate funds based on their performance in RS charts. Constituents of top performing funds can help us in identifying the leaders. All other methods of P&F analysis are applicable on Mutual fund and ETF P&F charts as well.

11.5: NIFTY PE

Price earning (PE) ratio is another important tool widely followed by many market participants. It is calculated by dividing the stock price of the company by its earnings per share and used as tool to check if the company is undervalued or overvalued.

Figure shown below is 0.25% × 3 Point & Figure chart of PE ratio of Nifty.

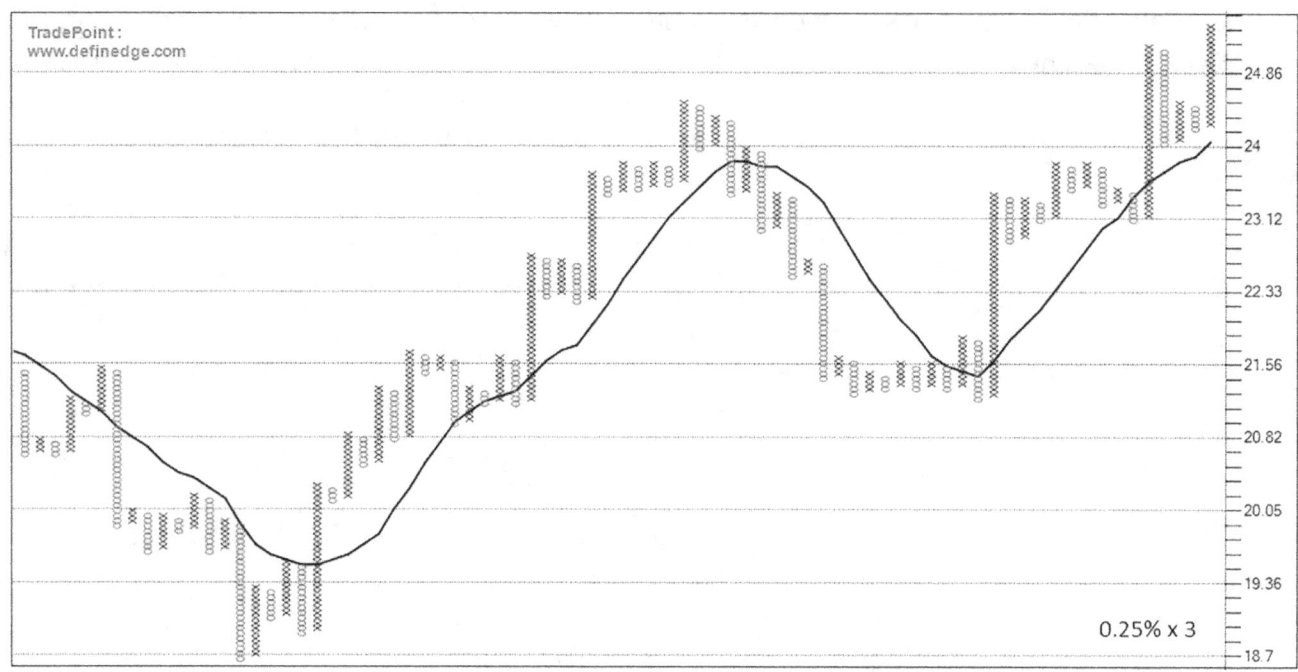

Figure 11.5.1: Nifty PE 0.25% × 3 Point & Figure chart

PE above moving average is bullish and below average is bearish. It is sufficient to tell us trend of PE. Let me pack the chart with more information. Below is a PE chart with trend lines, counts and XO zone.

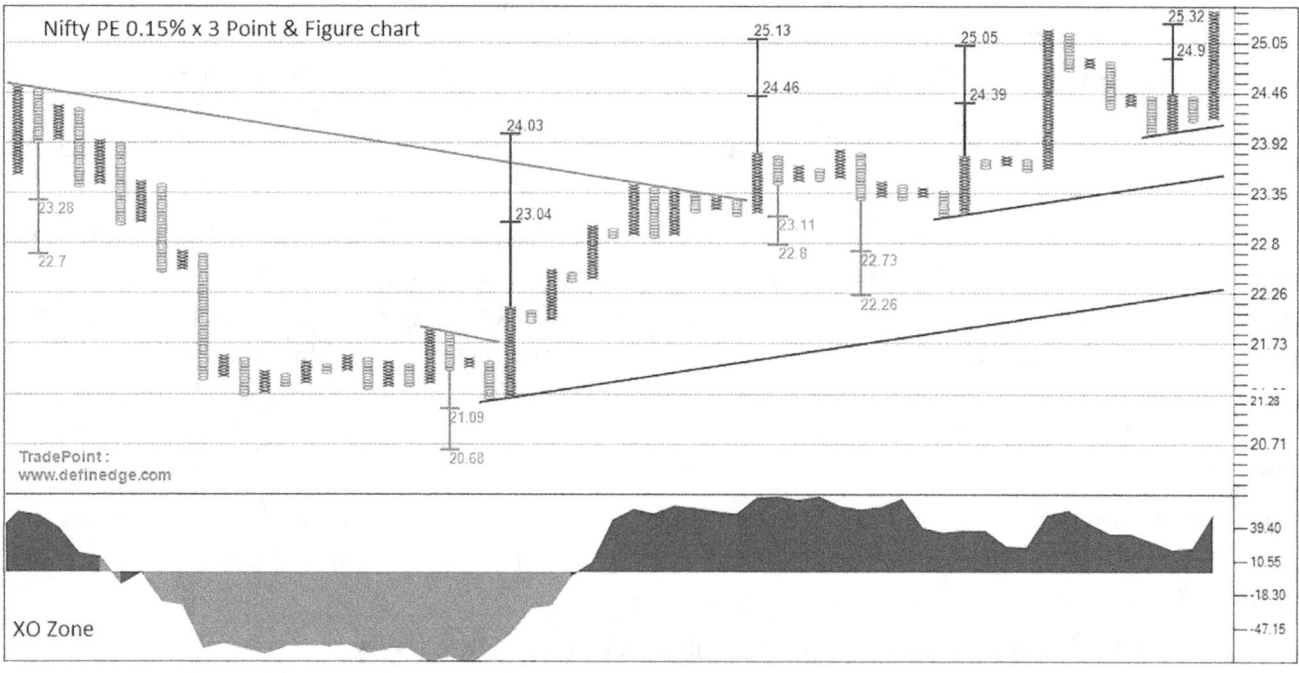

Figure 11.5.2: Nifty PE 0.15% × 3 Point & Figure chart

Trend, open counts and achievement or non-achievement of counts can be analyzed in chart plotted above.

Below is 1.50% × 3 Point & Figure chart of PE ratio of Nifty.

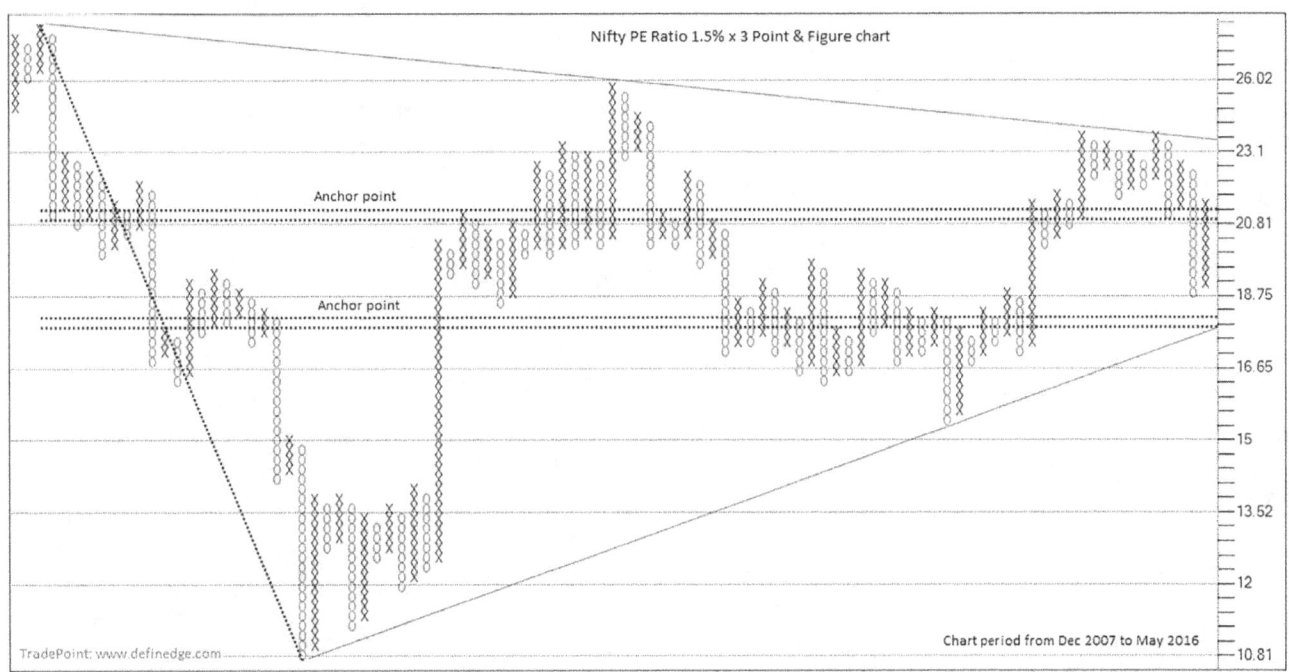

Figure 11.5.3: Nifty PE 0.1.5% × 3 Point & Figure chart

Converging formation is shown by the subjective trend lines on the chart. Anchor points are shown in the chart from the first leg. It is a useful tool to plot on such typically range-bound instruments. Approximately 20 is the Anchor point level of entire chart of PE. The most traded box-price in the entire tenure of the instrument can be identified by drawing the Anchor point from the first column of the chart to the current. It is a P&F mean or average point of an instrument; price is expected to hover around that level, when revisited.

The fun part is over and let's get back to the business of trading in the next chapter.

Chapter 12

TRADING

Various methods and techniques on P&F discussed throughout this book are applicable on all time frames and box-values. Even one or two things understood properly can make you trade any instrument successfully. A few strategies are discussed in this chapter from investing and trading perspective, to arm you with more ideas and use the ones that suit your approach.

12.1: INVESTING

Generally speaking, investment is made keeping larger time horizon in mind. It is a sensible approach to use higher box-values when time horizon is large. All P&F methods that we have discussed can be applied on larger box-value charts for medium-term or long-term investments; I am not repeating it unnecessarily. The earlier discussion about Slot 3 and Slot 4 box-value charts are sufficient to trade from a longer time horizon.

There are two specific methods of investments made objective and explained below.

3% Multi-Column Breakout

I recommend 3% box-value on three-box reversal charts, for trades and analysis for medium-term and long-term horizons, especially for mid-cap and small-cap stocks. Breakouts from large consolidation or horizontal formations like head and shoulders or cup and handle, etc. on daily-weekly bar charts show up as a simple Triple Top or multi-column breakout formation on these P&F charts.

Below is daily candlestick chart of Amarajabat. A price consolidation phase between February and August 2013 is shown in the chart.

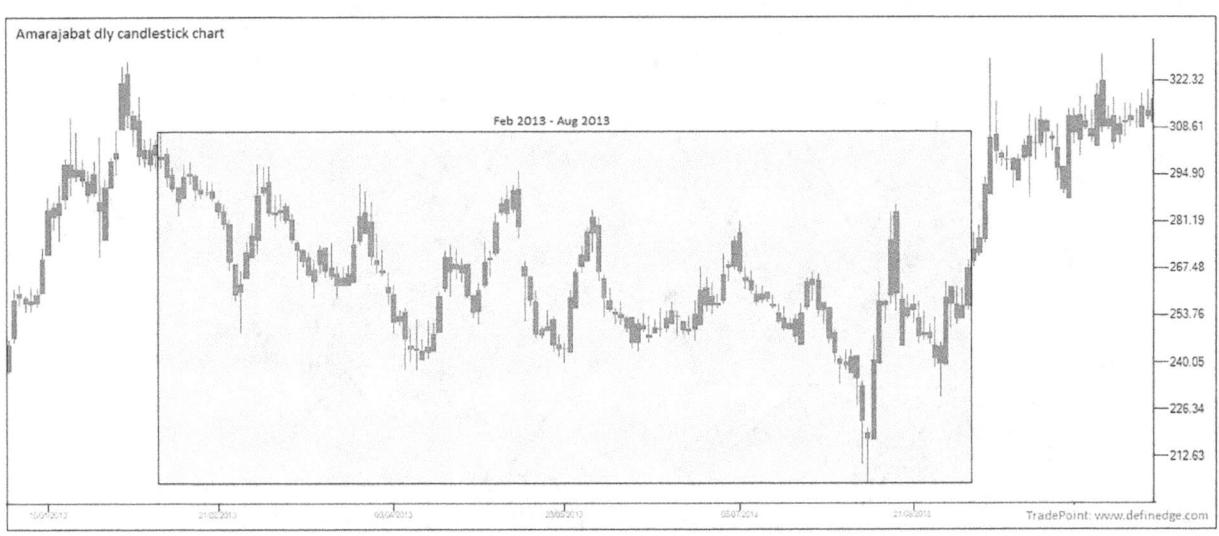

Figure 12.1.1: Amarrajabat daily candlestick chart

Same consolidation phase is also displayed in the box on P&F chart below plotted with 3% box-value. Such complex phase in the candle stick chart, comes across as a Quadruple Top breakout in the P&F chart.

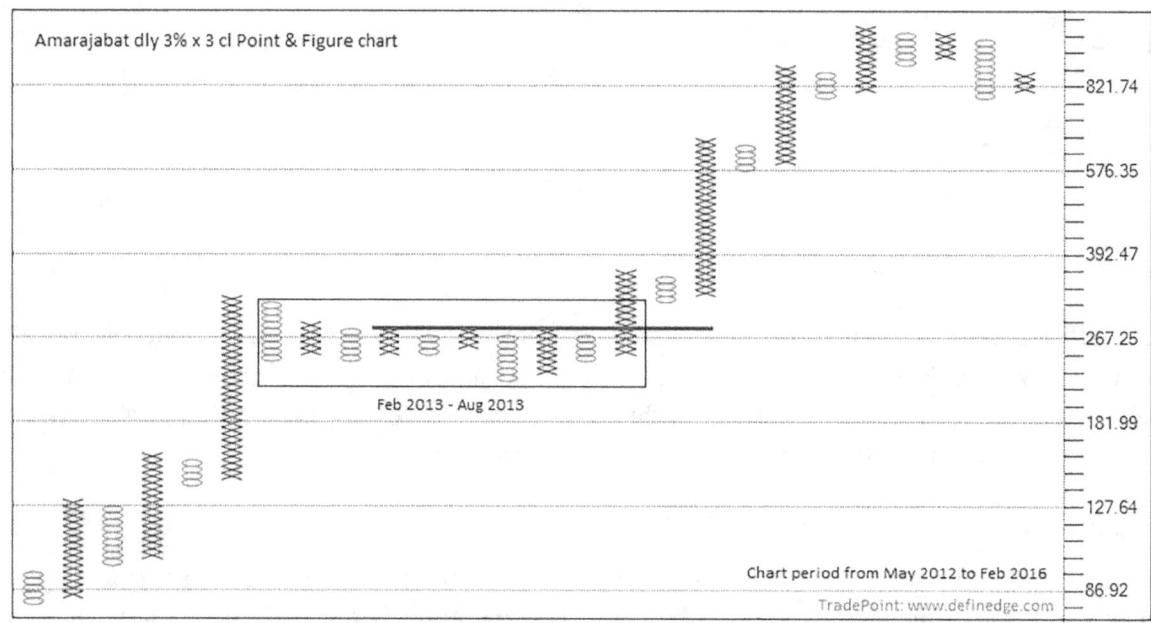

Figure 12.1.2: Amarrajabat daily 3% × 3 cl Point & Figure chart

It may not be a quadruple formation always, but multi-column breakouts or variations of it on this box-value chart represent a significant breakout from large and complex formations in the traditional time-based chart. While this was a Triple Top pattern as well, a Double Top pattern after retracement on these charts is also useful information. An investment can be made and ridden on this box-value as per the trailing methods that we have discussed.

To keep it simple, find Triple Top and diagonal top breakouts on 3% box-value charts. Such multi-column breakout P&F formations show that price is coming out of some serious consolidation spanning across a number of days or weeks or even months in some cases. Often, you will find that the breakout candidates identified from this method have consolidation breakout formations such as usual cup and handle or head and shoulder in traditional time-based charts.

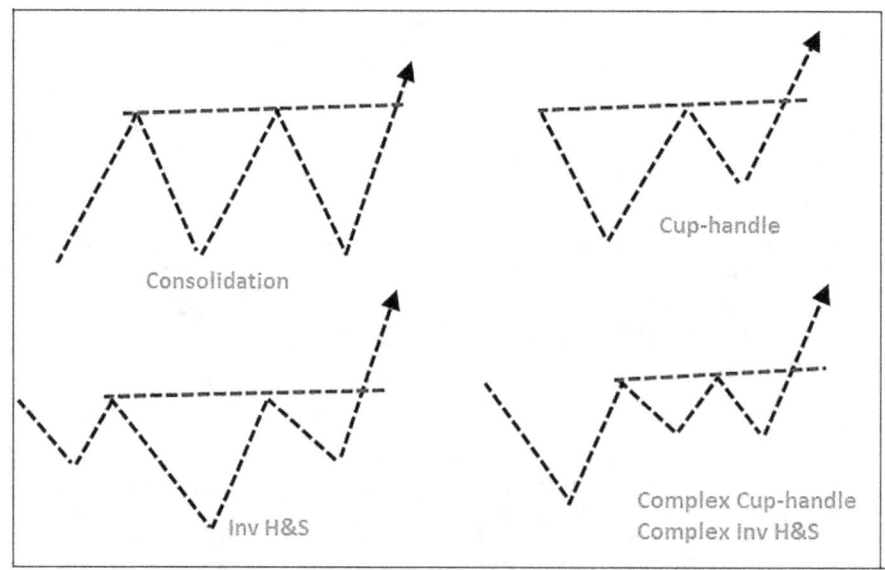

Image 12.1.1: Consolidation breakout patterns

Have a look at daily candlestick chart of Escorts shown below.

Figure 12.1.3: Escorts daily candlestick chart

It looks like inverted head and shoulders to me. Breakout from this kind of formations suggests accumulation or distribution and I always used to look for them on usual charts. The only issue is that it is very difficult to run a scan and shortlist such candidates in the traditional time-based charts. Have a look at 3% × 3 P&F chart of Escorts below.

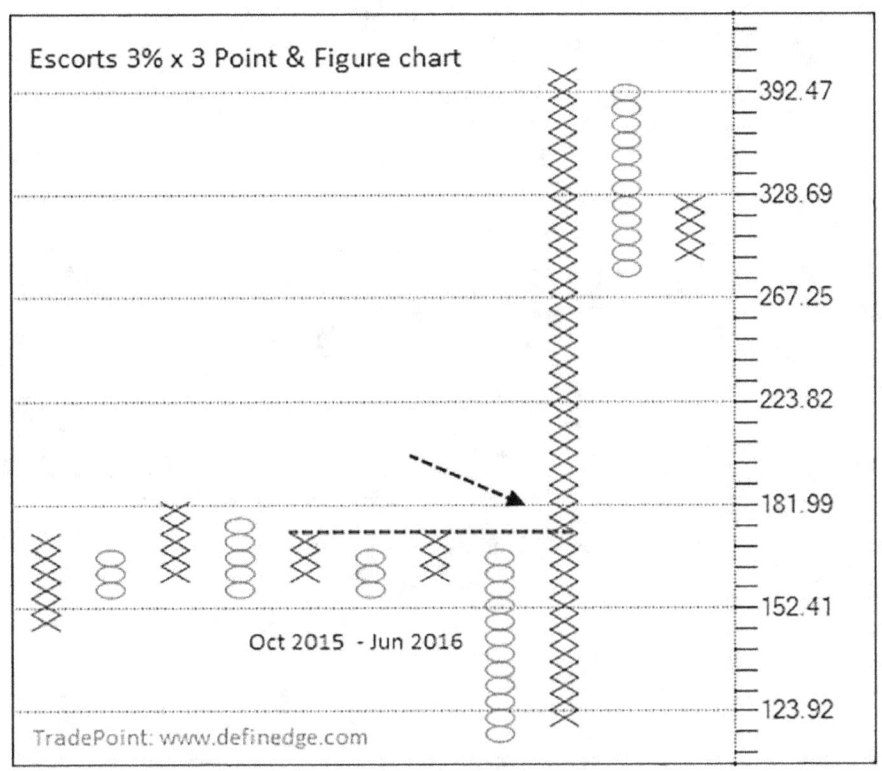

Figure 12.1.4: Escorts daily 3% × 3 cl Point & Figure chart

The Triple Top Buy pattern in the above chart suggested breakout from a 9 months accumulation pattern. Being an objective pattern, it can be scanned and the candidates where such breakouts happened can easily be identified and shortlisted. At times, it throws the list of stocks we get surprised to come across because we realize how difficult otherwise it be to identify such breakouts. Have a look at chart of VST industries shown below.

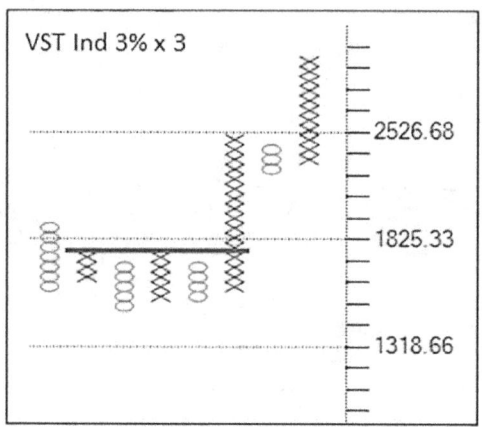

Figure 12.1.5: VST industries daily 3% × 3 cl Point & Figure chart

The above Triple Top Buy pattern duration was more than a year. Look at the accumulation pattern on candlestick chart shown below that immediately catches the eye.

Figure 12.1.6: VST industries daily candlestick chart

The stock delivered a 100% return in the following year. There are many such examples to share. But the best part with this method is that the pattern is objective and the failure point is also clearly defined. This makes it simple to estimate the initial risk if the pattern fails. The risk–reward will be very attractive if you ride the trend using basic P&F patterns.

In a nutshell, plot 3% box-value chart and scan for Triple Top Buy or diagonal Triple Top Buy patterns. Trade the candidates on that box-value if you are comfortable with the initial risk. Otherwise, identify the breakout candidates and trade them in a lower box-value that suits personal investment style.

The method is applicable on different box-values also. One can apply subjectivity and look for multi-column breakout instead of simple triple or diagonal, but keep things simple initially.

P&F Turtle Investment Method

We discussed the Turtle trading setup on Point & Figure charts in the first chapter. That knowledge can be applied for investment purpose with a long-only approach. For example, buy when price goes above highest price of last 20 'X's and exit if it falls below the lowest price of last 10 'O's. This should be applied on lower- or medium-term box-value charts such as 0.25% or 1%.

See the Sun Pharma chart shown below.

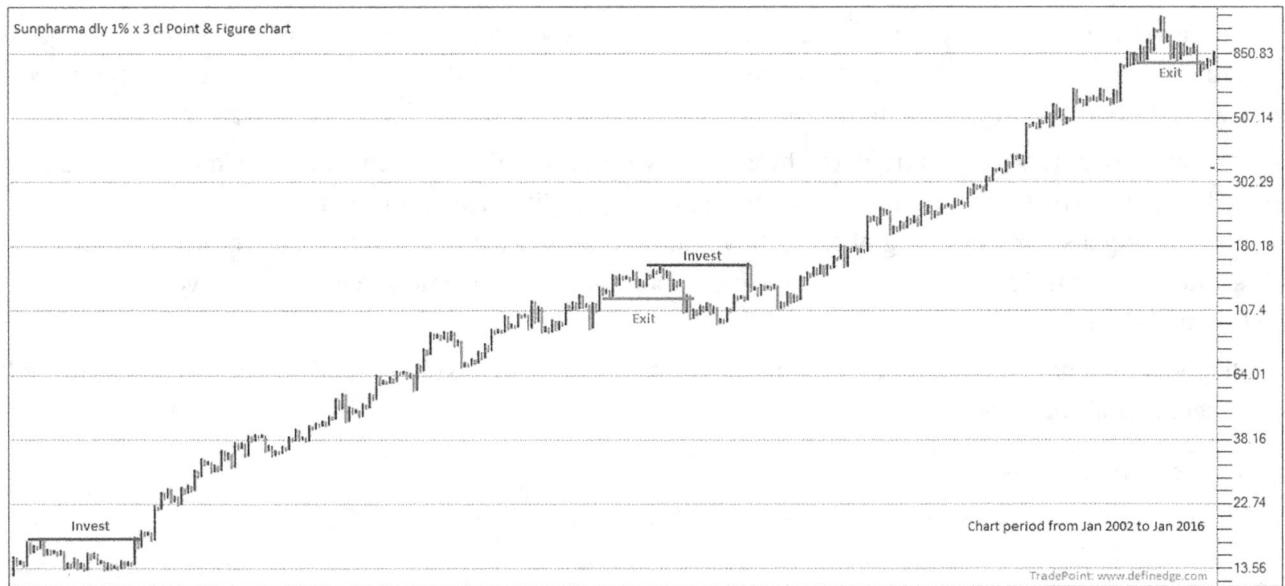

Figure 12.1.7: Sun Pharma daily 1% × 3 cl Point & Figure chart

Such strategies for investment have delivered attractive returns when back-tested. But again, that should not be the sole reason to adopt an investment strategy. This method is objective in nature and the signals are very infrequent and come with a well-defined exit mechanism. Stocks can be scanned based on multi-column breakout for investment.

Below is another stock from the pharma sector showing the breakouts on High–Low chart of 3% box-value.

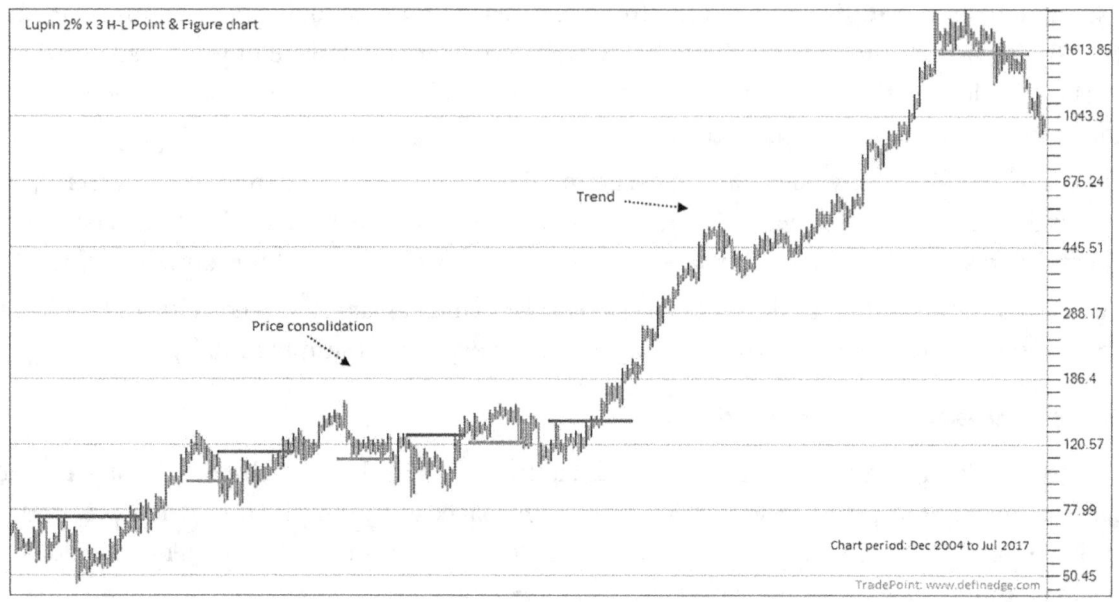

Figure 12.1.8: Lupin daily 2% × 3 H-L Point & Figure chart

There are about four trades in the chart shown above, two worked and two failed. Observe the gains from the profitable trades compared to the loss from the trades that didn't work. Hence, while the success ratio will be relatively moderate in this method, it scores handsomely in the risk–reward metric.

As stated earlier, whipsaws triggered by a strategy is unavoidable and must be viewed as premium paid for early exits to avert a significant erosion in the trading capital. Always remember that a re-entry is not banned. During a strong trending phase, a buy and hold strategy will deliver better returns compared to this strategy. But this method will outperform over a period of time, and safeguard the investments when the tide turns rough.

Below is the chart of Tata Steel showing the exit based on such simple method before the severe fall in the second half of 2008.

Figure 12.1.9: Tata Steel daily 1% × 3 cl Point & Figure chart

There are many such stocks that can be showcased as an example to show the importance of timely exits. Parameters can be tweaked based on personal preference but the key takeaway here is that a well-defined exit method shall outperform over a period. We have discussed in the chapter on Relative Strength that not all stocks perform even when the overall market trend is bullish.

Such types of sharp crash can happen even during an overall uptrend in the stock market. Similarly, certain set of stocks perform well even during bear markets. They can also be verified based on fundamental analysis and traded with this kind of a method or it can be the other way around too. Other methods of analysis will only complement P&F strategy.

I strongly believe that there must be value and base for price to go up, otherwise rallies are short-lived. The Triple Top or multiple top breakout pattern is a simple approach to find the breakout from base candidates. One can perform financial analysis to identify candidates that have value. I am a firm believer of fundamental analysis. I completely agree that one can invest confidently and significantly only if there is a story in the stock or sector supported by qualitative and quantitative analysis. One should study valuations, and invest in companies which have strong management and competitive advantage. But it is very difficult to keep track of macro- and micro-environment on a frequent basis and there is a risk of going wrong there as well. Price setups are often a lead indicator and help identify candidates on which further fundamental research may be conducted. There is no right or wrong way to select stocks. Just stick to the approach that makes sense to you. I believe in Funda-Techno approach, but if one is not well versed with fundamental analysis, investments then can be considered using the methods that we have discussed on P&F charts. Methods discussed in this chapter will not give frequent exits but will ensure that you exit before the situation worsens.

This shows that objective and simple systems can be designed on P&F. Notice that both methods are for medium to long-term investments, but one is applicable on higher box-values and the other is on lower. Hence, all box-values are useful; it depends on the method that we apply. Using the P&F patterns in conjunction with relative strength charts will help in improving trading or investment success.

The TradePoint software has capabilities of all types of back-testing. Try testing the above methods; you might be surprised to see what simple strategies can deliver. I could give this chapter a title such as *How to find multi-bagger* or *How to make millions using simple methods*.

Mini Top–Mini Bottoms, Anchor Top–Bottoms, Tweezers, Climax, etc. are other formations to name a few discussed in the book that can be applied from the investment perspective. Below are a few strategies discussed for short-term and medium-term trading.

12.2: SHORT-TERM AND MEDIUM-TERM TRADING

Analysis

Analyse the chart on different box-values and trade the patterns based on it. Look for the broader picture, plot objective 45-degree lines and treat breakouts as important when breadth is not at an extreme zone. Below are a few examples showing how patterns can be traded based on overall chart analysis.

Below is 0.25% × 3 P&F chart of Jisljaleqs.

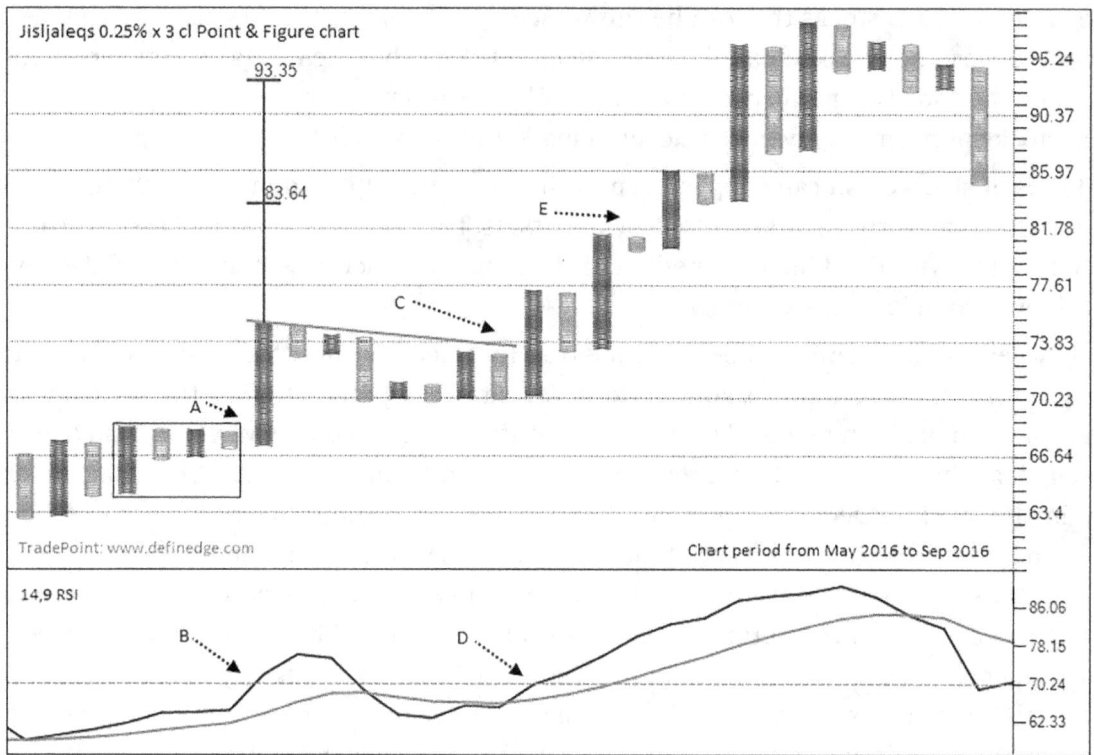

Figure 12.2.1: Jisljaleqs daily 0.25% × 3 cl Point & Figure chart

Pattern A is a four-column Triangle when RSI at point B is positive. Point C is bullish ABC setup when RSI at point D has turned positive after consolidation. Pattern E is super pattern that offers another opportunity to trade in the direction of the ABC setup count.

Below is 1% × 3 chart of Apollo Hospital

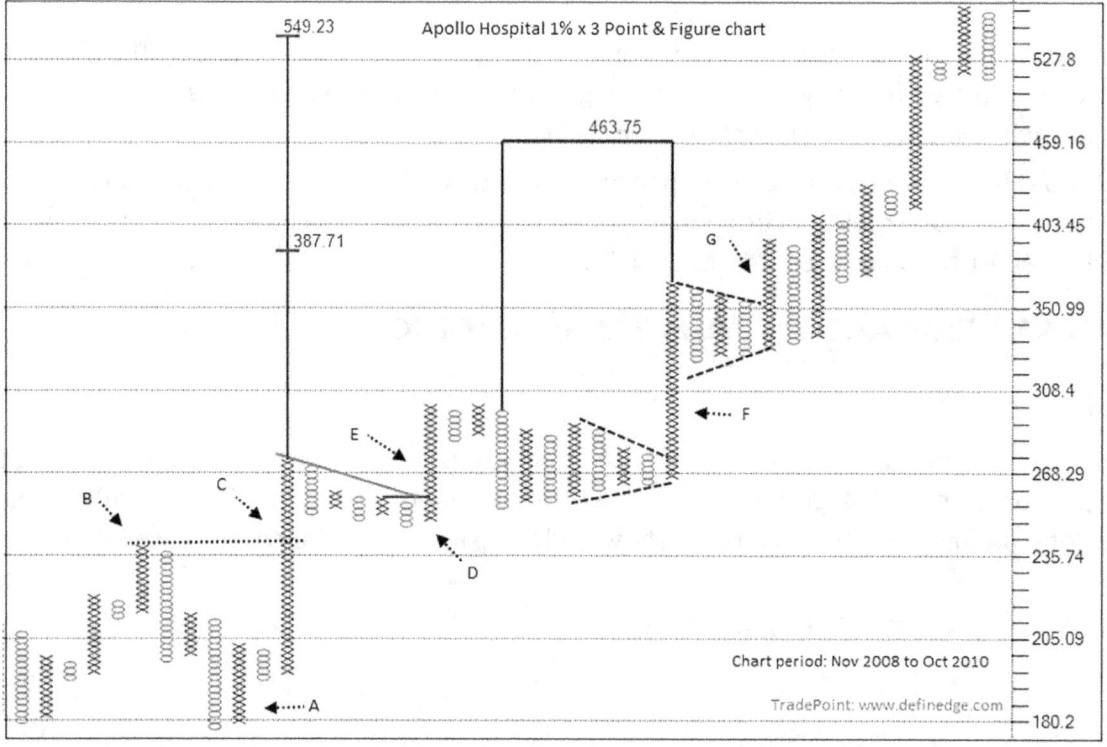

Figure 12.2.2: Apollo Hospital daily 0.25% × 3 cl Point & Figure chart

Point A is bullish double pattern retest. B is bearish 100% Pole; it was invalidated at point C that led to the chart turning bullish. Point D is Ziddi bulls pattern that also triggered ABC breakout at point E. F is four-column Triangle breakout that also resulted in a Tweezer pattern. Point G activated the Tweezer and happened to be a four-column Triangle breakout.

Practice will make you observe these formations on any P&F chart. The best advantage is that once the strength is identified in a instrument, patterns will keep giving opportunities to trade them continuously. Many traders identify a stock at the right time but exit early. The other typical mistake is that they don't trade its Continuation moves. P&F patterns will keep giving opportunities to trade Continuation signals in them.

Below is 0.25% × 3 chart of Reliance Industries.

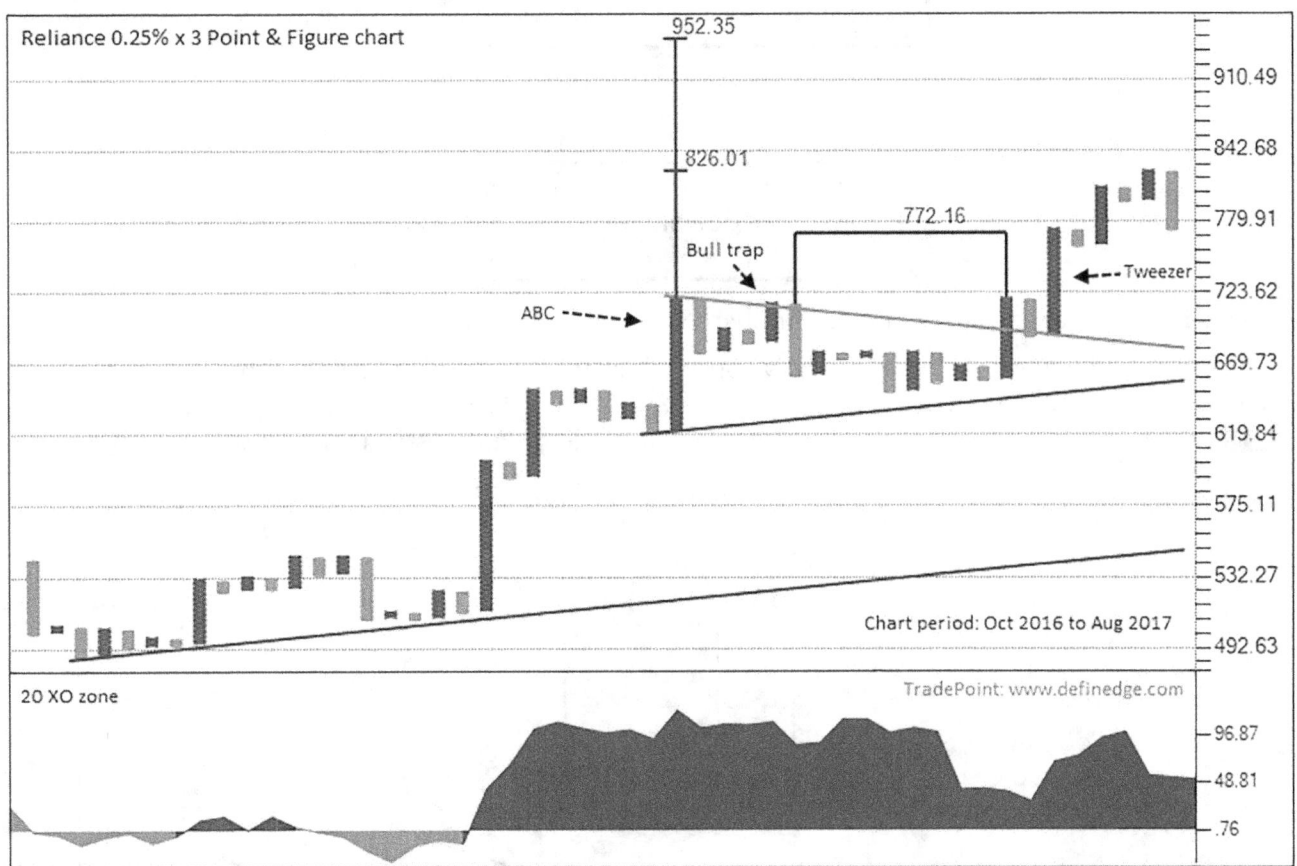

Figure 12.2.3: Reliance daily 0.25% × 3 cl Point & Figure chart

The chart above shows bullish 45-degree lines drawn from Mini Bottoms. Notice ABC and Tweezers when XO zone is showing the strength; there is no reason not to trade it. One more thing – Tweezer activation also negated the prior Bull Trap marked in the chart.

Top-Down Approach

The relative strength analysis can be the starting point in identifying a list of counters to be traded. Find the list of sectors outperforming the broader market index and then find the outperforming from those outperforming sectors. It is a top-down approach of finding out the list of stocks to be traded. The next step is to study the chart patterns in those shortlisted candidates to execute the trades.

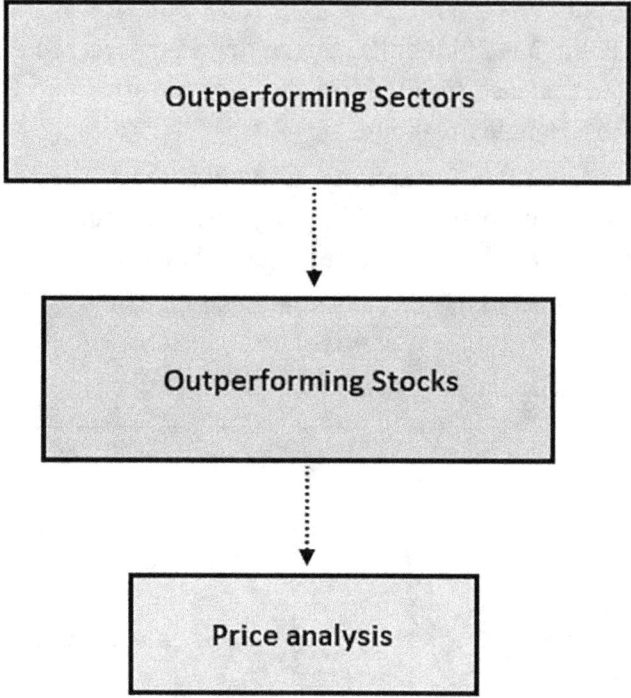

This method was explained in detail in Chapter 8. Below is an example.

Figure shown below is 0.25% × 3 Relative Strength chart of Bank Nifty against Nifty.

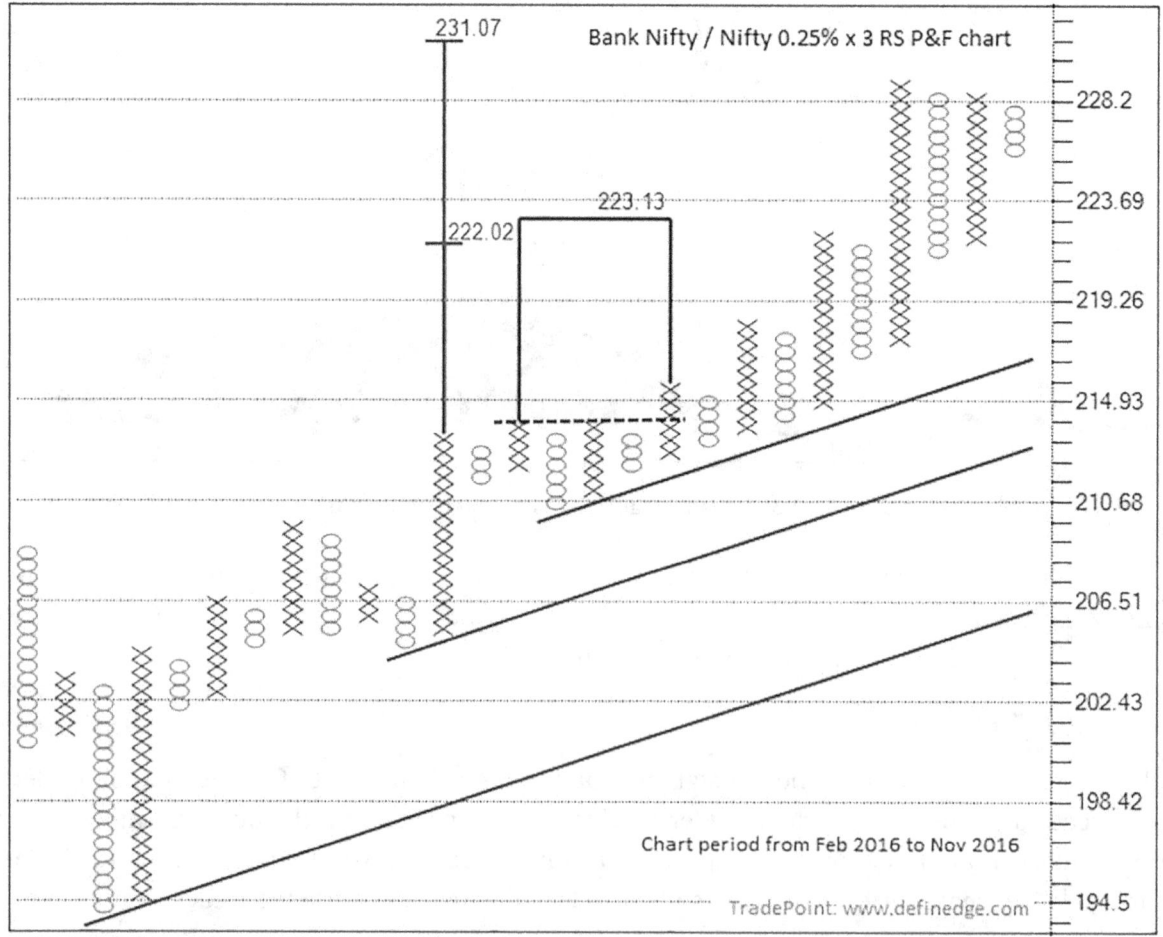

Figure 12.2.4: Bank Nifty/Nifty 0.25% × 3 daily Relative Strength Point & Figure chart

Triple Top Buy formation shown by the arrow indicates strength in the setup which is occurring above the objective trend lines. Aggressive horizontal count and bullish vertical counts derived from the pattern indicate that Bank sector may outperform broader market index.

Figure shown below is 0.25% × 3 P&F chart of HDFC bank for the same period.

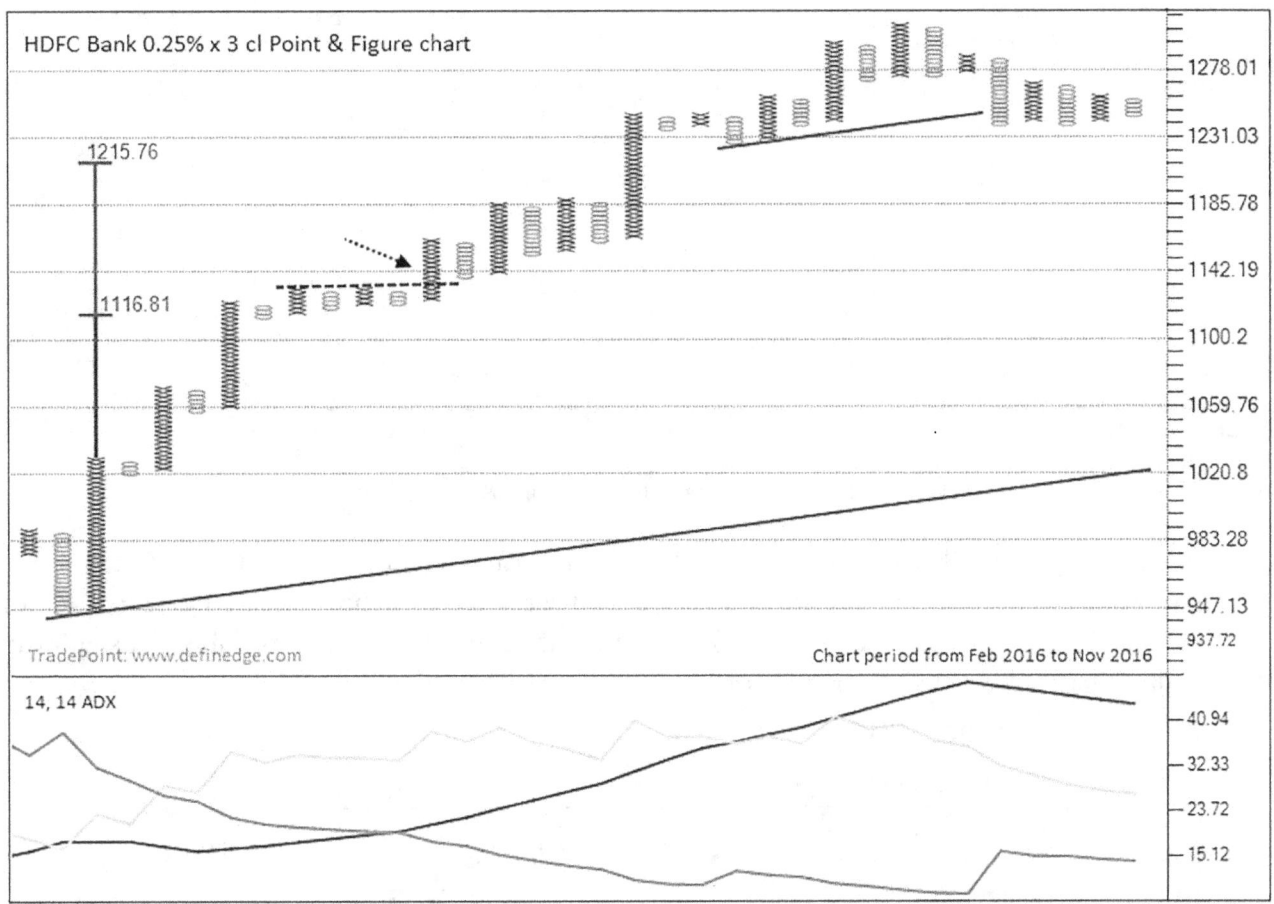

Figure 12.2.5: HDFC bank daily 0.25% × 3 cl Point & Figure chart

Triple Top formation in bullish environment when ADX also shows clear trend, indicates strength in the stock and shows that it is one of the leading candidates of the bank index, and outperforming the Nifty.

Keep track of stocks that fall less when markets correct, they tend to perform better when market recovers. Continuation patterns in those instruments offer high-probability trades.

Pattern Cluster

We discussed the concept of pattern cluster in Chapter 5. The best trades can be generated when there is a significant pattern visible across different box-values, especially when there is a breakout pattern on higher box-value and some failure formation in the lower box-value or time frame. When setup has got breakout and failure as an ingredient, chances of success are increased.

So find the stocks where there has been a major bullish formation on higher box-value charts such as 1% or 3%, and look for bullish setup on lower box-value chart that provides low-risk setup that can be traded.

Look at P&F charts of Engineers India shown below.

Engineers India

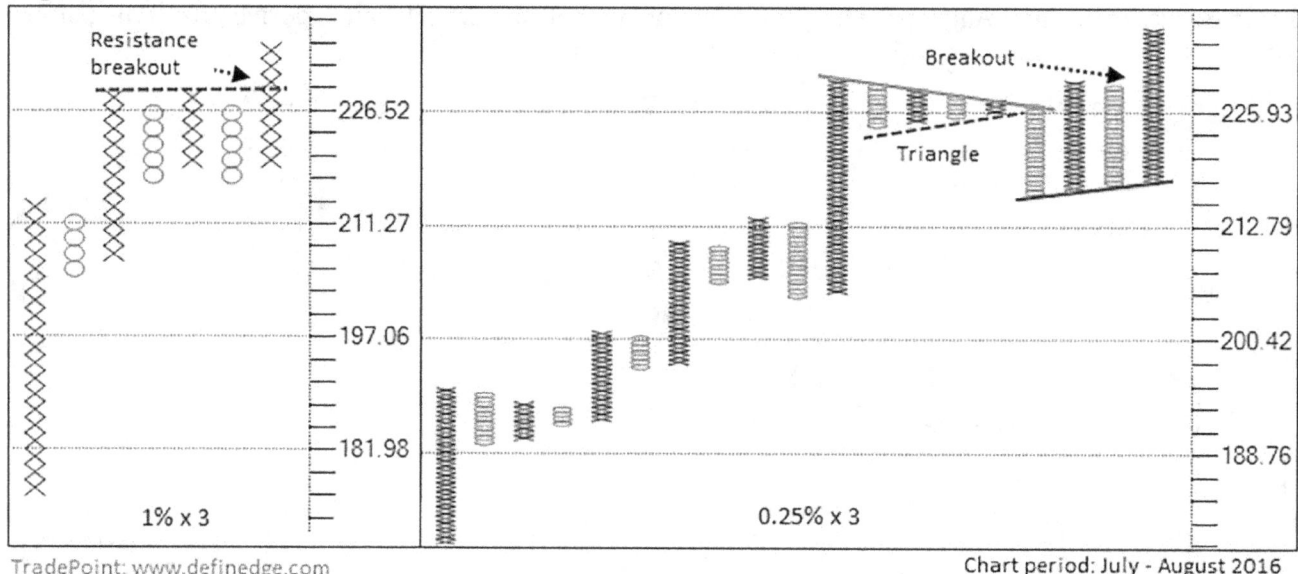

Figure 12.2.6: Engineers India daily Point & Figure charts

There was Triple Top Buy formation on 1% box-value formation and Triangle failure formation on 0.25% box-value followed by another Buy pattern. It is discernible that the attempts by bears in lower box-value failed when the price managed a significant breakout on the higher box-value is a significant information. Price witnessed 15% jump over the next few sessions.

Below is LIC housing finance P&F chart.

LIC Housing Finance

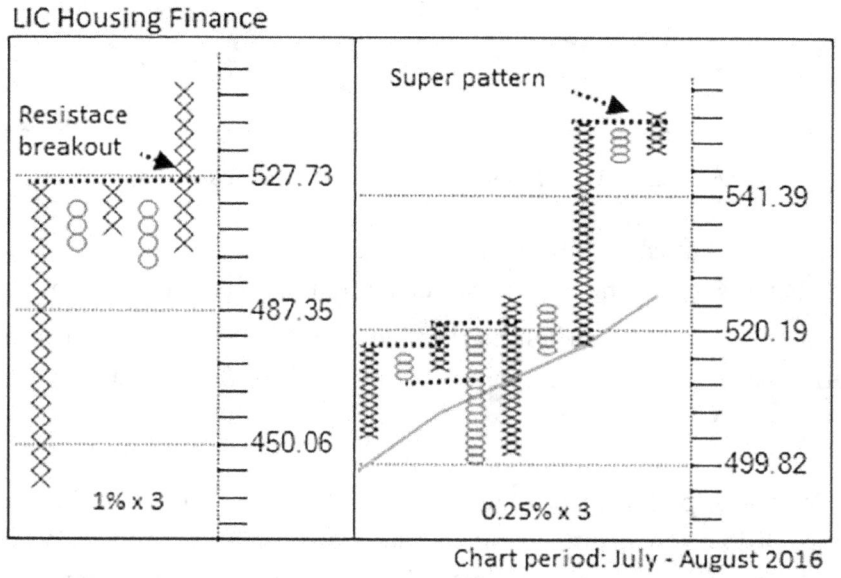

Figure 12.2.7: LIC housing finance daily Point & Figure charts

There was a Triple Top Buy formation on 1% chart and super pattern on 0.25% chart that offered a low-risk trade. It is better to know about larger degree setup while trading such breakout patterns on lower box-value charts and it helps in filtering out setups and increases the chances of success.

Below figure shows interesting setup in Canara bank.

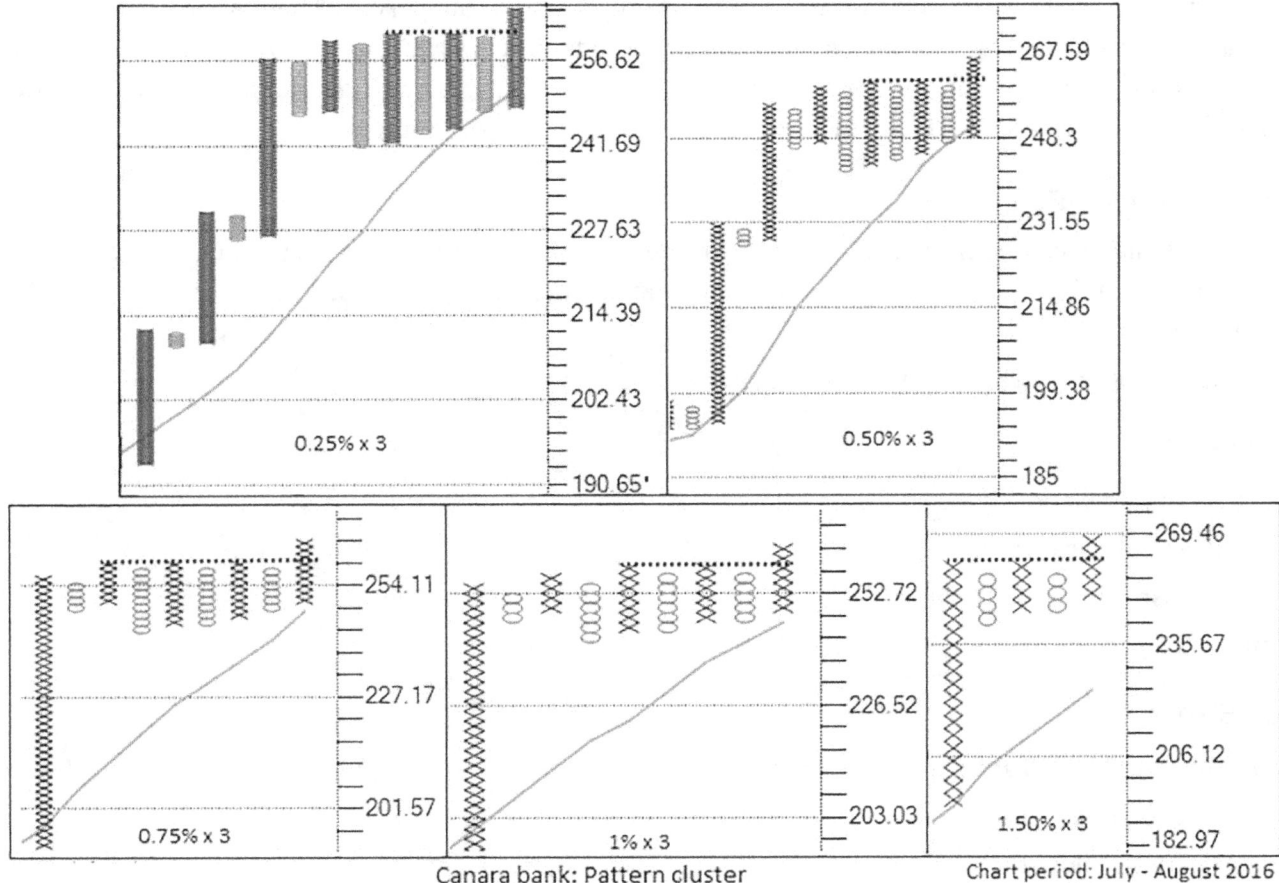

Canara bank: Pattern cluster   Chart period: July - August 2016

Figure 12.2.8: Canara bank daiy Point & Figure charts

It happened to be Triple Top Buy formation across box-values at the same time. It may not be the case all the time but breakout in multiple box-values or appearance of major patterns on different box-values at a same time present a good trading opportunity. Price went up by over 20% over next few trading sessions.

When there is major pattern cluster at multiple box-values, chances of a trade turning profitable is quite high. Box-values 0.25%, 1% and 3% are recommended to begin with this method of analysis. You may like to observe other tools like trend lines and indicators once pattern cluster is found.

One Setup Trading

One setup trading is one of the great advantages that P&F charts offer. Pattern following is a unique module that can be followed across time frames. For example, four-column Triangle breakout formation can be traded across groups of stocks whenever it occurs.

Pick one or two patterns that you are most comfortable with from the list and observe, back-test and practice them. Trade them upon occurrence in stocks across universe. It is a more useful approach than drifting aimlessly. P&F offers an edge due to its objectivity and noiselessness. Selecting one or two patterns and trading it continuously is far easier said than done, because more than trading them, it is ignoring the rest of the things that turns out to be more difficult. It is not very easy to become deaf to surrounding noise and concentrate on a few setups. But trading can be successful that way, on all time frames. Because, with this approach, we let the market tell us what to do instead of imposing our opinions on it. Trading becomes a process that makes it a sensible business, which can be scaled up. The entire focus is on execution rather than analysis.

People change their strategy when they go through a difficult period. Their mindless-style drift typically results in trading bad phases of multiple methods. Understand that no method is infallible and sticking to one is important. Accept a system or method with its drawbacks; understand the scenarios when it may not work well. The method that defines risk clearly, shall outperform in the longer run.

System Trading

Different systems can be designed on P&F with the help of patterns and indicators. Objective systems traded on a predefined universe can be effectively implemented on P&F as well; noise-free plotting is a big advantage with P&F method.

Example of one such system is given below.

For Long

RS chart should be positive

XO zone should be positive

Trade bullish Follow-through

Simple P&F patterns to be followed for exit

For Short

RS chart should be negative

XO zone should be negative

Trade bearish Follow-through

Simple P&F patterns to be followed for exit

The logic for above system is that I want to buy when there are more bullish prints than bearish and short a candidate where bearish prints are more. Follow-through is a smart pattern with predefined and usually affordable risk. Above system is just an example. Many other systems can be designed in the similar manner with combination of P&F patterns, tools and indicators.

Trend Reversal

Trend reversal or mean reversion trading is a contra-trend strategy where one is looking for setups against the trend in place. Below are the major triggers in P&F that can help contrarians:

- Reversal patterns when breadth is in extreme zone
- Anchor point
- Pattern retest
- RSI divergence
- Reversal formations when indicators are in exhaustion zone
- Reversal patterns at Bollinger band extremes
- Relative low–relative high

Combination of observations from above list offer best trading opportunities. Follow-through is the icing on the cake.

Figure shown below is a 1% × 3 chart of Ashok Leyland.

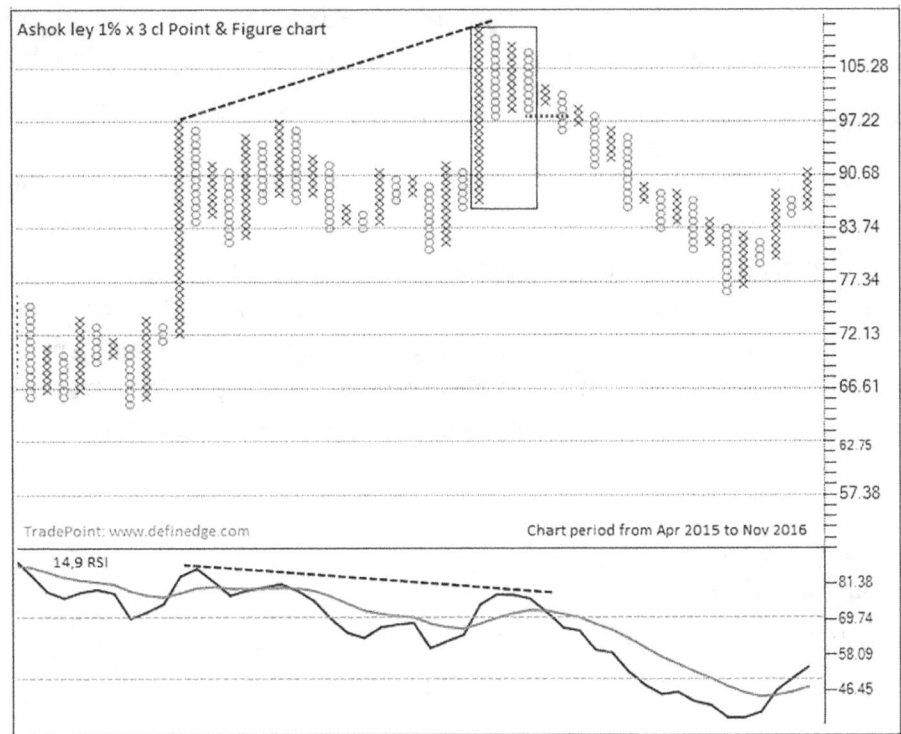

Figure 12.2.9: Ashok Leyland daily 1% × 3 cl Point & Figure chart

Weakness in new high was indicated by negative RSI divergence setup when Nifty breadth also entered overbought zone. Triangular pattern and its Follow-through bearish breakout when the breadth was overbought was a perfect setting to consider a counter-trend short trade.

Figure shown below is a 0.25% × 3 chart of PNB.

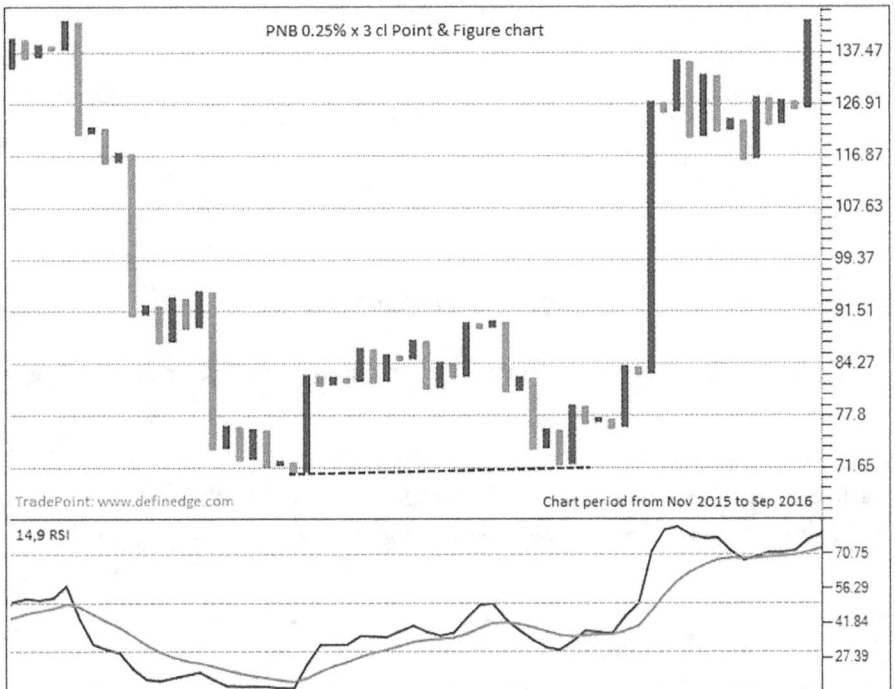

Figure 12.2.10: PNB daily 0.25% × 3 cl Point & Figure chart

Bullish double pattern when RSI was rising and breadth was in oversold zone triggered bullish mean reversion setup. Follow-through and Super pattern post also offered low-risk Continuation pattern trades.

Convergence–Expansion

Let me give you an idea how strategies can be designed using the traits and combinations of different patterns.

Trade four-column Triangle breakouts and Broadening Follow-through formations on your universe of stocks. The former is pattern of convergence and latter is expansion. They will produce trades with different traits in various market environments. Both are dependable and complementary in nature. They are already discussed in this book along with examples, so I will avoid repetition. But I have tried to trigger a spark in your thought process. Explore trading based on this pattern combination method of P&F charts.

P&F Setup

P&F setup is a very simple method designed using unique, simple yet smart features of P&F charts. It is applicable on all charts and all time frames.

P&F setup consists of two components: Pattern and Trend.

Patterns

Patterns in Point& Figure chart can be clearly defined as bullish or bearish. All major patterns are also basic Double Top Buy or Double Bottom Sell patterns except Poles. Hence, basic patterns and poles can be classified as bullish or bearish patterns.

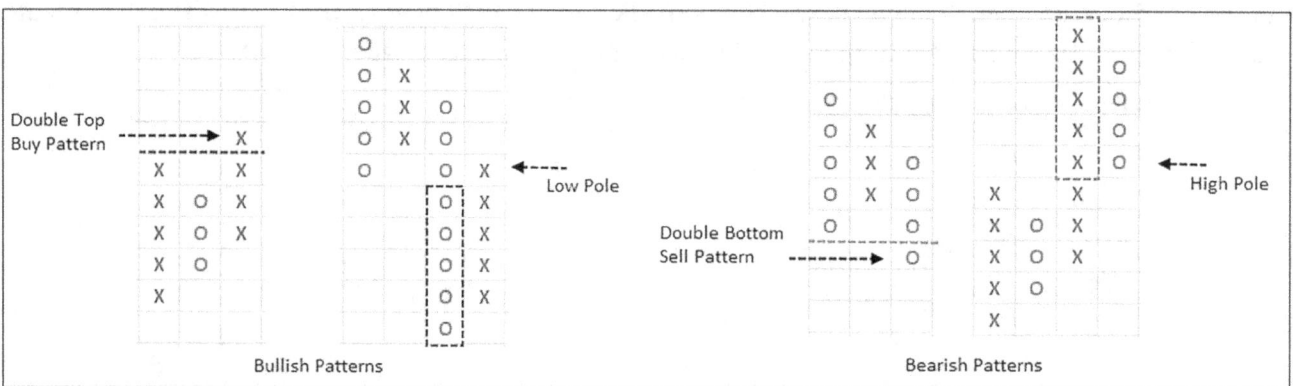

Image 12.2.1: P&F patterns

Triangle is a neutral pattern. All other patterns can be classified either as bullish or bearish.

Trend

Simple trend filtration criteria such as moving average help in identifying trend. The trend will be considered bullish if the price is trading above the moving average and vice versa

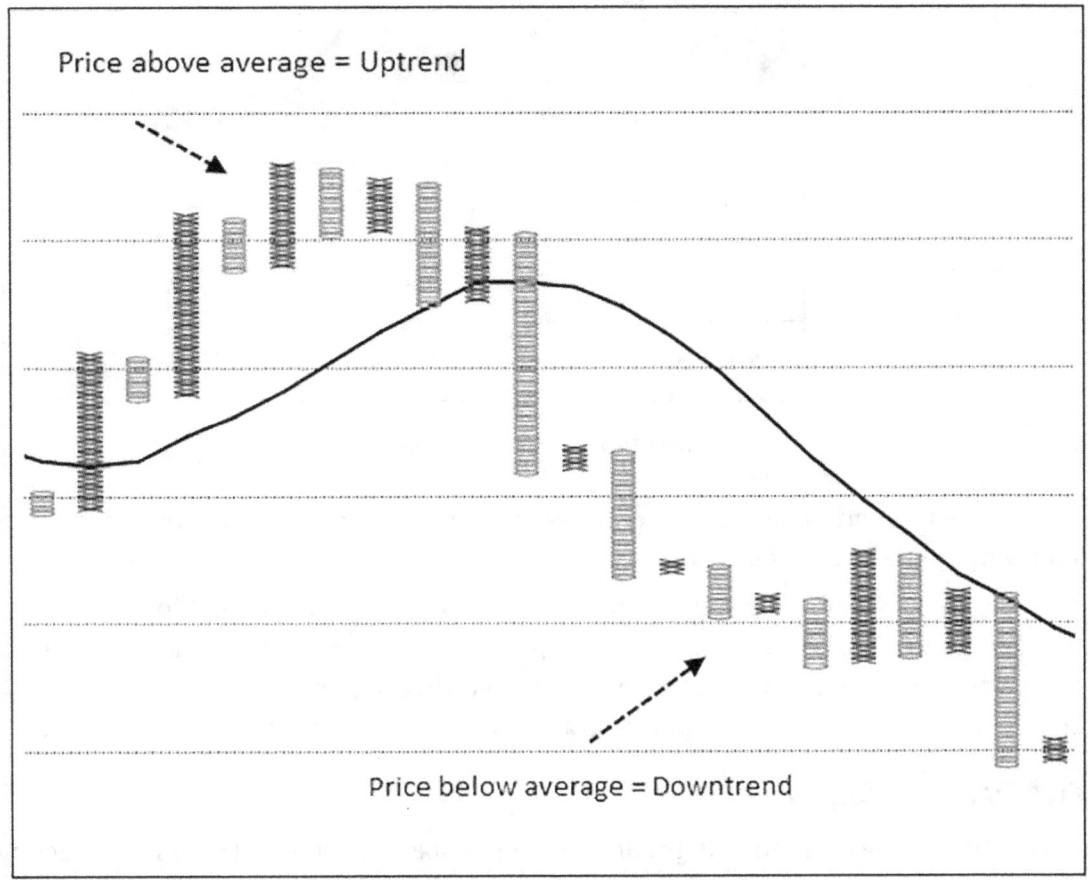

Image 12.2.2: Trend identification

We have now defined the two components : Pattern and Trend in a P&F chart. This can be used in any instrument and time frame. One may wonder why we have this differentiation between pattern and setup. Read on to understand the importance.

If the trend is bullish and pattern is also bullish, then the context is most ideal to focus on bullish trades. We call it a bullish setup. On the other hand, if the trend is bearish and pattern is also bearish, then the setup turns bearish and one should focus on bearish trades.

If the trend and pattern are not in sync, then the setup is considered neutral and it is advisable to apply neutral strategies. As a trader, it is very handy to know the context and market setup to decide the trading strategy. For instance, it is so very easy to lose money by shorting at each resistance in a rising markets or getting trapped buying at supports in a falling market. To avoid such situations, this delineation of trend and setup is useful. If setup is bullish, then buying on bullish breakouts and/or at supports is advisable. Similarly, bearish breakouts and selling at resistances are recommended if setup is bearish. And if setup is neutral, one should look for trend in the instrument concerned and then decide.

Below is a table that lists out various possibilities based on the pattern, trend and resultant setup.

Pattern	Trend	Setup
Bullish	Bullish	Bullish
Bearish	Bearish	Bearish
Bullish	Bearish	**Neutral**
Bearish	Bullish	**Neutral**

Image 12.2.3: P&F Setup table

One can apply own variations and use other box-values or indicators instead of moving average. That's okay. But follow one and beware of over-tweaking.

All techniques discussed above can be applied on time interval charts as well for very short-term or momentum trading. As mentioned earlier, one can plot various time interval charts but I recommend increasing box-value on 1 min time frame instead of plotting higher time interval charts. Usually, I recommend 0.15% × 3 P&F charts on 1 min time frame; adjust it as per your method and preference.

12.3: INTRADAY TRADING

Very short-term trading such as intraday trading requires a special skill set. There is so much noise out there that it is so easy to overtrade. The best advantage of P&F for trading time interval charts is that it reduces the number of trading signals.

Figure shown below is a P&F chart of Nifty showing Mini Tops and Bottoms, trend lines and vertical counts. Bullish formations in such cases should be traded.

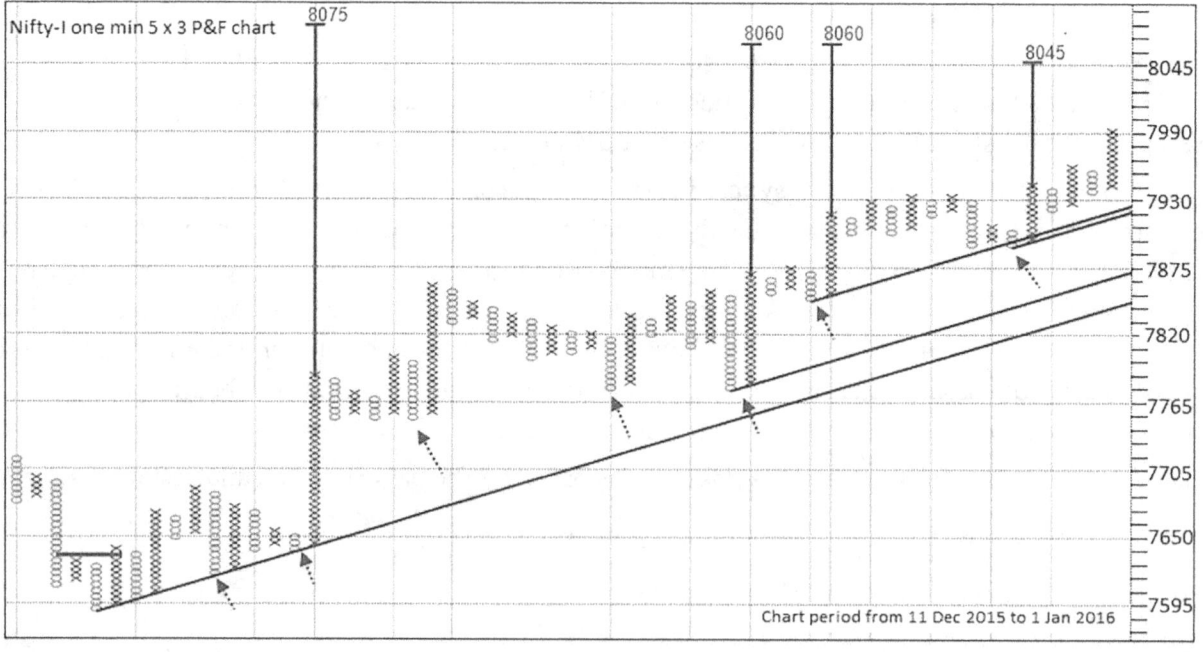

Figure 12.3.1: Nifty-I futures one min interval 5 × 3 cl Point & Figure chart

Have a look at the time interval chart of Jet Airways shown below.

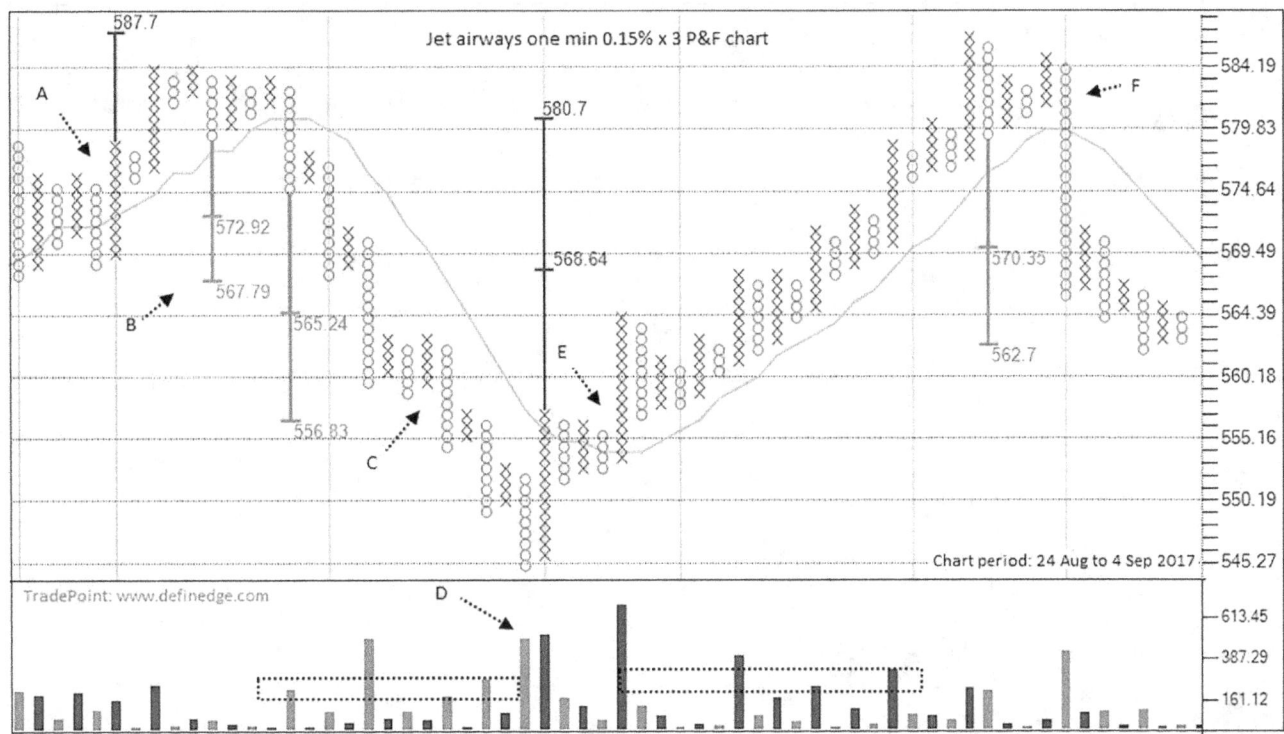

Figure 12.3.2: Jet Airways-I futures 1 min interval 0.15% × 3 cl Point & Figure chart

Above chart of Jet Airways is shown along with volume on 1 min time frame. Point A is Triple Top Buy pattern with bullish count. Point B is where price achieved bearish downside count and also invalidated the bullish count. Point C is where diagonal Triple Bottom Sell pattern was formed. Point D is selling volume climax followed by four-column Triangle breakout at point E that also activated bullish counts till 580. Point F is Bull Trap and Triangle failure formation with significant volume bar reiterating bearish open counts on the chart. Notice volume picture during Uptrend and Downtrend days on the chart.

This way, subjective analysis can be performed for intraday and momentum trading. Method such as one setup trading is a more sensible option in this time frame than random trading, which leads to emotional decisions most of the time. One setup can be traded throughout the day across instruments to yield best results over a period. Figure below is an example of Triple Top Buy formations on 1 min time interval chart of Nifty.

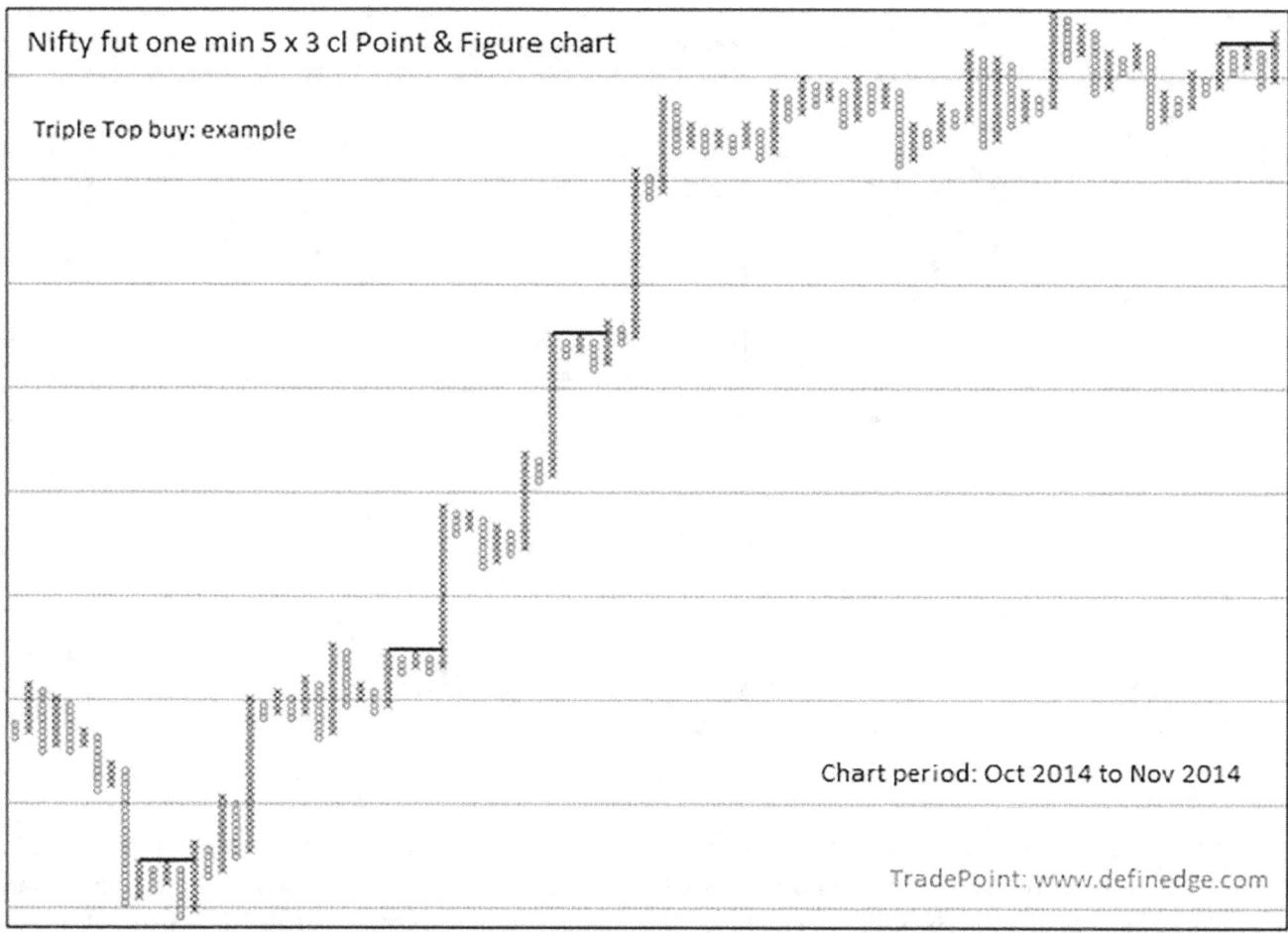

Figure 12.3.3: Nifty-I futures one min interval 5 × 3 cl Point & Figure chart

Triple Top pattern is an example. There can be any other pattern. Opt for one you are most comfortable with.

Super Pattern

If trend is strong, pull-backs will be brief, and price will bounce soon to new highs. For one setup trading, the super pattern offers well-defined pattern with Follow-through and risk control mechanism already built in. It is one of the best approaches I have ever come across for trading lower time frames. It may have 40–50% hit ratio, but risk–reward is extremely favorable and setup is very objective, making execution an easy task.

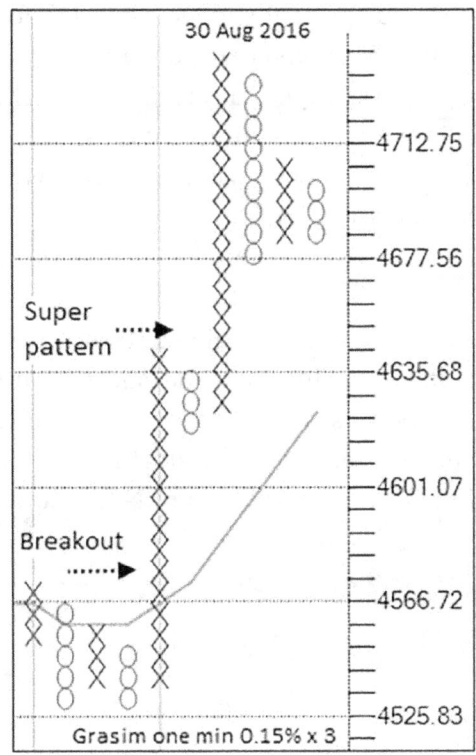

Figure 12.3.4: Grasim-I futures 1 min interval 0.15% × 3 cl Point & Figure chart

Below are 1 min time interval charts of MRPL and Bank India showing super pattern breakouts.

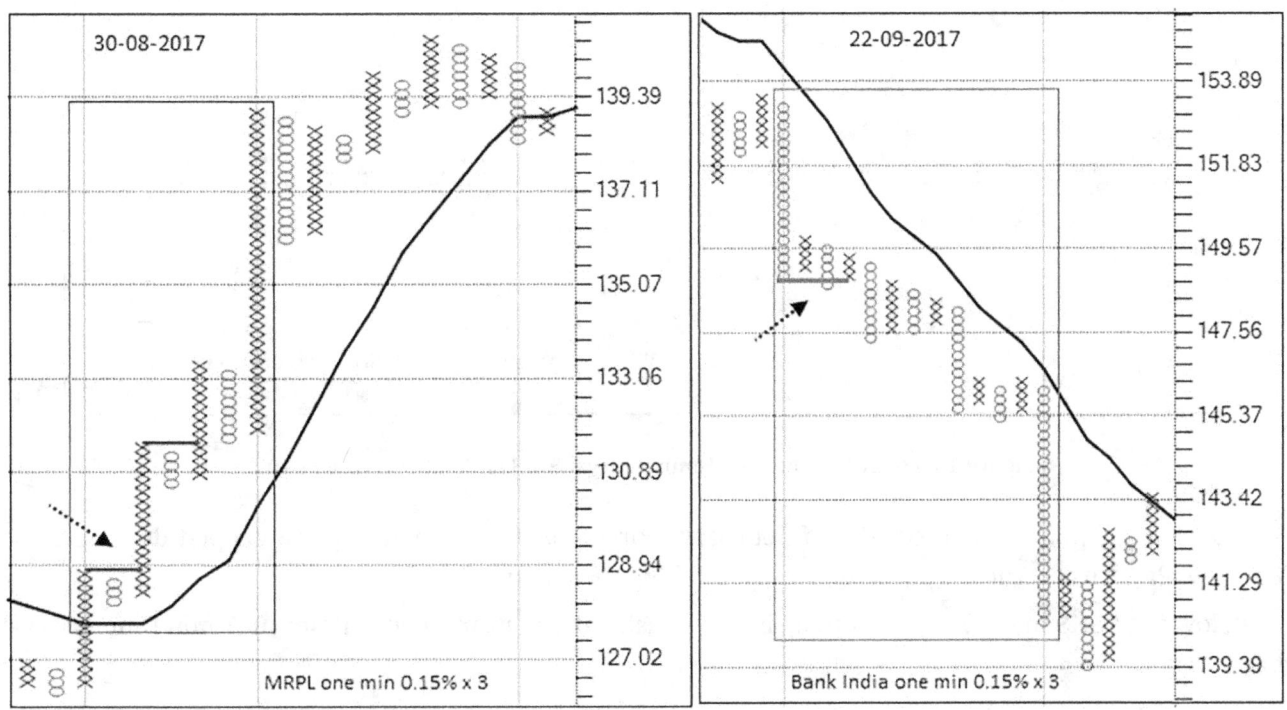

Figure 12.3.5: MRPL-I & Bank India-I futures 1 min interval 0.15% × 3 cl Point & Figure chart

Gap ups and gap downs are not in our control and we can't do much about those. But Continuation moves thereafter can prove very beneficial. Even during the day after a significant move, trading Continuation signals is a sensible approach. Super pattern is an objective method to identify candidates where there is a momentum which is the basic requirement of intraday trading. I recommend following a riding technique with P&F basic signals for exit; it will ensure that you make more when trade works in your favor and lose less when it goes against.

Anchor Points

Anchor points and Bollinger band are great tools to deal with trendless days. We discussed Anchor points on one-box reversal charts in Chapter 6 on intraday and short-term trading. They can be plotted on three-box charts also, especially on sessions of congestion or consolidation. Nonetheless, they can be applied on all sessions. Intraday Anchor points of consolidating days are important reference levels for coming sessions. Figure shown below is a 5 × 3 P&F chart of Nifty plotted on 1 min time frame.

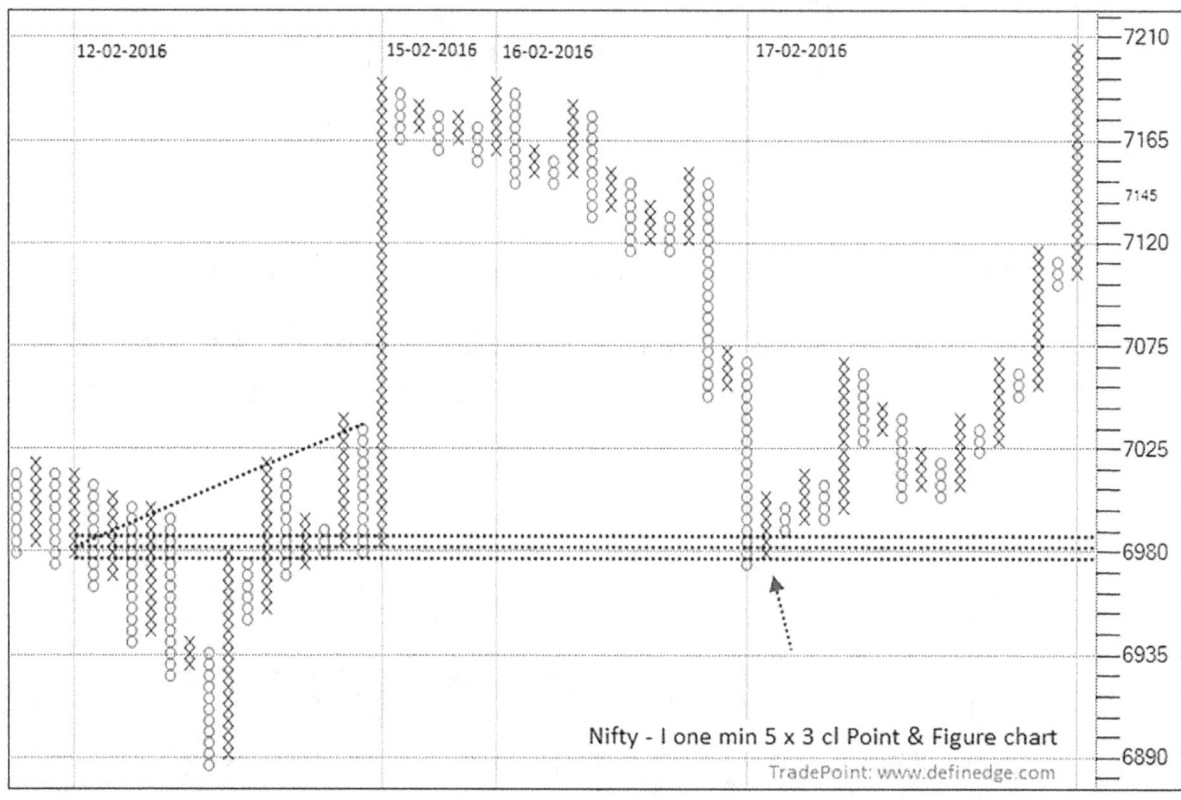

Figure 12.3.6: Nifty-I futures 1 min interval 5 × 3 cl Point & Figure chart

The Anchor point drawn on 12th of February worked as support when price gapped down on 17th February. Patterns at Anchor point level help in taking the trading decisions.

Below is an SKS micro P&F chart that shows bullish pattern near Anchor point on 1 min time interval chart.

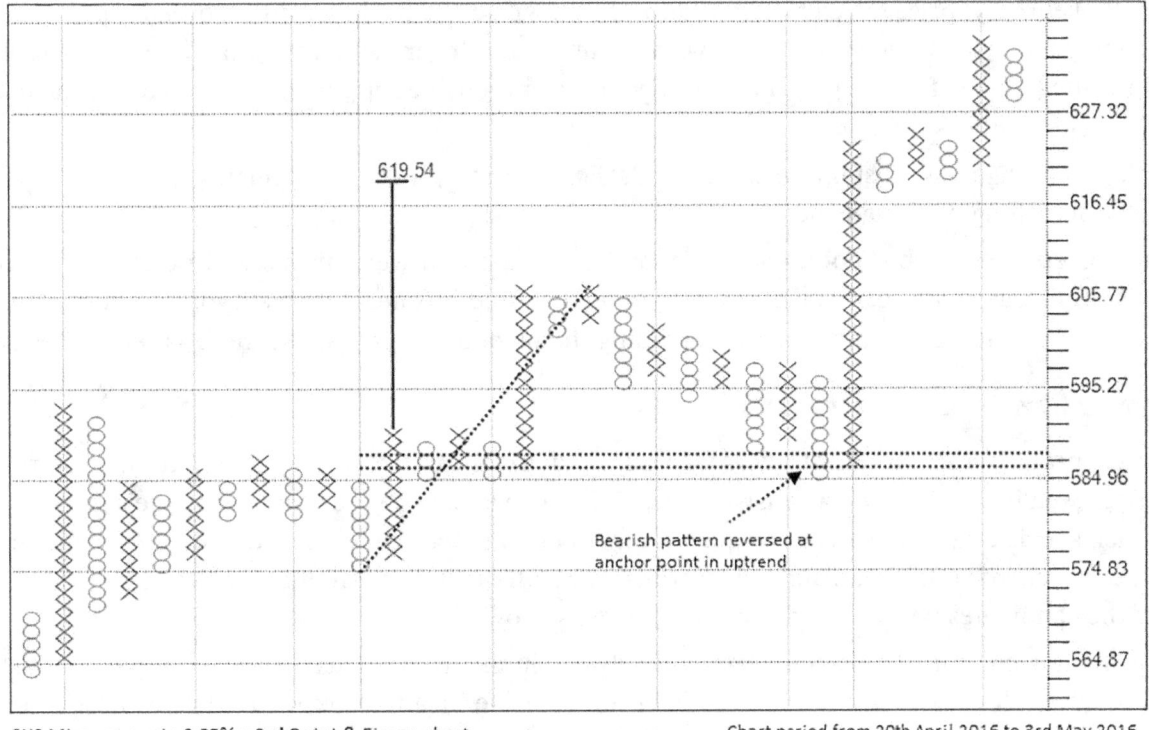

SKS Micro one min 0.25% x 3 cl Point & Figure chart   Chart period from 20th April 2016 to 3rd May 2016

Figure 12.3.7: SKS micro-I futures one min interval 0.25% × 3 cl Point & Figure chart

Buying on a bullish pattern near lower band when markets are not in bearish mode is a profitable strategy. Follow-through or Double Pattern coming along makes it a great setup and helps in short listing momentum picks.

Figure 12.3.8 is the 10 × 3 P&F chart of Bank Nifty showing the Anchor point, Bollinger band and Trend line.

Figure 12.3.8: Bank Nifty-I futures 1 min interval 10 × 3 cl Point & Figure chart

On 18th February, price tested the Anchor point drawn across the columns recorded on 16th February and this happened when price was flirting with the upper Bollinger band. In the same session, lower band near the 45-degree line from important Bottom will act as a reliable support. They played the role to tackle 19th February session as well.

Falling or rising bands display decisive trends. Follow-through and Continuation patterns make more money during falling or rising bands.

One-box running anchor point and horizontal count method were discussed in Chapter 6; I am not repeating the discussion here. If you have understood the three-box methods well, you can explore one-box chart setups. On this time frame, it helps in reading the pivotal points and use them as reference levels.

Column Buzz

The biggest problem that intraday traders face is in deciding the universe they should trade or settle down for trading fixed instruments on a consistent basis. One can decide on the universe of one's favorite stocks from which specific patterns can be traded, but that doesn't guarantee momentum. Every instrument goes through the cycle of contraction and expansion, or dull phase and a momentum phase. P&F can help you identify the candidates with momentum. Can you guess how?

Yes, Anchor column. The stocks having lengthy columns on the charts are the typical momentum candidates and tell us where the action is. Isn't it a sensible idea to look for trades in those stocks the following day? To make it objective and put things in simple words, any stock recording more than 25 boxes on 0.25% end-of-the-day chart qualifies as a column buzz. Make a list of all those stocks and trade their patterns next day. Trade bullish and bearish patterns in them filtered by trend, so that even exhaustion formation of daily time frames marked by column buzz can be handled and traded.

ORB

ORB (Open Range Breakout) is a popular technique followed for intraday trading. In ORB, the opening range of first 15 or 30 min candle is treated as range for the day, price remaining between the range is considered as consolidation and coming out from that range is known as an open rage breakout.

Same formation can be designed in P&F charts as well, where ORB will not be based on time but price. First column of the day is the opening column and the range of that column provides reference levels for the ORB technique. Price remaining within the columns is a consolidation and breaching the extreme price of the column is a breakout.

Figure shown below is a 5 × 3 chart of Nifty plotted using prices of every minute of 21st January 2016.

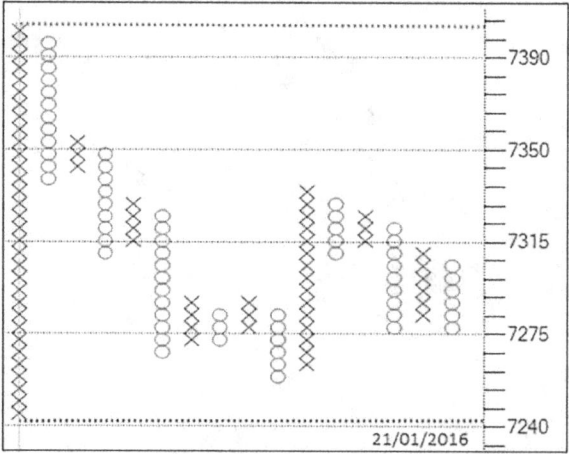

Figure 12.3.9: Nifty-I futures one min interval 5 × 3 cl Point & Figure chart

Horizontal lines from Top and Bottom of the first column show the opening range for the day. Price remained within the range for rest of the day in the above example. Below are examples of opening range breakouts by price during the day.

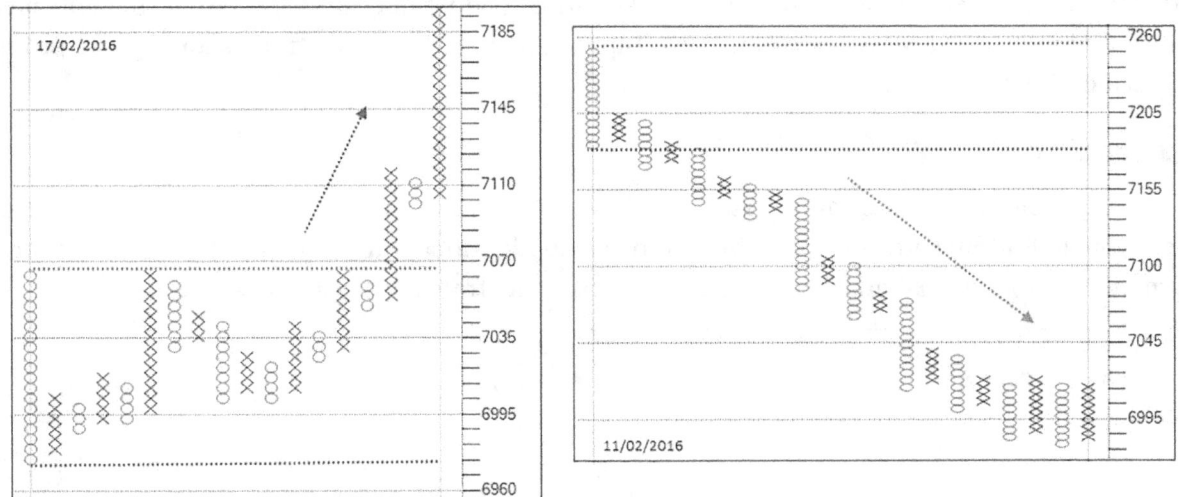

Figure 12.3.10: Nifty-I futures one min interval 5 × 3 cl Point & Figure charts

The first column reversal of the day decides the range of the day. And P&F patterns are guide to ride the trade. The patterns are traded in all cases.

On the other hand, many of the times the entire day is of three to four columns in P&F. In such cases there will be no signal. Though the number of columns during the day depends on the box-value that we use, more columns indicate more activity and fewer columns indicate dull phase or non-participation. Trend is smooth to ride when fewer columns are produced with Continuation signals, though that may not be the case always. The second chart in Figure 12.3.10 shown above is clear Downtrend with no Buy signal during the entire day. Trend is down but there were 21 columns. Figure shown below is a chart of 25th May 2016 of Nifty 5 × 3 P& F chart.

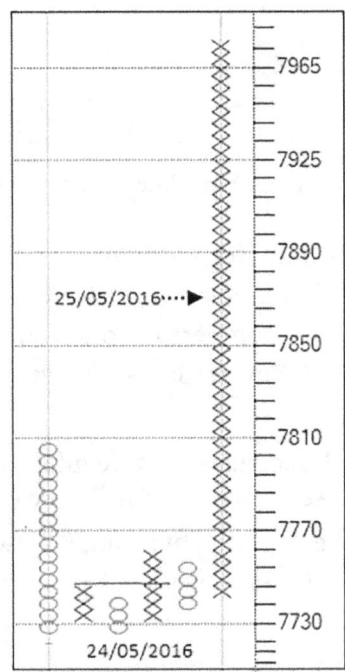

Figure 12.3.11: Nifty-I futures one min interval 5 × 3 cl Point & Figure chart

Price for the entire day remained in the same column. It is a very rare occurrence but displays clear Uptrend. Trend days are very well dealt with by P&F due to objective setups and clear riding techniques. But markets are dynamic; no strategy works every day and in all phases. Consistency is key. A trader should focus on exit methods so the limitation of any strategy does not hurt less than the benefits it gives. Like the ORB method, following the affordable setups in the direction of the trend should prove profitable over a period of time.

Index Trading

Nifty as per simple setup rules can be traded on lower time-frame charts. In other words, basic Double Top and Double Bottom patterns can be filtered by trend identification techniques like moving average. I recommend 5 absolute box-value for the same on 1 min time frame. Have a look at the chart below.

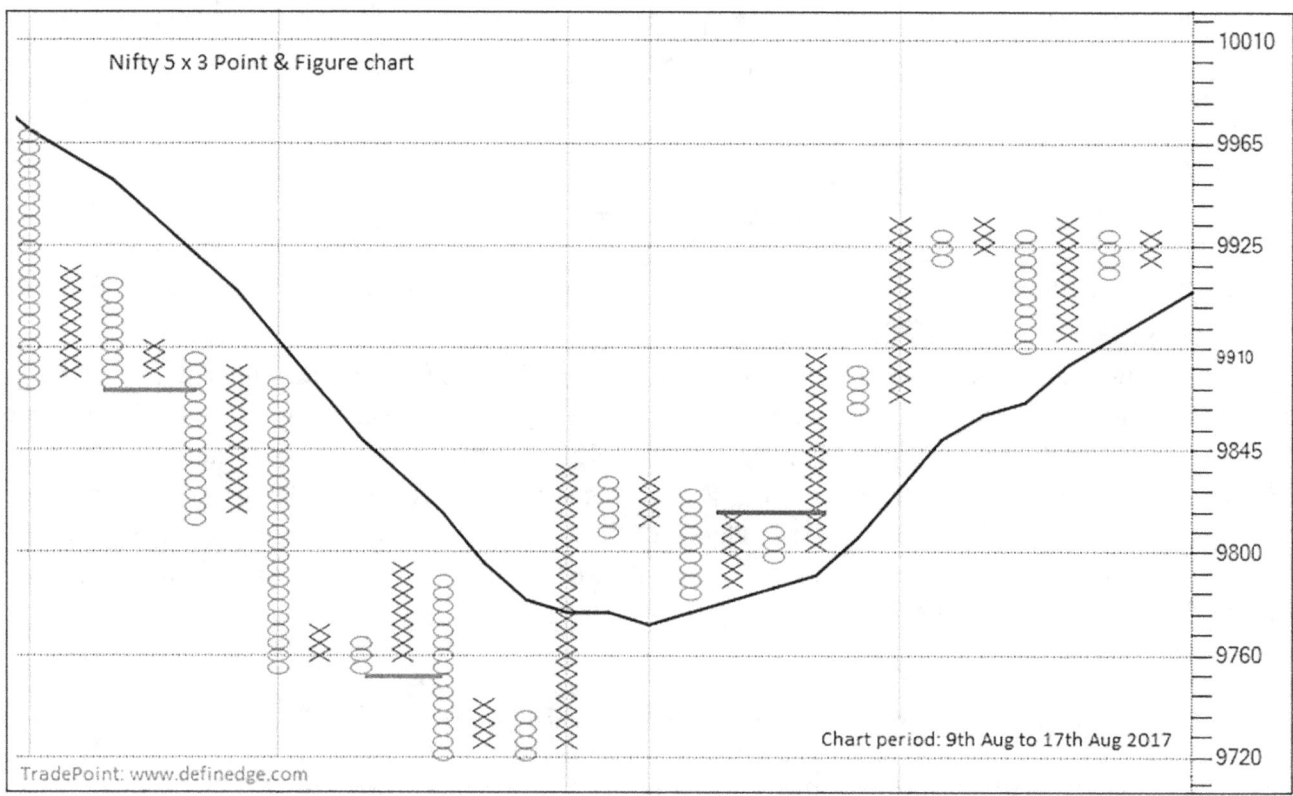

Figure 12.3.12: Nifty-I futures 1 min interval 5 × 3 cl Point & Figure chart

Same method can be followed on Bank Nifty with absolute box-value 10. Roughly, round number around 0.05% can be opted for plotting them. Vertical lines are day-separating lines in the above chart. Observe the noise that is reduced and fewer numbers of trades even on such a lower time interval chart. Trades using above box-values are momentum trades; box-value can be reduced for more number of trades.

Anchor days: If you can't follow these basic rules on a regular basis, you can do it on Anchor days. I define Anchor days as days when index has moved up or down by 0.50%. When that happens, open 1 min time-frame chart, and trade patterns in the direction of trend. Follow basic P&F rules for exit, decide initial risk to be taken for every trade and stop if index moves back below 0.50% requirement. If it happens to be a trend day, you might enjoy it.

Anchor instrument: It can be defined as instrument witnessing unusual move during the day. It is an anchor instrument for that day, and even basic signal breakout strategy filtered with trend indicator can be applied on them.

Setup-Breadth Strategy

Planning the strategy and preparing for the day is an important exercise for intraday trading. Here is an example of strategy designed using index trend to filter the trades.

State of the Nifty is important factor for an intraday trader to keep in mind while deciding the trading strategy of a particular day. Hence, begin with reading the daily three-box reversal P&F chart of Nifty: 0.10% or an absolute round number around that.

Define Nifty setup as bullish, bearish and neutral on daily time-frame chart as per setup rules explained earlier. Plot DT-percent breadth indicator of Nifty 50 index with 0.25% × 3 parameters. We discussed that breadth above 60% is overbought zone and below 20% is oversold zone. Any reading between them is a neutral zone of breadth. When the breadth is in neutral zone, look for bullish trade opportunities in stocks when the setup is bullish and bearish opportunities in stocks when setup is bearish. Use trend-riding techniques for exiting the trade.

When breadth is in extreme zone, reduce the position size and look actively to lock profits. I recommend to be a lazy trader when the breadth is at extremes. This way, we can define the days as bullish or bearish when trend in index is established and there is no exhaustion. Sharp reversals or volatility when breadth is in extreme zone may generate more whipsaws. Hence, avoiding trading or reducing allocation during such days proves effective. A column reversal in the P&F chart of the breadth indicator while at extreme zone is a sign to be cautious.

Simple setup rules can be applied on individual charts next day to decide bullish or bearish patterns. In this manner, we trade in the direction of patterns and trend when there is no exhaustion. We apply caution when there is euphoria or panic. Broader market index, index breadth, and individual trend are factored while determining the strategy for the day.

The method is explained to explore an idea; parameters and rules can be changed or tweaked as per requirement. Other methods of analysis such as Relative Strength, etc., can also be applied for filtering the setup. One can also design one's own universe of stocks to look for setups. When strategy for the day is decided, other methods and selected patterns can be traded on the selected group of stocks. The best part of defining rules is that we can define what not to do.

Money is made by knowing how and when not to trade. Extreme breadth zone is a tool to decide which markets are to be avoided or traded with caution and look for quick exits. Breakouts during extreme phases often turn out to be poor breakouts primarily because the broad market lacks the fuel to power ahead. Often poor highs or poor lows are recorded during such phases. Markets can remain in extreme zone during strong trends and P&F chart of breadth is better tool to be followed during such times because a column reversal or a pattern in extreme zone will be a reliable signal of exhaustion. The retracement that brings breadth back to the neutral zone would provide better opportunity.

When it is about intraday trading, money management and position-sizing strategies are very critical. Under-leverage and under-positioning is a far better approach. Overtrading is a big problem on this time frame and P&F will certainly help control that. Fixing a limit on the number of trades or turnover for the day is a must. Broadening days will make trend-following systems go for a toss, more allocation and trading on such days will result in major hit in the capital and also the morale. Remain very choosy and selective for trading, lazy trading is recommended.

Many traders suffer from obsessive trading disorder. It is okay to miss trending moves or days, it is fine to underperform at times and it is absolutely normal to exit early and see the price moving further. Don't chase. Markets open every day with infinite opportunities.

12.4: OPTIONS

Options are useful derivative trading instruments and they can be traded using technical analysis without having to understand the Greeks associated with them. P&F charts of options can be plotted and every P&F technique that we have discussed is applicable on them as well.

Time interval P&F charts of option premium should be plotted as other time frames are not very useful in India where next or far month contracts are illiquid. One minute is best time frame to view them but box-value should be higher than what is applied for analyzing the underlying. Normally, it should be multiplied by 5 for each slot of box-values we discussed; 2–3% box-values are useful for trading combination of patterns.

Figure shown below is 3% box-value P&F chart of 7200 strike price Put of Nifty of February 2016 expiry.

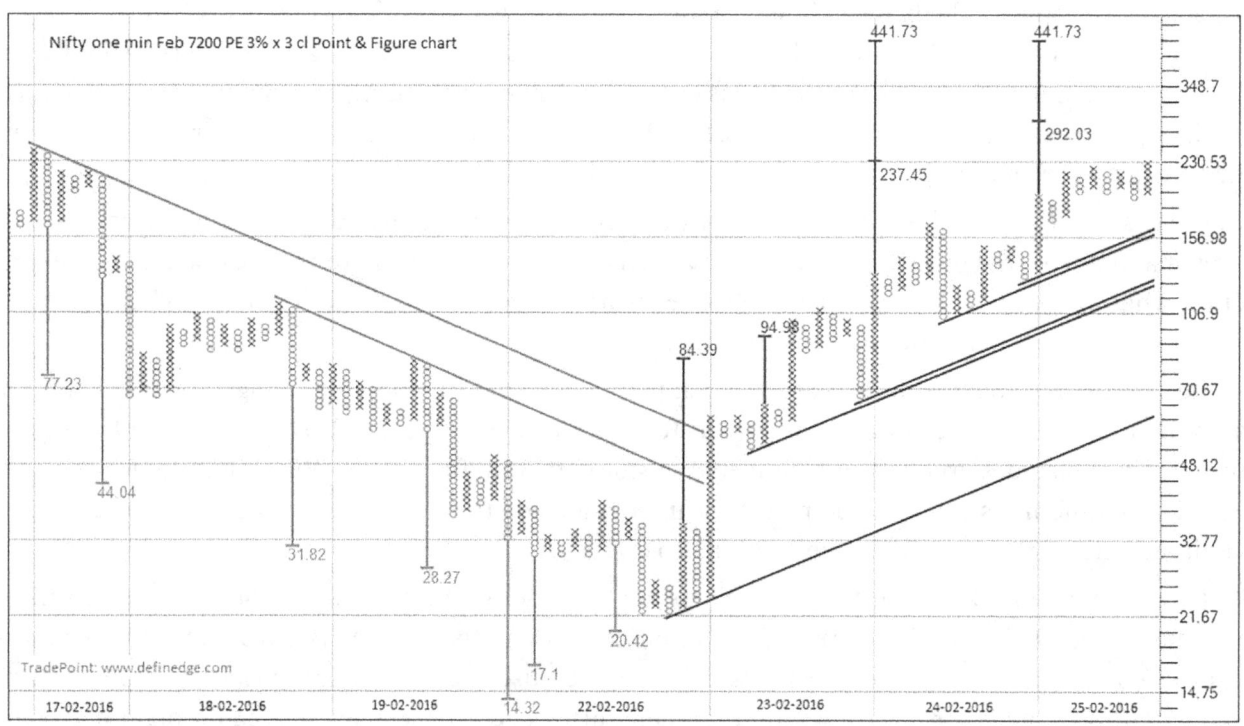

Figure 12.4.1: Nifty-I Feb 2016 7200 PE one min interval 3% × 3 cl Point & Figure chart

Trend lines and counts in the direction of trend are shown in the chart. Pattern in the direction of both provide a trading setup; they come with entry, exit and trailing mechanism.

Option is a tool that can be utilized for hedging by writing it against portfolio or some other position, which is popularly known as covered call strategy. Figure shown is the 2.5% box-value P&F chart of 7000 strike price Call option of Nifty of February 2016 expiry with 10-column Bollinger band superimposed on them.

Figure 12.4.2: Nifty-I Feb 2016 7000 CE 1 min interval 2.5% × 3 cl Point & Figure chart

Pattern retest formation shown at the higher level is followed by a downtrend. Sell strategy may be logical upon pattern confirmation at the upper band. It can turn out to be an effective pullback strategy.

When we can plot Option P&F charts, all methods we discussed in earlier sections are applicable on them as well. If you want to trade less, increase the box-value, and if you want more trades during the day, then just reduce the box-value.

For example, one setup trading is possible on option instruments as well. Have a look at below Option charts of Nifty and LT.

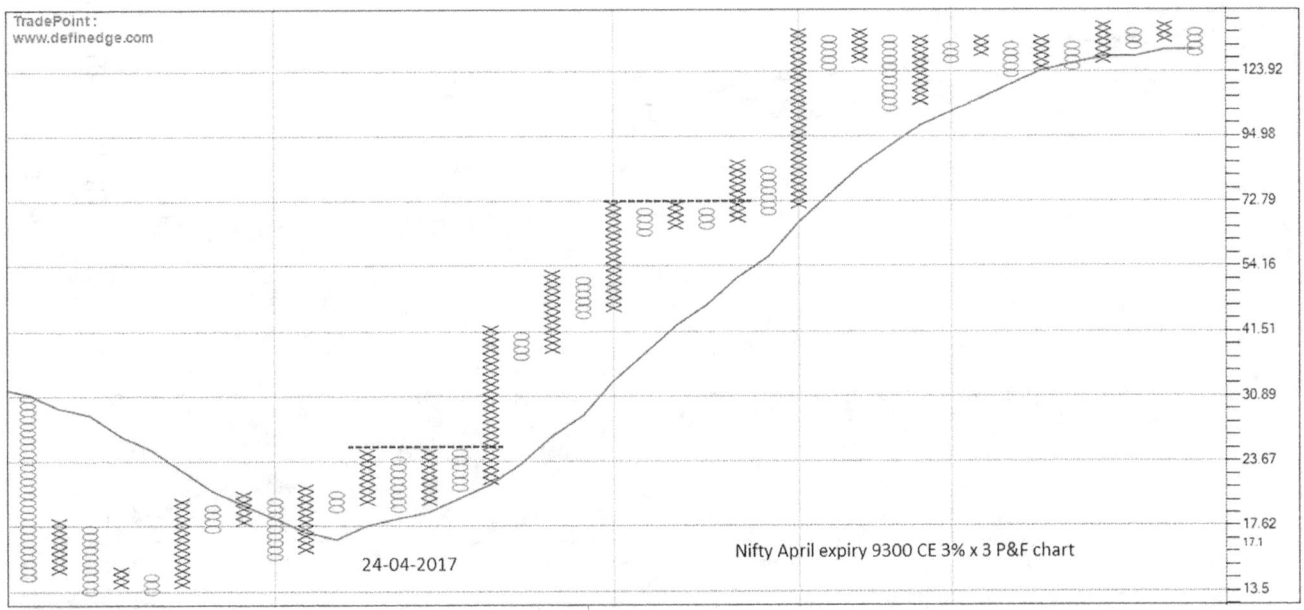

Figure 12.4.3: Nifty-I Apr 2017 9300 CE one min interval 3% × 3 cl Point & Figure chart

Figure 12.4.4: LT-I Apr 2017 1700 CE one min interval 3% × 3 cl Point & Figure chart

Systems can be designed for trading option instruments using P&F patterns and also by applying indicators on them, but you need to reduce box-value. Below is a chart showing triple MA, XO zone and volume on Option straddle chart of Nifty.

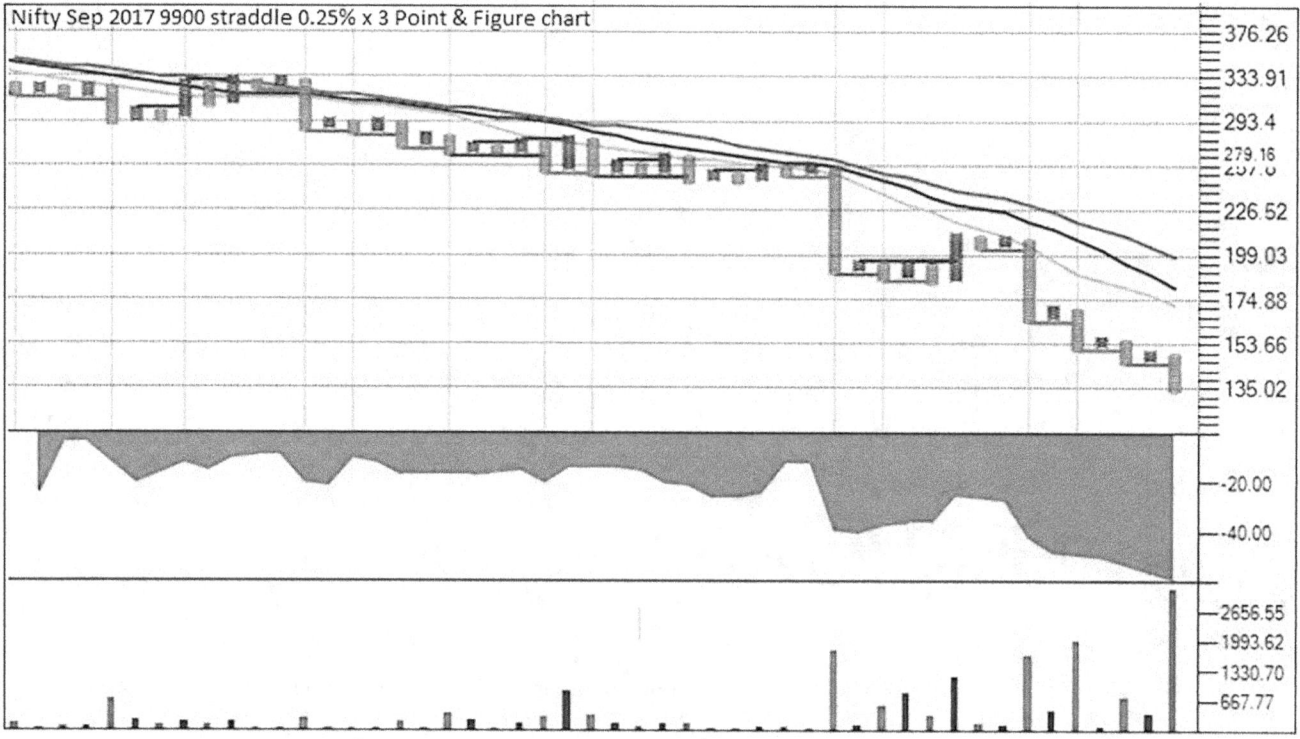

Figure 12.4.5: Nifty-I Sep 2017 9900 straddle one min interval 0.25% × 3 cl Point & Figure chart

Option straddle or strangle is a sum of two strike price premiums. They provide clues about the strength in the trend of the underlying. Recently, exchanges have introduced weekly expiry Bank Nifty option contracts. There are three possible outcomes after a breakout, either it will perform, won't perform or move Sideways. Imagine, Bank Nifty is in uptrend and sell signal is generated in weekly put option charts. Two from three possible outcomes are in our favor if we sell put option in such cases; vice versa for Downtrend. Selling option needs a lot of experience, hence caution is warranted while doing it. This is my attempt to talk about infinite possibilities of designing trading methods on P&F charts.

12.5: MORE ON TRADING

Art of Losing

Figure shown below is 0.15% × 3 cl P&F chart of UPL plotted on 1 min time interval chart.

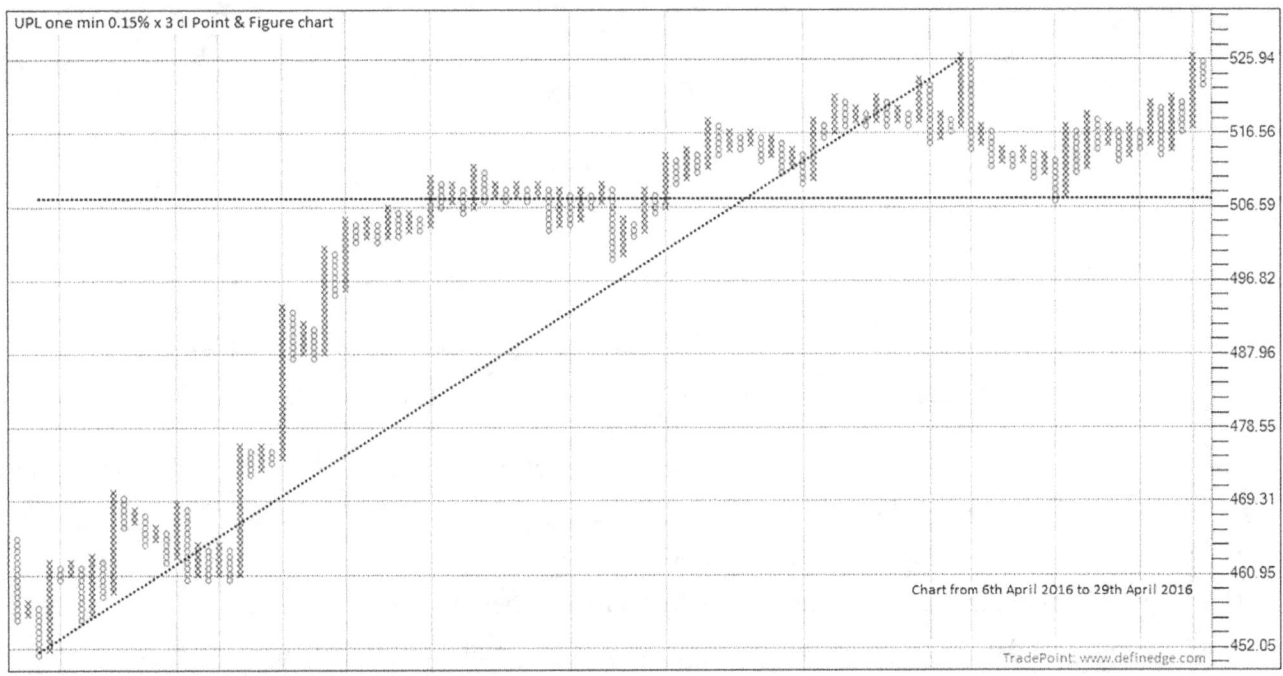

Figure 12.5.1: UPL-I futures 1 min interval 0.15% × 3 cl Point & Figure chart

The Anchor point is drawn by connecting the two major points on the chart in the Uptrend. Let's assume a trader has seen the chart when the support is taken at Anchor point when price formed Low Pole. Chart is magnified in figure shown below to drill into the formation at that point in time.

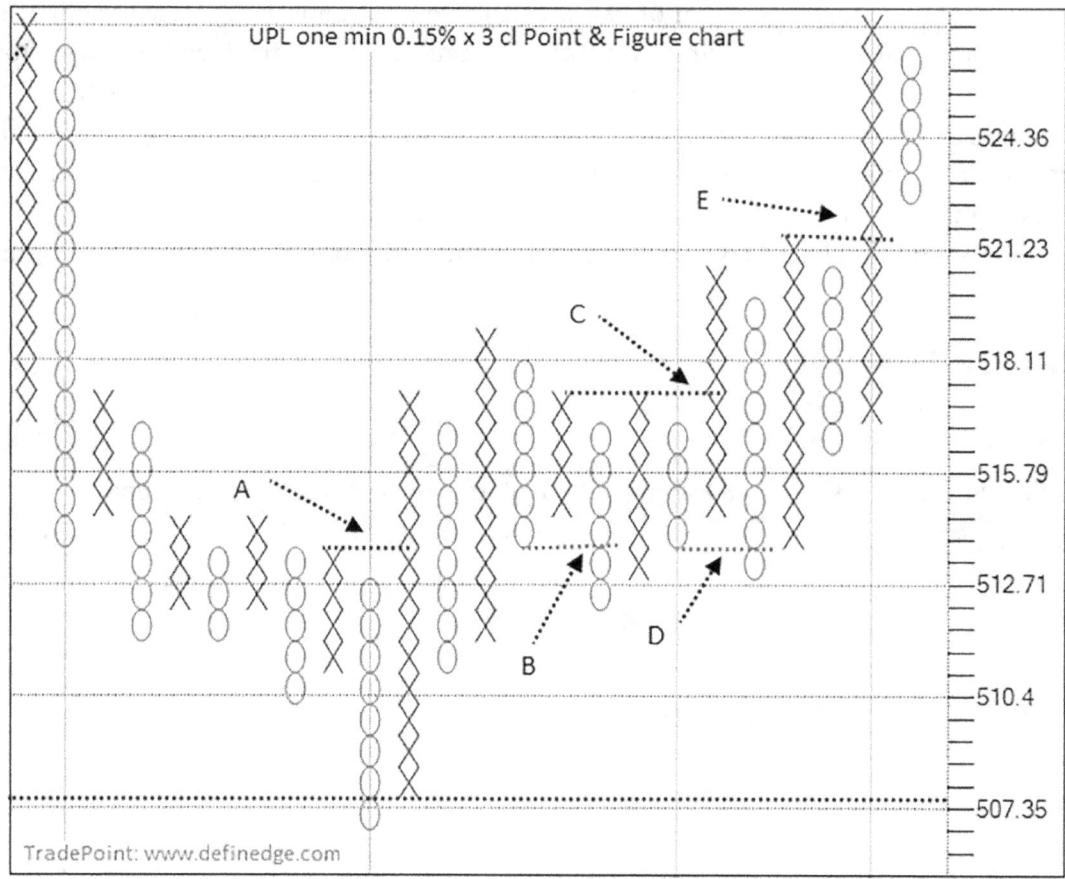

Figure 12.5.2: UPL-I futures one min interval 0.15% × 3 cl Point & Figure chart

A. Bullish 100% pole got formed at Anchor point. The setup is bullish. Column turned to 'O' but low of the formation is maintained.

B. Sell signal triggered. But it turned out to be a weak breakout.

C. Triple Top Buy Signal. Strong signal in bullish environment is a strong setup.

D. Breakout failed and generated the sell signal to trap the bulls. But it turned out to be weak as well and formed column of 'X' immediately, which turned out to be a Bullish Broadening formation.

E. Buy signal triggered, a Follow-through to Bullish Broadening.

I took this example because the ride was not smooth after price turned at support. Understand the setup; there could be different approaches to trade it. Two consecutive weak downside breakouts that maintained the bottom placed at anchor point. There could be different ways to trade it, column reversals after point B and D offered low-risk entries. The Follow-through formations can be traded and there were three Fresh signals in the chart if only basic signals were followed. Two of them failed and one of them is still on. Figure below shows the continuation to above chart.

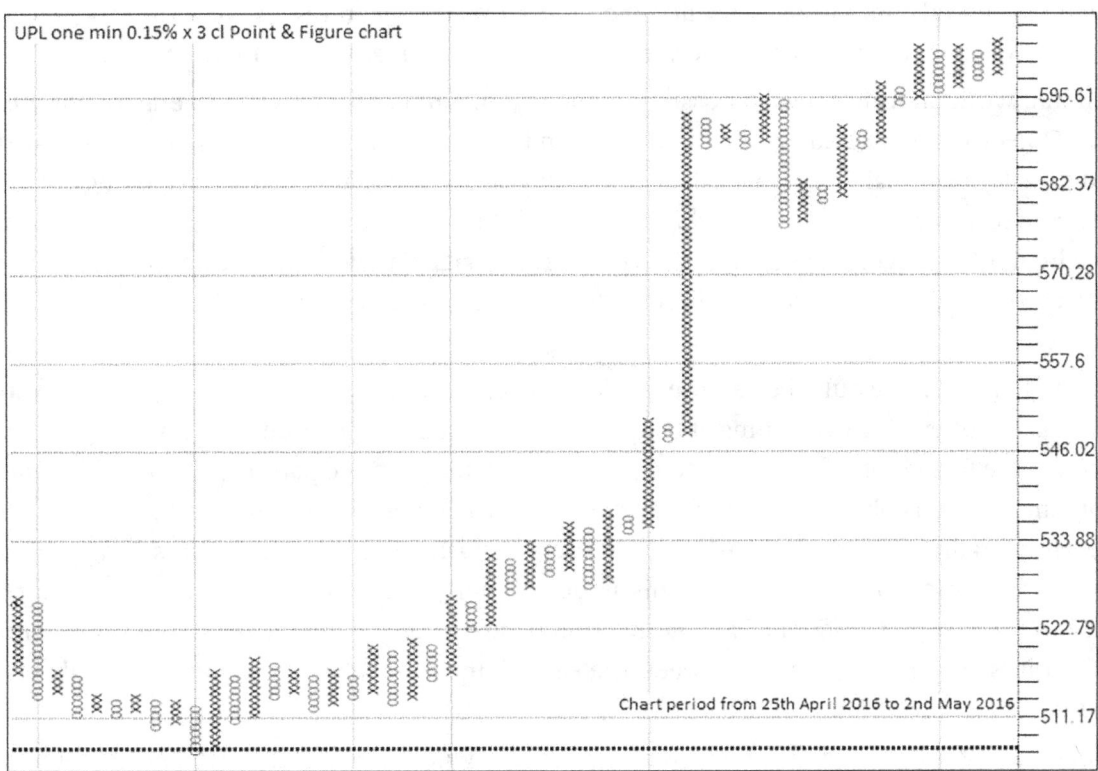

Figure 12.5.3: UPL-I futures 1 min interval 0.15% × 3 cl Point & Figure chart

Following the basic signals proves rewarding. Can the whipsaws be avoided? Methods like trend, Bollinger band or Follow-through rules can do it to a certain extent. The setup would become most easy to trade when I apply trend lines or indicators on it. Look at figure shown below.

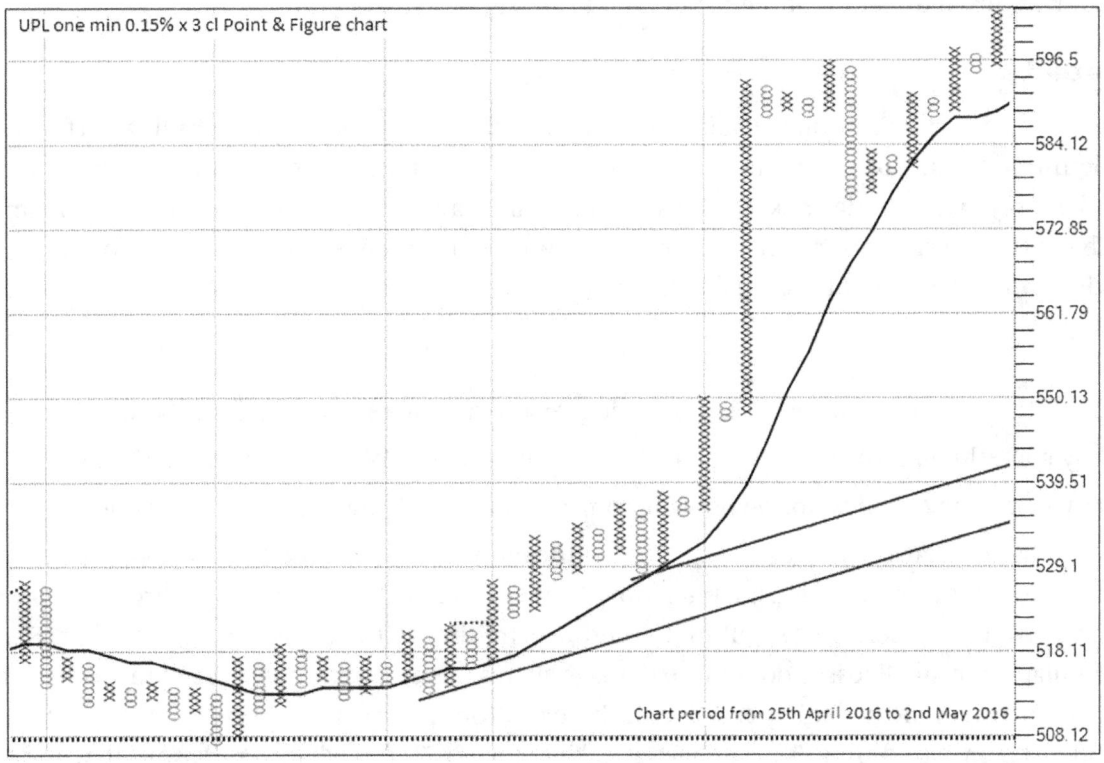

Figure 12.5.4: UPL-I futures 1 min interval 0.15% × 3 cl Point & Figure chart

Though we can take measures to reduce the number of trades and improve their efficiency, there is practically no way to avoid failures. Rather, they are an important aspect of analysis.

We should work on techniques to possibly reduce failure and focus on ways to ensure not missing out the trends. Objective setups help in dealing with them in a better manner. Besides, it is important to know when and how to lose small, to grab the big profit generating opportunity. It is this giving away which is important sometimes to judge and feel the strength of the formation. Weak negative breakouts turning out to be a higher bottom or traps against the trend are the signals that tell more about the strength of the trend. The stops could have been at Mini Tops /bottom or indicator-based. Wider stops result in better performance.

Position-sizing rules would better the performance. Adding at Follow-through and Continuation formation instead of putting everything at the initial signal is a nice approach to pyramiding. Many believe that the collective formation of all the participation is reflected on price patterns. But one becomes part of it the moment a trade is placed and having a detached involvement is not really a simple task thereafter. As said earlier, trading and analysis are separate sets of tasks. It is natural to be strongly opinionated but objective formations help in tackling this issue of being highly opinionated. Practice more to gain confidence in the setups. Confidence and conviction in setups play a big role in success. P&F charts have no noise, but it is very much present between the ears. Being calm and respecting the signals would help in making trading peaceful and noiseless.

No opportunity is ever lost. If a move is missed, there will always be another one as the markets are open every day and continuation signals would ensure ways to participate in the trend. But then not everyone is comfortable to buy something at say 150 when they saw it trading at 120 recently. As they say, it is all in the mind. Leave the fancy words like bloodbaths and catastrophic rallies for the media and the newsmakers.

The bottom line is: Accept losses, trade Continuation signals in the direction of the trend, and ride them. Major trades in direction of the major trend can pay rich dividends

Affordability

Have rules for initial risk that you will take. The singular way you can better your trading performance will be a trade filtered based on predefined and acceptable risk. The P&F boxes can help here. For example, place trades only when initial risk is of six boxes. This way you can run a scanner for patterns with permissible risk criteria. In real time, it can be very helpful because automatically a trade will not be placed without having prudent risk analysis.

Exit

We buy something, it goes up, we book profits, it goes further. We say we lack the patience.

We buy something, it goes up, we don't book, it comes down. We think we were greedy.

We buy something, it goes up, we book, it comes down. - Well...when does that happen?

Jokes apart, non-clarity of exit strategy is a significant problem that needs to be addressed. When and why to exit are important questions. Larger time frames offer wide stops but they are more productive. It saves you from the a series of small losses and overtrading as the signals are infrequent. Remember that accumulation of small losses does more damage than a larger stop. Analyse as many time frames and box-values but trade one, meaning exit should be based on one predefined box-value and time frame. If position is taken based on a 5 min chart and kept for BTST for whatever reason, it will eventually become a long-term investment as well. Often intraday positions get converted into long-term deliveries in this manner. Many portfolios are full of stocks not bought as a thoughtful investment but they come across as a bunch of failed short-term trades. No clear rules and frequent style drifts will lead us nowhere. Temptation of booking profits early make us miss out big trends and the inability to take the loss based on patterns make us keep holding weak stocks that turn out to be a bigger pain later. Mixing the time frames and no clear exit rules are biggest issues of a trader.

Patterns do fail and markets can change suddenly without prior notice. Sectors & products or commodities that were looking so promising at one point are not even relevant today. Be flexible and respect exit rules.

Market Wizards by Jack Schwager is a recommended book for all kinds of market traders. Successful traders have been interviewed in the book. Paul Tudor Jones is possibly one of the most successful traders of our time. He insists that a huge part of his success comes from cutting his losses quickly. If the price behavior is not in expected lines, then just get out. Also to quote Jesse Livermore, "One of the important keys to the success as a trader is understanding the market behavior and cutting the losing positions quickly."

The focus of most traders still remains on the entry. There are thousands of entry techniques and knowing as many of them is not important. I would like to reinforce that the focus should be on Exit strategies. Not much attention is paid to it even though so many books and all great traders have stressed enough on it. Understand that there may not be a perfect exit rule, everything has pros and cons. But to overcome emotional trading, it is very important to make exits very objective. Take complete charge and control over your rules of exiting the trade, which will make a world of a difference.

Profit Booking or Pattern Exit

Broadly, there are two types of exits that we discussed in the chapter on back-testing: riding and profit booking.

It is said that profit booking is not a sin. You often will catch people advising you, *"mil raha hai na, le lo"* (If you are getting something, take it). Profit booking is certainly an important part of trading. At times we wait for a bearish pattern to exit the long trade and end up losing the profits that could have been booked. It also happens that we book profits just to see price flying high and we end up missing a big move. Hence, which approach to be followed is a not a simple question to answer. Markets are dynamic; phases change and what worked yesterday may not work today.

The success ratio and risk–reward ratio have an inverse relationship. If you have found or experienced a technique having a high success ratio as well as risk–reward, it is perhaps a case where there is issue of smaller sample size associated with it. So if your strategy has scored handsomely in both aspects over a period of time, then think of tweaking it. This mathematics of trading applies to all methodologies. A value investor, picking the stocks based on business analysis and holding over a very long period may have a huge risk–reward ratio but a moderate success ratio, overall. Money is made when risk–reward is significant and trend is trailed. Success ratio doesn't matter much.

With such objective models, learn to treat trading as a business. And I think, like business, a trader should have multiple systems. A few systems with aggressive exits must be used for regular cash flow and systems on higher time frame with riding techniques for wealth creation.

Price Following–Pattern Following

The future is unknown and prediction is a different ball game. Prediction is not really important for successful trading; rather it can be harmful. The ability to handle different situations and be prepared for different outcomes is what is required. Flexibility and adaptability are to be learned and imbibed in trading techniques.

It is our nature to assume things. Being a trader, it is not easy to avoid prediction or being opinionated on the markets. But beware of over-analysis; it is a disease. No theory is complete and no theory is completely foolish. If you do more analysis, you can always come up with a reason or an excuse to buy or exit immediately after buying. Trading can be done based on intuition or assumption but needs to be tempered by discipline and objective trading criteria. Predictions are good only if you don't get obsessed with them or get biased. If not, they are a sure shot recipe for financial suicide.

To quote Paul Rotter here, "A trader should have no opinion. The stronger your opinion, the harder it is to get out of a losing position." Trend-following works on the simple philosophy of not guessing, and accepting that we don't know what tomorrow holds. A trend follower would not think whether we have corrected too much or less. But remember, trend-following systems have large drawdowns; they are very easy to design but difficult to follow.

There is nothing wrong in assuming things but it should be made executable. Study has proven that cycles exist. Though it is quite a complex subject and the cyclical phases and trends are visible everywhere. All these studies can be associated to simple price studies to only complement them. Associate all assumptions and analysis to price setups so that they can be traded. Otherwise, we will keep talking and gossiping about the markets but trading will not be successful.

The view of two analysts, be it technical or fundamental, or economists for that matter, may not be the same, though they may be brilliant. Analyses are important, but they are assumptions and price is the reality. Rules based on price patterns can help in trading our assumptions better.

Let me tell you a very small story. Ramesh is a good analyst friend of Suresh and he is excellent in prediction. He asked Suresh to sell a stock as he had a bearish view. The formation was still bullish and Suresh listened to him and waited for a bearish setup to take short trades. Ramesh is an experienced trader; he traded based on information but got stopped about twice while Suresh did not find the bearish pattern to sell. Eventually, Suresh found a bearish pattern and sold it. Ramesh did not enter the trade again but Suresh ended making money out the bearish view.

All internal sources that looked so smart in bull markets melt down during bear markets. Trading every information with certain rules will make us survive in the long run.

There is a question asked often: We may miss the first leg when we wait for the Buy signal or Follow-through on P&F charts, how can we avoid missing the first leg and try to catch them very early? I agree there can be a lag in entry, but this want to catch Tops and Bottoms is a dangerous game. Focus should be more on productivity or profitability of trades. I have seen some brilliant stock pickers who have bought a stock right at a bottom, but they ended up exiting very soon. A stock moves from 100 to 200 and someone gets it right at 100 but sells at 110. Another person may get in at 130 but keeps it till 180. What kind of approach will make money? Money is made by riding the swings, not by catching the Tops or Bottoms. A winning trade should not be exited until there is a good reason to do so.

When price is trading Sideways, we want to know when and in which direction it will trend. When they are trending we want to know how far it will go. Embrace unpredictability as an opportunity; it is more profitable and makes trading better. Separate the analyst in you from the trader. Objective formations help both the trader and analyst in you co-exist in harmony and bring the best out of both personalities. Objectivity helps in curbing our emotions; the biggest winning trades appear when we are least comfortable in taking them.

Have you seen people talking about some fictitious characters termed 'They' will take the market to some level and trap the retail traders. 'They' know everything is another common statement heard in market circles. I could never understand who constitute the 'They' category. Are 'They' operators, institutions and the big players? If we meant them, then they all don't operate in unison and they also go wrong and their shops also get shut. It is wrong to assume that all big money is smart money or all of them collectively operate the markets. We describe the price pattern we observe and believe that 'They' are creating it. 'They' is a figment of our imagination, and it is good for market gossip, but let's not trade based on our imaginations when we have charts reflecting objective price patterns.

The Best Strategy

I often come across a question: You have told us so many things on P&F, what's the best among all of them? You have done all these research, why do we do it again? You tell us the best working strategy and we will trade it.

After a lot of practice and experience, I found the best strategy: It is the one that suits your style and approach. I often say you give me the world's best system on 5 min candlestick chart and I will show you how to ruin it, because it is not meant for me. A pattern or method has no magic in itself. The magic is in practicing one of them consistently, and not getting distracted by noise. I work with lot of traders, and people successfully trade different methods. A system should suit your temperament so that you can execute it better; and knowing that by itself is a process. I could have picked a few strategies and written a book on how to make millions by trading them. I chose to have a comprehensive approach and provide you with many ideas on the subject to design a strategy that you are most comfortable with.

It is not possible for anyone to implement everything even though it is understood. I concede that there is an element of art in trading, but let's try to make it more of a science and as objective as possible. Consistent success in trading is possible only if trading is process-oriented. P&F charts are best suited for it. The patterns we discussed are objective in nature. Hence, they need no analytical skills, only execution needs to be focused upon. If your focus is on process, you can make money in the markets, but if focus is on money you may lose what you have.

Let's make it a process-oriented trading and engage in a profitable business. As great traders say, you should plan your trade and trade your plan. Below is a questionnaire you need to fill.

Trading Plan

1. What time frame will I trade?:
2. What box-value and reversal value will I trade?:
3. My trading universe:
4. My Entry setups:
5. My Exit setups:
6. My Re-entry setups:
7. How much will I allocate per trade?:
8. How much will I risk per trade?:
9. Will I use any hedging mechanism? If yes, what?:
10. Maximum positions that I will keep open at a time?:
11. If this is an intraday plan, how many trades will I take in a day?:

12. If this is an intraday plan, what is the max loss that I will take per day?:

13. What is the success rate and risk–reward ratio I expect?:

14. What is the review period?:

15. What is the weakness of this strategy?:

16. What is the strength of this strategy?:

17. What is the worst scenario if this strategy is traded?:

18. Am I comfortable with the strategy rules?:

There should be no ambiguity in answers. Answers like 'sometimes' or 'depends' have no place in trading plans. They should give you clear instructions while executing the trades. Review this plan periodically and don't tweak it often. We tend to tweak a plan easily and change it perhaps when it was most needed to be followed.

Chapter 13

FINALLY

A question that I frequently come across: Is this chart better than bar or candlestick? And another amazing question: What is its success ratio? These charts are not better or inferior to other charts – they are just different. And I am not explaining a system here to talk about its success ratio. P&F is a charting method where many systems can be built, each having different performance. There are unique features of these charts and they can certainly complement every kind of method and technique.

Tearing apart others' work doesn't prove us more intelligent. I don't need to stress on the disadvantages of any other method to prove P&F better. A trader should take the best out of everything. The arguments of one-versus-other is a waste of time and energy. Positivity is an essential aspect of achieving peace in life and trading is no different.

Charts never speak. Technical analysis is the best tool to regulate ourselves and manage the risk. After all, it teaches us what not to do, which is most important for successful trading. Success in trading has a lot to do with deciding what not to do. I think money is made not by doing something, but by not doing the rest of the things. It is not made by locking profits, but by booking losses. It is not made by precise entries, but by definite rule of exits. It is not made in one trade, but by practicing one technique consistently.

Markets are dynamic with no single factor controlling them. It is absolutely not possible and not necessary to know everything that is happening around the globe to be able to trade them. Simple rules shall beat complicated models in the longer run. It is impossible for any analyst to factor in all the possibilities before predicting. In fact, even knowing all variables will only add to confusion. Hence, never use aggressive or fancy words if you provide recommendations or express opinions as it may harm the amateurs and yourself. There is always a probability associated with anything including success in trading. Associating a reason to something can create false beliefs. A lot depends on luck, which is not in our control. But a lot depends on practice and beliefs which can be controlled and worked upon. I stress on patterns not because they are most profitable but because they come with clear cut entry and exit mechanism. I find this the most important aspect of trading.

Learn to have control over exits, which is stressed enough in this book. Make them as objective as possible and cut the crap. If you practice the techniques explained in the book, your ability to read the situation will improve. Lack of conviction stems from lack of practice. A good player knows the weakness of his techniques and develops the ability to handle it. Never change the approach depending upon the most recent results. Understand that the outcome of one trade is independent and will not influence the outcome of the next trade. Stop judging the methods based on a few trades and understand the implications of long-term thinking.

Develop playful approaches. It is okay to miss the trend, or not being there on the trend day or not participating in a move. Markets are open every day offering infinite opportunities. Delete SGX Nifty from the equation and avoid staring at overnight market. Invest time in better things; it is important to have a balanced life and a life outside of markets. Time with family is more important than gossiping about markets. Discussion should be on techniques rather than trades. You must have seen many of the times that after a wonderful seminar on techniques, people ask speaker's view on several stocks for the near term. The approach is short-term, which will lead one nowhere. I believe markets are enjoyed by practitioners and not by the tip seekers.

No person can trade all the time and win. Take breaks. Stay out and don't trade unless setup emerges. Willingness to be right all the time is dangerous; it is only possible for analysts and advisors. Observe more and trade less, people usually do otherwise. Don't fish for the trade, let it come to you. Learn new things, absorb and evolve your technique. Learn trading from your shocks and surprises, best trades come when we are least prepared for them. With random bets, it is difficult to produce consistent results. It is not easy to let go a trade when the trend is changing, but over a period, I have understood the importance of letting go. Trading is all about managing risk, rewards are not in our control. Time spent in the middle is important, be it cricket or trading. Time in the trade is more important than timing the trade. Focus on setups, and ride the trade once taken. Let not noise affect your trades. Understand that application is an open opportunity rather than a conclusion.

You can write to me at prashant.shah@definedge.com for feedback and discussion

There are brilliant traders and analysts out there and they can do wonders with Point & Figure charts. I wish more books are written on different trading systems and methods on P&F charts. I would feel highly motivated and content even if you manage to find just one thing to take home from this book that can benefit you in some way.

Understanding the market is a journey, not a destination. Read books mentioned in the Bibliography section for further study on the subject. What I have written is based on my learning from books, senior traders, colleagues and brilliant authors. I have filtered many things based on my practice and experience of trading over the years. Attempt has been made to keep it more relevant from the trading perspective. All mistakes in this work are entirely mine and credit of every good thing goes to the amazing practitioners who have worked so hard and kept the technique alive.

Take up one idea. Make that one idea your life. Think of it. Dream of it. Live on that idea. Let the brain, muscles, nerves, every part of the body be full of that idea and just leave every other idea alone. This is the way to success – Swami Vivekananda

– Prashant Shah

BIBLIOGRAPHY AND FURTHER STUDY

1. Aby, Carroll D. J. *Point & Figure Charting: The Complete Guide.* Grinville, SC: Traders Press Inc., 1996.

2. Bollinger, John. *Bollinger on Bollinger Bands.* New York, NY: McGraw-Hill, 2002.

3. Bulkowski, Thomas N. *Encyclopedia of Chart Patterns.* New York, NY: John Wiley & Sons, Inc., 2000.

4. Carney, Scott M. *Harmonic Trading, Volume One: Profiting from the Natural Order of the Financial Markets.* FT Press; 1 ed., April 22, 2010.

5. Dorsey, Thomas J. *Point & Figure charting: The Essential Applications for Forecasting and Tracking Market Prices.* Hoboken, New Jersey: John Wiley & Sons, Inc., 2007.

6. Du Plessis, Jeremy. *The Definitive Guide to Point and Figure: A comprehensive Guide to the Theory and Practical Use of the Point and Figure Charting Method,* Petersfield: Harriman House Publishing, 2006.

7. Edwards, R. and Magee, J. *Technical Analysis of Stock Trends,* 8th ed., 1948 ed. revised by W. H. C. Bassetti, St. Lucie Press, Boca Raton, FL, 2003.

8. Elder, Alexander. *Trading for Living.* New York, NY: John Wiley & Sons, Inc., 1993.

9. Gartley, H. M. Profits in the Stock Market, 3rd ed. (1981). Pomeroy, WA: Lambert-Gann Publishing Co., 1935.

10. Kaufman, Perry J. *Trading Systems and Methods,* 3rd ed. New York, NY: John Wiley & Sons, Inc., 1998.

11. Kirkpatrick, Charles D. and Dahlquist, Julie R. *The Complete Resource for Financial Market Technicians.* New Jersey: Pearson Education, Inc., 2007.

12. Murphy, John J. *Intermarket Analysis,* New Jersey: John Wiley & Sons, Inc., 2004.

13. Nison, Steve *Japanese Candlestick Charting Techniques,* New York, NY: New York Institute of Finance, 2001.

14. Pring, Martin J. *Technical Analysis Explained: The Successful Investor's Guide to Spotting Investment Trends and Turning Points,* McGraw-Hill, 2002.

15. Schwager, Jack D. *Market Wizards.* New York, NY: New York Institute of Finance, 1989.

16. Tharp, Van K. *Trade Your Way to Financial Freedom.* McGraw-Hill Education; 2 ed., 2006.

17. Wheelan, Alexander. *Study Helps in Point and Figure Technique, Morgan Rogers and Roberts,* New York, 1954 and Traders Press, Greenville, 1990.

18. Wilder, J. Welles Jr. *New Concepts in Technical Trading Systems.* Greensboro, SC: Trend Research, 1978.

19. Zieg, Kermit C. *Point & Figure Commodity & Stock Trading Techniques.* Traders Press, Greenville, 1997 c.